1265
675

The Nuclear Predicament

A Sourcebook

The Nuclear Predicament

A Sourcebook

Edited by

Donna Uthus Gregory

University of California,
Los Angeles

A Bedford Book

St. Martin's Press • New York

Library of Congress Catalog Card Number: 84-51681

Manufactured in the United States of America

9 8 7
f e d c

For information, write St. Martin's Press, Inc.,
175 Fifth Avenue, New York, N.Y. 10010
Editorial Offices: Bedford Books of St. Martin's Press,
29 Commonwealth Avenue, Boston, MA 02116

ISBN: 0-312-57972-1

Text design and typography: George McLean
Cover design: Dick Hannus
Cover photo: Joe Marvullo/Photomontage

Preface for Instructors

Early in the 1980s, the Reagan administration alarmed people all over the world with talk about fighting and winning nuclear wars. This book originated from this wave of public concern. It developed from the conviction that citizen involvement in public policy issues is a very good thing, that this involvement most decisively characterizes the freedom we equate with democracy—the freedom that nuclear weapons both promise to defend and threaten to destroy. To encourage public involvement thus affirms a value central to our society. To exercise responsibly and fully this cherished freedom, however, we must inform ourselves well. But as anyone who has tried to follow the policy debate knows, the complexity of nuclear weapons issues can be daunting; indeed, this complexity alone makes nuclear issues fit subjects for university courses.

As a teacher of literature and rhetoric, I wanted to help people become both more informed and especially, more articulate about nuclear issues. Nuclear weapons policy seemed to me to be a subject so compelling that it would certainly engage students, and that has proven to be true. Since we all learn faster and better how to write, argue, or think when our subject engages us, the present potential for nuclear holocaust and the debate about how to mitigate it provides—ironically enough—a subject through which writing, research, and critical thinking can be taught especially effectively.

The Nuclear Predicament developed out of a three-year trial in a UCLA freshman English course and in a university-wide interdisciplinary course. In addition, the book was influenced by my involvement in the University of California's Institute on Global Conflict and Cooperation that, among other activities, offers intensive seminars for college teachers. Such experience has shown me that nuclear weapons policy is not an easy subject to teach. This book tries to make it teachable.

The Nuclear Predicament provides an ideal introduction to the issues. It distills the vast amount of available material into one volume, highlighting the most significant data and points of debate. Although it was conceived primarily as a writing text for English classes, the book is designed to be a flexible resource that can serve a variety of courses. The four parts of the book can be read either sequentially or independently. Part 1 describes the types, numbers, and capabilities of nuclear weapons. Part 2 treats history, including the history of the arms race, arms control efforts, and nuclear strategy. Part 3 aims to enlarge our sense of the complex interrelationships between nuclear weapons and every aspect of our culture. Part 4 is a forum for the major positions in the current debate. Taken sequentially, the first three parts give students essential background for understanding the policy debate represented in Part 4. Taken independently, individual articles and sections are informative and stimulating, and many instructors will enjoy moving around in the material, guided by thematic, rhetorical, or disciplinary considerations. Care has been taken throughout the book, and particularly in Part 4, to represent all political perspectives.

Some instructors, both in English and in other disciplines, will want to use this book mainly as a research paper guide; others will prefer to use it primarily as a reader. The cross-curricular selections offer rich opportunities for students to write analytically or persuasively. Appendix 2, Suggested Research Topics, presents stimulating and important topics for essays and papers. As a reader, the book provides selections from every field of human endeavor except the arts; to remedy this omission, students are referred to relevant literature and films in Appendix 3, Further Research Sources.

To further assist readers, Appendix 4 includes a list of organizations that are active with respect to nuclear weapons issues. Two additional appendixes present tables pertaining to current arsenals of the United States and the USSR (Appendix 5) and a glossary (Appendix 6).

The Nuclear Predicament can serve a research-oriented course in two ways: it can be used as a sourcebook, a collection of both documentary evidence and expert opinion; or it can be used as background for, and a stimulus to, library research. The suggestions offered in Appendix 2 are designed for both of these possibilities. Guidelines for writing papers are presented in Appendix 1, Writing a Research Paper. Instructors who want to encourage research in this subject will find this appendix very helpful; the MLA system of documentation is explained and illustrated. The book tries to help students formulate good research questions. For this reason, both the Introduction and the research guidelines discuss the process by which we conceptualize problems.

Appendix 2 offers suggestions for fruitful activity outside the classroom, beginning with letters to editors and legislators and extending to a number of creative possibilities. This appendix makes explicit what the entire book implies, that the solution is going to be a many-faceted one, requiring all the fresh imagination that every varied segment of the society and every unique individual can bring to it. The pending nuclear crisis can turn out to be an opportunity for us to draw on perhaps the greatest strength of our society: its rich diversity of people, their perspectives, and their talents.

Many people contributed to this book. The University of California's Institute on Global Conflict and Cooperation has supported my work both financially and intellectually. UCLA Writing Programs, particularly Carol Hartzog and Lauren Cammack, provided essential departmental support. Lee Zimmerman and Gretchen Flesher tried out materials and ideas in their classrooms. Mal Kiniry and Pat Chittenden gave editorial help, often arcane. Hamilton Sterling, who catalyzed the project in the first place, provided the constant dialog and critique that makes books possible. The staff at Bedford Books was ever resourceful: Chuck Christensen early on saw the potential value of this book and deserves special thanks; Joan Feinberg, Elizabeth Schaaf, and Nancy Lyman all contributed their considerable expertise, patience, and good will.

Contents

PART 1

Where Are We?

Numbers, Types, and Effects of Nuclear Weapons *1*

JONATHAN SCHELL Hiroshima *3*

Drawing on firsthand accounts from Hiroshima, Jonathan Schell depicts some of the effects of a small atomic bomb, one equivalent to 13,000 tons of TNT.

ARMS CONTROL ASSOCIATION The Effects of Nuclear Weapons *10*

Briefly describes what would happen if one of today's medium-sized bombs—1 million tons of TNT, or 1 megaton (mt)—exploded over an urban center.

CARL SAGAN Nuclear Winter *13*

Carl Sagan reports on recent discoveries about the long-term consequences of exploding the equivalent of 100, 3,000, and 5,000 of these "medium-sized," 1-megaton bombs.

UNITED NATIONS SECRETARY-GENERAL Factual Information on Present Nuclear Arsenals *18*

Describes both the weapons and their configuration for the U.S. and the USSR, and other European countries. In addition, it introduces nuclear weapons jargon.

PART 2

How Did We Get Here?

Origins of the Arms Race *37*

Early History: Manhattan Project to A-Bomb *39*

ALBERT EINSTEIN Letter to President Roosevelt, August 2, 1939 *39*

Einstein's letter persuaded President Roosevelt that the Germans might develop the atomic bomb first, and as a result of this letter the Manhattan Project—the U.S. undertaking to develop the atomic bomb—was established.

NIELS BOHR Memorandum to President Roosevelt, July 1944 *41*

Bohr's memo is representative of many early attempts to prevent a nuclear arms race. Writing a full year before the weapons were even operational, Bohr warned that, without international agreements to control the use of nuclear weapons, a deadly competition in nuclear arms production would result.

JAMES FRANCK et al. The Franck Report: A Report to the Secretary of War, June 11, 1945 *43*

This report was written to express the deep concern of Manhattan Project scientists about how the bombs they were building would be used and about the risk of an arms race that they believed would threaten the world's existence.

LEO SZILARD A Petition to the President of the United States, July 17, 1945 *52*

One of the scientists to write and sign the Franck Report, Szilard wrote this petition opposing the targeting of Japanese cities on moral grounds.

HENRY L. STIMSON Letter and Memorandum, September 11, 1945 *54*

Secretary of War Stimson tells President Truman that he fears an impending arms race and proposes a radical step to prevent it: a nuclear partnership with Great Britain and the USSR.

DWIGHT D. EISENHOWER Letter to Bernard Baruch, June 14, 1946 *57*

In his letter regarding the world's first nuclear arms control proposal, General Eisenhower outlines what might be called the U.S. bargaining position.

BERNARD BARUCH The Baruch Plan *60*

On June 14, 1946, Bernard Baruch, an American financier, presented at the United Nations the first proposal for the international control of nuclear weapons.

BERTRAND RUSSELL The Russell-Einstein Manifesto *70*

By 1954 the arms race was a fact; moreover, the U.S. tested the first hydrogen bomb that year. Bertrand Russell first called upon scientists to attest the grave peril that nuclear weapons posed and then brought his pleas for an end to war to the people of the world.

Progress and Policy Since Hiroshima 74

RANDALL FORSBERG Nuclear Arms: A Brief History *74*

Forsberg sketches out the history of the arms race, showing how its continued escalation relates to foreign policies depending on the threat of nuclear force.

BARTON J. BERNSTEIN The Dropping of the A-Bomb *79*

The "decision" to drop the A-bombs was a matter of political, bureaucratic, and technological momentum.

DANIEL ELLSBERG How We Use Our Nuclear Arsenal *90*

Ellsberg believes that we actually use our nuclear arsenal as a means of implicit intimidation. He lists some occasions when the use of nuclear weapons was actually threatened.

G. ALLEN GREB and GERALD W. JOHNSON A History of Strategic Arms Limitations *96*

Tracing the history of arms control negotiations between the U.S. and the USSR, Greb and Johnson present some reasons why negotiations faltered during President Reagan's first term.

JEFFREY PORRO The Policy War: Brodie vs. Kahn *108*

Porro sketches out the history of weapons strategy—deterrence—by focusing on two men whose theories were at odds, using them to exemplify conflicts about strategy existing today.

COLIN S. GRAY AND KEITH PAYNE Victory Is Possible *115*

Gray and Payne agree with Kahn's view of strategy. This piece is admired by many people who take a "pro-weapons" position and is close to actual U.S. policy.

PART 3

How Are We Affected?

Perspectives on the Arms Race *125*

PAUL CHILTON Nukespeak: Nuclear Language, Culture, and Propaganda *127*

Chilton, a linguist, believes that propaganda is to a large degree responsible for our acceptance of vast nuclear arsenals. Chilton's ways of thinking about language can usefully be applied to many of the essays in this book.

MARY KALDOR The Weapons System *143*

Kaldor, a sociologist, explains how "weapons systems" may be seen as part of other complex social systems. She shows how the arms race has become embedded in our culture.

LISA PEATTIE Normalizing the Unthinkable *155*

Peattie, an anthropologist perplexed by people's ability to accommodate themselves to morally intolerable situations, discovers that the Nazi death camps shed some light on this phenomenon.

ROBERT W. DeGRASSE, Jr. The Military: Shortchanging the Economy *163*

DeGrasse argues that the defense budget affects the national economy in more ways than we realize.

JEROME D. FRANK Psychological Causes of the Nuclear Arms Race *172*

Frank, a psychiatrist, shows how certain mental processes keep policy-makers in the arms race.

INTERNATIONAL PHYSICIANS FOR THE PREVENTION OF NUCLEAR WAR What Soviet Children Are Saying about Nuclear War *178*

These interviews make us wonder why the Soviet people are better informed about nuclear issues than we generally suppose, and it shows their universal humanity.

MICHAEL FARRELL Leader Talks Détente, Religion *184*

Soviet scholars of American studies respond to some central questions about U.S.-USSR relations in an informal and lively interview.

LAWYERS COMMITTEE ON NUCLEAR POLICY Statement on the Illegality of Nuclear Weapons *198*

Basing their argument on international agreements, these lawyers claim that nuclear weapons are in fact illegal.

PART 4

What Should We Do?

Prospects for the Future *203*

Technological and Military Approaches *205*

COMMITTEE ON THE PRESENT DANGER Common Sense and the Common Danger *205*

This brief statement outlines the view of foreign policy held generally by the Reagan administration.

PRESIDENT RONALD REAGAN National Security: Address to the Nation March 23, 1983 *206*

President Reagan defends his defense budget and proposes the new missile defense system called the Strategic Defense Initiative (SDI), or "Star Wars." The speech shows the reasoning behind the Reagan military buildup.

WHITE HOUSE PAPER The President's Strategic Defense Initiative *215*

This White House Paper explains the Strategic Defense Initiative and shows how it is seen as a necessary part of deterrence.

CASPAR W. WEINBERGER To the Congress of the United States *224*

In the preface to his 1984 budget request, the secretary of defense under Reagan justifies his enormous and controversial budget—the largest ever in peacetime.

DEPARTMENT OF DEFENSE Department of Defense Views on Major Nuclear Issues and Proposals to Freeze Nuclear Forces at Current Levels *231*

This position paper explains the Department of Defense's reasons for opposing the Nuclear Freeze Initiative.

FEDERAL EMERGENCY MANAGEMENT AGENCY Shelter Management Handbook *236*

In 1982 Reagan authorized a seven-year program to assess and develop systems of protecting civilians in a nuclear attack. This publication is one result of that program.

Political Approaches 252

HERBERT SCOVILLE, Jr. The Currrent Situation and a Sketch of Its 36-Year History *252*

Scoville believes that negotiation is the answer but also believes that there cannot be serious attempts to negotiate without public involvement. Therefore, he thinks that public education on arms control issues is extremely important to the future of humanity.

RANDALL FORSBERG Call to Halt the Nuclear Arms Race—Proposal for a Mutual U.S.-Soviet Nuclear-Weapon Freeze *259*

The Nuclear Freeze Initiative is one of many kinds of arms control proposals but was the one that rallied the most intense public support.

JEROME B. WIESNER An Attack on "Nuclear Mythology" *266*

Wiesner condemns technical and military approaches to lessen the risk of nuclear war. He supports a freeze on new weapons production and some reductions in the present arsenals, to be negotiated in arms control talks held in good faith.

EDWARD ZUCKERMAN "This Area *Will* Be Evacuated" *269*

Zuckerman's book, The Day After World War III, *offers a critique of civil defense plans currently under discussion. Zuckerman's irony is an important feature of the selection.*

GEORGE F. KENNAN Cease This Madness *289*

Kennan's piece is an unusual and complex argument and a stirring piece of rhetoric. Kennan suggests that our increasing militarization makes us resemble our enemy.

LEON WIESELTIER A Defense of "Nuclear Realism" *295*

Though Wiesner and Wieseltier are critical in their proposals, Wieseltier levels his criticism at the peace movement, whereas Wiesner levels his at the Reagan administration.

McGEORGE BUNDY, GEORGE F. KENNAN, ROBERT S. McNAMARA, AND GERARD SMITH The President's Choice: Star Wars or Arms Control *297*

A detailed critique of SDI by four people with extensive experience in government service and national security affairs.

Long-Range Alternatives *310*

JONATHAN SCHELL The Choice *310*

In the long run, only social change—"reinventing the world"—and not a policy of nuclear deterrence can assure our safety from the threat of nuclear annihilation.

BEYOND WAR A New Way of Thinking *316*

This group represents a grass-roots effort to change our old habits of thinking, particularly about war.

E. P. THOMPSON Overthrowing the Satanic Kingdom *320*

Thompson claims that deterrence has warped our culture and that nothing less than total disarmament can heal it. Both Thompson's analysis and his views of the role that language plays in accommodating us to deterrence show George Orwell's influence.

MICHAEL NAGLER Redefining Peace *330*

Nagler borrows Martin Luther King, Jr.'s, terms—negative and positive peace—to explain important aspects of the nuclear weapons debate. Adopting the approach of "peace research" or "world order studies," Nagler explains why the opposite of "peace" is "violence," not "war."

RUTH LEGER SIVARD Opportunities *334*

Speaking from an international perspective, Sivard sketches out several opportunities for making "positive peace" a reality. She reminds us that nuclear weapons are not just a matter of U.S. or Soviet military policy but that they threaten the whole world.

APPENDIXES

1 Writing a Research Paper *343*
2 Suggested Research Topics *370*
3 Further Research Sources: Books, Periodicals, and Films *381*
4 What Can You Do? Directory of Organizations *389*
5 The Nuclear Arsenals of the United States and the USSR *394*
6 Glossary of Nuclear Terms *400*

Introduction for Students

Since the United States used atomic bombs on the Japanese cities of Hiroshima and Nagasaki in August 1945, humanity has lived under the shadow of nuclear weapons. In forty years our world has changed irrevocably. Debates about deterrence, arms control, military budgets, and disarmament have pervaded the 1980s. This book is the product of the concern and curiosity that has fueled those debates. It is intended to stimulate and encourage its readers' impulse to inquire—to help us take the measure of nuclear weapons' impact on our lives and on our whole civilization.

The material in this book has been chosen and organized to reflect the varied facets of the nuclear debate in America. The book's structure is straightforward. The selections in Part 1 describe the types and numbers of nuclear weapons and what they can do. Part 2 treats history, including the history of the arms race, arms control efforts, and nuclear strategy. Part 3 aims at enlarging our sense of the complex interrelationships between nuclear weapons and every aspect of our culture. Finally, Part 4 is a forum for the major positions and conflicts in the current debate.

To assist readers further, this book also includes a glossary (Appendix 6), a list of organizations active in nuclear weapons issues (Appendix 4), and a bibliography and filmography (Appendix 3). Appendix 2. Suggested Research Topics, recommends essay topics, some focusing on the material in the book and others using the book as a springboard to wider research. Guidelines for writing both types of paper are presented in Appendix 1, Writing a Research Paper, tailored specifically to nuclear issues. Appendix 5 provides a quantitative description of current arsenals in the United States and the USSR.

Background of the Nuclear Controversy

Nuclear weapons were conceived as an end to war by high-ranking military personnel, by political leaders, and by Manhattan Project scientists who developed the bomb. As America and its allies had hoped, the bombing of Hiroshima and Nagasaki hastened Japan's surrender and the end of World War II. Moreover, most of the scientists who helped to develop the first A-bombs believed that their work would prove that war itself was no longer feasible. With one nation able to wipe out another's cities in minutes, what choice did humanity have but peace?

However, as the past forty years have shown, the possibility of obliterating life as we know it has not made war obsolete. Though it is true that nuclear weapons have not been used again, still, millions of people have died in wars since World War II ended. Meanwhile, new generations now grow up with the ever present threat of nuclear annihilation. By the 1970s, enough warheads were in place around the world to destroy every city on the globe several times over. Yet the governments in charge of these warheads, far from pushing for an end to the arms buildup, continue to modernize and expand their arsenals every year. Not only could the nuclear weapons now in existence wipe out human civilization; they could also drastically alter the relationships among any surviving life forms. In a single hour, all human history could be stopped in its tracks, become ruins moldering on a radioactive planet. Within a single hour, a process of long-term ecological and genetic alteration could be set irrevocably in motion. The world has never before had a technology so powerful and so efficient.

This enormous destructive power has become part of the world in only four decades—half a human lifetime. We as individuals have been aware of it for even less time. All the assumptions our species makes about our own continuity, all the assumptions that ground our laws, our economic institutions, our philosophies, our art—assumptions about the endurance of the human spirit through times of strain and about the fulfillment of hopes after years of struggle—have suddenly been rendered tenuous. We have not yet fully comprehended this drastic change.

Current Concepts in the Nuclear Debate

The hope of ending war held by the people who created the world's first atomic bombs has metamorphosed into the political strategy of *deterrence:* we hope to prevent nuclear war by threatening to use our nuclear weapons in retaliation for another nation's using theirs. Everyone agrees, however, that deterrence is not foolproof. Therefore, a central issue in the nuclear debate is how to make deterrence safer. Some people believe that new weapons systems can add to the effectiveness of deterrence. Others strongly disagree, arguing that the dangers of new systems outweigh their benefits. Some people want to focus on arms control negotiations as a way to make deterrence more stable; but the question of which weapons systems to limit remains highly controversial.

An alternative to deterrence is *disarmament:* getting rid of nuclear weapons, either partly or completely. Advocates of disarmament have weighed the risks and costs of nuclear weapons against the role they play in promoting our national security goals and have concluded that deterrence is a risky bargain—even a dangerous illusion. The challenge disarmament advocates face is a dual one: they must not only present persuasive arguments against deterrence, but they must also suggest realistic ways to bring about disarmament. In a world dominated by the strategy of deterrence, both are difficult tasks. A realistic assessment of the difficulties leads most of those who favor disarmament to believe it is an impossible goal to achieve in the current political climate. Some people believe that a different climate might make disarmament, or even arms reductions, more possible. Others believe that the current political climate only exaggerates difficulties inherent in the culture, and that the basic ideas of our culture would have to change before nuclear weapons could be eliminated.

Views like these represent a shift in the scope of the nuclear debate. The goal of those who developed the first atomic bombs was very specific: a quick victory. There was little debate then. Even in the 1950s the debate—focusing on how nuclear weapons might help contain the potential expansion of the Soviet Union—was much narrower than it is now. Today, two dimensions have been added that did not exist in 1945 or 1955. One is the enormous size of the arsenals, coupled with their continual growth, and the impact these have on our daily lives. The other is that more countries are acquiring nuclear weapons every year—the problem is no longer restricted to the United States and the Soviet Union.

Not only are the issues in the nuclear debate more numerous today, but the participants as well have grown in both number and kind. People directly involved in national security issues are, of course, central participants in the policy debate—the military, presidential advisors, strategists, legislators, specialists in international relations. Now, however, people from other areas are also actively studying these problems and voicing their views. Scholars in the fields of anthropology, sociology, economics, psychology, law, history, linguistics, even philosophy and religion are concerned with issues regarding nuclear weapons. Their observations enable us to view nuclear weapons in varied contexts; and the more contexts in which we can place an idea or phenomenon, the more fully we can understand it.

Taking a Position on Nuclear Weapons

Thus, as nuclear weapons have proliferated, so have the complexity of the issues and the debate about them. So much has been written about the nuclear predicament in the last forty years that it would be virtually impossible for any individual, however committed, to read all of it. Yet, we cannot ignore this growing body of social, moral, and political analysis. Nor would we want to be in the dark about an issue so central to the survival of our nation, our world neighbors, our homes and families, and our values. As members of a democracy, we have not only the right but also the responsibility to hold opinions on nuclear weapons and to base our opinions on up-to-date information. One purpose of this book, then, is to distill the vast amount of available material into one volume that highlights the most significant data and points of debate, as well as to identify additional sources of information and arenas of potential action.

The complex dilemma of nuclear weapons offers us a compelling invitation to participate in the democratic process. The subject itself—our national security policy—reminds us that the strength of a nation rests first of all in the health of its institutions, and that health depends on the quality of thought and commitment individuals bring to those institutions. The true arsenal of democracy is the quality of our thinking. Ours is a tradition that has eagerly welcomed dissent and has insisted on making way for minority views. Our capacity to analyze and assess complex problems and then to act on our decisions defines us as autonomous, responsible political beings. Yet, at present, the quality of public thinking about these issues is alarmingly superficial.

Using This Book to Learn about Nuclear Weapons

The material in this book can help you get started toward becoming well informed about nuclear issues. Even more importantly, it is intended to help you develop some fundamental skills for thinking through any issue.

Let us briefly look again at the book's structure:

1. Where Are We? Numbers, Types, and Effects of Nuclear Weapons
2. How Did We Get Here? Origins of the Arms Race
3. How Are We Affected? Perspectives on the Arms Race
4. What Should We Do? Prospects for the Future

Because this book is meant to stimulate your inquiring impulse, its conceptual structure is as important as its surface structure. You will notice that the conceptual focus of the book is nuclear weapons—more specifically, nuclear weapons in American culture. As you read about the subject and perhaps write about it as well, you may want to investigate narrower topics within it, such as the arms race, deterrence, or disarmament. You can also use the book as a starting point for exploring broader topics, such as nuclear arsenals in other countries, the effects of nuclear proliferation on international attitudes, or the potential role of other nations in influencing the superpowers. You may even want to jump to a related topic, such as nuclear power or the danger of nuclear terrorism. Whatever the scope of your own investigation, you can use an approach similar to that of this book.

Each reading has been selected because it helps to answer at least one of the following questions:

1. What are nuclear weapons?
2. How have they come about?
3. How do we (as a culture) justify them?
4. How do we (as a culture) critique or assess them?
5. How can we reduce the risk of their annihilating our world?

The first two questions correspond closely to Part 1 and Part 2 of this book, and the fifth question corresponds to Part 4. Responses to questions 3 and 4—How do we justify nuclear weapons and how do we critique them?—are scattered throughout the book; Part 3 contains mostly assessments.

To clarify what we do, conceptually, when we try to understand an issue as complex as this one, let us look at these questions for a moment. In certain ways, each question is more demanding than the ones before. The first question—"What are nuclear weapons?"—basically asks for a definition. Here we are simply trying to identify what we are talking about: what the weapons' qualities are, what they do, how many exist, and so on. The second question—

"How have they come about?"—asks us to analyze historical or social processes. These include the history of nuclear weapons technology, the dynamics of the arms race, the process by which nuclear weapons are assimilated into a nation's consciousness, and the defense appropriations process.

Question 3—"How do we (as a culture) justify them?"—takes us into the more ambiguous realm of interpretation. We must consider concepts such as national security goals, experiences from past wars, the rivalry between the United States and the Soviet Union, constant technological advances, and deterrence strategy. Notice that the conceptual analysis called for by question 3 requires us to take account of some definitions (question 1) and some processes (question 2).

Question 4 is still more complex; "How do we (as a culture) critique or assess them?" Now we examine positive and negative responses to the concepts identified in question 3. We begin by scrutinizing the arguments put forth by both the attackers and the defenders of various positions: the effectiveness of deterrence, the need to modernize our arsenal with new technology, the danger of the Soviet threat, and so on. We can stop at this descriptive level, or we can go on to evaluate the strengths and weaknesses of each argument.

Ideally, all four kinds of thinking—defining, analyzing process (or cause), analyzing concepts, and assessment or critique—go into our approach to question 5: "How can we reduce the risk of their annihilating our world?" This question synthesizes what we have learned from investigating questions 1 through 4 into a proposal for action. When we first become aware of the terrifying potential of nuclear weapons, our natural tendency is to want to start with question 5. However, if we yield to the temptation to propose a solution before studying the problem, we will have only superficial—and probably useless—proposals. For instance, it may well be true that the world would be safest from nuclear destruction if no nuclear arsenals existed. But is this a realistic possibility? If so, why have all the attempts made thus far to bring about disarmament failed?

These five questions can serve as general guidelines as you approach any subject related to nuclear weapons. They are examined in more detail as a framework for the research and writing process in Appendix 1, Writing a Research Paper. These questions are also useful in evaluating other complex issues, for nearly every topic of controversy in modern life can benefit from careful evaluation and analysis.

What use you make of the information in this book is up to you. You may simply deal with it in the context of a class assignment; or you may choose to follow up your reading, thinking, research, and writing by taking action on your own. Appendix 4, What Can You Do? lists a variety of organizations involved in issues related to nuclear weapons. Whether or not you pursue the topic beyond this book, the skills you develop here should help you to function more effectively as an informed citizen.

The Nuclear Predicament

A Sourcebook

PART 1

Where Are We?

Numbers, Types, and Effects of Nuclear Weapons

JONATHAN SCHELL

Hiroshima

Jonathan Schell (b. 1943) has written two books on nuclear weapons and our culture: The Fate of the Earth *(New York: Knopf, 1982) and* The Abolition *(New York: Knopf, 1984). Schell, a primary voice in the disarmament movement, is a staff writer for the* New Yorker. *His Hiroshima narrative draws on firsthand accounts. The atomic bomb exploded over Hiroshima on August 6, 1945.*

The yardsticks by which one can measure the destruction that will be caused by weapons of different sizes are provided by the bombings of Hiroshima and Nagasaki and American nuclear tests in which the effects of hydrogen bombs with up to sixteen hundred times the explosive yield of the Hiroshima bomb were determined. The data gathered from these experiences make it a straightforward matter to work out the distances from the explosion at which different intensities of the various effects of a bomb are likely to occur. In the back of the Glasstone book,[1] the reader will find a small dial computer that places all this information at his fingertips. Thus, if one would like to know how deep a crater a twenty-megaton ground burst will leave in wet soil one has only to set a pointer at twenty megatons and look in a small window showing crater size to find that the depth would be six hundred feet—a hole deep enough to bury a fair-sized skyscraper. Yet this small circular computer, on which the downfall of every city on earth is distilled into a few lines and figures, can, of course, tell us nothing of the human reality of nuclear destruction. Part of the horror of thinking about a holocaust lies in the fact that it leads us to supplant the human world with a statistical world; we seek a human truth and come up with a handful of figures. The only source that gives us a glimpse of that human truth is the testimony of the survivors of the Hiroshima and Nagasaki bombings. Because the bombing of Hiroshima has been more thoroughly investigated than the bombing of Nagasaki, and therefore more information about it is available, I shall restrict myself to a brief description of that catastrophe.

On August 6, 1945, at 8:16 A.M., a fission bomb with a yield of twelve and a half kilotons was detonated about nineteen hundred feet above the central section of Hiroshima. By present-day standards, the bomb was a small one, and in today's arsenals it would be classed among the merely tactical weapons. Nevertheless, it was large enough to transform a city of some three hundred and forty thousand people into hell in the space of a few seconds. "It is no

---

exaggeration,'' the authors of ''Hiroshima and Nagasaki''[2] tell us, ''to say that the whole city was ruined instantaneously.'' In that instant, tens of thousands of people were burned, blasted, and crushed to death. Other tens of thousands suffered injuries of every description or were doomed to die of radiation sickness. The center of the city was flattened, and every part of the city was damaged. The trunks of bamboo trees as far away as five miles from ground zero—the point on the ground directly under the center of the explosion—were charred. Almost half the trees within a mile and a quarter were knocked down. Windows nearly seventeen miles away were broken. Half an hour after the blast, fires set by the thermal pulse and by the collapse of the buildings began to coalesce into a firestorm, which lasted for six hours. Starting about 9 A.M. and lasting until late afternoon, a ''black rain'' generated by the bomb (otherwise, the day was fair) fell on the western portions of the city, carrying radioactive fallout from the blast to the ground. For four hours at midday, a violent whirlwind, born of the strange meteorological conditions produced by the explosion, further devastated the city. The number of people who were killed outright or who died of their injuries over the next three months is estimated to be a hundred and thirty thousand. Sixty-eight percent of the buildings in the city were either completely destroyed or damaged beyond repair, and the center of the city was turned into a flat, rubble-strewn plain dotted with the ruins of a few of the sturdier buildings.

In the minutes after the detonation, the day grew dark, as heavy clouds of dust and smoke filled the air. A whole city had fallen in a moment, and in and under its ruins were its people. Among those still living, most were injured, and of these most were burned or had in some way been battered or had suffered both kinds of injury. Those within a mile and a quarter of ground zero had also been subjected to intense nuclear radiation, often in lethal doses. When people revived enough from their unconsciousness or shock to see what was happening around them, they found that where a second before there had been a city getting ready to go about its daily business on a peaceful, warm August morning, now there was a heap of debris and corpses and a stunned mass of injured humanity. But at first, as they awakened and tried to find their bearings in the gathering darkness, many felt cut off and alone. In a recent volume of recollections by survivors called ''Unforgetable Fire,'' in which the effects of the bombing are rendered in drawings as well as in words, Mrs. Haruko Ogasawara, a young girl on that August morning, recalls that she was at first knocked unconscious. She goes on to write:

> How many seconds or minutes had passed I could not tell, but, regaining consciousness, I found myself lying on the ground covered with pieces of wood. When I stood up in a frantic effort to look around, there was darkness. Terribly frightened, I thought I was alone in a world of death, and groped for any light. My fear was so great I did not think anyone would truly understand. When I came to my senses, I found my clothes in shreds, and I was without my wooden sandals.

Soon cries of pain and cries for help from the wounded filled the air. Survivors heard the voices of their families and their friends calling out in the gloom. Mrs. Ogasawara writes:

> Suddenly, I wondered what had happened to my mother and sister. My mother was then forty-five, and my sister five years old. When the darkness began to fade, I found that there was nothing around me. My house, the next door neighbor's house, and the next had all vanished. I was standing amid the ruins of my house. No one was around. It was quiet, very quiet—an eerie moment. I discovered my mother in a water tank. She had fainted. Crying out, "Mama, Mama," I shook her to bring her back to her senses. After coming to, my mother began to shout madly for my sister: "Eiko! Eiko!"
>
> I wondered how much time had passed when there were cries of searchers. Children were calling their parents' names, and parents were calling the names of their children. We were calling desperately for my sister and listening for her voice and looking to see her. Suddenly, Mother cried "Oh Eiko!" Four or five meters away, my sister's head was sticking out and was calling my mother. . . . Mother and I worked desperately to remove the plaster and pillars and pulled her out with great effort. Her body had turned purple from the bruises, and her arm was so badly wounded that we could have placed two fingers in the wound.

Others were less fortunate in their searches and rescue attempts. In "Unforgettable Fire," a housewife describes a scene she saw:

> A mother, driven half-mad while looking for her child, was calling his name. At last she found him. His head looked like a boiled octopus. His eyes were half-closed, and his mouth was white, pursed, and swollen.

Throughout the city, parents were discovering their wounded or dead children, and children were discovering their wounded or dead parents. Kikuno Segawa recalls seeing a little girl with her dead mother:

> A woman who looked like an expectant mother was dead. At her side, a girl of about three years of age brought some water in an empty can she had found. She was trying to let her mother drink from it.

The sight of people in extremities of suffering was ubiquitous. Kinzo Nishida recalls:

> While taking my severely wounded wife out to the riverbank by the side of the hill of Nakahiro-machi, I was horrified, indeed, at the sight of a stark naked man standing in the rain with his eyeball in his palm. He looked to be in great pain, but there was nothing that I could do for him.

Many people were astonished by the sheer sudden absence of the known world. The writer Yoko Ota later wrote:

> I just could not understand why our surroundings had changed so greatly in one instant. . . . I thought it might have been something which had nothing to do with the war—the collapse of the earth, which it was said would take place at the end of the world, and which I had read about as a child.

And a history professor who looked back at the city after the explosion remarked later, "I saw that Hiroshima had disappeared."

As the fires sprang up in the ruins, many people, having found injured family members and friends, were now forced to abandon them to the flames or to lose their own lives in the firestorm. Those who left children, husbands, wives, friends, and strangers to burn often found these experiences the most awful of the entire ordeal. Mikio Inoue describes how one man, a professor, came to abandon his wife:

> It was when I crossed Miyuki Bridge that I saw Professor Takenaka, standing at the foot of the bridge. He was almost naked, wearing nothing but shorts, and he had a ball of rice in his right hand. Beyond the streetcar line, the northern area was covered by red fire burning against the sky. Far away from the line, Ote-machi was also a sea of fire.
>
> That day, Professor Takenaka had not gone to Hiroshima University, and the A-bomb exploded when he was at home. He tried to rescue his wife, who was trapped under a roofbeam, but all his efforts were in vain. The fire was threatening him also. His wife pleaded, "Run away, dear!" He was forced to desert his wife and escape from the fire. He was now at the foot of Miyuki Bridge.
>
> But I wonder how he came to hold that ball of rice in his hand. His naked figure, standing there before the flames with that ball of rice, looked to me as a symbol of the modest hopes of human beings.

In "Hiroshima," John Hersey describes the flight of a group of German priests and their Japanese colleagues through a burning section of the city:

> The street was cluttered with parts of houses that had slid into it, and with fallen telephone poles and wires. From every second or third house came the voices of people buried and abandoned, who invariably screamed, with formal politeness, "*Tasukete kure!* Help, if you please!" The priests recognized several ruins from which these cries came as the homes of friends, but because of the fire it was too late to help.

And thus it happened that throughout Hiroshima all the ties of affection and respect that join human beings to one another were being pulled and rent by the spreading firestorm. Soon processions of the injured—processions of a kind that had never been seen before in history—began to file away from the center of the city toward its outskirts. Most of the people suffered from burns, which had often blackened their skin or caused it to sag off them. A Grocer who joined one of these processions has described them in an interview with Robert Jay Lifton which appears in his book "Death in Life":

> They held their arms bent [forward] . . . and their skin—not only on their hands but on their faces and bodies, too—hung down. . . . If there had been only one or two such people . . . perhaps I would not have had such a strong impression. But wherever I walked, I met these people. . . . Many of them died along the road. I can still picture them in my mind—like walking ghosts. They didn't look like people of this world.

The grocer also recalls that because of people's injuries, "you couldn't tell whether you were looking at them from in front or in back." People found it impossible to recognize one another. A woman who at the time was a girl of thirteen, and suffered disfiguring burns on her face, has recalled, "My face was so distorted and changed that people couldn't tell who I was. After a while I could call others' names but they couldn't recognize me." In addition to being injured, many people were vomiting—an early symptom of radiation sickness. For many, horrifying and unreal events occurred in a chaotic jumble. In "Unforgettable Fire," Torako Hironaka enumerates some of the things that she remembers:

1. Some burned work-clothes.
2. People crying for help with their heads, shoulders, or the soles of their feet injured by fragments of broken window glass. Glass fragments were scattered everywhere.
3. [A woman] crying, saying "Aigo! Aigo!" (a Korean expression of sorrow).
4. A burning pine tree.
5. A naked woman.
6. Naked girls crying, "Stupid America!"
7. I was crouching in a puddle, for fear of being shot by a machine gun. My breasts were torn.
8. Burned down electric power lines.
9. A telephone pole had burned and fallen down.
10. A field of watermelons.
11. A dead horse.
12. What with dead cats, pigs, and people, it was just a hell on earth.

Physical collapse brought emotional and spiritual collapse with it. The survivors were, on the whole, listless and stupefied. After the escapes, and the failures to escape, from the firestorm, a silence fell over the city and its remaining population. People suffered and died without speaking or otherwise making a sound. The processions of the injured, too, were soundless. Dr. Michihiko Hachiya has written in his book "Hiroshima Diary":

> Those who were able walked silently toward the suburbs in the distant hills, their spirits broken, their initiative gone. When asked whence they had come, they pointed to the city and said, "That way," and when asked where they were going, pointed away from the city and said, "This way." They were so broken and confused that they moved and behaved like automatons.
>
> Their reactions had astonished outsiders, who reported with amazement the spectacle of long files of people holding stolidly to a narrow, rough path when close by was a smooth, easy road going in the same direction. The outsiders could not grasp the fact that they were witnessing the exodus of a people who walked in the realm of dreams.

Those who were still capable of action often acted in an absurd or an insane way. Some of them energetically pursued tasks that had made sense in the intact Hiroshima of a few minutes before but were now utterly inappropriate. Hersey relates that the German priests were bent on bringing to safety a suitcase, containing diocesan accounts and a sum of money, that they had rescued from the fire and were carrying around with them through the burning city. And Dr. Lifton describes a young soldier's punctilious efforts to find and preserve the ashes of a burned military code book while people around him were screaming for help. Other people simply lost their minds. For example, when the German priests were escaping from the firestorm, one of them, Father Wilhelm Kleinsorge, carried on his back a Mr. Fukai, who kept saying that he wanted to remain where he was. When Father Kleinsorge finally put Mr. Fukai down, he started running. Hersey writes:

> Father Kleinsorge shouted to a dozen soldiers, who were standing by the bridge, to stop him. As Father Kleinsorge started back to get Mr. Fukai, Father LaSalle called out, "Hurry! Don't waste time!" So Father Kleinsorge just requested the soldiers to take care of Mr. Fukai. They said they would, but the little, broken man got away from them, and the last the priests could see of him, he was running back toward the fire.

In the weeks after the bombing, many survivors began to notice the appearance of petechiae—small spots caused by hemorrhages—on their skin. These usually signalled the onset of the critical stage of radiation sickness. In the first stage, the victims characteristically vomited repeatedly, ran a fever, and developed an abnormal thirst. (The cry "Water! Water!" was one of the few sounds often heard in Hiroshima on the day of the bombing.) Then, after a few hours or days, there was a deceptively hopeful period of remission of symptoms, called the latency period, which lasted from about a week to about four weeks. Radiation attacks the reproductive function of cells, and those that reproduce most frequently are therefore the most vulnerable. Among these are the bone-marrow cells, which are responsible for the production of blood cells. During the latency period, the count of white blood cells, which are instrumental in fighting infections, and the count of platelets, which are instrumental in clotting, drop precipitously, so the body is poorly defended against infection and is liable to hemorrhaging. In the third, and final, stage, which may last for several weeks, the victim's hair may fall out and he may suffer from diarrhea and may bleed from the intestines, the mouth, or other parts of the body, and in the end he will either recover or die. Because the fireball of the Hiroshima bomb did not touch the ground, very little ground material was mixed with the fission products of the bomb, and therefore very little local fallout was generated. (What fallout there was descended in the black rain.) Therefore, the fatalities from radiation sickness were probably all caused by the initial nuclear radiation, and since this affected only people within a radius of a mile and a quarter of ground zero, most of the people who received lethal doses were killed more quickly by the thermal pulse and the blast wave. Thus, Hiroshima did not experience the mass radiation sickness that can be expected if a weapon is ground-burst. Since the Nagasaki bomb was also burst in the air, the effect of widespread lethal fallout on large areas, causing the death by radiation sickness of whole populations in the hours, days, and weeks after the blast, is a form of nuclear horror that the world has not experienced.

In the months and years following the bombing of Hiroshima, after radiation sickness had run its course and most of the injured had either died of their wounds or recovered from them, the inhabitants of the city began to learn that the exposure to radiation they had experienced would bring about a wide variety of illnesses, many of them lethal, throughout the lifetimes of those who had been exposed. An early sign that the harm from radiation was not restricted to radiation sickness came in the months immediately following the bombing, when people found that their reproductive organs had been temporarily harmed, with men experiencing sterility and women experiencing abnormalities in their menstrual cycles. Then, over the years, other illnesses, including cataracts of the eye and leukemia and other forms of cancer, began to appear in larger than normally expected numbers among the exposed population. In all these illnesses, correlations have been found between nearness to the explosion and incidence of the disease. Also, fetuses exposed to the bomb's radiation in utero exhibited abnormalities and developmental retardation. Those exposed within the mile-and-a-quarter radius were seven times as likely as unexposed fetuses to die in utero, and were also seven times as likely to die at birth or in infancy. Surviving children who were exposed in utero tended to be shorter and lighter than other children, and were more often mentally retarded. One of the most serious abnormalities caused by exposure to the bomb's radiation was microcephaly—abnormal smallness of the head, which is often accompanied by mental retardation. In one study, thirty-three cases of microcephaly were found among a hundred and sixty-nine children exposed in utero.

Notes

[1]Samuel P. Glasstone and Philip J. Dolan, eds., *The Effects of Nuclear Weapons,* 3rd ed. (Washington, D.C.: U.S. Dept. of Defense and U.S. Dept. of Energy, 1977). [Editor's note]

[2]Hiroshima-shi Nagasaki-shi Gembaku Saigaishi Henshu Iinkai, *Hiroshima and Nagasaki: The Physical, Medical, and Social Effects of the Atomic Bombings.* The Committee for the Compilation of Materials on Damage Caused by the Atomic Bombs in Hiroshima and Nagasaki. Translated by Eisii Ishikawa and David L. Swain (New York: Basic Books, 1981) [Editor's note]

ARMS CONTROL ASSOCIATION

The Effects of Nuclear Weapons

The Arms Control Association, a public education group that was founded in 1971, is composed of scientists, policy analysts, and other experts on nuclear weapons. "The Effects of Nuclear Weapons" describes what would happen if a 1-megaton bomb exploded over a city.

Could you literally "run for your life" if a one megaton (1 Mt) warhead was launched in a surprise attack against your town?

Though more warning time is generally assumed, the distance you can run from the explosion point, called "ground zero," in the thirty minutes it takes for a Soviet warhead to reach the United States, helps illustrate the destructive potential of a single nuclear warhead. [See Table 1.]

Without transportation available, imagine you start running at the first sound of alarm. If you can sprint a 6-minute mile, by the time the weapon explodes you will be 5 miles from ground zero. At this point, the heat is so intense that exposed skin is charred and clothing ignites; winds blowing at 130 miles per hour spray the landscape with debris and broken glass; the roof on a nearby hospital flies off and windows shatter. The immediate radiation dose will eventually kill over one-half of those in the area (who do not die from the other effects).

For slower runners, those averaging a ten-minute mile, the surroundings are far more dangerous. At 3 miles from ground zero, typical concrete office buildings are collapsing all around; people and objects in buildings not crushed are blown out of windows by 250-mile winds. Those not killed by the direct effects would receive lethal radiation doses and die in six weeks' time.

These scenes illustrate the local primary effects of nuclear weapons: initial nuclear radiation, thermal radiation pulse, and blast. (Note that conventional weapons have only one destructive effect, which is the blast or shock wave.)

Initial nuclear radiation comes from invisible, highly-penetrating gamma rays which are emitted in the first minute of the explosion when atoms fission (fly apart) and fusion (join together) in a typical nuclear reaction. This radiation alters or destroys human cells. It is so penetrating that people surrounded by 24 inches of concrete one mile from a 1 Mt blast would perish. The radiation effect is a significant difference from conventional weapons which is generally not appreciated.

Arms Control Association, "The Effects of Nuclear Weapons." In *Arms Control and National Security: An Introduction* (Washington, D.C.: Arms Control Association, 1982), pp. 18–19. Reprinted by permission of the Arms Control Association.

TABLE 1 Biological Effects of Thermal Radiation

Type of Burn	Distance from Ground Zero
Third degree: pain experienced only in region surrounding burn as nerve damage occurs in area directly burned; all layers of skin affected, hence long heal time and slow scab formation.	0–5 miles
Second degree: intense and persistent pain, blisters, and scabs form; danger of infection, outer layers of skin affected.	5–7 miles
First-degree: mild pain and redness of afflicted area; only superficial layers of skin affected.	7–12 miles

Source: The Effects of Nuclear War. The Office of Technology Assessment.

The second primary effect, thermal radiation, is more familiar. It is the tremendous energy released in the form of heat and light during the nuclear explosion. Unlike a conventional weapon, which releases energy from a chemical reaction, the punch from nuclear weapons comes from the forces which bind all matter together in atoms. These forces are so powerful that, when released, their energy is millions of times greater than conventional weapons per pound of explosive material. Consequently, temperatures reach tens of millions of degrees, or superstellar level, in the nuclear fireball, as opposed to a few thousand degrees in a conventional bomb. The thermal pulse will cause third-degree burns on persons eight miles from ground zero in a 1 Mt explosion, or over an area of 250 square miles. [See Table 2.]

The hot gaseous materials created by the nuclear burst expand rapidly and form the final primary effect: a pressure wave, known as blast or shock. The shock front races like a wall of compressed air outward from the fireball (which, at a distance of 50 miles from a 1 Mt burst, appears many times more brilliant than the sun at noon). High winds, still 70 mph even six miles from ground zero, will accompany the blast wave. In addition, great pressures are created, enough to crush frame houses several miles out.

These primary effects by no means tell the whole story. Residual radiation and fallout, which is radioactive debris, remain after the explosion, and can carry great distances depending on the wind. (The Office of Technology Assessment believes survivors should remain indoors for two weeks to a month after an attack to assure safety from fallout.) Also, massive fires would result from the tremendous winds and heat.

In addition, there is an electromagnetic pulse (EMP) effect, something crudely like radio transmissions, which was only recognized in 1960 as a serious nuclear effect. EMP from a single burst high over the United States could damage computers, solid-state components, electrical, and communications equipment over the entire country.

TABLE 2 Blast Effects of a 1-Mt Explosion 8,000 ft Above the Earth's Surface

Distance From Ground Zero (ml)	Peak Overpressure	Peak Wind Velocity (mph)	Typical Blast Effects
0.8	20 psi	470	Reinforced concrete structures leveled.
3.0	10 psi	290	Most factories and commercial buildings collapsed. Small wood-frame and brick residences destroyed.
4.4	5 psi	160	Lightly constructed commercial buildings and typical residences destroyed; heavier construction severely damaged.
5.9	3 psi	95	Walls of typical steel-frame buildings blown away; severe damage to residences. Winds sufficient to kill people in the open.
11.6	1 psi	35	Damage to structures; people endangered by flying glass debris.

Source: The Effects of Nuclear War. The Office of Technology Assessment.

These primary and residual effects of nuclear weapons are well documented from U.S. Government tests, but also from the two atomic bombs the U.S. dropped on Hiroshima and Nagasaki in 1945. In an instant, a teeming Hiroshima of 340,000 people turned to rubble, swallowing a third of the population. Survivors of the blast depict a nightmare more vivid than mere statistics can express.

How would this nightmare take shape in the U.S.? Because there are so many uncertainties about nuclear war, predictions on exact conditions are hard to gauge. But deaths from a "limited" attack on U.S. land missiles could range up to 20 million. Even this "small" civilian loss would bring tremendous economic, psychological, and long-term genetic effects. For a full-scale attack, the disaster would increase immeasurably. Some 160 million could perish, and those who survive would have little if any medical attention, food, and the means to support life.

Finally, what would be the effect if all nuclear weapons, more powerful than a million Hiroshimas, exploded in a world war? Would it mean the end of the earth? Though the planet would not expire in a strict sense, the earth's ecology could be irrevocably altered. In the words of one writer, the U.S. would become "a republic of insects and grass."

CARL SAGAN
Nuclear Winter

Carl Sagan (b. 1934), professor of astronomy and space sciences at Cornell University, has long been active in attempts to curb nuclear weapons. He was among the group of scientists who recently publicized their discovery of the "nuclear winter" effect. Sagan addressed this subject in "Nuclear Winter: Global Consequences of Multiple Nuclear Explosions" (Science *222, Dec. 23, 1983, 1283–1292), which he authored with R. P. Turco, O. B. Toon, T. P. Ackerman, and J. B. Pollack (called the TTAPS article), and in "Nuclear War and Climactic Consequences: Some Policy Implications"* (Foreign Affairs *62[2], 1984, 257–292). He is perhaps best known as the author and narrator of the television series "Cosmos," a Public Broadcasting System production that was first aired in 1980. In this essay, written for the general public, he describes what could happen if 300, 3,000, or 5,000 1-megaton bombs were detonated; 5,000 megatons equals about half the world's present arsenals.*

> "Into the eternal darkness, into fire, into ice."
>
> –Dante, *The Inferno*

Except for fools and madmen, everyone knows that nuclear war would be an unprecedented human catastrophe. A more or less typical strategic warhead has a yield of 2 megatons, the explosive equivalent of 2 million tons of TNT. But 2 million tons of TNT is about the same as all the bombs exploded in World War II—a single bomb with the explosive power of the entire Second World War but compressed into a few seconds of time and an area 30 or 40 miles across. . . .

In a 2-megaton explosion over a fairly large city, buildings would be vaporized, people reduced to atoms and shadows, outlying structures blown down like matchsticks, and raging fires ignited. And if the bomb were exploded on the ground, an enormous crater, like those that can be seen through a telescope on the surface of the Moon, would be all that remained where midtown once had been. There are now more then 50,000 nuclear weapons, more than 13,000 megatons of yield, deployed in the arsenals of the United States and the Soviet Union—enough to obliterate a million Hiroshimas.

But there are fewer than 3000 cities on the Earth with populations of 100,000 or more. You cannot find anything like a million Hiroshimas to obliterate. Prime military and industrial targets that are far from cities are comparatively rare.

Thus, there are vastly more nuclear weapons than are needed for any plausible deterrence of a potential adversary.

Nobody knows, of course, how many megatons would be exploded in a real nuclear war. There are some who think that a nuclear war can be "contained," bottled up before it runs away to involve much of the world's arsenals. But a number of detailed analyses, war games run by the U.S. Department of Defense, and official Soviet pronouncements all indicate that this containment may be too much to hope for: Once the bombs begin exploding, communications failures, disorganization, fear, the necessity of making in minutes decisions affecting the fates of millions, and the immense psychological burden of knowing that your own loved ones may already have been destroyed are likely to result in a nuclear paroxysm. Many investigations, including a number of studies for the U.S. government, envision the explosion of 5000 to 10,000 megatons—the detonation of tens of thousands of nuclear weapons that now sit quietly, inconspicuously, in missile silos, submarines, and long-range bombers, faithful servants awaiting orders.

The World Health Organization, in a recent detailed study chaired by Sune K. Bergstrom (the 1982 Nobel laureate in physiology and medicine), concludes that 1.1 billion people would be killed outright in such a nuclear war, mainly in the United States, the Soviet Union, Europe, China, and Japan. An additional 1.1 billion people would suffer serious injuries and radiation sickness, for which medical help would be unavailable. It thus seems possible that more than 2 billion people—almost half of all the humans on Earth—would be destroyed in the immediate aftermath of a global thermonuclear war. This would represent by far the greatest disaster in the history of the human species and, with no other adverse effects, would probably be enough to reduce at least the Northern Hemisphere to a state of prolonged agony and barbarism. Unfortunately, the real situation would be much worse.

In technical studies of the consequences of nuclear weapons explosions, there has been a dangerous tendency to underestimate the results. This is partly due to a tradition of conservatism which generally works well in science but which is of more dubious applicability when the lives of billions of people are at stake. In the Bravo test of March 1, 1954, a 15-megaton thermonuclear bomb was exploded on Bikini Atoll. It had about double the yield expected, and there was an unanticipated last-minute shift in the wind direction. As a result, deadly radioactive fallout came down on Rongelap in the Marshall Islands, more than 200 kilometers away. Almost all the children on Rongelap subsequently developed thyroid nodules and lesions, and other long-term medical problems, due to the radioactive fallout.

Likewise, in 1973, it was discovered that high-yield airbursts will chemically burn the nitrogen in the upper air, converting it into oxides of nitrogen; these, in turn, combine with and destroy the protective ozone in the Earth's stratosphere. The surface of the Earth is shielded from deadly solar ultraviolet radiation by a layer of ozone so tenuous that, were it brought down to sea level, it would be only 3 millimeters thick. Partial destruction of this ozone layer can have serious consequences for the biology of the entire planet.

These discoveries, and others like them, were made by chance. They were largely unexpected. And now another consequence—by far the most dire—has been uncovered, again more or less by accident.

The U.S. Mariner 9 spacecraft, the first vehicle to orbit another planet, arrived at Mars in late 1971. The planet was enveloped in a global dust storm. As the fine particles slowly fell out, we were able to measure temperature changes in the atmosphere and on the surface. Soon it became clear what had happened.

The dust, lofted by high winds off the desert into the upper Martian atmosphere, had absorbed the incoming sunlight and prevented much of it from reaching the ground. Heated by the sunlight, the dust warmed the adjacent air. But the surface, enveloped in partial darkness, became much chillier than usual. Months later, after the dust fell out of the atmosphere, the upper air cooled and the surface warmed, both returning to their normal conditions. We were able to calculate accurately, from how much dust there was in the atmosphere, how cool the Martian surface ought to have been.

Afterwards, I and my colleagues, James B. Pollack and Brian Toon of NASA's Ames Research Center, were eager to apply these insights to the Earth. In a volcanic explosion, dust aerosols are lofted into the high atmosphere. We calculated by how much the Earth's global temperature should decline after a major volcanic explosion and found that our results (generally a fraction of a degree) were in good accord with actual measurements. Joining forces with Richard Turco, who has studied the effects of nuclear weapons for many years, we then began to turn our attention to the climatic effects of nuclear war. [The scientific paper, "Global Atmospheric Consequences of Nuclear War," is written by R. P. Turco, O. B. Toon, T. P. Ackerman, J. B. Pollack and Carl Sagan. From the last names of the authors, this work is generally referred to as "TTAPS."]

We knew that nuclear explosions, particularly groundbursts, would lift an enormous quantity of fine soil particles into the atmosphere (more than 100,000 tons of fine dust for every megaton exploded in a surface burst). Our work was further spurred by Paul Crutzen of the Max Planck Institute for Chemistry in Mainz, West Germany, and by John Birks of the University of Colorado, who pointed out that huge quantities of smoke would be generated in the burning of cities and forests following a nuclear war.

Groundbursts—at hardened missile silos, for example—generate fine dust. Airbursts—over cities and unhardened military installations—make fires and therefore smoke. The amount of dust and soot generated depends on the conduct of the war, the yields of the weapons employed, and the ratio of groundbursts to airbursts. So we ran computer models for several dozen different nuclear war scenarios. Our baseline case, as in many other studies, was a 5000-megaton war with only a modest fraction of the yield (20 percent) expended on urban or industrial targets. Our job, for each case, was to follow the dust and smoke generated, see how much sunlight was absorbed and by how much the temperatures changed, figure out how the particles spread in longitude and latitude, and calculate how long before it all fell out of the air back onto the surface. Since the radioactivity would be attached to these same fine particles, our calculations also revealed the extent and timing of the subsequent radioactive fallout.

Some of what I am about to describe is horrifying. I know, because it horrifies me. There is a tendency—psychiatrists call it "denial"—to put it out of our minds, not to think about it. But if we are to deal intelligently, wisely, with the nuclear arms race, then we must steel ourselves to contemplate the horrors of nuclear war.

The results of our calculations astonished us. In the baseline case, the amount of sunlight at the ground was reduced to a few percent of normal—much darker, in daylight, than in a heavy overcast and too dark for plants to make a living from photosynthesis. At least in the Northern Hemisphere, where the great preponderance of strategic targets lies, an unbroken and deadly gloom would persist for weeks.

Even more unexpected were the temperatures calculated. In the baseline case, land temperatures, except for narrow strips of coastline, dropped to minus 25° Celsius (minus 13° Fahrenheit) and stayed below freezing for months—even for a summer war. (Because the atmospheric structure becomes much more stable as the upper atmosphere is heated and the lower air is cooled, we may have severely *under*estimated how long the cold and the dark would last.) The oceans, a significant heat reservoir, would not freeze, however, and a major ice age would probably not be triggered. But because the temperatures would drop so catastrophically, virtually all crops and farm animals, at least in the Northern Hemisphere, would be destroyed, as would most varieties of uncultivated or undomesticated food supplies. Most of the human survivors would starve.

In addition, the amount of radioactive fallout is much more than expected. Many previous calculations simply ignored the intermediate time-scale fallout. That is, calculations were made for the prompt fallout—the plumes of radioactive debris blown downwind from each target—and for the long-term fallout, the fine radioactive particles lofted into the stratosphere that would descend about a year later, after most of the radioactivity had decayed. However, the radioactivity carried into the upper atmosphere (but not as high as the stratosphere) seems to have been largely forgotten. We found for the baseline case that roughly 30 percent of the land at northern midlatitudes could receive a radioactive dose greater than 250 rads, and that about 50 percent of northern midlatitudes could receive a dose greater than 100 rads. A 100-rad dose is the equivalent of about 1000 medical X-rays. A 400-rad dose will, more likely than not, kill you.

The cold, the dark, and the intense radioactivity, together lasting for months, represent a severe assault on our civilization and our species. Civil and sanitary services would be wiped out. Medical facilities, drugs, the most rudimentary means for relieving the vast human suffering, would be unavailable. Any but the most elaborate shelters would be useless, quite apart from the question of what good it might be to emerge a few months later. Synthetics burned in the destruction of the cities would produce a wide variety of toxic gases, including carbon monoxide, cyanides, dioxins, and furans. After the dust and soot settled out, the solar ultraviolet flux would be much larger than its present value. Immunity to disease would decline. Epidemics and pandemics would be rampant, especially after the billion or so unburied bodies began to thaw. Moreover, the combined influence of these severe and simultaneous stresses on life are likely to produce even more adverse consequences—biologists call them synergisms—that we are not yet wise enough to foresee.

So far, we have talked only of the Northern Hemisphere. But it now seems—unlike the case of a single nuclear weapons test—that in a real nuclear war, the heating of the vast quantities of atmospheric dust and soot in northern midlatitudes will transport these fine particles toward and across the Equator. We see just this happening in Martian dust storms. The Southern Hemisphere would experience effects that, while less severe than in the Northern Hemisphere, are nevertheless extemely ominous. The illusion with which some people in the Northern Hemisphere reassure themselves—catching an Air New Zealand flight in a time of serious international crisis, or the like—is now much less tenable, even on the narrow issue of personal survival for those with the price of a ticket.

But what if nuclear wars *can* be contained, and much less than 5000 megatons is detonated? Perhaps the greatest surprise in our work was that even small nuclear wars can have devastating climatic effects. We considered a war in which a mere 100 megatons were exploded, less than one percent of the world arsenals, and only in low-yield airbursts over cities. This scenario, we found, would ignite thousands of fires, and the smoke from these fires alone would be enough to generate an epoch of cold and dark almost as severe as in the 5000-megaton case. The threshold for what Richard Turco has called The Nuclear Winter is very low.

Could we have overlooked some important effect? The carrying of dust and soot from the Northern to the Southern Hemisphere (as well as more local atmospheric circulation) will certainly thin the clouds out over the Northern Hemisphere. But, in many cases, this thinning would be insufficient to render the climatic consequences tolerable—and every time it got better in the Northern Hemisphere, it would get worse in the Southern.

Our results have been carefully scrutinized by more than 100 scientists in the United States, Europe, and the Soviet Union. There are still arguments on points of detail. But the overall conclusion seems to be agreed upon: There are severe and previously unanticipated global consequences of nuclear war—subfreezing temperatures in a twilit radioactive gloom lasting for months or longer.

Scientists initially underestimated the effects of fallout, were amazed that nuclear explosions in space disabled distant satellites, had no idea that the fireballs from high-yield thermonuclear explosions could deplete the ozone layer, and missed altogether the possible climatic effects of nuclear dust and smoke. What else have we overlooked?

Nuclear war is a problem that can be treated only theoretically. It is not amenable to experimentation. Conceivably, we have left something important out of our analysis, and the effects are more modest than we calculate. On the other hand, it is also possible—and, from previous experience, even likely—that there are further adverse effects that no one has yet been wise enough to recognize. With billions of lives at stake, where does conservatism lie—in assuming that the results will be better than we calculate, or worse?

Many biologists, considering the nuclear winter that these calculations describe, believe they carry somber implications for life on Earth. Many species of plants and animals would become extinct. Vast numbers of surviving humans would starve to death. The delicate ecological relations that bind together organisms on Earth in a fabric of mutual dependency would be torn, perhaps irreparably. There is little question that our global civilization would be destroyed. The human population would be reduced to prehistoric levels, or less. Life for any survivors would be extremely hard. And there seems to be a real possibility of the extinction of the human species.

It is now almost 40 years since the invention of nuclear weapons. We have not yet experienced a global thermonuclear war—although on more than one occasion we have come tremulously close. I do not think our luck can hold forever. Men and machines are fallible, as recent events remind us. Fools and madmen do exist, and sometimes rise to power. Concentrating always on the near future, we have ignored the long-term consequences of our actions. We have placed our civilization and our species in jeopardy.

Fortunately, it is not yet too late. We can safeguard the planetary civilization and the human family if we so choose. There is no more important or more urgent issue.

UNITED NATIONS SECRETARY-GENERAL

Factual Information on Present Nuclear Arsenals

United Nations Secretary-General. The United Nations, an international organization established by charter in 1945, has done exten-

"Factual Information on Present Nuclear Arsenals" from the report of the Secretary-General of the United Nations entitled *General and Complete Disarmament: Comprehensive Study on Nuclear Weapons: Report of the Secretary-General,* presented Fall 1980. Reprinted by permission.

sive research on nuclear weapons and publishes studies useful for people who want to inform themselves about these issues. Table 1 and Figures 2 and 3 at the end of the article were designed by the Stockholm International Peace Research Institute (SIPRI), a Swedish institution dedicated to lessening the dangers inherent in the arms race. SIPRI publications are key sources of information on Soviet weaponry.

The exact number of nuclear warheads in the world today is probably not known by any single person or institution, and estimates cannot be verified officially. Published figures indicate, however, that the total may be in excess of 40,000. In explosive power these warheads are reported to range from about 100 tons up to more than 20 million tons equivalent of chemical high explosive. The largest weapon ever tested released an energy approximately 4,000 times that of the atomic bomb that leveled Hiroshima, and there is in principle no upper limit to the explosive yield that may be attained. The total strength of present nuclear arsenals may be equivalent to about 1 million Hiroshima bombs, i.e., some 13,000 million tons of TNT. It is often pointed out that this is equivalent to more than 3 tons for every man, woman, and child on earth. The arsenals of the United States and the Soviet Union contain most of these weapons, with the known remainder belonging to China, France, and the United Kingdom.

A measure of the resources claimed by nuclear-weapon programs is the amount of natural uranium they consume. It is estimated that 4 to 5 percent of the uranium believed to be available in the ground in the United States and Canada (between 2 and 3 million metric tons) has already been processed for the extraction of enriched uranium-235 for military purposes. Additional uranium has been converted to plutonium, of which the bulk so far has been used to fabricate nuclear weapons.

In terms of defense expenditure, the budgetary demands for equipment and labor to make these vast numbers of nuclear warheads are now stated to be in the range of $2,000 to $2,500 million annually for the United States and believed to be about the same for the Soviet Union. This may be less than 1 percent of the total defense budgets of the two superpowers, but the delivery systems claim 10 times as much and when research and development costs are included, the amount for nuclear forces comes to about 20 percent of the entire defense budget, according to United States estimates.

The Nuclear Weapon

The energy released by a nuclear weapon originates in the nucleus of the atom. In the fission bomb, the process involved is the splitting of uranium or plutonium nuclei into lighter fragments, fission products. In a thermonuclear or hydrogen bomb, nuclei of heavy hydrogen isotopes—deuterium and tritium—

are fused together at the very high temperatures triggered through the fission process.

The speed of the nuclear reactions is enormous. Both in a fission and a fusion explosive, the entire nuclear energy is released in about one millionth of a second. With today's technique, it is thus possible to release by one weapon more energy in one microsecond than that from all conventional weapons in all wars of history.

In order to sustain the chain reaction in a fission explosion, it is necessary to have more than a certain minimum amount of fissile material, the critical mass. This mass depends upon the purity and density of the material, its geometrical shape, the possible presence of neutron reflecting materials, and other factors. The fissile material has to be brought together very quickly if the weapon is to explode with great force. Conventional explosives are used for this purpose and the fissile material put together, with or without compression, to a size which, for a plutonium bomb, needs to be no larger in volume than a man's fist. At this time the chain reaction is initiated. The 1968 United Nations study on nuclear weapons set 8 kg. of plutonium containing 90 to 95 percent of plutonium-239 and 25 kg. of highly enriched uranium-235 as the amounts necessary to achieve an explosion with a yield corresponding to 20 kt. of high explosive. Depending on the design sophistication and with high quality material, this mass can range from 15 to 25 kg. for uranium-235 and from 4 to 8 kg. for plutonium-239.[1]

If a fission device is accompanied by the heavy isotopes of hydrogen, the high temperature and pressure triggered by the explosion can cause the fusion of these isotopes into heavier ones, thereby releasing vast amounts of energy. Even though one fusion reaction releases less energy than one fission reaction, the amount of energy released per kilogram of nuclear explosive material can be more than four times as large in a fusion device as in a fission device.

The energy is usually expressed in units of kiloton (kt.) or megaton (Mt.) corresponding to the energy release in a thousand or a million metric tons of TNT (trinitrotoluene). The atomic bomb dropped on Hiroshima on 6 August 1945 derived its energy from a chain reaction fissioning the nuclei of uranium-235 atoms and had a yield of 13 kt. The critical size was achieved using a "gun" to shoot one piece of uranium into another. In contrast, the Nagasaki bomb of 9 August 1945 utilized plutonium-239 and had a yield of 22 kt. The plutonium was arranged as a spherical shell which was crushed together by a surrounding shell of chemical explosive. This is referred to as a "nuclear implosion weapon."

The design of a thermonuclear weapon is publicly less well known in all its details. The energy released comes both from the fission "trigger" and the fusion materials. There may also be added a considerable amount of fission energy by surrounding the fusion weapon with a shell of uranium-238. The fission reactions give rise to much larger amounts of radioactivity than the fusion reactions. For this reason, thermonuclear weapons are sometimes spoken of as "clean" or "dirty," depending on what fraction of their total energy release derives from fission. Even a "clean" weapon generates some radioactivity, however, both as debris from the fission trigger and tritium and as "induced activity" caused by the massive outflux of neutrons from the explosion.

Long-Range Delivery Systems

The nuclear explosive can be carried to the intended target by various delivery vehicles. Among them, the land-based intercontinental ballistic missile (ICBM) is considered highly reliable and accurate, i.e., a large fraction is ready to be launched at any time and would be able to reach and destroy their targets. The carriers are multistage rockets with an intercontinental range of up to 13,000 km. or 7,000 nautical miles (one nmi is 1.852 km.), based in "hardened" silos and linked up to an elaborate system of command and control. The term "ballistic" derives from the motion of the re-entry vehicle (RV) which is governed by inertia and gravity after separation from the rocket. The shape of the RV is chosen to minimize drag upon re-entry into the atmosphere, so as to maintain accuracy under variable winds and to render the high-speed RV difficult to defend against. The transit time of the ICBM over its intercontinental range is about 30 minutes. . . .

The rocket may carry one or several warheads, which may be independently targeted. The multiple independently targetable re-entry vehicle (MIRV) system was developed by the United States in the late 1960s and is deployed also by the Soviet Union. In a MIRVed system, the separate re-entry vehicles are usually carried on a "bus" which releases the RVs one by one after making preselected changes in speed and orientation so as to direct the RVs to their separate targets. These RVs can reportedly land inside an area of perhaps 150 km. by 500 km. Thus, they are not as completely independent in arrival time or location as they would be were they on different ICBMs, and they provide less targeting flexibility.

With increasing missile accuracy and many RVs per missile, MIRV has raised the specter that a fraction of one side's ICBM forces may in a "first strike" destroy the opponent's ICBMs still housed in their hardened silos. This would be possible with sufficient accuracy and reliability of the attacking RVs, and if the ICBMs to be attacked were not launched before they were destroyed. This situation is therefore considered to be potentially unstable, since in time of crisis each side may consider launching its missiles rather than risk their destruction.

If a target is vulnerable to a particular pressure level of the air blast, its destruction may be achieved within a certain maximum area around the point of detonation. The size of this area increases with the weapon yield (e.g., by a factor 4 for an 8-fold increase in yield or a factor 100 for a 1,000-fold increase in yield). By contrast, the area of destruction due to blast increases in proportion to the number of weapons. This means in practice that the destruction is increased by increasing the number of warheads and lowering their individual RV yield; i.e., one large warhead is not so effective as several smaller ones of the same total yield spread out over the target area. This is also illustrated by Figure 1.

In order to destroy a "hard" target an attacker will use a powerful warhead, unless he has a missile of high accuracy. Missile accuracy is usually given in terms of the circular error probable (CEP), defined as the distance from the target within which, on the average, half the re-entry vehicles will land if aimed directly at the target. For example, a 1 Mt. nuclear warhead may be needed on a missile with a CEP of 1 km. in order to destroy a particular hardened structure. The same effect could result from a 125 kt. warhead with a 0.5 km. CEP missile accuracy, or a 40 kt. warhead with a 0.33 km. CEP. Megatonnage alone is thus a very misleading measure of one side's capability. Of equal or more importance is missile accuracy.

Definite CEP values for different existing missile systems are not available, for reasons both of secrecy and, presumably, insufficient basic knowledge. However, several open sources give estimates for many of these systems. The indications are that both United States and Soviet ICBMs are approaching a CEP of about 200 m.

Another delivery vehicle for nuclear weapons is the submarine-launched ballistic missile (SLBM). Even though an individual submarine may be vulnerable to attack, this system as a whole has the powerful advantage of virtual invulnerability as long as the submarines are traveling undetected under the ocean surface. At present, no nation is known to have an anti-submarine capability that threatens this invulnerability. In comparison with the ICBM, however, the SLBMs are considered to have a more tenuous communication link with the national command authority, particularly under wartime conditions. Also, they are for the time being less accurate than their land-based counterpart, partly because of the uncertainty of the submarine's determination of its location, orientation, and velocity. Thus the SLBM is not at present suited to attack small "hard" targets (e.g., missile silos), but could be utilized against larger and "softer" targets, such as military bases, air fields, and population centers. They are thus not considered destabilizing in the sense that the accurate MIRVed ICBMs may be. However, because of the possibility that the attacking submarine may come quite close to some targets, warning of an attack could be considerably less than for ICBM missiles. The SLBMs are therefore considered to be a serious threat to bombers which might have time to fly out from under an ICBM attack.

A third method of nuclear-weapon delivery, emphasized more by the United States than the USSR, is by long-range bomber. With sufficient warning, the United States bomber force would carry between one fourth and one third of all deliverable United States strategic nuclear weapons, adding up to perhaps half the total megatonnage, while the Soviet strategic nuclear payload is con-

FIGURE 1 Relationship Between Weapon Yield and Area Destroyed by Blast

The circles illustrate how the size of the area destroyed by blast increases with weapon yield. This is accounted for by the introduction of "equivalent megatonnage." . . . In the lower part of the figure are three examples of the equivalent megatonnage when the nominal yield 1 Mt is delivered in three different ways.

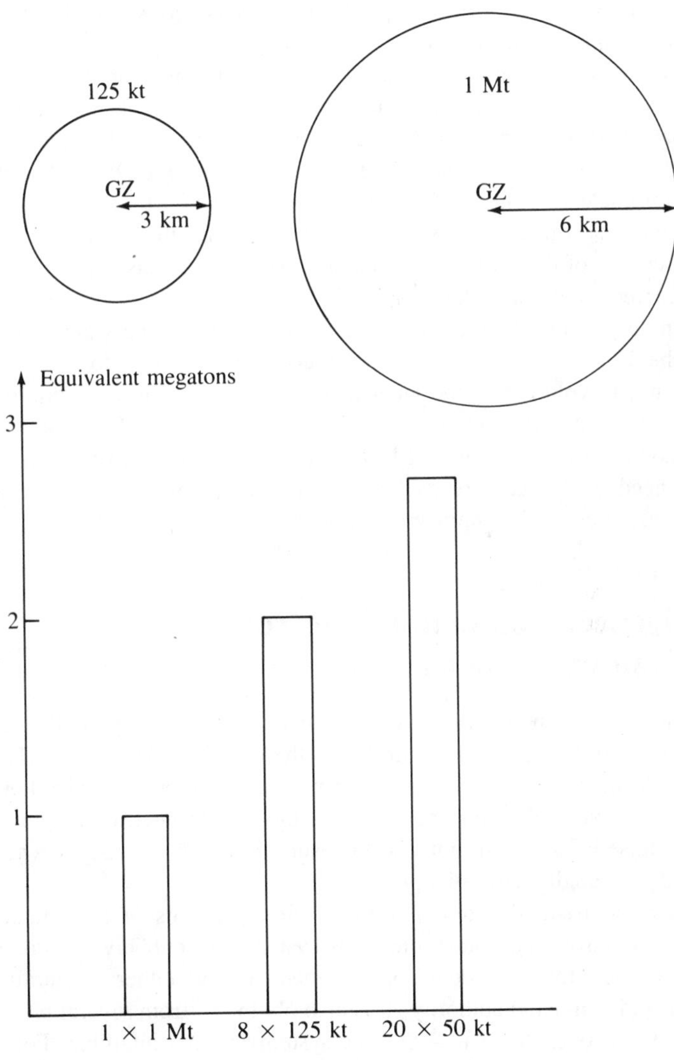

centrated in its ICBMs. The bombers could carry either gravity bombs or various aerodynamic or "cruise" missiles. The latter can be fired from a "standoff" position, i.e., without the bomber penetrating the enemy's air defenses, which enhances the operational survivability of the system. The manned bomber force may be recalled after dispatch, or retargeted en route. This flexibility in addition to the large payload possible is considered the main advantage of the strategic bomber force, while the disadvantages are its vulnerability and low speed, as compared with ICBMs.

Cruise missiles, as defined by the SALT II treaty, are "unmanned, self-propelled guided weapon delivery vehicles which sustain flight through the use of aerodynamic lift over most of their flight path." With an advanced navigation and guidance system, . . . the cruise missile may have a CEP of less than 100 m. With a nuclear warhead of moderate yield, it would be capable of destroying the hardest targets. The speed is subsonic and the flight time may be many hours. Because of this, it has been maintained that the cruise missile should not be considered as a first strike weapon.

Technological development has increased the effectiveness of nuclear weapons in the 12 years since the earlier United Nations report, to some extent by the continued evolution of the nuclear explosive but mainly by improvements in the accuracy and flexibility of delivery. To retain in 1980 the same destructive capability, particularly against hard targets, as in 1968, fewer weapons would thus be needed. As has already been pointed out, however, nuclear weapons have greatly increased in numbers since 1968.

Intelligence, Command, Control, and Communications

The nuclear-weapon States have instituted systems—reportedly of a very elaborate nature—to maintain control over their large nuclear forces. These systems would have a dual purpose: to prevent unintentional or unauthorized release of weapons and to ensure that decisions to use nuclear weapons are not based on false information, but also to ensure that such a decision, when made, is carried out rapidly and reliably.

Neither the basic structure nor the technical details of such intelligence, command, control, and communications systems are publicly known. It is obvious, however, that they could be designed to serve either a centralized or a decentralized command authority. It is also obvious—from several press reports of false alarms over the years—that the systems are not infallible. For this reason there is a growing concern that control may some day fail, under the influence of, for example, a false message or a misunderstood command, and that nuclear war is thus triggered inadvertently.

The Main Strategic Arsenals of the Super-Powers[2]

In the proposed SALT II treaty[3] between the United States and the Soviet Union, there is an exchange of data on the strategic nuclear forces of both sides. The forces in question are those with capability to threaten the super-Powers' own homelands, i.e., what is sometimes referred to as "central strategic systems." In the "Memorandum of Understanding Regarding Establishment of a Data Base" the two countries for the first time have declared their possession of the following numbers of such strategic arms as at 18 June 1979:

	United States	USSR
Launchers of ICBMs	1,054	1,398
Fixed launchers of ICBMs	1,054	1,398
Launchers of ICBMs equipped with MIRVs	550	608
Launchers of SLBMs	656	950
Launchers of SLBMs equipped with MIRVs	496	144
Heavy bombers	573	156
Heavy bombers equipped for cruise missiles capable of range in excess of 600 km.	3	0
ASBMs (air-to-surface ballistic missiles)	0	0

Of the 1,054 missile launchers in the United States ICBM force, 550 have MIRVed Minuteman-III missiles with three warheads, each of 170 kt. yield. The remaining ICBMs are all single-warhead type, 450 of which are the Minuteman II, having a yield of 1–2 Mt., and 54 Titan II, with 5–10 Mt. warheads.

The Minuteman III is the most accurate missile in the United States arsenal, with a CEP reported to be better than 300 m. With the installation of a new warhead of 350 kt. yield in 300 of the Minuteman III, as well as completed guidance improvements, the missile will have a higher probability to destroy an adversary's hardened silos, although it is stated that this probability would still be "modest."

On the Soviet side there are many classes of ICBMs deployed, . . . with up to 8 warheads of 500 kt. each, deployed on the MIRVed SS-18 mod. 2.[4] The largest deployed warhead is on the single-warhead SS-18 and has a yield of about 20 Mt. The CEP of the SS-18 is believed to be about equal to that of the Minuteman III.

For a number of years the United States has had 41 SLBM-equipped submarines, with a total of 656 missiles. About 500 of these are MIRVed Poseidon missiles with an average of 10 warheads, each with a yield of 40 kt. The remaining somewhat older missiles are of the multiple warhead type, but are not independently targetable. This means that they would separate in flight and have different impact points, which, however, cannot be pre-selected according to their strategic value. Each of these warheads has a yield of 200 kt., with a missile range of 4,000 to 5,000 km.

The new Trident submarine will first be deployed late in 1980 or early in

1981 with the Trident I (also denoted Trident C-4) MIRVed missile of more than 7,000 km. range, which will also have been substituted in the Poseidon submarines. This Trident submarine will carry 24 MIRVed missiles, be quieter and faster, and will have an expanded operating area. At the same time, it needs less operating area to remain within range of its targets.

Most Soviet deployed SLBMs are presently non-MIRVed, except for the SS-N-18 which has 3 warheads of about 200 kt. yield and a range believed to be similar to that of Trident. Soviet missile-launching submarines equipped with these missiles have a vastly expanded operating area and are less vulnerable to anti-submarine warfare.

On the United States side, the bomber force contains 300 to 350 B-52 long-range bombers. The United States bomber force is kept at a high level of ground alert, as it is vulnerable to SLBM attack, of which only a few minutes' warning would be available. The two Soviet corresponding types of long-range bombers are the Tupolev 95 and the Myasishchev, known in the West as the Bear and the Bison, respectively. There are about 150 of these aircraft.

According to the official United States Department of Defense estimates, independently targetable weapons in ICBMs, SLBMs and long-range bombers add up to over 9,000 for the United States side and about 6,000 for the Soviet Union. (The total numbers of weapons in the strategic stockpiles could be considerably larger, as is indicated in Table 1. . . .) These numbers are expected to increase in the next few years by at least 40 percent with continued MIRVing, introduction of new cruise missiles, and the deployment of the Trident submarine.

The power and number of these strategic weapons is difficult to grasp. Consider that a single Poseidon submarine with its 16 MIRVed missiles can deliver warheads to 160 separate targets; these warheads have a total explosive yield of 6.4 Mt., a larger explosive power than that of all the munitions fired in the Second World War; still, this megatonnage is of the order of one or a few thousandths of the megatonnage in either the United States or the Soviet strategic arsenal.

Regional Nuclear Forces (Nuclear Weapons of Medium or Intermediate Range)

In addition to these central strategic forces, both superpowers have many weapon systems with somewhat shorter ranges. These systems (and similar weapons belonging to other nuclear-weapon States) are sometimes referred to as "gray area" weapons or, in a European context, as "Eurostrategic" weapons. If the word "strategic" is used in its ordinary military sense, then indeed most nuclear weapons can be used for strategic purposes. If "gray area" weapons are sometimes thought of as a special category, it is mainly because they could reach not only targets in countries other than those of the superpowers

TABLE 1 Rough Estimates of Current Nuclear Arsenals[a] (Total number of warheads and total yield in Mt)

Nation	"Central Strategic" Warheads[c]	"Central Strategic" Mt[d]	Other Systems Warheads[d]	Other Systems Mt[d]	Total[b] Warheads	Total[b] Mt
United States of America	9,000–11,000	3,000–4,000	16,000–22,000	1,000–4,000	25,000–33,000	4,000– 8,000
USSR	6,000– 7,500	5,000–8,000	5,000– 8,000	2,000–3,000	11,000–15,000	7,000–11,000
United Kingdom					200– 1,000	200– 1,000
China					<300	200– 400
France					<200	<100
				Rounded grand total	37,000–50,000	11,000–20,000

[a] These estimates were made for this report by the Swedish National Defense Research Institute in co-operation with the Institute for Defense and Disarmament Studies, Brookline, Mass. They are based on available open sources. Among these are *SIPRI Yearbook 1980* as well as *The Military Balance, 1979–1980*. As is apparent from the table, there are substantial uncertainties in all the estimates. The largest single source of uncertainty is lack of knowledge regarding numbers and powers of weapons for aircraft delivery. In addition, some of these weapons are believed to have variable yields. Other uncertainties are introduced by the fact that different sources refer to different times, by differing assumptions as to the state of various systems under conversion, etc. Multiple re-entry vehicles have been counted separately, and assumptions have been made regarding possible reserves of certain weapons. It should be noted that calculations based on estimates of the amount of fissile material that could have been produced might lead to considerably higher figures for the possible number of warheads.

[b] Figures for the two superpowers are rounded to the nearest thousands; for other nations, to the nearest hundreds.

[c] Figures rounded to the nearest five hundreds.

[d] Figures rounded to the nearest thousands.

but also, by forward deployment, targets on the territories of the superpowers themselves.

There is no clear borderline between these weapons and, for instance, the SLBM forces already described. It is common practice, however, to single out medium-range (800–2,400 km.) ballistic missiles (MRBM), intermediate-range (2,400–6,400 km.) ballistic missiles (IRBM), and medium-range bomber aircraft as particularly important for non-central strategic employment.

The Soviet Union has some 700 MRBMs and IRBMs deployed both in the western USSR and east of the Urals. Among them is the new, mobile SS-20 missile with a 3-MIRV payload. It is believed that over 100 of these have been deployed so far. Also the USSR possesses about 500 medium-range bombers, e.g., of the types Tu-16 "Badger" and Tu-22M "Backfire," capable of nuclear delivery. On the United States side there are 65 FB-111A medium-range bombers and 300–400 forward based short-range, nuclear capable strike aircraft of types F-4, F-111, and others. The United States arsenal has no IRBMs.

Strategic Arsenals of Other Countries

Britain has 4 nuclear ballistic missile submarines, each with 16 Polaris A-3 missiles (3 x 200 kt., not independently targetable), with an operational radius of about 3,000 km. The Vulcan bomber fleet, formerly considered as a strategic nuclear component, is no longer listed as such in available sources. It has been reported recently that the British Government has decided to buy the American Trident C-4 submarine-launched ballistic missile, which will be equipped with British "Chevaline" warheads.

France possesses at present 64 SLBMs in 4 nuclear-powered submarines, 18 IRBMs, and 6 squadrons of some 30 Mirage-IVA medium-range bombers. A fifth SLBM submarine is scheduled to be operational before 1985. The SLBMs have about a 5,000 km. range and 1 Mt. single warheads; the IRBMs, a range of some 3,000 km. and single warheads of 150 kt. yield.

China is estimated to have deployed 50 to 70 intermediate-range ballistic missiles, 40 to 50 medium-range ballistic missiles, and two limited-range ICBMs. A flight test of a Chinese ICBM was conducted in the middle of May 1980. Also in China's strategic force are Tu-16 and Tu-4 medium-range bombers. China's stockpile of weapons, fission and fusion, probably amounts to 225–300 with fission warhead yields in the 20–40 kt. range and fusion warheads of 3–4 Mt.

Tactical Nuclear Forces

Tactical nuclear weapons are common terms for those nuclear weapons systems which, by virtue of their range and yield as well as the way they are incorporated in a military organization, have been designed or can be used for employment against military targets in a theater of war.[5] Such weapons are artillery shells; ground mobile rockets and missiles; air-launched bombs, rockets, and missiles (with aircraft operating from carriers as well as land bases); and atomic demolition munitions ("land mines"). Naval forces of this kind comprise submarine-launched cruise or ballistic missiles; torpedoes; and short-range, submarine-launched anti-submarine warfare rockets. Ground-based systems have ranges from about 15 km. (artillery) to several hundreds of km. (heavy missiles). Yield may vary from less than 0.1 to more than 100 kt.

As for short-range (under 800 km.) ballistic missiles (SRBM), the United States has deployed in Europe some 108 Pershing in the high-kiloton range and some 36 Lance in the low-kiloton range, while the Soviet Union has some 1,300 "Frog" 7, SS-1b, SS-1c, SS-12, and SS-21, some of which are believed to have megaton-yield warheads. France has a tactical nuclear force equipped with 32 short-range (about 120 km.) ballistic missiles called Pluton. These are believed to have about 20 kt. warheads.

Some of the non-nuclear-weapon States which are members of NATO, as well as Warsaw Pact States other than the Soviet Union, have in their armed forces short-range ballistic missiles which are capable of nuclear delivery. These are some 200 Pershing, Honest John, and Lance missiles on the NATO side and about 330 SS-1b, SS-1c, and "Frog" 7 missiles on the Warsaw Pact side. However, all nuclear warheads for these missiles are in United States and Soviet custody, respectively.

Aside from the strategic submarine-launched missiles already mentioned, the Soviet Union has about 80 older short-range ballistic missiles (SS-N-4 and SS-N-5, with warheads of megaton yield) based on submarines. There are also one or a few hundred sea-launched aerodynamic missiles (SS-N-3, with a kiloton-yield warhead) deployed on cruisers and submarines. No other State is known to possess this type of system.

The United States has some 1,000 aerodynamic air-launched missiles of short range with warheads of 100 to 200 kiloton yield. These are denoted SRAMs (short-range attack missiles). On the Soviet side, approximately the same number of AS-3 "Kangaroo," AS-4 "Kitchen," and AS-6 "Kingfish" missiles of kiloton yield have long been available, probably for use against surface ships.

In addition to the medium-range bombers already enumerated, there are many types of aircraft in many nations which are or could be made nuclear-capable for short-range missions. The land-based strike aircraft of the United States deployed in Europe comprise 300 to 400 nuclear-capable aircraft, where the Soviet Union has about 1,000. The United States also possesses 100 to 200 carrier-based strike aircraft capable of delivering nuclear weapons against targets on sea or land. It is not clear how many of the large force of F-104 and F-4 in the other NATO States or Su-7 and Su-20 on the Warsaw Pact side actually have a nuclear role.

In principle, artillery pieces of 155 mm. caliber or larger are nuclear-capable. Both the Soviet Union and the United States have in their regular army units several hundred such artillery pieces, as they are primarily intended to fire conventional shells. Nuclear artillery shells for 155 mm. and 203 mm. pieces have been developed in the United States and are also deployed in Europe. They are generally believed to have yields from a fraction of a kiloton up to a few kilotons. Some sources state without qualification that the Soviet Union also has these nuclear munitions.

Atomic demolition munitions (ADMs) are designed to function somewhat like conventional land mines, creating craters and other obstacles to an advancing enemy. Only the United States is known to have manufactured this type of nuclear explosive, but any nuclear charge of suitable size could probably be quickly adapted for the purpose. No emplacement is known to have taken place.

Very few data are available on some naval nuclear-weapon systems, which have for many years been said to exist at least in the United States arsenal. Most frequently mentioned are the American ASROC and SUBROC ASW rocket-torpedoes with an alleged yield of 1 kt.[6] Reportedly, there are also nuclear depth-charges with 5 to 10 kt. yield. Whether or not nuclear sea mines are at present available anywhere is unclear.

Europe is a zone of very high concentration of tactical nuclear weapons. An often quoted figure is that the United States disposes of about 7,000 such weapons in Europe, in many depots in the territories of several countries. The Soviet Union is believed to possess more than 3,000 weapons of this kind for use in Europe.

Techniques and Costs of Acquiring Nuclear Weapons

The previous United Nations study on nuclear weapons contained an analysis of the cost of the acquisition and further development of these weapons. Since then some further studies which provide data about the availability of nuclear technology have become available, notably from the International Conference on Nuclear Power and Its Fuel Cycle held at Salzburg, Austria, under the auspices of the International Atomic Energy Agency (1977) and the International Fuel Cycle Evaluation (INFCE, 1980). These studies have been utilized to update the previous analyses.[7]

To be a nuclear-weapon State, a nation must necessarily possess an explosive device based on the nuclear fission of either uranium or plutonium. Uranium, as found in nature, is a mixture of several isotopes which differ by only about 1 percent in weight, but greatly in nuclear properties. The fissile isotope uranium-235 forms only 0.7 percent of natural uranium, the rest being uranium-238. Uranium-238 is fissile only by very high-energy neutrons and cannot be used to make a fission weapon. The uranium-235 fraction must therefore be increased in an isotope enrichment facility to in principle more than 5 percent, in practice say 20 percent or more. For technical and economical reasons, the "weapon-grade" uranium used in nuclear weapons will contain 90–95 percent uranium-235. This enrichment process is very expensive and requires advanced technology. As an example of the cost, the three United States separation plants (based on gaseous diffusion) required an investment cost of about $4,500 million (in 1980 dollars). Annual maintenance and operation costs are estimated at $500 to 600 million. These United States plants could produce about 100,000 kg. of 90 percent uranium-235 annually, enough for some 4,000 fission weapons. It should be noted that these plants also enrich uranium for civil purposes. Enrichment plants of comparable size exist in the Soviet Union and smaller plants have been built in France, the United Kingdom, and China. A large plant is presently under construction in France with the participation of Belgium, Italy, and Spain for the production of low-enriched uranium for peaceful use in power-producing reactors.

Uranium-235 can also be enriched by aerodynamic processes, most importantly by centrifugation. The production of a few weapons per year would require a centrifuge enrichment plant with an investment cost of about $50 million. The construction time could be estimated as about 5 to 7 years, for a State with no previous experience with this technology. A larger plant, giving material sufficient for 200 weapons annually, would require an investment of about $500 million and 6 or 7 years' construction time for an industrialized nation. Operation and maintenance costs as a percentage of capital costs are in the 25 to 30 percent range. Centrifuge enrichment plants are known to exist or to be under construction in the United States, the Soviet Union, the United Kingdom, Japan, and the Netherlands. The plant in the Netherlands is a joint project between several European countries, including the United Kingdom and the Federal Republic of Germany. A pilot plant based on a different aerodynamic concept, the vortex tube, exists in South Africa. Among non-aerodynamic methods, laser enrichment is attracting increasing interest.

Plutonium-239 is normally produced in a nuclear reactor. A production line for plutonium requires the capability to refine uranium, the fabrication of reactor fuel, a nuclear reactor, and a chemical plant for plutonium extraction from the spent fuel elements (reprocessing).

It is easier to construct and operate a dedicated plutonium production reactor than an electrical power producing reactor. Investment costs for the simplest type of graphite moderated reactor giving enough plutonium-239 for one or two weapons annually (10 kg. plutonium) are estimated to be in the range of $13 to $26 million (1976 dollars). The capital cost of a reprocessing plant to extract plutonium from the irradiated fuel would amount to an additional $25 million (1976 dollars). Personnel requirements for construction and operation are modest and plutonium could be produced 4 years after the start of the construction. In order to obtain plutonium for 10 to 20 weapons per year with a safe and reliable reactor, investment costs would range from $250 to $500 million and require some 50 to 75 engineers and 150 to 200 skilled technicians. The time span until the first output of plutonium would be 5 to 7 years.

According to some estimates, the total amount worldwide of weapon-grade uranium produced since the Second World War ranges between 1,000 and 2,000 tons. Similarly, the total quantity of weapon-grade plutonium produced worldwide amounts to 100–200 tons.

A problem of growing concern has been the possibility of using plutonium produced in ordinary nuclear-power reactors as the explosive material in atomic bombs. The core of the matter is the presence of other plutonium isotopes, particularly plutonium-240, which increase in abundance with the time of exposure in the reactor. While it is clear that so-called reactor-grade plutonium, i.e., with a concentration of plutonium-240 higher than, say, 10 percent, might be used to produce a nuclear explosive, it is also clear that such an explosive is more difficult to design and fabricate, and will generally have a very low yield which cannot be predicted with the accuracy possible if weapon-grade plutonium had been used. It would thus be considered less suitable to use reactor-grade plutonium in military nuclear weapons, while a device based on such plutonium could still be very destructive.

It should be pointed out in this connection that it might be possible to manipulate the operation of some power reactors to produce weapon-grade plutonium, even if a country contemplating the manufacture of nuclear weapons might prefer, for reasons of cost and operational simplicity, to install separate reactors for production of weapon-grade plutonium. It should also be pointed out that some research reactors do produce small but significant quantities of weapon-grade plutonium, and that some others are fueled with weapon-grade uranium. Finally, it should be noted that it is not possible to make a weapon out of the uranium content of commercial light-water reactor fuel, as this contains only 3 percent of the isotope uranium-235 and thus can never attain a fast critical mass.

Uranium-233, which can be produced by irradiating thorium with neutrons, is a third fissile isotope theoretically suitable for fission weapons. No weapons are known to have been constructed from uranium-233, however, partly due to gamma radiation hazards of material containing uranium-233.

For the production of nuclear weapons there are further expenses of warhead-assembly and weapon-testing. The previous United Nations study estimated that a plutonium-weapon program that produced ten 20 kt. devices over ten years would cost around $200 million or $20 million per warhead. A program that produced 100 such warheads would cost $375 million or about $3.8 million per warhead.

The costs connected with an advanced delivery system for the weapon are typically in the range of many thousands of millions of dollars. There is a need for ensuring the reliability of the delivery vehicles and their protection against attack, which can add substantially to the cost. On the other hand, simpler and cheaper solutions might be considered by a State contemplating the buildup of a small, perhaps secret, nuclear-weapon capability. Because of the evolution of technology, including nuclear power, electronics, chemical engineering, and the like, the real cost of developing nuclear weapons is now less than it was in 1945.

Notes

[1] *Nuclear Proliferation Factbook,* prepared by the Congressional Research Service, Library of Congress, United States Government Printing Office, 23 September 1977, p. 382.

[2] Figures pertaining to numbers and characteristics of weapons quoted in this chapter are based on data given in *SIPRI Yearbook 1980* or *The Military Balance* (1979–1980), International Institute for Strategic Studies, London, unless otherwise stated.

[3] As at 12 July 1980 this treaty had not been ratified.

[4] Note that this chapter uses primarily the Western designators for both United States and Soviet missiles because they have long been familiar under those titles and because Soviet designators are generally not published. The correspondence between Soviet and NATO designators for Soviet missiles specified in the SALT II treaty is as follows: RS—16 = SS—77; RS—18 = SS—19; RS—20 = SS—18; RSM—50 = SS—N—18.

[5] Whereas "battlefield" usually refers only to the zone of ground combat, "theater" encompasses rear areas containing for instance air bases, reserve forces, and supply depots. In some cases, a corresponding distinction is made between "tactical" and "theater" weapons. This distinction is now upheld in this report.

[6] Figures quoted from "Tactical Nuclear Weapons: European Perspectives," edited by SIPRI (London: Taylor and Francis, 1978).

[7] Some other works in the abundant literature on issues related to nuclear proliferation have also been used in preparing this section. Of particular importance is the report entitled "Nuclear Proliferation and Safeguards" by the Congress of the United States (Office of Technology Assessment, 1977).

FIGURE 2 The US and Soviet Strategic Nuclear Weapon Capability

The nuclear balance is not delicate. There is no military need for parity. There is no rational military use which could be made of some margin of superiority.

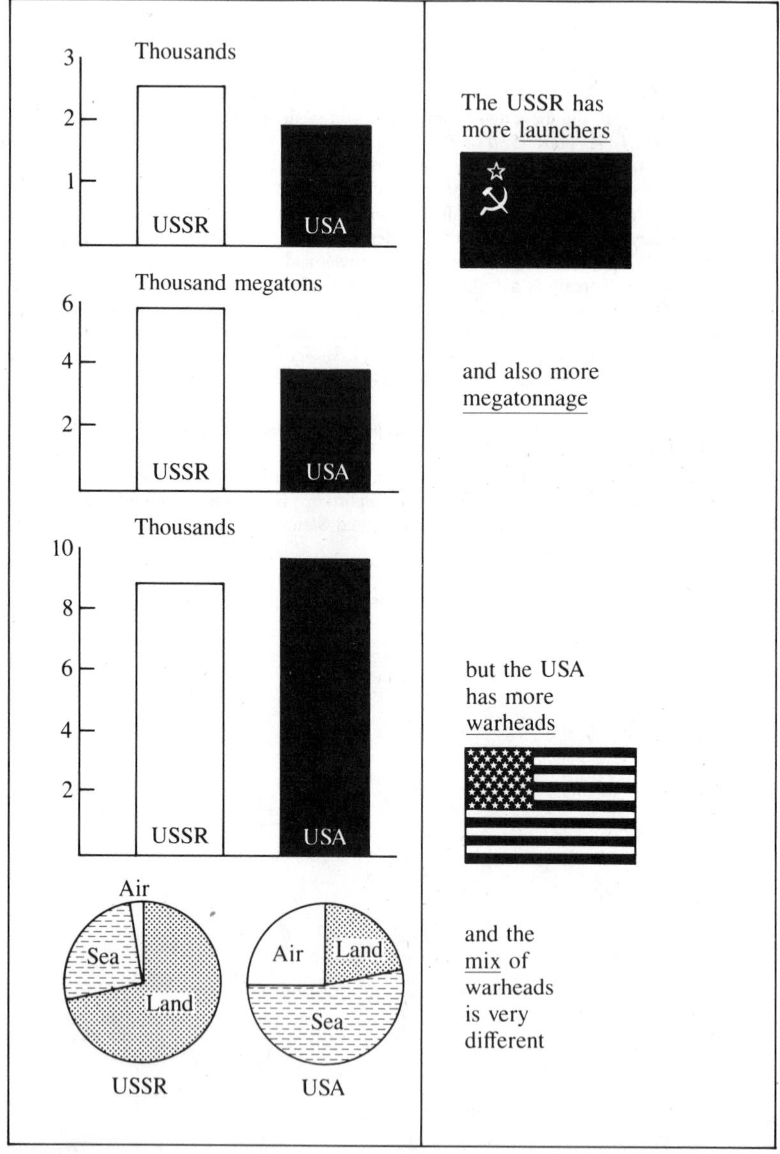

Source: From Stockholm International Peace Research Institute, *The Arms Race and Arms Control 1984: The Shorter SIPRI Yearbook.* Reprinted by permission of the publisher, Taylor and Francis, Ltd.

FIGURE 3 World Military Expenditure

The massive diversion of resources for military consumption is a growing problem for most countries. In the longer term it can be expected that current procurement policies and cost trends will result in a redistribution of resources in favor of the military sector.

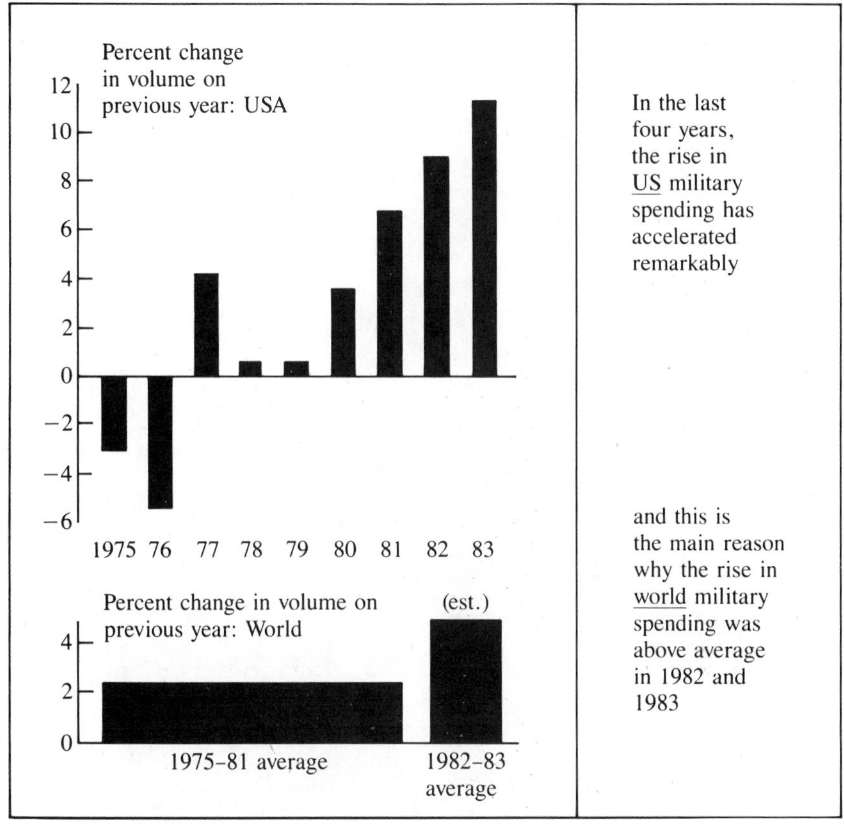

Source: See Figure 2.

PART 2

How Did We Get Here?

Origins of the Arms Race

Early History: Manhattan Project to A-Bomb

Progress and Policy Since Hiroshima

Early History: Manhattan Project to A-Bomb

ALBERT EINSTEIN

Letter to President Roosevelt, August 2, 1939

Albert Einstein (1879–1955). Aware of German research on nuclear fission, an international group of scientists convinced Albert Einstein—during World War II the most eminent physicist in the world—to write to President Franklin D. Roosevelt. The Einstein letter persuaded Roosevelt to initiate the Manhattan Project—the intensive American effort to develop the atomic bomb. Einstein, a pacifist, became active after the war in efforts to stop production of nuclear weapons.

Albert Einstein
Old Grove Rd.
Nassau Point
Peconic, Long Island
August 2nd, 1939

F. D. Roosevelt
President of the United States
White House
Washington, D.C.

Sir:

Some recent work by E. Fermi and L. Szilard, which has been communicated to me in manuscript, leads me to expect that the element uranium may be turned into a new and important source of energy in the immediate future.

Reprinted in Spencer R. Weart and Gertrude Weiss Szilard, *Leo Szilard: His Version of the Facts* (Cambridge, Mass.: MIT Press, 1978), pp. 94–95.

Certain aspects of the situation which has arisen seem to call for watchfulness and, if necessary, quick action on the part of the Administration. I believe therefore that it is my duty to bring to your attention the following facts and recommendations:

In the course of the last four months it has been made probable—through the work of Joliot in France as well as Fermi and Szilard in America—that it may become possible to set up a nuclear chain reaction in a large mass of uranium by which vast amounts of power and large quantities of new radium-like elements would be generated. Now it appears almost certain that this could be achieved in the immediate future.

This new phenomenon would also lead to the construction of bombs, and it is conceivable—though much less certain—that extremely powerful bombs of a new type may thus be constructed. A single bomb of this type, carried by boat and exploded in a port, might very well destroy the whole port together with some of the surrounding territory. However, such bombs might very well prove to be too heavy for transportation by air.

The United States has only very poor ores of uranium in moderate quantities. There is some good ore in Canada and the former Czechoslovakia, while the most important source of uranium is the Belgian Congo.

In view of this situation you may think it desirable to have some permanent contact maintained between the Administration and the group of physicists working on chain reactions in America. One possible way of achieving this might be for you to entrust with this task a person who has your confidence and who could perhaps serve in an inofficial capacity. His task might comprise the following:

a) to approach Government Departments, keep them informed of the further development, and put forward recommendations for Government action, giving particular attention to the problem of securing a supply of uranium ore for the United States,

b) to speed up the experimental work, which is at present being carried on within the limits of the budgets of University laboratories, by providing funds, if such funds be required, through his contacts with private persons who are willing to make contributions for this cause, and perhaps also by obtaining the co-operation of industrial laboratories which have the necessary equipment.

I understand that Germany has actually stopped the sale of uranium from the Czechoslovakian mines which she has taken over. That she should have taken such early action might perhaps be understood on the ground that the son of the German Under-Secretary of State, von Weizsäcker, is attached to the Kaiser-Wilhelm-Institut in Berlin where some of the American work on uranium is now being repeated.

Yours very truly, A. Einstein

NIELS BOHR

Memorandum to President Roosevelt, July 1944

Niels Bohr (1885—1962) was an eminent Danish physicist deeply concerned about the risks of an arms race. This memorandum to President Franklin D. Roosevelt warns of the dangers of a nuclear arms race a full year before the weapons were built and used. A month after writing the memorandum he met with Roosevelt—one of many attempts by him and other scientists to establish international control over nuclear weapons. Bohr received a Nobel Prize in physics in 1922.

It certainly surpasses the imagination of anyone to survey the consequences of the project in years to come, where, in the long run, the enormous energy sources which will be available may be expected to revolutionize industry and transport. The fact of immediate preponderance is, however, that a weapon of an unparalleled power is being created which will completely change all future conditions of warfare.

Quite apart from the question of how soon the weapon will be ready for use and what role it may play in the present war, this situation raises a number of problems which call for most urgent attention. Unless, indeed, some agreement about the control of the use of the new active materials can be obtained in due time, any temporary advantage, however great, may be outweighed by a perpetual menace to human security.

Ever since the possibilities of releasing atomic energy on a vast scale came in sight, much thought has naturally been given to the question of control, but the further the exploration of the scientific problems concerned is proceeding, the clearer it becomes that no kind of customary measures will suffice for this purpose, and that the terrifying prospect of a future competition between nations about a weapon of such formidable character can only be avoided through a universal agreement in true confidence.

In this connection it is particularly significant that the enterprise, immense as it is, has still proved far smaller than might have been anticipated, and that the progress of the work has continually revealed new possibilities for facilitating the production of the active materials and of intensifying their efforts.

The prevention of a competition prepared in secrecy will therefore demand

---

Niels Bohr, "Memorandum to President Roosevelt, July 1944." Reprinted in Robert Jungk, *Brighter Than a Thousand Suns* (New York: Harcourt, Brace, 1958), pp. 344–347.

such concessions regarding exchange of information and openness about industrial efforts, including military preparations, as would hardly be conceivable unless all partners were assured of a compensating guarantee of common security against dangers of unprecedented acuteness.

The establishment of effective control measures will of course involve intricate technical and administrative problems, but the main point of the argument is that the accomplishment of the project would not only seem to necessitate but should also, due to the urgency of mutual confidence, facilitate a new approach to the problems of international relationship.

The present moment where almost all nations are entangled in a deadly struggle for freedom and humanity might, at first sight, seem most unsuited for any committing arrangement concerning the project. Not only have the aggressive powers still great military strength, although their original plans of world domination have been frustrated and it seems certain that they must ultimately surrender, but even when this happens, the nations united against aggression may face grave causes of disagreement due to conflicting attitudes toward social and economic problems.

A closer consideration, however, would indicate that the potentialities of the project as a means of inspiring confidence under these very circumstances acquire real importance. Moreover, the present situation affords unique possibilities which might be forfeited by a postponement awaiting the further development of the war situation and the final completion of the new weapon. . . .

In view of these eventualities the present situation appears to offer a most favorable opportunity for an early initiative from the side which by good fortune has achieved a lead in the efforts of mastering mighty forces of nature hitherto beyond human reach.

Without impeding the immediate military objectives, an initiative, aiming at forestalling a fateful competition, should serve to uproot any cause of distrust between the powers on whose harmonious collaboration the fate of coming generations will depend.

Indeed, it would appear that only when the question is raised among the united nations as to what concessions the various powers are prepared to make as their contribution to an adequate control arrangement, will it be possible for any one of the partners to assure himself of the sincerity of the intentions of the others.

Of course, the responsible statesmen alone can have insight as to the actual political possibilities. It would, however, seem most fortunate that the expectations for a future harmonious international co-operation, which have found unanimous expressions from all sides within the united nations, so remarkably correspond to the unique opportunities which, unknown to the public, have been created by the advancement of science.

Many reasons, indeed, would seem to justify the conviction that an approach with the object of establishing common security from ominous menaces, without excluding any nation from participating in the promising industrial development which the accomplishment of the project entails, will be welcomed, and be met with loyal co-operation in the enforcement of the necessary far-reaching control measures.

It is in such respects that helpful support may perhaps be afforded by the world-wide scientific collaboration which for years has embodied such bright promises for common human striving. Personal connections between scientists of different nations might even offer means of establishing preliminary and unofficial contact.

It need hardly be added that any such remark or suggestion implies no underrating of the difficulty and delicacy of the steps to be taken by the statesmen in order to obtain an arrangement satisfactory to all concerned, but aims only at pointing to some aspects of the situation which might facilitate endeavors to turn the project to the lasting benefit of the common cause.

JAMES FRANCK et al.

The Franck Report: A Report to the Secretary of War, June 11, 1945

James Franck (1882–1964). Many scientists working within the Manhattan Project were concerned about how the weapons they were designing might actually be used, and they worried about the prospects of a runaway competition in the production of nuclear arms. Other scientists, however, believed that it was not the proper role of the scientist to offer advice or to make moral assessments about political policy. Thus, the action of the Franck group in writing to Secretary of War Henry L. Stimson was surrounded by great controversy.

I. Preamble

The only reason to treat nuclear power differently from all other developments in the field of physics is the possibility of its use as a means of political pressure in peace and sudden destruction in war. All present plans for the organization of research, scientific and industrial development, and publication in the field of nucleonics are conditioned by the political and military climate in which one expects those plans to be carried out. Therefore, in making suggestions for the postwar organization of nucleonics, a discussion of political prob-

---

James Franck et al., "The Franck Report: A Report to the Secretary of War, June 11, 1945." Reprinted in Robert Jungk, *Brighter Than a Thousand Suns* (New York: Harcourt, Brace, 1958), pp. 348–360.

lems cannot be avoided. The scientists on this Project do not presume to speak authoritatively on problems of national and international policy. However, we found ourselves, by the force of events, during the last five years, in the position of a small group of citizens cognizant of a grave danger for the safety of this country as well as for the future of all the other nations, of which the rest of mankind is unaware. We therefore feel it is our duty to urge that the political problems, arising from the mastering of nuclear power, be recognized in all their gravity, and that appropriate steps be taken for their study and the preparation of necessary decisions. We hope that the creation of the Committee by the Secretary of War to deal with all aspects of nucleonics, indicates that these implications have been recognized by the government. We believe that our acquaintance with the scientific elements of the situation and prolonged preoccupation with its world-wide political implications, imposes on us the obligation to offer to the Committee some suggestions as to the possible solution of these grave problems.

Scientists have often before been accused of providing new weapons for the mutual destruction of nations, instead of improving their well-being. It is undoubtedly true that the discovery of flying, for example, has so far brought much more misery than enjoyment and profit to humanity. However, in the past, scientists could disclaim direct responsibility for the use to which mankind had put their disinterested discoveries. We feel compelled to take a more active stand now because the success which we have achieved in the development of nuclear power is fraught with infinitely greater dangers than were all the inventions of the past. All of us, familiar with the present state of nucleonics, live with the vision before our eyes of sudden destruction visited on our own country, of a Pearl Harbor disaster repeated in thousand-fold magnification in every one of our major cities.

In the past, science has often been able to provide also new methods of protection against new weapons of aggression it made possible, but it cannot promise such efficient protection against the destructive use of nuclear power. This protection can come only from the political organization of the world. Among all the arguments calling for an efficient international organization for peace, the existence of nuclear weapons is the most compelling one. In the absence of an international authority which would make all resort to force in international conflicts impossible, nations could still be diverted from a path which must lead to total mutual destruction, by a specific international agreement barring a nuclear armaments race.

II. Prospects of Armaments Race

It could be suggested that the danger of destruction by nuclear weapons can be avoided—at least as far as this country is concerned—either by keeping our discoveries secret for an indefinite time, or else by developing our nuclear armaments at such a pace that no other nations would think of attacking us from fear of overwhelming retaliation.

The answer to the first suggestion is that although we undoubtedly are at present ahead of the rest of the world in this field, the fundamental facts of nuclear power are a subject of common knowledge. British scientists know as much as we do about the basic wartime progress of nucleonics—if not of the specific processes used in our engineering developments—and the role which French nuclear physicists have played in the pre-war development of this field, plus their occasional contact with our Projects, will enable them to catch up rapidly, at least as far as basic scientific discoveries are concerned. German scientists, in whose discoveries the whole development of this field originated, apparently did not develop it during the war to the same extent to which this has been done in America: but to the last day of the European war, we were living in constant apprehension as to their possible achievements. The certainty that German scientists were working on this weapon and that their government would certainly have no scruples against using it when available was the main motivation of the initiative which American scientists took in urging the development of nuclear power for military purposes on a large scale in this country. In Russia, too, the basic facts and implications of nuclear power were well understood in 1940, and the experience of Russian scientists in nuclear research is entirely sufficient to enable them to retrace our steps within a few years, even if we should make every attempt to conceal them. Even if we can retain our leadership in basic knowledge of nucleonics for a certain time by maintaining secrecy as to all results achieved on this and associated Projects, it would be foolish to hope that this can protect us for more than a few years.

It may be asked whether we cannot prevent the development of military nucleonics in other countries by a monopoly on the raw materials of nuclear power. The answer is that even though the largest now known deposits of uranium ores are under the control of powers which belong to the "western" group (Canada, Belgium, and British India), the old deposits in Czechoslovakia are outside this sphere. Russia is known to be mining radium on its own territory; and even if we do not know the size of the deposits discovered so far in the USSR, the probability that no large reserves of uranium will be found in a country which covers one-fifth of the land area of the earth (and whose sphere of influence takes in additional territory) is too small to serve as a basis for security. Thus, we cannot hope to avoid a nuclear armament race either by keeping secret from the competing nations the basic scientific facts of nuclear power or by cornering the raw materials required for such a race.

We now consider the second of the two suggestions made at the beginning of this section, and ask whether we could not feel ourselves safe in a race of nuclear armaments by virtue of our greater industrial potential, including greater diffusion of scientific and technical knowledge, greater volume and efficiency of our skilled labor crops, and greater experience of our management—all the factors whose importance has been so strikingly demonstrated in the conversion of this country into an arsenal of the Allied Nations in the present war. The answer is that all that these advantages can give us is the accumulation of a larger number of bigger and better atomic bombs.

However, such a quantitative advantage in reserves of bottled destructive power will not make us safe from sudden attack. Just because a potential enemy will be afraid of being "outnumbered and outgunned," the temptation for him may be overwhelming to attempt a sudden unprovoked blow—particularly if he should suspect us of harboring aggressive intentions against his security of his sphere of influence. In no other type of warfare does the advantage lie so heavily with the aggressor. He can place his "infernal machines" in advance in all our major cities and explode them simultaneously, thus destroying a major part of our industry and a large part of our population, aggregated in densely populated mteropolitan districts. Our possibilities of retailiation—even if retaliation should be considered adequate compensation for the loss of millions of lives and destruction of our largest cities—will be greatly handicapped because we must rely on aerial transportation of the bombs, and also because we may have to deal with an enemy whose industry and population are dispersed over a large territory.

In fact, if the race for nuclear armaments is allowed to develop, the only apparent way in which our country can be protected from the paralyzing effects of a sudden attack is by dispersal of those industries which are essential for our war effort and dispersal of the populations of our major metropolitan cities. As long as nuclear bombs remain scarce (i.e., as long as uranium remains the only basic material for their fabrication), efficient dispersal of our industry and the scattering of our metropolitan population will considerably decrease the temptation to attack us by nuclear weapons.

At present, it may be that atomic bombs can be detonated with an effect equal to that of 20,000 tons of TNT. One of these bombs could then destroy something like 3 square miles of an urban area. Atomic bombs containing a larger quantity of active material but still weighing less than one ton may be expected to be available within ten years which could destroy over ten square miles of a city. A nation able to assign 10 tons of atomic explosives for a sneak attack on this country, can then hope to achieve the destruction of all industry and most of the population in an area from 500 square miles upwards. If no choice of targets, with a total area of five hundred square miles of American territory, contains a large enough fraction of the nation's industry and population to make their destruction a crippling blow to the nation's war potential and its ability to defend itself, then the attack will not pay, and may not be undertaken. At present, one could easily select in this country a hundred areas of five square miles each whose simultaneous destruction would be a staggering blow to the nation. Since the area of the United States is about three million square miles, it should be possible to scatter its industrial and human resources in such a way as to leave no 500 square miles important enough to serve as a target for nuclear attack.

We are fully aware of the staggering difficulties involved in such a radical change in the social and economic structure of our nation. We felt, however, that the dilemma had to be stated, to show what kind of alternative methods of protection will have to be considered if no successful international agreement is reached. It must be pointed out that in this field we are in a less favorable position than nations which are either now more diffusely populated and whose industries are more scattered, or whose governments have unlimited power over the movement of population and the location of industrial plants.

If no efficient international agreement is achieved, the race for nuclear armaments will be on in earnest not later than the morning after our first demonstration of the existence of nuclear weapons. After this, it might take other nations three or four years to overcome our present head start, and eight or ten years to draw even with us if we continue to do intensive work in this field. This might be all the time we would have to bring about the relocation of our population and industry. Obviously, no time should be lost in inaugurating a study of this problem by experts.

III. Prospects of Agreement

The consequences of nuclear warfare, and the type of measures which would have to be taken to protect a country from total destruction by nuclear bombing, must be as abhorrent to other nations as to the United States. England, France, and the smaller nations of the European continent, with their congeries of people and industries would be in a particularly desperate situation in the face of such a threat. Russia and China are the only great nations at present which could survive a nuclear attack. However, even though these countries may value human life less than the peoples of Western Europe and America, and even though Russia, in particular, has an immense space over which its vital industries could be dispersed and a government which can order this dispersion the day it is convinced that such a measure is necessary—there is no doubt that Russia, too, will shudder at the possibility of a sudden disintegration of Moscow and Leningrad, almost miraculously preserved in the present war, and of its new industrial cities in the Urals and Siberia. Therefore, only lack of mutual trust, and not lack of desire for agreement, can stand in the path of an efficient agreement for the prevention of nuclear warfare. The achievement of such an agreement will thus essentially depend on the integrity of intentions and readiness to sacrifice the necessary fraction of one's own sovereignty, by all the parties to the agreement.

One possible way to introduce nuclear weapons to the world—which may particularly appeal to those who consider nuclear bombs primarily as a secret weapon developed to help win the present war—is to use them without warning on appropriately selected objects in Japan.

Although important tactical results undoubtedly can be achieved by a sudden introduction of nuclear weapons, we nevertheless think that the question of the use of the very first available atomic bombs in the Japanese war should be weighed very carefully, not only by military authorities, but by the highest political leadership of this country.

Russia, and even allied countries which bear less mistrust of our ways and intentions, as well as neutral countries may be deeply shocked by this step. It may be very difficult to persuade the world that a nation which was capable of secretly preparing and suddenly releasing a new weapon, as indiscriminate as the rocket bomb and a thousand times more destructive, is to be trusted in its proclaimed desire of having such weapons abolished by international agreement. We have large accumulations of poison gas, but do not use them, and recent polls have shown that public opinion in this country would disapprove of such a use even if it would accelerate the winning of the Far Eastern war. It is true that some irrational element in mass psychology makes gas poisoning more revolting than blasting by explosives, even though gas warfare is in no way more "inhuman" than the war of bombs and bullets. Nevertheless, it is not at all certain that American public opinion, if it could be enlightened as to the effect of atomic explosives, would approve of our own country being the first to introduce such an indiscriminate method of wholesale destruction of civilian life.

Thus, from the "optimistic" point of view—looking forward to an international agreement on the prevention of nuclear warfare—the military advantages and the saving of American lives achieved by the sudden use of atomic bombs against Japan may be outweighed by the ensuing loss of confidence and by a wave of horror and repulsion sweeping over the rest of the world and perhaps even dividing public opinion at home.

From this point of view, a demonstration of the new weapon might best be made, before the eyes of representatives of all the United Nations, on the desert or a barren island. The best possible atmosphere for the achievement of an international agreement could be achieved if America could say to the world, "You see what sort of a weapon we had but did not use. We are ready to renounce its use in the future if other nations join us in this renunciation and agree to the establishment of an efficient control."

After such a demonstration the weapon might perhaps be used against Japan if the sanction of the United Nations (and if public opinion at home) were obtained, perhaps after a preliminary ultimatum to Japan to surrender or at least to evacuate certain regions as an alternative to their total destruction. This may sound fantastic, but in nuclear weapons we have something entirely new in order of magnitude of destructive power, and if we want to capitalize fully on the advantage their possession gives us, we must use new and imaginative methods.

It must be stressed that if one takes the pessimistic point of view and discounts the possibility of an effective international control over nuclear weapons at the present time, then the advisability of an early use of nuclear bombs against Japan becomes even more doubtful—quite independently of any humanitarian considerations. If an international agreement is not concluded immediately after the first demonstration, this will mean a flying start towards an unlimited armaments race. If this race is inevitable, we have every reason to delay its beginning as long as possible in order to increase our head start still further.

The benefit to the nation, and the saving of American lives in the future, achieved by renouncing an early demonstration of nuclear bombs and letting the other nations come into the race only reluctantly, on the basis of guesswork and without definite knowledge that the "thing does work," may far outweigh the advantages to be gained by the immediate use of the first and comparatively inefficient bombs in the war against Japan. On the other hand, it may be argued that without an early demonstration it may prove difficult to obtain adequate support for further intensive development of nucleonics in this country and that thus the time gained by the postponement of an open armaments pace will not be properly used. Furthermore one may suggest that other nations are now, or will soon be, not entirely unaware of our present achievements, and that consequently the postponement of a demonstration may serve no useful purpose as far as the avoidance of an armaments race is concerned, and may only create additional mistrust, thus worsening rather than improving the chances of an ultimate accord on the international control of nuclear explosives.

Thus, if the prospects of an agreement will be considered poor in the immediate future, the pros and cons of an early revelation of our possession of nuclear weapons to the world—not only by their actual use against Japan but also by a prearranged demonstration—must be carefully weighed by the supreme political and military leadership of the country, and the decisions should not be left to the considerations of military tactics alone.

One may point out that scientists themselves have initiated the development of this "secret weapon" and it is therefore strange that they should be reluctant to try it out on the enemy as soon as it is available. The answer to this question was given above—the compelling reason for creating this weapon with such speed was our fear that Germany had the technical skill necessary to develop such a weapon and that the German government had no moral restraints regarding its use.

Another argument which could be quoted in favor of using atomic bombs as soon as they are available is that so much taxpayers' money has been invested in these Projects that the Congress and the American public will demand a return for their money. The attitude of American public opinion, mentioned earlier, in the matter of the use of poison gas against Japan, shows that one can expect the American public to understand that it is sometimes desirable to keep a weapon in readiness for use only in extreme emergency; and as soon as the potentialities of nuclear weapons are revealed to the American people, one can be sure that they will support all attempts to make the use of such weapons impossible.

Once this is achieved, the large installations and the accumulation of explosive material at present earmarked for potential military use will become available for important peacetime developments, including power production, large engineering undertakings, and mass production of radioactive materials. In this way, the money spent on wartime development of nucleonics may become a boon for the peacetime development of national economy.

IV. Methods of International Control

We now consider the question of how an effective international control of nuclear armaments can be achieved. This is a difficult problem, but we think it soluble. It requires study by statesmen and international lawyers, and we can offer only some preliminary suggestions for such a study.

Given mutual trust and willingness on all sides to give up a certain part of their sovereign rights, by admitting international control of certain phases of national economy, the control could be exercised (alternatively or simultaneously) on two different levels.

The first and perhaps the simplest way is to ration the raw materials—primarily, the uranium ores. Production of nuclear explosives begins with the processing of large quantities of uranium in large isotope separation plants or huge production piles. The amounts of ore taken out of the ground at different locations could be controlled by resident agents of the international Control Board, and each nation could be allotted only an amount which would make large-scale separation of fissionable isotopes impossible.

Such a limitation would have the drawback of making impossible also the development of nuclear power for peacetime purposes. However, it need not prevent the production of radioactive elements on a scale sufficient to revolutionize the industrial, scientific, and technical use of these materials, and would thus not eliminate the main benefits which nucleonics promises to bring to mankind.

An agreement of a higher level, involving more mutual trust and understanding, would be to allow unlimited production, but keep exact bookkeeping on the fate of each pound of uranium mined. If in this way, check is kept on the conversion of uranium and thorium ore into pure fissionable materials, the question arises as to how to prevent accumulation of large quantities of such materials in the hands of one or several nations. Accumulations of this kind could be rapidly converted into atomic bombs if a nation should break away from international control. It has been suggested that a compulsory denaturation of pure fissionable isotopes may be agreed upon—by diluting them, after production, with suitable isotopes to make them useless for military purposes, while retaining their usefulness for power engines.

One thing is clear: any international agreement on prevention of nuclear armaments must be backed by actual and efficient controls. No paper agreement can be sufficient, since neither this or any other nation can stake its whole existence on trust in other nations' signatures. Every attempt to impede the international control agencies would have to be considered equivalent to denunciation of the agreement.

It hardly needs stressing that we as scientists believe that any systems of control envisaged should leave as much freedom for the peacetime development of nucleonics as is consistent with the safety of the world.

Summary

The development of nuclear power not only constitutes an important addition to the technological and military power of the United States but also creates grave political and economic problems for the future of this country.

Nuclear bombs cannot possibly remain a "secret weapon" at the exclusive disposal of this country for more than a few years. The scientific facts on which construction is bases are well known to scientists of other countries. Unless an effective international control of nuclear explosives is instituted, a race for nuclear armaments is certain to ensue following the first revelation of our possession of nuclear weapons to the world. Within ten years other countries may have nuclear bombs, each of which, weighing less than a ton, could destroy an urban area of more than ten square miles. In the war to which such an armaments race is likely to lead, the United States, with its agglomeration of population and industry in comparatively few metropolitan districts, will be at a disadvantage compared to nations whose populations and industry are scattered over large areas.

We believe that these considerations make the use of nuclear bombs for an early unannounced attack against Japan inadvisable. If the United States were to be the first to release this new means of indiscriminate destruction upon mankind, she would sacrifice public support throughout the world, precipitate the race for armaments, and prejudice the possibility of reaching an international agreement on the future control of such weapons.

Much more favorable conditions for the eventual achievement of such an agreement could be created if nuclear bombs were first revealed to the world by a demonstration in an appropriately selected uninhabited area.

In case chances for the establishment of an effective international control of nuclear weapons should have to be considered slight at the present time, then not only the use of these weapons against Japan, but even their early demonstration, may be contrary to the interests of this country. A postponement of such a demonstration will have in this case the advantage of delaying the beginning of the nuclear armaments race as long as possible.

If the government should decide in favor of an early demonstration of nuclear weapons, it will then have the possibility of taking into account the public opinion of this country and of the other nations before deciding whether these weapons should be used against Japan. In this way, other nations may assume a share of responsibility for such a fateful decision.

Composed and signed by: J. Franck, D. Hughes, L. Szilard, T. Hogness, E. Rabinowitch, G. Seaborg, and C. J. Nickson

LEO SZILARD

A Petition to the President of the United States, July 17, 1945

Leo Szilard (1898–1964). A physicist with the Chicago group of Manhattan Project scientists and one of those who signed The Franck Report, Leo Szilard has been called the first moral philosopher of the nuclear age. After the German surrender, the reason that the United States developed the bomb in the first place vanished, and Szilard objected to our changing the target. Szilard, who founded the Council for a Livable World in 1962, remained active in nuclear disarmament efforts until his death.

Discoveries of which the people of the United States are not aware may affect the welfare of this nation in the near future. The liberation of atomic power which has been achieved places atomic bombs in the hands of the Army. It places in your hands, as Commander-in-Chief, the fateful decision whether or not to sanction the use of such bombs in the present phase of the war against Japan.

We . . . have been working in the field of atomic power. Until recently we have had to fear that the United States might be attacked by atomic bombs during this war and that her only defense might lie in a counterattack by the

---

Leo Szilard, "A Petition to the President of the United States." Reprinted in *The Atomic Age: Scientists in National and World Affairs*, edited by Morton Grodzins and Eugene Rabinowitch (New York: Basic Books, 1963), pp. 28–29.

same means. Today, with the defeat of Germany, this danger is averted and we feel impelled to say what follows:

The war has to be brought speedily to a successful conclusion and attacks by atomic bombs may very well be an effective method of warfare. We feel, however, that such attacks on Japan could not be justified, at least not unless the terms which will be imposed after the war on Japan were made public in detail and Japan were given an opportunity to surrender.

If such public announcement gave assurance to the Japanese that they could look forward to a life devoted to peaceful pursuits in their homeland and if Japan still refused to surrender, our nation might then, in certain circumstances, find itself forced to resort to the use of atomic bombs. Such a step, however, ought not to be made at any time without seriously considering the moral responsibilities which are involved.

The development of atomic power will provide the nations with new means of destruction. The atomic bombs at our disposal represent only the first step in this direction and there is almost no limit to the destructive power which will become available in the course of their future development. Thus a nation which sets the precedent of using these newly liberated forces of nature for purposes of destruction may have to bear the responsibility of opening the door to an era of devastation on an unimaginable scale.

If after this war a situation is allowed to develop in the world which permits rival powers to be in uncontrolled possession of these new means of destruction, the cities of the United States as well as the cities of other nations will be in continuous danger of sudden annihilation. All the resources of the United States, moral and material, may have to be mobilized to prevent the advent of such a world situation. Its prevention is at present the solemn responsibility of the United States—singled out by virtue of her lead in the field of atomic power.

The added material strength which this lead gives to the United States brings with it the obligation of restraint, and if we were to violate this obligation our moral position would be weakened in the eyes of the world and in our own eyes. It would then be more difficult for us to live up to our responsibility of bringing the unloosened forces of destruction under control

In view of the foregoing, we, the undersigned, respectfully petition: first, that you exercise your power as Commander-in-Chief to rule that the United States shall not resort to the use of atomic bombs in this war unless the terms which will be imposed upon Japan have been made public in detail and Japan, knowing these terms, has refused to surrender; second, that in such an event the question whether or not to use atomic bombs be decided by you in the light of the considerations presented in this petition as well as all the other moral responsibilities which are involved.

HENRY L. STIMSON

Letter and Memorandum, September 11, 1945

Henry L. Stimson (1867–1950) was secretary of war—equivalent to our secretary of defense—under Franklin D. Roosevelt and Harry S. Truman. One of the policymakers who set in motion the Manhattan Project and approved the Japanese targeting plans, Stimson, after the war, had been convinced by the Franck Report, among other factors, that to risk an arms race would set us on a very dangerous course. Here he tries to prevail upon Truman to set U.S.-Soviet cooperation above the temptation to continue U.S. nuclear superiority.

The Secretary of War (Stimson) to President Truman

Washington, September 11, 1945

Dear Mr. President: In handing you today my memorandum[1] about our relations with Russia in respect to the atomic bomb, I am not unmindful of the fact that when in Potsdam I talked with you about the question whether we could be safe in sharing the atomic bomb with Russia while she was still a police state and before she put into effect provisions assuring personal rights of liberty to the individual citizen.[2]

I still recognize the difficulty and am still convinced of the importance of the ultimate importance of a change in Russian attitude toward individual liberty but I have come to the conclusion that it would not be possible to use our possession of the atomic bomb as a direct lever to produce the change. I have become convinced that any demand by us for an internal change in Russia as a condition of sharing in the atomic weapon would be so resented that it would make the objective we have in view less probable.

I believe that the change in attitude toward the individual in Russia will come slowly and gradually and I am satisfied that we should not delay our approach to Russia in the matter of the atomic bomb until that process has been completed. My reasons are set forth in the memorandum I am handing you today. Furthermore, I believe that this long process of change in Russia is more likely to be expedited by the closer relationship in the matter of the atomic bomb which I suggest and the trust and confidence that I believe would be inspired by the method of approach which I have outlined.

Faithfully yours, [Henry L. Stimson]

Henry L. Stimson, "Memorandum, September 11, 1945." Reprinted in Henry L. Stimson and McGeorge Bundy, *On Active Service in Peace and War* (New York: Octagon Books, 1948), pp. 642–646.

Memorandum by the Secretary of War (Stimson) to President Truman[3]

[Washington,] 11 September, 1945

Subject: Proposed Action for Control of Atomic Bombs

The advent of the atomic bomb has stimulated great military and probably even greater political interest throughout the civilized world. In a world atmosphere already extremely sensitive to power, the introduction of this weapon has profoundly affected political considerations in all sections of the globe.

In many quarters it has been interpreted as a substantial offset to the growth of Russian influence on the continent. We can be certain that the Soviet government has sensed this tendency and the temptation will be strong for the Soviet political and military leaders to acquire this weapon in the shortest possible time. Britain in effect already has the status of a partner with us in the development of this weapon. Accordingly, unless the Soviets are voluntarily invited into the partnership upon a basis of cooperation and trust, we are going to maintain the Anglo-Saxon bloc over against the Soviet in the possession of this weapon. Such a condition will almost certainly stimulate feverish activity on the part of the Soviet toward the development of this bomb in what will in effect be a secret armament race of a rather desperate character. There is evidence to indicate that such activity may have already commenced.

If we feel, as I assume we must, that civilization demands that some day we shall arrive at a satisfactory international arrangement respecting the control of this new force, the question then is how long we can afford to enjoy out momentary superiority in the hope of achieving our immediate peace council objectives.

Whether Russia gets control of the necessary secrets of production in a minimum of say four years or a maximum of twenty years is not nearly as important to the world and civilization as to make sure that when they do get it they are willing and cooperative partners among the peace loving nations of the world. It is true that if we approach them now, as I would propose, we may be gambling on their good faith and risk their getting into production of bombs a little sooner than they would otherwise.

To put the matter concisely, I consider the problem of our satisfactory relations with Russia as not merely connected with but as virtually dominated by the problem of the atomic bomb. Except for the problem of the control of that bomb, those relations, while vitally important, might not be immediately pressing. The establishment of relations of mutual confidence between her and us could afford to await the slow progress of time. But with the discovery of the bomb, they become immediately emergent. These relations may be perhaps irretrievably embittered by the way in which we approach the solution of the bomb with Russia. For if we fail to approach them now and merely continue to negotiate with them, having this weapon rather ostentatiously on our hip, their suspicions and their distrust of our purposes and motives will increase. It will inspire them to greater efforts in an all out effort to solve the problem. If the solution is achieved in that spirit, it is much less likely that we will ever get the kind of covenant we may desperately need in the future. This risk is, I believe, greater than the other, inasmuch as our objective must be to get the best kind of international bargain we can—one that has some chance of being kept and saving civilization not for five or for twenty years, but forever.

The chief lesson I have learned in a long life is that the only way you can make a man trustworthy is to trust him; and the surest way to make him untrustworthy is to distrust him and show your distrust.

If the atomic bomb were merely another though more devastating military weapon to be assimilated into our pattern of international relations, it would be one thing. We could then follow the old custom of secrecy and nationalistic military superiority relying on international caution to prescribe *[proscribe?]* the future use of the weapon as we did with gas. But I think the bomb instead constitutes merely a first step in a new control by man over the forces of nature too revolutionary and dangerous to fit into the old concepts. I think it really caps the climax of the race between man's growing technical power for destructiveness and his psychological power of self-control and group control—his moral power. If so, our method of approach to the Russians is a question of the most vital importance in the evolution of human progress.

Since the crux of the problem is Russia, any contemplated action leading to the control of this weapon should be primarily directed *to* Russia. It is my judgment that the Soviet would be more apt to respond sincerely to a direct and forthright approach made by the United States on this subject than would be the case if the approach were made as a part of a general international scheme, or if the approach were made after a succession of express or implied threats or near threats in our peace negotiations.

My idea of an approach to the Soviets would be a direct proposal after discussion with the British that we would be prepared in effect to enter an arrangment with the Russians, the general purpose of which would be to control and limit the use of the atomic bomb as an instrument of war and so far as possible to direct and encourage the development of atomic power for peaceful and humanitarian purposes. Such an approach might more specifically lead to the proposal that we would stop work on the further improvement in, or manufacture of, the bomb as a military weapon, provided the Russians and the British would agree to do likewise. It might also provide that we would be willing to impound what bombs we now have in the United States provided the Russians and the British would agree with us that in no event will they or we use a bomb as an instrument of war unless all three Governments agree to that use. We might also consider including in the arrangement a covenant with the U.K. and the Soviets providing for the exchange of benefits of future developments whereby atomic energy may be applied on a mutually satisfactory basis for commercial or humanitarian purposes.

I would make such an approach just as soon as our immediate political considerations make it appropriate.

I emphasize perhaps beyond all other considerations the importance of taking this action with Russia as a proposal of the United States—backed by Great Britain—but peculiarly the proposal of the United States. Action of any international group of nations, including many small nations who have not demonstrated their potential power or responsibility in this war would not, in my opinion, be taken seriously by the Soviets. The loose debates which would surround such proposal, if put before a conference of nations, would provoke but scant favor from the Soviet. As I say, I think this is the most important point in the program.

After the nations which have won this war have agreed to it, there will be ample time to introduce France and China into the covenants and finally to incorporate the agreement into the scheme of the United Nations. The use of this bomb has been accepted by the world as the result of the initiative and productive capacity of the United States, and I think this factor is a most potent lever toward having our proposals accepted by the Soviets, whereas I am most skeptical of obtaining any tangible results by way of any international debate. I urge this method as the most realistic means of accomplishing this vitally important step in the history of the world.

[Henry L. Stimson]

Notes

[1] A manuscript note indicated that this letter and the accompanying memorandum, *infra*, were handed to and discussed with the President by Mr. Stimson on September 12.

[2] See *Conference of Berlin (Potsdam)*, vol. II, p. 1155.

[3] See note 1.

DWIGHT D. EISENHOWER

Letter to Bernard Baruch, June 14, 1946

Dwight D. Eisenhower (1890–1969), commander in chief of Allied forces during World War II, was widely credited with the Allied victory over Germany. After the war, he remained the army chief of staff and was both influential and highly respected. Eisenhower was elected president in 1953 and remained in office through 1960. Bernard Baruch was the man who would present to the United Nations

---

U.S Department of State, *Foreign Relations of the United States*, vol. I (Washington, DC: U.S. Government Printing Office, 1972), pp. 854–856.

the U.S. proposal for international control of atomic energy and weapons. Eisenhower's letter reveals much about U.S. security thinking at the time, and it amounts to a statement of our "bargaining position."

The Chief of Staff of the United States Army (Eisenhower) to the United States Representative on the Atomic Energy Commission (Baruch)

SECRET Washington, 14 June 1946

Dear Mr. Baruch: The Joint Chiefs of Staff have agreed that their views on the complex questions raised in your letters of 24 May 1946 can best be dealt with individually. My personal views follow.

General. I completely agree with you that only through effective international control of atomic energy can we hope to prevent atomic war. Arriving at the methods for such control is, of course, the difficult task. The national security requires that those methods be tested and proven before the U.S. can enter any international agreement limiting the production or use of atomic bombs.

Approach to the Problem. The procedures outlined in the Acheson report° appear to offer the most practicable initial steps towards international control, provided that in the step by step accomplishment of those procedures, the U.S. does not recede from its position of advantage faster than realistic and practical reciprocal concessions are made by other powerful nations. We must not further unbalance against us world power relationships.

Inspection, the First Step. An essential primary step is to establish, and prove in operation, a system of free and complete inspection. We must satisfy ourselves of complete good faith on the part of the other great powers; their past and current policies are not altogether reassuring. In this connection, as I understand present atomic energy production techniques, no system of inspection can be expected to guarantee completely against the construction of some atomic bombs.

Preventive Measures. For the present, I am sure you agree that there must be force behind any system for *preventing* aggression. There must exist for deter-

---

°**Acheson report** Dean Acheson, undersecretary of state, and David Lilienthal, then chairman of the Tennessee Valley Authority and soon the first director of the Atomic Energy Commission, chaired a committee of scientists and political advisors appointed by President Truman. The committee's task was to develop a plan for the regulation of atomic energy. Their report, simply called "The Acheson-Lilienthal Report," was read on national radio on April 23, 1946. Excerpts are printed in the *State Department Bulletin,* April 7, 1946, 553ff. The report stressed the utter necessity for international agreements and provided the basis for the Baruch Plan. However, President Truman, Secretary of State James Byrnes, and Bernard Baruch were not entirely happy with the report, and Truman and Byrnes urged Baruch to make the changes that characterized the Baruch Plan. [Editor's note]

rent purposes, provisions for *retaliation* in the event other control and prevention devices should fail. Further, the sanctions employed against a willful aggressor by law-abiding nations can be no less effective in character than the weapons the aggressor nation is capable of using. To my mind, this means, for the present, that to *prevent* the use of atomic weapons there must exist the capability of employing atomic weapons against the recalcitrant.

Decisive Weapons in War. Biological, chemical, and other as yet unforseen weapons may prove no less effective than the atomic bomb, and even less susceptible to control. Another major war may see the use of such destructive weapons, however horrible, including the atomic bomb. The problem of controlling, and finally preventing, the use of atomic bombs (and other decisive weapons) thus becomes the problem of preventing war itself.

The Dilemma. If we enter too hurriedly into an international agreement to abolish all atomic weapons, we may find ourselves in the position of having no restraining means in the world capable of effective action if a great power violates the agreement. Such a power might, in fact, deliberately avoid the use of atomic weapons and embark on aggression with other equally decisive weapons. If, on the other hand, we enter into agreements providing for the maintenance of atomic weapons under international control, we face extraordinary difficulties. First, in providing adequate control and inspection systems and second, the possibility that the national leaders of a totalitarian state, possessing a supply of the weapons, might choose to strike first rather than to compromise. This dilemma, unless other approaches to a solution come to hand, must be solved before we should proceed to any treaty, abolishing atomic weapons.

Fundamental National Interest. The U.S. should be party to no control treaty which militates against our vital security interests. I have touched upon aspects of this scarcely debatable point. However, the fundamental interest and security of the American people is bound up with a solution to the problem you face. We can yield much, even certain points of our sovereignty, to reach this solution. Whether our people could be brought to see this necessity at present is a question. There will exist practical difficulties in keying up the American people to accept even the necessity for immediate preventive military action with conventional weapons in case an aggressor violates measures for inspection and control. Historically, in the face of threats of unmistakable import and seriousness, our practice has been to indulge in wishful thinking rather than to undertake decisive action.

To summarize:

a. The existence of the atomic bomb in our hands is a deterrent, in fact, to aggression in the world. We cannot at this time limit our capability to produce or use this weapon.

b. We must move, by steps, toward international control of atomic energy if we are to avoid an atomic war. The Acheson report is a practicable suggestion for an approach to such control. A first step is to *prove* a system of inspection.

c. Atomic weapons are only a part of the problem. There will be other equally terrible weapons of mass destruction. The whole problem must be solved concurrently with the problem of controlling atomic energy. To control atomic weapons, in which field we are preeminent, without provision for equally adequate control of other weapons of mass destruction can seriously endanger our national security.

I will continue to consider this problem and will communicate to you any ideas which might assist your difficult decisions.

Sincerely, Dwight D. Eisenhower

BERNARD BARUCH

The Baruch Plan

Bernard Baruch (1870–1965), a financier, was chosen by President Harry S. Truman to present the U.S. proposal for international control of nuclear weapons at the United Nations. Baruch was an arrogant man whom the Soviets already knew to be difficult to work with. Baruch's Soviet counterpart was Andrei Gromyko, a statesman who until recently was centrally involved in U.S.-Soviet arms negotiations.

This United Nations meeting was the first nuclear weapons negotiation meeting. It did not go well. Five days after Baruch presented the U.S. proposal, Gromyko presented the Soviet response. The Soviets said they would not talk about how the controls over nuclear materials could be created until the United States first destroyed its existing stockpile of atomic bombs. The United States refused, as Eisenhower had advised (see Dwight D. Eisenhower's "Letter to Bernard Baruch, June 14, 1946"), and the talks stalemated. In 1949 the Soviets tested their first atomic bomb, and the talks dissolved shortly thereafter.

Bernard Baruch, "The Baruch Plan." Reprinted in *The Atomic Age: Scientists in National and World Affairs,* edited by Morton Grodzins and Eugene Rabinowitch (New York: Basic Books, 1963), pp. 45–46.

Proposals for an International Atomic Development Authority

By The United States Representative to the Atomic Energy Commission[1]

My Fellow Members of the United Nations Atomic Energy Commission, and My Fellow Citizens of the World:

We are here to make a choice between the quick and the dead.

That is our business.

Behind the black portent of the new atomic age lies a hope which, seized upon with faith, can work our salvation. If we fail, then we have damned every man to be the slave of Fear. Let us not deceive ourselves: We must elect World Peace or World Destruction.

Science has torn from nature a secret so vast in its potentialities that our minds cower from the terror it creates. Yet terror is not enough to inhibit the use of the atomic bomb. The terror created by weapons has never stopped man from employing them. For each new weapon a defense has been produced, in time. But now we face a condition in which adequate defense does not exist.

Science, which gave use this dread power, shows that it *can* be made a giant help to humanity, but science does *not* show us how to prevent its baleful use. So we have been appointed to obviate that peril by finding a meeting of the minds and the hearts of our peoples. Only in the will of mankind lies the answer.

It is to express this will and make it effective that we have been assembled. We must provide the mechanism to assure that atomic energy is used for peaceful purposes and preclude its use in war. To that end, we must provide immediate, swift, and sure punishment of those who violate the agreements that are reached by the nations. Penalization is essential if peace is to be more than a feverish interlude between wars. And, too, the United Nations can prescribe individual responsibility and punishment on the principles applied at Nürnberg by the Union of Soviet Socialist Republics, the United Kingdom, France, and the United States—a formula certain to benefit the world's future.

In this crisis, we represent not only our governments but, in a larger way, we represent the peoples of the world. We must remember that the peoples do not belong to the governments but that the governments belong to the peoples. We must answer their demands; we must answer the world's longing for peace and security.

In that desire the United States shares ardently and hopefully. The search of science for the absolute weapon has reached fruition in this country. But she stands ready to proscribe and destroy this instrument—to lift its use from death to life—if the world will join in a pact to that end.

In our success lies the promise of a new life, freed from the heart-stopping fears that now beset the world. The beginning of victory for the great ideals for which millions have bled and died lies in building a workable plan. Now we approach fulfillment of the aspirations of mankind. At the end of the road lies the fairer, better, surer life we crave and mean to have.

Only by a lasting peace are liberties and democracies strengthened and deepened. War is their enemy. And it will not do to believe that any of us can escape war's devastation. Victor, vanquished, and neutrals alike are affected physically, economically, and morally.

Against the degradation of war we can erect a safeguard. That is the guerdon for which we reach. Within the scope of the formula we outline here there will be found, to those who seek it, the essential elements of our purpose. Others will see only emptiness. Each of us carries his own mirror in which is reflected hope—or determined desperation—courage or cowardice.

There is a famine throughout the world today. It starves men's bodies. But there is a greater famine—the hunger of men's spirit. That starvation can be cured by the conquest of fear, and the substitution of hope, from which springs faith—faith in each other, faith that we want to work together toward salvation, and determination that those who threaten the peace and safety shall be punished.

The peoples of these democracies gathered here have a particular concern with our answer, for their peoples hate war. They will have a heavy exaction to make of those who fail to provide an escape. They are not afraid of an internationalism that protects; they are unwilling to be fobbed off by mouthings about narrow sovereignty, which is today's phrase for yesterday's isolation.

The basis of a sound foreign policy, in this new age, for all the nations here gathered, is that anything that happens, no matter where or how, which menaces the peace of the world, or the economic stability, concerns each and all of us.

That, roughly, may be said to be the central theme of the United Nations. It is with that thought we begin consideration of the most important subject that can engage mankind—life itself.

Let there be no quibbling about the duty and the responsibility of this group and of the governments we represent. I was moved, in the afternoon of my life, to add my effort to gain the world's quest, by the broad mandate under which we were created. The resolution of the General Assembly, passed January 24, 1946, in London, reads:

> *Section V. Terms of Reference of the Commission*
>
> The Commission shall proceed with the utmost despatch and enquire into all phases of the problems, and make such recommendations from time to time with respect to them as it finds possible. In particular the Commission shall make specific proposals:
>
> (a) For extending between all nations the exchange of basic scientific information for peaceful ends;

> (b) For control of atomic energy to the extent necessary to ensure its use only for peaceful purposes;
>
> (c) For the elimination from national armaments of atomic weapons and of all other major weapons adaptable to mass destruction;
>
> (d) For effective safeguards by way of inspection and other means to protect complying States against the hazards of violations and evasions.
>
> The work of the Commission should proceed by separate stages, the successful completion of each of which will develop the necessary confidence of the world before the next stage is undertaken. . . .[2]

Our mandate rests, in text and in spirit, upon the outcome of the Conference in Moscow of Messrs. Molotov of the Union of Soviet Socialist Republics, Bevin of the United Kingdom, and Byrnes of the United States of America. The three Foreign Ministers on December 27, 1945 proposed the establishment of this body.[3]

Their action was animated by a preceding conference in Washington on November 15, 1945, when the President of the United States, associated with Mr. Attlee, Prime Minister of the United Kingdom, and Mr. Mackenzie King, Prime Minister of Canada, stated that international control of the whole field of atomic energy was immediately essential. They proposed the formation of this body. In examining that source, the Agreed Declaration, it will be found that the fathers of the concept recognized the final means of world salvation—the abolition of war. Solemnly they wrote:

> We are aware that the only complete protection for the civilized world from the destructive use of scientific knowledge lies in the prevention of war. No system of safeguards that can be devised will of itself provide an effective guarantee against production of atomic weapons by a nation bent on aggression. Nor can we ignore the possibility of the development of other weapons, or of new methods of warfare, which may constitute as great a threat to civilization as the military use of atomic energy.[4]

Through the historical approach I have outlined, we find ourselves here to test if man can produce, through his will and faith, the miracle of peace, just as he has, through science and skill, the miracle of the atom.

The United States proposes the creation of an International Atomic Development Authority, to which should be entrusted all phases of the development and use of atomic energy, starting with the raw material and including—

1. Managerial control or ownership of all atomic-energy activities potentially dangerous to world security.
2. Power to control, inspect, and license all other atomic activities.
3. The duty of fostering the beneficial uses of atomic energy.
4. Research and development responsibilities of an affirmative character intended to put the Authority in the forefront of atomic knowledge and thus to enable it to comprehend, and therefor to detect, misuse of atomic energy. To be effective, the Authority must itself be the world's leader in the field

of atomic knowledge and development and thus supplement its legal authority with the great power inherent in possession of leadership in knowledge.

I offer this as a basis for beginning our dicussion.

But I think the peoples we serve would not believe—and without faith nothing counts—that a treaty, merely outlawing possession or use of the atomic bomb, constitutes effective fulfillment of the instructions to this Commission. Previous failures have been recorded in trying the method of simple renunciation, unsupported by effective guaranties of security and armament limitation. No one would have faith in that approach alone.

Now, if ever, is the time to act for the common good. Public opinion supports a world movement toward security. If I read the signs aright, the peoples want a program not composed merely of pious thoughts but of enforceable sanctions—an international law with teeth in it.

We of this nation, desirous of helping to bring peace to the world and realizing the heavy obligations upon us arising from our possession of the means of producing the bomb and from the fact that it is part of our armament, are prepared to make our full contribution toward effective control of atomic energy.

When an adequate system for control of atomic energy, including the renunciation of the bomb as a weapon, has been agreed upon and put into effective operation and condign punishments set up for violations of the rules of control which are to be stigmatized as international crimes, we propose that—

1. Manufacture of atomic bombs shall stop;
2. Existing bombs shall be disposed of pursuant to the terms of the treaty; and
3. The Authority shall be in possession of full information as to the know-how for the production of atomic energy.

Let me repeat, so as to avoid misunderstanding: My country is ready to make its full contribution toward the end we seek, subject of course to our constitutional processes and to an adequate system of control becoming fully effective, as we finally work it out.

Now as to violations: In the agreement, penalties of as serious a nature as the nations may wish and as immediate and certain in their execution as possible should be fixed for—

1. Illegal possession or use of an atomic bomb;
2. Illegal possession, or separation, of atomic material suitable for use in an atomic bomb;
3. Seizure of any plant or other property belonging to or licensed by the Authority;
4. Wilful interference with the activities of the Authority;
5. Creation or operation of dangerous projects in a manner contrary to, or in the absence of, a license granted by the international control body.

It would be a deception, to which I am unwilling to lend myself, were I not to say to you and to our peoples that the matter of punishment lies at the very heart of our present security system. It might as well be admitted, here and now, that the subject goes straight to the veto power contained in the Charter of the United Nations so far as it relates to the field of atomic energy. The Charter permits penalization only by concurrence of each of the five great powers—the Union of Soviet Socialist Republics, the United Kingdom, China, France, and the United States.

I want to make very plain that I am concerned here with the veto power only as it affects this particular problem. There must be no veto to protect those who violate their solemn agreements not to develop or use atomic energy for destructive purposes.

The bomb does not wait upon debate. To delay may be to die. The time between violation and preventive action or punishment would be all too short for extended discussion as to the course to be followed.

As matters now stand several years may be necessary for another country to produce a bomb, *de novo*. However, once the basic information is generally known, and the Authority has established producing plants for peaceful purposes in the several countries, an illegal seizure of such a plant might permit a malevolent nation to produce a bomb in 12 months, and if preceded by secret preparation and necessary facilities perhaps even in a much shorter time. The time required—the advance warning given of the possible use of a bomb—can only be generally estimated but obviously will depend upon many factors, including the success with which the Authority has been able to introduce elements of safety in the design of its plants and the degree to which illegal and secret preparation for the military use of atomic energy will have been eliminated. Presumably no nation would think of starting a war with only one bomb.

This shows how imperative speed is in detecting and penalizing violations.

The process of prevention and penalization—a problem of profound statecraft—is, as I read it, implicit in the Moscow statement, signed by the Union of Soviet Socialist Republics, the United States, and the United Kingdom a few months ago.

But before a country is ready to relinquish any winning weapons it must have more than words to reassure it. It must have a guarantee of safety, not only against the offenders in the atomic area but against the illegal users of other weapons—bacteriological, biological, gas—perhaps—why not?—against war itself.

In the elimination of war lies our solution, for only then will nations cease to compete with one another in the production and use of dread "secret" weapons which are evaluated solely by their capacity to kill. This devilish program takes us back not merely to the Dark Ages but from cosmos to chaos. If we succeed in finding a suitable way to control atomic weapons, it is reasonable to hope that we may also preclude the use of other weapons adaptable to mass destruction. When a man learns to say "A" he can, if he chooses, learn the rest of the alphabet too.

Let this be anchored in our minds:

Peace is never long preserved by weight of metal or by an armament race. Peace can be made tranquil and secure only by understanding and agreement fortified by sanctions. We must embrace international cooperation or international disintegration.

Science has taught us how to put the atom to work. But to make it work for good instead of for evil lies in the domain dealing with the principles of human duty. We are now facing a problem more of ethics than of physics.

The solution will require apparent sacrifice in pride and in position, but better pain as the price of peace than death as the price of war.

I now submit the following measures as representing the fundamental features of a plan which would give effect to certain of the conclusions which I have epitomized.

1. General. The Authority should set up a thorough plan for control of the field of atomic energy, through various forms of ownership, dominion, licenses, operation, inspection, research, and management by competent personnel. After this is provided for, there should be as little interference as may be with the economic plans and the present private, corporate, and state relationships in the several countries involved.

2. Raw Materials. The Authority should have as one of its earliest purposes to obtain and maintain complete and accurate information on world supplies of uranium and thorium and to bring them under its dominion. The precise pattern of control for various types of deposits of such materials will have to depend upon the geological, mining, refining, and economic facts involved in different situations.

The Authority should conduct continuous surveys so that it will have the most complete knowledge of the world geology of uranium and thorium. Only after all current information on world sources of uranium and thorium is known to us all can equitable plans be made for their production, refining, and distribution.

3. Primary Production Plants. The Authority should exercise complete managerial control of the production of fissionable materials. This means that it should control and operate all plants producing fissionable materials in dangerous quantities and must own and control the product of these plants.

4. Atomic Explosives. The Authority should be given sole and exclusive right to conduct research in the field of atomic explosives. Research activities in the field of atomic explosives are essential in order that the Authority may keep in the forefront of knowledge in the field of atomic energy and fulfill the objective of preventing illicit manufacture of bombs. Only maintaining its position as the best-informed agency will the Authority be able to determine the line between intrinsically dangerous and non-dangerous activities.

5. ***Strategic Distribution of Activities and Materials.*** The activities entrusted exclusively to the Authority because they are intrinsically dangerous to security should be distributed throughout the world. Similarly, stockpiles of raw materials and fissionable materials should not be centralized.

6. ***Non-Dangerous Activities.*** A function of the Authority should be promotion of the peacetime benefits of atomic energy.

Atomic research (except in explosives), the use of research reactors, the production of radioactive tracers by means of non-dangerous reactors, the use of such tracers, and to some extent the production of power should be open to nations and their citizens under reasonable licensing arrangements from the Authority. Denatured materials, whose use we know also requires suitable safeguards, should be furnished for such purposes by the Authority under lease or other arrangement. Denaturing seems to have been overestimated by the public as a safety measure.

7. ***Definition of Dangerous and Non-Dangerous Activities.*** Although a reasonable dividing line can be drawn between dangerous and non-dangerous activities, it is not hard and fast. Provision should, therefore, be made to assure constant reexamination of the questions and to permit revision of the dividing line as changing conditions and new discoveries may require.

8. ***Operations of Dangerous Activities.*** Any plant dealing with uranium or thorium after it once reaches the potential of dangerous use must be not only subject to the most rigorous and competent inspection by the Authority, but its actual operation shall be under the management, supervision, and control of the Authority.

9. ***Inspection.*** By assigning intrinsically dangerous activities exclusively to the Authority, the difficulties of inspection are reduced. If the Authority is the only agency which may lawfully conduct dangerous activities, then visible operation by others than the Authority will constitute an unambiguous danger signal. Inspection will also occur in connection with the licensing functions of the Authority.

10. ***Freedom of Access.*** Adequate ingress and egress for all qualified representatives of the Authority must be assured. Many of the inspection activities of the Authority should grow out of, and be incidental to, its other functions. Important measures of inspection will be associated with the tight control of raw materials, for this is a keystone of the plan. The continuing activities of prospecting, survey, and research in relation to raw materials will be designed not only to serve the affirmative development functions of the Authority but also to assure that no surreptitious operations are conducted in the raw-materials field by nations or their citizens.

11. Personnel. The personnel of the Authority should be recruited on a basis of proven competence but also so far as possible on an international basis.

12. Progress by Stages. A primary step in the creation of the system of control is the setting forth, in comprehensive terms, of the functions, responsibilities, powers, and limitations of the Authority. Once a charter for the Authority has been adopted, the Authority and the system of control for which it will be responsible will require time to become fully organized and effective. The plan of control will, therefore, have to come into effect in successive stages. These should be specifically fixed in the charter or means should be otherwise set forth in the charter for transitions from one stage to another, as contemplated in the resolution of the United Nations Assembly which created this Commission.

13. Disclosures. In the deliberations of the United Nations Commission on Atomic Energy, the United States is prepared to make available the information essential to a reasonable understanding of the proposals which it advocates. Further disclosures must be dependent, in the interests of all, upon the effective ratification of the treaty. When the Authority is actually created, the United States will join the other nations in making available the further information essential to that organization for the performance of its functions. As the successive stages of international control are reached, the United States will be prepared to yield, to the extent required by each state, national control of activities in this field to the Authority.

14. International Control. There will be questions about the extent of control to be allowed to national bodies, when the Authority is established. Purely national authorities for control and development of atomic energy should to the extent necessary for the effective operation of the Authority be subordinate to it. This is neither an endorsement nor a disapproval of the creation of national authorities. The Commission should evolve a clear demarcation of the scope of duties and responsibilities of such national authorities.

And now I end. I have submitted an outline for present discussion. Our consideration will be broadened by the criticism of the United States proposals and by the plans of the other nations, which, it is to be hoped, will be submitted at their early convenience. I and my associates of the United States Delegation will make available to each member of this body books and pamphlets, including the Acheson-Lilienthal report, recently made by the United States Department of State, and the McMahon Committee Monograph No. 1 entitled ‘‘Essential Information on Atomic Energy'' relating to the McMahon bill recently passed by the United States Senate, which may prove a value in assessing the situation.[5]

All of us are consecrated to making an end of gloom and hopelessness. It will not be an easy job. The way is long and thorny, but supremely worth traveling. All of us want to stand erect, with our faces to the sun, instead of being forced to burrow into the earth, like rats.

The pattern of salvation must be worked out by all for all.

The light at the end of the tunnel is dim, but our path seems to grow brighter as we actually begin our journey. We cannot yet light the way to the end. However, we hope the suggestions of my Government will be illuminating.

Let us keep in mind the exhortation of Abraham Lincoln, whose words, uttered at a moment of shattering national peril, form a complete text for our deliberation. I quote, paraphrasing slightly:

> We cannot escape history. We of this meeting will be remembered in spite of ourselves. No personal significance or insignificance can spare one or another of us. The fiery trial through which we are passing will light us down in honor or dishonor to the latest generation.
>
> We say we are for Peace. The world will not forget that we say this. We know how to save Peace. The world knows that we do. We, even we here, hold the power and have the responsibility.
>
> We shall nobly save, or meanly lose, the last, best hope of earth. The way is plain, peaceful, generous, just—a way which, if followed, the world will forever applaud.

My thanks for your attention.

Notes

[1]Bernard M. Baruch, who delivered this address at the opening session of the United Nations Atomic Energy Commission in New York, N.Y., on June 14. The address was released to the press by the U.S. Delegation to the United Nations on the same date.

[2]Department of State *Bulletin* of Feb. 10, 1946, p. 198.

[3]Department of State *Bulletin* of Dec. 30, 1945, p. 1031.

[4]Department of State *Bulletin* of Nov. 18, 1945, p. 781.

[5]Department of State publication 2498; for excerpts from the Acheson-Lilienthal report see *Bulletin* of Apr. 7, 1946, p. 553. The text of the McMahon bill is S. Rept. 1211, 79th Cong.

BERTRAND RUSSELL

The Russell-Einstein Manifesto

Bertrand Russell (1872–1970) was an eminent British philosopher and mathematician deeply concerned about the spiraling arms race, particularly its newest development, the hydrogen bomb. This essay was a radio address Russell made on July 9, 1955 to the people of the world informing them of the dangers of nuclear weapons and urging them to avoid all war. It was signed by a dozen Nobel Prize-winning scientists. The Russell-Einstein Manifesto, as it was called, was presented at the first meeting of the Pugwash movement, an international group of scientists. The group, which first met in the village of Pugwash, Nova Scotia, in 1957, for what are formally called Conferences on Science and World Affairs, pledged to lessen the dangers of nuclear weapons, and is still active today. The Federation of American Scientists and the Union of Concerned Scientists are the two active scientific groups in the United States.

In the tragic situation which confronts humanity, we feel that scientists should assemble in conference to appraise the perils that have arisen as a result of the development of weapons of mass destruction, and to discuss a resolution in the spirit of the appended draft.

We are speaking on this occasion, not as members of this or that nation, continent, or creed, but as human beings, members of the species Man, whose continued existence is in doubt. The world is full of conflicts; and, over-shadowing all minor conflicts, the titanic struggle between Communism and anti-Communism.

Almost everybody who is politically conscious has strong feelings about one or more of these issues; but we want you, if you can, to set aside such feelings and consider yourselves only as members of a biological species which has had a remarkable history, and whose disappearance none of us can desire.

We shall try to say no single word which should appeal to one group rather than to another. All, equally, are in peril, and, if the peril is understood, there is hope that they may collectively avert it.

We have to learn to think in a new way. We have to learn to ask ourselves, not what steps can be taken to give military victory to whatever group we prefer, for there no longer are such steps; the question we have to ask ourselves is: what steps can be taken to prevent a military contest of which the issue must be disastrous to all parties?

The general public, and even many men in positions of authority, have not

---

realized what would be involved in a war with nuclear bombs. The general public still thinks in terms of the obliteration of cities. It is understood that the new bombs are more powerful than the old, and that, while one A-bomb could obliterate Hiroshima, one H-bomb could obliterate the largest cities, such as London, New York, and Moscow.

No doubt in an H-bomb war great cities would be obliterated. But this is one of the minor disasters that would have to be faced. If everybody in London, New York, and Moscow were exterminated, the world might, in the course of a few centuries, recover from the blow. But we now know, especially since the Bikini test, that nuclear bombs can gradually spread destruction over a very much wider area than had been supposed.

It is stated on very good authority that a bomb can now be manufactured which will be 2,500 times as powerful as that which destroyed Hiroshima. Such a bomb, if exploded near the ground or under water, sends radioactive particles into the upper air. They sink gradually and reach the surface of the earth in the form of a deadly dust or rain. It was this dust which infected the Japanese fishermen and their catch of fish.

No one knows how widely such lethal radio-active particles might be diffused, but the best authorities are unanimous in saying that a war with H-bombs might quite possibly put an end to the human race. It is feared that if many H-bombs are used there will be universal death—sudden only for a minority, but for the majority a slow torture of disease and disintegration.

Many warnings have been uttered by eminent men of science and by authorties in military strategy. None of them will say that the worst results are certain. What they do say is that these results are possible, and no one can be sure that they will not be realized. We have not yet found that the views of experts on this question depend in any degree upon their polities or prejudices. They depend only, so far as our researches have revealed, upon the extent of the particular expert's knowledge. We have found that the men who know most are the most gloomy.

Here, then, is the problem which we present to you, stark and dreadful and inescapable: Shall we put an end to the human race; or shall mankind renounce war?[1] People will not face this alternative because it is so difficult to abolish war.

The abolition of war will demand distasteful limitations of national sovereignty.[2] But what perhaps impedes understanding of the situation more than anything else is that the term "mankind" feels vague and abstract. People scarcely realize in imagination that the danger is to themselves and their children and their grandchildren, and not only to a dimly apprehended humanity. They can scarcely bring themselves to grasp that they, individually, and those whom they love are imminent danger of perishing agonizingly. And so they hope that perhaps war may be allowed to continue provided modern weapons are prohibited.

This hope is illusory. Whatever agreements not to use H-bombs had been reached in time of peace, they would no longer be considered binding in time of war, and both sides would set to work to manufacture H-bombs as soon as war broke out, for, if one side manufactured the bombs and the other did not, the side that manufactured them would inevitably be victorious.

Although an agreement to renounce nuclear weapons as part of a general reduction of armaments[3] would not afford an ultimate solution, it would serve certain important purposes. First: any agreement between East and West is to the good in so far as it tends to diminish tension. Second: the abolition of thermonuclear weapons, if each side believed that the other had carried it out sincerely, would lessen the fear of a sudden attack in the style of Pearl Harbor, which at present keeps both sides in a state of nervous apprehension. We should, therefore, welcome such an agreement, though only as a first step.

Most of us are not neutral in feeling, but as human beings, we have to remember that, if the issues between East and West are to be decided in any manner that can give any possible satisfaction to anybody, whether Communist or anti-Communist, whether Asian or European or American, whether White or Black, then these issues must not be decided by war. We should wish this to be understood, both in the East and in the West.

There lies before us, if we choose, continual progress in happiness, knowledge, and wisdom. Shall we, instead, choose death, because we cannot forget our quarrels? We appeal, as human beings, to human beings: remember your humanity, and forget the rest. If you can do so, the way lies open to a new Paradise; if you cannot, there lies before you the risk of universal death.

Resolution

We invite this Congress, and through it the scientists of the world and the general public, to subscribe to the following resolution:

> In view of the fact that in any future world war nuclear weapons will certainly be employed, and that such weapons threaten the continued existence of mankind, we urge the Governments of the world to realize, and to acknowledge publicly, that their purpose cannot be furthered by a world war, and we urge them, consequently, to find peaceful means for the settlement of all matters of dispute between them.

Professor Max Born (Professor of Theoretical Physics at Berlin, Frankfurt, and Göttingen, and of Natural Philosophy, Edinburgh; Nobel Prize in physics).

Professor P. W. Bridgman (Professor of Physics. Harvard University; Nobel Prize in physics).

Professor Albert Einstein.

Professor L. Infeld (Professor of Theoretical Physics, University of Warsaw).

Professor J. F. Joliot-Curie (Professor of Physics at the Collège de France; Nobel Prize in chemistry).

Professor H. J. Muller (Professor of Zoology at University of Indiana; Nobel Prize in physiology and medicine).

Professor Linus Pauling (Professor of Chemistry, California Institute of Technology; Nobel Prize in chemistry).

Professor C. F. Powell (Professer of Physics, Bristol University; Nobel Prize in physics).

Professor J. Rotblat (Professor of Physics, University of London; Medical College of St. Bartholomew's Hospital).

Bertrand Russell.

Professor Hideki Yukawa (Professor of Theoretical Physics, Kyoto University, Nobel Prize in physics).

Notes

[1] Professor Joliot-Curie wishes to add the words: "as a means of settling differences between States."

[2] Professor Joliot-Curie wishes to add that these limitations are to be agreed by all and in the interests of all.

[3] Professor Muller makes the reservation that this be taken to mean "a concomitant balanced reduction of all armaments."

Progress and Policy Since Hiroshima

RANDALL FORSBERG

Nuclear Arms: A Brief History

Randall Forsberg (b. 1943) did graduate work in political science at the Massachusetts Institute of Technology, during which time she conceived and wrote the Nuclear Freeze Resolution (see p. 259). She is presently executive director of the Institute for Defense and Disarmament Studies.

What is the relationship of the nuclear arms race to the various roles of conventional military forces?

Most people in the United States believe that the purpose of US nuclear weapons is to deter a nuclear attack on the United States by the Soviet Union by threatening retaliation in kind.

This is undoubtedly one of the functions of U.S. nuclear weapons, but it is not the only function, nor the function that motivates the continuation of the nuclear arms race between the United States and the Soviet Union.

The purpose of the on-going nuclear arms race, to the extent that there is any rational purpose, is to back up U.S. uses of conventional armed forces overseas and to deter such uses of Soviet conventional forces. This connection between the roles of nuclear and conventional military forces is illustrated throughout the history of the nuclear arms race.

Initially, the United States developed nuclear weapons because we believed that there might be a nuclear program in Germany during World War II. We wanted to be able to respond to a potential nuclear threat with a nuclear response.

However, toward the end of World War II it became clear that Germany did not have a nuclear program; and that there was no nuclear threat to the Western

---

Randall Forsberg, "Nuclear Arms: A Brief History." Originally titled "A Nuclear Freeze and Non-Interventionary Conventional Policy" (Brookline, Mass.: Institute for Defense and Disarmament Studies, 1982). Reprinted by permission of the author and the Institute for Defense and Disarmament Studies.

allies. At that point the U.S. nuclear program did not end. With great momentum, it continued right ahead.

During the four-year wartime Manhattan project, the United States produced enough fissionable uranium and plutonium to make just three nuclear bombs. We tested one of them in the desert, and we used the other two on Hiroshima and Nagasaki.

This use of nuclear weapons had nothing to do with deterring a nuclear attack on the United States or anyone else. The United States used nuclear weapons that had been produced for two reasons.

One was to end a conventional war with, it was argued, less loss of life than would occur if the war continued. It was claimed that it might take 500,000 American lives to recapture all of the Pacific islands from the Japanese, in bloody, over-the-beach warfare. The bombs dropped on Hiroshima and Nagasaki killed, immediately, about 100,000 persons each. So nuclear weapons were seen as a means of decreasing death and violence and ending the war more quickly. They were intimately interrelated with the pursuit of conventional warfare goals.

The second reason probably played a great role in the dropping of the second bomb on Nagasaki. For the bomb on Hiroshima should have been enough (if even that was needed) to make the Japanese sue for total surrender, which were the only terms permitted to them.

The function of the second bomb, if not the first, was to intimidate the Soviet Union: as a precedent for the post-war environment, to make clear that the United States not only had a nuclear monopoly, but was prepared to use it. The demonstration was intended to show that, if the Soviet Union used its conventional forces in a manner objectionable to the United States, the USA would not hesitate to respond with nuclear weapons. Thus, again, nuclear policy was inextricably intertwined with conventional war and power politics.

Post-War Nuclear Policies

During the period from 1945 to 1955 the United States continued to have a virtual monopoly on nuclear weapons. U.S. policy in this period was called "massive retaliation." Its purpose was to deter Soviet uses of conventional military force by threatening simply to wipe out the major cities of the Soviet Union in response. In 1950 the United States had 300 nuclear bombs on 300 propeller-driven planes. Those were all the nuclear weapons in the world. They were not very many by present day standards; and they might well have been used against population targets because they were, relatively speaking, so few in number.

By 1960, the Soviet Union had acquired nuclear weapons and the means to deliver them to the United States. It had at that time 150 strategic bombers that could reach this country, together with several hundred nuclear missiles and about 500 bombers that could reach Western Europe.

In the interval, the United States had deployed 2000 strategic bombers, loaded, ready-to-go, and aimed at the Soviet Union: 600 B52s and 1400 shorter-range B47s stationed at overseas bases. The USA had also built up a force of about 10,000 tactical nuclear weapons. These are short-range nuclear weapons aimed primarily at military targets: anti-aircraft missiles with nuclear tips; antisubmarine torpedoes with nuclear tips; and surface-to-surface missiles to use on the battlefield against oncoming enemy tank formations, including missiles with a range of 400 miles that would go from West Germany to East Germany, as well as missiles with a range of 70 miles, missiles with a range of 30 miles, and even 8-inch howitzers with a range of 15 miles, for use on the battlefield in West Germany. (The neutron bomb is an antitank weapon that is designed to emit enough radiation not merely to kill the men driving the tanks but to make them die in a matter of minutes or hours rather than days or weeks.)

Accompanying the deployment of tactical nuclear weapons, the United States maintained the policy in effect since the end of World War II of posing a threat of first use of nuclear weapons. If the USA became involved in a conventional war with the Soviet Union, and the war was going against this country, we would be ready (on someone else's territory) to escalate up to the use of our tactical nuclear weapons against Soviet conventional forces.

Until the mid-1960s, the United States still had such a marked superiority in both intercontinental and Europe-oriented nuclear weapons that it could continue to pose this threat with some confidence. The USA built up its original strategic missile force much sooner than the Soviet Union did. Both on land and on submarines the main force of invulnerable U.S. missiles was deployed between 1960 and 1967. At that time, the Soviet Union was still relying on its few intercontinental bombers and on 200 vulnerable ICBMs. Neither the Soviet bombers nor the ICBMs were ready to launch, and both could have been destroyed in a preemptive strike.

The Soviet Union first began to acquire nuclear forces that gave it an invulnerable, second-strike deterrent in 1965. This is when the USSR started building ICBMs in steel-reinforced concrete underground silos. The Soviet Union deployed 1400 such ICBMs over the period 1965–1971. It started building submarines with long-range missiles deployed in range of the United States only in 1967; and it built up a force of sixty-two strategic submaries between 1967 and 1977.

Thus, it is only in this last 15 years that U.S. cities have become unavoidably hostage to a Soviet missile strike that could take place in half an hour. It is only because we failed to stop the arms race in 1960 that we are exposed to this threat today.

During the last decade there has been widespread recognition of parity between the USA and USSR in nuclear forces. What this means is not that the Soviet Union can match all the esoteric nuclear capabilities of the United States, but that, for the first time, it can match the all-important, "bottom-line" second-strike capability: it can retain the forces to obliterate the USA in a second strike, no matter what sort of counterforce attack the United States undertakes first.

While the Soviet Union was still building up its main generation of strategic missiles, between 1970 and 1977, the United States took out most of the missiles that it had on land and on submarines and replaced them with new missiles with multiple nuclear warheads or MIRVs (multiple, independently-targetable re-entry vehicles).

In 1976, in a program that was perfectly predictable, the USSR started doing the same thing: replacing its main ICBM and submarine-launched missiles with new MIRVed missiles. The Soviet MIRV program has now been completed on land but is still under way on submarines, where it probably will not be completed until 1985.

Effort to Recapture Superiority

The response of the United States to Soviet acquisition of an invulnerable deterrent force over the last 15 years is to try to recapture the clear superiority that it had until the mid-1960s. The attempt to do this is being made by developing and deploying the MX missile, which will have the ability to destroy Soviet ICBMs in their silos; and by adding a new submarine-based missile, the Trident II, and a new type of missile, the cruise missile, which will provide thousands of additional nuclear warheads with precision attack capability.

In addition to these new offensive nuclear forces, the United States already has an extraordinary antisubmarine warfare (ASW) capability built, as described earlier, in response to Soviet conventional submarines. The U.S. ASW capability has been strengthened for operations against strategic submarines. The United States has large sonar towers off the coast of Norway, off the Azores, and off the Japanese Islands. These are attached by cable to a giant computer processing center, which can dampen out all of the other noises in the ocean and leave in only the noises of Soviet submarines. Under good conditions, Soviet submarines can actually be tracked all the way across the Atlantic by means of these sonar towers. Soviet submarines come out of narrow port exits. They are rather poorly designed and noisy. The port exits are surrounded by U.S., Japanese, and British antisub submarines and aircraft.

As a result of this ASW capability, when the United States acquires the MX in the late 1980s, it will be back in a position similar to that of the 1950s and 1960s, when it could threaten a preemptive strike against most Soviet medium-range and intercontinental nuclear forces.

There will be very important differences, though, between the earlier situation and that in 1990. When the USA threatened a preemptive strike earlier, the number of targets (airfields and missile groups) that it would strike was relatively small, a few hundred; and the Soviet Union had no capability to launch its missiles on warning of an incoming attack. Today and in the future that will not be the case. The Soviet generals can now launch their missiles, just as the United States can, when their radar screens show that the opponent's missiles have been launched. In addition, current U.S. counterforce attack scenarios provide for the use of several thousand nuclear warheads against the large Soviet Missile forces. The Soviets could send back to the United States a retaliatory attack of equal magnitude.

The effect of even a limited counterforce exchange between the two superpowers, with nuclear warheads directed against the nuclear forces of the opposing side, has been calculated to be between three and twenty million dead in the United States and a like number in the USSR, simply from downwind fallout of the explosions on missile sites.

This is the most easily predictable effect. No one has the faintest notion of what would happen to the global ecology if 4000–8000 nuclear weapons were exploded in a very short space of time.[1] The ozone layer would be blown away. The fallout would increase the background level of radiation and darken the sky worldwide. Tremendous firestorms would be created. These things combined would create changes in the world's climate which could be cumulative and synergistic. . . .

The main region for nuclear deterrence of conventional war is Europe. But this is a very stable region, in which conventional war between East and West is highly unlikely: both sides have too little to gain and too much to lose. Where conventional war remains quite likely, and thus, where the nuclear backup may acutally be believed to play an active role in shaping the course of events, is in the third world. In this sense, the purpose of the on-going nuclear arms race is, from the point of view of the USA, to give the United States greater freedom to intervene in developing countries without risking a conventional challenge on the part of the Soviet Union; and to inhibit Soviet conventional intervention. From the point of view of the USSR, the purpose of trying to match U.S. nuclear developments is to nullify the nuclear factor in global power politics.

The U.S. generals calculate that, if they can show on paper that a direct conventional confrontation between the two superpowers could escalate to a local or intercontinental nuclear exchange that would leave the U.S. ahead by some measure, then the Soviet generals will not risk sending in conventional forces in the first place; nor with they feel free to intervene themselves in developing countries where Western stakes are high, which was not the case in Afghanistan.

Note

[1]This article was written in 1982, before the nuclear winter phenomenon had been widely discussed. [Editor's note]

BARTON J. BERNSTEIN

The Dropping of the A-Bomb

Barton J. Bernstein (b. 1936) is a professor of history at Stanford University. He has written extensively on the history of the nuclear arms race. He specializes in the history of the Truman period.

How Decisions Are Made When a Nation Is at War

> "I know that Japan is a terribly cruel and uncivilized nation in warfare but I can't bring myself to believe that, because they are beasts, we should ourselves act in the same manner."
>
> –Harry S. Truman, August 10, 1945

On August 6, 1945, the Enola Gay, a B-29, dropped an atomic bomb on Hiroshima, a major Japanese city. That bomb killed at least eighty thousand; injured many more; and, unknown to Americans then, killed some American prisoners of war. Most of the immediate Japanese deaths were from flash burns, blast, and falling debris. Ultimately thousands more died from radiation. "Hiroshima was uniformly and extensively devastated," an American bombing survey later reported. "Practically the entire densely or moderately built-up portion of the city was leveled by blast or swept by fire." Americans enthusiastically welcomed the news of the atomic bombing.

When President Harry S. Truman announced the atomic destruction of Hiroshima, which he described only as "an important Japanese army base," he warned Japan of "a rain of ruin" unless it surrendered on American terms. Three days later, on the 9th, America dropped another A-bomb, this time on Nagasaki. That bomb killed at least forty-five thousand, injured over fifty thousand, and again killed some allied prisoners of war. The next day, when Japan offered conditional surrender, Truman decided to halt the atomic bombing. He told his Cabinet, according to an associate's diary, "the thought of wiping out another one hundred thousand people was too horrible. He didn't like the idea of killing, as he said, 'all those kids.' " On August 14th, Japan finally surrendered and the third A-bomb, which could have been delivered on the 18th or 19th, was placed in the stockpile.

Since 1945, and especially with the renewed anxiety about nuclear war, many

---

Barton J. Bernstein, "The Dropping of the A-Bomb: How Decisions Are Made When a Nation Is at War," *The Center Magazine* (March/April 1983), pp. 7–15. Reprinted with permission from *The Center Magazine*, a publication of The Center for the Study of Democratic Institutions, and from the author.

have asked important questions about the nuclear attacks on Hiroshima and Nagasaki: Why weren't alternatives first tried? Would they have produced a speedy Japanese surrender? Why were the bombs used? Why were cities chosen, and why those cities? Weren't American leaders appalled by the likely Japanese deaths? On the basis of newly available information, some have asked additional questions: If the war had not ended in mid-August, would Truman have dropped a third atomic bomb and possibly more? Why didn't the government later admit the nuclear deaths of the POWs?

I

In late 1941, when President Franklin D. Roosevelt launched the top-secret A-bomb project, inspired largely by the fear that Germany was also racing to build the dread weapon, American leaders assumed that the bomb would be a legitimate weapon in the war. Throughout the war, they never questioned that assumption. Building on that assumption, they slowly came to define the target as Japan, not Germany, and to plan to use the weapon on a city, not a purely military installation.

On May 5, 1943, when the evidence was still unclear whether Germany was successfully pursuing its A-bomb project, a high-level American committee, including General Leslie Groves, director of the American project, and Vannevar Bush and James Conant, top scientist-administrators then advising FDR, concluded that the first bomb should be dropped on Japan. "[T]he general view," according to the minutes, was that the bomb's "best point of use would be on a Japanese fleet concentration in the Harbor of Truk." General Wilhelm Styer, the representative of the War Department, "suggested Tokyo but it was pointed out that the bomb should be used where, if it failed to go off, it would land in water of sufficient depth to prevent easy salvage. The Japanese were selected as they would not be so apt to secure knowledge from it as would the Germans."

The committee members never discussed in moral terms the issue of selecting a target: Should the bomb be used against a clearly military target, like a fleet or troops, or against a city, where civilians and industry were intertwined and thousands of civilians would be killed? In this discussion, the committee disposed of the issue on narrow tactical grounds—what was the best way of using the bomb and of keeping the technology secret if the bomb did not explode? Hence, they did not have to face directly the question of whether America should follow Britain and Germany and use "terror" bombing—the intentional killing of civilians.

Apparently, the choice of targets did not receive systematic attention until late April, 1945. By then, the war against Germany was nearly over and scientists estimated that the first A-bombs would be ready in August and might be equivalent to about five thousand tons of TNT. On April 27th, a special Target

Committee, including General Groves; General Lauris Norstad, later the commander of the North Atlantic Treaty Organization; and John Von Neumann, the famous mathematician, considered which Japanese cities would be good targets.

The good targets were being destroyed, the group lamented. As the minutes stated, "the 20th Air Force is operating primarily to laying waste all the main Japanese cities, . . . with the prime purpose in mind of not leaving one stone lying on another."

"Consideration [of targets for the A-bomb] is to be given," they concluded, "to large urban areas of not less than three miles in diameter existing in the larger populated areas [and the] target and/or aiming point should have a high strategic value." They wanted the bomb to kill civilians. They picked seventeen places for further study: Tokyo Bay (the port area), Kawasaki, Yokohama, Nagoya, Osaka, Kobe, Kyoto, Hiroshima, Kure, Yawata, Kokura, Shimosenka, Yamaguchi, Kumamoto, Fukuoka, Nagasaki, and Sasebo.

Two weeks later, at their meeting on May 10th and 11th, held this time in the Los Alamos Laboratory office of its director, J. Robert Oppenheimer, the notable physicist, they discussed where to drop the bomb. They talked about bombing the Emperor's palace but, according to the minutes, agreed "that we should not recommend it but that any action for this bombing should come from authorities on military policy." They focused on five targets: Kyoto, Hiroshima, Yokohama, Kokura Arsenal, and Niigata. They rejected Niigata, classified as only a "B" target, but retained the other four, since Kyoto and Hiroshima were "AA" targets and Yokohama and Kokura Arsenal "A" targets.

They stressed that "psychological factors in the target selection were of great importance [, especially] obtaining the greatest psychological effect against Japan and . . . making the initial use sufficiently spectacular for the importance of the weapon to be internationally recognized. . . ." Kyoto, the former Japanese capital, they emphasized, "has the advantage of the people being more highly intelligent and hence better able to appreciate the significance of the weapon. Hiroshima has the advantage of being such a size and with possible focusing from nearby mountains that a large fraction of the city may be destroyed. The Emperor's palace in Tokyo has a greater fame than any other target but is of less strategic value."

When the Target Committee met on May 28th, they revised their list of target cities and selected Kyoto, Hiroshima, and Niigata. They decided the bomb should be dropped in the center of the city since the industrial areas of each city were "small, spread on fringes . . . and dispersed."

Three days later, on May 31st, the high-level Interim Committee met to discuss how—not whether—to use the bomb. It was a blue-ribbon panel, appointed by Secretary of War Henry L. Stimson, including Conant and Bush, the two scientist-administrators; James F. Byrnes, the next Secretary of State; Karl Compton, the physicist; William L. Clayton, Assistant Secretary of State; Ralph Bard, Under-Secretary of the Navy; and George Harrison, Stimson's representative. According to the minutes, Stimson "expressed the conclusion, on which there was general agreement, that we could not give the Japanese any warning; that we could not concentrate on a civilian area; but that we should seek to make a psychological impression on as many inhabitants as possible. At the suggestion of Dr. Conant, the Secretary [Stimson] agreed that the most desirable target would be a vital war plant employing a large number of workers and *closely surrounded by workers' houses*" (emphasis added). Three weeks later, the committee reaffirmed this recommendation.

They were not looking for a way to avoid the use of the bomb, nor did they only want to kill civilians. Rather, as a logical extension of the policy of large-scale strategic bombing, they wished to destroy industrial targets and kill civilians. They saw no reason to discuss the trade-offs between a war plant and civilians, for the major plants employed many workers and could be selected to assure that nearby workers' families would also die.

On the 31st, at the Interim Committee lunch, Ernest O. Lawrence, a Nobel physicist and inventor of the cyclotron, suggested that America should first try a warning and noncombat demonstration of the bomb. Others at the lunch table speedily rejected that notion, for the bomb might be a dud and hence the warning would embarrass the United States and embolden the Japanese, or Japan might move allied POWs into the target area and the bomb would kill them. A few weeks later, when some A-bomb scientists recommended a noncombat demonstration, their proposal was speedily rejected by the four-member scientific advisory panel of Lawrence; Oppenheimer; Enrico Fermi, an Italian Nobel laureate in physics; and Arthur Holly Compton, an American Nobel physicist. They explained, "We can propose no technical demonstration likely to bring an end to the war; we see no acceptable alternative to direct military use."

Secretary of War Stimson, though uneasy about the mass killing of civilians in the Air Force's area bombing against Japan, was not seeking to avoid the use of the A-bomb or to drop it on the exclusively military target. On June 6th, in discussing conventional and atomic bombing with Truman, Stimson revealed the moral tensions in his own thought. "I . . .was anxious about this feature [area bombing] of the war for two reasons: first, because I did not want to have the United States get the reputation of outdoing Hitler in atrocities; and second, I was a little fearful that before we could get ready the Air Force might have Japan so thoroughly bombed out that the new weapon would not have a background to show its strength." According to Stimson, Truman "laughed and said he understood."

To later-day readers, Stimson may seem hypocritical. How could he be sincerely troubled about area bombing, which killed thousands of enemy citizens, and yet want to use the A-bomb, which would kill many thousands of citizens? He was not hypocritical. He was inconsistent. He was torn between an older morality, which deemed it wrong to try to kill civilians, and a new morality, which made it an acceptable way of war. He was too close to events, too harried by the need for decisions, and too enamored to the top-secret A-bomb project to resolve the tension or even to define the problem clearly.

Stimson had compelled the military planners to delete Kyoto, the former capital and famous shrine city, from their list of A-bomb targets. Its elimination was not to save lives but to save the shrines. As Stimson recorded in his diary, Truman agreed strongly that if Kyoto was not eliminated from the targets, "the bitterness which would be caused by such a wanton act [atomic bombing of the shrines] might make it possible during the long postwar period to reconcile the Japanese to us in that area rather than to the Russians." Both men feared that an angered Japan might otherwise ally with the Soviet Union, and both comfortably accepted the substitution of Nagasaki for Kyoto.

II

On July 16th, at Alamogordo, America tested the first A-bomb. It was a great success. On the basis of that test, Oppenheimer informed General Groves that the total energy released by the first bombs on Japan would be equivalent to between twelve thousand and twenty thousand tons of TNT, and the blast's power would be between eight thousand and fifteen thousand tons. Because the bombs would be exploded about a third of a mile in the air, "it is not expected that radioactive contamination will reach the ground," Oppenheimer wrote, though "lethal radiation will, of course, reach the ground from the bomb itself." The implication, tucked away in scientific, impersonal language, was that radiation would help kill residents of the city but not persist very long.

General Groves promptly informed Oppenheimer, "It is necessary to drop the first Little Boy [uranium gun weapon] and the first Fat Man [implosion plutonium weapon] and probably a second one in accordance with our original plans. It may be that as many as three of the latter [will be necessary]."

Truman was then at Potsdam for the conference with Prime Minister Winston Churchill and Premier Joseph Stalin, a meeting that the President had delayed a few weeks so that he would know the results of the Alamogordo test. On July 16th, Truman received the report on Alamogordo that he was anxiously awaiting. "Operated on this morning," the coded message announced. "Diagnosis not yet complete but results seem satisfactory and already exceed expectations." The next day, when more details arrived about the bomb's awesome power, Truman expressed his delight. "The President was evidently very greatly re-enforced over the message," Stimson happily recorded in his diary.

On the 21st, the President received a full report on the Alamogordo test. The blast was equivalent to at least fifteen to twenty thousand tons of TNT, evaporating a one-hundred-foot steel tower, leaving a crater with a diameter of 1,200 feet, knocking over at a half-mile a seventy-foot steel tower anchored in concrete, and knocking over observers at six miles. "The effects on the [seventy-foot] tower indicate,'' Groves reported, ''that, at that distance, unshielded permanent steel and masonry buildings would have been destroyed. I no longer consider the Pentagon a safe shelter from such a bomb.'' The bomb would be more powerful than American experts had foreseen.

So impressed was Truman that he summarized the report in his private diary. Both Truman and Secretary of State Byrnes ''were immensely pleased,'' Stimson noted in his own diary. ''The President was tremendously pepped up by it and spoke to me of it again and again. . . . He said it gave him an entirely new feeling of confidence.'' Churchill, when he saw the report, stated that he now understood why Truman had seemed suddenly emboldened at the negotiating table and pushed matters through with a new confidence and authority. The bomb made Truman tougher in negotiating with the Soviets, for, as he realized, its power might intimidate them.

When Stimson received from Groves the formal military order listing the target cities—Hiroshima, Kokura, Niigata, and Nagasaki (replacing Kyoto)—Truman easily approved the directive. He did not call in other advisers for consultation. Truman was simply implementing the shared assumption, recently confirmed by the Interim Committee, that the bomb would be used. He felt no need to discuss alternatives. ''The weapon is to be used against Japan between now [July 25th] and August 10th,'' Truman recorded in his private diary.

''I have told . . . Stimson,'' Truman wrote in his diary, ''to use it so that military objectives and soldiers and sailors are the target and not women and children. Even if the Japs are savages, ruthless, merciless, and fanatic, we as the leader for the common welfare cannot drop the terrible bomb on the old capital [Kyoto] or the new [Tokyo]. He and I are in accord. The target will be a purely military one. . . .''

None of the target cities was a purely military one, and in the case of Hiroshima the aiming point was not a military target but the center of the city itself. Indeed, as the recently declassified documents show, the cities were chosen partly because of their vulnerable civilian populations. The mass killing of civilians was a major goal.

Yet Truman had privately described the targets as ''purely military.'' Why? Probably he was engaging in a necessary self-deception, for he could not admit to himself that the bomb would kill many thousands of civilians. The great power of the weapon and the earlier criteria for the choice of targets made the mass deaths inevitable.

''The attack [on Hiroshima],'' according to the official Air Force history, ''was directed against a densely built-up area, a mixture of residential, commercial, military, and small industrial buildings. . . . Planners, calculating on a 7,500-foot radius of destruction, thought that a bomb exploding [there] would wreck all important parts of the city except the dock areas. In this they were eminently correct.''

World War II had transformed morality. The mass bombings of Dresden, Hamburg, and Tokyo had been designed to destroy morale and industry, and to kill workers and other civilians, all sinews of war, in what had become total war. Most of the citizens of the civilized world—in German, Britain, Russia, Japan, and ultimately America—had become inured to the intentional mass killing of civilians.

America had held out longer than Britain or Germany before following such tactics, but by 1945 all the civilized nations at war had adopted such tactics. Very few in America openly protested, and most Americans disregarded their arguments. War had come to justify virtually any weapons and tactics.

III

On July 31, 1945, General Carl Spaatz, commanding general of the Strategic Air Force in the Pacific, anxiously cabled the Pentagon that "prisoner of war sources, not verified by photos, give location of allied prisoner of war camp [near] center of . . . Nagasaki. Does this influence the choice of this target for initial [A-bomb] operation?" Before Washington replied, Spaatz sent a second message, "Hiroshima [, according to prisoner of war reports,] is the only one of four target cities for [the A-bomb] that does not have allied prisoner of war camps."

General Groves briefly considered substituting Osaka, Amagasaki, and Omuta for Nagasaki. But after drafting that cable, he discarded it and simply replied, "Targets previously assigned . . . remain unchanged. However if you consider your information reliable Hiroshima should be given first priority . . . Information available here indicates that there are prisoner of war camps in practically every major Japanese city." The cable concluded by informing Spaatz that the "best available information here" is a special study, most recently revised on July 1st, on the location of POW camps in Japan. That study, as Washington and Spaatz knew, listed a camp within Hiroshima, on the basis of a 1944 British report.

Spaatz decided to disregard that dated British report and thus concluded that Hiroshima was the best target. On the 6th, at 8:15 A.M., forty-five minutes after a previous air-raid alert, with most factory workers on the job and schoolchildren outdoors, "Little Boy" exploded over Hiroshima. Among the many victims were at least eleven Americans, mostly from the crew of the recently downed Lonesome Lady, and maybe as many as twenty-three American POWs. They were not housed in the British-reported camp, which had been closed, but elsewhere in the city.

No American leader expected a speedy Japanese surrender, and so three days later, after scientists had rushed through the night to get the second bomb ready before bad weather set in for a few days, "Fat Man" was ready for delivery. That day, the primary target, Kokura, was clouded over, so Bock's Car, the B-29 carrying the deadly weapon, flew on with its short fuel supply to Nagasaki, the secondary target. The bombardier dropped the weapon at 11:01 A.M.

Because there had been an earlier air-raid warning that morning and the warning of this one came eight minutes *after* "Fat Man," few Japanese had taken cover. Most were at work, at home, or on the streets. The plutonium bomb, equivalent to about twenty-two thousand tons of TNT, destroyed much of the city but did less damage than the comparatively weaker Hiroshima bomb (12,500 tons) because the hills of Nagasaki blunted the impact of the bomb, and fire storms did not rip through the city. Among the areas destroyed was a small POW camp with sixteen Dutch and two Americans. All the Dutch were killed. Allegedly the two Americans escaped injury.

The aiming point for the bomb, according to the mission planning survey, "was placed east of Nagasaki Harbor in the commercial district of the city. Based upon a 7,500 feet radius, it was believed that an accurate blow would destroy the bulk of the city east of the harbor and possibly carry across to the western shore." The bomb had missed this aiming point by more than a mile because the city was clouded over and the bombardier, according to his report, had not found a break in the clouds until the last thirty seconds of the bombing run. Luis Alvarez, a physicist then at Tinian, the Pacific outpost from which Bock's Car had departed, later told Groves that the error was so substantial because the bomb was dropped by radar, contrary to orders, and that the official report concealed this violation of orders.

Regardless of how one explains the bombing error, the fact remains that if the bombardier had erred about two miles in the opposite direction, "Fat Man" would have destroyed a large POW camp, then unknown to planners, with about 1,400 POWs, including 1,290 Americans. If they had been killed, the news would have leaked out after the war and American officials would have been compelled to admit the atomic slaying of allied POWs at Nagasaki.

The Nagasaki bombing was probably unnecessary. There is no evidence that it speeded the end of the war. The bomb did not change the thinking of the militarists in Japan nor lead the Emperor to intervene in the deliberations to ask his ministers to seek peace on the 10th. He was already privately committed to calling for an end to the war. Even after the Nagasaki bombing, the militarists in the Japanese Cabinet opposed the quest for peace until the Emperor pleaded for peace. The available evidence indicates that the war would probably have ended in about the same way, maybe even on the same day, if the second bomb had never been used.

Why was it dropped? The process had been automatic. The second bomb had seemed necessary. American leaders believed that the Hiroshima bomb, Soviet entry into the war on the 8th, and even the second bomb might not produce an imminent Japanese surrender. They even assumed that more A-bombs would be necessary. Above all, they wanted to end the war on acceptable terms before November 1, 1945, the date for the so-called "small" invasion of Japan, with about 775,000 troops and casualties estimated nearly thirty-one thousand in the first month. No American leader ever considered delaying the second bomb to await the changes in Japanese policy produced by the trip-hammer blows of "Little Boy" on the 6th and Soviet entry on the 8th. The original order to the Air Force had said, ''[use bombs] as soon as made ready.'' The Air Force and the Scientists who assembled the bomb in the Pacific eagerly followed those orders.

IV

If the second bomb was almost definitely unnecessary, what about the first bomb? Why was it used? Why weren't alternatives first tried?

Ever since FDR had initiated the secret project, American leaders had assumed that the bomb would be used in the war. Truman inherited that assumption and the advisers who shared it. It fit his own inclinations, and he never questioned it.

Because most American leaders were not deeply troubled by the prospective use of the A-bomb, they did not seek alternatives and they easily rejected tactics that later critics would cite as ''missed opportunities,'' as ways of avoiding the combat use of the A-bomb. There were at least four: a warning and noncombat demonstration; pursuit of Japan's peace feelers; a guarantee of the Emperor; and a delay until Soviet entry into the Pacific war.

According to Truman and some key advisers, these tactics risked prolonging the war and making the scheduled invasion of November 1st necessary. Only if Truman and his major advisers had viewed the bomb as a radical evil, as a weapon to be avoided, might they have been tempted to try one or more of these tactics. Instead, they deemed the bomb attractive because it offered a potential bonus: its combat use might intimidate the Soviets and make them more tractable in the postwar period. The quest for retribution—retaliation for Pearl Harbor and the mistreatment of POWs—may have also constituted a subtle influence, for Truman stressed these themes in later justifying his decision.

In view of what we know about the course of events immediately after Hiroshima, when the Japanese militarists sought to minimize the A-bomb and still wished to continue the war, it is unlikely that a warning and noncombat demonstration or pursuit of peace feelers would have ended the war on American terms in the next few months. Japan's militarists were too obdurate and the peace group too timid. Japan's peace feelers ranged between vague and arrogant, and they never approached American expectations.

Even an American guarantee of the Emperor would not have met the Japanese militarists' demands and might have emboldened these men to hold out for more concessions—no postwar occupation, self-disarmament, and Japanese-conducted trials of their own war criminals. Perhaps Soviet entry would have crushed the militarists' hopes and led them to accept a reasonable peace before November 1st. Such speculation remains ''iffy,'' especially since both the Hiroshima bombing and Soviet entry did not promptly alter the demands of the militarists. They had held out through various meetings even after the Nagasaki bombing, until the Emperor himself had intervened.

Since the Soviets had promised that they would enter the Pacific war on about

August 21st, there would have been only ten weeks for the impact of their entry to produce a Japanese surrender before the scheduled invasion of November 1st. American leaders had not believed that Soviet entry could be so critical and they were unwilling to gamble on its effect by delaying the bomb. Some, like Secretary of State James Byrnes and Secretary of the Navy James Forrestal, even hoped that the war might end before the Soviets could get into it and grab parts of Manchuria. But none ever viewed the A-bomb and Soviet entry as competing ways to end the war. And many viewed the atomic bombings and Soviet entry as essential to speed the end of the war.

Given the widespread American hatred of the Japanese—spurred by official American propaganda—and the likely anger if Truman had sacrificed American lives to avoid using the bomb in order to save Japanese lives, the President's decision was virtually inevitable. "No man, in our position and subject to our responsibilities, holding in his hand a weapon of such possibilities," Stimson later wrote, "could have failed to use it and afterwards looked his countrymen in the face." It would have been morally unacceptable and politically disastrous, he argued, not to have dropped the A-bomb on Japan.

V

No American leader had foreseen an imminent Japanese surrender. They assumed that the A-bombs would be powerful supplements to, not substitutes for, large-scale conventional bombing. Accordingly, in the days between the Hiroshima and Nagasaki bombings, the Air Force continued to pound Japan with incendiaries and high explosives. After the Nagasaki bombing, the Air Force continued this "rain of ruin." On August 14th, the day of the Japanese surrender, about one thousand American planes bombed Japan.

So unexpected was Japan's offer of conditional surrender on the 10th that Stimson was headed at the time to the airport for a much-needed vacation. Abruptly canceling his plans, he rushed to the White House where American leaders split over whether they should accept Japan's conditional surrender, with its stipulation that the imperial system be continued. Urging speedy acceptance, Stimson and Forrestal, the two service secretaries, stressed that they wished to end the bloodshed. Stimson emphasized that continuation of the Emperor would be useful in guaranteeing the surrender of the Japanese armies. But Secretary of State James Byrnes, a shrewd politician, warned Truman that such a concession, marking a retreat from explicit American terms, could mean "crucifixion of the President." "I cannot understand," Byrnes complained, "why we should go further than we were willing to go at Potsdam when we had no atomic bomb, and Russia was not in the war."

"Let the Japs know unqualifiedly what unconditional surrender means. Let the dirty Japs squeal," one bloodthirsty congressman telegraphed the White House. Of the 170 telegrams sent to the President, 153 urged the harsh terms of unconditional surrender. "No concession [should] be made that will continue the rule of Hirohito," some liberal organizations insisted, for he is "as much a symbol of the super-race theory as Hitler."

Truman, fearful of a political backlash at home, where many linked Hirohito and Hitler, refused to accept Japan's single condition. His advisers accordingly phrased an ambiguous message that neither accepted nor rejected continuation of the imperial system. That message briefly shattered the peace coalition in Japan, emboldened some of the militarists, compelled the Emperor to intervene again on behalf of peace, and nearly unleashed a successful military coup. Had General Korechika Anami, Japan's war minister, supported the coup, it probably would have won support from the Japanese Army, and succeeded.

Against the advice of Stimson and Forrestal, Truman decided on the 10th to continue the heavy conventional bombing of Japan's cities. He wanted to pressure the Japanese into accepting America's terms. But he ordered, in the words of an associate, that the A-bomb "is not to be released on Japan without express authority from the President." No longer would the process of dropping A-bombs be automatic.

The third bomb, Groves had reported, "should be ready for delivery . . . after 17 or 18 August." It was a weapon that Truman did not want to use, for, as he explained to his Cabinet, he did not want to kill another one hundred thousand people, including "all those kids." When one prominent Democratic senator pleaded for more A-bombings, Truman replied, "I know that Japan is a terribly cruel and uncivilized nation in warfare but I can't bring myself to believe that, because they are beasts, we should ourselves act in the same manner. For myself, I certainly regret the necessity of wiping out whole populations because of the 'pigheadedness' of [their] leaders . . . I am not going to do it unless it is absolutely necessary."

The use of the third atomic bomb would have been popular in America. If the war had dragged on much beyond the 17th, Truman might have had great difficulty resisting the political pressures for its use. How could he have justified dropping the first two and then explained that new moral doubts deterred him from using a third and even more? It would not have been an easy argument to sell to an often bloodthirsty electorate which had come to hate the Japanese.

Fortunately, Japan accepted America's ambiguous terms and surrendered on August 14th. In their enthusiasm over peace and their anxiety over reconversion, few Americans paid much attention to the continuation of the Japanese imperial system. It never became a political issue in postwar America. Nor did the combat use of the two A-bombs.

Even had Americans learned that the Hiroshima bomb had killed some American POWs, it is unlikely that citizens would have raised political and moral questions about the use of these powerful weapons. American officials, probably anxious about a domestic backlash, concealed the information about the dead POWs. Probably officials did not want to risk unleashing a dialogue that might challenge government decisions, threaten careers, and make future combat use of the A-bomb more difficult. Ironically, just as Truman was morally more concerned about using a third bomb than were most Americans, officials worried unduly after Hiroshima and Nagasaki that citizens might question the A-bombings of Japan. Not for many years would substantial numbers of Americans criticize those momentous actions of 1945.

DANIEL ELLSBERG

How We Use Our Nuclear Arsenal

Daniel Ellsberg (b. 1931), formerly a defense analyst for the Rand Corporation, the Department of Defense, and the State Department, now writes and teaches about nuclear weapons and United States foreign policy. Most recently, he has held professorial posts at the University of California and at Stanford University. Ellsberg became internationally known in the 1970s for his release to the press of a set of classified documents, published by the New York Times in 1971 as The Pentagon Papers. *These documents revealed, among other things, that the United States was seriously considering using nuclear weapons in the Vietnam War. Ellsberg's essay is excerpted from his introduction to a collection of essays advocating nuclear disarmament.*

The notion common to nearly all Americans that "no nuclear weapons have been used since Nagasaki" is mistaken. It is not the case that U.S. nuclear weapons have simply piled up over the years—we have over 30,000 of them now, after dismantling many thousands of obsolete ones—unused and unusable, save for the single function of deterring their use against us by the Soviets. Again and again, generally in secret from the American public, U.S. nuclear weapons have been used, for quite different purposes: in the precise way that a gun is used when you point it at someone's head in a direct confrontation, whether or not the trigger is pulled.

By Harry Truman's own telling, it was just seven months after Nagasaki that he so used the Bomb in the "postwar" world. As he recalled, the effect was immediately as successful as on the first occasion, with no need this time to pull the trigger.

The issue was, as it happens, Russian influence in northern Iran, where the

---

Daniel Ellsberg, "How We Use Our Nuclear Arsenal." From *Protest and Survive*, E. P. Thompson and Dan Smith, eds. (New York: Monthly Review Press, 1981).

Soviets were prolonging their wartime occupation and supporting separatist regimes in Azerbaijan and Kurdistan, in pursuit of Russian oil leases in that area comparable to those of the British in the south. One version of Truman's account was revealed to Time by Senator Henry Jackson in January 1980, the week, by no coincidence, that the Carter Doctrine was announced. Time gave the story the heading, "Good Old Days for the Middle East":

> In a little-known episode of nuclear diplomacy that Jackson said he had heard from Harry Truman, the President summoned Soviet Ambassador Andrei Gromyko to the White House. Truman told Gromyko that Soviet troops should evacuate Iran within 48 hours—or the U.S. would use the new superbomb that it alone possessed. "We're going to drop it on you," Jackson quoted Truman as saying. They moved in 24 hours.

Truman's memory may be faulty in this recounting; Barry Blechman, who believes it was, reports at least seven public or private occasions when Truman discussed what he called his "ultimatum" over Iran, the earliest of these in 1950, but there are inconsistencies and a lack of any supporting evidence. This is not the case with any other of the episodes to be discussed below, for which this anecdote is, in the form Truman presented it, nevertheless archetypal.

The most recent of these, thirty-five years later, brings us back to the very same region and adversary. When outgoing Secretary of Defense Harold Brown told interviewers in January 1981, and President Ronald Reagan reiterated in February—using the same words—that what will keep Russia out of northern Iran and other parts of the Middle East in the 1980s is "the risk of World War III," the threat-strategy each was at the same time describing and implementing was somewhat more complex than that which Truman recollected, but not by much.

And there is no lack, this time, of corroborating elucidations of the nuclear component to the policy. A year earlier, in the weeks before and after Carter's State of the Union message announcing his "doctrine" for the Middle East, the White House almost jammed Washington talk shows and major front pages with authorized leaks, backgrounders, and official spokesmen all carrying the message that the president's commitment to use "any means necessary, including military force" against a further Soviet move into the Persian Gulf region was, at its heart, a threat of possible initiation of tactical nuclear warfare by the United States.

Just after the president's speech, Richard Burt of the New York Times (now a high Reagan official), was shown a secret Pentagon study, "the most extensive military study of the region ever done by the government," which lay behind the president's warning. It concluded, as he summarized it, "that the American forces could not stop a Soviet thrust into northern Iran and that the United States should therefore consider using 'tactical' nuclear weapons in any conflict there" (New York Times, February 2, 1980).

Even before the president spoke, this same conclusion was reflected in White House backgrounders given to Los Angeles Times reporters Jack Nelson and

Robert Toth. Heralding the president's message, "White House and other senior officials dealing with national security" told them that "if the Soviet Union carried its expansionism into Iran or Pakistan, the United States would have little choice but to oppose it militarily." These officials went on to say what the president, speaking to the public a few days later, did not put into words: such a war with the Soviet Union "would almost certainly become a nuclear war" (*Los Angeles Times,* January 18, 1980). This information was the lead front-page story, under the headline "Russia vs. Iran: U.S. Ponders Unthinkable." The same story reprinted next day in the *San Francisco Chronicle* bore the headline, "Doomsday Talk in Washington."

The revelation in *Time* of Senator Jackson's old conversation with Truman, appearing on newsstands the day before the president's speech, was part of this same chorus. It was particularly well suited to administration purposes—evident in the unusual publicity given to threats usually kept highly secret—of legitimizing and gaining public acceptance for the president's own policy. The Truman anecdote displayed a precedent of nuclear threats against the Russians, involving Iran (or really, in both cases, the transcendent issue of Middle East oil), invoking just the image of feisty, now-popular Harry Truman (re-elected against all odds, now enshrined in history after the lowest ratings in popular support until Jimmy Carter) that the president sought to associate with his own shift to a new Cold War: above all, a precedent of success.

But there was still another reason to evoke the memory of Harry Truman in this context. For all the talk and posturing, for all the military analyses, plans, and recommendations, even the deployments, the question remained: Could the Russians, could anyone, come to believe that the president of the United States, if challenged, might really carry out such threats, accepting the prospects at best—if the war, improbably, stayed regionally limited—of annihilating the local population along with troops? Indeed, was he not bound to the contrary—as most Americans still imagine, quite falsely—by an explicit or at least tacit "no first-use" commitment, never to be the first to use nuclear weapons in a crisis or non-nuclear conflict?

It was the official function of William Dyess, assistant secretary of state for public information, to interpret the president's meaning to the public in the week following the speech, and to address in particular just these questions. In an arresting exchange on television (*Newsmakers,* NBC Television, February 3, 1980) one day after Burt's leak of the Pentagon study, Dyess answered the second question crisply and correctly, and the first as well:

> Q: In nuclear war are we committed not to make the first strike?
>
> Dyess: No Sir.
>
> Q: We could conceivably make an offensive. . . .
>
> Dyess: We make no comment on that whatsoever, but the Soviets know that this terrible weapon has been dropped on human beings twice in history and it was an American president who dropped it both times. Therefore, they have to take this into consideration in their calculus.

But the Soviets, better than most, know a good deal more than this about past uses and near-uses of U.S. nuclear weapons. What Dyess might have mentioned (but almost surely does not know) is that in the thirty-six years since Hiroshima, every president from Truman to Reagan, with the possible exception of Ford, has felt compelled to consider or direct serious preparations for possible imminent U.S. initiation of tactical or strategic nuclear warfare, in the midst of an ongoing, intense, non-nuclear conflict or crisis.

The Soviets know this because they were made to know it—often by explicit threats from the Oval Office, even when White House considerations of use of nuclear weapons was secret from other audiences—since they or their allies or client states were the intended targets of these preparations and warnings. Moreover, the Soviets will recall that the U.S. Strategic Air Command was established in early 1946 with the function of delivering nuclear attacks upon Russia when so directed, at a time when it was publicly proclaimed by the president and high military that the Soviet Union was not expected to possess operational nuclear weapon systems for a decade or longer. SAC's *only* mission in that initial period—which included the formation of NATO— was to threaten or carry out a U.S. first strike: *not at all* to deter or retaliate for a nuclear attack on the United States or anywhere else.

It is not the Russians but the rest of us who need to learn these hidden realities of the nuclear dimension to U.S. foreign policy. As important background for the essays that follow and for much else, here, briefly listed, are more of the actual nuclear crises that can now be documented from memoirs or other public sources (in most cases after long periods of secrecy. . . .):

- Truman's deployment of B-29s, officially described as "atomic-capable," to bases in Britain and Germany at the outset of the Berlin Blockade, June 1948.
- Truman's press conference warning that nuclear weapons were under consideration, the day after marines were surrounded by Chinese Communist troops at the Chosin Reservoir, Korea, November 30, 1950.
- Eisenhower's secret nuclear threats against China, to force and maintain a settlement in Korea, 1953.
- Secretary of State Dulles' secret offer to Prime Minister Bidault of three tactical nuclear weapons in 1954 to relieve the French troops besieged by the Indochinese at Dienbienphu.
- Eisenhower's secret directive to the Joint Chiefs during the "Lebanon Crisis" in 1958 to prepare to use nuclear weapons, if necessary, to prevent an Iraqi move into the oilfields of Kuwait.
- Eisenhower's secret directive to the Joint Chiefs in 1958 to plan to use nuclear weapons, imminently, against China if the Chinese Communists should attempt to invade the island of Quemoy, occupied by Chiang's troops, a few miles offshore mainland China.
- The Berlin crisis, 1961.

- The Cuban Missile Crisis, 1962.
- Numerous "shows of nuclear force" involving demonstrative deployments or alerts—deliberately visible to adversaries and intended as a "nuclear signal"—of forces with a designated role in U.S. plans for strategic nuclear war.
- Much public discussion, in newspapers and in the Senate, of (true) reports that the White House had been advised of the possible necessity of nuclear weapons to defend marines surrounded at Khe Sanh, Vietnam, 1968.
- Nixon's secret threats of massive escalation, including possible use of nuclear weapons, conveyed to the North Vietnamese by Henry Kissinger, 1969–72.
- The Carter Doctrine on the Middle East (January 1980) as explained by Defense Secretary Harold Brown, Assistant Secretary of State William Dyess, and other spokesmen, reaffirmed, in essence, by President Reagan in 1981.

Although the current warnings and preparations for nuclear war in the Middle East are the most public threats since the crises over Berlin and Cuba a generation ago, it follows from this listing that there has been no thirty-six-year moratorium upon the active consideration and use of nuclear weapons to support "nuclear diplomacy." Indeed, many of the recurrent circumstances were remarkably similar to the first use at Hiroshima.

In none of these cases, any more than in 1945, was there apprehension among U.S. officials that nuclear war might be initiated by an adversary or needed urgent deterring. In most of them, just as against Japan, the aim was to coerce in urgent circumstances a much weaker opponent that possessed no nuclear weapons at all. In the remaining cases the object—already important in August 1945—was to intimidate the Soviet Union in an otherwise non-nuclear conflict.

And even against the Soviets most of these threats were seen as effective, just as the first two bombs were. U.S. marines, who had fought their way out of Chinese encirclement at the Chosin Reservoir without carrying out Truman's 1950 warning, were never finally assaulted at Khe Sanh, in 1968. The Chinese accepted and kept our 1953 armistice terms in Korea; in 1958, they ceased abruptly their daily shelling of Quemoy. The Russians backed down over Berlin in 1961 and again, spectacularly, in Cuba the next year.

Whether the nuclear component of U.S. threats to escalate the level of hostilities was actually critical to the behavior of opponents is not the issue here. (That question is still hotly controversial for the 1945 case itself.) What matters, if we are to understand this record, is that presidents *believed* that past and current threats had succeeded: this was why, as they understood it, they or their predecessors had not been forced to carry them out, and why they and their successors kept making such threats, and buying more and more first-use and first-strike nuclear weapon systems to maintain and increase the credibility and effectiveness of threats they expected to make in the future. It is why, after all, each president has refused to make a ''no first-use'' commitment, even when the Soviet Union has proposed such a commitment bilaterally.

The objection to these tactics is not that such threats cannot possibly ''work.'' However, it is important to observe that most of these known incidents—*and all of the apparently successful ones* (except Khe Sanh)—occurred under earlier conditions of American strategic nuclear superiority so overwhelming as to amount to monopoly.

Thus, in mid-1961, the year of the projected ''missile gap'' favoring the Russians, the United States had within range of Russia about 1000 tactical bombers and 2000 intercontinental bombers, 40 ICBMs, 48 Polaris missiles, and another 100 intermediate range missiles based in Europe. The Soviets had at that time some 190 intercontinental bombers and exactly *four* ICBMs: four ''soft,'' nonalert, liquid-fueled ICBMs at one site at Plesetsk that was vulnerable to a small attack with conventional weapons.

When Kennedy urged the American people to prepare fall-out shelters during the Berlin crisis that year, it was not for a nuclear war that would be started by the Soviets. Nor was it to avert Soviet superiority, nor to deter a Soviet nuclear first strike, that Kennedy fixed on the figure of 1000 missiles as the projected size of the Minuteman force in November of that year, well *after* the intelligence community had concurred on the conclusive estimate that the Soviets possessed less than ten ICBMs.

Officially, the precise figure cited above for Soviet ICBMs in the period from early 1960 to early 1962—four—is guarded as a classified secret today just as it was twenty years ago: the number presented in nearly all public sources—''about fifty''—is wrong by an order of magnitude. The true figure remains secret for the same reason as before: because public knowledge of the *scale* of the ''missile gap'' hoax would undercut the recurrently-necessary tactic of whipping up public fears of imminent U.S. ''inferiority'' to mobilize support for vastly expensive arms spending intended, in fact, to assure continued and increased—or in the present instance, regained—U.S. superiority.

The Soviets did acquire a large and growing ability to devastate Western Europe from the mid-fifties on (with short- and medium-range bombers and rockets). But (a) the ability to disarm the opposing superpower of its strategic forces in a first strike, and (b) the ability to retailiate against the homeland of the opposing superpower in a second strike, were both capabilities strictly monopolized by the United States until the late sixties. Not until 1967 did the Russians begin to put their ICBMs into ''hardened'' concrete silos and deploy advanced missile submarines, thereby acquiring the second capability and depriving the U.S. of the first.

For most of two decades, it is now clear, the Soviets chose not to seriously challenge what amounted to U.S. strategic monopoly. But the cost to U.S. security interests of *using* that monopoly repeatedly, most dramatically over Quemoy, Berlin, and Cuba—while increasing spending sharply to maintain it and refusing to put a ceiling on U.S. technological superiority by a comprehensive, bilateral test ban on warheads or missiles—was to discredit Khrushchev's reliance on cheap bluffs and to help him lose his job. Brezhnev, displacing Khrushchev in 1964, seems to have promised the Soviet military to spend whatever it would take to eliminate inferiority. The Soviets proceeded to outspend the U.S. in the seventies, as they finally duplicated the huge investments in strategic capabilities that the U.S. had made in the fifties and sixties. In the course of the decade, they succeeded in buying "rough equivalence" or parity, thus drastically eroding the credibility of the U.S. first-strike threat, and along with it, the credibility of threats to escalate lesser levels of conflict if necessary to avoid tactical defeat or stalemate.

Americans are now being mobilized for a massive attempt to buy back these two lost pillars of U.S. foreign policy. The damaged credibility is to be partially restored by adding to our sizeable (and unique) antisubmarine capability the highly precise counterforce capabilities for a disarming first strike against landbased forces represented by the MX, Trident II, Pershing, and cruise missiles (with antiballistic missile systems and civil defense as logical and likely complements, when the public is ready). So far (July 1981) Congress is not balking at a projected price tag of several hundred billion dollars, even though the significant superiority sought (under the consciously deceptive public slogan of "avoiding inferiority") seems most unlikely to be achieved, in face of the evident Soviet determination to deny it.

G. ALLEN GREB and
GERALD W. JOHNSON

A History of Strategic Arms Limitations

G. Allen Greb (b. 1948) and Gerald W. Johnson (b. 1927). G. Allen Greb is a research historian in the Program in Science, Technology, and Public Affairs at the University of California at San Diego and also serves as the Assistant Director of the Institute for Global Conflict and Cooperation. Gerald W. Johnson was part of the negotiating team to SALT II and the Comprehensive Test Ban Negotiations. He is presently a scientist with TRW, an aerospace corporation.

G. Allen Greb and Gerald W. Johnson, "A History of Strategic Arms Limitations," *Bulletin of the Atomic Scientists* (January 1984), pp. 30–37. Reprinted by permission of the *Bulletin of the Atomic Scientists*, a magazine of science and world affairs.

SALT I, the Vladivostok accord, SALT II, START—more has been said and written about these superpower forays into arms control than any other set of agreements or negotiations of the nuclear era. Included in this vast literature are several book-length accounts by participants, volumes of Congressional testimony, and analyses by government experts and scholars.

Yet, while familiar with the acronyms, most Americans would be hard pressed to discuss the substance of these efforts to limit strategic nuclear arms. Our aim here is to help demystify this historic set of negotiations.

Although the Strategic Arms Limitation Talks (SALT) constitute the most important, most intense, and longest-running attempt to curb the arms race, they do not stand alone. In fact, SALT would not have come into existence at all if its most famous antecedent, the so-called Baruch plan, had been implemented, On June 14, 1946, at the very outset of the nuclear age, the United States introduced this plan to ban forever all atomic weapons and place nuclear technology under international control. The men behind the plan were a diverse group of scientific and government experts: the atomic scientist Robert Oppenheimer, who originally conceived it; U.S. Atomic Energy Chairman David Lilienthal and Secretary of State Dean Acheson, who substantially modified it; and financier Bernard Baruch, who presented it before the United Nations.

The proposal called for the creation of an international nuclear development authority. This authority would have the power to control all atomic energy activities and to establish inspection procedures not subject to U.N. Security Council veto. The United States promised to dismantle its nuclear bombs once this agency was established. The Soviet reply, presented by Deputy Foreign Minister Andrei Gromyko, came only five days later; because the United States enjoyed a nuclear monopoly, the Soviets called for the destruction of existing atomic arsenals *before* any discussion of inspection and control procedures could take place. This fundamental difference blocked all progress toward any form of arms control or disarmament for a dozen years.

The roots of this U.S.-Soviet failure went deeper than disagreement on the specifics of the Baruch plan. Growing tension between East and West rendered any agreement on atomic energy highly unlikely. The authors of the plan, especially Oppenheimer, were well aware of this hostile political climate. They believed, however, that the uniqueness and magnitude of the problem demanded extraordinary measures:

> The program we propose will undoubtedly arouse skepticism when it is first considered. It did among us, but thought and discussion have converted us.
>
> It may seem too idealistic. It seems time we endeavor to bring some of our expressed ideals into being.
>
> It may seem too radical, too advanced, too much beyond human experience. All these terms apply with peculiar fitness to the atomic bomb.
>
> In considering the plan . . . one should ask oneself, "What are the alternatives?" We have, and we find no tolerable answer.[1]

These words proved all too prophetic. As many anticipated, the Soviet Union soon acquired the bomb. The Cold War deepened and intensified, and the nuclear arsenals of both sides grew in both numbers and sophistication. It was two stormy decades before the superpowers could again address the issue of arms limitation, if only partially, through the medium of SALT.

An early approach to negotiation proposed by Secretary of War Henry Stimson to President Harry Truman and the Cabinet one month after the nuclear attacks on Hiroshima and Nagasaki has recently come to light. Although Truman did not follow Stimson's suggestion, it did outline a bold and possibly attractive alternative to the Baruch plan. Stimson suggested that the United States, in concert with the United Kingdom, enter into direct discussions with the Soviet Union, warning that a multinational approach could create the impression of "ganging up" on the Soviets. He noted that the atomic bomb was a uniquely dangerous weapon that must be brought under control, and that traditional diplomatic procedures might not suffice to meet the challenge. In his view, *when* the Soviets acquired the bomb—whether it be four or 20 years—was less important than the superpowers having a peaceful cooperative relationship when they did.

In November 1969, the United States and the Soviet Union in essence adopted such an approach, formally initiating bilateral negotiations on strategic nuclear arms. This followed a number of abortive overtures and initiatives made during the 1950s and 1960s: one by Soviet Premier Nikolai Bulganin in 1955 and several by U.S. President Lyndon B. Johnson. In 1964 Johnson proposed a "verified freeze" on strategic weapons; in 1966 a limit on anti-ballistic missile (ABM) deployment; and in 1967 restrictions on both offensive and defensive systems. Finally, in mid-1968, each side publicly committed itself to enter negotiations. But that summer the Soviet Union invaded Czechoslovakia. As so often has happened in the history of SALT, it was an unrelated political action, but it rudely changed the course of events. The 1968 presidential elections made for further delay. Talks formally began on November 17, 1969, after President Nixon and his special assistant Henry Kissinger reviewed and approved the SALT idea.

What put arms limitation on the political and diplomatic agendas of each side at this time? One fact stands above all others: stockpiles of nuclear weapons and the means to deliver them had reached such levels that Soviet and U.S. leaders independently concluded that their national security lay in some degree of mutual arms restraint. Washington and Moscow cited both the risks of nuclear war and the prohibitive cost of carrying on an unbridled strategic competition.

Each side had its own variations of this common theme. For the United States, arms limitation had become more attractive because of a fundamental change in the global strategic environment. For the first time, U.S. nuclear dominance was clearly and irrevocably ended, as a result of a determined Soviet buildup following the Cuban missile crisis of 1962. Each side now possessed—or perceived itself and the other to possess—a nuclear retaliatory force that could inflict unacceptable damage after a first strike. This tenuous balance seemed to promise new possibilities in arms control.

The person primarily responsible for rethinking and retooling U.S. strategic goals in light of this new international reality was President Lyndon Johnson's Defense Secretary, Robert S. McNamara. Backed by an army of "systems analysts," McNamara persuasively demonstrated to the President and the Joint Chiefs of Staff the absurdity of engaging in a strategic arms competition that no one could win. He also successfully conveyed his concerns about anti-ballistic missiles (ABMs). This developing technology, he argued, offered no sure guarantees of safety and might completely destabilize the deterrent system by acting as a stimulus to offensive countermeasures. ABM curbs became the prime target of the U.S. negotiating position.

For the Soviet Union, catching up with the United States in nuclear weaponry made negotiations attractive for different reasons. The Soviets had always been haunted by feelings of inferiority in comparison with their capitalist adversaries. The leaders who took over in the wake of the 1962 Cuban fiasco, Leonid Brezhnev and Alexei Kosygin, were, in the view of prominent Kremlinologists, particularly "obsessed by the notion of inequality."[2] And SALT offered confirmation of their country's status as a superpower. The Brezhnev-Kosygin regime also saw an opportunity to check the U.S. technological lead in new weapons systems, including ABMs, even though the Soviets had been first to deploy these, and multiple independently-targeted re-entry vehicles (MIRVs). American advances in multiple warheads in particular threatened to undermine the hard-fought Soviet gains in the numerical strength and capabilities of its Strategic Rocket Forces.

Beyond these strategic considerations, domestic pressures played a major role in both U.S. and Soviet decisions to negotiate. In the United States, negative reaction to the Vietnam War and a growing public and Congressional interest in national security matters produced demands for reductions in defense spending. Some officials worried that Congress would legislate unilateral restraints on strategic forces in the absence of mutual agreements. For the Soviet Union, discussion and negotiation became a way to avoid costly global confrontations while consolidating power at home and within the Soviet sphere. The deepening Sino-Soviet breach, dating from the late 1950s and fully confirmed after 1964; persistent nationalism in East European countries; and the allure of trade and credits with the West caused the new Kremlin regime to initiate what Brezhnev and Kosygin termed an "opening to the West."

Both superpowers were also motivated by the desire to build upon a series of arms control agreements achieved during the previous decade: the Antarctic Treaty, the Hot-Line agreement, the Limited Test Ban Treaty, the Outer Space Treaty, and the Non-Proliferation Treaty. Article VI of the 1968 Non-Proliferation Treaty, for example, specifically committed the two giants "to pursue negotiations in good faith on effective measures relating to cessation of the nuclear arms race."[3]

Thus, with the strategic forces and psychology of both countries "in phase," as the chief U.S. negotiator, Gerard Smith, put it, SALT began. Neither side, however, entered into these initial negotiations with much optimism. "Although overall political relations had mellowed slightly in the 1960s," Ambassador Smith remembers, "American and Soviet SALT negotiators were under no illusions that they were involved in anything but an adversary relationship, representing two superpowers tentatively searching for a less risky and costly way to maintain the balance of nuclear terror."[4] Nevertheless, after two-and-a-half years of hard bargaining involving both formal negotiations and important behind-the-scenes maneuvering between Henry Kissinger and Soviet Ambassador A. F. Dobrynin, Washington and Moscow forged two accords, together known as SALT I.

The 1972 ABM Treaty and its companion 1974 Protocol severely restrict ballistic missile defense systems, allowing each side only one deployment site and placing qualitative restraints on ABM technology. Considered by many to be the most significant result of SALT, the Treaty was described by one expert as "a classic case of both sides agreeing not to build something that neither side wanted but that each would have probably ended up building in the absence of an agreement."[5] Though of unlimited duration, the pact is subject to review every five years. Each side reaffirmed its support for the Treaty at the 1982 review, but ballistic missile defense is again being considered seriously. President Reagan in fact recently announced a long-term research and development program to explore all possible non-nuclear avenues to provide for an effective missile defense.

The SALT I interim Agreement on Offensive Arms essentially imposes a five-year quantitative freeze on the superpowers' intercontinental ballistic missiles (ICBMs) and submarine-launched ballistic missiles (SLBMs), the first set of actual limits on strategic hardware ever achieved. Much more controversial and difficult to negotiate than the ABM Treaty, the Interim Agreement is a series of compromises—or trade-offs—between adversaries. The agreement left the Soviet Union with several hundred more launchers than the United States had—2,347 to 1,710. And within this aggregate, the Soviets were allowed about 300 "modern large" or "heavy" ICBMs while the United States had none. The U.S. research and development community much earlier had turned away from large missiles in favor of Minuteman, a smaller, more accurate, more efficient rocket. But this discrepancy worried many Pentagon planners nonetheless.

For their part, the Soviets could point to a number of important compromises which compensated for asymmetries in the aggregate force level: First, it was significant that they accepted *any* restrictions on their offensive missiles. The Kremlin had resisted including such forces for a year and a half, an indication of internal pressure from the military establishment. Even more important, the Soviets agreed to defer consideration of several key issues: U.S. technological superiority, U.S. forward-based systems capable of delivering a nuclear attack on Soviet territory from outside the United States, and the U.S. advantage of approximately three-to-one in long-range strategic bombers.

Neither side was fully satisfied by the Interim Agreement, but both recognized it as a temporary measure, with the potential to produce more meaningful future limits on strategic forces. In addition, both governments welcomed it and the ABM Treaty as significant political achievements. During the negotiations SALT acquired an institutional life of its own that has fundamentally altered the superpower relationship.

> Soviet and American officials sat across from each other at long tables, sipped mineral water and discussed military matters that used to be the stuff that spies were paid and shot for. . . . The process was the product. There emerged SALT bureaucrats in Washington and SALT *apparatchiks* in Moscow. SALT became a career in the civil service. The process acquired an institutional mass . . . that served as a kind of deep-water anchor in Soviet-American relations.[6]

The American public and Congress also greeted SALT I with much initial enthusiasm, reflected most vividly in the Senate ratification vote of 88-to-2. Gerald Ford, then a Congressman, best summarized the national mood: ''What it all comes down to is this,'' Ford told a middle-America audience in June 1972. ''We did not give anything away, and we slowed the Soviet momentum in the nuclear arms race.''[7] Support was not unconditional, however. Congress overwhelmingly approved the SALT I accords in September but added an amendment sponsored by Senator Henry Jackson requesting ''the President to seek a future treaty that . . . would not limit the United States to levels of intercontinental strategic forces inferior to the limits provided for the Soviet Union.''[8]

Foreshadowed by the Jackson amendment and the debate over Soviet ''superiority,'' the problems rather than the promise of SALT dominated the next phase of discussions. Between November 1972 and November 1974, the negotiations stalled over familiar issues: What systems to include in a permanent, comprehensive agreement; how to deal with qualitative as well as quantitative limits, especially with regard to MIRV; and how to keep outside political events—''linkage''—from influencing the discussions.

By far the greatest impediment to progress in this period was the continued improvement of Soviet and U.S. strategic nuclear forces within SALT I limits. During the 1970s the military, industrial, and scientific bureaucracies on both sides kept pressure on policy-makers to modernize strategic systems. Working from worst-case analyses, they warned about the possibility of technological ''breakout'' and worried about the uncertainties and unknowns of a possible SALT II agreement, all of which created a difficult and uncomfortable situation for SALT negotiators.

The Soviet military buildup was particularly dramatic, especially in the eyes of U.S. defense planners. Of gravest concern was a new generation of hardened Soviet ICBMs with improved accuracy, increased throw-weight (payload capacity), and MIRV capabilities. The Soviets also introduced new submarine-launched ballistic missiles; a new intermediate-range ballistic missile, the SS-20; and a new bomber, the Tu-22M Backfire. And they continued to improve air defense and civil defense systems. According to political analyst Thomas Wolfe, during the 1970s the "Soviet R&D establishment . . . was continuing to operate at its own cyclical rhythm, little affected by SALT."[9]

Reacting to these moves, President Nixon's defense secretary, James R. Schlesinger, suggested in 1974 that the Soviets were creating a "major one-sided counterforce [hard-target] capability against the United States ICBM force" that was "impermissible from our point of view."[10] This became the major justification for the continuing modernization of U.S. nuclear forces. In addition to proceeding with MIRV deployment, which helped maintain the substantial U.S. advantage in numbers of warheads, Washington expanded the existing Trident missile and B-1 intercontinental bomber programs and initiated numerous other research and development projects. These included the MX missile, the long-range cruise missile, the increased yield MK-12A warhead, and MARV, a maneuverable re-entry vehicle that was the technological successor of MIRV. Wolfe's observation about Soviet research and development could as easily apply to U.S. programs.

Negotiators also found themselves adversely affected by the deterioration of international relations. SALT I had bolstered U.S.-Soviet political accommodation, but SALT II fell victim to political trouble between the superpowers. The Soviets' backing of the October 1973 Arab attack on Israel and their adventurism elsewhere in the Third World noticeably strained the Geneva negotiations.

Still, both sides had a great deal invested in SALT and the preservation of detente. Hence the talks continued, surviving the shifts in the U.S. Administration after Watergate. Finally in November 1974, President Gerald Ford and General Secretary Brezhnev met at Vladivostok where they hammered out an "agreed framework" for SALT II. Henry Kissinger, utilizing his talents at personal diplomacy, was largely responsible for engineering this major breakthrough.

Like SALT I, the Vladivostok accord was a mixture of superpower compromises. Meeting a central U.S. concern, the Kremlin accepted the principle of equal overall ceilings on delivery vehicles and agreed to drop the contentious forward-based-systems issue. However, the specific force level aggregate set by Ford and Brezhnev—2,400 strategic nuclear delivery vehicles, including for the first time, strategic bombers—was higher by about 300 than the United States would have preferred. Within this aggregate, moreover, each side would be permitted to mix and modernize its forces in any way it saw fit (which left unresolved the issue of Soviet heavy missiles). Also, bowing to U.S. pressure for "parity," the two leaders established a sub-ceiling of 1,320 MIRVed missile launchers for each side, but placed no specific limits on throw-weight, in which the Soviets had a large advantage.

Despite having a treaty "90 percent" completed by the end of 1975, according to Kissinger, and despite a January 1976 "near miss" by Kissinger to find that 10 percent solution, SALT II would not be signed for another three years.[11] There were several reasons for this renewed stalemate. For the sake of agreement, the negotiators at Vladivostok once more left the hardest strategic questions for future discussion. They underestimated the dynamism of new technology. And they met a formidable roadblock in the U.S. political process.

The two particularly controversial new technologies were the Soviet Backfire bomber and the U.S. long-range cruise missile. The Backfire is a modern supersonic airplane intended for use primarily as a medium-range bomber but which could also be employed for strategic missions. The modern cruise missile is a small, pilotless aircraft. It can be launched from the air, land, or sea, and its sophisticated guidance system permits it to fly at very low altitudes. The fact that the Backfire bomber and the cruise missile are both capable of strategic as well as tactical roles made each attractive to their respective military establishments, even while posing almost insurmountable difficulties for negotiators. Whether to include the Backfire as a strategic system and how to count cruise missiles in a new SALT agreement became the almost impossible arms control task.

In 1977 the Carter Administration came to power, deeply committed to arms control and determined to resolve the difficult remaining SALT issues. In March Carter sent Secretary of State Cyrus Vance to Moscow with a comprehensive package of SALT proposals they were confident would break the impasse. In a typically bold but rash move, Carter and his national security advisor, Zbigniew Brzezenski, had included several provisions that went far beyond the Vladivostok equal-aggregates formula. As Paul Warnke, the Administration's chief arms negotiator, later recalled, Carter and Brzezinski hoped "to shortcut the arms control negotiating process and move in one single giant step toward very significant reductions in numbers and toward a whole series of qualitative restraints."[12] Predictably, the proposal shocked Soviet bureaucrats who had a built-in distaste for surprises or changes. Brezhnev summarily rejected it.

Thus, what seemed at first to be a giant leap toward arms limitation turned out to be step backward. But despite continuing Soviet uneasiness over Carter's idealism, his open style of diplomacy, and his unpredictability, the two sides narrowed their differences and adopted a compromise negotiating framework in September 1977. At the same time, they issued unilateral statements agreeing to abide by the SALT I Interim Agreement while the SALT II process continued. On June 18, 1979, Carter and Brezhnev met in Vienna and signed the three-part SALT II accords.

What is SALT II? At first glance, the accords appear to be a complex mass of documents describing the minutiae of nuclear arsenals. They include the basic Treaty on the Limitation of Strategic Offensive Arms to run through 1985, a protocol of three years' duration, and a bewildering jumble of Joint and Agreed Statements, Common Understandings, and Memoranda totaling more than 100 pages. Buried in this legalistic and technical jargon, however, is a working, viable agreement.

At the heart of the Treaty are the aggregate numerical limits and sublimits: on total launchers (2,400 initially, 2,250 within a year, which would require the Soviets to dismantle 250 existing systems); on MIRV launchers, including missiles and cruise-missile-carrying bombers (1,350); on MIRVed missiles alone (1,200); on MIRVed land-based ICBMs alone (820); and on "heavy" ICBMs (308). The Treaty also established limits on numbers of warheads or reentry vehicles per missile (10 for each MIRVed ICBM, 14 for each SLBM) and on the number of long-range cruise missiles per heavy bomber (an average of 28). The parties also agreed to several important bans: on the flight-testing or deployment of new types of ICBMs, except for one new type of "light" missile for each side; on heavy mobile ICBMs and heavy SLBMs; on the construction of additional fixed ICBM launchers; and on rapid reload systems. Restrictions on the Backfire bomber are less clear, but the Soviets did add an official statement that limits its production rate to 30 per year. Finally, the agreement includes detailed definitions and counting rules for the weapons systems it covers as well as an agreed data base.

The spirit of compromise was very evident in the Treaty. The Joint Chiefs of Staff explicitly recognized this in 1979 and consequently supported SALT II as a "modest but useful step in a long-range process which must include the resolve . . . to maintain strategic equivalence coupled with vigorous efforts to achieve further substantial reductions."[13] Many former national security officials and members of Congress, however, did not see it this way. Led by Senator Henry Jackson and Paul Nitze, a former SALT I negotiator and co-founder of the Committee on the Present Danger, domestic critics mounted a massive campaign against SALT II during 1978 and 1979 which intensified during the ratification process.

Nitze became the intellectual driving force behind the anti-SALT movement. He and his Committee on the Present Danger attacked the Treaty itself as "fatally flawed" and President Carter as soft on national security issues. Nitze emphasized the persistent question of the Soviet heavy missile advantage, stressing the hypothetical threat it posed for U.S. ICBMs and creating ingenious scenarios in which the Soviets might use this advantage in a post-SALT II world for political blackmail. Nitze, Jackson, and other Treaty detractors noted another "fatal flaw"—the non-inclusion of the Backfire bomber as a strategic system—and also raised questions about the ability to monitor Soviet compliance with the treaty.

Political analysts and Senate-watchers were still giving SALT II at least a 50-50 chance of ratification when a series of world events in the latter months of 1979 threw the agreement into limbo. In August, the United States discovered a Soviet troop brigade in Cuba; in November, Iranians seized the U.S. Embassy in Teheran; and in December, the Soviet Union invaded Afghanistan. The overall effect of these actions was to both divert attention from SALT and deepen public distrust of the Soviets. In January 1980, Carter asked the Senate to "delay consideration" of the Treaty.[14]

The present U.S. Administration has yet another approach to arms limitation. President Reagan came to office with a strong public mandate to "get tough" with the Soviets. He initially took this mandate to heart, adopting a policy of "arms now—talk later" in his dealings with the Soviets. For nearly a year and a half, high-level Administration officials paid almost no attention to the issue of arms control. But responding in part to a growing international and national anti-nuclear movement, Reagan's advisors have expressed renewed interest in arms control even while emphasizing the need to bolster the military.

What does this mean for SALT? Nearly all members of the national security team, including the President, have been extremely critical of the SALT agreement. Eugene Rostow, former director of the Arms Control and Disarmament Agency, for example, has stated that the benefits of SALT I and SALT II "have turned to ashes in our mouths."[15] Thus when forced to formulate their own policies and goals, these advisors proposed going beyond the SALT regime to achieve "truly substantial" reductions in nuclear arsenals.[16] SALT became START—Strategic Arms Reduction Talks—and was conducted in coordination with the new intermediate Range Nuclear Forces talks, dealing with European theater systems.

The START deep-cut strategy envisions downgrading the importance of equal numbers of delivery vehicles and emphasizing instead restraints on the "destructive capacity" of strategic weapons—throw-weight, megatonnage, warhead and missile accuracy. Whether this approach can actually lead to agreement is questionable. As a Carnegie Endowment Study notes, the task is formidable: "Any scheme must deal with the wide differences in current forces and consider how to move from the current regimes toward a significantly different one without creating new instabilities."[17] Still, the Soviets have not rejected the Reagan proposals outright (as they did Carter's in 1977), and talks have resumed.

The Reagan Administration first proposed at START to cut each side's total force of submarine and land-based missiles to 850. [See Table 1.] Warheads on those missiles would be reduced to 5,000 each, with no more than 2,500 on land-based ICBMs. This would cut U.S. missiles by half and Soviet missiles by two-thirds. Moscow countered with an offer to make an overall reduction in the missile and strategic bomber forces to 1,800 for each side, but Soviet negotiators carefully avoided proposing restrictions on any of the separate strategic weapons systems. Responding to the Scowcroft Commission report and congressional suggestions on arms control, Reagan has since slightly modified the original U.S. START position. While maintaining the proposed 5,000-warhead limitation, the President has directed negotiators to abandon the ceiling of 850 missiles for each side and called for "measured flexibility" in the negotiations.

SALT II survives as a *de facto* observance by both sides. But Reagan's defense officials continue to explore the ICBM vulnerability problem in ways that threaten to unravel existing elements of SALT—for example, using ABMs to

TABLE 1 Reductions Required by Phase I START Proposals

	United States	Soviet Union
U.S. proposal		
Total warheads	7128 to 5000: −2128	6735 to 5000: −1735
ICBM and SLBM launchers	1564 to 850: −714	2415 to 850: −1565
ICBM warheads	2152 to 2500: +348	5302 to 2500: −2802
Soviet proposal		
All delivery vehicles	1940 to 1800: −140	2650 to 1800: −850

Source: Stockholm International Peace Research Institute, *1983 SIPRI Yearbook* (London and New York: Taylor & Francis Ltd.), Table 3.3, p. 61. Copyright 1983. Reprinted by permission of the publisher.

protect the MX, which would require abrogation or "technical adjustment" of the 1972 ABM Treaty. "Dense pack" would also have been inconsistent with the terms of SALT II.

What do we stand to lose if SALT I and SALT II are gradually eroded or even scrapped? To be sure, SALT has left both sides with huge nuclear arsenals. And certain negotiating tactics that can be traced back to the Nixon-Kissinger years have actually accelerated weapons procurement. The utilization of "bargaining chips"—new weapons systems employed to gain negotiating leverage—is perhaps the most disturbing of these practices. "The bargaining chip," one study notes, "cannot always be cashed in."[18] Or as another puts it, "Weapons initially justified as bargaining chips soon become building blocks—weapons systems which become permanent parts of the arsenal."[19]

Benefits from SALT far outweigh its costs, however. Apart from the specific restrictions of individual agreements which act as a control mechanism, however imperfect, on the East-West arms race, the overall SALT process has resulted in some general benefits to U.S. security. Heading this list are advances in verification procedures and apparatus which both increase our knowledge about the other side and build mutual confidence. The 1972 agreements explicitly legitimize, and SALT II reaffirms, the unimpeded use of "national technical means of verification," a euphemism for satellite reconnaissance and other non-intrusive information-gathering techniques, such as radar and electronic monitors. SALT II builds upon this basic achievement with several new verification measures: "counting rules" for hard-to-inspect systems, among them MIRVed missiles (adopting the standard "once tested [as a particular type], always counted"); "type definitions" of systems, for example, of "heavy" missiles; and an "agreed data base" on ten categories of strategic forces to be updated at regular intervals.

Together these provisions represent a significant gain for U.S. intelligence and a marked change in Soviet attitudes about secrecy. After agreeing to the data base exchange, for example, chief Soviet negotiator Vladimir Semyenov reportedly said to Paul Warnke that 400 years of Russian history had just been "repealed." "But on reflection," he added, "maybe that's not a bad thing."[20] Not only have Soviet leaders agreed to reveal more to the West; they have in the process opened a flow of information within their own bureaucracy. Apparently, the military is no longer the sole custodian of strategic facts and doctrine. New constituencies, in particular foreign policy experts, have taken their place in the internal decision-making process through the negotiations themselves, and such special SALT bodies as a jointly-run ad hoc group within the Ministry of Defense.

Another valuable product of the SALT process is the Standing Consultative Commission. Set up originally by the ABM Treaty to monitor problems and complaints about compliance, the Commission has quietly evolved into an important force for continuing dialogue and accommodation on nuclear issues. Since its inception in 1973, it has met at least twice a year in Geneva, in sessions completely separate from the formal negotiations. In the past, the U.S. delegation has been represented by a civilian commissioner from the Arms Control and Disarmament Agency, a military deputy, and a staff of advisors from various government agencies. Today both top officials are military officers. The Kremlin also has civilian and military personnel on its delegation, led since the outset by Major General G. I. Ustinov of the General Staff and Viktor P. Karpov of the Ministry of Foreign Affairs, who now also heads the START negotiations. According to one SALT scholar, the Commission's most significant contribution to date has been the "successful . . . defusing [of] several public accusations of Soviet cheating by American critics of the SALT process."[21] This confidence-building role will expand under SALT II and START since the Commission will be responsible for maintaining the data base, supervising any dismantling of strategic weapons that may be called for, and even considering new arms limitation strategies.

Thus, each side is now playing the strategic armaments game by a new set of rules which make the game more predictable and enhance stability. They should not be sacrificed or discarded in the interests of short-term military goals. SALT is not a panacea for our national security problems; neither is it the main cause of U.S. strategic deficiencies. Rather, it provides a valuable framework in which the superpowers can work toward further progress in negotiated arms limitation.

Notes

[1]Chester I. Barnard, J. R. Oppenheimer, Charles A. Thomas, Harry A. Winne, David E. Lilienthal, *A Report on the International Control of Atomic Energy,* prepared for the Secretary of State's Committee on Atomic Energy (Washington, D.C.: March 16, 1946), p. 31.

[2]Helmut Sonnenfeldt and William G. Hyland, *Soviet Perspectives on Security,* Adelphi Paper No. 150 (Spring 1979), p. 14.

[3]ACDA *Arms Control and Disarmament Agreements: Texts and Histories of Negotiations* (Washington, D.C.: Aug. 1980), p. 92.

[4]Gerard Smith, *Doubletalk: The Story of the First Strategic Arms Limitation Talks* (New York: Doubleday, 1980), pp. 35, 37.

[5]Richard J. Barnet, *The Giants: Russia and America* (New York: Simon and Schuster, 1977), p. 102.

[6]Strobe Talbott, *Endgame: The Inside Story of SALT II* (New York: Harper and Row, 1980), p. 20.

[7]Representative Gerald R. Ford, Address before the VFW State Convention, Grand Rapids, Michigan (June 17, 1972).

[8]See Michael B. Donley, ed., *The SALT Handbook* (Washington, D.C.: The Heritage Foundation, 1979), p. 15.

[9]Thomas W. Wolfe, *The SALT Experience* (Cambridge, Massachusetts: Ballinger, 1979), p. 123.

[10]*Report of Secretary of Defense James R. Schlesinger to the Congress on the FY 1975 Budget and FY 1975–1979 Defense Program* (March 4, 1974), p. 6.

[11]New York Times, Oct. 13, 1975.

[12]Paul C. Warnke, "The SALT Process," Department of State News Release (Jan. 19, 1978), p. 3.

[13]David C. Jones, Chairman, Joint Chiefs of Staff, "SALT II: The Opinion of the Joint Chiefs of Staff," *Vital Speeches of the Day,* 45 (Aug. 15, 1979), p. 655.

[14]Talbott, *Endgame,* p. 290.

[15]Los Angeles Times, Jan. 24, 1982.

[16]New York Times, May 1, 1982.

[17]Carnegie Panel on U.S. Security and the Future of Arms Control, *Challenges for U.S. National Security: Nuclear Strategy Issues of the 1980s,* Third Report (Washington, D.C.: Carnegie Endowment for International Peace, 1982), p. 68.

[18]John H. Barton and Lawrence D. Weiler, eds., *International Arms Control: Issues and Agreements* (Stanford, California: Stanford University Press, 1976), p. 226.

[19]Robert J. Bresler and Robert C. Gray, "The Bargaining Chip and SALT," *Political Science Quarterly,* 92 (1977/78), p. 86.

[20]Talbott, *Endgame,* p. 98; Wolfe, *SALT Experience,* p. 261.

[21]Jane M. O. Sharp, "Restructuring the SALT Dialogue," *International Security,* 6 (Winter 1981/82), p. 149.

JEFFREY PORRO

The Policy War: Brodie vs. Kahn

Jeffrey Porro (b. 1947), a writer concerned with nuclear issues, has been associated with Arms Control Today, *a publication of the Arms Control Association. He is presently assistant editor of the National Academy of Sciences publication,* Issues in Science and Technology.

Jeffrey D. Porro, "The Policy War: Brodie vs. Kahn," *Bulletin of the Atomic Scientists* (June/July 1982), pp. 16–19. Reprinted by permission of the *Bulletin of the Atomic Scientists,* a magazine of science and world affairs.

The "countervalue" position associated with Kahn is close to our present defense policy.

Fifteen years of public apathy about nuclear war have ended. Membership in arms control organizations is up. The nuclear freeze movement is growing. The national and local media regularly carry stories and features about arms control and the nuclear danger.

Most of the people newly concerned about arms control have, quite simply, been scared by the Reagan Administration. Vice President Bush's statement that a nuclear war is winnable, Secretary Haig's comments on a nuclear demonstration shot, President Reagan's musings on a European nuclear war, and recent quotes from Administration civil defense officials on the survivability of a nuclear war seem to add up to a radically new and dangerous policy.

People are right to be scared; the Administration's attitude is dangerous. But it is nothing new. Moreover, turning out the Reagan Administration will not, in itself, lessen the dangers of nuclear war.

American policy toward nuclear weapons has been shaped by a relatively small group of men, mostly civilians. During the last 20 years, most of these men have come to believe that we must think about nuclear war in the way we think about other kinds of war; that is, we must develop the plans and weapons necessary to fight. This nuclear warfighting strategy overlaps labels like Democratic and Republican, liberal and conservative.

This strategy has evolved from a conflict between the ideas of two men—Bernard Brodie and Herman Kahn. Educated as a political scientist at the University of Chicago, Bernard Brodie began his professional life before World War II with a number of well-received works on naval strategy. He turned his attention to atomic war after 1945, first at Yale and later at the Rand Corporation and the University of California at Los Angeles. The conclusions he drew about nuclear strategy were revolutionary.

Immediately after World War II, most strategists—civilian and military—agreed that the atomic bomb had not altered military strategy fundamentally. But in a remarkable essay written within months of Hiroshima and Nagasaki, Brodie took exception: "Thus far the chief purpose of our military establishment has been to win wars. From now on its chief purpose must be to prevent them. It can have almost no other useful purpose."[1] Brodie reasoned from Clausewitz's key insight that war is a *means* to a *political* objective. If the costs of war outweighed the benefits of the political objective, war was senseless.

In his early essays, Brodie focused on the likely costs of war. Since atomic bombs could be acquired in large numbers and were so tremendously powerful, even if only a small percentage got through, hundreds of cities and millions of people would be destroyed. Brodie's conclusion: The costs to each side in an atomic war would be so high they would far outweigh any meaningful political goal. Neither side would be able to achieve "victory" in any valid sense. Atomic weapons could be used only to prevent general war, not "win" it.

To show just how atomic weapons should be used to prevent war, Brodie dusted off an old concept, "deterrence." In the atomic age, Brodie said, the key to deterrence was to guarantee that a potential attacker fear retaliation.

> If it must fear retaliation, the fact that it destroys its opponents' cities some hours or even days before its own are destroyed may avail it little. . . . Thus, the first and most vital step in any American security program for the age of atomic bombs is to take measures to guarantee to ourselves in case of attack the possibility of retaliation in kind.[2]

Throughout the 1950s, Brodie made it clear in his writings that deterrent strategy was very different from win-the-war strategies: The latter required superiority in numbers of weapons; deterrence did not. A relatively small number of bombers and missiles—as long as they could survive—could damage an attacker enough to outweigh any conceivable political gain. In a war-winning strategy, military might was used to destroy the enemy's weapons, forcing him to surrender. In a deterrent strategy military might should be directed against cities, not military forces, for two reasons:

"Limiting damage" in any politically meaningful sense was impossible, given the destructive power of even a few nuclear weapons.

More importantly, aiming at military forces could weaken deterrence and increase the chances of massive destruction. Any potential attacker "cares more for his cities intrinsically than he does for a few airfields."[3] If the Soviets believed they would suffer only the loss of some military bases after they attacked us, they might be tempted. They would be much less tempted if they knew an attack would mean the loss of their cities.

Brodie's ideas—first published in 1946 and elaborated in the 1950s—dominated published works by civilian strategists until the early 1960s. But a significant minority of civilian strategic thinkers rejected them from the start. Many of these, interestingly enough, were Brodie's colleagues at Rand, but they also included some hard-line government officials like Paul Nitze, and Harvard's Henry Kissinger. Herman Kahn, however, most forcefully presented these anti-Brodie views.

Unlike Brodie, Kahn did not come to the analysis of nuclear warfare from studying military strategy in the pre-atomic era. Kahn studied physics and turned to strategy when he joined Rand in 1948. Kahn quantified and applied abstract logic to nuclear war. He translated deaths, destruction, and even chromosome damage into columns of numbers, added up those on one side, compared them to those on the other, and decided who came out ahead. He dreamed up scenarios in which national leaders reasoned like chess players, trading off cities or millions of people, to place the enemy at a disadvantage on the board.

Kahn published *On Thermonuclear War* in 1960, resting his disagreement with Brodie on two points. First, nuclear war, like all other kinds of war, could be won or lost. Second, Brodie's version of deterrence was an insufficient strategy for the United States.

On his first point, Kahn claimed that, while a nuclear war was quite likely to be an "unprecedented catastrophe," it would not mean the end of civilization. In fact, "the limits of the magnitude of the catastrophe seem to be closely dependent on what kinds of preparations have been made, and how the war is started and fought."[4] As he said, "If proper preparations have been made, it would be possible for us or the Soviets to cope with all of the effects of a thermonuclear war in the sense of saving most people and restoring something close to the previous standard of living in a relatively short time."[5]

Since one side could cope better with nuclear war than the other, Brodie, according to Kahn, was wrong. Questions of victory or defeat were not irrelevant. The purpose of the military establishment remained what it always had been: to win the war.

Given this line of argument, it is not surprising that Kahn rejected Brodie's version of deterrence, which Kahn labeled Type I. Instead, Kahn called for what he labeled "Type II," deterring the Soviets by giving the United States the capability to fight and win a nuclear war. In Kahn's mind, there were a number of scenarios where the United States, if it lacked Type II deterrence, would be faced with a choice of "oblivion or surrender." One key example Kahn cited was a Soviet attack only on our nuclear forces, avoiding our cities.

The way out of this was for the United States to target our missiles not against Soviet cities but against their bomber and missile bases and—in some cases—to retain a first strike option. Kahn labeled a strike against the enemy's military forces "counterforce"; a strike against cities was "counter value." At the very least, a strategy based on a first strike option, plus counterforce, could spare cities, Kahn said. At the most it could allow the United States to win a nuclear war.

Throughout his work, Kahn the physicist never asked the questions that bothered Brodie: What possible political goal could justify the loss of a hundred cities or even a "few" million people? Could the people of a nation which suffered even "limited" nuclear damage be expected, in Brodie's words, to "show much concern for the further pursuit of political-military objectives?"

Not all experts, at Rand and elsewhere, who rejected Brodie's view of nuclear strategy agreed completely with Kahn. Some were much less sanguine about the prospects of recovery from nuclear war. But they agreed that Brodie's view of deterrence was insufficient, and that it would be more advantageous for us if our forces could fight a nuclear war by attacking the Soviet military.

The Kahn view was given a tremendous boost in 1960 with the election of John F. Kennedy and the appointment of Robert McNamara as Secretary of Defense.

McNamara was briefed on counterforce by the nuclear warfighters at Rand a few weeks after taking office. Impressed, he brought many of them to Washington. (Kahn was not invited, probably because he had become a lightning rod for public worry about nuclear war. Brodie was also conspicuously left behind.)

They began at once to work on a new strategy, which McNamara announced in early 1962. While McNamara, unlike Kahn, repeatedly stressed the terrible dangers of nuclear war, in the end, like the Rand people, he came down hard on Kahn's side of the argument:

> The U.S. has come to the conclusion that to the extent feasible, basic military strategy in a possible general nuclear war should be approached in much the same way that more conventional military operations have been regarded in the past. That is to say, principal military objectives, in the event of a nuclear war stemming from a major attack on the Alliance, should be the destruction of the enemy's military forces, not of his civilian population.[6]

At about the same time, President Kennedy himself made statements implying that the United States might strike first if its vital interests were threatened, and the Administration embarked on a massive nuclear buildup.

The more McNamara studied nuclear war, however, the clearer it became to him that, with Soviet nuclear forces growing and becoming more difficult to destroy, it would not be possible to limit damage in a meaningful way. Moreover, he found that a "damage-limiting" strategy helped the Air Force drive for ever-larger strategic forces. In the middle 1960s, McNamara began to move toward Brodie. By 1967 he could say, "It is our ability to destroy an attacker . . . that provides the deterrent not our ability to potentially limit damage to ourselves."[7] McNamara never completely abandoned damage limitation; but the Brodie form of deterrence, now labelled "assured destruction," was publicly given top priority by McNamara during his last years.

Kahn's temporary victory had lasting effects, however. The United States increased its submarine-launched ballistic missiles and ICBMs 18-fold, a buildup which the Soviets soon began to match. A significant number of U.S. nuclear weapons were now "counterforce targeted," that is, aimed, not at Soviet cities and economic assets, but at military targets including airfields and missile bases.

The boost from McNamara in the mid-1960s helped Brodie's views continue to dominate the writing and thinking of expert civilians. But the minority who supported a Kahn-like view, especially the analysts at Rand, was stronger and more vocal.

The complete victory of Kahn's ideas came in the early 1970s, the result of the public statements by another Secretary of Defense, James Schlesinger.

Schlesinger, who took office in 1973, had been at Rand during the middle and late 1960s, serving for a few years as Director of Strategic Studies. He had published a number of scathing attacks on assured destruction, and soon after he was appointed head of the Pentagon, he returned publicly to counterforce and nuclear warfighting. In 1973 and 1974 Schlesinger announced "a change in the strategies of the United States with regard to hypothetical implementation of central strategic forces." In particular, the United States would obtain "the forces to execute a wide range of options in response to particular action by an enemy, including a capability for precise attacks on both soft and hard [military] targets, while at the same time minimizing unintended collateral damage.''[8] Schlesinger's successor, Donald Rumsfeld, echoed Kahn even more clearly, rejecting the notion that nuclear war would inevitably wipe out a major portion of the American population and calling for a greater U.S. warfighting capability.

The Schlesinger-announced changes, like McNamara's helped push the arms race forward. To allay Congressional worries about his new strategy, Schlesinger first said it required no higher levels of spending and no new nuclear weapons. But this announcement was soon followed by an increase in the number of U.S. warheads, a major improvement in the accuracy of U.S. ICBMs and the go-ahead for new, more powerful and accurate systems, including the MX.

Among civilian experts, Schlesinger's public move away from assured destruction provoked a storm of controversy, with the pendulum swinging Kahn's way.

The most influential blasts at views in agreement with Brodie's came from Paul Nitze. (Now the Reagan Administration's chief negotiator of nuclear weapons in Europe, Nitze had held high office in both the Defense and State Departments.) In 1975 and 1976, he published two articles using arguments that were basically ''Kahn brought up to date,'' with more clarity and coherence.

Nitze began by attacking assured destruction. Like Kahn, he argued that fighting nuclear war the right way, with the correct preparations, could reduce damage significantly. He also argued that, in nuclear war, questions of victory or defeat were not irrelevant. The Soviets, Nitze said, knew this, but we did not. Since 1973, the Soviets had been ''gaining the military capability to end an exchange in their favor.'' In spelling out exactly how the Soviets might do this, Nitze revived one of Kahn's scenarios. He feared the Soviets could avoid our cities and attack just our nuclear forces. Since the United States relied on assured destruction, Nitze claimed, it would then have to choose between suicide or surrender.[9]

To be sure, the supporters of Brodie's version of deterrence were far from silent during this period. But they no longer had their former impact, either on the non-government experts or on the Republican Administration. By late 1976, even the ''moderates'' writing about nuclear arms accepted the need for increased warfighting capabilities.

Some in what had become the minority Brodie school placed their hopes in the election of Jimmy Carter, and in Carter's appointment of Harold Brown as Secretary of Defense. As recently as 1975, Brown had warned that contingency planning to fight a nuclear war could ''increase the likelihood of catastrophe.''[10]

Before long, however, the new Secretary of Defense began to sound like the others. In 1978 he said: ''We cannot afford to make a complete distinction between deterrence forces and what are so awkwardly called warfighting forces.''[11] Over the next two years he elaborated what he called a ''countervailing strategy,'' which meant having plans ''to attack the targets which comprise the Soviet military force structure and political power structure, and to hold back a significant reserve.''[12] The new strategy, codified in Presidential Directive 59, anticipated prolonged nuclear battles and required more accurate missiles and beefed-up civil defense.

To be sure, Brown and most of the others in the Carter Administration did not go as far in the direction of Kahn as did Nitze and some others. They were much less optimistic about the prospects of either side surviving a nuclear war and conceded it was unlikely that nuclear wars could remain limited. Nor did they support the same kind of arms buildup advocated by most of the vehement critics of assured destruction; and they strongly supported the SALT II Treaty. But they let Kahn-Nitze scenarios affect their thinking. In the end they agreed that the United States must develop plans and weapons that would allow us to avoid cities and strike Soviet military forces.

The Reagan Administration has not gone much further in Kahn's direction than did its predecessors. Indeed, by deciding to cut MX deployments from the Carter-planned level, they may have diminished U.S. warfighting capabilities. Yet Reagan officials have scared people simply because they have brought to public notice what nuclear war theorists have been saying for a long time.

As long as Kahn's ideas hold sway, the defeat of one President and election of a new one will not lessen the dangers of nuclear war. Democratic warfighters are no better than Republican ones. What is needed is a counterrevolution in nuclear strategy, a return to Brodie's ideas on nuclear war. This is the true challenge for the growing arms control movement.

Notes

[1]Bernard Brodie, ''Implications for Military Policy,'' in *The Absolute Weapon*, ed. Bernard Brodie (New York: Harcourt, Brace & Co., 1946), p. 74.

[2]Bernard Brodie, ''Implications,'' pp. 73–76.

[3]Bernard Brodie, *Strategy in the Missile Age* (Princeton, New Jersey: Princeton University Press, 1965), p. 292.

[4]Herman Kahn, *On Thermonuclear War* (New York: Free Press, 1969), pp. 10–11.

[5]Herman Kahn, *On Thermonuclear War*, p. 78.

[6]Quoted in Desmond Ball, *Politics and Force Levels: The Strategic Missile Program of the Kennedy Administration* (Berkeley: University of California Press, 1980), p. 197.

[7]Robert S. McNamara, Statement before the House Armed Services Committee on the FY 1968–72 and 1968 Defense Budget, p. 39.

[8]James Schlesinger, ''Flexible Strategic Options and Deterrence,'' *Survival* (March/April 1974), pp. 86–90.

[9]Paul Nitze, ''Assuring Strategic Stability in an Era of Detente,'' *Foreign Affairs* (Jan. 1976), pp. 223–26.

[10]''Strategic Force Structure and Strategic Arms Limitation,'' *Civil Preparedness and Limited Nuclear War*. Hearings before the Joint Committee on Defense Production, (April 28, 1976), p. 133.

[11]Department of Defense *Annual Report, FY 1979*, p. 54.

[12]Department of Defense *Annual Report, FY 1981*, pp. 66–69.

COLIN S. GRAY and KEITH PAYNE

Victory Is Possible

Colin S. Gray and Keith Payne are both strategic analysts formerly with the Hudson Institute, the conservative think tank founded by Herman Kahn. Gray writes extensively, particularly in the literature of professional strategists, advocating "nuclear warfighting" doctrines. He also is a strong advocate of Strategic Defense Initiative (SDI). This piece, written in 1980, reflects the direction U.S. policy is moving during the Reagan administration.

Nuclear war is possible. But unlike Armageddon, the apocalyptic war prophesied to end history, nuclear war can have a wide range of possible outcomes. Many commentators and senior U.S. government officials consider it a nonservivable event. The popularity of this view in Washington has such a pervasive and malign effect upon American defense planning that it is rapidly becoming a self-fulfilling prophecy for the United States.

Recognition that war at any level can be won or lost, and that the distinction between winning and losing would not be trivial, is essential for intelligent defense planning. Moreover, nuclear war can occur regardless of the quality of U.S. military posture and the content of American strategic theory. If it does, deterrence, crisis management, and escalation control might play a negligible role. Through an inability to communicate or through Soviet disinterest in receiving and acting upon American messages, the United States might not even have the option to surrender and thus might have to fight the war as best it can. Furthermore, the West needs to devise ways in which it can employ strategic nuclear forces coercively, while minimizing the potentially paralyzing impact of self-deterrence.

If American nuclear power is to support U.S. foreign policy objectives, the United States must possess the ability to wage nuclear war rationally. This requirement is inherent in the geography of East-West relations, in the persisting deficiencies in Western conventional and theater nuclear forces, and in the distinction between the objectives of a revolutionary and status quo power.

U.S. strategic planning should exploit Soviet fears insofar as is feasible from the Soviet perspective; take full account of likely Soviet responses and the willingness of Americans to accept those responses; and provide for the protection of American territory. Such planning would enhance the prospect for effective deterrence and survival during a war. Only recently has U.S. nuclear targeting policy been based on careful study of the Soviet Union as a distinct political

---

Colin S. Gray and Keith Payne, "Victory Is Possible," *Foreign Policy* 39 (Summer 1980), pp. 14–27. Reprinted with permission from *Foreign Policy*.

culture, but the U.S. defense community continues to resist many of the policy implications of Soviet responses to U.S. weapons programs. In addition, the U.S. government simply does not recognize the validity of attempting to relate its freedom of offensive nuclear action and the credibility of its offensive nuclear threat to the protection of American territory.

Critics of such strategic planning are vulnerable in two crucial respects: They do not, and cannot, offer policy prescriptions that will insure that the United States is never confronted with the stark choice between fighting a nuclear war or surrendering, and they do not offer a concept of deterrence that meets the extended responsibilities of U.S. strategic nuclear forces. No matter how elegant the deterrence theory, a question that cannot be avoided is what happens if deterrence mechanisms fail? Theorists whose concept of deterrence is limited to massive retaliation after Soviet attack would have nothing of interest to say to a president facing conventional defeat in the Persian Gulf or in Western Europe. Their strategic environment exists only in peacetime. They can recommend very limited, symbolic options but have no theory of how a large-scale Soviet response is to be deterred.

Because many believe that homeland defense will lead to a steeper arms race and destabilize the strategic balance, the U.S. defense community has endorsed a posture that maximizes the prospect for self-deterrence. Yet the credibility of the extended U.S. deterrent depends on the Soviet belief that a U.S. president would risk nuclear escalation on behalf of foreign commitments.

In the late 1960s the United States endorsed the concept of strategic parity without thinking through what that would mean for the credibility of America's nuclear umbrella. A condition of parity or essential equivalence is incompatible with extended deterrent duties because of the self-deterrence inherent in such a strategic context. However, the practical implications of parity may be less dire in some areas of U.S. vital interest. Western Europe, for example, is so important an American interest that Soviet leaders could be more impressed by the character and duration of the U.S. commitment than by the details of the strategic balance.

A Threat to Commit Suicide

Ironically, it is commonplace to assert that war-survival theories affront the crucial test of political and moral acceptability. Surely no one can be comfortable with the claim that a strategy that would kill millions of Soviet citizens and would invite a strategic response that could kill tens of millions of U.S. citizens would be politically and morally acceptable. However, it is worth recalling the six guidelines for the use of force provided by the "just war" doctrine of the Catholic Church: Force can be used in a just cause; with a right intent; with a reasonable chance of success; in order that, if successful, its use offers a better future than would have been the case had it not been employed;

to a degree proportional to the goals sought, or to the evil combated; and with the determination to spare noncombatants, when there is a reasonable chance of doing so.

These guidelines carry a message for U.S. policy. Specifically, as long as nuclear threat is a part of the U.S. diplomatic arsenal and provided that threat reflects real operational intentions—it is not a total bluff—U.S. defense planners are obliged to think through the probable course of a nuclear war. They must also have at least some idea of the intended relationship between force applied and the likelihood that political goals will be achieved—that is, a strategy.

Current American strategic policy is not compatible with at least three of the six just-war guidelines. The policy contains no definition of success aside from denying victory to the enemy, no promise that the successful use of nuclear power would insure a better future than surrender, and no sense of proportion because central war strategy in operational terms is not guided by political goals. In short, U.S. nuclear strategy is immoral.

Those who believe that a central nuclear war cannot be waged for political purposes because the destruction inflicted and suffered would dwarf the importance of any political goals can construct a coherent and logical policy position. They argue that nuclear war will be the end of history for the states involved, and that a threat to initiate nuclear war is a threat to commit suicide and thus lacks credibility. However, they acknowledge that nuclear weapons cannot be abolished. They maintain that even incredible threats may deter, provided the affront in question is sufficiently serious, because miscalculation by an adversary could have terminal consequences; because genuinely irrational behavior is always possible; and because the conflict could become uncontrollable.

In the 1970s the U.S. defense community rejected this theory of deterrence. Successive strategic targeting reviews appeared to move U.S. policy further and further from the declaratory doctrine of mutual assured destruction adopted by former Secretary of Defense Robert S. McNamara. Yet U.S. defense planners have not thoroughly studied the problems of nuclear war nor thought through the meaning of strategy in relation to nuclear war. The U.S. defense community has always tended to regard strategic nuclear war not as war but as a holocaust. Former Secretary of Defense James R. Schlesinger apparently adopted limited nuclear options (LNOs)—strikes employing anywhere from a handful of several dozen warheads—as a compromise between the optimists of the minimum deterrence school and the pessimists of the so-called war-fighting persuasion. By definition, LNOs apply only to the initial stages of a war. But what happens once LNOs have been exhausted? If the Soviets retaliated after U.S. LNOs, the United States would face the dilemma of escalating further or conciliating.

Deterrence may fail to be restored during war for several reasons: The enemy may not grant, in operational practice, the concept of intrawar deterrence and simply wage the war as it is able; and command, control, and communications may be degraded so rapidly that strategic decisions are precluded and both sides execute their war plans. Somewhat belatedly, the U.S. defense community has come to understand that flexibility in targeting and LNOs do not constitute a strategy and cannot compensate for inadequate strategic nuclear forces.

LNOs are the tactics of the strong, not of a country entering a period of strategic inferiority, as the United States is now. LNOs would be operationally viable only if the United States had a plausible theory of how it could control and dominate later escalation.

The fundamental inadequacy of flexible targeting, as presented in the 1970s, is that it neglected to take proper account of the fact that the United States would be initiating a process of competitive escalation that it had no basis for assuming could be concluded on satisfactory terms. Flexible targeting was an adjunct to plans that had no persuasive vision of how the application of force would promote the attainment of political objectives.

War Aims

U.S. strategic targeting doctrine must have a unity of political purpose from the first to the last strikes. Strategic flexibility, unless wedded to a plausible theory of how to win a war or at least insure an acceptable end to a war, does not offer the United States an adequate bargaining position before or during a conflict and is an invitation to defeat. Small, preplanned strikes can only be of use if the United States enjoys strategic superiority—the ability to wage a nuclear war at any level of violence with a reasonable prospect of defeating the Soviet Union and of recovering sufficiently to insure a satisfactory postwar world order.

However, the U.S. government does not yet appear ready to plan seriously for the actual conduct of nuclear war should deterrence fail, in spite of the fact that such a policy should strengthen deterrence. Assured-destruction reasoning is proclaimed officially to be insufficient in itself as a strategic doctrine. However, a Soviet assured-destruction capability continues to exist as a result of the enduring official U.S. disinterest in strategic defense, with potentially paralyzing implications for the United States. No matter how well designed and articulated, targeting plans that allow an enemy to inflict in retaliation whatever damage it wishes on American society are likely to prove unusable.

Four interdependent areas of strategic policy—strategy, weapons development and procurement, arms control, and defense doctrine—are currently treated separately. Theoretically, strategy should determine the evolution of the other three areas. In practice, it never has. Most of what has been portrayed as war-fighting strategy is nothing of the kind. Instead, it is an extension of the American theory of deterrence into war itself. To advocate LNOs and targeting flexibility and selectivity is not the same as to advocate a war-fighting, war-survival strategy.

Strategists do not find the idea of nuclear war fighting attractive. Instead, they believe that an ability to wage and survive war is vital for the effectiveness of deterrence; there can be no such thing as an adequate deterrent posture unrelated to probable wartime effectiveness; victory or defeat in nuclear war is possible, and such a war may have to be waged to that point; and, the clearer the vision of successful war termination, the more likely war can be waged intelligently at earlier stages.

There should be no misunderstanding the fact that the primary interest of U.S. strategy is deterrence. However, American strategic forces do not exist solely for the purpose of deterring a Soviet nuclear threat or attack against the United States itself. Instead, they are intended to support U.S. foreign policy, as reflected, for example, in the commitment to preserve Western Europe against aggression. Such a function requires American strategic forces that would enable a president to initiate strategic nuclear use for coercive, though politically defensive, purposes.

U.S. strategy, typically, has proceeded from the bottom up. Such targeting does not involve any conception of the war as a whole, nor of how the war might be concluded on favorable terms. The U.S. defense community cannot plan intelligently for lower levels of combat, unless it has an acceptable idea of where they might lead.

Most analyses of flexible targeting options assume virtually perfect stability at the highest levels of conflict. Advocates of flexible targeting assert that a U.S. LNO would signal the beginning of an escalation process that the Soviets would wish to avoid in light of the American threat to Soviet urban-industrial areas. Yet it seems inconsistent to argue that the U.S. threat of assured destruction would deter the Soviets from engaging in escalation following an LNO but that U.S. leaders could initiate the process despite the Soviet threat. What could be the basis of such relative U.S. resolve and Soviet vacillation in the face of strategic parity or Soviet superiority?

Moreover, the desired deterrent effect would probably depend upon the Soviet analysis of the entire nuclear campaign. In other words, Soviet leaders would be less impressed by American willingness to launch an LNO than they would be by a plausible American victory strategy. Such a theory would have to envisage the demise of the Soviet state. The United States should plan to defeat the Soviet Union and to do so at a cost that would not prohibit U.S. recovery. Washington should identify war aims that in the last resort would contemplate the destruction of Soviet political authority and the emergence of a postwar world order compatible with Western values.

The most frightening threat to the Soviet Union would be the destruction or serious impairment of its political system. Thus, the United States should be able to destroy key leadership cadres, their means of communication, and some of the instruments of domestic control. The USSR, with its gross overcentralization of authority, epitomized by its vast bureaucracy in Moscow, should be highly vulnerable to such an attack. The Soviet Union might cease to function if its security agency, the KGB, were severely crippled. If the Moscow bureaucracy could be eliminated, damaged, or isolated, the USSR might disintegrate into anarchy, hence the extensive civil defense preparations intended to insure the survival of the Soviet leadership. Judicious U.S. targeting and weapon procurement policies might be able to deny the USSR the assurance of political survival.

Once the defeat of the Soviet state is established as a war aim, defense professionals should attempt to identify an optimum targeting plan for the accomplishment of that goal. For example, Soviet political control of its territory in Central Asia and in the Far East could be weakened by discriminate nuclear targeting. The same applies to Transcaucasia and Eastern Europe.

The Ultimate Penalty

Despite a succession of U.S. targeting reviews, Soviet leaders, looking to the mid-1980s, may well anticipate the ability to wage World War III successfully. The continuing trend in the East-West military balance allows Soviet military planners to design a theory of military victory that is not implausible and that may stir hopes among Soviet political leaders that they might reap many of the rewards of military success even without having to fight. The Soviets may anticipate that U.S. self-deterrence could discourage Washington from punishing Soviet society. Even if the United States were to launch a large-scale second strike against Soviet military and economic targets, the resulting damage should be bearable to the Soviet Union given the stakes of the conflict and the fact that the Soviets would control regions abroad that could contribute to its recovery.

In the late 1960s the United States identified the destruction of 20–25 percent of the population and 50–75 percent of industrial capacity as the ultimate penalty it had to be able to inflict on the USSR. In the 1970s the United States shifted its attention to the Soviet recovery economy. The Soviet theory of victory depends on the requirement that the Soviet Union survive and recover rapidly from a nuclear conflict. However, the U.S. government does not completely understand the details of the Soviet recovery economy, and the concept has lost popularity as a result. Highly complex modeling of the Soviet economy cannot disguise the fact that the available evidence is too rudimentary to permit any confidence in the analysis. With an inadequate data base it should require little imagination to foresee how difficult it is to determine targeting priorities in relation to the importance of different economic targets for recovery.

Schlesinger's advocacy of essential equivalence called for a U.S. ability to match military damage for military damage. But American strategic development since the early 1970s has not been sufficient to maintain the American end of that balance. Because the U.S. defense community has refused to recognize the importance of the possibility that a nuclear war could be won or lost, it has neglected to think beyond a punitive sequence of targeting options.

American nuclear strategy is not intended to defeat the Soviet Union or insure the survival of the United States in any carefully calculated manner. Instead, it is intended to insure that the Soviet Union is punished increasingly severely. American targeting philosophy today is only a superficial improvement over that prevalent in the late 1960s, primarily because U.S. defense planners do not consider anticipated damage to the United States to be relevant to the integrity of their offensive war plans. The strategic case for ballistic missile defense and civil defense has not been considered on its merits for a decade.

In the late 1970s the United States targeted a range of Soviet economic entities that were important either to war-supporting industry or to economic recovery. The rationale for this targeting scheme was, and remains, fragile. War-supporting industry is important only for a war of considerable duration or for a period of post-war defense mobilization. Moreover, although recovery from war is an integral part of a Soviet theory of victory, it is less important than the achievement of military success. If the USSR is able to win the war, it should have sufficient military force in reserve to compel the surviving world economy to contribute to Soviet recovery. Thus, the current trend is to move away from targeting the recovery economy.

To date, the U.S. government has declined to transcend what amounts to a deterrence-through-punishment approach to strategic war planning. Moreover, the strategic targeting reviews of the 1970s did not address the question of self-deterrence adequately. The United States has no ballistic missile defense and effectively no civil defense, while U.S. air defense is capable of guarding American air space only in peacetime. The Pentagon has sought to compensate for a lack of relative military muscle through more imaginative strategic targeting. Review after review has attempted to identify more effective ways in which the USSR could be hurt. Schlesinger above all sought essential equivalence through a more flexible set of targeting options without calling for extensive new U.S. strategic capabilities. Indeed, he went to some pains to separate the question of targeting design from procurement issues.

The United States should identify nuclear targeting options that could help restore deterrence, yet would destroy the Soviet state and enhance the likelihood of U.S. survival if fully implemented. The first priority of such a targeting scheme would be Soviet military power of all kinds, and the second would be the political, military, and economic control structure of the USSR. Successful strikes against military and political control targets would reduce the Soviet ability to project military power abroad and to sustain political authority at home. However, it would not be in the interest of the United States actually to implement an offensive nuclear strategy no matter how frightening in Soviet perspective, if the U.S. homeland were totally naked to Soviet retaliation.

Striking the USSR should entail targeting the relocation bunkers of the top political and bureaucratic leadership, including those of the KGB; key communication centers of the Communist party, the military, and the government; and many of the economic, political, and military records. Even limited destruction of some of these targets and substantial isolation of many of the key personnel who survive could have revolutionary consequences for the country.

The Armageddon Syndrome

The strategic questions that remain incompletely answered are in some ways more difficult than the practical problems of targeting the political control structure. Is it sensible to destroy the government of the enemy, thus eliminating the option of negotiating an end to the war? In the unlikely event that the United States identifies all of the key relocation bunkers for the central political leadership, who would then conduct the Soviet war effort and to what ends? Since after a large-scale counter-control strike the surviving Soviet leadership would have little else to fear, could this targeting option be anything other than a threat?

The U.S. defense community today believes that the political control structure of the USSR is among the most important targets for U.S. strategic forces. However, just how important such targeting might be for deterrence or damage limitation has not been determined. Current American understanding of exactly how the control structure functions is less than perfect. But that is a technical matter that can in principle be solved through more research. The issue of whether the Soviet control structure should actually be struck is more problematic.

Strategists cannot offer painless conflicts or guarantee that their preferred posture and doctrine promise a greatly superior deterrence posture to current American schemes. But, they can claim that an intelligent U.S. offensive strategy, wedded to homeland defenses, should reduce U.S. casualties to approximately 20 million, which should render U.S. strategic threats more credible. If the United States developed the targeting plans and procured the weapons necessary to hold the Soviet political, bureaucratic, and military leadership at risk, that should serve as the functional equivalent in Soviet perspective of the assured-destruction effect of the late 1960s. However, the U.S. targeting community has not determined how it would organize this targeting option.

A combination of counterforce offensive targeting, civil defense, and ballistic missile and air defense should hold U.S. casualties down to a level compatible with national survival and recovery. The actual number would depend on several factors, some of which the United States could control (the level of U.S. homeland defenses); some of which it could influence (the weight and character of the Soviet attack); and some of which might evade anybody's ability to control or influence (for example, the weather). What can be assured is a choice between a defense program that insures the survival of the vast majority of Americans with relative confidence and one that deliberately permits the Soviet Union to wreak whatever level of damage it chooses.

No matter how grave the Soviet offense, a U.S. president cannot credibly threaten and should not launch a strategic nuclear strike if expected U.S. casualties are likely to involve 100 million or more American citizens. There is a difference between a doctrine that can offer little rational guidance should deterrence fail and a doctrine that a president might employ responsibly for identified political purposes. Existing evidence on the probable consequences of nuclear exchanges suggests that there should be a role for strategy in nuclear war. To ignore the possibility that strategy can be applied to nuclear war is to insure by choice a nuclear apocalypse if deterrence fails. The current U.S. deterrence posture is fundamentally flawed because it does not provide for the protection of American territory.

Nuclear war is unlikely to be an essentially meaningless, terminal event. Instead it is likely to be waged to coerce the Soviet Union to give up some recent gain. Thus, a president must have the ability, not merely to end a war, but to end it favorably. The United States would need to be able to persuade desperate and determined Soviet leaders that it has the capability, and the determination, to wage nuclear war at ever higher levels of violence until an acceptable outcome is achieved. For deterrence to function during a war each side would have to calculate whether an improved outcome is possible through further escalation.

An adequate U.S. deterrent posture is one that denies the Soviet Union any plausible hope of success at any level of strategic conflict; offers a likely prospect of Soviet defeat; and offers a reasonable chance of limiting damage to the United States. Such a deterrence posture is often criticized as contributing to the arms race and causing strategic instability, because it would stimulate new Soviet deployments. However, during the 1970s the Soviet Union showed that its weapon development and deployment decisions are not dictated by American actions. Western understanding of what determines Soviet defense procurement is less than perfect, but it is now obvious that Soviet weapon decisions cannot be explained with reference to any simple action-reaction model of arms-race dynamics. In addition, highly survivable U.S. strategic forces should insure strategic stability by denying the Soviets an attractive first-strike target set.

An Armageddon syndrome lurks behind most concepts of nuclear strategy. It amounts either to the belief that because the United States could lose as many as 20 million people, it should not save the 80 million or more who otherwise would be at risk, or to a disbelief in the serious possibility that 200 million Americans could survive a nuclear war.

There is little satisfaction in advocating an operational nuclear doctrine that could result in the deaths of 20 million or more people in an unconstrained nuclear war. However, as long as the United States relies on nuclear threats to deter an increasingly powerful Soviet Union, it is inconceivable that the U.S. defense community can continue to divorce its thinking on deterrence from its planning for the efficient conduct of war and defense of the country. Prudence in the latter should enhance the former.

PART 3

How Are We Affected?

Perspectives on the Arms Race

PAUL CHILTON

Nukespeak: Nuclear Language, Culture, and Propaganda

Paul Chilton is a linguistics scholar at the University of Warwick, England, where he teaches in the Department of French. He has written an important book on fifteenth-century French poetry. He is presently working on a full-length study of the language of nuclear propaganda.

In totalitarian regimes, official state propaganda fills the hole of silence left by the censor. It is clearly and recognizably framed off from all other writing and talk. For that very reason it may not be heeded; people may even develop a healthy art of skeptical reading between the lines. Of course, propaganda in totalitarian states does not need to be effective: the army and the secret police are a more impressive short-term silencer.

In Western democracies, though you may be watched, you will probably not be imprisoned for expressing dissident views or unpalatable facts, and few people, I imagine, would question that this is a preferable state of affairs. However, contrary to conventional wisdom, this does not mean that in Western societies, censorship and propaganda do not operate, and operate effectively, despite the fact that there is no official censor or propaganda office. Noam Chomsky has pointed out that "state censorship is not necessary, or even very effective, in comparison to the ideological controls exercised by systems that are more complex and more decentralized."[1] Indeed ideological control may be more effective for not being recognizably framed off from the rest of discourse. To quote Chomsky further:

> A totalitarian state simply enunciates official doctrine—clearly, explicitly. Internally, one can think what one likes, but one can only express opposition at one's peril. In a democratic system of propaganda no one is punished (in theory) for objecting to official dogma. In fact dissidence is encouraged. What this system attempts to do is to fix the limits of possible thought: supporters of official doctrine at one end, and the critics . . . at the other. . . . No doubt a propaganda system is more effective when its doctrines are insinuated rather than asserted, when it sets the bounds for possible thought rather than simply imposing a clear and easily identifiable doctrine that one must parrot—or suffer the consequences.[2]

Chomsky is referring here to the way the American press excluded certain views on Vietnam in the 1970s, but parallels can be drawn with the manipula-

Paul Chilton, "Nukespeak: Nuclear Language, Culture, and Propaganda." From *Nukespeak: The Media and the Bomb,* Crispin Aubrey, ed. (London: Comedia Publishing Group, 1982). Reprinted by permission of the Comedia Publishing Group.

tion of the nuclear debate in the British media. . . . Alongside simple exclusion, of course, there are the equally effective techniques of ridicule, deemphasis, smear, and so on.

In addition to these methods of censorship, there is also a likelihood that "the bounds for possible thought" about the nuclear issue are influenced in a more positive way—in the sense that both official and popular utterances about nuclear weapons and war use language in such a way that nuclear weapons and war are familiarized and made acceptable. This is the basic idea of "nukespeak".

To coin the term "nukespeak" itself is to make three main claims. First, that there exists a specialized vocabulary for talking about nuclear weapons and war together with habitual metaphors, and even preferred grammatical constructions. Secondly, that this variety of English is not neutral and purely descriptive, but ideologically loaded in favor of the nuclear culture; and thirdly, that this *matters,* insofar as it possibly affects how people think about the subject, and probably determines to a large extent the sort of ideas they exchange about it.

Granted that nukespeak exists, one is led to ask who is responsible for it. Clearly not some Orwellian grammarian rewriting the English language in the Ministry of Truth. One way of answering the question is to seek nukespeak as a symptom of the nuclear culture we have forged for ourselves, as an indication of the depth of its penetration into our mentality. The post-Hiroshima world has had to create new images and vocabulary to encapsulate the inconceivable—literally inconceivable—phenomenon of nuclear fission/fusion and its moral implications. The development of the atomic bomb was not a smooth transition from existing weaponry, but a catastrophic jump to a new order of experience in science, politics and everyday life. In 1945 it was popular to refer to this jump as a "revolution" which would itself "revolutionize" human behavior, and to communicate about such matters on the fringe of experience and imagination places strain on our symbolic systems. The language used to talk about the new weapons of mass extermination was partly a reflection of an attempt to slot the new reality into the old paradigms of our culture. It was also no doubt a language that served the purpose of those who were concerned to perpetuate nuclear weapons development and deployment.

This is the second way of looking at nukespeak, to see it not just as a kind of mass response to a crisis of comprehension, but as a controlled response directed by the state in conjunction with other interested parties, and to see it as a means of constraining possible thought on the nuclear phenomenon. In the consolidation and dissemination of nukespeak the media are crucial, their function being to pass on nuclear language from producer to consumer along a one-way channel.

Once you begin to look closely at nuclear language, you get the strong impression that in spite of the scientific background, in spite of the technical theorizing, most talk about nuclear war and weapons reflects irrational, not to say, superstitious, processes of thought. Myths, metaphors, paradoxes, and contradictions abound. There is no time here to unravel all the complexities: I aim merely to point out some of the features and landmarks in the linguistic control of nuclear ideology.

The Birth of the Bomb

The first atomic explosion was at Alamogordo in the New Mexico desert on July 16, 1945. It appears that many of the scientists involved were genuinely overwhelmed by the spectacle and deeply disturbed by the implications. Many more people, scientists and nonscientists alike, were overwhelmed and disturbed when atomic explosions destroyed Hiroshima and Nagasaki later the same year. One soldier who saw the first test is reported to have said: "The long-haired boys have lost control." Others too have been impressed by the fact that the people behind the "atomization" (as it was sometimes popularly called in 1945) of Hiroshima and Nagasaki were civilized and cultured men.[3] Patriotic fervor, political naivety, and the myopia of scientific specialization doubtless played a part.

But after the explosion, what sense did they and the general public make of the experience? Nicholas Humphrey has recently stated the question like this: "I do not see how any human being whose intelligence and sensibilities have been shaped by traditional facts and values could possible understand the nature of these unnatural, other-worldly weapons."[4] One explanation—the one I want to outline here—is that it is precisely certain traditional patterns of thought which make it possible to come to terms with, if not strictly to "understand," nuclear explosions. We have traditional ways of talking, myths, symbols, metaphors, which provide safe pigeonholes for what is "unnatural" or "otherworldly." This is a dangerous tendency in human culture, one which perhaps helps to explain the spellbound ambivalence of our attitudes toward the bomb.

One of the physicists who left the atom bomb project when it no longer seemed necessary, Joseph Rotblatt, points to a related tendency:

> While everybody agrees that a nuclear war would be an unmitigated catastrophe, the attitude towards it is becoming similar to that of potential natural disaster, earthquakes, tornadoes, and other Acts of God. . . .[5]

Robert Oppenheimer, the director of the first tests, seems to have handled his own experience of the explosions in terms of traditional images. He called the first test site "Trinity"—that most mysterious of theological concepts. (Interestingly, the sacred threesome has reappeared in the form of "the Triad," that is the "convention," the nuclear "strategic" and the nuclear "theater" forces of NATO). It is said that he had been reading John Donne's sonnet "Batter my heart, three personed God. . . ." At the moment of detonation, so the story continues, a passage from sacred Hindu literature "flashed" across his mind:

> If the radiance of a thousand suns
> were to burst into the sky,
> that would be like the
> splendour of the Mighty One . . .

And on beholding the monstrous mushroom cloud he recalled another line: "I am become Death, the shatterer of worlds."

This was not an idiosyncratic response. After Trinity an official report was rushed to President Truman, who was then meeting at Potsdam with Churchill and Stalin:

> It [the explosion] lighted every peak, crevasse and ridge of the nearby mountain range with a clarity and beauty that cannot be described. . . . It was the beauty the great poets dream about . . . . Then came the strong, sustained, awesome roar which warned of doomsday and made us feel that we puny things were blasphemous to dare to tamper with the forces heretofore reserved to the Almighty.[6]

The religious vocabulary and phrasing are unmistakable, and are typical of the way the politicians and the press spoke later. In religious cultures the awful and the anomalous are allied with the supernatural, and the supernatural is both dangerous and sacred. Such familiar patterns of thought and talk somehow seem to have made the bomb both conceivable and acceptable. There is also another deep-seated cultural stereotype that has served to mythologize the sorry history of Oppenheimer himself, as well as to alleviate the guilt of the physicists. This is the stereotype of Faust, the overweening genius with dangerous access to the secrets of the universe.

Oppenheimer declared, Faust-like, in 1956: 'We did the Devil's work." To what extent did he act out the role? He certainly appears, or is portrayed as, a late Renaissance stereotype—like Faust ambitious, individualistic, immersed in science and culture.

Some of the scientists may indeed have been mythologizing themselves. Wiseman thinks that "what they really were doing, and they must have been aware of it as they were doing it, was challenging the whole system of God and the whole of the Judeo-Christian morality that up to then said certain things are prohibited by God."[7] Others have cast them in the traditional roles. Lord Zuckerman speaks of the "alchemists of our times, working in secret ways which cannot be divulged, casting spells . . ." In one recent film about Oppenheimer, his scientist-biographer explicitly describes him as a Faust figure.[8] In traditional cultures such figures are dangerous; they have to be purged. It's therefore not surprising that in the McCarthyite witch hunts Oppenheimer was ritualistically cast out of the body politic. My point is that the recycling of symbolic thought, talk, and actions has helped to bring us to terms with the invention of the bomb. It is a dangerous game to play in the nuclear age.

It is important to realize that this recycling was fostered by politicians and the press. In August 1945 there emerged a new consensus language, speaking of the atomic bomb in terms of religious awe and evoking simultaneously the forces of life and death. One useful consequence of such language, if not one of its actual motivations, was to appear to diminish human control, responsibility, and guilt. Its immediate political function was to obscure the fact that, strictly, the bomb project need never have been completed, and the bomb itself never dropped.

The problem, for the press, linguistically speaking, was what words to use to refer to the new thing, how to capture a new concept, but also how to conceal from the many the horror that had been glimpsed by the few. There is a kind of gruesome poetry in the resulting style. Rarely is the atomic bomb described in totally negative terms. When the *Times* called it "the new and terrible weapon of annihilation,"[9] this was exceptional. Some letter writers criticized it vigorously, but the contrary was evidently the editorial policy of the established papers.

Like the scientists, journalists expressed themselves in terms of incomprehension and ineffable awe. The *Times* called the scale of destruction "stupendous," "beyond belief," and declared its "bewilderment."[10] The verbal reactions of eyewitnesses of Hiroshima and Nagasaki were dutifully reported: " 'My God,' burst out every member of the crew as the bomb struck." "The whole thing was tremendous and awe-inspiring" said a Captain Parsons of the U.S. Navy.[11] The *Daily Mail* spoke of the problem for the human mind in confronting what human minds had produced: "The test for our survival . . . is whether the solution of the problems raised by the splitting of the atom lies within the human brain." This was dismissed by the *Daily Worker* as "mumbo jumbo," "medieval superstition," and "mysticism." Actually, both papers were making a valid point. At the end of the week the *Observer* gave a sermon on what it called "a week of wonders," mystified the bomb by referring to it simply as "A" (for "atom," but also for alpha, source of creation), and compounded the mystification by calling it "destruction's masterpiece." Such paradoxical expressions abound in the press rhetoric of that week.

There emerged a small set of evocative, positively valued words for describing the bomb and its effects. They are interesting for the notion of nukespeak not only because they stretch existing meanings but also because their use often seems to originate in specific sources—politicians' speeches, and the public utterances of the military. The papers picked them up both in reporting and in comment, and not only repeated them incessantly, but spawned on them a whole network of associations and metaphors.

The press did not in fact, in the first instance, report Hiroshima and Nagasaki direct; it reported official utterances *about* them. The speeches of Truman and Churchill on August 6, 1945, were quoted verbatim, but they also provided the core of the subsequent bomb rhetoric developed in the papers. Two key passages in Truman's speech were seized upon:

> It is an atomic bomb. It is the *harnessing of the basic power of the universe*. . . .

and

> The *force* from which *the sun* draws *its power* has been *loosed*. . . .

The key words here seem to have triggered off a whole series of associations which have their basis in the language of religion and myth. Churchill, reported verbatim in the *Times* of August 7, provides an example of this, one that was to yield still more reverberations:

> *By God's mercy* British and American science outpaced all German efforts. . . . This *revelation of the secrets of nature,* long mercifully *withheld from man,* should arouse the most solemn reflections in the mind and conscience of every human being capable of comprehension. We must indeed *pray* that these awful *agencies* will indeed *be made to conduce to peace* among the nations, and instead of wreaking measureless havoc upon the entire globe they may become *a permanent fountain* of world *prosperity.*

So the select few capable of comprehending the problem are let off with "solemn reflections"—that is, pious platitudes well illustrated in the surrounding verbiage, and copiously regurgitated by editorialists. How do the rhetorical tricks work?

Churchill does not refer directly to the event that inspired the speech, but instead to the "revelation of the secrets of nature." In the next few days it became commonplace to describe the development and dropping of the bomb in such a way as to make it a natural (or supernatural) process somehow outside human control. That perspective is underscored by a grammatical tactic—using the passive construction with no mention of the causative agent. The "secrets of nature" have been "long withheld." By whom? When agents are omitted readers and hearers normally have to make an inference from context, if possible, and if not possible, make speculative guesses that are plausible in some framework of belief. Or, more conveniently, they can just leave the question unasked. Here readers are strongly encouraged (by words like "pray" and "revelation") to suppose that God was the agent. In fact, what Churchill left implicit was to be amplified for *Times* readers by the Dean of Salisbury in a letter on August 10: "God made the atom and gave the scientists the skill to release its energy. . . ." More "solemn reflections" followed. A letter of August 13 actually amplifies Churchill's phrase "God's mercy": "By the same token it might be claimed that through divine grace English-speaking scientists were able to make their original discoveries of the vast source of energy. . . ."

Thus one is left with the supposition that men were not ultimately responsible for the invention and use of the atomic bomb; it was given to them by some outside force. This is not all. In Churchill's phrase "will be made to conduce to peace," there is no clear reference to who will do the making (God again?). Moreover, the atomic bombs ("these awful agencies") themselves, and not humans, are presented as the agents of peace or destruction. It is the bombs that "conduce to peace" (whatever that means) or "wreak havoc." The final image ("perennial fountain") of life-giving water is a potent symbol in traditional culture, and is used to insinuate the belief that the bomb is a "power" for good.

The *Times*'s leading article for August 8 gives some idea of how the catch phrases and grammatical tricks could be used to construct a kind of poetic pseudosolution to the problem. The mushroom cloud becomes a metaphor—and an excuse:

> An impenetrable *cloud* of dust and smoke . . . still *veils* the undoubtedly stupendous destruction wrought by the first impact in war of the atomic bomb. . . . A *mist* no less impenetrable is likely for a long time to *conceal* the full significance in human affairs of the *release* of the *vast and mysterious power locked* within the infinitesimal units of which the material structure of the universe is built up. . . . All that can be said with certainty is that the world stands in the presence of a *revolution in earthly affairs* at least as big with potentialities of good and evil as when the *forces* of steam and electricity were *harnessed* for the first time. . . . Science itself is neutral, like the *blind forces of nature* that it studies and aspires to control. . . . *The fundamental power of the universe,* the power *manifested* in the *sunshine* that has been recognized from the remotest ages as the sustaining *force* of *earthly life,* is *entrusted* to earthly hands . . . the new *power* [must] be *consecrated* to peace not war. . . .

It isn't difficult to spot the verbal and thematic similarities between this passage and the sources cited earlier. The methods are similar—the exploitation of familiar traditional images evoking supernatural activity, and the subtle manipulation of grammatical forms; and so is the general presentation of the atomic bomb as something paradoxically good and evil but predominantly good, and as something outside human responsibility.

One of the most prominent words in the speeches and press reports is "power," closely followed by "force." Religious associations are never far beneath the surface. Here's a sample: *Basic Power of the Universe, the fundamental power of the universe, the new power, the irresistible power, vast and mysterious power, mighty power, power manifested in the sunshine, power for healing and industrial application, mighty force, new force, powerful and forceful influence*. . . . All these phrases are elicited by the news of the destruction of Hiroshima and Nagasaki. The advantage of intoning the word "power" lay in the fact that it implied both supernatural forces and at the same time beneficial technological applications. This way of talking, together with the failure to report the full horrific details (reports of Hiroshima and Nagasaki casualties were at first presented as Japanese propaganda), made it possible to conceive that the atomic bomb and its use had been a good thing. A *Sunday Times* book reviewer thought Nagasaki should be remembered as "A-B" day," but the ambivalence of current attitudes towards the bomb was such that he did not know whether it should be celebrated "with universal rejoicing as heralding Man's entrance into a Kingdom of Power and Glory, or with a dirge".[12]

The Naming of the Bomb

Describing the architects of the atomic bomb, Lord Zuckerman has said that "the men in the nuclear laboratories on both sides have succeeded in creating a world with an irrational foundation." This is usually taken to mean that the highly rational activities of scientists have led to the production of weapons with no clear rational purpose—weapons as technical solutions in search of a problem. It can mean too that the strategic doctrine based on, even generated by such weapons, is paradoxical or self-contradictory—MAD. And it can mean, as E. P. Thompson has written, that "mystery envelops the operation of the technological "alchemists," "Deterrence" has become normal . . . and within this normality, hideous cultural abnormalities have been nurtured and are growing to full girth." The naming of weapons systems, seemingly trivial, well illustrates this last point.

The accumulation of nuclear weapons beyond the point strictly required in a theory of mutual destruction has been said to serve a symbolic purpose, in the sense of creating political and diplomatic advantage. But there may be more to it than this. I want to suggest that the publicly known nicknames given to weapons systems are a symptom of their progressive assimilation into our culture, and also that such names serve to advertise this fact to the domestic population. The way they do it is something like this. There are deeply ingrained patterns of symbolic thought (some researchers think they are innate tendencies of the human mind) which are used to organize, classify, and "normalize" our experiences of the world. Such patterns are present in mythology, religion, and many other domains. "When a human mind, even a scientist's mind, is overcome by bewilderment, it runs for shelter to the archetypes of pre-scientific thought. . . .[13] Thus, while nuclear weapons represent the most advanced scientific thinking, their role in human affairs is handled in a subrational, mythological fashion.

The Cold War itself is deeply subrational, and the symbols used to express it reflect the fact. In a common image two tribes oppose one another—the Eagle and the Bear. To see how this is ideologically loaded, consider the contrasting attributes of these two totems: one soars to the skies, is wise, and all-seeing; the other is heavy, clumsy, stupid, and half blind. Weapon names are the mythological insignia of the two tribes, and there is a similar relationship between the two sets of names we have given them. Not quite all, but most of the NATO weapons are given two names: LGM-30F/G is also called Minuteman, for example. The nicknames come from Greco-Roman and Scandinavian mythology, and from the more recent "mythology" of national history. They form a meaningful pattern. The nicknames given to Soviet weapons, on the other hand, are generally based on an initial letter and are designed to diaparage or to be meaningless: Saddler, Sasin, Scarp, Sego, Savage, Bison, Blinder, Bear . . .

As we saw earlier, atomic and nuclear weapons were perceived as awesome and incomprehensible. A slot in our classification of reality had to be found for them, and to chirsten them was the first step. Rites of naming are rites of incorporation into social life; the officially unnamed in many cultures, including Christian, are in a state of nature (as opposed to society) and sin; they are perceived as dangerous. But even before naming them, weapons are humanized. They have fathers (Edward Teller, "father of the H-bomb"), though no mothers; they grow from infants ("baby nukes") to old age (NATO's allegedly "aging" forces) in a family ("the ICBM family"); they retire ("retiring Polaris force") and make way for the young ("new generation MX ICBMs").

The pattern of development of the names is itself revealing. There are four categories: human types and roles (less popular now); artefacts of human culture—tools, hand weapons (increasingly popular); animals (never very much used); and gods and heroes (most prominent). The early atom-test scientists under Oppenheimer referred to the first atomic device as "the gadget"—not strictly a name, but a synonym that made the momentous experiment feel familiar, homely, and useful. And when the "gadget" was accepted into the life of the nation in the form of a usable bomb, it acquired a name. The uranium bomb detonated over Hiroshima was called "Little Boy", the plutonium bomb dropped on Nagasaki, "Fat Man." They were thus familiarized as amiable human stereotypes. But that was *before* the deed was done and the cataclysmic effects brought home. After the event there were new naming tendencies which reflected the sense of supernatural awe. The human designations lingered on, however, though their effect is now not only to familiarize but also to confer a military status and a patriotic role.

The 1960s saw "Little Boy" promoted to "Corporal," and later to "Sergeant" (both of these were tactical, short-range missiles). At about the same time "Honest John" also appeared in Europe, equipping BAOR° and the French forces. Then there were the "Minutemen," intercontinental ballistic missiles of which we have now had three "generations," the latest having been "MIRVed" with 200-kiloton warheads. The word "Minuteman" may not mean much to a European. To an American patriot it refers to the heroic militiamen of the American Revolutionary War who were trained to turn out at a minute's warning. Thus this inconceivably devastating weapon is given a place in national folklore. And if you didn't know about that, there is also the odd fact that the name of this particular missile also spells "minute [small] man"—odd because that too scales down the weapon's size, and recalls "Little Boy."

Animal names are not much used. They seem to be largely reserved to designate Soviet weapon systems. But one is worth mentioning because it illustrates the often bizarre way in which nuclear planners elaborate their semicoded talk. In the 1960s a system was investigated which could dodge ABMs (Anti-Ballistic Missiles). It was nicknamed "Antelope"—a beast that is agile at high altitudes. A further refinement was called "Super-Antelope." This had the notorious successor "Chevaline," a name which ought to mean (in French)

BAOR Reference to British Air Force operations.

''horselike.'' Its popularity may owe more to its streamlined sound to the English ear, but it had to have a meaning too, and Lawrence Freedman notes that ''there is a belief in the Ministry of Defense that Chevaline refers to a species of antelope which is akin to a mountain goat and is supposed to share with the new warhead the ability to move in a variety of directions at high altitudes.''[14]

The symbolism of height as well as of depth, the symbolism of sky and earth, life and death, is contained in the structure of many traditional myths. But the system is plainer in the imposing *classical* names that accommodate our weapons of mass annihilation in the structures of traditional culture. There are the gods of the sky, thunder, blinding light, who are both creators and destroyers. ''Polaris'' (submarine launched ballistic missile dating from 1950s) is the ''stella polaris,'' the pole star, traditional top of the celestial sphere. ''Skybolt'' was a missile project canceled in 1962. ''Thor'' (an American IRBM kept in Turkey in the 1950s and early 1960s) was the Scandinavian god of thunder. ''Jupiter'' (another IRBM, accompanying ''Thor'') was the Latin sky-god of rain, storms, and thunder. ''Atlas'' (an American missile of the 1950s) was a Titan, condemned to stand in the west to stop the sky falling down—an uncannily apt expression of ''deterrence'' dogma. The ''Titans'' themselves (the largest of the American ICBMs, carrying a nine-megaton warhead) were a ''monstrous and unconquerable race of giants with fearful countenances and the tails of dragons.''[15] Then there are the gods of the depths. The largest of the American submarine-launched ballistic missiles is called ''Poseidon,'' the Greek god of earthquakes and of the sea, who calls forth storms. Poseidon had a brother Pluto, the ruler of the Underworld, and the French have a mobile nuclear missile called ''Pluton,'' and a new ''generation'' in gestation known as ''Super-Pluton.''

These names enable us to classify the ''unnatural, otherworldly'' weapons, though the actual mythological classification still keeps them precisely in that category. But the more recent trend is to mythically classify them as a part of human cluture rather than as part of nature (or supernature), which is alien, terrifying, and dangerous. This is a return to the era of ''the gadget.'' Nuclear weapons appear again with the names of human artefacts, though this time they are predominantly tools of combat with strong associations in national folklore.

''Trident'' (the Mark II Tridents are high-precision MIRVed and MARVed systems which will arm Poseidon submarines) is not only the god Poseidon's weapon, but also Britannia's. The symbolism may not be without impact on some British minds. There is also a smaller, ''tactical'' surface-to-surface ''Harpoon.'' The highly significant technical innovation in the arms race represented by the cruise missile is called a ''Tomahawk''—though this one can travel 1,500 miles with a 200-kiloton warhead. From medieval military history we have the ''Mace,'' an early form of cruise missile developed in the 1960s. NATO forces in Europe are armed with ''Lances''—artillery missiles that can deliver conventional, nuclear, or neutron shells up to 75 miles. And the neutron shell itself has been variously christened in ways that illustrate the present point. The term ''enhanced radiation weapon'' is a rather unsubtle euphemism, and when Reagan's decision to deploy the thing in Europe was announced in 1981, the popular British press did its best to justify it. They did so in a way very similar to the naming process that produced lances, maces, and the rest.

The *Sun* (August 10, 1981) said: "It [the neutron weapon] will give Europe a *shield*. . . ." Who would object to a purely defensive shield? We would, after all, not need a shield if there were no aggression. The *Daily Express's* Denis Lehane, in a piece entitled "This Chilling but Vital Evil," shows how spurious arguments can be spun out from logically weak but emotionally powerful analogies. Lehane says he is seeking to rebut the charge that "the neutron bomb is a moral evil . . . because it kills people but leaves buildings largely intact." Here is his response:

> Well, so does the *bow and arrow!* The neutron weapon is for Western Europe today what the English long bow was for Henry V and his army at Agincourt in 1415.
>
> It is a weapon of shilling efficiency and destructive power which counter-balances the enemy's superiority in sophisticated armour. . . .

There is a crude logic here which goes something like this. The neutron weapon destroys people, not property. The longbow destroys people, not property. Therefore, the neutron weapon "is" a longbow. But the longbow is good (and picturesque). Therefore, the neutron weapon is good.

Comparison with accepted primitive weapons is not the only way in which nuclear weapons are classified as part of human culture, and thus as nondangerous. The neutron "gadget" has reportedly been referred to in some quarters as a "cookie cutter." Now to associate it with the kitchen and cooking is significant, because in our myths it is the cooked as opposed to the raw that marks human culture out from the untamed forces of nature. The natural and supernatural is also mythically associated with noise, culture and quiet, and "Cruise" and "Pershing," aside from their referential meaning, may well use sound symbolism to convey speed and civilized silence. "Pershing," apart from being historically apt (he was the U.S. commander who established the American Expeditionary Force in Europe against the initial opposition of the French and British in 1917) may well be onomatopoeic ("purr" in the first syllable) for some hearers. With these points in mind note finally that it has been said of the American nuclear superpower: "You must speak *softly* when you carry a *big stick.*"[16]

There is then a trend in the "naturalization," or rather the *acculturation,* of the nuclear phenomenon. Instead of being symbolically classified as objects of supernatural awe, nuclear weapons now tend to be classified as safe and usable instruments. This shift has clearly accompanied the gradual shift in strategic doctrine toward a more pronounced doctrine of warfighting, of which the nicknames are the public propaganda face.

The Bomb Made Safe

Like advertising, propaganda in western democracies has to sell a product. "Deterrents," like detergents, also have to be sold. Taxpayers buy weapons in the sense that they choose the governments who buy them—though in terms of defense policies the choice has not been too broad. Of course, governments can spend your money without telling you (as in the Chevaline development and the Trident decision), but if the arms race is at all "democratized," and facts about cruise, for instance, become known, then specific propaganda becomes necessary. When propaganda is not concealed in "objective" and "balanced" reporting in the media, it may take the guise of respectable advertising. One is reminded of cigarette advertising. Once people come to believe that cigarettes and missiles might be dangerous for them, the producers have to work hard to modify, eliminate, or repress that belief.

When the plans to deploy cruise missiles became known during 1980, the population in and near the proposed bases received glossy brochures.[17] On the front is a drawing of a sleek windowless aircraft sailing through azure skies. It has no military markings. Unlike the familiar image of the missile pointed toward the heavens, this one is horizontal and has no tail of fire and smoke. Because of the way it is drawn, it appears to cruise silently past your left ear as you read the text. The first thing the pamphlet does, then, is not to explain the technical facts but to trigger a vague emotional response to the word "cruise." The dominant metaphor of the pamphlet is not, however, that of the travel agent, but rather the insurance broker. Beneath the drawing, in bold type, is the following statement: "A vital part of the West's Life Insurance." This odd metaphor is actually quite common in the parlance of nuclear strategists and those who advocate deterrence theory. Indeed, metaphors and analogies of all kinds are disturbingly prevalent in what is often claimed to be highly rational discourse.

It is not just that the association of "Life" with weapons of death and destruction is bizarre. The expression "life insurance" is odd to start with. You insure against theft or fire and you can insure against death too but you then have to call it not "death insurance," but life insurance. The advantage of doing so is first that you suppress the taboo word, and second that you read the phrase (unconsciously no doubt) as "that which insures, ensures or assures life." Perhaps it is some such irrationality that makes the phrase effective in relation to missiles, since it scarcely makes sense as a literal analogy. If you buy an insurance policy, someone will benefit when you die; but it won't deter death from striking you, though you may have a superstitious feeling that it will. The supposedly rational argument that the cruise deterrent will ward off the death of the West is thus sustained by a doubly irrational metaphor.

The rest of the pamphlet follows the pattern of a commercial brochure. There is a series of questions and answers, or rather pseudoquestions and pseudoanswers, of which more below, and a wallet flap containing a separate leaflet, which does little more than repeat the material written on its glossy container. On the flap itself, however, is a color photograph of a Transporter Erector Launcher (TEL) ("about the same weight and size as large commercial vehicles" according to the legend). Its raised pod forms one side of a triangle; a line of fir trees forms the other. The foreshortening reduces the impression of the length of the vehicle. A man in green and dark glasses leans against the cab, and the line projected by his arms as well as the direction of his gaze intersects very low with the missile pod, to reduce the impression of height.

The back page is devoted to other aspects of making the weapon seem civilized and convenient. "What will the Cruise Missiles do in peacetime?" We are assured that "the exercises will be arranged to cause the least inconvenience to the public" and that "busy road traffic periods will be avoided." But "Are Nuclear Weapons Safe? What happens if there is an accident?" You will be reassured to know that "Nuclear Weapons are designed to the highest safety standards and [that] the greatest care is taken in their handline and storage." The same might be claimed of television sets and electric light bulbs. However, in case any reader had some other notion of "safe" in mind, he has the appropriate question asked for him: "Will Basing of Cruise Missiles in this Country make us a Special Target if there is a War?" This and the preceding question are the only ones that expect a yes/no answer. The answer is "No," and the reason is the "sad truth . . . that no part of this country . . . will be safe from danger whether we have Cruise Missiles or not." There is a good deal of fudging and hedging here, if not actual self-contradiction, and the fuzziness starts with the formulation of the question. Who is supposed to be asking the questions? Any British inhabitant, or specifically those near the bases at Molesworth and Greenham Common? Who is the "Special Target"? "Us" in Molesworth or "us . . . in this Country"? What the pamphlet seems to be doing is to deny that the bases are "special" or "priority" targets, and offering the cold comfort of a sort of randomized danger in time of war.

It is interesting that this, the most curcial question of the cruise controversy, is handled in this way. It is not just ignored, but raised at the end of the pamphlet, sandwiched between a "question" on "safety" and one on cost (in general, questions relating to wartime and peacetime matters are alternated and thus associated throughout the pamphlet). Moreover, the contradictions are scarcely veiled. But what carries weight in the act of reading is that emphatic "No," which establishes an intention to deny and reassure: the reader will use that perceived intention to interpret the rest of the confusing text. This is a species of doublespeak and its significance is clear in the light of the 1980 civil defense exercises, which included the cruise bases on their list of nuclear strikes.

The technique in the pamplhet as a whole is reminiscent of the distortions of "balanced" reporting and discussion. Opposition as such is not silenced, but what constitutes opposition is predefined—the "limits of possible thought" are fixed in advance, and the permitted degree of opposition is handled in such a way by those who control the medium that it is neutralized or marginalized.

The cruise pamphlet sets up dissident questions on its own terms and knocks them down without possibility of reply. Most of the questions are phrased in such a way that they presuppose an assertion of the official view. The supposed questioner is made to say not "Are nuclear weapons necessary?" which is the fundamental question, but "Why are nuclear weapons necessary?" This presupposes the statement "nuclear weapons are necessary," and places the "questioner" in the role of tentative enquirer approaching someone with superior knowledge and authority. Similarly, (s)he does not say "Does NATO need more nuclear weapons?" but has the question "Why does NATO need more nuclear weapons?" put in their mouth.

No one will buy an insurance policy unless they are convinced that they are at risk. Hence the front page of the borchure is devoted to insinuating the Russian threat. This does not mean that there is no threat or risk—clearly there is—but the situtation cannot be rationally appraised by dealing in half-truths and innuendo; the verbal techniques draw on the inherent (and necessary) vagueness of human language. When a hearer or reader interprets an utterance he assumes that the speaker has a specific intention and that he is speaking in relation to some shared context. This means that speakers can make indirect assertions, leaving readers to draw relevant inferences, while speakers can disclaim responsibility. There is the added bonus that insinuated propaganda is probably more effective than bald declarations.

Consider the principal actors in the front page text. On the one hand "We." In English this word is ambiguous: "we" including "you," and "we" excluding "you." The actual situation is that "we" (Ministry of Defense propaganda writers) are addressing "you," but the reader is clearly intended to assume the "we" includes her or him. Otherwise (s)he is committed to assuming that (s)he does not "want to live at peace." "We" who "want to live in peace" are then indirectly and directly identified with "The United Kingdom," with "We in the West," and with "NATO." Interestingly, there is no reference to the United States. The pronouns "we" and "us" are also defined in relation to "they" and "them," those outside the "we" group. In "we want to live at peace," the reader may be prompted by a number of contextual cues to stress the "we," thus simultaneously inferring that "*they*" do *not* want peace. And the phrase "But it takes two to make agreements and progress has been slow" infers that "they" have been recalcitrant but "we" have not.

Consider now the actions and mental states attributed to the principal actors in the various verb phrases. The vocabulary is not peculiar to the pamphlet, but is typical of the current rhetoric of the arms race. It is characterized by evocative vagueness, though a persuing reader may be left with the general impression of detailed definiteness.

Modal verbs expressing possibility, necessity, desire are most frequently attributed to "us." So "we" "*want* to live," *seek* to disarm, "*must* be stronger," "*need* to strengthen" (implying that "we" are not currently "strong"). Cruise missiles "*can* go a long way to achieving this aim"—"this aim" being a tortuous back reference to the equally vague "need to strengthen." All this strongly suggests passivity, lack, and inaction. "We" also "persuade"—a verbal activity; our military activities are limited to "basing", and "we" "have been falling behind," in a modally ambiguous sentence, the Russians "see we are weak."

"They," on the other hand, are not characterized by needs, wants, and lacks, but by definite actions and possessions. "They" "have been rapidly building up their military strength"; the Soviet Union "spends 12% of its national wealth each year on its armed forces," and "This is over twice the proportion spent by the NATO allies." This sounds both authoritative and precise (all the more so because of the "about"), but it is a misleading piece of noninformation. Accurate information on Soviet military spending and valid methods of comparison are notoriously difficult to come by. The figures given are in any case relative—they take no account of the absolute difference in "national wealth."[18] The main aim is not to inform but to induce the reader to infer aggressive Soviet intentions.

Note also the prevalence of the present and perfect tenses, which imply definiteness, reinforced by repetition: "the Russians . . . have been rapidly building up. . . . The Soviet Union spends. . . . The Warsaw Pact countries have massive forces. . . . They have large conventional forces. . . . They also have. . . . Finally they have. . . ." "Their" weapons are described as "massive," "large," "very large," "modern," whereas existing NATO weapons are not mentioned at all. If "they" is read with contrastive stress, as it might well be, the reader might infer from the statement "*They* also have short and medium-range nuclear weapons" that "*we*" do not have such weapons. However, the cunning pamphleteer has included an ambiguous "also"; so that if challenged, he could always claim that he meant it to mean "they as well as us." Finally, notice the phrases "to start a war" and to "risk a war against us"; it is "they," the Russians again, who are the logical subjects of these actions.

The distribution of vocabulary and grammatical devices is systematic, but will probably go unnoticed. Most readers seem to store *meanings* in memory rather than words and phrases, and may not question the details. They will be left with the impression of a powerful alien threat to "us," to their group. On these irrational premises is laid a spuriously rational logic. We are peaceful and weak. The Russians are warlike and strong. Conclusion: "NATO *therefore* needs to strengthen its defenses." How? "By basing Cruise Missiles, etc."

This is the first statement about these mysterious objects, or indeed the first mention of any NATO armaments. But we are not yet told what cruise missiles are or how they operate. We are told merely (for the second time) that "the Cruise Missile is a vital part of the West's life insurance," whatever that can mean. More succinctly, we are then told that "Cruise Missiles are (not 'would be' or 'might be,' but *are*) a deterrent."

The fact that they are classified as "a deterrent," before their characteristics are divulged, is a significant ploy. It predisposes the reader to think of them in a certain fashion. In the first place "deterrent" seems to have become for many people in certain contexts a synonym—and a dangerous one—for "nuclear missile." So Cruise is classified first of all as just another nuclear missile—without the word "nuclear" ever having to be used about "our" weapons. (Equally the nuclear warhead and its explosive yield are never mentioned in the semitechnical details provided inside the brochure: the missiles just "hit their targets.") In the second place, in the single word "deterrent" an important claim is made—namely, that the things do, as a matter of actual fact, "deter." That is to say, they prevent or hold back (depending on your individual use of the term) some enemy (the Russians, clearly) from doing something they are claimed, as a matter of fact, to be about to do—attack us. All that appears to be implied, in context, in the semantic structure of the term. Indeed, as this potent single word is habitually used, it encapsulates the whole cold war ideology.

The cruise missiles pamphlet is not an isolated example. Its rhetorical ploys are typical of current official discourse concerning defense matters and relations with the Soviet Union. Such discourse is scarcely conducive to a rational evaluation either of Soviet policy or of our own defense needs. Rather it is the typical stuff of which western propaganda is made. And it is all-pervasive. That is why much of this article has had to be written in inverted commas.

Notes

[1] *Language and Responsibility,* Harvester Press, 1979, p. 20. Chomsky is specifically discussing Vietnam, but what he says applies equally to official doctrines on the cold war and nuclear weapons.

[2] As above, pp. 38–9.

[3] Cf. Thomas Wiseman, referred to in *The Guardian,* Nov. 5, 1981, p. 10.

[4] The Bronowski Memorial Lecture. See *The Listener,* Dec. 29, 1981, p. 494.

[5] Cited in *Overkill* by John Cox, Pelican, 1981, p. 10.

[6] Quoted by Nicholas Humphrey, see *The Listener,* Dec. 29, 1981, p. 498.

[7] Quoted in *The Guardian,* Nov. 5, 1981.

[8] *After Trinity* by John Else.

[9] Aug. 10, 1945, p. 5.

[10] Aug. 8, 1945, p. 5; Aug. 9, p. 4; Aug. 13, p. 4.

[11] *Daily Worker,* Aug. 8, 1945, p. 1, and other papers.

[12] Aug. 12, 1945.

[13] *Robert Oppenheimer* by M. Rouze, Souvenir Press, 1962, p. 23.

[14] *Britain and Nuclear Weapons,* MacMillan, 1980, p. 48.

[15] *Dictionary of Greek and Roman Biography and Mythology,* edited by W. Smith.

[16] Denis Healey, reported in *The Guardian,* Nov. 6, 1981.

[17] Available from the Ministry of Defense.

[18] See *SIPRI Yearbook 1981,* pp. 147–169 ("World military expenditure and the current situation") for further comments on this kind of distortion, e.g.: "One constantly finds, in Western discussions of Soviet military expenditure, that military spokesmen and others use the *dollar* estimate for the level of military expenditure, since that gives you a very high figure, and the *rouble* estimate for the rate of growth in that expenditure, since that method gives the higher figure for the rate of growth. This is, of course, not the only problem in producing sensible, and comparable, figures for rates of growth; one of the other main problems [is] the measurement of quality change.

Using constant price figures (rather than the misleading proportion of national wealth), SIPRI notes "that there is a rough parity of resources devoted to military purposes. . . ." It also points out that "the one country in NATO Europe which had a military spending boom is the UK, with an average annual volume increase each year over the three years from 1977 to 1980 of 4.5%. This is an extraordinarily high figure. . . ."

MARY KALDOR

The Weapons System

Mary Kaldor (b. 1946) is a British sociologist who writes extensively on matters related to nuclear weapons. "The Weapons System" is a chapter from her book, The Baroque Arsenal. *A faculty member of the University of Sussex in England, Kaldor is a Fellow of the Science Policy Research Unit and the Institute of Development Studies. Her other works include* The Disintegrating West *(New York: Allen Lane, 1978) and* The World Military Order: The Impact of Military Technology on the Third World *(New York: Macmillan, 1979).*

It has become commonplace to compare the command of an army with the management of a large corporation. But there is one essential difference. It is easier to persuade men to work than to kill or to risk getting killed. The basis of persuasion in the armed forces has varied according to time and place. It has involved such things as personal loyalty, the appeal to ideas like patriotism and democracy, and discipline. Yet is it probably true to say that in modern society the persuasive techniques used by military officers have more nearly come to resemble the techniques adopted in industry. Except during the Vietnam War, when . . . the inadequacies of military persuasion were acutely revealed, the output of the armed forces, the business of killing has become more remote, and the production of armed forces, the organization of men and machines, has become more and more of an industrial undertaking.

Morris Janowitz, in his seminal book *The Professional Soldier,* which was published in 1960, described "the shift from authoritarian domination to greater reliance on manipulation, persuasion and group consensus."[1] And he ascribed this shift to modern technology:

> The technology of warfare is so complex that the coordination of a complex group of specialists cannot be guaranteed simply by authoritarian discipline. Members of a military group recognize their greater mutual dependence on the technical proficiency of the team members, rather than on the formal authority structure.[2]

In industry the embodiment of technology is the machine, and much has been written about the domination of man by machine in the twentieth century. The military equivalent of the machine is the weapons system. The weapons system combines a weapons platform: ship, aircraft or tank; a weapon: gun, missile,

---

Mary Kaldor, "The Weapons System." From *The Baroque Arsenal* by Mary Kaldor (New York: Hill and Wang, 1981), pp. 11–28.

or torpedo; and the means of command and communication. The concept of the weapons system emerged in the late nineteenth century with the Anglo-German naval arms race and came to fruition in World War II as the aircraft and the tank came of age, although the term was not used until the 1950s. It was associated, as we shall see, with the entry of capitalist industry into the arms market; shipbuilding and heavy engineering in Britain in the 1880s, aircraft and automobiles in the 1940s.

As the term is used in this book, the "weapons system" is more than just a military classification of hardware. It is a classification of people as well. The weapons system implies the existence of an entire supporting cast—scientist to invent the weapons, workers to build them, soldiers to use them, and technicians to repair them. Indeed, the concept was developed by the U.S. Air Force in the 1950s as a tool of management, in order to organize this ever-growing cast. The institutions and language of "systems," however, served eventually to conceal the relationship between government and industry, which underlies the very concept of the weapons system.

In most Western countries, the procurement of armaments, what one might call the fixed capital of warfare, accounts for about half the military budget. Moreover, the procurement budget is dominated by a few major weapon systems. In the United States, for example, the Trident submarine and the new nuclear-powered aircraft carrier, together with their missiles and aircraft, account for about 60 percent of the naval procurement budget. The latest Air Force fighters, F-15 and F-16, account for more than 40 percent of the Air Force procurement budget, while the XM-1 battle tank accounts for a major share of the Army budget. The same is true in Western Europe. In Britain, the Multi Role Combat Aircraft (MRCA) Tornado accounts for around 40 percent of the Royal Air Force budget; the three antisubmarine warfare cruisers, with their associated escort and support ships, probably account for a fifth to a quarter of the British naval procurement budget.

The major weapons system defines, by and large, the lines of command in modern armed forces. Navies, for example, are organized by ship, with groups of ships organized hierarchially into task forces. At the apex of the U.S. surface navy is the aircraft carrier, requiring destroyers and a submarine or two for protection, aircraft to fly from its deck, and supply ships of various kinds. The bomber and the battle tank have a similar role in the Air Force and Army. The Air Force is divided into bomber, fighter, and transport commands. The Army is made up of armor, artillery, parachute, and infantry units. But the armored units are, to quote Colonel Vernon Pizer, "the mailed fist that strikes hard, fast and deep,"[3] the core of the combined arms team. The House Armed Services Committee of the U.S. Congress recently reasserted its belief that "the tank is—and will continue to be—the heart of land warfare."[4] The independence of individual services or military units is achieved through independent strategies associated with particular weapons systems. This would explain why strategic bombing is so central to the U.S. Air Force or why the British Navy remains committed to an oceangoing role associated with carriers, long after the abandonment of overseas commitments.

The growing capital intensity of warfare is also reflected in the composition of skills. The direct labor of war, which includes infantrymen, tank crews, artillerymen, fighter and bomber crewmen, fighting ships' personnel, who actually do the fighting, has declined dramatically as a proportion of total military manpower. It is known as the declining ''teeth to tail'' ratio.

> In all the [U.S.] services fewer than one out of every six persons in uniform—360,000 out of 2,200,000—currently serve in a combat specialty. By way of historical comparison, better than nine of every ten persons serving in the Union forces during the American Civil War had combat specialties.[5]

The lone fighter pilot, who was the heroic individual of World War II, was in fact part of a team that serviced, operated, and maintained his aeroplane; a team which today has grown to seventy people. The tendency to substitute ''the firepower and mobility of improved war machines for manpower''[6] is also reflected in what is known as ''grade creep,'' the increase in middle-level officers—the white-collar military technicians—so that the traditional pyramid shape of the military hierarchy has come to look like a diamond.

The role of the individual is thus defined in relation to the weapons system, and the lower his position in the hierarchy, the more specialized is his job. At the base of any modern military organization is the small group of about ten to thirty enlisted men, identified by occupation (e.g., a division of ship's cooks) or by function (e.g., a gun crew). Modern military sociologists argue that the individual thinks of himself as a member of a specific skill group rather than of a social class and that his motivation is based on technical pride in his work. There is a powerful ideology of team spirit in the well-integrated, technically efficient military unit, which, combined with modern awe for technology, is supposed to supplement, if not supplant, traditional techniques of command and control. According to Morris Janowitz, this is symbolized in the uniform of the soldier. In the past, smart uniforms were an expression of the military idea of honor. Today, the occupational uniform of both the U.S. Army and U.S. Air Force is the fatigue suit.

> The uniform which obscures the differences between ranks similarly obliterates the difference between the military and the industrial. It is a persistent expression of the thought that military men are not only representative men, but representative of the technical contemporary society rather than of a previous historical period.[7]

The link between the military and the industrial is not only an idea, it is materialized in the weapons system. Like the machine, the weapons system is both an object of use and an object of production. The military capabilities of a particular weapons system, which define its role in a particular military unit, reflect the manufacturing capabilities of a particular defense company. Thus, there are parallels, which have become closer over time, between military organization and industrial structure.

The design, development, and production of weapons systems is, by and large, undertaken by a handful of companies known as prime contractors. With a few significant exceptions . . . the prime contractors are generally the manufacturers of weapons platforms—aircraft, shipbuilding, automobile, or engineering companies.° They assemble the complete weapons system, subcontracting subsystems, like gun or missile, the engine and the electronics and components, and so create an interdependent network of big and small companies. The prime contractors are generally among the largest industrial companies. Since World War II, between forty and fifty companies have regularly appeared both on *Fortune*'s list of the top one hundred United States companies and on the Pentagon's list of the one hundred companies receiving the highest prime contract awards. The stability of the primes has been widely noted. Since the war, firms have disappeared through merger or, in Europe, through nationalization, but there have been virtually no closures and virtually no new entrants.

Each of the primes specializes in types of weapons systems. Boeing, General Dynamics, and Rockwell are bomber enterprises. Grumman and Vought make fighters for the Navy; McDonnell Douglas and General Dynamics make fighters for the Air Force: Lockheed makes heavy air transports as well as submarine-based missiles. Chrysler and General Motors are the prime contractors for battle tanks. Dassault in France, MBB in Germany, and British Aerospace in Britain make combat aircraft. Fokker in Holland makes transport aircraft. Westland, in Britain, like Sikorsky (now a division of United Technologies), Bell, or Boeign Vertol in America, or Sud Aviation (now Aerospatiale) in France, are the manufacturers of helicopters. Electric Boat, now owned by General Dynamics, has made submarines since the 1890s, when it was purchased by the British company Vickers. Today Electric Boat is building the Trident submarine, the projected system for the American underwater nuclear forces in the 1980s. Newport News makes aircraft carriers. And so on.

Each of these companies represents a manufacturing experience, a particular combination of plant, equipment, and people, a specific mix of skills and techniques, a hierarchical organization of people, of relationships with customers (the military units) and suppliers (the subcontractors). The president of Newport News, when justifying financial claims on the government to a congressional committee, explained:

> What we have built at Newport News is a unique ship-manufacturing complex—the only one in the United States that has the facilities, equipment and human resources to build, repair, overhaul and refuel the full range of Navy vessels and the only one now building nuclear-powered surface ships. Newport News is truly a national asset.[8]

Literally thousands of subcontractors are dependent on the primes. Some are very large and are prime contractors themselves. These would include the en-

---

In Europe tanks are made by engineering companies rather than by automobile companies.

gine companies like Rolls Royce, Pratt and Whitney (now United Technologies), and General Electric, or the electronic companies like Texas Instruments, Raytheon, Westinghouse in the United States, or Ferranti and Marconi-Elliot in Britain. There are also many small suppliers; some are established by the primes to produce a particular component. The small subcontractors are not at all stable. Their composition varies along with technology, and in the lean years it is they who go bankrupt.

Very often, prime contractors and their families of subcontractors dominate a region, so that the economic impact of producing a weapons system may be very great. Boeing is the biggest company in the state of Washington. Several aircraft companies—Lockheed, Rockwell, Douglas, for example—are located in Southern California. McDonnell dominates manufacturing in St. Louis, while Bath Ironworks, which makes destroyers, is the most important employer in Maine. Hundreds and thousands of people may work on a single contract. At Electric Boat in Groton, Connecticut, 31,000 people are estimated to work on the Trident submarine. And this does not include the people employed by subcontractors or the ripple effect on the producers of consumer goods purchased by the people employed or the capital goods acquired by the contractors. At Rockwell, 13,000 people were working on the B-1 bomber project when it was canceled in 1977, and about 40,000 people were said to have been employed by Rockwell's subcontractors throughout the nation. Had the B-1 bomber gone into production, many thousands more would have been employed. In the 1960s, it was estimated that, although military contracts account directly for only 8 percent of California's employment, the total impact including indirect employment by subcontractors and indirect employment among producers of consumer and capital goods was 40 percent.[9] And if we also take into account the fact that many small firms which produce both military and civil goods are dependent on the military market to ensure their survival, then it is evident that the whole defense industry is deeply embedded in the economy as a whole.

The weapons system is subject to a technological dynamic characteristic of its industrial environment. As the social structure of industry and the armed forces converge, the competition which epitomizes private industrial enterprise pervades the various institutions which make up the organization of defense. The National Security Industrial Association, an organization of American defense contractors, reports:

> Within DoD [the U.S. Department of Defense] itself, competition is a very active force. This is reflected in DoD's drive to stay ahead of our potential enemies by fielding weapons which incorporate the latest possible technology; in DoD's relationships with other governmental departments; in the efforts of the military services to protect and expand their respective roles and missions and to obtain a larger share of the defense budget; in the relationship between the military services and the Office of the Secretary of Defense; and in the competition among the branches, commands, arsenals, yards, centers, and laboratories of the military services.
>
> For industry, competition is keen because the overall total of defense business is

> seldom adequate to support the available capacity of even the hard-core defense contractors, thus forcing the companies into a continuous life-and-death struggle to obtain defense contracts. Defense programs often are of gigantic magnitude, which results in competition more intensely concentrated than is typically encountered in the commercial marketplace.[10]

The consequence of this competition is rapid technical change, in which every component part of successive weapons systems is pushed up to and beyond the "state of the art." It is the fantastic space-age dimensions of much modern weaponry which so awes the soldier and the civilian observer. And yet the direction of technical change, it can be argued, is confined within limits that are defined by the persistence of military and industrial institutions. The stability of prime contractors and their customers has helped to preserve traditions about the kind of military equipment that is considered appropriate. Indeed, the very sophistication and complexity of hardware may be a sign of conservatism and narrow perspective. In peacetime, in the absence of external necessity imposed by war, decisions about what constitutes technical advance are necessarily subjective. They tend to be taken by people who make and use the weapons systems, whose ideas are necessarily shaped by institutional experience and interest in survival. "We have," writes John Downey, an eminent British soldier,

> a situation in which the nature of present strategy (deterrence) precludes the acid test of war, while complexity invalidates the rough and ready evaluations of public opinion.[11]

The consequence is that

> the system is almost completely introverted, concentrating on the perpetual perfection of itself against some future day of judgement. The dynamic tensions, commonly regarded as necessary in all systems, must also be generated internally and can only come from debate between vigorous minds. But although the system strives hard to recruit able people, it chooses and trains them in its own image.[12]

Morris Janowitz makes much the same point when he emphasizes the routinization of innovation in the military establishment, with the consequence that

> traditional thinking has more often than not led to trend thinking, to a concern with gradually perfecting technical instruments, rather than strategic re-evaluation of weapons systems. This orientation in itself is a form, though a modified one, of technological conservatism whether the problem is missiles or manpower, planning toward the future tends to be a perfection of trends rather than an imaginative emphasis on revolutionary development.[13]

This is what we mean by baroque technology. "Baroque" technical change consists largely of improvements to a given set of "performance characteristics." Submarines are faster, quieter, bigger, and have longer ranges. Aircraft have greater speed, more powerful thrust, and bigger payloads. All weapons systems have more destructive weapons, particularly missiles, and greatly improved capabilities for communication, navigation, detection, identification, and weapon guidance. Even the development of nuclear weapons can be regarded as an extension of strategic bombing. While the basic technology of the delivery system has not changed much, such marginal improvements have often entailed the use of very advanced technology; e.g., radical electronics innovations such as microprocessors or nuclear power for submarines, and this has greatly increased the complexity of the weapons system as a whole.

Any "improvement" to a particular performance characteristic tends to beget others, and any "improvement" to a particular weapons system as a whole tends to infect whole families of weapons systems. Witness this description of the carrier:

> To achieve greater air capability . . . the individual naval aircraft and the ships' complement have grown in size and complexity. . . .
>
> These trends have caused growth in the carrier itself, because of the need for more aviation fuel, more hangar-deck space, greater strength and size of the landing deck to support the heavier aircraft with higher landing speeds and so forth. As all parts of the design move together, the carrier, its power plant, its auxiliary services, and its crew have all grown. . . .[14]

Baroque technical change may also lead to versatility, the development of multipurpose weapons systems. Competition tends to promote institutional expansion. Military branches, services, and commands poach the roles of others; corporations imitate the capabilities of competitors. The Army emphasizes the development of amphibious and airborne missions. The Navy clings to the ability to fly aircraft and land Marines. The Air Force, in order to retain its organizational autonomy through its bombing role, insists that fighter aircraft be able to strike deep into enemy territory. Prime contractors tend to diversify into a wider range of defense products. Lockheed, Litton, and General Dynamics, aerospace companies, have purchased shipyards. North American Aviation merged with Rockwell, the company which makes axles for army trucks. The Ford Motor Company has acquired an aerospace subsidiary. At the same time, the growing cost of individual weapons systems has tended to result in a decline in their number and variety so that military units have had to share the same systems and contractors have learned to collaborate in development and production.

The consequence is the all-rounded weapons system: the number of "performance characteristics" specified for a weapons system is increased. The different characteristics that were formerly specified for several individual systems are now combined into one. The F-111, which was to have been the main combat aircraft of the American Air Force and Navy during the 1970s, was expected by Tactical Air Command to have to take off from short and rough landing strips and to fly the Atlantic nonstop,

> to travel extremely long distances, carrying a load of nuclear weapons and fly at treetop level . . . engage in aerial combat at high altitudes and at speeds in excess of 1,700 miles per hour . . . [and to have] a large ordnance carrying capacity.[15]

These were the characteristics which defined the Air Force missions of interdiction, air superiority, and ground support. In addition, the Navy wanted a plane for fleet air defense. For this, the plane had to be able to circle "a fleet of ships at high altitudes for long periods [and] to locate and destroy up to twenty miles away an enemy aircraft approaching the fleet."[16] It turned out to be very difficult to make one plane which could do all these things well, and in the end, the Navy version was cancelled.

The British cruiser *Invincible* and its sister ships *Indefatigable* and *Ark Royal* are expected to combine the roles of command, control, and coordination of British and NATO maritime forces, the deployment of antisubmarine warfare aircraft, and the capacity to carry one thousand commando troops—tasks which were formerly carried out by several different ships. The European Multi Role Combat Aircraft, which is jointly developed and produced by Britain, Germany, and Italy, has been described as the "egg-laying, wool-producing, milk-giving sow."[17] Britain wants MRCA for long-range strike and strategic air defense (against bombers). Germany wants MRCA for close air support. Italy wants MRCA for air superiority (against fighters). . . . these requirements are not easy to reconcile; MRCA has ended up primarily as an expensive low-level bomber for nuclear strike.

These features of baroque technical change—trend improvement and multiplication of roles—are designed to preserve the military-industrial structure. But technical change demands organizational change. What occurs is a kind of regroupment for survival. More and more men are required to produce and operate a particular type of weapons system, increasing the size of military and industrial teams, as well as the degree of individual specialization. As the variety of weapons systems declines, the tactics of different military missions, and even the broader land, sea, and air strategies, are more closely integrated. The number of prime contractors for each type of weapons system falls and the interdependence of companies is increased through mergers, collaboration, and an interlocking set of contractual relationships. The smaller subcontractors become more fragmented and more specialized; duplicate suppliers for particular components are squeezed out, while the total number of components increases. Essentially, these changes mean greater hierarchy and less individual autonomy; a narrowing of the apex of the pyramid in both military and industrial spheres. Transnational projects like MRCA or the Anglo-French Jaguar, or even the American and German attempt to achieve "commonality" in tank design, represent the development of multinational forms of military and industrial organization.

The consequence of this elaborate combination of conservatism and technical dynamism is what economists call "diminishing returns": more and more effort is expended for smaller improvements in military effectiveness. As military and industrial teams grow bigger and more hierarchical, the relationship of the individual to the whole is at once narrower and more remote; the inability to see beyond the design of a component, the repair of a part, or the wrath of an immediate superior may impair the ability to consider the industrial technology or the military mission in its entirety. Conflict and compromise are increasingly built into the design of weapons systems as formerly competing users and producers join in a single project. A former Litton employee describes the problems that were encountered when two hundred people were assigned the task of preparing a proposal for the series production of Spruance class destroyers for the Navy:

> Scarce top engineering talent was siphoned into management roles, from which positions they had little time to actually work on, or even think about, the actual problem. Instead, they became embroiled in jurisdictional fights and empire-building. If a job got behind, the group involved automatically claimed it didn't have enough people. More people were supplied, and management problems compounded.
>
> Efforts at communication took up much of the time. This was aggravated by the fact that group managers sometimes withheld information if this was judged to be in the individual group's parochial interest. . . . Thus a technical mistake . . . could proceed for some time without being noticed. . . .
>
> Finally, a group this size presents severe problems in motivating the people who actually do the work to operate in accordance with the goal of the overall project. The people who actually did the work were so far removed from the corporate reward system that their own goal became minimizing the risk that their individual subsystem be judged infeasible. . . . The result was consistent overdesign and conservatism. The lowest level would design an individual system element with plenty of margin, his boss would throw in another margin just to make sure, and so on.[18]

The problem was compounded by the size of the Navy evaluation team:

> Litton realized that whatever the merits of its basic concept, unless the proposal defined such subsystems as, say, the galley in great detail, whoever was evaluating the galley part of the proposal would give the proposal low marks. Since there were many such subsystems, a disproportionate amount of Litton's effort was devoted to routine subsystem design.[19]

Similar problems have been recounted for the design of other systems. On the F-111, for example, Graham Allison, in a summary of a study by Robert Coulam, describes how the contractor and the Air Force organized their engineering teams "in parallel fashion with horizontal communications quite strong between counterpart contractor and Air Force civilian engineers." This greatly hampered the ability to make technical trade-offs.

> If results at one level of design indicated the need to trade among higher order objectives, the whole elaborate hierarchy of specification detail—detail which coordinated the engineering efforts of thousands of contractors and government officials—stood in the way. . . . Even relatively minor reformulations would require the concurrence of layer upon layer of contractor and government authorities.[20]

The outcome of this contradictory process, in which technology is simultaneously promoted and restrained, is gross, elaborate, and very expensive hardware. The Trident program will cost the American taxpayer over $30 billion (in 1980 prices). The latest nuclear-powered aircraft carrier, the subject of controversy between Congress and President Carter, will cost, together with its associated ships and aircraft, more than $60 billion. An Air Force F-15 fighter costs $19 million; the Navy F-14 costs $22 million. The Air Force F-16 and Navy F-18, which were originally designed as cheap, lightweight fighters, are currently estimated to cost $11 million and $18 million, respectively. These costs are several times greater than the cost of World War II predecessors, even when inflation is taken into account. One well-known estimate suggests that if current trends continue, the U.S. Air Force will be able to afford only one plane in 2020.[21] Bombers cost two hundred times as much as they did in World War II. Fighters cost one hundred times or more than they did in World War II. Aircraft carriers are twenty times as expensive and battle tanks are fifteen times as expensive as in World War II. A Gato class submarine cost $5,500 per ton in World War II, compared with $1.6 million per ton for the Trident submarine.[22]

These costs primarily reflect amazing sophistication and technical complexity. And complexity means thousands and thousands of parts, each part a servicing and logistical problem. The F-4, for example, the predecessor to F-14 and F-15, required 70,000 spare parts. In Vietnam, despite the most extensive logistical operation ever mounted, there were always shortages. All military aircraft are much less reliable than commercial aircraft. They break down more often; they require more maintenance, more repairs, more spares, and more fuel. Tanks are much less reliable than tractors, and warships are much less reliable than merchant ships. As weapons systems become complex, particularly as they incorporate more electronic equipment, reliability declines and operational costs increase at an exponential rate (despite the increased reliability of solid-state devices and improved automated maintenance). According to Captain O'Rourke, a U.S. Navy officer:

> Expensive airplanes are complex airplanes, and complex airplanes, over the past ten to fifteen years, have been the bane of our existence. The costs of keeping a stable of these complex machines in fighting trim is astronomical—in terms of people. Our maintenance and support people have repeatedly fallen behind the heavy demands which these complex, sophisticated systems have made. The Navy supply system; bound up in red tape of its own space age bureaucratic computerdom, has rarely been able to stay apace with the ever-increasing demands for high cost, one-of-a-kind spare parts for the sophisticated systems.[23]

Complex weapons systems are also complex to operate. And yet training hours, combat exercises, and firing practice are reduced because of high operating cost as well as the risk of an expensive accident. And families of weapons systems are increasingly dependent on complex systems of communication which are also costly to operate and maintain.

Nor is it at all clear that cost and complexity are justified by increased performance. First of all, measurable improvements in performance characteristics are rarely proportionate to the increase in costs. In particular, all-roundedness, as we have seen, tends to *reduce* the efficiency of any one role. Second, improvements in the accuracy and lethality of munitions have greatly increased the vulnerability of all weapons systems and their associated communication and support systems. As a result, many of the performance characteristics so dear to the services and contractors have become irrelevant in modern warfare. The classic examples are aircraft speed, which reduces the accuracy of pinpoint bombing, and speed of surface vessels, which cannot reduce vulnerability to aircraft and submarines. A recent Pentagon exercise, known as Air Missile Intercept Evaluation, demonstrated that numbers were more important than sophistication in air warfare. In close engagements, F-5s, F-14s, and F-15s consistently destroyed one another. Major General Frederick C. Blesse (USAF ret), who observed the exercise, explained: "it doesn't make much difference how fast your airplane is or how high it will fly. Once you get inside your enemy's missile envelope, you're not likely to escape."[24] The more sophisticated aircraft, F-14 and F-15, imposed great strain on the pilots, who were unable to make use of the many theoretical capabilities of the planes.

The Trident, perhaps, is the best example, because most people would think that nuclear-firing missile submarines represent just about the best that modern military technology has to offer. The Trident submarine is huge. It is 560 feet long, longer than the Washington Monument, and six inches too deep to get out of the Thames Channel in Connecticut from its building site to the sea. It is faster than its predecessors, the Polaris/Poseidon submarines. It carries more missiles with a longer range. It has a natural circulation nuclear reactor which is significantly quieter at normal patrol speeds. Its size and its large complement of missiles, however, may actually increase its vulnerability, since it will be easier to detect than its predecessors. Its top underwater speed (25 knots) is still significantly lower than that of attack submarines (30 knots), and in any case, it is so noisy at top speed that it would have to go slowly to escape detection. The increased missile range is of dubious advantage since, for the foreseeable future, Soviet antisubmarine warfare forces cannot detect submarines within the operating area of the current Poseidon submarine.

Similar criticisms can be made of the main systems now under development in the United States: the XM-1 Main Battle Tank, the new MX intercontinental missile, the new class of Air Force and Navy fighters, the cruise missile carriers, and the latest aircraft carriers. William W. Kaufman, an adviser to James Schlesinger when he was Secretary of Defense, said of the aircraft carrier that

> no more costly method of keeping a limited number of airplanes at a forward base has ever been devised by the mind of man. The Navy cannot define circumstances in which these very expensive sorties will make a significant difference in a situation where we care.[25]

It is equally difficult to explain why some of the European systems like MRCA or Invincible will be better than their predecessors.

In short, the weapon system, in perfecting itself along the lines projected by users and producers, seems to have overreached itself. It has become big, costly, elaborate, and less and less functional. It serves a certain social purpose, in creating an ever more complicated set of connections between soldiers, sailors, officers, managers, designers, workers, and bureaucrats. And it retains a certain grandeur, a certain ability to instill social awe, that is often to be found in the baroque, whether art, architecture, or technology—a grandeur that may portend degeneration.

Notes

[1] New York: Free Press, 1960, p. 8.

[2] *Ibid.*, p. 41.

[3] Vernon Pizer (Lt. Colonel, U.S.A. Ret.), *The U.S. Army* (New York: Praeger, 1967), p. 39.

[4] Quoted in Jonathan E. Medalia and A. A. Tinajero, "XM-1 Main Battle Tank Program," *Issue Brief Number IB 75052,* Washington, D.C.: Library of Congress, Congressional Research Service, July 1975, updated May 1978.

[5] William D. White, *U.S. Tactical Air Power: Missions, Forces and Costs* (Washington, D.C.: The Brookings Institution, 1974), p. 5.

[6] *Ibid.*

[7] Janowitz, *op.cit.*, p. 320.

[8] *U.S. Congressional Record,* 95th Cong., 1st Sess., CXXIII, Part 8, p. 9269, March 28, 1977.

[9] Charles M. Tiebout, "The Regional Impact of Defense Expenditures: Its Measurement and Problems of Adjustment," in Roger E. Bolton, *Defense and Disarmament: The Economics of Transition* (Englewood Cliffs, N.J.: Prentice-Hall, 1966).

[10] Quoted in J. R. Fox, *Arming America: How the U.S. Buys Weapons* (Cambridge, Mass.: Harvard University, 1974), pp. 100–1.

[11] *Management in the Armed Forces: An Anatomy of the Military Profession* (London: McGraw-Hill, 1977), p. 195.

[12] *Ibid.*, p. 198.

[13] *Op.cit.*, pp. 27–28.

[14] Seymour J. Deitchman, *New Technologies and Military Power: General Purpose Forces for the 1980s and Beyond* (Boulder, Colo.: Westview Press, 1979), p. 107.

[15] Robert J. Art, *The TFX Decision: McNamara and the Military* (Boston: Little, Brown & Co., 1968), p. 15.

[16] *Ibid.*, p. 25.

[17] Ulrich Albrecht, *et al.*, "Das ender des MRCA?" in Studiengruppe Militärpolitik, *Ein Anti-Weisbuch Materialien für eine Alternative Militärpolitik* (Hamburg: Rowohlt, 1974), author's translation, p. 83.

[18] J. W. Devanney in "The DX Competition," *U.S. Naval Institute Proceedings* (August 1975), pp. 25–26.

[19] *Ibid.*

[20] "The F-111," in *Commission on the Organization of the Government for the Conduct of Foreign Policy* (Murphy Commission) (Washington, D.C., June 1975), *Volume 4, Appendix K: Adequacy of Current Organization: Defense and Arms Control,* pp. 131–2.

[21] Norman R. Augustine, "One Plane, One Tank, One Ship: Trend for the Future," *Defense Management Journal* (April 1975).

[22] Aerospace Systems Analysis, McDonnell Douglas Astronautics Corp., *Cost of War Index* (Santa Monica, Calif.: September 1968).

[23] "Two Views on Navy Fighters," *Armed Forces Journal* (November 1974).

[24] Quoted in Jo. L. Husbands, "The Long Long Pipeline. Arms Sales and Technological Dependence," unpublished, Center for Defense Information, Washington, D.C., 1978.

[25] Quoted in John Wicklein, "The Oldest Establishment Permanent Floating Anachronism in the Sea," *Washington Monthly* (February 1970).

LISA PEATTIE

Normalizing the Unthinkable

Lisa Peattie (b. 1924), a professor of urban anthropology at the Massachusetts Institute of Technology, has worked with the MIT Disarmament Study Group—where Randall Forsberg was a colleague.She is coauthor of a book entitled Women's Claims: A Study of Political Economy *(New York: Oxford University Press, 1983). Her other works include* Thinking about Development *(New York: Plenum, 1981) and* Making Work *(New York: Plenum, 1983).*

An environmental Protection Agency study of "Evacuation Risks" argues energetically against the "panic image" of human behavior in an emergency situation: "People will often stay in a potentially threatening situation rather than move out of it," the report declares. "Human beings have very strong tendencies to continue on-going lines of behavior in preference to initiating new courses of action."[1]

Current planning for the management of a nuclear war in itself constitutes an examplary confirmation of this principle. The situation which the planners address is the most dreadful conceivable. It involves at the minimum the deaths of a substantial number of the human beings whom we love and with whom we share a common fate, the destruction of the physical places where we live and to which we are attached, the disorganization of our society. It may mean the end of human life on Earth, and thus the very sensibleness of planning. But the tone of the planning studies is entirely normal and normalizing.

One approach is to work from analogies with the familiar. A study of the consequences of "incidents" involving nuclear power plants draws from human actions and reactions in floods, fires, and earthquakes. The data are deaths from motor vehicle accidents; costs for food and housing; salaries and wages for national guardsmen, policemen and firemen; loss of wages per day per evacuee.[2] Such analogies appear also in planning for nuclear war.

Nuclear war, however, even in the world of civil defense research, appears somewhat off the scale of analysis by analogy to the ordinary. Therefore resort is made to rendering the situation playfully, via models and games. One study, for example, declares that "Like war games and business games the post-attack problems for which a single city model might be used are characterized by both rich environments and incomplete sets of decision rules."[3] Such a gaming approach deals in "weapons impacts," "resource availability," "cumulating costs

---

Lisa Peattie, "Normalizing the Unthinkable," *Bulletin of the Atomic Scientists* (March 1984): 32–36. Reprinted by permission of the *Bulletin of the Atomic Scientists,* a magazine of science and world affairs.

of items or modules damaged beyond repair,'' and ''vulnerability indexes.'' Dividing reduced resources by a greatly reduced population, it is possible to conclude that ''Considering resources alone, a moderate level attack on the nation might reduce consumption to the equivalent of that of the Great Depression.''[4]

The principle is correct. There appears to be no situation so abnormal—experientially, socially, morally—that human beings, if not totally stunned out of all reactivity, will not at least strive to assimilate it to normal practice.

Even at Hiroshima, there became apparent a certain mad orderliness which we might interpret as the behavioral counterpart of the intellectual processes which would equate the effects of nuclear war with those of the Great Depression:

> Those who were able walked silently towards the suburbs and the distant hills. . . . They were so broken and confused that they moved and behaved like automatons. Their reactions had astonished outsiders who reported with amazement the spectacle of long files of people holding stolidly to a narrow, rough path when close by was a smooth, easy road going in the same direction. The outsiders could not grasp the fact that they were witnessing the exodus of a people who walked in the realm of dreams.[5]

Let us consider what we know of human behavior in the concentration camp. Jean François Steiner's account of life in Treblinka describes how, even as the scale and atrociousness of the extermination process advanced, the institutions and social organization of the camp came more and more to parallel those of a normal society.[6] The technology improved; the original clumsy experiments with killing Jews by exhaust fumes in the trucks which brought them from Warsaw were supplanted by the developed technology of the gas chambers. The Germans found it inconvenient to work with a perpetually inexperienced labor force. Thus, from an initial strategy of gassing those who had been forced to strip their fellow victims of clothing, valuables, hair, and gold teeth, they established a set of longer-term workers who would only at extended intervals be sent to the chambers.

Relationships, both bureaucratic and personal, came into being. The longer-term inmates found particular niches in the organization and learned to work the system for their own personal well-being and protection and, when they could, to protect their friends. A prisoners' orchestra was formed, and when the trains unloaded a new set of victims, musicians were pulled out of the ranks to join the music makers. Prizefights became another form of entertainment, and another principle of selection. A park and zoo were built.

Toward the end, when the Germans began to realize that they were likely to lose the war, a goal became that of concealing the evidence. The prisoner-workers were set to digging up, by heavy machinery, bodies which had been piled into deep pits, so that they could be burnt. It took a little time to evolve the techniques for cremating this mountain of bodies, but eventually a regular procedure was developed, and the slow, smoky burning of the old bodies became part of the normal functioning of the camp.

Meanwhile, a new institution came into being: a cabaret, shared by the Germans and some of the more established, and therefore privileged, inmates. Weddings were held and celebrated with festivities.

In the latter period of the camp's operation, the long-term inmates, now able to function on a more extended basis, began to organize an uprising. In Steiner's account of this process—which ended with a bloody battle and the capture and death of almost all of those prisoners who had escaped—the most painful part of the story is the difficulty experienced by the leaders in starting the revolt.

They kept putting it off, although they knew that time was running out for them. They made calculations: the original Jewish population of Warsaw; the thousands who passed through the gas chambers; the numbers that must be left; the weeks it would take to process the remaining Jews into extinction. They knew that at the moment the death factory ran out of raw material they too would go into the gas chambers. But no given day seemed quite right. Steiner wrote that it was as though they were stuck in a dream: the dream of the daily routine, of the normality of ordinary behavior. The camp, with its bureaucracy, its personalities, its roles, its smoking bodies, had become normal.

Steiner's description of Treblinka is particularly rich in recording the normalizing of an atrocious institution, but the theme is in all the personal accounts of concentration camp experience by those who survived for any time in one or the other. There was the daily routine of blows and roll call and soup. There was the barter economy of bread, turnips, scraps of cloth, gold teeth.[7] There were specializations: prison plumbers laid the water pipe in the crematorium and prison electricians wired the fences.[8] The camp managers maintained standards and orderly process. The cobblestones which paved the crematorium yard at Auschwitz had to be perfectly scrubbed.[9]

Germany was not a backward country. On the contrary, it was a world leader in modern music, philosophy, high technology, and the social institutions we call the welfare state. Thus, to normalize the unthinkable, the world of the concentration camp had available to it not only the simple techniques of every human society—the establishment of routine, of social ties and of exchange relationships muting conflict through shared commitment and individual rewards for participation. It also had the sophisticated techniques of technological elaboration and bureaucratic rationality. The inhabitants of Treblinka were able to normalize the atrocious by elaborating around it not only music and art but also technology and management.

Every prisoner had his or her number tattooed on the arm, and this number was carried through in the files and records. The day before Auschwitz was abandoned a new sort of "columns of smoke could be seen rising in all parts of the camp."[10] The SS were burning their card indexes and files.

When we hear of "scientific" experiments performed on inmates in the concentration camp setting we tend to recoil in horror. But is the pretense of science any more horrifying than the rest of it? Indeed, it seems that we must understand these experiments as arising not out of pure sadism, but out of that same human tendency to normalize any setting that generated the concentration camp infirmaries, to which they were often connected. It was quite in keeping with the spirit of it all that these "experimental" tortures constituted the basis for papers read at scientific meetings where, although the source of the data must have been evident, apparently no protest was made. "Science" in the concentration camp was yet another manifestation of the human normalizing tendency, both noble and horrifying, which came to link victims and torturers in the creation of a shared society based on the production of death.

Are we not today engaged in a similar enterprise?

The SS men watched the crumbling of the German Reich, and the prisoners counted the numbers of Jews in the transports and calculated how many weeks it must be before their turn would come. Yet together, day by day, they scrubbed the cobblestones or ordered the cobblestones scrubbed; went to roll call to count and be counted, maintaining the world of Treblinka. Like them, we collaborate day by day in maintaining the institutions of the warfare state which seems more and more plausibly set to destroy us. We are caught in the human endeavor to create daily life: to normalize the unthinkable.

The devices which we use are roughly similar: the division of labor, which separates, in understanding and potential for collective organization, what it makes interdependent in functioning; the structure of rewards and incentives which makes it to individuals' personal and familiar interest to undermine daily, in countless small steps, the basis of common existence; and the legitimating use of bureaucratic formalism and of scientific and technological elaboration.

The division of labor serves most obviously to normalize the atrocious when it takes the form of institutions specialized for purposes which we must assume that normal people would abhor. We might be somewhat less inclined to out-of-hand rejection of the claims of "good" Germans that they did not know what those crematoria were burning when we consider that Bishop Leroy Matthiesen—now a particularly outspoken opponent of the nuclear arms race—served for nine years as a parish priest, two miles from the Pantex plant at Amarillo, Texas, without realizing that its output is nuclear bombs. Pantex covers 10,000 acres and employs 2,400 people; it does final assembly of the entire nuclear arsenal.[11]

But even within the institutions of death, the division of labor continues in a multitude of ways to normalize operation. At the structural level, it divides participants in the organization into groups with specialized interests, less likely to combine against the higher authorities. So at Treblinka an absolute separation of work, housing, and communication was maintained between the group of workers who received the Jews from the trains and marshaled them into the gas chambers and those at the other side who removed hair and gold teeth and disposed of the bodies.[12]

A more central issue for war planners is the separation of planning from execution. Adolph Eichmann was a thoroughly responsible person, according to his understanding of responsibility. For him it was clear that the heads of state set policy. His role was to implement, and fortunately, he felt, it was never part of his job actually to have to kill anyone.[13]

There are gradations of distance from execution which constitute varying levels of protection from responsibility and render the moral problem exceedingly fuzzy. During the debates in the late 1960s at MIT with respect to its role in weapons development, the head of the main military research laboratory argued that their concern was development, not use, of technology. The university administration eventually undertook to sever operational weapons systems research from the Institute, but it still permitted on-campus work, which was funded mainly because of its potential military application.[14]

Even while diffusing responsibility by separating planning from execution and one element of execution from another, the division of labor produces complicity through the functional interdependence of the specializations. In Treblinka "the Jews themselves had to become responsible for output as well as for discipline." "Experience with the ghettos had taught [the Germans] that a man who had knowingly compromised himself did not revolt against his masters, no matter what idea had driven him to collaboration: too many mutual skeletons in the closet."[15]

The division of labor brings with it an organizational sociology of specialization, hierarchy, and differential rewards. Material rewards are allocated on the basis of active and skillful participation in the system. Defense contractors can bid for the most highly skilled engineers and scientists and pay them handsomely. Weapons research and war planning become the path to material success. In the underworld of the concentration camp, the "low numbers"—those who had survived for relatively long periods—were all specialists. Only they ate enough to keep alive.[16]

The work-Jews at Treblinka ate well and were well-clothed because of the goods which came with the "transports"; there are accounts of storerooms knee-deep in valuables. The transports of persons to the gas chambers were also the camp's lifeline. A survivor of Treblinka described how deep the economic base of complicity came to be:

> Things went from bad to worse that month of March. There were no transports—in February just a few, remnants from here and there, then a few hundred gypsies—they were really poor; they brought nothing. In the storehouses everything had been packed up and shipped. . . . And suddenly everything—clothes, watches, spectacles, shoes, walking-sticks, cooking-pots, linen, not to speak of food—everything went. . . . You can't imagine what we felt when there was nothing there. You see, the things were our justification for being alive. If there were no things to administer, why would they let us stay alive? On top of that we were, for the first time, hungry. We were eating the camp food now, and it was terrible and, of course, totally inadequate. . . . In the six weeks of almost no transports, all of us had lost an incredible amount of weight and energy. . . .

> It was just about when we had reached the lowest ebb in our morale that . . . Kurt Franz walked into our barracks, a wide grin in his face. "As of tomorrow," he said, "transports will be rolling in again." And do you know what we did? We shouted, "Hurrah, hurrah." It seems impossible now. Every time I think of it I die a small death; but it's the truth. That is what we did; that is where we had got to. And sure enough, the next morning they arrived.[17]

Along with material success comes prestige. Salaries and positions translate into dinner parties with important people, heads that turn when one enters the conference room. A former research analyst at the Department of Defense recalls:

> When I was "chosen" for a special clearance, my immediate feeling was one of achievement and pleasure. I also remember the earlier feeling when I was not cleared for special intelligence and how important it seemed to me to be one of the three or four who were cleared among the twenty or so analysts in the Political and Economics Section.[18]

Primo Levi brags at Auschwitz: "In the whole camp there are only a few Greeks who have a [food pot] larger than ours. Besides the material advantages, it carries with it a perceptible improvement in our social standing."[19]

Specialization brings with it the possibility of developing the peculiarly human satisfactions in problem-solving, expertise, and the exercise of skill. High technology is the creative frontier. The development of the atomic bomb is one of the great dramas of creativity of our time, and the subsequent elaboration of the technology has provided, and continues to provide, opportunities for the intellectual excitement of stretching the mind to its limits.

In 1947, James Killian, then vice president of MIT and later its president, said of the Institute during wartime:

> The concentration of war research on its campus, the presence here of a great assemblage of gifted scientists from hundreds of institutions and the remarkably varied activities of its own staff contributed . . . to the establishment of a fresh and vigorous post-war program. . . . No one at MIT during this period can fail to be impressed by the ferment of ideas.[20]

The concentration camp may seem like an unpropitious environment for skill and discovery, but even there it had its role in the experiments on human subjects. At Treblinka, when they solved the problem of how to burn the bodies, they broke out champagne; it was a technological breakthrough. And in the underworld of the prisoners, Primo Levi boasts again from Auschwitz: "And I would not like to be accused of immodesty if I add that it was our idea, mine and Alberto's, to steal the rolls of graph-paper from the thermographs of the Desiccation Department."[21]

Paul Loeb, studying the community developed around plutonium production at Hanford, Washington, shows how organizational process within the enterprise, and family, and community life around it, give the production of bombs the most peaceful of settings. As one informant explained:

> We were proud to work for a major company like General Electric. We felt we were part of a well-run industrial enterprise with good management practices, good cost control and a good competitive feeling because the AEC [Atomic Energy Commission] would be comparing our cost and productivity figures with those of Savannah River. Some of us even went on recruiting trips, visiting different colleges along with other people from GE divisions around the country—and we explained plutonium as simply our product, just as light bulbs or turbines were someone else's.[22]

In his work on Treblinka, Steiner makes a general point which seems strongly relevant to the movement toward nuclear war: It is not simply the attachment to going concerns which makes it difficult to stop; it is the very seriousness of the situation. An outcome of sufficient dreadfulness becomes, in effect, inconceivable. "One fact played into the hands of the 'technicians': the monstrosity of the truth. The extermination of a whole people was so unimaginable that the human mind could not accept it."[23] Similarly, nuclear war has been designated "the unthinkable."[24]

This is why the character of civil defense planning is critically important. It is not nuclear war which is unthinkable; it is its consequences. And generally we do not deal with consequences. Policy focuses on purposes; research and development and military planning deal with means. Civil defense has to deal with consequences.

The problems of having, in some way, to confront consequences are increased by the fact that civil defense planning must to some extent be brought before the public. The information most accessible to the public is found in the evacuation plans prepared for each city and town. According to these plans, millions of people will gather their children; arrange to leave their pets with food and water; assemble shovels, clothing, credit cards, and sanitary napkins. Then, affixing the proper Civil Defense stickers to their automobiles, they will move smoothly over bridges, through tunnels and down highways—normally clogged to a standstill by any holiday weekend—to predesignated areas in smaller communities.

Nothing in this picture has any of the characteristics of an emergency situation. Indeed, to remove from the picture any semblance of a real nuclear war situation, all other real-world characteristics have also been removed. There are no traffic jams, no people searching for others, no one demanding to be taken along, or insisting on taking their pets or guns.

Most dreamlike is the absence of any dimension of time. Anyone who has ever tried to pack a picnic, assemble a family, and drive to the country on a Fourth of July weekend is likely to see such a description as lacking verisimilitude. The plans, for this reason, have not been well received. A reading of the Cambridge plan in the City Council chambers stimulated the Council to distribute a pamphlet declaring the concept worthless and urging political activity directed at stopping the arms race. And what happens after the bombs have fallen, when the survivors emerge from the shelters with their credit cards in hand? The plans offer neither description nor instruction.

It is as though these planners had fallen into the same solution as the description of the Jewish Holocaust provided by those who designed the Toronto World's Fair Israeli pavilion. Fairgoers learned about Jewish history by passing down a long corridor lined with photographs and objects. At the point in the story where the Holocaust takes place, the fairgoer turned a sharp corner and found himself facing a blank wall—a blank wall, one pair of battered baby shoes and a photograph of a small boy staring up in terror.

There are those who argue that preparation for nuclear war is necessary for reasons of national security. I believe, and have tried to show, that the continuation of weapons production and military planning can be explained without recourse to any argument involving national interest. And about the argument as it relates to national purpose, I would say that:

- there now exist descriptions of the consequences of nuclear war sufficiently apocalyptic to show that there is no conceivable national purpose for which the triggering of nuclear war would be sufficient justification;
- the continuing institutionalized preparation for nuclear war brings us continually closer to the precipice of its occurrence;
- we ought to move immediately to eliminate preparation for nuclear war from its current place as an instrument of national policy. Even the brutalized and complicitous prisoners of Treblinka eventually rose up against normalization of the unthinkable.

Some of us, confronted with our present situation, are ready to consign the very notion of national purpose to the dustbin of history, along with Hitler's Third Reich.

Notes

[1]Environmental Protection Agency, "Evacuation Risks—An Evaluation" (EPA 520/6-74 -002), p. 45.

[2]*Ibid.*

[3]John Dewitt Norton, *Economic Models: Methods, Uses, Prospects* (Washington, D.C.: National Planning Association, Economic Programming Center, 1969), p. viii.

[4]*Ibid,* p. 111.

[5]M. Hachiga, *Hiroshima Diary* (Chapel Hill: University of North Carolina Press, 1983), pp. 54–55.

[6]Jean François Steiner, *Treblinka* (New York: Simon and Schuster, 1967).

[7]Primo Levi, *Survival in Auschwitz* (New York: Collier Books, 1961).

[8]Filip Muller, *Eyewitness Auschwitz: Three Years in the Gas Chambers* (New York: Stein and Day, 1979), p. 40.

[9]*Ibid.*, p. 43.

[10]*Ibid.*, p. 165.

[11]"The Bishop at Ground Zero," *Life,* 5, No. 7 (July 1982), pp. 62–66.

[12]Steiner, *Treblinka.*

[13]Hannah Arendt, *Eichmann in Jerusalem: A Report on the Banality of Evil* (New York: Viking Press, 1964).

[14]Dorothy Nelkin, *The University and Military Research: Moral Politics at MIT* (Ithaca, New York: Cornell University Press, 1972).

[15]Steiner, *Treblinka,* pp. 68, 69.

[16]Levi, *Survival,* p. 102.

[17]Gitta Sereny, *Into That Darkness: An Examination of Conscience* (New York: Random House, 1982), pp. 212–13.

[18]Henry T. Nash, "The Bureaucratization of Homicide," *Bulletin*, 36 (April 1980), pp. 22–27.

[19]Paul Loeb, *Nuclear Culture: Living and Working in the World's Largest Complex* (New York: Coward, McCann and Geoghegan, Inc., 1982).

[20]Quoted in Dorothy Nelkin, *The University*, p. 17.

[21]Levi, *Survival*, p. 98.

[22]Steiner, *Treblinka*, p. 136.

[23]*Ibid.*

[24]Herman Kahn, *Thinking about the Unthinkable* (New York: Horizon Press, 1962).

ROBERT W. DEGRASSE, JR.

The Military: Shortchanging the Economy

Robert W. DeGrasse, Jr. (b. 1954), a Fellow at the Council on Economic Priorities, is the author of Military Expansion, Economic Decline: The Impact of Military Spending on U.S. Economic Performance *(Armonk, N.Y.: M. E. Sharpe, 1983). He is currently enrolled in the mid-career program at the Kennedy School of Government at Harvard University. DeGrasse also coauthored* South Africa, Foreign Investment and Apartheid *(Washington, D.C.: Institute for Policy Studies, 1978).*

Politicians have cited the economic benefits of military spending ever since World War II jolted the nation out of the Great Depression. Defense programs, it is argued, create jobs, boost the economy, and result in technological spin-offs. The Reagan Administration also has stressed the claim that military spending creates jobs.

Recently the Council on Economic Priorities has closely examined these claims and has found that a large, rapid arms increase could induce serious economic distortions and long-range damage. Comparing 17 advanced industrial nations, we found that those devoting large portions of gross domestic product to arms typically had weakening economies, decreasing technological progress, and spreading industrial lethargy associated with low investment rates. We also found that military spending is not the best way to solve our unemployment problem.

Robert DeGrasse, Jr., "The Military: Shortchanging the Economy," *Bulletin of the Atomic Scientists* (May 1984): 37–40. Reprinted by permission of the *Bulletin of the Atomic Scientists*, a magazine of science and world affairs.

FIGURE 1 Jobs Created Per Billion Dollars of Final Demand, Direct and Indirect (constant 1981 dollars)

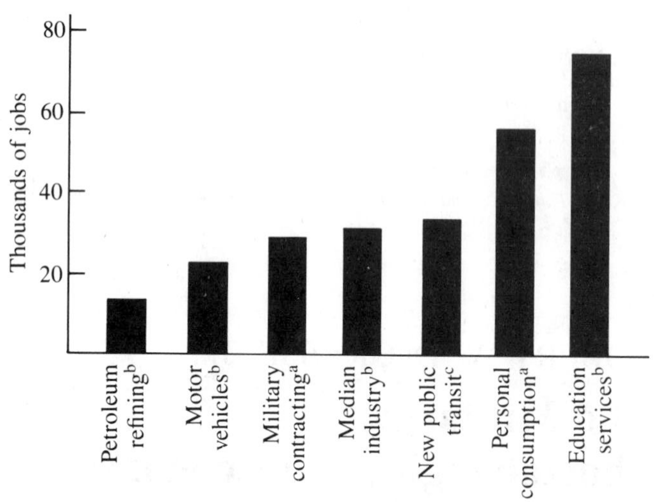

Source:
[a]Marion Anderson, Jeb Brugmann and George Erickcek, "The Price of the Pentagon: The Industrial and Commercial Impact of the 1981 Military Budget" (Lansing, Michigan: Employment Research Associates, 1982).
[b]U.S. Department of Labor. Bureau of Labor Statistics, "Employment Matrix for 1972 in 1972 dollars," unpublished. Inflated to 1981 dollars using appropriate implicit price deflator from *Economic Report of the President* (Washington, D.C.: U.S. Government Printing Office, Feb. 1983), pp. 166–167.
[c]U.S. Department of Labor, Bureau of Labor Statistics, phone conversation with Karen Horowitz.

Pentagon officials correctly point out that cuts in military spending mean job cuts in the short run. The Council study, however, shows that compared to other uses of the same money, military spending is one of the least effective ways to quickly stimulate job creation, especially sorely needed blue-collar jobs. Extrapolations from U.S. Labor Department data show that:

- About 28,000 jobs are created for every billion dollars spent on military procurement (Figure 1).
- The same billion dollars would create 32,000 jobs if spent for public transit, 57,000 jobs if spent for personal consumption, or 71,000 jobs if spent for education.

While in the long run the employment induced by military production workers spending their higher salaries will even out these differences, the immediate impact of arms spending does not help those who most need assistance.

Who gets the jobs? Weapons builders employ mainly the highly skilled, a group whose 3.7 percent unemployment rate at the height of the recent recession was the lowest of any occupational category. At the same time, blue-collar workers, who receive less employment from arms producers than other manufacturers, had a 20 percent unemployment rate. Eleven of the 15 principal military-oriented manufacturing industries employ a significantly lower portion of production workers than the average U.S. manufacturing industry. Four of the five top military industries employ significantly more professional and technical workers than the national average (Table 1).

The U.S. standard of living has been declining relative to other industrial nations since the Vietnam War years, as manufacturing industries have become less competitive internationally.

Comparative data over two decades (1960–1980) from 17 noncommunist, advanced industrial nations indicate that nations which have devoted a larger share of output to civilian investment have experienced faster overall economic growth and, prior to the energy crisis, higher productivity growth as well. Greater civilian investment also coincided with higher employment. Conversely, the larger the military's demand for resources, both financial and human, the poorer a nation's economic performance. Indeed, of the 17 countries studied the United States had the lowest level of civilian investment and productivity growth, while bearing the heaviest military burden (Figure 2).

Military spending, however, is not the only reason for poorer performance. The 1973 oil crisis forced many manufacturers to invest heavily in new, energy-efficient plant and machinery. Countries such as the United States with old, inefficient operations had relatively greater replacement costs. Economic growth was also related to industrial maturity. The less developed industrial nations enjoyed higher rates of investment and faster gains in economic and productivity growth (see Box A).

A. Civilian Government and Labor Costs Compared

The Council on Economic Priorities' analysis indicates that:

- Government spending in the civil sector does not explain why the United States performed poorly. Among 17 nations studied the United States ranked thirteenth in the share of gross domestic product spent on civilian government consumption. It ranked thirteenth among 14 nations in the share of gross domestic product transferred from one income group to another through the government.
- Labor costs did not seem to play a significant role in comparative economic performance. Nations with higher labor costs tended to offset this disadvantage with higher rates of output per employee. Manufacturing labor costs also have converged over the past 20 years. By 1980 the United States ranked fifth among 10 nations in compensation for manufacturing production workers.
- Labor force growth does not explain the decrease in manufacturing productivity during the 1970s either. The U.S. manufacturing labor force actually grew more slowly after 1973 than during the 1960s.

TABLE 1 Percentage of Work Force in Each Occupational Category, 1980

Occupation	Aircraft and Parts	Communications Equipment	Guided Missiles	Ordnance	Shipbuilding and Repair	All Manufacturing
Professional and Technical	25.4	32.3	55.7	15.2	7.0	9.1
Engineers	11.5	15.0	31.1	5.1	4.8	2.9
Managers	7.4	7.3	7.2	5.3	3.1	5.9
Sales	0.8	0.7	0.2	0.4	0.4	2.2
Clerical	13.9	15.7	12.3	10.9	7.3	11.3
Craft	21.3	12.4	10.8	22.5	40.9	18.5
Operatives	27.3	27.3	11.2	33.5	31.6	43.4
Service	2.0	1.5	2.1	5.0	1.5	2.0
Laborers	2.0	2.9	.6	7.3	8.3	7.7

Source: U.S. Department of Labor, Bureau of Labor Statistics, ''Employment by Industry and Occupation, 1980 and Projected 1990 Alternatives,'' unpublished data.

FIGURE 2 **Investment vs. Military Spending, Selected Nations, 1960–1980**

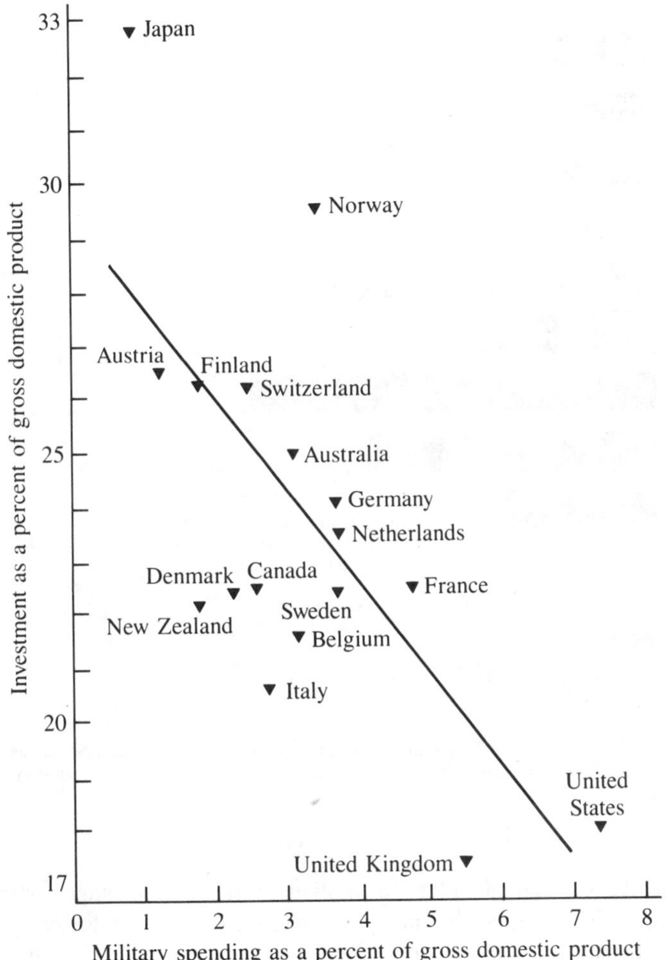

Supporters of higher Pentagon budgets argue that military spending directly benefits commercial technology. And it is true that the Pentagon has influenced the course and content of U.S. technological development. Its research, development, and procurement projects employed roughly 30 percent of the nation's engineers and scientists during the 1960s, about 20 percent during the 1970s. The percentages are significantly higher for fields directly related to aerospace and electronics. For example, at least 60 percent of aeronautical engineers and more than 35 percent of electronics engineers worked primarily on national defense in 1978, when the share of gross national product devoted to the military was at its lowest point since 1950 (Figure 3).

FIGURE 3 Scientists and Engineers Working Primarily on National Defense and Space Projects, 1978

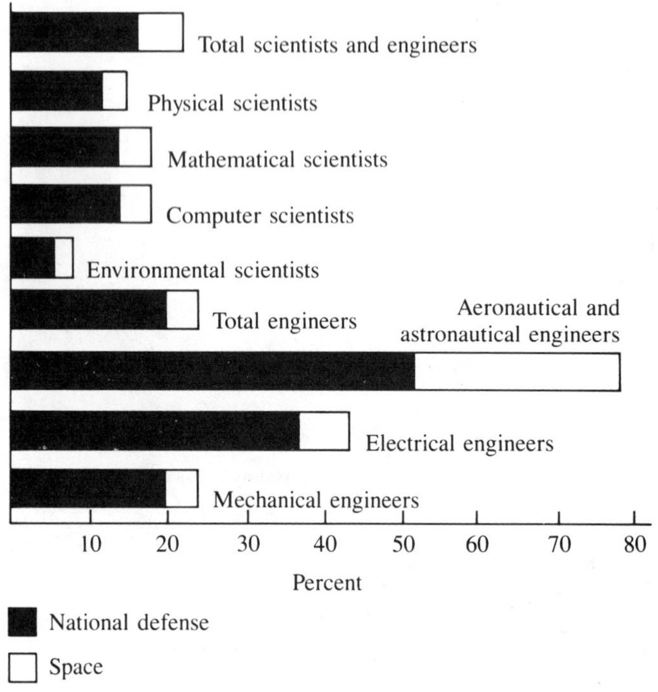

Source: U.S. National Science Foundation, "Characteristics of Experienced Scientists and Engineers, 1978, Detailed Statistical Tables," (Washington, D.C.: U.S. Government Printing Office, 1978), Table B-13.

Despite the substantial influence implied by those percentages, strong evidence suggests that military spending has stunted U.S. technological growth in commercial markets. The Council examined the electronics, aircraft, and machine tool industries, assuming that if commercial industries benefit from military research, then firms serving the Pentagon should have maintained or expanded their overall market shares. In each case the contrary proved true. Japanese industries have significantly penetrated markets for electronic memory chips and for computer-controlled machine tools. European firms have expanded their share of the machine tool market. And Airbus Industrie, a European consortium, is challenging U.S. dominance in the commercial airline market. The Council's case study of the electronics industry shows that Pentagon contracts, once a commercial stimulus, now inhibit commercial success (see Box B).

To many who recall the World War II and Korean War eras, Reagan Administration plans for military expansion along with economic growth may not seem mutually exclusive. Yet historical comparisons suggest that the proposed

B. Pentagon's Effect on Semiconductor Development

While military programs contributed significantly to the early development of the electronics industry, the costs now seem to outweigh the benefits:

• The end products developed for military use, such as missile guidance systems and electronic warfare devices, have few commercial applications.

• Military research and development have a mixed record in supporting projects that have led to significant innovations. It is hard for military personnel to judge the most promising projects. And the Pentagon tends to support larger, established firms rather than the newer, smaller firms that have proved more innovative.

• Military subsidies for new products are increasingly unnecessary. As the cost of electronic circuits has rapidly fallen, massive industrial and commercial markets have overshadowed the military's role as "creative first user."

• The Pentagon's current attempts to guide the development of semiconductor and machine tool technology raise serious economic and political issues. Military subsidies for semiconductor technology may hinder its development rather than nurture new products. Defense Department programs designed to increase factory automation are financing a narrow approach without input from the workers who will be affected.

$1.6 trillion arms buildup will have serious adverse effects on the U.S. economy.

The planned military expansion is the largest in U.S. peacetime history, only somewhat smaller than that engendered by the Vietnam War. Between fiscal years 1982 and 1985 military expenditures are slated to grow 32.4 percent in constant dollars. During a comparable three-year period of the Vietnam War (fiscal years 1965 to 1968), the military budget rose 42.7 percent.

While the buildup planned by the Reagan Administration is less dramatic than that of the Vietnam era, there is little reason to believe that its economic impact will be lighter or comparatively beneficial. The Vietnam conflict required fewer new resources than did the Korean War, yet the economic problems it caused were greater, triggering the series of price and wage increases that still plagues the economy. Unlike the Korean, the Vietnam War was financed by deficit spending. Those deficits occurred when the economy was functioning at peak capacity. And there were no wartime economic controls to dampen inflation.

Measured as a share of gross national product, the projected Reagan Administration deficits will exceed those of the Vietnam War peak in each of the next three years (Figure 4). The fiscal stimulus of deficit spending did not hurt the economy during the just past recession, but during the current recovery massive deficits could fuel inflation or provoke extreme competition in the credit markets, depending on the nation's monetary policy.

Since the government does not plan peacetime wage and price controls, the Federal Reserve Board can be expected to control inflationary pressure by slow-

FIGURE 4 Unified Budget Deficits as a Share of Gross National Product

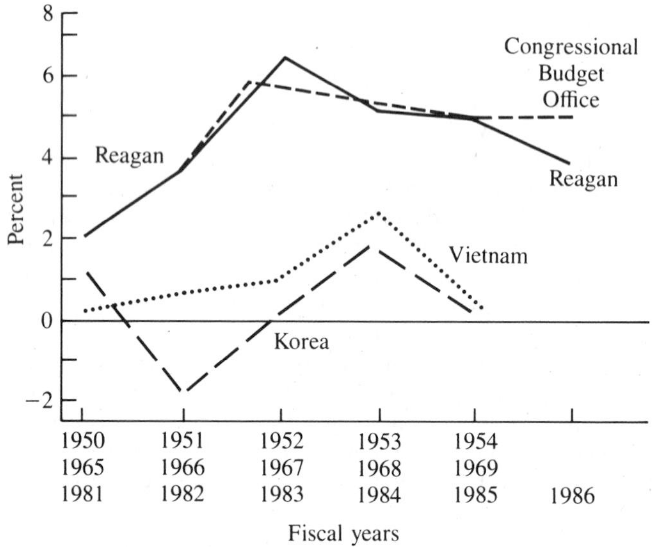

ing growth of the money supply. With money tight, the vast government borrowing now foreseen would push interest rates ever higher, choking off recovery.

Military spending would be largely responsible for such dangerous deficits. After subtracting such self-funding programs as social security from the federal budget and adding all military-related costs to the national defense function, we find that nearly 49 percent of the federal government's general funds were spent on the military in fiscal 1981 (Table 2). In fiscal 1986 the Pentagon is expected to use more than 56 percent of the government's general funds.

Inflation escalators and delays in delivering military products also could add to inflation in some industrial sectors. That likelihood is considerable since between fiscal 1982 and 1985 over 55 percent of the growth in military outlays will be for procurement and research and development, both infamous for costly backlogs. By comparison, procurement and research and development accounted for but 40 percent of the growth during the Vietnam War, and 43 percent during the Korean War. During past buildups, a larger share of the defense budget increase paid for soldiers and spare parts than in the current situation.

Commerce Department analysts have predicted that the current buildup might require such a large portion of the output of advanced industries as to slow export of high-technology goods. Further, the value of unfilled orders for military products has risen until it is now greater (in constant dollars) than at the height

TABLE 2 Total Military Spending Budget, Fiscal Years 1981 and 1986 (Millions of Dollars)

Agency or Program	1981 Outlays	Percent of Federal Funds	1986 Outlays	Percent of Federal Funds
National defense function	$159,765	33.6	$310,550	42.1
Military-related programs				
Veterans' benefits	22,988	4.8	27,808	3.8
Foreign military assistance	793	0.2	950**	0.1
National Aeronautics and Space Admin.	1,084	0.2	1,560**	0.2
Coast Guard	341	0.1	500**	*
Merchant Marine	13	*	10	*
Aid to federally impacted areas	172	*	200	*
Interest payments on military-related debt	45,565	9.6	75,000	10.2
Subtotal of additions	70,956	14.9	106,028	14.4
Total military budget	$230,721	48.6	$416,578	56.5
Total federal funds	$475,171	100.0	$737,865	100.0

*Less than 0.1 percent
**Estimates

of the Vietnam War. And unfortunately, as Pentagon demands mount, the ability to deliver goods on time may decrease because of an inadequate supply of skilled labor, such as engineers and machinists. Thus, an economic simulation by Data Resources, Inc., suggests that the present buildup could result in bottlenecks throughout the economy by 1985. Production bottlenecks and skilled labor shortages time and again have inflated the costs of products purchased by the Pentagon. Indeed, during the past five years, inflation in the cost of military equipment as been substantially higher than in the economy as a whole.

The United States can afford whatever is needed to provide for its security. However, a diversion of government resources to the military on the scale planned by the Reagan Administration will seriously weaken the nation's ability to meet the challenges of unemployment, foreign market losses, diminishing technological leadership, and industrial obsolescence. The question we must ask is: Does the military power created by the buildup justify the economic price we will pay for it?

JEROME D. FRANK

Psychological Causes of the Nuclear Arms Race

Jerome D. Frank (b. 1909), a psychologist who has written extensively on the psychology of the arms race and international relations, is best known in this field for his edition of a collection of essays entitled Sanity and Survival: Psychological Aspects of War and Peace *(New York: Random House, 1967). Frank combines his work as a professional psychologist with writing and speaking about nuclear issues.*

Leaders of the nuclear powers are behaving in a self-contradictory fashion. All agree that an all-out nuclear exchange would be an incalculable, perhaps irretrievable, catastrophe for all nations involved; yet they pursue policies that steadily increase the probability that it will occur.

We psychiatrists can contribute to the prevention of nuclear war by calling attention to certain mental processes that prevent national decision makers from breaking out of the nuclear arms race. Let me emphasize immediately that although psychiatrists learn by studying mental patients, these mental processes are in no sense abnormal. They are universal and under most conditions are necessary for survival. Only under rare and unprecedented circumstances such as those created by nuclear weapons do they become dangerous.

I will only mention four of the many mental processes that contribute to this paradoxical behavior.

- First is inability to change habits of thinking and behavior rapidly and drastically enough to adapt to sudden, profound changes in the international scene created by the emergence of nuclear weapons. This is made easier by the psychological unreality of these weapons.
- Second is the propensity to resort to violence when frustrated or frightened.
- Third is the inevitable mutual formation of the image of the enemy by groups in conflict.
- Fourth is the primitivizing effect of emotions on thought, which contributes to the instability of deterrence.

A major psychological obstacle to coping with nuclear weapons is that they are psychologically unreal. In contrast to previous weapons, which most hu-

---

Jerome D. Frank, "Psychological Causes of the Nuclear Arms Race," *Chemtech* 12 (August 1982): 466–469. Reprinted with permission from *Chemtech*. Copyright 1982 American Chemical Society. Reprinted also with permission of the author.

mans have seen in action either personally or on film, the magnitude of the destructive power of nuclear weapons corresponds to nothing in previous human experience, except perhaps major volcanic eruptions, and these have been experienced by only a small fraction of humanity. Except for the remaining survivors of Hiroshima, Nagasaki, and the few who have seen films of their devastation, as well as the even fewer who have actually witnessed atmospheric nuclear tests, the destructive power of these weapons exists only in imagination. To my knowledge, none of today's national leaders have ever actually seen a nuclear explosion. Since nuclear weapons in distant countries poised for annihilation cannot be seen, heard, smelled, tasted, or touched, we must constantly use our imaginations to keep in mind how threatening they are. Perhaps some of those Americans who speak so calmly about limited, contained nuclear war do so because no living American has experienced the devastation wrought by any weapon of war on American soil.

All of today's national leaders started their climb to power in a world of conventional weapons; they are masters of the prenuclear international game, in which war is the final resort and the nation possessing more and better arms wins. Therefore, the appropriate national behavior is to try to outarm one's rivals in the hope of deterring them from resorting to force and defeating them if deterrence fails.

When humans face an entirely new and unprecedented problem, they try to make it appear like a familiar one, and handle it with methods that have worked in the past. So national leaders still try to accumulate more and better nuclear weapons than their adversaries, even though they know intellectually that, as Harold Brown, former Secretary of Defense under Carter, wrote: "Comprehensive military supremacy for either side is a military and economic impossibility."

Here we see that mere intellectual insight is virtually powerless to change maladaptive behavior, especially when, as with war, it has been ingrained over millennia, linked to a biological drive (in this case self-preservation), and supported by strong emotions. Our intellect may tell us what we should do, but our emotions too often prevent us from doing it.

Unfortunately, our thinking and behavior are guided more by events as we perceive them than as they are in actuality. Prenuclear weapons from spears and clubs to bombs and shells have conferred strength on their possessors both in appearance and in actual fact. The image of strength projected by nonnuclear weapons was based on real strength. The more a nation possessed, the stronger and more secure it really was. Therefore, it was realistic for national leaders to accumulate them to reassure themselves, intimidate their actual or potential enemies, and hold the loyalty of their allies. Nuclear weapons have abruptly and permanently broken the connection between weaponry and strength in one respect, but not in another. Perceived and actual reality still coincide in that the strategic nuclear weapons of one adversary gravely menace the other. They differ sharply, however, in that beyond a level long since passed by the U.S. and the USSR, accumulating more powerful and sophisticated strategic weapons decreases the security of all nations, including the possessor. The more persons who have hands on these weapons within and among nations, the greater the likelihood that one will be fired by malice or by accident, thereby triggering the computers poised to launch a strategic nuclear exchange. With these weapons, one cannot afford a single mistake.

It's Us or Them

As long as the world's leaders perceive nuclear weapons as simply bigger conventional ones, however, the country that has a smaller or less technically advanced stockpile will see itself as weaker and will be seen as weaker by its opponents and allies. So it will act as if it actually were weaker—that is, it will be more easily intimidated, will act less decisively in crises, and will be in danger of losing its allies and tempting its opponents to seize the initiative. As Adm. Stansfield Turner put it: "But whatever we do, it must not only correct the actual imbalance of [nuclear] capability; it must also correct the perception of imbalance. . . . Changing the world's perception that we are falling behind the Soviet Union is as important as not falling behind in fact." Reference to "actual imbalance" and "falling behind in fact," of course, means that he still views nuclear weapons as simply bigger conventional ones.

In short, the pursuit of security through illusory nuclear superiority is in reality more a race for prestige than actual strength. The nuclear arms race is an especially costly and dangerous form of psychological warfare.

Behind the arms races and wars lies a trait humans share with all social animals: fear and distrust of members of groups other than their own. When two human groups compete for the same goal, this distrust rapidly escalates into the mutual "image of the enemy."

The power of group relationships to determine how members of groups perceive each other has been neatly shown by the vicissitudes of this image, which always arises when two nations are in conflict and which is always the same no matter who the conflicting parties are. Enemy-images mirror each other—that is, each side attributes the same virtues to itself and the same vices to the enemy. "We" are trustworthy, peace-loving, honorable, and humanitarian; "they" are treacherous, warlike, and cruel. In surveys of Americans conducted in 1942, the first five adjectives chosen to characterize both Germans and Japanese (enemies) included warlike, treacherous, and cruel, none of which appeared among the first five describing the Russians (allies); in 1966 all three had disappeared from American characterizations of the Germans ad Japanese (allies), but now the Russians (no longer allies, although more rivals than enemies) were warlike and treacherous. In 1966 the mainland Chinese, predictably, were seen as warlike, treacherous, and sly. After President Nixon's visit to China, these adjectives disappeared from our characterization of the Chinese, whom we now see as hard-working, intelligent, artistic, progressive, and practical.

The image of the enemy creates a self-fulfilling prophecy by causing enemies to acquire the evil characteristics they attribute to each other. In combating what they perceive to be the other's cruelty and treachery, each side becomes more cruel and treacherous itself. The enemy-image nations form of each other thus more or less corresponds to reality. Although the behavior of the enemy may be motivated by fear more than aggressiveness, nations failing to recognize their enemies as treacherous and warlike would not long survive.

Unfortunately, this mutual perception, however justified, aggravates mutual hostilities and impedes resolution of conflict in several ways. It leads to progressive restriction of communication (after all, why bother to communicate with a chronic liar?), thus increasing the likelihood of serious misunderstandings of the enemy's intentions. Moreover, the enemy-image acts like a distorting lens, which overemphasizes information that confirms it and filters out information that is incompatible with it. Thus the mass media play up incidents of an enemy's treachery or cruelty, and ignore examples of humanitarian or honorable behavior. The same behavior is seen positively if performed by our side and negatively if performed by an enemy. For example, although in wartime both sides always commit atrocities, the enemy's atrocities are evidences of his evil nature, whereas ours are portrayed as regrettable necessities.

Finally, because anything the enemy wants must by definition be bad for us, the enemy-image blinds both sides to interests they might have in common. Thus when the Soviet Union stresses the horrors of nuclear war, many Americans perceive this as a ruse to cause us to stop our nuclear arms buildup. They cannot entertain the possibility that mutual reduction of nuclear stockpiles would benefit both countries.

Faced with an adversary perceived as treacherous and implacably malevolent in a world without effective international peacekeeping institutions, the only recourse is to confront the adversary with superior force in the hope that this will deter hostile acts through threat of retaliation, or enable us to defeat him should deterrence fail. Since resorting to nuclear weapons would be suicidal, nuclear powers are forced to rely on the hope of maintaining deterrence indefinitely. There are strong psychological grounds for believing that such a hope will continue to be vain in the future, as it always has been in the past.

Deterrence is the attempt of one party to control another by threat of punishment should the latter attempt to perform a forbidden act. This creates an inherently unstable system. It breaks down when one of the parties calculates, correctly or incorrectly, that the potential benefits of the forbidden action outweigh the probable costs, or when emotional tensions reach such a pitch that leaders throw caution to the winds. This is the point when, as Bertrand Russell put it, the desire to destroy the enemy becomes greater than the desire to stay alive oneself. In the grip of strong emotions, a person's thinking becomes more primitive—that is, he or she perceives fewer alternatives, simplifies issues, and focuses exclusively on combating the immediate threat without sufficiently considering remote or long-term consequences. Strong emotion impels to impulsive action. There is nothing harder, when under emotional stress, than to do nothing.

We can, perhaps, derive some comfort from the recognition that most national leaders would not have survived the struggle to reach the top unless they were able to preserve good judgment under stress. Yet the graveyard of history is littered with the remains of societies whose leaders' judgments failed under emotional pressure. As Robert Kennedy indicated in his book on the Cuban missile crisis, even some of the "best and brightest" can reach a breaking point: ". . . some [of the decision makers], because of the pressure of events, even appeared to lose their judgment and stability."

It's Us and Them

So much for some of the psychological forces propelling the world's leaders toward nuclear disaster. To turn now to new hopes for survival, we must start by recognizing that from now on any war can escalate into a nuclear one. And since humans will never forget how to make nuclear weapons, the only ultimate solution requires the elimination of war itself.

Before considering some hopeful psychological steps toward this distant and difficult goal, we must pause to consider the biological argument that the elimination of war is impossible. This asserts that war is an inevitable manifestation of the biological human impulse to respond to threat or frustration with violence. It is true that programs of violent behavior are built into the human central nervous system, but they are released inappropriately only when the brain is diseased. Since human individuals and groups are self-aggrandizing, however, they will always push until they come up against frustrating obstacles, of which the most common are other individuals or groups pursuing conflicting goals. Group conflicts are inevitable. This does not mean, however, that wars are inevitable, for there is no direct link between biological drives and learned, complex social behaviors such as war.

The expression of biological needs is channeled and shaped by cultural values and institutions. To claim that because humans are innately violent, war is inevitable would be like saying that because they are violent, human sacrifice in religious rites is inevitable; or that because humans are innately carnivorous, cannibalism is inevitable. Social institutions wither away when they cease to perform useful social functions. Nuclear weapons are destroying the usefulness of war for resolving international conflicts. Since Hiroshima, no war except one that could involve the nuclear superpowers has been fought to victory. That war was Vietnam, and the superpower lost. In this, I believe, lies the hope that, like slavery, human religious sacrifices, cannibalism, and dueling, war will eventually wither away.

Societies have found internal ways of keeping domestic violence within tolerable bounds. They have accomplished this by developing rules for peacefully resolving conflicts, enforced by appropriate institutions. Analogously, international anarchy must eventually be replaced by an effective world government. The authority of all peacekeeping institutions within nations depends on a consensus of those who support them. Jurists have pointed out that even in dictatorships no law can be enforced unless more than 90% of the citizens comply voluntarily.

Similarly, from a psychological standpoint, developing international peacekeeping institutions requires the creation of a sense of community of all the world's peoples transcending their national allegiances. This would make it possible for each nation to relinquish some of its national sovereignty to international peacekeeping organizations. The achievement of this distant goal lies primarily in the realm of political science, jurisprudence, economics, and similar disciplines. One aspect to which students of human behavior could contribute, however, lies in the very first step, the reduction of mutual fear and mistrust among nations.

The same technological advances that have created the new dangers to survival have produced new means for progress toward this goal. These include means of constant electronic communication between national decision makers without the distorting effects of intermediaries. I speak of the hotline, and direct surveillance by satellites. Both of these methods increase the accuracy and completeness of information concerning the opponents' intentions and capabilities. In itself, this reduces fears generated by mutual uncertainty by imposing restraints on preparations for hostilities by both sides.

Television and radio are by far the most powerful communication tools ever devised for combating mutual fears and promoting mutual understanding. Transistor radios are widely distributed throughout the world; even small villages often have television receivers set up in the village square. Thus for the first time the same message can be sent to everyone in the world by satellites simultaneously—a message that jumps the literacy barrier and is more powerful than the written word. Although often used to inflame antagonisms, the untapped constructive potentials of electronic audiovisual communication are boundless.

The greatest hope for fostering a sense of world community, however, probably lies in the new incentives and opportunities for nations to work together toward the achievement of superordinate goals—goals that all nations want, but that can be achieved only by international cooperation.

These are not idle dreams. Smallpox has been eradicated, and nations have undertaken highly successful joint ventures, such as the International Geophysical Year and the Barcelona conference on cleaning up the Mediterranean. In this conference, Turks and Greeks, Arabs and Israelis worked together. Such examples raise hopes for the tension-reducing potentials of other cooperative international activities.

These considerations are for the long range. The problem is how to get from here to there. A concrete beginning that lies within the realm of the possible would be to institute a freeze on production of nuclear weapons coupled with a comprehensive test ban, followed by unilateral tension-reducing initiatives. A major impetus to the nuclear arms race today is the breakneck pace of weapons development. Leaders of both nuclear nations fear that the other might just possibly achieve a breakthrough that for a brief period would enable it to attack with relative impunity, which would be an almost irresistible temptation. Moreover, the speed of technological innovation makes agreements for arms control impossible by far outstripping the snail-like pace of the negotiating process. By the time agreements are reached, they are already obsolete. A comprehensive test ban, by slowing the creation of new weapons, would create more hope for negotiations. These are also stymied at present, however, by the high level of mutual mistrust. Unilateral scrapping of a few weapons, which in view of the superfluity of stockpiles on both sides could be done without danger, could initiate what Khrushchev called a "policy of mutual example" that might eventually bring tensions down to the point where negotiations would have some hope of success.

In conclusion, to turn again to a broad perspective, some of the behaviors of today's youth that we elders automatically deplore may prove to be gropings toward the new values and behavior required by the nuclear age. For example, many youngsters are participating in new experiments in social living ranging from transcendental cults like Hare Krishna to a variety of secular communes, all of which counterattack the more destructive features of contemporary society by espousing behavior patterns and values such as noncompetitiveness, reverence for all life, and nonmaterialism. It may not be too much to hope that from these crucibles of change will emerge ways of living compatible with survival in the nuclear world.

INTERNATIONAL PHYSICIANS FOR THE PREVENTION OF NUCLEAR WAR

What Soviet Children Are Saying about Nuclear War

International Physicians for the Prevention of Nuclear War (IPPNW) was founded by an international group of physicians; the current co-presidents are cardiologists Bernard Lown of Boston and Yevgeni

International Physicians for the Prevention of Nuclear War, "What Soviet Children Are Saying about Nuclear War." Reprinted by permission of International Physicians for the Prevention of Nuclear War, Inc.

Chazov of Moscow. Its purpose is to focus international attention on the medical consequences of nuclear war. The five-year-old organization won the 1985 Nobel Peace Prize.

Transcript of 21-Minute Videotape of Interviews with Soviet Children

A joint project of International Physicians for the Prevention of Nuclear War and Harvard Medical School, Department of Psychiatry, Research Program for the Study of Human Continuity.

Eric Chivian: This study was done to parallel similar studies done in the U.S. by many investigators over the past several years that have demonstrated that American children know a lot about nuclear weapons and are deeply affected by this knowledge. We wanted to learn whether Soviet children were similarly informed and affected.

The project was carried out at two Pioneer Camps. Pioneers are Soviet children between the ages of 10 and 15. They number between 20 and 24 million in the Soviet Union. They can be most likened to American Scouts. During the summer, they attend camps throughout the Soviet Union. Of the two camps that we visited, one was named after the Soviet cosmonaut, Gargarin. It was near Moscow, had 350 children, whose parents mostly worked at a domestic airport near Moscow. The other camp was called Orlyonok, which means "little eagle." It was a much larger camp, 2800 children, and it was located on the Black Sea in the Caucasus. Orlyonok was a different type of camp in that children came from all over the Soviet Union and were eligible to come to the camp after winning academic, athletic, artistic, or citizenship competitions.

The children were interviewed either singly or in groups. In all, approximately 60 children between the ages of 10 and 15 were interviewed. The tapes that you will see represent interviews with five of these groups totaling 25 children.

We wanted to learn at what age Soviet children found out about the effects of nuclear weapons. We wanted to learn how they found out this information. We wanted to investigate what Soviet children knew about the subject of nuclear weapons and nuclear war. We wanted to know whether they believed a nuclear war would occur in their lifetime. We wanted to know whether they thought it would be possible to survive a nuclear war and, in particular, we wanted to know whether they thought shelters would help them survive. We wanted to know how this subject made them feel. We wanted to know whether they thought there were things that children could do to prevent nuclear war. And we wanted to know, finally, whether they had any messages they wanted to send to American children.

Because we wished to ensure that the children's responses reflected their own thoughts and feelings, we brought our own translator to verify that the questions asked and responses obtained were accurately and completely translated. We did not discuss beforehand what we would ask in the interviews and we carefully designed the selection and interview processes to ensure that the children were neither prompted nor prepared. Finally, although the videotapes were recorded by Soviet TV crews, we brought back all the unedited videotapes to the United States for translation and technical preparation.

Eric Chivian: "At what age have you learned about these effects? About?"

Boris (Minsk, age 13): "I found out about it first when I was seven years old, when I saw the television show, 'Vremya.' It was on the sixth of August commemorating the bombing of Hiroshima and Nagasaki, and they showed the atomic bombardment of the city."

Irina (Estonia, age 13): "I was eight years old and in second grade when I saw the show 'International Panorama.' In one of the sections of the program, I learned about the existence of nuclear weapons. After that, I began to read newspapers, and I became convinced that, about the consequences of nuclear weapons, what a threat they present."

Sveta (Georgievskoye, age 11): "I was seven years old, in my eighth year and in school they told us, and I also saw a documentary film. My mother and father talk about it often."

Oskana (Moscow, age 11): "I was seven years old. In school, they talk about it and I also saw a film."

Oleg (Yakutsk, age 14): "When I was little, my parents told me about it. That nuclear war is a disastrous horror and if it begins, there won't be anything left on this earth."

Eric Chivian: "How have other people heard about nuclear weapons?"

Irina (Moscow, age 13): "I learned about nuclear war from the television shows 'Vremya' and 'International Panorama.' A lot is said on these shows about this, almost every day. And this television show is on almost every day."

Olga (Moscow, age 13): "I saw the television show, 'Today in the World,' and they showed a desert with a rocket-launching platform. And they said that from one of those rockets, the entire earth could turn into a lifeless desert."

Vovo (Moldavia, age 12): "I think about it almost every other, every day because I watch the television show, 'Vremya.' They constantly show, and they show how there shouldn't be any nuclear weapons."

Alla (Minsk, age 12): "I saw a book, even, about Hiroshima and Nagasaki and saw the destruction there. There were illustrations in the book and I particularly noticed a picture of a baby, a child, all his skin was, was burned and radiated and I felt very uncomfortable."

Katya (Moscow, age 12): "In the literary gazette, there were photographs of simulated explosions in laboratories. And they showed the nearest houses to, nothing was left of the houses, but dust. In Hiroshima, I remember seeing a film, on a, on a bridge that was located not far from the epicenter of the explosion and the only thing that was left of people were their shadows. And an explosion that would happen now, an explosion that would be so much more powerful than that one, it is hard to imagine what would, I can't imagine what would become of people, if one such explosion could destroy so many people and to this day people suffer so much from that.''

John Mack: ''If there were a nuclear war, what would happen?''

Oksana (Moscow, age 11): ''The atomic bombs were dropped a fairly long time ago, but children are still being born with the effects of radiation.''

Sergei (Moscow, age 13): ''Many casualties, many, many casualties. And they will principally be people who want peace, children, old people, men, men are stronger of course than children. And many, many people will perish.''

Andrei (Moscow, age 15): ''If the atomic bomb killed in Hiroshima and Nagasaki killed, I don't, I don't even know how many, these nuclear weapons will kill a hundred times more.''

Elena (Moscow, age 13): ''And if a war like that starts, it will be absolutely terrible. Nobody will be needed, not teachers, doctors. Everything, everything around will die.''

Alexei (Tambovskaya, age 13): ''The entire earth will become a wasteland. All buildings will be destroyed or buildings will remain, but all living things will perish—no grass, trees, no greenery.''

Eric Chivian: ''Do any of you ever think that there might be a nuclear war in your lifetimes?''

Irina (Estonia, age 13): ''Yes, but that is a horrible thought.''

Boris (Minsk, age 13): ''We hope that never happens. The consequences are terrible.''

Irina (Estonia, age 13): ''We don't like to believe things like that. The Soviet Union struggles for peace.''

Larisa (Serov, age 13): ''We can't let war happen, because it affects too many innocent people.''

Sveta (Riazan, age 13): ''War will never happen because the Soviet Union and America will, will, will come to terms.''

Larisa (Serov, age 13): ''And they will understand that there shouldn't be nuclear war. No countries in the world want war and they're struggling for peace and they always will.''

Valery (Moscow, age 14): ''Technology has reached a high level at the rocket installation stage. It seems to me that one person could do it all. Could push the button and that would be it. Rockets would be launched at us and we would launch rockets back.''

''It could start any time.''

Sasha (Byelorussia, age 14): ''I think everything will be smoothed out. Well, if people really wanted it, it will happen.''

Oleg (Yakutsk, age 14): "All peoples of the world are against war and that's why, it seems to me, war will never begin."

Oleg (Ukraine, age 15): "If all humanity gathers together, they can curtail the nuclear war. And that's why I don't think it will happen, not in our lifetime or after our lifetime."

Kira (Minsk, age 14): "Nuclear war is very possible. It could start from any simple accident. If an American computer or our computer made a mistake, there would be war, accidentally."

Eric Chivian: "Would it be possible to survive this nuclear war?"

Katya (Moscow, age 14): "What can I say. If American rockets can reach us in half an hour, there won't be even time to hide or defend oneself."

Oksana (Moscow, age 11): "some will live, but become diseased from the radiation and there is very little chance that they could be cured."

Eric Chivian: "But some people believe that you could hide underground or in a shelter and then it would be O.K."

Irina (Estonia, age 13): "No. The air would be destroyed. The atmosphere would be destroyed."

Larisa (Serov, age 13): "It would be impossible to live. And when you come out of the bomb shelter after that kind of catastrophe, in the city there wouldn't be anything left alive. And how can that be. You'd have to start life all over again."

Sergei (Moscow, age 13): "You couldn't survive a nuclear strike. The nuclear radioactivity remains for a very long time. And even if a person goes underground, no matter how much he wants to live, he wouldn't."

Alla (Minsk, age 14): "If such an explosion were to happen somewhere, then for tens and hundreds of kilometers around the atomic particles will be distributed and everything will be destroyed. The planet will turn into a wasteland."

Eric Chivian: "No animals?"

Alla (Minsk, age 14): "No."

Eric Chivian: "Plants?"

Alla (Minsk, age 14): "Of course not. Everything will be diseased."

Eric Chivian: "In the whole earth?"

Alla (Minsk, age 14): "Yes."

John Mack: "How does this question we're talking about make you feel inside yourselves?"

Vovo (Moldavia, age 12): "I feel pain, because when I watched a film about Hiroshima and Nagasaki, how people suffered from the radiation, how they died."

Boris (Minsk, age 13): "We can't imagine life without our parents, friends, brothers and sisters, relatives."

Larisa (Serov, age 13): "To think about it is bad enough, but to imagine it is even worse."

Sveta (Riazan, age 13): "It's hard to picture living by yourself without friends or parents."

Oleg (Ukraine, age 15): "There is a film that tells how a war almost broke out between America and the Soviet Union, and after that I didn't sleep for several nights thinking about this, about how war almost broke out and how our existence is hanging on a thread."

Sveta (Georgievskoye, age 11): "When I watch films or listen to the radio, I can imagine immediately how bombs will fall on my village. And sometimes at night, I cover myself with the blankets, because I'm afraid."

Oskana (Moscow, age 11): "If war starts, we might all be without parents."

Eric Chivian: "And you all feel that there are things that children can do to help prevent a nuclear war?"

Larisa (Serov, age 13): "Yes, of course. Because children will live longer; they will live."

Irina (Estonia, age 13): "They're the ones that have to live and grow and collect information."

Oleg (Yakutsk, age 14): "Everyone thinks about their children. And we can help them by struggling against nuclear, nuclear war—by sending letters, designing banners. These are the things that we can contribute to the struggle against nuclear war. Then they will understand that their children don't want war either."

Eric Chivian: "Is there anything that you would like to say to American people, or to American young people like yourselves?"

Elena (Moscow, age 13): "I would like to wish American children, I'd like to wish that they'd struggle and fight against nuclear war and that they don't believe that it will happen. And that if in some event it does happen, that we will try very hard to stop it. And a very warm welcome from Soviet children."

Valery (Moscow, age 14): "I don't want them to believe the bad things that are said about the Soviet Union. We are the same type of people as they. We also want peace."

Andrei (Moscow, age 15): "And this film could help very much by telling them much more about the Soviet Union than they already know."

Olga (Moscow, age 13): "American people are exactly like we are, exactly the same. The children are the same, and they don't want war either."

Irina (Estonia, age 13): "We'd like to tell the children of America and the children of the world—we say 'Hello' to them."

Data

1. Do you think a nuclear war between the U.S. and the USSR will happen during your lifetime?

	Soviet	American
Yes	11.8%	38.5%
No	54.5%	16.0%
Uncertain	33.7%	44.5%

2. If there were a nuclear war, do you think that you and your family would survive?

	Soviet	American
Yes	2.9%	16.5%
No	80.7%	41.5%
Uncertain	16.4%	41.1%

3. If there were a nuclear war, do you think that the U.S. and the USSR would survive it?

	Soviet	American*
Yes	6.1%	22.0%
No	78.9%	38.0%
Uncertain	15.0%	39.5%

*American children were asked only about survival of the U.S.

4. Do you think nuclear war between the U.S. and the USSR can be prevented?

	Soviet	American
Yes	93.3%	65.0%
No	2.8%	14.5%
Uncertain	3.9%	20.0%

MICHAEL FARRELL

Leader Talks Détente, Religion

Michael Farrell (b. 1935). Foreign editor for the National Catholic Reporter, *Farrell visited the Soviet Union in order to get firsthand information for his readers. Readers of* NCR *are, for the most part, liberal Catholics.*

Michael Farrell, "Leader Talks Détente, Religion," *National Catholic Reporter,* July 15, 1983. Reprinted by permission of the *National Catholic Reporter,* P.O. Box 281, Kansas City, MO 64141.

[When trends and reviews editor Michael Farrell visited Russia recently, *NCR* asked Soviet leader Yuri Andropov for an interview. He was not available but delegated Georgy Arbatov to talk to Farrell. Arbatov, a member of the Supreme Soviet and the Central Committee of the Communist party, is also director of the Institute of U.S. and Canadian Studies. He is a leading Soviet expert on the United States.

Arbatov began with a personal message from Chairman Andropov, expressing the latter's desire for "normalizing relations . . . and a return to détente." And he went on: "[Andropov] has a high opinion of the efforts which are being made by many representatives of different churches in the United States, including American Catholics, to bring this very urgent message to humanity to do something now. It is really an urgent task to stop this race to oblivion toward which we are heading."

For the interview/conversation which follows, Arbatov called in three of his colleagues: Yuri Zanoshkin, a department head at the institute; Vitaly Zhurkin, deputy director; and Vladimir Krestianov, secretary for international relations at the institute. Only minor editorial changes have been made from the taped session, for purposes of grammar or to compensate for words eclipsed by the clinking of teacups.]

Farrell: What do you most admire about the United States?

Arbatov: I am a professional in this field, so my answer may not be very typical. I would say Americans are very human, with all the assets and liabilities of almost any other people. I admire their achievements. They made the country. Their history is full of nice pages and very cruel pages, as is the history of each people. Of course Americans have made a very significant contribution to human civilization, which is admirable. I see also many weaknesses. . . .

Zanoshkin: The United States of America is one of the greatest nations in the world and it has an interesting history, full of democracy, freedom, a very interesting experiment in making such a big country. I would admire many things in American history, and of course some of these traditions stay today. [I admire] the democracy. Not the rhetoric of democracy which has been used against other countries and which shows the snobbishness of America, and lack of understanding of different cultures, but the democratic conditions which express these cultures as they exist. I would admire some features of political realism in the United States. At the same time. . . .

Arbatov: A lot of them are at the grass roots, not very much higher up. . . .

Zanoshkin: Well, there is some political realism higher up, but there is some ideological rhetoric today which doesn't show realism at all, which shows mythology, nostalgia for the past, unwillingness to accept reality, which I don't admire. This is the country which was organized by immigrants, so the unification of different cultures was there. But at the same time I don't admire the lack of knowledge about other cultures which sometimes I find today in the United States, parochialism and the lack of understanding of the great traditions of other countries which have millions of years behind them. So there are some things which I admire and some things which I don't admire. Yes, there was always an interest in technology and science, but there is also a fetishism aligned with fanaticism, like Jerry Falwell—I heard his speech recently when I was in the United States—which I don't admire.

And there was, of course, in the history of America, the witch-hunting in many ways, which I don't admire. And the anti-Darwin trial, which I don't admire. But a great deal of science and literature, which I do admire, and art and music, which benefited the world very much. . . . I could go on and on. So I would say there are some types of American national character which I don't like, and some types which I do like. And I see the United States as a system of different types which are quite contradictory and many opposite each other.

Farrell: Do you admire the elements that are more prominently represented in government at this time—the conservative elements?

Zanoshkin: I don't, actually. I don't like conservatives myself. But I wouldn't like to criticize the president.

Arbatov: He's [Zanoshkin] very shy!

Zanoshkin: I'm very shy, but I don't like some of the ideas he has. This crusade, by the way, of rhetoric is very risky and dangerous.

Arbatov: I would propose that you make an experiment. Ask some youngsters whom you meet during your trip, maybe four or five, what do they know about American literature. And then ask the same number of youngsters in the U.S. what they know about Soviet literature.

Zanoshkin: That would be a very good experiment.

Farrell: If I can find the youngsters here who will talk to me. . . .

Arbatov: Why not?

Farrell: I had great trouble finding you here [at the institute]. Nobody I asked could understand me.

Krestianov: And we had great trouble finding you.

Farrell: Let me ask *you* what American literature you most admire.

Arbatov: My favorite writer is [Ernest] Hemingway, if you take all time.

Farrell: You mean, in the English language?

Arbatov: I mean, from America.

Zanoshkin: All his novels are translated into Russian.

Farrell: And still popular?

Arbatov: Very popular. From contemporary writers, I prefer [Kurt] Vonnegut.

Zanoshkin: Also, his novels are translated into Russian, three of them.

Farrell: Who else is popular now?

Zanoshkin: Thomas Wolfe. Two of his novels are translated now. I like him very much. [William] Faulkner—five or six of his novels are translated. Updike. . . .

Arbatov: [John] Updike, [J. D.] Salinger.

Zanoshkin: Salinger was popular. . . .

Arbatov: And [Ray] Bradbury. And Isaac Asimov.

Zanoshkin: And [Richard] Heller. *Something Happened* was translated recently and became quite popular. So it's a great variety.

Arbatov: Three plays of Tennessee Williams are now being staged.

Zanoshkin: Not less than four. I know four.

Arbatov: Here it is not comparable. Maybe it is not fair that I ask you to make such an experiment. And it is not only for Americans, but for Germans and French. And Zanoshkin put his finger on it, that one of the bad traits of America—it is understandable—is due to their history: they really were never too much interested in other countries, and never cared too much about them. We were never in such a favorable situation that we could even allow ourselves to withdraw. And therefore there are in Russia outstanding traditions. I think we translate maybe 10 or 12 times more American writers than the United States translates our writers. The same is true for movies and theater and many other things.

I have this question: whom do you know from contemporary [Russian] writers? They know [Alexander] Solzhenitsyn, but only because of the political scandal around him. And otherwise, I was told, perhaps [Leo] Tolstoy, [Fedor] Dostoevsky . . .

Zanoshkin: Some of the poets maybe. Yevtuschenko and [Andrei] Voznesensky, but only the elite.

Arbatov: I told them [Americans] they were not particularly Soviet writers, you know.

Farrell: I want to hear somebody say something about Solzhenitsyn. Is he not a Soviet writer?

Arbatov: He is an anti-Soviet writer!

Farrell: And he is a Russian.

Zanoshkin: And he's a Russian. He was published before he emigrated, you know.

Farrell: Is he a great disappointment to you?

Arbatov: Yes.

Farrell: Do you think his writing is literature?

Arbatov: Of course it is literature. When his first things were published, they were controversial even from the point of view of form; not everybody liked his style. But it was seen as some event in literary life and it was never denied. What he did afterward, from the ideological point of view, from the point of view of [his] understanding of the country, everything is, I think, more than conservative. Just calling back to some . . .

Zanoshkin: Some Russian notion of the church as the embodiment of the state, you know, antiscience, antitechnology.

Arbatov: Monarchy. He's a monarchist.

Zanoshkin: He embodies Russian chauvinism, anti-Semitism and anti–other nations.

Farrell: If it's any consolation, he's almost equally anti-American, as America stands at the moment.

Arbatov: Oh, he likes himself! He has some ideas about how things should go, but they are. . . . Anyway, none of us is a specialist in literature.

Farrell: You can't get out of it like that.

Arbatov: And if we are, then more in American literature than Russian literature.

Zanoshkin: I wouldn't agree.

Farrell: You don't have to be a specialist in any case to have definite views about Solzhenitsyn. . . . I should say at this stage I am not American, I am Irish.

Arbatov: But all Americans are somebody else, aside from the poor Indians, whom you rarely meet in America.

Farrell: Have you met any?

Arbatov: Yes, I was on a couple of reservations.

Farrell: You made a point of going there?

Arbatov: We were in such states [where there are Indians], and I was interested to go there.

Zanoshkin: And, of course, we like Bernard Shaw. And [James] Joyce.

Krestianov: Shaw is not American.

Zanoshkin: I mean, Irish.

Arbatov: We have only 25 minutes left, so stop this literature. I think you are interested in other subjects.

Farrell: Let's talk about the freeze. As you know, there is a strong peace movement in the United States, and there are the Greens in Europe, and others. Does it seep through in Russia that this is happening?

Arbatov: Of course. Here we have maybe an even bigger asymmetry than in the attitude toward the world, because you are a nation living beyond two oceans, with rather weak neighbors, and we spent all our history on the crossroads between East and West. We were overrun many times, and so people here have different feelings about war. This is a nation which lost 20 million lives in the last war, and not only the generation which fought—and we belong to that generation—but also our children and our grandchildren, we don't know yet, they feel it also as their problem very much, because they were educated to this.

For this nation, of course, war and peace is the number one priority. For Americans, as I noticed, the most tragic experience in their history was the great Depression. And if you are in Leningrad, visit the Piskaryovskoye cemetery. It is a cemetery where only the war dead are buried, civilian—because there was a siege—and also military. And there in this single cemetery, I think, more war dead are buried than America has lost in all wars.

Therefore, the existence of the peace movement is widely reported and read with great interest.

Zanoshkin: That's why the Catholic bishops' statement was noticed.

Arbatov: Oh, yes, it was noticed. And that is why Mr. Andropov asked me—

he wanted me to emphasize that these efforts are highly respected, both of the Catholic bishops and other religious leaders in the United States.

Farrell: Was there any disappointment that they didn't go far enough?

Arbatov: It is very difficult to say how far they could go. . . . In our political analysis it meant that the attitude of the center of the political spectrum felt the change, because as I personally understand it the Catholic church represents the center and partially of course both sides, mainly to the right of center traditionally.

Farrell: What do you think otherwise of the church's role?

Arbatov: What is striking for me—it's just a matter of personal curiosity, of course—is that now we see such a development in the American church and a very passive attitude in most of the European churches. Our church, by the way, is also rather active.

Farrell: Had the Russian Orthodox church made a statement such as the American bishops made, how would it be received in this country?

Zhurkin: The Russian Orthodox church made statements many times, and long before one was made by American bishops.

Arbatov: What do you have in mind?

Farrell: I have in mind the possibility of its being critical of its own government's policy.

Krestianov: What for to criticize what the government is fighting for, the reduction of armaments? If it is proposing the freeze that your government is rejecting, what for our church should criticize the government, if it's for nuclear arms reduction?

Arbatov: I think, just at the moment, we have such different policies on both sides, with regards to arms control and armaments and relations with each other, that you would hardly be successful in finding symmetry in reactions to these policies.

We are for normal relations with the United States, for normal trade with the United States. We don't try to press our allies not to give credits or to introduce trade barriers or impede trade with the U.S. We are open to all proposals, which are proposals and not political maneuvers. We propose a nuclear free Europe. We propose to resume negotiations on many items where we almost had agreement, like a comprehensive test ban treaty, which is very important, or—what we have begun and which becomes more important now—the demilitarization of outer space, and many others. So just now, I think, many people just find an intellectual escape in trying to put both governments on the same level, so that it becomes easier to criticize. "Nobody can blame you because you are just in favor of the Soviets." But now we have shown strikingly that we have different policies and positions on these subjects. But it's not we who are introducing new weapons systems. And actually we were not in the same position all along.

Zhurkin: You were the first to introduce nuclear weapons, and even to use them. You had the means of delivery, we hadn't. If you take all the major weapons systems since 1945, all of them were made by the U.S.; then we had to follow. So there is just no symmetry. Therefore you cannot expect such mass movements in our country to [our] policies as exist in some European countries or in the U.S. I hope our church is in normal relations with the government. This doesn't mean they have the same opinion on all points.

Zanoshkin: Ideologically they are tremendously different.

Farrell: It is often said the Russian Orthodox church is not free to criticize the government.

Arbatov: I will not judge. You have to ask the churchmen. To be quite honest, we had a not very easy history of relations with the church. When the revolution happened, it was not only a matter of us being atheists. It was mainly, I think, political. The Russian church was not separated from the [former] government. It was an official czarist church. The church was the biggest landowner, which was deprived of ownership. Everything was nationalized. The church took a tremendously active part, most of the church, and the church made civil war against the government, and the relations were very bad.

Then, from the first institution of the state, the church was never forbidden as such, but it was limited very seriously. Then, beginning from the Great Patriotic War, the Second World War, our relations again began to become better. Old grudges were forgotten, and old attitudes. Most clergymen showed themselves very patriotic, and this helped to improve the relations very rapidly.

Farrell: Abroad, when people want to be derogatory about it, they say "godless Communism." That doesn't please you, or does it?

Zanoshkin: It was one of the popes who said that atheists also may be good and respectable and noble people who are guided by the noble principle. It was in one of the encyclicals. . . .

Arbatov: You know, Mr. Farrell, I think it is very curious that this topic was brought to the surface of the discussion at the end of the 20th century. If we go on in the same way in the 21st century, we will discuss the pros and cons of cannibalism. Because this was solved a long time ago by history. We know Ivan the Terrible was a tremendously religious man. And Henry VIII as well. And Alexander Borgia was even the pope. . . .

Zanoshkin: And when the Irish were slaughtered by the English, they were slaughtered in the name of the church. . . .

Arbatov: So the watershed doesn't go between those who believe and those who do not believe.

Zhurkin: All the mass movements of the previous centuries had also a religious color. They believed in different religions, the shades were different, and they all tried to destroy each other.

Arbatov: I think you can judge that, in the USSR, we respect the beliefs of others, but we believe that we have the right to believe or not to believe. And when we are called "godless," if it is meant simply as a statement of fact, that Communists are atheists, then we take it as a statement of fact. If it is used in a derogatory sense, just to show that we are immoral, then we take it as a slander, and we think this is just not right. You have a lot of very religious scoundrels, you know, and just as many very noble atheists.

Zanoshkin: By the way, public opinion polls in Sweden show the majority now do not believe in God. So Sweden can be called godless as well. And many other countries as well. With the amount of people who don't believe in God, the world is becoming more and more godless.

Farrell: But the common perception of Communism is that on principle the state and the philosophy behind it are anti-God. You say you're free to believe or not to believe. If, tomorrow, you said, "I want to become a Greek Orthodox Catholic—or a follower of Jerry Falwell, for that matter—would it cause any problems with your life?

Zhurkin: No.

Arbatov: As party members, yes.

Zanoshkin: Only as a party member.

Arbatov: Because to belong to the party you have to share its philosophy, its ideology. Its philosophy is materialistic, and one of its starting points is that there are no supernatural forces which have created earth, society and which rule the society. If you don't believe in that, then you are a bad Communist. Just to be honest, you have either to be a Communist—but it doesn't mean you cannot be a perfect Soviet citizen, and be absolutely okay, in full order, and be promoted, and at the same time profess religion.

Farrell: Do you not feel that with this materialistic philosophy, as you call it, a great deal more than the idea of God has been taken away, that you have removed all the possibility of idealism and transcendence?

Zanoshkin: Americans use the term "materialism" in a different way, oriented for the consumer, goods, you know, oriented for the fetishism of commodities and so on, which we reject utterly. The materialism you use is very different from the term "materialism" we use.

Arbatov: I know very well not only this generation of Communists but also the former one. I think they were the most idealistic people in the world, in the sense of idealism as belief in ideals, ascetic, very intolerant to immoral things, very demanding, sometimes even too demanding on the behavior of others—actually that was typical of the whole moral and intellectual atmosphere of the country for the first 15 or 20 years.

Farrell: Has that gone away?

Arbatov: No.

Zanoshkin: Now there is much more freedom for using one's own talents or using one's own tastes, you know. Why not? It goes together with humanistic ideals.

Arbatov: It is unbelievable. You Americans would hardly be able to understand what we went through in our history since after the civil war, the real hunger from which millions of people [died], and then the Second World War; awful, due to some mistakes we made ourselves; nobody is guaranteed against that.

Zanoshkin: So high moral standards can go together with a variety of human individuality in the development of your tastes, in the development of your needs.

Arbatov: I think we are pretty much idealistic even now, in this good sense that people don't consider it normal that somebody is not honest, that people can complain about some things publicly.

Zanoshkin: I would say promiscuity and pornography are out of the question.

Farrell: Are they out of the question because they are not allowed? Because, if I brought in *Playboy* to the country—actually they didn't look in my cases, so you don't know whether I did or not—but if I did, it would have been confiscated and I may have had a few questions to answer.

Krestianov: Because here there are laws against it.

Farrell: So when you say they are more moral, maybe it is because they have no opportunity to be otherwise.

Arbatov: I think, essentially, all people are the same, Americans and Russians, so if somebody becomes very fallible to pornography or drugs or something else, it is due to something, including maybe sometimes very lax attitudes of the society. And I think on some points your country is maybe too lax. They should be a bit stricter. The attitude toward violence, for example.

Zanoshkin: The commercialization of the vices. A lot of people make money from pornography. Everything becomes big business.

Farrell: On the other hand, can you legislate morality, as some would say you are trying to do?

Arbatov: No. This is understood here.

Farrell: But isn't that what you are doing?

Zhurkin: But the deterioration of morality you can stop to a certain degree by laws.

Zanoshkin: For example, in a war propaganda is prohibited by law in our country. So it's a kind of legislation.

Arbatov: Pornography is also forbidden. Of course, the understanding of pornography—it is not such a strict word, so that you can move it one side or the other side. We are a young society. When the society matures, the standards can become broader.

Farrell: How can you talk about a young society? America is a young society.

Arbatov: From 1917, after the revolution.

Farrell: Did people change that much?

Arbatov: Society changed tremendously. The people changed. All of you are also a very old society in this sense—the old Indians lived for a lot of years.

Zanoshkin: Your revolution was 200 years ago. Ours was 60-some.

Arbatov: The society was created [out of] a monarchic, very aristocratic society, with big landlords with private ownership, very backward, 85 percent of the population illiterate in rural areas, and a very primitive agriculture which was maybe 100 years behind German or Austrian agriculture. You must also understand that Russians comprise a little bit more than half of our population.

Zanoshkin: I assure you they are much less, 100 million, less than half.

Farrell: I have heard that this makes some people nervous.

Krestianov: In the United States maybe!

Farrell: I would think, on the contrary, that the United States should be happy about it.

Arbatov: We think it is bad that the birthrate remains so low in some parts of the country. . . .

Zanoshkin: Because we lack the labor.

Arbatov: But that is not because we are afraid of something. When he [Zanoshkin] says the Russians are less than half—I meant, together with [Soviet] Europeans and Belorussians, which are very close culturally.

Zanoshkin: And then, of course, we are the biggest nation in the Soviet Union. We have 75 nationalities.

Farrell: If one of the others, Georgia, for example, wanted to secede, wouldn't this cause a problem?

Arbatov: It has a right under the constitution.

Farrell: And there would be no interference from Moscow?

Arbatov: If the majority decided. It has to be a plebiscite.

Zanoshkin: Of course it is speculation, because they never expressed this desire.

Arbatov: It is a legal right. It is most improbable that it will happen due to many reasons, cultural, economic, political.

Zanoshkin: And there is tremendous cultural integration, by the way, going on.

Farrell: Is the rumor I hear, that some of the republics would like to secede, totally untrue?

Zanoshkin: Wishful thinking!

Arbatov: In each of the republics you can find some people who are not satisfied. But in each republic the majority are working people who think about the facts of life and are not daydreaming. I don't think it is a subject which interests them very much.

Zanoshkin: They have tremendous benefits being a part of the Soviet Union.

Farrell: Are we all going to survive until the 21st century?

Arbatov: We have to.

Farrell: But that's not the question I asked you. Do you think we will?

Zanoshkin: I think we will, somehow.

Arbatov: I feel that the dangers are there. And we really can commit mistakes which are irretrievable. I think our generation has a unique responsibility before mankind, before all the previous history and the future history of mankind, I don't think any nation will start war by its conscious decision and intention. But I think it must be understood that the policies certain nations are practicing now can make war possible, maybe even probable, under some situations inevitable.

This is a situation which has to be caught in the correct time. Therefore I think what was understood by the Catholic bishops of the U.S. and by many others was a very timely thing: that if we drift in the same direction, even if nobody wants war, but we have an unlimited arms race, we have such hatred in our relations, unlimited hostility in our relations, and we have uncontrollable hotbeds of conflict all around the world, sometime something will very probably happen which will really be a finite holocaust.

And for the first time it came to mind last year. I was 18 when I had to go to war. And I remember at this time there were many studies published about some pilots of ours whose planes were shot down; their parachutes didn't open, but they survived. The plane hit the ground and the shock wave from the explosion softened the fall, or deep snow, or something—and these were facts of life, there were names of people. But if somebody would make of these facts of life the conclusion that somebody can jump out of a plane, it would be insanity. Just almost such insanity would be to think that we can live as we lived these 37 years of the nuclear age. . . .

Farrell: The logical conclusion of what you're saying is, not only must we not increase but we have to roll back nuclear arms.

Arbatov: Of course. The danger is already there, tremendous danger.

Farrell: Is it possible *all* nuclear arms could be abolished? There's still the question of other nations than the two superpowers.

Arbatov: I think, yes. It can look absolutely improbable now. But we are living in a very strange world. The arms race usually was a product of bad political relations. Now the arms race is a source of bad political relations.

Actually we have no real controversies with Americans. Our major source of distrust is the arms race itself. Why are you building the MX? Why are you trying to bring the Pershing II close to our borders? Such suspicions could also be on the American side, I can understand that. And we have to act [to change this].

And I think it happened. Chemical weapons looked so enticing but they were never used. So you cannot win. I think the whole notion about war has changed. Now war doesn't pay. You cannot win from a big war. And as we noticed also, it was the case even in smaller wars. The cost or something has started to change.

Farrell: Where do you begin to solve this: at arms talks in Geneva, or sitting around tables like this? Is it people interaction or high-level negotiations or both together?

Arbatov: Many governments, I am afraid, would never do anything without pressure.

Zhurkin: We had examples when both nations wanted something, for instance, the ABM treaty. Both sides decided not to construct this new ABM system, and it was not created. And we could live in a very dangerous world if we did not do this. Take the SALT I treaty. It was agreed that neither the United States nor the Soviet Union would construct new silos for intercontinental ballistic missiles, and no silos were constructed since 1972. For 10 years they were constructed, and for more than 10 years not a single one was created. So there is a possibility of progress, but certainly the public should participate. The public should raise its voice and demand that more and more drastic measures should be taken. The Soviet public is quite outspoken. . . .

Arbatov: And I would say that peace and war are too important subjects to be left to the generals and politicians. The fate of everybody depends on it.

Farrell: How is the Soviet voice heard? In the U.S. it's heard because people are out there on the streets.

Zanoshkin: Here they are on the streets. Last year there were about 60 million who participated in demonstrations.

Arbatov: Yesterday there was a big demonstration against missiles in Europe . . . I think, 50,000 people.

Zanoshkin: There was an international peace march which started in Norway, Sweden, Helsinki, then came to Moscow. In Moscow 300,000 people participated. It was international.

Farrell: Against whom was it directed?

Arbatov: Against nuclear weapons in the East and West. This was last summer.

Zhurkin: Last summer there were thousands of demonstrations all over the country.

Farrell: Who organizes these? The Communist party?

Zhurkin: No. Peace committees, women's organizations, trade unions, the church, youth organizations.

Arbatov: You must excuse me, gentlemen. If you want to go on, go on in the next room. I have to work.

Zanoshkin: Wait. There is another aspect in which Arbatov participates very much, dispersion of information about the catastrophic characteristics of nuclear war. All of us participated, and you [to Arbatov] participated very much with physicians. . . .

Arbatov: We had a lot of letters. There are more than a million letters written to the Central Committee of the party in a year. . . . On this subject, if you talk with anybody—I remember many times [Leonid] Brezhnev has told me this is a factor of substance. He asked about complaints, which is difficult. Well, he's told, there's housing, there's kindergarten or something. You know, there are a lot of problems we have, but the major problem is that there be peace. All other problems, we could solve them—please care about this. This is the attitude in this country because, I told you, this, together with maybe a few other European countries, has a special national memory.

Zhurkin: About the demonstrations, I think one thing only should be said. To an extent they are different from a demonstration in the West. They are spontaneous demonstrations. You cannot order people, after their work, to go and demonstrate somewhere. But they are not anti-Communist demonstrations. They are demanding disarmament, but they are at the same time supporting the peaceful policy of the government.

Zanoshkin: But they are, by the way, pushing the government in the direction they want [it to go].

Arbatov: I think the government consists of people who also had war experiences, were families, you know. In this country, to see that there are more important things than peace would be political suicide for any leader.

Farrell: Did I understand you to say, just a minute ago, that Mr. Andropov's first priority is peace?

Arbatov: Of course. Of course. And Brezhnev's was. And Andropov's is. And it is demanded of them. And it is the decision of the party congress, which is the highest body we have, that this is the first priority.

Zanoshkin: He [Arbatov] is a member of the parliament, he can tell you.

Arbatov: I can find you quotations.

Farrell: I'll take your word.

Arbatov: Because everybody knows that all other things would simply have no sense if there is no peace. . . .

Zanoshkin: And the economic burden of the arms race for us is very great.

Farrell: Tell me what to tell the people of the United States that would make a difference, in one word.

Arbatov: In one word you hardly can say. But I think that we now are living in the time of the greatest lies in history, the most dangerous lies, about the military balance. There simply cannot be such a balance in favor of the Soviet Union. We comprise maybe 20 or 25 percent of the gross national product of our possible adversaries taken together. And 16 percent of their population. We simply cannot have it. If we speak about parity we are very generous. And not a single general or politician in the U.S. would exchange weapons and geopolitical situation and everything with us. So it is a big lie. The Soviet Union never dreamed about having a military victory or superiority. It is just not what we are concerned about.

Farrell: Would *you* swap arsenals with the U.S.?

Zhorkin: I personally would prefer to reduce both of them.

Krestianov: And destroy big parts of the rest.

Zanoshkin: We are asymmetrical in many ways. It is difficult to say.

Arbatov: This is what fools the Americans. The U.S. all the time is comparing itself with the Soviet Union. But the United States has it allies. And its allies have a bigger economy, have a big army. The Germans have maybe a better army than the United States, more than a bit better. They produce their own weapons. Two of them are nuclear.

Farrell: On the other hand, the U.S. is very nervous about your getting in through Cuba to Nicaragua at the moment, for example.

Arbatov: You see! And *they* are all around *us*. They must have better feelings about this. They are in Turkey. They were in Iran. . . .

Zanoshkin: They are in South Korea.

Arbatov: We are just as near to Japan, you know, as you to Cuba.

Farrell: And I'm sure you're nervous about their being in Turkey and round about. Do you see why they would be nervous?

Zanoshkin: Of course.

Arbatov: It is just another big lie. Because the source of what happens in Nicaragua is not what we [do]. We are unable to do it. It is *your* policy.

Zanoshkin: Of course, if you [still] had Somoza, you would have Nicaragua.

Arbatov: You created such an economic situation in those banana republics. You supported the most bloody regimes everywhere. Batista in Cuba. Somoza.

Zanoshkin: Guatemala.

Arbatov: And, you know, you must have learned it from Iran already, that it just brings an explosion sooner or later. And until you learn it, you won't have sound policy toward those countries.

Farrell: And—my last shot—you don't think this is similar to Afghanistan? This, many Americans would say, was the last straw.

Arbatov: No, Poland was the last!

I don't know what they wanted from us in Poland—that we make a *coup d'état* and throw away General [Wojciech] Jaruzelski and put instead of him [Lech] Walesa? But we would never do it. What bad things did we do in Poland?

Zanoshkin: We gave away [to Poland] $400 million just in food and other ways—which we need—to pay their debts.

Arbatov: The situation in Afghanistan, as we see it, was absolutely different. It was not the last straw. In Afghanistan we made the decision when the assessment of the situation was absolutely different. NATO had already taken the decision about the missiles in Europe. The SALT II ratification process was already torpedoed. You had a lot of your warships assembled in the Persian Gulf which were intended to do something either in Iran or Afghanistan. And there were, supported by the U.S. and China, permanent incursions of big groups of armed people to Afghanistan. And they asked us 12 times. We refused to introduce our troops. We agreed the 12th time because the assessment of threat was different. This is on our border. I don't expect you to support us in Afghanistan, but what we want there is a political solution. And Andropov has stressed it several times, to the general secretary of the United Nations, in his interviews and speeches everywhere. When the camps where these people are trained are closed and the border is closed, then we will pull away the troops from Afghanistan.

LAWYERS COMMITTEE ON NUCLEAR POLICY

Statement on the Illegality of Nuclear Weapons

The Lawyers Committee on Nuclear Policy, founded in 1981, is a New York-based group dedicated to the prevention of nuclear war and the abolition of nuclear weapons. The group works to educate lawyers and the public about nuclear weapons and disarmament from the standpoint that nuclear weapons are illegal under existing international law.

Humanity has entered a critical period in its history as a species. Today's nuclear arsenals have the potential for annihilating a large segment of the world's populations, for devastating and contaminating vast areas of the earth's surface, and for producing unpredictable and uncontrollable biological and environmental consequences. In short, nuclear weapons threaten human survival itself.

Yet, the use of nuclear weapons once considered unthinkable is increasingly being contemplated by U.S. policymakers. In fact, with Presidential Directive 59, the United States has officially adopted a counterforce strategy that envisions the use (including the first use) of nuclear weapons in a variety of conventional as well as nuclear settings. This shift in nuclear strategy is all the more troubling given the Reagan administration's position that the United States must be prepared to intervene, using nuclear capabilities if necessary, to protect U.S. interests wherever threatened. Thus there has developed in U.S. official policy a dangerous acceptance of the legitimacy and efficacy of using nuclear weapons to reverse international situations considered adverse to U.S. national interests.

Rather than preserving international peace as claimed, this nuclear strategy is likely to bring us closer to nuclear war. The insistence on a limited nuclear war option increases dramatically the prospect that nuclear weapons will be used in a crisis situation. Furthermore, the notion that the use of nuclear weapons can be kept from escalating into an all-out nuclear exchange is, as many experts have argued, highly questionable. Consequently, we believe there is a growing specter of nuclear war, which requires us to undertake a fundamental rethinking of the status of nuclear weapons under international law.

The prevalent belief among the general public as well as policymakers is

---

Lawyers Committee on Nuclear Policy, "Statement on the Illegality of Nuclear Weapons." In *Toward Nuclear Disarmament and Global Security* Burns H. Weston, ed. (Boulder, Colo.: Westview Press, 1984), pp. 146–151. Reprinted by permission of Westview Press from *Toward Nuclear Disarmament and Global Security*.

that nuclear weapons are legal. This belief is based on the assumption that a state may do whatever it is not expressly forbidden from doing. The legality of nuclear weapons, however, cannot be judged solely by the existence or non-existence of a treaty rule specifically prohibiting or restricting their use. Any reasonable legal analysis must take into account all the recognized sources of international law—international treaties, international custom, general principles of law, judicial decisions, and the writings of the most qualified publicists. Of particular relevance to the legality of nuclear weapons are the many treaties and conventions which limit the use of any weapons in war, the traditional distinction between combatant and noncombatant, and the principles of humanity including the prohibition of weapons and tactics that are especially cruel and cause unnecessary suffering. A review of these basic principles supports a conclusion that the threat and use of nuclear weapons is illegal under international law.

A basic source of the laws of war are the Hague Conventions of 1907, particularly the Regulations embodied in Hague Convention IV. The United States Air Force, in its most recent official publication (1976) on international law and armed conflict, states that these Regulations "remain the foundation stones of the modern law of armed conflict." A fundamental tenet of these Regulations is the prohibition of wanton or indiscriminate destruction. The Regulations forbid, for example, "the attack or bombardment, by whatever means, of town, villages, [and even individual] dwellings or buildings which are undefended."

The universally accepted Geneva Conventions of 1949 updated and greatly strengthened the 1907 Regulations. In particular, the Convention on "the Protection of Civilian Persons in Time of War" imposes additional detailed obligations on all belligerents to ensure the essential requirements for the health, safety, and sustenance of the civilian population. A primary objective of these Conventions is to assure that "disinterested [outside] aid [can be] given without discrimination to all victims of war including members of the armed forces who on account of their wounds, capture or shipwreck cease to be enemies but become suffering and helpless human beings." The use of nuclear weapons of any type would inevitably result in massive violations of both the 1907 and 1949 rules.

Furthermore, restraints on the conduct of hostilities are traditionally not limited to those given explicit voice in specific treaty stipulations. Aware of the continuous evolution of war technology, the 1907 Hague Regulations contain a general yardstick intended exactly for situations where no specific treaty rule exists to prohibit a new type of weapon or tactic. In such cases, "the inhabitants and the belligerents remain under the protection and the rule of the principles of the laws of nations, as they result from the usages established among civilized peoples, from the laws of humanity, and the dictates of public conscience." In short, this general rule, known as the Martens clause, makes civilized usages, the demands of humanity, and the dictates of public conscience obligatory by themselves—without the formulation of a treaty specifically prohibiting a new weapon. Any specific convention solemnly prohibiting a specific new weapon or tactic, of course, would serve to reconfirm and strengthen the existing body of law.

Historically, the principles of humanity have been one of the primary sources of law limiting the violence permissible in war. Ever since the Declaration of St. Petersburg of 1868, the principles of humanity have been asserted as a constraint upon military necessity. The Declaration embodies what may be the twin ground rules of the laws of war: that "the right to adopt means of injuring the enemy is not unlimited" and that "the only legitimate object which States should endeavor to accomplish during a war is to weaken the military forces of the enemy."

The protection of civilians and neutral countries flows logically from the elementary distinction between combatant and noncombatant. The commitment to protect civilians and neutral countries also implies that weapons must be used selectively, and only against military targets. As stated by the International Red Cross Committee in its commentary on the 1949 Geneva Conventions, "the civilian population can never be regarded as a military objective. That truth is the very basis of the whole law of war." Without differentiating between military and nonmilitary targets, the fundamental distinction between combatant and noncombatant becomes meaningless.

It is clear that the use of nuclear weapons in populated areas would result in the indiscriminate and massive slaughter of civilians. Moreover, even if nuclear weapons were used only against an enemy's strategic nuclear forces, the annihilation and extermination of the civilian population of the enemy would be an inevitable by-product. As the experiences of Hiroshima and Nagasaki amply demonstrate, the effects of nuclear weapons because of their very awesome nature cannot be limited to military targets.

The 1949 Geneva Conventions were adopted four years after the advent of the "nuclear age." It would therefore be illogical to assume that their provisions are not applicable to nuclear weapons. Nor did any nuclear-weapons State or any of the 130-odd other States that ratified or acceded to the Geneva Conventions make any reservation to such effect. However, it would be impossible under conditions of nuclear warfare to carry out the obligations of the Geneva Conventions, just as it would also be impossible to live up to the universally binding rules of the Hague Conventions of 1907, all of which aim at preserving the minimum requirements for the continued survivability and viability of all societies involved in armed conflict. Hence, the use of nuclear weapons would inevitably result in the commission of war crimes on an enormous scale. This fact alone is sufficient to prohibit the use of nuclear weapons.

The use of nuclear weapons would also result, directly or indirectly, in the indiscriminate destruction of people of a particular nationality. If, for example, the stated objective were the destruction of a nation-state, then the threat or use of nuclear weapons toward this end would violate at least the spirit of the Genocide Convention of 1948—which made the destruction of groups on racial, religious, or nationality grounds an international crime. To assume the legality of a weapon with the distinct capability to terrorize and to destroy an entire civilian population would make meaningless the entire effort to limit combat through the laws of war. As fragile as the laws of war may be, they must be supported, especially in the present setting where the risks to human survival are so great.

One of the most important law-making treaties, the United Nations Charter, establishes a legal duty for all states to refrain from the threat or use of force in their international relations except in self-defense or under the authority of the United Nations. Furthermore, the principle that a war of aggression warrants the highest degree of international opprobrium, namely, to be branded as an international crime, was affirmed by the Nuremberg Tribunals. These two principles have so often been unanimously reaffirmed by the General Assembly as to have become undisputed axioms of international law.

On the basis of these unquestioned principles of international law, the United Nations has repeatedly condemned the use of nuclear weapons as an "international crime." On November 24, 1961, for example, the General Assembly declared in Resolution 1653 (XVI) that "any State using nuclear or thermonuclear weapons is to be considered as violating the Charter of the United Nations, as acting contrary to the law of humanity, and as committing a crime against mankind and civilization." In Resolution 33/71-B of December 14, 1978, and in Resolution 35/152-D of December 12, 1980, the General Assembly again declared that "the use of nuclear weapons would be a violation of the Charter of the United Nations and a crime against humanity." As evidenced by these actions of the General Assembly, a consensus has been clearly emerging that the use of nuclear weapons contradicts the fundamental humanitarian principles upon which the international law of war is founded.

Yet, there is an influential school of thought which would deny the applicability of the existing laws of war to nuclear warfare. This school asserts that in an era of "total war" even the most fundamental rules can be disregarded if this enhances the chances for victory. This argument was urged in another context by some of the Nuremberg defendants, and indignantly rejected by the international Tribunal. The Tribunal's judgment warns that this "Nazi conception" of total war would destroy the validity of international law altogether. Ultimately, the legitimacy of such a view would exculpate Auschwitz.

In sum, if the goal of the laws of war—to set limits on permissible violence—is to be realized to any serious degree, and if the fundamental principles of humanity are to be of continuing relevance to their interpretation, then it must be concluded that any threat of use of nuclear weapons is illegal. Global "survivability" is so elemental that the prohibition can be reasonably inferred from the existing laws of war. To conclude differently would be to ignore the barbaric and nefarious character of the use of nuclear weapons. As the laws of war embody the minimum demands of decency, exempting nuclear weapons from that body of laws would be abandoning even this minimum standard.

The genetic and environmental effects resulting from the use of nuclear weapons, alone, provide a compelling moral and humanitarian argument against their legality. But, as indicated above, this is not the only basis for concluding that the threat or use of nuclear weapons is illegal. The unnecessary and disproportionate suffering resulting from their use; the indiscriminate nature of their effects for civilians and combatants alike; the uncontrollable radioactive fallout they set off; and their similarity in terms of effects to poision, poison gas, or bacteriological weapons (all of which are prohibited by the Hague Convention of 1907 and the Geneva Gas Protocol of 1925)—each is a sufficient basis for concluding that the threat or use of nuclear weapons is prohibited under existing international law. When taken together, these arguments provide overwhelming support for the conclusion that any threat or use of nuclear weapons is contrary to the dictates of international law.

So too, these arguments provide a sound legal basis for delegitimating and criminalizing the manufacture, possession, and ownership of nuclear weapons. If a course of action is illegal, then the planning and preparation for such an action are, by legal and moral logic, also forbidden. Moreover, the attack on the legality of manufacturing and possessing nuclear weapons is all the more necessary given the increasing prospects for the "accidental" use of nuclear weapons arising out of today's dangerous first-strike strategies.

Our intention is not to score points in a battle of legal wits. What we wish to present to fellow lawyers, to governmental decision makers, and to the public is the view that nuclear warfare would lead to results incompatible with fundamental rules of international law, elementary morality, and contrary to any rational conception of national interest and world order. In short, the very nature of nuclear warfare is destructive of all the values which law obligates us to preserve. While it is accurate to say that international law has not been as effective as it should have been in regulating state acts, international law is important to preserve our sense of humanity and to enhance the prospects for peace.

Reducing the likelihood of nuclear war must obviously, then, be the highest priority of our profession. To this end, the legal community needs to give its urgent attention to the study and implementation of the international law relating to nuclear weapons.

PART 4

What Should We Do?

Prospects for the Future

Technological and Military Approaches

Political Approaches

Long-Range Alternatives

Technological and Military Approaches

COMMITTEE ON THE PRESENT DANGER

Common Sense and the Common Danger

The Committee on the Present Danger (CPD) was formed in the late 1970s by a group of highly influential conservatives. One of the founding members was Ronald Reagan, and sixteen of the original group received appointments in his administration, including Jeane Kirkpatrick, former ambassador to the UN; Paul Nitze, former head of the U.S. delegation, INF negotiations; and Max Kampelman, chief negotiator, START (Strategic Arms Reduction Talks). The Committee advocates a 1950s type of containment policy toward the Soviet Union, believing that only a vast nuclear arsenal can prevent Soviet expansion.

Our country is in a period of danger, and the danger is increasing. Unless decisive steps are taken to alert the nation, and to change the course of its policy, our economic and military capacity will become inadequate to assure peace with security.

The principal threat to our nation, to world peace, and to the cause of human freedom is the Soviet drive for dominance based upon an unparalleled military buildup.

The scope and sophistication of the Soviet campaign have been increased in recent years, and its tempo quickened.

For more than a decade, the Soviet Union has been enlarging and improving both its strategic and its conventional military forces far more rapidly than the United States and its allies. Soviet military power and its rate of growth cannot be explained or justified by considerations of self-defense. The Soviet Union is consciously seeking what its spokesmen call ''visible preponderance'' for the

---

Committee on the Present Danger, ''Common Sense and the Common Danger.'' A policy statement reprinted by permission of The Committee on the Present Danger®, issued 11 November 1976 in Washington, D.C.

Soviet sphere. Such preponderance, they explain, will permit the Soviet Union "to transform the conditions of world politics" and determine the direction of its development.

The process of Soviet expansion and the worldwide deployment of its military power threaten our interest in the political independence of our friends and allies, their and our fair access to raw materials, the freedom of the seas, and in avoiding a preponderance of adversary power. These interests can be threatened not only by direct attack but also by envelopment and indirect aggression.

To sustain an effective foreign policy, economic strength, military strength, and a commitment to leadership are essential.

If we continue to drift, we shall become second best to the Soviet Union in overall military strength; our alliances will weaken; our promising rapprochement with China could be reversed. Then we could find ourselves isolated in a hostile world, facing the unremitting pressures of Soviet policy backed by an overwhelming preponderance of power. Our national survival itself would be in peril, and we should face, one after another, bitter choices between war and acquiescence under pressure.

PRESIDENT RONALD REAGAN

National Security: Address to the Nation, March 23, 1983

Ronald Reagan (b. 1911), President of the United States (1981–). In this, the famous "Star Wars Speech," President Reagan justifies his defense budget and announces his intention to promote an elaborate ballistic missile defense system. This system, called the Strategic Defense Initiative (SDI), is essentially President Reagan's own idea (scientists had decided prior to the speech that such a system was still unrealizable). The speech tells us a good deal about President Reagan's attitudes toward defense issues.

My fellow Americans, thank you for sharing your time with me tonight.

The subject I want to discuss with you, peace and national security, is both timely and important. Timely, because I've reached a decision which offers a new hope for our children in the 21st century, a decision I'll tell you about in a few minutes. And important because there's a very big decision that you must

---

Reprinted from the "Weekly Compilation of Presidential Documents," vol. 19, no. 12 (Washington, D.C.: U.S. Government Printing Office, 1983).

make for yourselves. This subject involves the most basic duty that any President and any people share, the duty to protect and strengthen the peace.

At the beginning of this year, I submitted to the Congress a defense budget which reflects my best judgment of the best understanding of the experts and specialists who advise me about what we and our allies must do to protect our people in the years ahead. That budget is much more than a long list of numbers, for behind all the numbers lies America's ability to prevent the greatest of human tragedies and preserve our free way of life in a sometimes dangerous world. It is part of a careful, long-term plan to make America strong again after too many years of neglect and mistakes.

Our efforts to rebuild America's defenses and strengthen the peace began 2 years ago when we requested a major increase in the defense program. Since then, the amount of those increases we first proposed has been reduced by half, through improvements in management and procurement and other savings.

The budget request that is now before the Congress has been trimmed to the limits of safety. Further deep cuts cannot be made without seriously endangering the security of the Nation. The choice is up to the men and women you've elected to the Congress, and that means the choice is up to you.

Tonight, I want to explain to you what this defense debate is all about and why I'm convinced that the budget now before the Congress is necessary, responsible, and deserving of your support. And I want to offer hope for the future.

But first, let me say what the defense debate is not about. It is not about spending arithmetic. I know that in the last few weeks you've been bombarded with numbers and percentages. Some say we need only a 5-percent increase in defense spending. The so-called alternate budget backed by liberals in the House of Representatives would lower the figure to 2 to 3 percent, cutting our defense spending by $163 billion over the next 5 years. The trouble with all these numbers is that they tell us little about the kind of defense program America needs or the benefits and security and freedom that our defense effort buys for us.

What seems to have been lost in all this debate is the simple truth of how a defense budget is arrived at. It isn't done by deciding to spend a certain number of dollars. Those loud voices that are occasionally heard charging that the Government is trying to solve a security problem by throwing money at it are nothing more than noise based on ignorance. We start by considering what must be done to maintain peace and review all the possible threats against our security. Then a strategy for strengthening peace and defending against those threats must be agreed upon. And, finally, our defense establishment must be evaluated to see what is necessary to protect against any or all of the potential threats. The cost of achieving these ends is totaled up, and the result is the budget for national defense.

There is no logical way that you can say, let's spend *x* billion dollars less. You can only say, which part of our defense measures do we believe we can do without and still have security against all contingencies? Anyone in the Congress who advocates a percentage or a specific dollar cut in defense spending should be made to say what part of our defenses he would eliminate, and he should be candid enough to acknowledge that his cuts mean cutting our commitments to allies or inviting greater risk or both.

The defense policy of the United States is based on a simple premise: The United States does not start fights. We will never be an aggressor. We maintain our strength in order to deter and defend against aggression—to preserve freedom and peace.

Since the dawn of the atomic age, we've sought to reduce the risk of war by maintaining a strong deterrent and by seeking genuine arms control. "Deterrence" means simply this: making sure any adversary who thinks about attacking the United States, or our allies, or our vital interests, concludes that the risks to him outweigh any potential gains. Once he understands that, he won't attack. We maintain the peace through our strength; weakness only invites aggression.

This strategy of deterrence has not changed. It still works. But what it takes to maintain deterrence has changed. It took one kind of military force to deter an attack when we had far more nuclear weapons than any other power; it takes another kind now that the Soviets, for example, have enough accurate and powerful nuclear weapons to destroy virtually all of our missiles on the ground. Now, this is not to say that the Soviet Union is planning to make war on us. Nor do I believe a war is inevitable—quite the contrary. But what must be recognized is that our security is based on being prepared to meet all threats.

There was a time when we depended on coastal forts and artillery batteries, because, with the weaponry of that day, any attack would have had to come by sea. Well, this is a different world, and our defenses must be based on recognition and awareness of the weaponry possessed by other nations in the nuclear age.

We can't afford to believe that we will never be threatened. There have been two world wars in my lifetime. We didn't start them and, indeed, did everything we could to avoid being drawn into them. But we were ill-prepared for both. Had we been better prepared, peace might have been preserved.

For 20 years the Soviet Union has been accumulating enormous military might. They didn't stop when their forces exceeded all requirements of a legitimate defensive capability. And they haven't stopped now. During the past decade and a half, the Soviets have built up a massive arsenal of new strategic nuclear weapons—weapons that can strike directly at the United States.

As an example, the United States introduced its last new intercontinental ballistic missile, the Minute Man III, in 1969, and we're now dismantling our even older Titan missiles. But what has the Soviet Union done in these intervening years? Well, since 1969 the Soviet Union has built five new classes of ICBM's, and upgraded these eight times. As a result, their missiles are much more powerful and accurate than they were several years ago, and they continue to develop more, while ours are increasingly obsolete.

The same thing has happened in other areas. Over the same period, the Soviet Union built 4 new classes of submarine-launched ballistic missiles and over 60 new missile submarines. We built 2 new types of submarine missiles and actually withdrew 10 submarines from strategic missions. The Soviet Union built over 200 new Backfire bombers, and their brand new Blackjack bomber is now under development. We haven't built a new long-range bomber since our B-52's were developed about a quarter of a century ago, and we've already retired several hundred of those because of old age. Indeed, despite what many people think, our strategic forces only cost about 15 percent of the defense budget.

Another example of what's happened: In 1978 the Soviets had 600 intermediate-range nuclear missiles based on land and were beginning to add the SS-20—a new, highly accurate, mobile missile with 3 warheads. We had none. Since then the Soviets have strengthened their lead. By the end of 1979, when Soviet leader Brezhnev declared "a balance now exists," the Soviets had over 800 warheads. We still had none. A year ago this month, Mr. Brezhnev pledged a moratorium, or freeze, on SS-20 deployment. But by last August, their 800 warheads had become more than 1,200. We still had none. Some freeze. At this time Soviet Defense Minister Ustinov announced "approximate parity of forces continues to exist." But the Soviets are still adding an average of 3 new warheads a week, and now have 1,300. These warheads can reach their targets in a matter of a few minutes. We still have none. So far, it seems that the Soviet definition of parity is a box score of 1,300 to nothing, in their favor.

So, together with our NATO allies, we decided in 1979 to deploy new weapons, beginning this year, as a deterrent to their SS-20's and as an incentive to the Soviet Union to meet us in serious arms control negotiations. We will begin that deployment late this year. At the same time, however, we're willing to cancel our program if the Soviets will dismantle theirs. This is what we've called a zero-zero plan. The Soviets are now at the negotiating table—and I think it's fair to say that without our planned deployments, they wouldn't be there.

Now, let's consider conventional forces. Since 1974 the United States has produced 3,050 tactical combat aircraft. By contrast, the Soviet Union has produced twice as many. When we look at attack submarines, the United States has produced 27 while the Soviet Union has produced 61. For armored vehicles, including tanks, we have produced 11,200. The Soviet Union has produced 54,000—nearly 5 to 1 in their favor. Finally, with artillery, we've produced 950 artillery and rocket launchers while the Soviets have produced more than 13,000—a staggering 14-to-1 ratio.

There was a time when we were able to offset superior Soviet numbers with higher quality, but today they are building weapons as sophisticated and modern as our own.

As the Soviets have increased their military power, they've been emboldened to extend that power. They're spreading their military influence in ways that can directly challenge our vital interests and those of our allies.

The following aerial photographs, most of them secret until now, illustrate this point in a crucial area very close to home: Central America and the Caribbean Basin. They're not dramatic photographs. But I think they help give you a better understanding of what I'm talking about.

This Soviet intelligence collection facility, less than a hundred miles from our coast, is the largest of its kind in the world. The acres and acres of antennae fields and intelligence monitors are targeted on key U.S. military installations and sensitive activities. The installation in Lourdes, Cuba, is manned by 1,500 Soviet technicians. And the satellite ground station allows instant communications with Moscow. This 28-square-mile facility has grown by more than 60 percent in size and capability during the past decade.

In western Cuba, we see this military airfield and its complement of modern, Soviet-built Mig-23 aircraft. The Soviet Union uses this Cuban airfield for its own long-range reconnaissance missions. And earlier this month, two modern Soviet antisubmarine warfare aircraft began operating from it. During the past 2 years, the level of Soviet arms exports to Cuba can only be compared to the levels reached during the Cuban missile crisis 20 years ago.

This third photo, which is the only one in this series that has been previously made public, shows Soviet military hardware that has made its way to Central America. This airfield with its MI-8 helicopters, anti-aircraft guns, and protected fighter sites is one of a number of military facilities in Nicaragua which has received Soviet equipment funneled through Cuba, and reflects the massive military buildup going on in that country.

On the small island of Grenada, at the southern end of the Caribbean chain, the Cubans, with Soviet financing and backing, are in the process of building an airfield with a 10,000-foot runway. Grenada doesn't even have an air force. Who is it intended for? The Caribbean is a very important passageway for our international commerce and military lines of communication. More than half of all American oil imports now pass through the Caribbean. The rapid buildup of Grenada's military potential is unrelated to any conceivable threat to this island country of under 110,000 people and totally at odds with the pattern of other eastern Caribbean States, most of which are unarmed.

The Soviet-Cuban militarization of Grenada, in short, can only be seen as power projection into the region. And it is in this important economic and strategic area that we're trying to help the Governments of El Salvador, Costa Rica, Honduras, and others in their struggles for democracy against guerrillas supported through Cuba and Nicaragua.

These pictures only tell a small part of the story. I wish I could show you more without compromising our most sensitive intelligence sources and methods. But the Soviet Union is also supporting Cuban military forces in Angola and Ethiopia. They have bases in Ethiopia and South Yemen, near the Persian Gulf oil fields. They've taken over the port that we built at Cam Ranh Bay in Vietnam. And now for the first time in history, the Soviet Navy is a force to be reckoned with in the South Pacific.

Some people may still ask: Would the Soviets ever use their formidable military power? Well, again, can we afford to believe they won't? There is Afghanistan. And in Poland, the Soviets denied the will of the people and in so doing demonstrated to the world how their military power could also be used to intimidate.

The final fact is that the Soviet Union is acquiring what can only be considered an offensive military force. They have continued to build far more intercontinental ballistic missiles than they could possibly need simply to deter an attack. Their conventional forces are trained and equipped not so much to defend against an attack as they are to permit sudden, surprise offensives of their own.

Our NATO allies have assumed a great defense burden, including the military draft in most countries. We're working with them and our other friends around the world to do more. Our defensive strategy means we need military forces that can move very quickly, forces that are trained and ready to respond to any emergency.

Every item in our defense program—our ships, our tanks, our planes, our funds for training and spare parts—is intended for one all-important purpose: to keep the peace. Unfortunately, a decade of neglecting our military forces had called into question our ability to do that.

When I took office in January 1981, I was appalled by what I found: American planes that couldn't fly and American ships that couldn't sail for lack of spare parts and trained personnel and insufficient fuel and ammunition for essential training. The inevitable result of all this was poor morale in our Armed Forces, difficulty in recruiting the brightest young Americans to wear the uniform, and difficulty in convincing our most experienced military personnel to stay on.

There was a real question then about how well we could meet a crisis. And it was obvious that we had to begin a major modernization program to ensure we could deter aggression and preserve the peace in the years ahead.

We had to move immediately to improve the basic readiness and staying power of our conventional forces, so they could meet—and therefore help deter—a crisis. We had to make up for lost years of investment by moving forward with a long-term plan to prepare our forces to counter the military capabilities our adversaries were developing for the future.

I know that all of you want peace, and so do I. I know too that many of you seriously believe that a nuclear freeze would further the cause of peace. But a freeze now would make us less, not more, secure and would raise, not reduce, the risks of war. It would be largely unverifiable and would seriously undercut our negotiations on arms reduction. It would reward the Soviets for their massive military buildup while preventing us from modernizing our aging and increasingly vulnerable forces. With their present margin of superiority, why should they agree to arms reductions knowing that we were prohibited from catching up?

Believe me, it wasn't pleasant for someone who had come to Washington determined to reduce government spending, but we had to move forward with the task of repairing our defenses or we would lose our ability to deter conflict now and in the future. We had to demonstrate to any adversary that aggression could not succeed, and that the only real solution was substantial, equitable, and effectively verifiable arms reduction—the kind we're working for right now in Geneva.

Thanks to your strong support, and bipartisan support from the Congress, we began to turn things around. Already, we're seeing some very encouraging results. Quality recruitment and retention are up dramatically—more high school graduates are choosing military careers, and more experienced career personnel are choosing to stay. Our men and women in uniform at last are getting the tools and training they need to do their jobs.

Ask around today, especially among our young people, and I think you will find a whole new attitude toward serving ehrir country. This reflects more than just better pay, equipment, and leadership. You the American people have sent a signal to these young people that it is once again an honor to wear the uniform. That's not something you measure in a budget, but it's a very real part of our nation's strength.

It'll take us longer to build the kind of equipment we need to keep peace in the future, but we've made a good start.

We haven't built a new long-range bomber for 21 years. Now we're building the B-1. We hadn't launched one new strategic submarine for 17 years. Now we're building one Trident submarine a year. Our land-based missiles are increasingly threatened by the many huge, new Soviet ICBM's. We're determining how to solve that problem. At the same time, we're working in the START and INF negotiations with the goal of achieving deep reductions in the strategic and intermediate nuclear arsenals of both sides.

We have also begun the long-needed modernization of our conventional forces. The Army is getting its first new tank in 20 years. The Air Force is modernizing. We're rebuilding our Navy, which shrank from about a thousand ships in the late 1960's to 453 during the 1970's. Our nation needs a superior navy to support our military forces and vital interests overseas. We're now on the road to achieving a 600-ship navy and increasing the amphibious capabilities of our marines, who are now serving the cause of peace in Lebanon. And we're building a real capability to assist our friends in the vitally important Indian Ocean and Persian Gulf region.

This adds up to a major effort, and it isn't cheap. It comes at a time when there are many other pressures on our budget and when the American people have already had to make major sacrifices during the recession. But we must not be misled by those who would make defense once again the scapegoat of the Federal budget.

The fact is that in the past few decades we have seen a dramatic shift in how we spend the taxpayer's dollar. Back in 1955, payments to individuals took up only about 20 percent of the Federal budget. For nearly three decades, these payments steadily increased and, this year, will account for 49 percent of the budget. By contrast, in 1955 defense took up more than half of the Federal budget. By 1980 this spending had fallen to a low of 23 percent. Even with the increase that I am requesting this year, defense will still amount to only 28 percent of the budget.

The calls for cutting back the defense budget come in nice, simple arithmetic. They're the same kind of talk that led the democracies to neglect their defenses in the 1930's and invited the tragedy of World War II. We must not let that grim chapter of history repeat itself through apathy or neglect.

This is why I'm speaking to you tonight—to urge you to tell your Senators and Congressmen that you know we must continue to restore our military strength. If we stop in midstream, we will send a signal of decline, of lessened will, to friends and adversaries alike. Free people must voluntarily, through open debate and democratic means, meet the challenge that totalitarians pose by compulsion. It's up to us, in our time, to choose and choose wisely between the hard but necessary task of preserving peace and freedom and the temptation to ignore our duty and blindly hope for the best while the enemies of freedom grow stronger day by day.

The solution is well within our grasp. But to reach it, there is simply no alternative but to continue this year, in this budget, to provide the resources we need to preserve the peace and guarantee our freedom.

Now, thus far tonight I've shared with you my thoughts on the problems of national security we must face together. My predecessors in the Oval Office have appeared before you on other occasions to describe the threat posed by Soviet power and have proposed steps to address that threat. But since the advent of nuclear weapons, those steps have been increasingly directed toward deterrence of aggression through the promise of retaliation.

This approach to stability through offensive threat has worked. We and our allies have succeeded in preventing nuclear war for more than three decades. In recent months, however, my advisers, including in particular the Joint Chiefs of Staff, have underscored the necessity to break out of a future that relies solely on offensive retaliation for our security.

Over the course of these discussions, I've become more and more deeply convinced that the human spirit must be capable of rising above dealing with other nations and human beings by threatening their existence. Feeling this way, I believe we must thoroughly examine every opportunity for reducing tensions and for introducing greater stability into the strategic calculus on both sides.

One of the most important contributions we can make is, of course, to lower the level of all arms, and particularly nuclear arms. We're engaged right now in several negotiations with the Soviet Union to bring about a mutual reduction of weapons. I will report to you a week from tomorrow my thoughts on that score. But let me just say, I'm totally committed to this course.

If the Soviet Union will join with us in our effort to achieve major arms reduction, we will have succeeded in stabilizing the nuclear balance. Nevertheless, it will still be necessary to rely on the specter of retaliation, on mutual threat. And that's a sad commentary on the human condition. Wouldn't it be better to save lives than to avenge them? Are we not capable of demonstrating our peaceful intentions by applying all our abilities and our ingenuity to achieving a truly lasting stability? I think we are. Indeed, we must.

After careful consultation with my advisers, including the Joint Chiefs of Staff, I believe there is a way. Let me share with you a vision of the future which offers hope. It is that we embark on a program to counter the awesome Soviet missile threat with measures that are defensive. Let us turn to the very strengths in technology that spawned our great industrial base and that have given us the quality of life we enjoy today.

What if free people could live secure in the knowledge that their security did not rest upon the threat of instant U.S. retaliation to deter a Soviet attack, that we could intercept and destroy strategic ballistic missiles before they reached our own soil or that of our allies?

I know this is a formidable, technical task, one that may not be accomplished before the end of this century. Yet, current technology has attained a level of sophistication where it's reasonable for us to begin this effort. It will take years, probably decades of effort on many fronts. There will be failures and setbacks, just as there will be successes and breakthroughs. And as we proceed, we must remain constant in preserving the nuclear deterrent and maintaining a solid capability for flexible response. But isn't it worth every investment necessary to free the world from the threat of nuclear war? We know it is.

In the meantime, we will continue to pursue real reductions in nuclear arms, negotiating from a position of strength that can be ensured only by modernizing our strategic forces. At the same time, we must take steps to reduce the risk of a conventional military conflict escalating to nuclear war by improving our non-nuclear capabilities.

America does possess—now—the technologies to attain very significant improvements in the effectiveness of our conventional, non-nuclear forces. Proceeding boldly with these new technologies, we can significantly reduce any incentive that the Soviet Union may have to threaten attack against the United States or its allies.

As we pursue our goal of defensive technologies, we recognize that our allies rely upon our strategic offensive power to deter attacks against them. Their vital interests and ours are inextricably linked. Their safety and ours are once. And no change in technology can or will alter that reality. We must and shall continue to honor our commitments.

I clearly recognize that defensive systems have limitations and raise certain problems and ambiguities. If paired with offensive systems, they can be viewed as fostering an aggressive policy, and no one wants that. But with these considerations firmly in mind, I call upon the scientific community in our country, those who gave us nuclear weapons, to turn their great talents now to the cause of mankind and world peace, to give us the means of rendering these nuclear weapons impotent and obsolete.

Tonight, consistent with our obligations of the ABM treaty and recognizing the need for closer consultation with our allies, I'm taking an important first step. I am directing a comprehensive and intensive effort to define a long-term research and development program to begin to achieve our ultimate goal of eliminating the threat posed by strategic nuclear missiles. This could pave the way for arms control measures to eliminate the weapons themselves. We seek neither military superiority nor political advantage. Our only purpose—one all people share—is to search for ways to reduce the danger of nuclear war.

My fellow Americans, tonight we're launching an effort which holds the promise of changing the course of human history. There will be risks, and results take time. But I believe we can do it. As we cross this threshold, I ask for your prayers and your support.

Thank you, good night, and God bless you.

Note: The President spoke at 8:02 PM from the Oval Office at the White House. The address was broadcast live on nationwide radio and television.

Following his remarks, the President met in the White House with a number of administration officials, including members of the Cabinet, the White House staff, and the Joint Chiefs of Staff, and former officials of past administrations to discuss the address.

WHITE HOUSE PAPER

The President's Strategic Defense Initiative

White House Paper. This white paper, an official statement offering the government's rationale on a particular issue, explains SDI and indicates that it is believed to enhance the deterrent effect of our nuclear arsenal.

White House Paper, "The President's Strategic Defense Initiative." Washington, D.C.: U.S. President, 1985. 10 pp.

> What if free people could live secure in the knowledge that their security did not rest upon the threat of instant U.S. retaliation to deter a Soviet attack, that we could intercept and destroy strategic ballistic missiles before they reached our own soil or that of our allies?
>
> —President Reagan, March 23, 1983 speech

The President's Vision

In his March 23rd address to the nation, the President described his vision of a world free of its overwhelming dependence on nuclear weapons, a world free once and for all of the threat of nuclear war. The Strategic Defense Initiative, by itself, cannot fully realize this vision nor solve all the security challenges we and our allies will face in the future; for this we will need to seek many solutions—political as well as technological. A long road with much hard work lies ahead of us. The President believes we must begin now. The Strategic Defense Initiative takes a crucial first step.

The basic security of the United States and our allies rests upon our collective ability to deter aggression. Our nuclear retaliatory forces help achieve this security and have deterred war for nearly forty years. Since World War II, nuclear weapons have not been used; there has been no direct military conflict between the two largest world powers, and Europe has not seen such an extended period of peace since the last century. The fact is, however, that we have no defense against nuclear ballistic missile attack. And, as the Soviet building program widens the imbalance in key offensive capabilities, introducing systems whose status and characteristics are more difficult to confirm, our vulnerability and that of our allies to blackmail becomes quite high. In the event deterrence failed, a President's only recourse would be to surrender or to retaliate. Nuclear retaliation, whether massive or limited, would result in the loss of millions of lives.

The President believes strongly that we must find a better way to assure credible deterrence. If we apply our great scientific and engineering talent to the problem of defending against ballistic missiles, there is a very real possibility that future presidents will be able to deter war by means other than threatening devastation to any aggressor—and by a means which threatens no one.

The President's goal, and his challenge to our scientists and engineers, is to identify the technological problems and to find the technical solutions so that we have the option of using the potential of strategic defenses to provide a more effective, more stable means of keeping the United States and our allies secure from aggression and coercion. The Joint Chiefs of Staff, many respected scientists, and other experts believe that, with firm leadership and adequate funding, recent advances in defensive technologies could make such defenses achievable.

What Is the President's Strategic Defense Initiative

The President announced his Strategic Defense Initiative (SDI) in his March 23, 1983, address to the nation. Its purpose is to identify ways to exploit recent advances in ballistic missile defense technologies that have potential for strengthening deterrence—and thereby increasing our security and that of our allies. The program is designed to answer a number of fundamental scientific and engineering questions that must be addressed before the promise of these new technologies can be fully assessed. The SDI research program will provide to a future President and a future Congress the technical knowledge necessary to support a decision in the early 1990's on whether to develop and deploy such advanced defensive systems.

As a broad research program, the SDI is not based on any single or preconceived notion of what an effective defense system would look like. A number of different concepts, involving a wide range of technologies, are being examined. No single concept or technology has been identified as the best or the most appropriate. A number of non-nuclear technologies hold promise for dealing effectively with ballistic missiles.

We do feel, however, that the technologies that are becoming available today may offer the possibility of providing a layered defense—a defense that uses various technologies to destroy attacking missiles during each phase of their flight.

- Some missiles could be destroyed shortly after they launch as they burn their engines and boost their warheads into space. By destroying a missile during this boost phase, we would also destroy all of the nuclear warheads it carries at the same time. In the case of ICBMs, they would probably be destroyed before leaving the territory of the aggressor.
- Next, we could destroy those nuclear warheads that survive the boost phase by attacking them during the post-boost phase. During this phase we would target the device that sits on top of the missile and is used to dispense its warheads while it is in the process of releasing its cargo. By destroying this device, the post-boost vehicle, we can destroy all the warheads not yet released.
- Those warheads that have been released and survive, travel for tens of minutes in the void of space on their ballistic trajectories towards their targets. While we would now have to locate, identify, and destroy the individual nuclear warheads themselves, this relatively long mid-course phase of flight again offers us time to exploit advanced technologies to do just that.
- Finally, those warheads that survive the outer layers of defense, could be attacked during the terminal phase as they approach the end of their ballistic flight.

The concept of a layered defense could be extremely effective because the progressive layers would be able to work together to provide many opportunities to destroy attacking nuclear warheads well before they approach our territory or that of our allies. An opponent facing several separate layers of defenses would find it difficult to redesign his missiles and their nuclear warheads to penetrate all of the layers. Moreover, defenses during the boost, post-boost and mid-course phases of ballistic missile flight make no distinction in the targets of the attacking missiles—they simply destroy attacking nuclear warheads, and in the process protect people and our country. The combined effectiveness of the defense provided by the multiple layers need not provide 100% protection in order to enhance deterrence significantly. It need only create sufficient uncertainty in the mind of a potential aggressor concerning his ability to succeed in the purposes of his attack. The concept of a layered defense certainly will help do this.

There have been considerable advances in technology since U.S. ballistic missile defenses were first developed in the 1960's. At the time the ABM Treaty was signed (1972), ballistic missile defense prospects were largely confined to the attacking nuclear warheads during the terminal phase of their flight using nuclear-tipped interceptor missiles. Since that time, emerging technologies offer the possibility of non-nuclear options for destroying missiles and the nuclear warheads they carry in all phases of their flight. New technologies may be able to permit a layered defense by providing sensors for identifying and tracking missiles and nuclear warheads; advanced ground and spaceborne interceptors and directed energy weapons to destroy both missiles and nuclear warheads; and, the technology to permit the command, control, and communications necessary to operate a layered defense.

In the planning that went into the SDI research program, we consciously chose to look broadly at defense against ballistic missiles as it could be applied across all these phases of missile flight: boost, post-boost, mid-course, and terminal. Although it is too early to define fully those individual technologies or applications which will ultimately prove to be most effective, such a layered approach maximizes the application of emerging technology and holds out the possibility of destroying nuclear warheads well before they reach the territory of the United States or our allies.

As President Reagan made clear at the start of this effort, the SDI research program will be consistent with all U.S. treaty obligations, including the ABM Treaty. The Soviets, who have and are improving the world's only existing anti-ballistic missile system (deployed around Moscow), are continuing a program of research on both traditional and advanced anti–ballistic missile technologies that has been underway for many years. But while the President has directed that the United States effort be conducted in a manner that is consistent with the ABM Treaty, the Soviet Union almost certainly is violating that Treaty by constructing a large ballistic missile early warning radar in Siberia (at Krasnoyarsk) which is located and oriented in a manner prohibited by the Treaty. This radar could contribute significantly to the Soviet Union's considerable potential to rapidly expand its deployed ballistic missile defense capability.

The United States has offered to discuss with the Soviet Union the implications of defensive technologies being explored by both countries. Such a discussion would be useful in helping to clarify both sides' understanding of the relationship between offensive and defensive forces and in clarifying the purposes that underlie the United States and Soviet programs. Further, this dialogue could lead to agreement to work together toward a more stable strategic relationship than exists today.

Why SDI?

SDI and Deterrence. The primary responsibility of a government is to provide for the security of its people. Deterrence of aggression is the most certain path to ensure that we and our allies survive as free and independent nations. Providing a better, more stable basis for enhanced deterrence is the central purpose of the SDI program.

Under the SDI program, we are conducting intensive research focused on advanced defensive technologies with the aim of enhancing the basis of deterrence, strengthening stability, and thereby increasing the security of the United States and our allies. On many occasions, the President has stated his strong belief that "a nuclear war cannot be won and must never be fought." U.S. policy has always been one of deterring aggression and will remain so even if a decision is made in the future to deploy defensive systems. The purpose of SDI is to strengthen deterrence and lower the level of nuclear forces.

Defensive systems are consistent with a policy of deterrence both historically and theoretically. While today we rely almost exclusively on the threat of retaliation with offensive forces for our strategic deterrence, this has not always been the case. Throughout the 1950's and most of the 1960's, the United States maintained an extensive air defense network to protect North America from attack by Soviet bomber forces. At that time, this network formed an important part of our deterrent capability. It was allowed to decline only when the Soviet emphasis shifted to intercontinental ballistic missiles, a threat for which there was previously no effective defense. Recent advances in ballistic missile defense technologies, however, provide more than sufficient reason to believe that defensive systems could eventually provide a better and more stable basis for deterrence.

Effective defenses against ballistic missiles have potential for enhancing deterrence in the future in a number of ways. First, they could significantly increase an aggressor's uncertainties regarding whether his weapons would penetrate the defenses and destroy our missiles and other military targets. It would be very difficult for a potential aggressor to predict his own vulnerability in the face of such uncertainties. It would restore the condition that attacking could never leave him better off. An aggressor will be much less likely to contemplate initiating a nuclear conflict, even in crisis circumstances, while lacking confidence in his ability to succeed.

Such uncertainties also would serve to reduce or eliminate the incentive for first strike attack. Modern, accurate ICBMs carrying multiple nuclear warheads—if deployed in sufficiently large numbers relative to the size of an opponent's force structure, as the Soviets have done with their ICBM force—could be used in a rapid first strike to undercut an opponent's ability to retaliate effectively. By significantly reducing or eliminating the ability of ballistic missiles to attack military forces effectively, and thereby rendering them impotent and obsolete as a means of supporting aggression, advanced defenses could remove this potential major source of instability.

Finally, in conjunction with air defenses, very effective defenses against ballistic missiles could help reduce or eliminate the apparent military value of nuclear attack to an aggressor. By preventing an aggressor from destroying a significant portion of our country, an aggressor would have gained nothing by attacking in the first place. In this way, very effective defenses could reduce substantially the possibility of nuclear conflict.

If we take the prudent and necessary steps to maintain strong, credible military forces, there is every reason to believe that deterrence will continue to preserve the peace. However, even with the utmost vigilance, few things in this world are absolutely certain, and a responsible government must consider the remote possibility that deterrence could fail. Today, the United States and our allies have no defense against ballistic missile attack. We also have very limited capability to defend the United States against an attack by enemy bombers. If deterrence were to fail, without a shield of any kind, it could cause the death of most of our population and the destruction of our nation as we know it. The SDI program provides our only long-term hope to change this situation.

Defenses also could provide insurance against either accidental ballistic missile launches or launches by some future irrational leader in possession of a nuclear armed missile. While such events are improbable, they are not inconceivable. The United States and other nuclear-capable powers have instituted appropriate safeguards against inadvertent launches by their own forces and together have formulated policies to preclude the proliferation of nuclear weapons. Nonetheless, it is difficult to predict the future course of events. While we hope, and expect that our best efforts will continue to be successful, our national security interests will be well served by a vigorous SDI research program that could provide an additional safeguard against such potentially catastrophic events.

Today our retaliatory forces provide a strong sword to deter aggression. However, the President seeks a better way of maintaining deterrence. For the future, the SDI program strives to provide a defensive shield which will do more than simply make that deterrence stronger. It will allow us to build a better, more stable basis for deterrence. And, at the same time, that same shield will provide necessary protection should an aggressor not be deterred.

Insurance against Soviet Defensive Technology Program. While we refer to our program as the President's Strategic Defense Initiative some have the misconception that the United States alone is pursuing an increased emphasis on defensive systems—a unilateral U.S. action which will alter the strategic balance. This is not the case. The Soviet Union has always considered defense to be a central and natural part of its national security policy. The extensive, advanced Soviet air defense network and large civil defense program are obvious examples of this priority.

But in addition to this, the Soviets have for many years been working on a number of technologies, both traditional and advanced, with potential for defending against ballistic missiles. For example, while within the constraints of the ABM Treaty, the Soviet Union currently is upgrading the capability of the only operational ABM system in the world today—the Moscow ABM defense system.

The Soviets are also engaged in research and development on a rapidly deployable ABM system that raises concerns about their potential ability to break out of the ABM Treaty and deploy a nationwide ABM defense system within the next ten years should they choose to do so. Were they to do so, as they could, deterrence would collapse, and we would have no choices between surrender and suicide.

In addition to these ABM efforts, some of the Soviet Union's air defense missiles and radars are also of particular concern. The Soviet Union already possesses an extensive air defense network. With continued improvements to this network, it could also provide some degree of ABM protection for the Soviet Union and its Warsaw Pact allies—and do so all nominally within the bounds prescribed by the ABM Treaty.

Since the late 1960's, the Soviet Union also has been pursuing a substantial, advanced defensive technologies program—a program which has been exploring many of the same technologies of interest to the United States in the SDI program. In addition to covering a wide range of advanced technologies, including various laser and neutral particle beams, the Soviet program apparently has been much larger than the U.S. effort in terms of resources invested—plant, capital, and manpower. In fact, over the last two decades, the Soviet Union has spent roughly as much on defense as it has on its massive offensive program.

The SDI program is a prudent response to the very active Soviet research and development activities in this field and provides insurance against Soviet efforts to develop and deploy unilaterally an advanced defensive system. A unilateral Soviet deployment of such advanced defenses, in concert with the Soviet Union's massive offensive forces and its already impressive air and passive defense capabilities, would destroy the foundation on which deterrence has rested for twenty years.

In pursuing the Strategic Defense Initiative, the United States is striving to fashion a future environment that serves the security interests of the United States and our allies, as well as the Soviet Union. Consequently, should it prove possible to develop a highly capable defense against ballistic missiles, we would envision parallel United States and Soviet deployments, with the outcome being enhanced mutual security and international stability.

Requirements for an Effective Defense

To achieve the benefits which advanced defensive technologies could offer, they must, at a minimum, be able to destroy a sufficient portion of an aggressor's attacking forces to deny him confidence in the outcome of an attack or deny an aggressor the ability to destroy a militarily significant portion of the target base he wishes to attack. The level of defense system capability required to achieve these ends cannot be determined at this time, depending as it does on the size, composition, effectiveness, and passive survivability of U.S. forces relative to those of the Soviet Union. Any effective defensive system must, of course, be survivable and cost-effective.

To achieve the required level of survivability, the defensive system need not be invulnerable, but must be able to maintain a sufficient degree of effectiveness to fulfill its mission, even in the face of determined attacks against it. This characteristic is essential not only to maintain the effectiveness of a defense system, but to maintain stability.

Finally, in the interest of discouraging the proliferation of ballistic missile forces, the defensive system must be able to maintain its effectiveness against the offense at less cost than it would take to develop offensive countermeasures and proliferate the ballistic missiles necessary to overcome it. ABM systems of the past have lacked this essential capability, but the newly emerging technologies being pursued under the SDI program have great potential in this regard.

Current Programs

Today, deterrence against Soviet aggression is grounded almost exclusively in the capabilities of our offensive retaliatory forces, and this is likely to remain true for some time. Consequently, the SDI program in no way signals a near-term shift away from the modernization of our strategic and intermediate-range nuclear systems and our conventional military forces. Such modernization is essential to the maintenance of deterrence while we are pursuing the generation of technologically feasible defensive options. In addition, in the event a decision to deploy a defensive system were made by a future President, having a modern and capable retaliatory deterrent force would be essential to the preservation of a stable environment while the shift is made to a different and enhanced basis for deterrence.

Arms Control

As directed by the President, the SDI research program will be conducted in a manner fully consistent with all U.S. treaty obligations, including the 1972 ABM Treaty. The ABM Treaty prohibits the development, testing, and deployment of ABM systems and components that are space-based, air-based, sea-based, or mobile land-based. However, as Gerard Smith, chief U.S. negotiator of the ABM Treaty, reported to the Senate Armed Services Committee in 1972, that agreement does permit research short of field testing of a prototype ABM system or component. This is the type of research that will be conducted under the SDI program.

Any future national decision to deploy defensive systems would, of course, lead to an important change in the structure of United States and Soviet forces. We are examining ways in which the offense/defense relationship can be managed to achieve a more stable balance through strategic arms control. Above all, we seek to ensure that the interaction of offensive and defensive forces removes first-strike options from either side's capability.

The United States does not view defensive measures as a means of establishing military superiority. Because we have no ambitions in this regard, deployments of defensive systems would most usefully be done in the context of a cooperative, equitable, and verifiable arms control environment that regulates the offensive and defensive developments and deployments of the United States and Soviet Union. Such an environment could be particularly useful in the period of transition from a deterrent based on the threat of nuclear retaliation, through deterrence based on a balance of offensive and defensive forces, to the period when adjustments to the basis of deterrence are complete and advanced defensive systems are fully deployed. During the transition, arms control agreements could help to manage and establish guidelines for the deployment of defensive systems.

The SDI research program will complement and support U.S. efforts to seek equitable, verifiable reductions in offensive nuclear forces through arms control negotiations. Such reductions would make a useful contribution to stability, whether in today's deterrence environment or in a potential future deterrence environment in which defenses played a leading role.

A future decision to develop and deploy effective defenses against ballistic missiles could support our policy of pursuing significant reductions in ballistic missile forces. To the extent that defensive systems could reduce the effectiveness and, thus, value of ballistic missiles, they also could increase the incentives for negotiated reductions. Significant reductions in turn would serve to increase the effectiveness and deterrent potential of defensive systems.

SDI and the Allies

Because our security is inextricably linked to that of our friends and allies, the SDI program will not confine itself solely to an exploitation of technologies with potential against ICBMs and SLBMs, but will also carefully examine technologies with potential against shorter-range ballistic missiles.

An effective defense against shorter range ballistic missiles could have a significant impact on deterring aggression in Europe. Soviet SS-20's, SCALEBOARDs, and other shorter-range ballistic missiles provide overlapping capabilities to strike all of NATO Europe. Moreover, Soviet doctrine stresses the use of conventionally-armed ballistic missiles to initiate rapid and wide-ranging attacks on cruciel NATO military targets throughout Europe. The purpose of this tactic would be to reduce significantly NATO's ability to resist the initial thrust of a Soviet conventional force attack and to impede NATO's ability to resupply and reinforce its combatants from outside Europe. By reducing or eliminating the military effectiveness of such ballistic missiles, defensive systems have the potential for enhancing deterrence against not only strategic nuclear war, but against nuclear and conventional attacks on our allies as well.

Over the next several years, we will work closely with our allies to ensure that, in the event of any future decision to deploy defensive systems (a decision in which consultation with our allies will play an important part), allied, as well as U.S. security against aggression would be enhanced.

CASPAR W. WEINBERGER

To the Congress of the United States

Caspar W. Weinberger (b. 1917), Secretary of Defense in the Reagan administration, has spent much of his career dealing with budgetary issues for Republican administrations. He is trained as a lawyer. Each year the secretary addresses Congress to present the new defense budget.

Reprinted from the *Annual Report to the Congress, Fiscal Year 1985* (Washington, D.C.: U.S. Government Printing Office, 1984), pp. 3–9.

Three years ago a newly inaugurated President Ronald Reagan stood at the West Front of the Capitol and promised that "when action is required to preserve our national security, we will act." Recognizing that the preservation of peace required more than just rhetoric or good intentions, he committed his Administration to take the steps necessary to deter aggression and promote stability and freedom in a complex and changing world.

For a President taking office in January 1981, this was not a pledge to be given lightly. By the beginning of this decade, a majority of Americans were expressing their concern, indeed their fear, that the world had become a more dangerous place. They recognized that we faced a crisis of leadership, as the impression grew both at home and abroad that the United States was a superpower on the decline, unable to protect its citizens or its interests against a growing threat.

The 1980 election sent a clear signal that the American people wanted to reverse this dangerous slide and to restore America's position in the world. They recognized that we must regain the strength of our armed forces and restore the military balance so essential for preserving deterrence. They recognized that we must begin again the quest for genuine arms reductions, not settling for negotiations that resulted in merely codifying the growth in nuclear arsenals. We seek agreements that will *reduce* armaments of all kinds to lower, equal, and verifiable levels. Finally, they recognized that the United States, while it could not and should not be the world's policeman, nevertheless needed to reassume a leadership role recognized by our allies and friends, and our foes and potential enemies.

The American people entrusted responsibility for fulfilling this mandate to Ronald Reagan, and he and his Administration accepted that responsibility. Today, we have firm leadership to keep us steady on our course—leadership that combines a realistic understanding of the dangers and complexities of our world with a firm commitment to do what is necessary to preserve peace.

In this year's *Annual Report to the Congress,* we present our defense program for preserving peace in a dangerous world. We also assess this Administration's three-year stewardship of our nation's defenses, and the progress we have made toward fulfilling the mandate entrusted by the American people to Ronald Reagan in 1980.

A Realistic Approach to Peace

"A safer world," President Reagan told the American Legion last August, "will not be realized simply through honorable intentions and good will. . . . No, the pursuit of the fundamental goals our nation seeks in world affairs—peace, human rights, economic progress, national independence, and international stability—requires a dedicated effort to support our friends and defend our interests. Our commitment as peacemaker is focused on those goals."

In making this statement, President Reagan confronted the paradox of peace—that to preserve it, the peacemaker must be prepared to use force and use it successfully. Only if we can convince any potential adversary that the cost of aggression would be far greater than any possible benefit, can we be certain that aggression will be deterred and peace preserved.

We had to begin with a hard look at the challenges facing this nation as it entered a new decade. Our alliances were being subjected to new strains, as expanding Soviet military power required greater defense efforts by all members to restore the military balance. In the Third World, we saw the reach and intensity of conflict fueled by increased Soviet support for terrorism, insurgency, and aggression. Above all, at the beginning of this decade we were confronted by a Soviet Union increasingly capable of upsetting the stability of nuclear deterrence, of projecting power well beyond its borders, and of conducting offensive operations with larger, technologically sophisticated, and increasingly flexible forces.

This renewed sense of realism about the challenges we faced only strengthened our resolve to work for peace. Indeed, by directly facing the dangers posed by the erosion in the military balance with the Soviet Union, and by demonstrating in Grenada and Lebanon that the United States would not be held hostage to terrorism, President Reagan's leadership enhanced deterrence by strengthening the confidence of our friends and allies and complicating the calculations of potential aggressors.

Similarly, a realistic appraisal of Soviet negotiating behavior—an appraisal that does not rely on assumptions of Soviet good will—has improved the prospects for arms reductions. We recognized that the Soviets would accept genuine, significant, verifiable arms reductions only if they became convinced that the alternative was not Soviet superiority, but an American determination to maintain the strategic balance. By demonstrating the capability and the will to restore that balance, we are offering the Soviets a strong incentive to join us in reaching a negotiated "build-down" of the most dangerous arsenal ever to threaten mankind.

Restoring America's Defenses

In facing up to the realities of a dangerous world, we also had to confront the serious deterioation of our own military posture. Any one of the problems we faced—low levels of readiness and sustainability, difficulty recruiting and retaining qualified personnel, shortfalls and obsolescence of military hardware, and higher costs from inefficient management of defense resources—would have required immediate attention. This Administration had little choice but to address them simultaneously if we were to fulfill President Reagan's pledge and, indeed, the American people's mandate to *act* to preserve our national security. And so, with the bipartisan support of the Congress, we started a major effort to restore the strength of our defenses.

Readiness and Sustainability. By the beginning of this decade, the readiness of our forces to meet a crisis and sustain operations had seriously eroded. In a speech from the Oval Office last March, President Reagan recalled from the early days of his Administration that "I was appalled by what I found: American planes that could not fly and American ships that could not sail for lack of spare parts and trained personnel, and insufficient fuel and ammunition for essential training." Depleted stores of vital military supplies were inadequate for combat operations, encouraging potential aggressors to calculate they could outlast us in a conventional conflict.

We acted immediately to improve the readiness and sustainability of our forces. Today, three years later, 39% more of our major military units are categorized as fully or substantially ready for combat. At the same time, our capability to sustain our forces in the field will have increased by almost 50% when the munitions and secondary items procured by the FY 1985 budget are delivered.

Personnel. When this Administration took office, morale in the armed forces was dangerously low, the result of a failure to give our men and women in uniform the compensation, the tools, or the respect they needed and deserved. The quality of new recruits declined, while experienced personnel left the military in droves. Fewer than ten years after its establishment, many were claiming that the All-Volunteer Armed Forces was a failed experiment, and calling for a return to conscription.

Today, people are our biggest success story. Retention and recruiting are up dramatically. The Navy and Air Force attained record high reenlistment rates last year, and all the Services are meeting their recruiting quotas. Moreover, 91% of the new recruits are high school graduates, up from 68% in 1980. And these retention and recruiting successes are coming at a time when the economy is improving, a time when skeptics said young Americans would turn their backs on the military.

Conventional Modernization. This Administration also had to confront a major shortfall in weapons and equipment. Much of what we did have, moreover, was aging and increasingly obsolete compared with new Soviet hardware. The 1960s-era tanks, artillery, and armored vehicles in our ground forces were threatened with block obsolescence; the number of ships in our Navy had fallen by more than half; and our aircraft needed upgrading to counter dramatic improvements in Soviet aircraft and air defenses. Although the previous Administration had announced a new commitment to defend our access to resources in Southwest Asia, we lacked the airlift, sealift, and amphibious capabilities to move our forces quickly in time of crisis, or to support them if they became involved in combat.

It would be a heavy responsibility for any President or Secretary of Defense to have to order American troops into battle facing Soviet equipment that was known to be superior to ours. That is a responsibility the previous Administration would have had to face. We had to change that situation. Now, we can be confident that should war break out, our men will have equipment that is at least equal to, and in many cases superior to, that of the Soviets. For that very reason, it is increasingly unlikely we will have to test any of it in combat.

The FY 1982 budget and associated five-year plan of the previous Administration were not only inadequate for the rebuilding task we confronted; they were also gravely underfunded and could not have been carried out as planned. During the past three years, we have restored funding for several vitally needed programs, and are now successfully embarked on a long-term program to modernize our forces for the future.

Our ground forces are now receiving the modern weapons they need to deter quantitatively superior and increasingly sophisticated Soviet forces. The M-1 tank recently proved its tremendous capability in NATO's annual tank competition, performing better than any other U.S. tank in history. The Army's new Bradley fighting vehicle gives the infantry the mobility and firepower to fight alongside the tanks. And giving support and protection to those ground forces is the new multiple-launched rocket system (MLRS), which provides long-range artillery fire.

The Navy fleet now stands at 516 ships, as 23 modern, more capable ships were delivered in 1983. The saga of one of these ships—the battleship *New Jersey*—since she was recommissioned by President Reagan in December 1982 points out the timeliness of our naval expansion. Having left San Diego last summer on a shakedown cruise to Asia and the South Pacific, the *New Jersey* was then called back to Central America to support U.S. forces training there. She was next sent to the Eastern Mediterranean, where she remains on station supporting the multinational peacekeeping force. In her first year, the *New Jersey* put 30,000 miles under her keel.

The Marine Corps, with longer-range 155-m howitzers, CH-53E helicopters, and F/A-18 fighter and attack aircraft, will have even greater mobility and greater firepower to accomplish the wide range of missions it must be prepared to undertake. We are also revitalizing our amphibious assault capability with the construction of new amphibious ships and air cushion landing craft.

Over the past ten years, the Soviets have significantly increased both the quantity and quality of their aircraft. To maintain our qualitative edge in airpower, we are now producing advanced versions of the F-15 and F-16 tactical fighters, two of the finest aircraft in the world. We have also begun a large-scale acquisition program that will increase our intertheater airlift capability by 75% by the end of the decade.

Strategic Modernization. Dangerous obsolescence threatened all three legs of our strategic triad in 1980, challenging the stability of deterrence. When President Reagan took office, our *newest* long-range bomber was 19 years old. Our newest strategic submarine was 15 years old, and did not have missiles capable of destroying hardened Soviet targets. Our land-based missiles were increasingly threatened by huge, new, accurate Soviet ICBMs, while our own lacked the accuracy and destructive force we needed for continued deterrence.

Our strategic modernization program is now strengthening all three legs of the strategic triad, as well as our strategic command, control, and communications (C^3) systems.° Three successful tests of the Peacekeeper missile have now been completed. Our first new strategic bomber in more than thirty years is in production; and Trident II missiles now under development will provide our submarine force the increased payload and improved accuracy needed to assure effective retaliation against hardened targets. Finally, our C^3 systems are being modernized and upgraded.

At President Reagan's behest, we are also embarking on a bold new effort to develop a reliable defense against ballistic missiles. This will require many years, during which we will assess different technological options and secure the means to adopt the best. I believe it is the most significant step we can and will take to preserve peace with freedom and to pass on to our children the legacy of a safer world. It is a program that offers the hope of rendering nuclear missiles impotent. Removing this horror from the future is one of our highest priorities.

Management Reform. Upon taking office, we also discovered that the outdated defense procurement system contained few incentives to reduce costs or improve efficiency and failed to take full advantage of competition. Likewise, as investments in ammunition, spare parts, and new weapons and equipment were canceled, postponed, or stretched out, cost-efficient production became impossible. Many businesses decided to leave defense contracting altogether, further reducing competition and limiting our ability to mobilize resources in an emergency.

This Administration undertook a wide-ranging management reform program that included a thorough and forthright audit program to identify the sources of waste and inefficiency and a comprehensive acquisition improvement program to instill sound business practices in defense procurement. The extensive procurement reforms begun in 1981 are now paying dividends.

We are aggressively combating fraud and inefficiency. In the past fiscal year alone, 657 convictions and $14 million in fines, restitutions, and recoveries resulted from DoD and Justice Department cooperation. Our auditors, likewise, identified $1.6 billion in potential savings associated with greater efficiency.

We have taken firm steps to end the spare parts pricing abuses that we uncovered and reported. These reforms include tightening contracts, challenging high prices, obtaining refunds, continuing audits, and enhancing competition. Besides taking very firm and strict measures against irresponsible contractors and negligent employees, we are also rewarding those employees who come up with ways to save the taxpayers money.

C^3 Pronounced *c-cubed,* an abbreviation for command, control, and communications—various procedures to ensure that the president and the military have adequate communications during a nuclear encounter and that chains of command are clearly delineated to meet alternative attack possibilities. When intelligence operations are included in the procedure, the term is C^3I.

To obtain lower costs and better quality, we are stressing greater competition in defense procurement; and advocates of competition are now working in all buying commands to challenge noncompetitive purchases. Already we are seeing results; for example, competition to supply aircraft spare parts has tripled. To assure continued competition, new contracts include provisions designed to provide the data necessary to seek second sources of supply in purchasing parts.

To maintain control over costs, the Defense Department is enforcing realistic budget estimates in order to halt the past practice of over-optimistic estimates that made a weapon system appear affordable, but left a legacy of cost overruns. The Department is also making the tough decisions necessary to eliminate marginal programs and maintain high-priority programs at stable and efficient rates.

Meeting the Challenges of the Future

In 1984, we will continue our long-term defense program, all the wiser for the lessons we have learned in the past three years, and confident that we are on the right course. But let us have no illusions: the next few years will be as crucial for America's defense program as they will be difficult.

In weighing the investments we must make, we cannot forget that the costs of maintaining a strong defense are easily measured. But the benefits are not. When we spend our savings on a new car, or a new home, we have acquired a tangible good. When we spend tax dollars on food stamps or federal highways, we have created a tangible result for all to see. But although we can count our missiles, or our tanks, or our men in arms, we can never really measure how much aggression we have deterred, or how much peace we have preserved. These are intangibles—until they are lost.

Indeed, it is a paradox of deterrence that the longer it succeeds, the less necessary it appears. As time passes, the maintenance of peace is attributed not to a strong defense, but to a host of more facile assumptions: some imagined newfound "peaceful intent" of the opponent, or the spirit of détente, or growing economic interdependency.

As the bills that we as a nation put off too long continue to come due, it will be tempting to search for excuses to avoid the reckoning once more. We must not yield to that temptation. Already the Congress has cut back on our operations and maintenance budgets, threatening our improvements in readiness, and slowed down several programs, increasing the cost of what all agree we will need—and courting the dangers inherent in taking too long to secure an effective deterrent. Already critics of the defense budget are discovering a new enthusiasm for weapons that are—conveniently—still on the drawing boards, even as they oppose procurement of hardware available now to strengthen our forces.

Unfortunately, we cannot make up for a decade of neglect in only three years of higher defense budgets. Restoring—and then maintaining—the military balance requires a determined and sustained effort. If we stop in midcourse, we will only endanger the progress we have made in recent years, and invite speculation by friends and adversaries alike that the United States can sustain neither its will nor its leadership.

By the same token, if we are allowed to continue on the path we have set, we can look forward to a time, only two fiscal years from now, when defense increases can begin to slow dramatically.

The Fiscal Year 1985 *Annual Report to the Congress* presents a prudent and responsible defense budget, and provides a thorough rationale for that budget. It shows that we arrived at this budget not by picking a budget number arbitrarily, but by weighing the threats and challenges to our interests, by refining our strategy for meeting those threats, and by identifying the capabilities we need to fulfill that strategy. The report also analyzes the resources available for acquiring those capabilities, and describes in detail the specific programs for which we are requesting funds.

Most importantly, the report is a document to help members of Congress in this coming year as they confront important—and difficult—budgetary decisions that will shape America's security through the end of this century. Over the past three years, the Congress and this Administration have worked together to rebuild America's defenses and restore our leadership in the world. We have made great progress. This year, let us again work together to preserve our gains and move closer to our goal of a stronger and more secure America, which is the best guarantee of a lasting peace.

[Caspar W. Weinberger]

DEPARTMENT OF DEFENSE

Department of Defense Views on Major Nuclear Issues and Proposals to Freeze Nuclear Forces at Current Levels

The Department of Defense (DoD), the successor agency to the National Military Establishment and the Department of War, was cre-

---

Department of Defense, Office of the Assistant Secretary of Defense—Public Affairs, "Department of Defense Views on Major Nuclear Issues and Proposals to Freeze Nuclear Forces at Current Levels." Unpublished, August 1985.

ated by the National Security Act of 1947 and in 1949 became a part of the executive branch of the government. The Central headquarters of the DOD is the Pentagon. The DOD occasionally issues position statements on matters of public controversy, as it did in 1982 when the Freeze Initiative came before Congress. The following paper represents their views as of August 1985.

Background on the Administration Approach to Major Nuclear Issues

The primary security objective of the U.S. is to reduce the risk of war while maintaining our right, and that of our allies in Europe and Asia, to live in freedom. To achieve this objective, the Reagan Administration is proceding along several tracks:

Strengthening Deterrence. The essential purpose of our military forces is to deter aggression and coercion directed at the U.S. or our allies. For the foreseeable future, offensive nuclear forces will remain the key element of U.S. deterrence strategy because they hold open the prospect of imposing unacceptable costs on a potential aggressor. Over the past 15 years, however, the Soviet Union has eroded the stability of mutual deterrence by undertaking a massive expansion and modernization of its strategic nuclear forces, thereby posing an increasing threat to the survivability of our retaliatory forces. In response to serious and growing imbalances between Soviet and U.S. forces, the Reagan Administration has begun a strategic force modernization program that will strengthen our deterrent, enhance stability, and provide incentives to the Soviet Union to join with us in achieving real arms reduction.

Seeking Arms Reduction. Consistent with the Administration's objective of strengthening deterrence and improving stability, we are vigorously pursuing the negotiation of equitable and verifiable agreements leading to radical reductions in the existing nuclear arsenals of the U.S. and Soviet Union. To this end, the U.S. has proposed to the Soviets at the Nuclear and Space Talks in Geneva that we reduce ballistic missile warheads by about one-third (to a limit of 5,000 warheads on each side). Our negotiators also have proposed—as an interim step toward our goal of eliminating U.S. and Soviet longer-range intermediate nuclear forces (LRINF) in Europe—that we agree to equal global limits on LRINF missile warheads at the lowest possible level. The President has given our negotiators in Geneva great latitude and flexibility to find common ground with the Soviets and to explore possible trade-offs between areas of U.S. and Soviet advantage.

Insisting on Compliance. As part of this Administration's efforts to put the arms reduction process on a firm and lasting foundation, we have paid close attention to the question of compliance. The U.S. has complied fully with existing arms control obligations, whereas the Soviets have not. Among the arms control agreements which the Soviets have violated or probably violated are the unratified Strategic Arms Limitation Talks agreement (SALT II), the Anti-Ballistic Missile (ABM) Treaty, the Geneva Protocol on chemical weapons, the Limited Test Ban Treaty, and the nuclear testing limit of the unratified Threshold Test Ban Treaty. Despite our long and repeated efforts to resolve our serious compliance concerns, the Soviets have neither provided satisfactory explanations nor undertaken corrective action. While the U.S. is willing to go the extra mile in giving the Soviets the opportunity to correct their activities involving noncompliance, we cannot accept a double standard that amounts to unilateral treaty compliance by the U.S. and, in effect, unilateral disarmament. To do so would undermine U.S. security and wreck any chance for real, equitable, and verifiable arms control agreements in the future.

Confidence-Building Measures. The Reagan Administration has backed a broad range of confidence-building measures (CBMs) designed to: reduce the possibility of an accidental East-West confrontation, miscalculation, or failure of communication; inhibit opportunities for surprise attack; and increase stability in times of both calm and crisis. Of particular relevance to our efforts to reduce the risk of nuclear war is the July 1984 U.S.-Soviet agreement (first proposed by this Administration) to upgrade the technical capabilities of the "Hotline" that enables the President to communicate rapidly and directly with the Soviet leadership. Another Administration initiative came to fruition in June, 1985, when the U.S. and Soviet Union concluded an agreement (within the framework of the 1971 U.S.-USSR Agreement on Measures to Reduce the Risk of Outbreak of Nuclear War) designed to facilitate exchanges in the event of a nuclear incident involving unauthorized parties. Other nuclear-related CBMs proposed by this Administration in recent years include: prior notification of ballistic missile launches; expanded exchanges of data on U.S. and Soviet forces; and a U.S.-Soviet Joint Military Communications Link that would, among other things, serve to complement Hotline exchanges and avoid or resolve any potentially serious incident involving the two countries.

Exploring New Technologies. New advanced technologies hold considerable potential for strengthening various elements of our nuclear deterrence posture. For example, in response to the Soviet buildup of offensive nuclear forces and to their large and longstanding programs to develop and improve strategic defenses—including the capability to deploy a territorial ballistic missile defense—the Reagan Administration has established a Strategic Defense Initiative (SDI). The SDI is a research program designed to study whether new defensive technologies could be used in a reliable, survivable, and cost-effective system to defend the U.S. and our allies against the threat of nuclear-armed and conventionally-armed ballistic missiles of all ranges. The SDI research program is being conducted in full compliance with the ABM Treaty. If new defensive technologies prove feasible, they could serve to strengthen deterrence and enhance stability by reducing the role of ballistic missile weapons and by placing greater reliance on defenses which threaten no one.

Freeze Proposals: A Counterproductive Approach

The Administration, as noted above, is committed to pursuing radical cuts in the nuclear arsenals of the U.S. and Soviet Union through equitable and verifiable arms reduction agreements. Advocates of various nuclear freeze proposals generally maintain that a freeze today would facilitate such agreements—or perhaps even serve as an alternative to the slow-moving negotiating process—with little or no risk to the security of the U.S. or its allies. While the Administration shares the desire of freeze advocates to see rapid progress toward real arms reductions, we believe the freeze approach is counterproductive and, if accepted, would seriously harm our shared goals of ensuring a strong deterrent and reducing the risk of nuclear war.

The Administration's position is based on several concerns:

A Freeze Would Reward the Soviets for Their Unprecedented Military Buildup During a Period of Relative U.S. Restraint and Would Lock in Appreciable Soviet Advantages. The facts demonstrate the breadth and depth of Soviet efforts to gain a strategic advantage. For example, the Soviets today have a monopoly in prompt hard target capability and a 3-to-1 advantage in ballistic missile throwweight. A freeze would not only perpetuate these and other Soviet offensive nuclear advantages, it also would magnify the importance of Soviet strategic defense and conventional force advantages that would be unconstrained by a nuclear freeze. In addition to sanctioning the potentially destabilizing military effects of significant and, in some areas, growing imbalances between U.S. and Soviet strategic forces, a freeze would send worldwide a dangerous political signal that the U.S. may be unable to resist aggressive Soviet behavior even short of nuclear intimidation.

A Freeze Today Would Prevent the U.S. from Undertaking Necessary Steps to Modernize Our Forces and Thereby Stop the Erosion of the Basis of Deterrence. All three legs of the U.S. strategic triad—intercontinental ballistic missiles (ICBMs), submarine launched ballistic missiles (SLBMs), and heavy bombers—need to be modernized if we are to continue to have a credible deterrent force. Roughly 75 percent of U.S. strategic nuclear weapons are on launch systems over 15 years old, whereas over half of comparable Soviet weapons are on launch systems that are 5 years old or less. For example, the U.S. has not deployed a new type of ICBM since 1970, but the Soviets have replaced nearly half of their ICBMs since 1972 with 3 new types of missiles and 10 variations. Similarly, our youngest B-52 bomber was built 23 years ago and has become increasingly vulnerable to modernized Soviet defenses. Moreover, some 31 Poseidon ballistic missile submarines (SSBNs) constructed in the mid-1960s face obsolescence in the mid-1990s, whereas the Soviets have deployed more than 50 new SSBNs in 6 new or improved classes since 1972. A nuclear freeze today therefore would weaken our deterrent by preventing vital modernization programs including the Trident SSBN, the B-1 bomber, and the Peacekeeper ICBM. It also would hasten the obsolescence of aging U.S. systems by inhibiting necessary improvements to maintain safe, operational, and cost-effective systems.

A Freeze Would Divide the U.S. from Its Allies and Friends. One serious consequence of a freeze would be to undercut the U.S. commitment to its NATO allies in 1979 to deploy new longer-range intermediate nuclear forces (LRINF) in Western Europe–specifically Pershing II ballistic missiles and ground-launched cruise missiles–unless the Soviets agree to reduce their growing arsenal of LRINF systems, including the SS-20. A freeze would leave the Soviets with an overwhelming advantage in LRINF warheads of about 8-to-1 and reward their efforts to "decouple" the U.S. from its longstanding commitment to European defense.

Contrary to the Assertions of Freeze Advocates, a Freeze Could Not be Effectively Verified. The U.S. cannot effectively monitor important aspects of the complete range of Soviet efforts—research, development, production, testing, stockpiling, and deployment—to modernize and expand their nuclear offensive and strategic defense capabilities. To accept a freeze which, in fact, cannot be effectively verified is to ensure that the Soviets will not face real restraints in the future while the U.S. does.

A Freeze Would Derail—Not Facilitate—Opportunities For Real Arms Reductions. Experience demonstrates that the Soviets will not negotiate seriously and will continue their present policies unless they see proof that the U.S. is 1) determined to rectify existing imbalances, and 2) insistent on achieving equitable and verifiable mutual reductions. U.S. negotiators at Geneva have put on the table specific proposals for such reductions and have been authorized by the President to explore possible trade-offs with the Soviets. If the U.S. were to shift its attention to negotiating a freeze with the Soviets, the problem of U.S. and Soviet force imbalances would be left untouched and the possibility of real and mutual reductions—which remains our primary objective—would be postponed again, perhaps indefinitely.

FEDERAL EMERGENCY MANAGEMENT AGENCY

Shelter Management Handbook

The Federal Emergency Management Agency (FEMA), a federal agency established in the executive branch as an independent agency in 1978–79, includes all nonmilitary agencies concerned with providing services or restoring order in any kind of crisis. Thus, it is charged with developing defensive plans in the event of nuclear disaster as well as with providing flood-crisis assistance and crowd control at large political events. FEMA's nuclear attack management plans are very controversial.

The Importance of Shelter Management

- Effective shelter management can add millions of survivors, nationwide, in a nuclear attack.
- In YOUR shelter, effective management can:

  1. Prevent deaths from fallout radiation, and prevent radiation sickness, anywhere in the U.S.
  2. Prevent deaths from blast effects, if your shelter is in a "risk area." (A risk area is a city of 50,000 or greater population—or a city near an important military base or industry.)

- Shelter Management can save lives by assuring that the people in the shelter:

  1. Stay (if possible) in the basement of the shelter building—which provides the best protection against *fallout*.
  2. In risk areas:
  - Stay in the *parts* of the basement that provide the best protection against *blast* (near the sides of the basement—not under unsupported parts of the basement's ceiling).
  - Take fire prevention actions (close curtains and window blinds throughout the building) *immediately* after entering the shelter.
  - If a nuclear explosion occurs, *immediately* check for burning materials throughout the building. Stamp out smoldering curtains. Throw smoldering furniture out the window. Then return to the shelter area in the building.

Federal Emergency Management Agency, "Shelter Management Handbook." Washington, D.C.: U.S. Government Printing Office, May 1984.

3. Stay *in the shelter* for several days up to two weeks—when fallout levels have fallen enough that people can leave shelters.

Note to Local Civil Defense Directors

In Time of Emergency Take This Handbook to the Local Newspaper(s) for Printing, or Duplicate in Large Numbers and Distribute.

Immediate Actions for Survival

Actions

1. Place people in the basement and, if necessary, in the central core of the building (beginning with the first floor).
2. Take immediate preattack actions—especially closing blinds throughout building to reduce fire vulnerability. Also, put shelterees in best protective posture against fallout and (in risk areas) blast.
3. Organize to operate shelter.
4. If a weapon detonates nearby:
   a. Extinguish fires
   b. Repair damage
5. Determine available resources, including food, water, utility services, communications equipment, and take steps to use them effectively.

Operational Requirements

Your Responsibility

As Shelter Manager, you are responsible to the local Civil Defense Director. You have complete authority for operating this shelter, including organizing the shelter layout and staff, and enforcing rules and procedures.

The first regular staff member to arrive shall be in charge, and shall be succeeded by any other member of higher listing. If none of the listed regular staff members arrive, any person in shelter who is capable of assuming leadership should do so at once.

At Time of Shelter Entry

Turn off heat. If blast is not immediately expected, turn on any existing ventilation.

Entry into shelter should be orderly and rapid, with shelterees placed in the safest areas. The basement area and center core of the building are the best shelter spaces. Fill parts of shelter farthest from entrance first.

People should be advised to bring into the shelter only those items which increase shelter habitability and create no extra management problem. Special health foods and medicines should be retained by the shelterees. The Shelter Manager may later want to place them under centralized control for safekeeping. If any shelterees are familiar with the building, ask them to bring in vital supplies (first-aid kits, fire extinguishers) that are in rooms or corridors near the shelter area.

Procedures for Shelter Use

Getting Organized

You cannot do all the organizing and managing yourself. Appoint people or get volunteers to assist you. Appoint an Administrative Assistant, an Advisory Committee, and three Deputies for: (1) Operations, (2) Information, and (3) Supply and Maintenance. The Deputies for Information and Supply and Maintenance will be in charge of single functional teams; and the Deputy for Operations will be in charge of several functional teams. Your Administrative Assistant is to maintain daily logs, prepare reports, and supervise any clerical aides.

Protective Actions

A. *Immediate Preattack—High-Risk Areas*. In high-risk areas where blast and heat effects may occur:

1. Send parties to *close all window blinds and curtains IMMEDIATELY,* throughout the building, to reduce fire vulnerability to nuclear weapon heat flash.

2. Place people in the best-protected places; that is, in below-ground space if possible. Crowd people in best-protected areas, if necessary, until after the attack has taken place, *or* local authorities advise that further attack on the U.S. is not expected.

a. In basement areas instruct the people to:

(1) Go to the corners and/or exterior walls of the basement that have the least exterior exposure, or around columns. Stay away from parts of the basement where the ceiling is unsupported.

(2) Stay away from windows and doorways that open to the outside of the building.

(3) Lie face down on the floor with arms in a protective position on the head; or sit about two feet from (not touching) the walls in rows back to back.

b. In aboveground areas instruct the people to:

(1) Go to the central area of the designated shelter floor.

(2) Stay away from the windows. Close all window blinds and curtains, if not already done. (Open all windows to minimize hazard of flying glass.)

(3) Lie face down on the floor out of line of flying glass, with arms in a protective position on the head.

(4) Resist looking outside (the flash of a nuclear burst can cause blindness at distances of several miles).

(5) Cover as much of the body as possible, to prevent burns, with clothing or other materials (light-colored materials, if available, are best).

(6) Remain in protective position after the flash (the blast wave may arrive a number of seconds after the flash).

3. Organize teams to check preattack fire prevention measures, such as closing blinds and curtains, and be prepared to carry out rapid inspection of the entire shelter building if detonations occur nearby. Firefighting equipment should be collected from all parts of the building. Locate and put out fires (or throw smoldering furniture out the windows) before uncontrollable fires can start. After a fire watch is organized, the emergency exits should be noted, and shelterees drilled in evacuation procedures as soon as possible, in case fire forces evacuation of the shelter.

4. Organize a ventilation team to monitor the shelter environmental conditions and existing ventilation systems. Set up manual ventilation devices° if needed.

5. Organize a shelter radiological monitoring capability so that monitoring of fallout can be started as soon as possible after the detonation of a nuclear weapon. Inventory any radiological equipment available. Radiological monitoring instruments should be checked for operability, and monitors should be appointed and acquainted with their duties. (If trained monitors are present in shelter, they should take planned actions.)

6. Turn off, unplug, and disconnect electrical equipment to protect against the electromagnetic pulse effects of a nuclear detonation.

7. If a weapon detonates nearby, turn off controls for gas (to prevent possible fires) and water (to prevent possible loss of trapped water in building).

8. Disseminate information on the emergency situation.

9. When the capacity of the shelter is reached, attempt to send additional people to other nearby shelters.

B. *Immediate Preattack—Low-Risk Areas.* In low-risk areas, where fallout radiation will be the principal danger:

1. Place shelterees in safest designated areas within the shelter.

a. In basement areas, instruct the people to:

Ventilation equipment such as manually operated blowers and fans may be stored in the shelter area. The equipment should be unpacked and set up according to instructions on the containers.

(1) Go to the corners and/or exterior walls of the basement that have the least exterior exposure. (The most important factors in fallout protection are distance from the source of fallout radiation, and the amount of dense, heavy materials between the shelteree and the source of radiation.)

(2) Stay away from windows and doorways that open to the outside of the building.

b. In aboveground areas, instruct the people to:

(1) Go to the central area of the designated shelter floor.

(2) Stay away from windows.

2. Ready safety supplies and ventilation equipment for possible use, including radiological monitoring instruments (see item A5 above).

3. Reduce potential fire hazards by controlling smoking, keeping area free of trash, etc.

4. If a weapon detonates nearby, turn off controls for gas (to prevent possible fires) and water (to prevent possible loss of trapped water in building).

5. Disseminate pertinent information relative to the crisis situation.

6. When the capacity of the shelter is reached, attempt to send additional people to other nearby shelters.

C. *Preattack—If Time Permits*

If attack is not imminent, provide expedient blast and/or fallout protection improvement (e.g., shoring up joists and ceilings, piling dirt or sandbags around exterior walls—except for ventilation outlets). Protect and secure equipment and movable items from effects of shock and displacement.

In risk area shelters which are aboveground, in building cores, or in large basements, it may be difficult to close off the shelter area. Because the force of the blast can turn hastily constructed barriers and barricades within the shelter area into dangerous missiles, it is recommended that makeshift or free-standing blast protection not be improvised.

Shelter Operations

A. *Initial Actions*

1. Organize the shelter and establish a complete schedule for shelter activities.
2. Maintain a 24-hour watch and communications log.
3. Use available furniture, equipment, etc., as necessary to improvise a more desirable environment.
4. Control smoking. Prohibit it if necessary.
5. Control the distribution of food and water supplies.
6. Monitor radiological conditions and ventilation on a 24-hour basis.
7. Enforce health, sanitation, and safety rules.
8. Keep shelterees occupied to the extent possible through work details and recreational activities, while considering shelter temperature and ventilation.

9. Radiological monitoring personnel should study or review the shelter radiological monitoring handbook. Additional personnel should be recruited as monitors for around-the-clock monitoring. Dosimeters, if available, should be distributed to unit leaders and procedures established for maintaining a radiation exposure record for each shelteree.

B. *Immediately After the Attack*

1. Assess damage from blast, which can vary from light (e.g., glass breakage, broken light fixtures, false ceilings falling to the floor, etc.) to more severe structural damage. Fires may have started and should be quickly suppressed. *Throw smoldering materials outside.* Help the injured.

2. Repair damage which severely affects the habitability of the shelter area, and clear blocked exits. For exterior repairs in particular, speed will be of the utmost urgency; fallout from a nearby detonation may begin to fall within 15–30 minutes.

3. Commence radiological monitoring to determine if and when fallout arrives and to keep the exposure of the shelterees as low as possible. (See radiation handbook.)

4. If instruments are not available, shelterees should still try to locate in the best-protected areas possible. The best-protected areas are generally below ground areas first, and the central core areas of larger buildings, second (except for the top couple of floors and the 1st or 2nd floors up from ground level).

5. Do not abandon the shelter unless an inspection indicates that evacuation is called for, e.g., an uncontrollable fire situation or rising flood waters.

Operational Procedures

A. *Initial Procedures*

1. Report to the local headquarters on number of shelterees and the condition of the shelter.

2. Organize the shelter into units based upon the layout, such as by floors or other specific sections of the facility, and possibly in units of 10 each. Each shelter area or unit should select its leader.

3. Assign sleeping areas, operating services areas, and other areas as needed.

4. Select shelter management staff from those best qualified.

5. Implement safety and fire regulations.

6. Implement law-and-order regulations.

7. Implement health and sanitation rules.

8. Have the shelterees select representatives to serve as a Shelter Manager's Advisory Committee.

B. *Orientation of Shelterees*

1. Identify and introduce (if not already done) the Shelter Management staff. Explain their responsibilities and functions.

2. Explain the organization and management structure.
3. Explain the policies concerning personal possessions.
4. Stress the need for shelterees to assist each other and the need for cooperation for their common health and welfare.
5. Issue instructions for the use of facilities.
6. Explain the procedures for operating the shelter.
7. Permit the shelterees to ask questions to clarify instructions.

C. *Registration*

1. Distribute registration forms to each family group and unaccompanied person. If forms are unavailable, improvise registration forms from any paper supply on hand and request the shelterees to provide the information listed on the example form.
2. The shelter management staff will use the registration to:
   a. Ascertain useful skills and interests.
   b. Make work assignments.
   c. Determine sleeping arrangements.
   d. Determine special requirements.
   e. Maintain and report number of shelterees to headquarters.
   f. Provide data for possible post-shelter use.
   g. Identify persons needing special care.

D. *Facility Administration*

1. Test operation of:
   a. Commercial power, water, and sanitation facilities.
   b. Heating and ventilating kits, if available.
   c. Communications equipment.
   d. Radiological monitoring instruments.
   e. Safety equipment.
   f. Emergency lighting, if available.
2. Inventory health and sanitation supplies.
3. Inventory supplies, including food and water, and develop procedures for distribution. Also check sanitation facilities and arrangements for use.
4. Inventory supplies brought into shelter by the public, and store for safekeeping bulk articles and items which can endanger safety, such as guns and knives.

Continuing Actions

The Shelter Manager is responsible for providing information to the local government headquarters regarding the condition and needs of the shelter and the health and welfare of the shelterees. A detailed daily log of operations should be maintained.

1. The first report, to be made as soon as possible after shelter capacity has been reached or people stop arriving in the shelter, should cover the following:
   a. Time of shelter activation.
   b. Condition of the shelter.
   c. Number of shelterees.
   d. Estimates of the supply situation.
2. Subsequent reports should cover the following:
   a. Condition of the shelterees; health, morale, special requirements, etc.
   b. Radiological monitoring (when appropriate).
   c. Supply situation.
   d. Special problems or situations.

Shelter Management Teams

Shelter management teams and their functions are as follows:

A. *Feeding (Food and Water)*

1. Advise the Shelter Manager daily of the quantity of food and water on hand. Next to good air, water is the most essential requirement of your facility's population.

- Healthy people can survive for quite some time without food, but most of your population will die after 4 to 5 days without water. Physical damage to the body caused by lack of water may become irreversible. It is essential, therefore, that you and your water supply team act quickly to determine how much water will be available to your facility.
- One 150-pound man needs about 2.2 quarts of water each day to maintain body functions. Pregnant women, persons doing physical work, diabetics, the very young and very old, and ill persons all require more water, and should be encouraged to drink it.
- Physical damage to the body becomes irreversible after a certain amount of time without water; increasing water intake after this will not help people recover.
- Symptoms of water deprivation range from the mild symptoms of impatience, emotional instability, fatigue, and apathy, through the more severe symptoms of headache, labored breathing and increasing weakness, to the extreme symptoms of mental confusion and hallucination. Death can follow.
- Water requirements are another reason to be concerned with air temperature in your facility. The warmer the temperature, the more people must perspire (and thus lose water) to reduce body heat. If your facility's temperature rises above 82°F., the water needed by each person increases rapidly above normal body requirements.
- Salty or other thirst-provoking foods raise water requirements. Foods high

in protein and fat greatly increase the amount of drinking water required to eliminate waste from the body.

- Vigorous physical exercise increases water requirements.
- How you distribute water will depend upon how large your population is; what water supply and alternate sources are available to you. Your population needs to drink water at regular intervals throughout the day, at least five times. To control its use, you may have to turn off fountains and control access to rest rooms in your building.
- If a shelter is not stocked, supplies may be available elsewhere in the building or nearby. Shelter management should be prepared to obtain initial or supplementary supplies prior to attack if conditions permit.
- Drinkable water that has been stored in a closed system or closed container for any length of time may taste bad and appear undrinkable to many people. Exposing it to fresh air will improve its taste: carefully pour it from one container into another several times.

2. How to purify water that may be contaminated if it is not from the regular water supply system.

- The three most probable impurities are: bacteria; foreign bodies; such toxics as anti-rust chemicals.

a. To purify against bacteria: Use water purification tablets; or several drops of chlorine household bleach or tincture of iodine added to each quart of water; or boil water for at least one minute.

b. To purify against foreign bodies: Filter water through filter paper, gauze, fiberglass, or finely woven fabric; or allow water to stand until any sediment settles and then pour off ''clean'' water.

3. Should inspection of food and water supplies obtained from outside the shelter reveal the presence of radioactive particles, simple remedial procedures should be followed. In general, fallout on food should be treated much as any grit or sand that one might encounter on one's food, at the beach, for instance. The normal tendency would be to remove as many of the grit or sand particles as possible before consuming the food item. The same procedure should be adopted in dealing with fallout.

If food is contaminated, remove as much of the fallout as is feasible from it. If noncontaminated food is available, consume it first. If all the available food is contaminated, and shelterees are hungry, serve this food after decontaminating it as thoroughly as is feasible.

Procedures for dealing with contaminated water are identical to that for fallout on food: (1) Serve uncontaminated water first, if available. (2) Apply simple decontamination procedures to water which contains fallout particles. Allow water to stand until fallout settles to the bottom and then siphon off the uncontaminated upper layer. Filtering water through paper towels or layers of fine cloth is another approach. Boiling or chlorination will not remove contaminations. (3) Serve water, if it is potable from a medical standpoint, even though it may contain some radioactive material, if necessary. Because water is vital for survival, it is important that the manager not deny water to the shelter population unnecessarily, in the name of radiological protection.

4. Special health foods should be kept by individuals unless it is desirable to turn them over to Supply for storage and safekeeping.

5. Strict controls should be maintained to minimize waste and to assure equitable distribution of available supplies. A daily status report should be made to the Shelter Manager to determine the need for any changes in distribution or procedures. This report should include the amount of each item used and on hand and the length of time the supply should last at the current usage rate.

If there is no food or water in the shelter or supplies run out, request for supplies should be made to the local government headquarters; or, as conditions permit (absence or diminishing of fallout or fire hazards), personnel may be assigned to go outside to obtain initial supplies or replenish stocks. (Radiation exposures must be considered.)

6. Check water containers for leakage or contamination. Take measures to prevent damage to containers or contamination of water.

B. *Sleeping*

1. Assign available sleeping equipment and bedding as necessary.

2. Establish sleeping schedules that provide the best possible quiet periods for the shelterees.

C. *Safety*

1. Establish fire and evacuation procedures and conduct daily drills.

2. Enforce safety and fire regulations.

3. Enforce law-and-order regulations. Police officers, if present, will enforce regulations; otherwise, the shelter management staff is responsible.

D. *Health and Sanitation*

1. Determine whether any of the shelterees are experienced in medical and health matters and establish a Health and Sanitation Team.

2. Enforce health and sanitation rules.

3. Maintain a clean and sanitary environment.

4. Maintain checks on water and food for contamination or spoilage.

5. Control medical supplies and equipment. Medical supplies should be issued only to the shelter unit leaders, not directly to individuals. A daily status report should be made to the Shelter Manager.

6. Conduct and schedule daily sick call to check and treat shelterees for illnesses or injuries. Isolate the seriously ill.

E. *Radiological*

1. Minimize the exposure of shelterees to fallout radiation by:

a. Assuring their stay in safest areas of the shelter. If lack of space pro-

TABLE 1 Radiation Exposure Table

	Accumulated Radiation Exposures (R) in Any Period of		
Medical Care Will Be Needed By	a. One Week	b. One Month	c. Four Months
A None	150	200	300
B Some (5 percent may die)	250	350	500
C Most (50 percent may die)	450	600	—

An average adult will not need medical care when the whole body is exposed to the quantities of radiation listed in Row A when the exposure is spread out over the listed periods of time. Rows B and C are intended to be used for making decisions on performing urgent missions which may require extra radiation exposure. For most shelter occupants, the exposures in row A should not be exceeded.

hibits locating the entire shelter population into areas offering the highest protection, management should consider using the best-protected area for pregnant women, infants, children, and those who will be performing emergency missions. Radiation exposure of all shelterees should be kept as low as practicable. Table 1 provides general guidance on the expected effects if accumulated radiation exposures are kept below certain doses during certain periods of time. If the radiation levels throughout the shelter vary significantly, some rotation of the shelterees may be required to minimize the overall exposure to everyone.

b. Periodic monitoring to detect radiation, and radiation levels, within the shelter, if instruments are available.

c. Taking measures to prevent entry of fallout into the shelter.

2. Check shelterees to see if fallout particles have lodged on them (particularly in the hair) or on their clothing.

a. Decontaminate, if necessary.

b. **Refer to the Health and Sanitation Team for treatment if symptoms of radiation exposure develop. (See Table 2.)**

3. Follow instructions in radiological monitor handbook, if available.

F. *Communications*

1. Messages to and from shelter must be restricted to essential information and filed or kept in as short form as possible.

2. Maintain a log of all messages sent or received by time and date.

3. Assign person or persons to telephone(s) and monitor radio receiver (if available) continuously. Log significant information for referral to the Shelter Manager. Information of concern to all those in shelter should be posted by the Manager, or at his direction, on a bulletin board (if available).

4. As directed by the Shelter Manager, transmit messages by telephone, radio, or any available means to headquarters.

TABLE 2 Effects of Brief (2-Week) Radiation Exposure

50–200 R
- Less than half experience nausea and vomiting.
- Possible increased fatigue.
- Decrease in white blood cell count.
- Possible complications due to infection, blast, and thermal injuries.

200–450 R
- More than half experience nausea and vomiting.
- Acute illness for a few days.
- Symptoms disappear for 1–3 weeks; changes in blood cell counts.
- Illness then returns.
- Possible hair loss.
- Moderately severe illness; infection, sore throat.
- Most require medical care.
- More than half will survive without therapy.
- Survival rate improves with medical care.

450–600 R
- Initial acute gastric distress more severe and prolonged.
- Latent period shortened to 1–2 weeks.
- Main illness characterized by oral, pharyngeal, dermal hemorrhages.
- Infections commonplace; sore throat, pneumonia, intestinal inflammation.
- Intensive medical care and hospitalization required for survival.
- Fewer than half survive even with best care.

600–1000 R
- Accelerated illness.
- Vomiting begins soon after exposure.
- Gastric distress can continue for several days or until death.
- Damage to the gastrointestinal tract causes severe cramps and bloody diarrhea.
- Death can occur anytime during the second week without appearance of hemorrhage or loss of hair.
- Unlikely that many can survive even with extensive medical care.

Note: In an attack environment, medical facilities and the availability of extensive medical care would be severely limited.

5. Use only one radio at a time to conserve battery power.

6. Locate the broadcast radio in an area where it can be heard by the largest number of shelterees.

G. *Information, Recreation, and Religious Affairs*

1. Keep shelterees informed of the attack and post-attack situations as directed by the Shelter Manager. This will help prevent rumors, which could adversely affect morale and shelter management control.

2. To keep up morale and maintain good physical condition among shelterees, conduct educational and recreational activities as temperature and space allows. Encourage religious activities.

H. *Supply and Maintenance*

1. Receive and inventory supplies and equipment brought into the shelter. Maintain the inventory as items are used.
2. Maintain shelter facility and mechanical equipment.
3. Assist the Health and Sanitation team in:
   a. Disposing of the dead.
   b. Disposing of refuse.
   c. Maintaining sanitary standards.

Shelter Emergence

A. *Temporary Emergence*

When authorized by the Civil Defense Director or other competent authority, the Shelter Manager, where necessary, may direct or permit temporary emergence; for example, to obtain needed food, water, medical, or other supplies. In the absence of communications with headquarters, the Shelter Manager must obtain advice from the Radiological Team to determine whether it is safe to permit temporary emergence.

If fallout is visible, then radiation readings from radiological instruments are necessary to avoid serious radiation overexposure. The estimate of time to be spent outside the shelter must be based upon instrument readings of the outside exposure rates. The estimate of the time should contain a safety factor to allow for significant variations in fallout accumulation, inaccuracy in measurements, or unexpected problems that would delay their return to shelter. In addition, since radiation exposure will continue to be accumulated even after the shelter occupancy period, every effort should be made to keep the total exposure as low as reasonably practical and certainly below those amounts that would be expected to result in medical care being needed (see Table 1).

Temporary emergence may also be necessary for:

1. Radiological monitoring.
2. Movement of the seriously ill.
3. Avoidance of fire, smoke, or other life-threatening hazards within the shelter.
4. Morale purposes.

Note: If temporary emergence from shelters is necessary, it is important to remember that even radiation exposures that are so low as to cause no physical effects may nevertheless pose a long-term health risk, such as increased susceptibility to leukemia and other cancers 10 to 30 years in the future and genetic disorders in future offspring.

B. *Permanent Emergence*

When authorized by the Civil Defense Director or other responsible authority, the Shelter Manager will allow people to leave the shelter when:

1. Danger has lessened to an acceptable level or no longer exists.
2. Temporary lodging is available or people can return to their homes.
3. People may move safely from shelter to another place (if emergency controls allow such movement).
4. Hospitalization is available for those requiring medical care.

In the absence of communications with headquarters and shelter radiological monitoring sets, it will probably be advisable to prepare for a shelter stay of two weeks, provided that fallout has been visually observed (as sandlike or gritty particles on window sills or outside the shelter).

Before people leave the shelter, they should be informed of conditions existing in the community and of provisions made for their safety and well-being.

They should be advised of the importance of continuing actions to minimize radiation exposure (e.g., sleep in protected areas, undertake decontamination measures).

In areas that have experienced heavy fallout, it will often be necessary to move shelterees as a group to less contaminated areas, perhaps 20 or 40 miles away. The need for such movement should be ascertained from the local government headquarters before considering release of shelterees.

If movement to a relatively distant area is required, the local headquarters will issue the necessary instructions to the shelter manager—who will be responsible for organizing the movement of his or her shelterees as a group. The Shelter Manager will return personal possessions to the shelterees.

Closing the Shelter

When the shelter is closed (deactivated), the Shelter Manager should contact the local Civil Defense Director for instructions concerning disposition of supplies and equipment, reporting requirements, and other activities desired by the local government.

Using the Shelter

. . . Brief instructions to be given by shelter managers when shelterees enter the shelter are on pages 240 to 242.

Best Shelter Areas

The best shelter areas are (1) belowground, (2) on the ground floor, and (3) on the second and third floors. No one should be sheltered above the third floor in a high-risk area.

Since belowground areas are by far the safest, temporary overcrowding, with people lying face down or sitting near the exterior walls of the shelter area (but not touching the walls), is recommended. People can adapt to crowding for several hours. Six hours is likely to be the period of maximum threat from detonations in the vicinity, although this cannot be guaranteed.

Description of Safest Areas

In belowground areas, which should be *first choice,* the best shelter spaces are located near the walls and corners away from windows. When an exterior basement wall is partially or completely exposed, the better shelter areas are located farthest from the exposed wall. On aboveground floors, the best shelter is in the central area of the building or wing, away from outside walls and windows.

Once the fallout has arrived, the Shelter Manager should use radiological instruments, if available, to make the final determinations of where to locate the people to be sheltered within a particular facility (i.e., which areas have the lowest measured radiation exposure rates).

Ventilation

Adequate ventilation is critical to the well-being of the shelterees. Aboveground, the provision of ventilation may simply be a matter of opening (or breaking) available windows and doors. However, in belowground areas additional measures are necessary for maximum shelter utilization. If mechanical ventilation is operable it should be used along with any portable fans. Also, any manually operated blowers or fans, which might be stored in the shelter, should be unpacked and set up according to the instructions on the equipment package. Lacking mechanical ventilation, the maximum advantage should be made of natural ventilation by creating a "chimney effect" and/or making use of outside winds. To optimize the "chimney effect," windows or areaway openings into the lowest floor and windows on the upper floors should be opened. This procedure allows the hot air, created by the shelterees, to rise and be replaced by fresh air. If a wind is blowing, the air flow can be maximized by opening the windward side windows on the lower floor and the leeward side windows on the upper floor. Experiment will quickly show the best combination.

If, despite efforts to improve ventilation, high effective temperatures are approached, then other remedial action is necessary. Effective temperature is a composite measure of temperature, humidity, and air movement. At a given effective temperature with sufficient air movement, the environment might be quite comfortable. However, with no perceptible air movement and high humidity, the same effective temperature would be considerably uncomfortable. If body temperatures rise about 2° F. above normal, action should be taken to relieve the situation through air exchange or by moving all or part of the sheltered group to another part of the building for a short period. Similar action should be taken whenever it appears that there is a buildup of excess amounts of carbon dioxide. This can be assumed if a number of persons complain of shortness of breath, dizziness, or nausea which cannot readily be attributed to other aspects of the shelter environment.

Trapped Water

Most buildings have a sizable quantity of potable water trapped within the plumbing system. This includes water in water heaters, boilers, fire standpipes, distribution pipes, etc. To use this water, it is only necessary to follow a few simple steps. First, if water service to the building is no longer functioning, the main valve should be located and turned off to prevent water already in the building from being drained away by a possible outside break in the line. Next, in order to relieve any vacuum created within the lines, open one or more faucets on the top floor of the building. Water can then be drawn off the system being available at the lowest floor. Storage tanks such as water heaters will usually have a drain valve near the bottom. Although water from such tanks may initially be muddy, the water is still drinkable after allowing the particles to settle.

Political Approaches

HERBERT SCOVILLE, JR.

The Current Situation and a Sketch of Its 36-Year History

Herbert Scoville, Jr. (1915–1985), was intimately involved with the nuclear world. A scientist at Los Alamos, he held many key positions in the Pentagon, the CIA, and the Arms Control and Defense Agency. In the past several years he had actively worked to curb the arms race. He was president of the Arms Control Association, a non-profit public education institute, and sat on the boards of the Council for a Livable World and the Center for Defense Information. This piece is the transcript of a speech he gave to college professors interested in developing courses in nuclear education.

I am going to talk about where we are today in terms of the United States and the Soviet Union's strategic programs. Looking objectively at the state of the nuclear confrontation and the risks of a nuclear war breaking out, the prospects are gloomy. Arms control and the nuclear-weapons programs on both sides are going in the wrong direction. Arms-control negotiations are virtually at a standstill, and the United States and the Soviet Union are adding daily to their nuclear-weapons stockpiles. The numbers are now so high as to have no real meaning regarding the damage they can do; a small fraction could create such devastating consequences that civilization as we know it would be ended.

What especially concerns me is that both countries are acquiring strategic nuclear-weapon delivery systems which make nuclear war more likely. These systems provide incentives for each side to launch first in a preemptive strike, as their capabilities threaten to undermine the strategy of deterrence for both sides. We may not like the psychology of having to depend on deterrence, but we have to live with nuclear weapons, and the only situation which makes sense is when mutual deterrence is stable. Nuclear weapons serve no military purpose; they only serve to deter the other side from using their weapons.

Herbert Scoville, Jr., "The Current Situation and a Sketch of Its 36-Year History." From *Proceedings of the Symposium, The Role of the Academy in Addressing the Issues of Nuclear War* (Washington, D.C., March 25–26, 1982), pp. 12–19. Reprinted by permission.

A major danger of first-strike weapons is that they are only useful if you want to use them first. They encourage both sides to adopt a posture of launch-on-warning or launch-under-attack, which means that, when one side's computers detect a launch from the other side, they automatically launch their missiles so they won't be destroyed. This may seem to be a sure way of protecting the missiles, but in effect, this strategy has to short-circuit virtually the whole command and control structure and to rely solely on computers.

U.S. procurement of the *MX* missile may lead the Soviets to adopt this dangerous posture. President Reagan said last October that he wants the *MX* as quickly as possible, to have what he called a prompt threat to Soviet ICBMs in their silos. That prompt threat from those *MX* missiles is *so* prompt that it is only a threat if we launch them in a first strike. Of course, the Soviet Union knows that, so that what we are doing with the *MX* program is pushing them into a position where they will adopt a launch-on-warning posture.

I don't want my security or the security of this country or the security of the world to depend on whether the United States' computers work properly and don't give false alarms, and the last thing in the world that I want is to have everyone's security depend on whether or not Soviet computers work correctly. However, that is the kind of position that we are pushing the world into today, a posture in which computers may decide the fate of the world rather than, at least, leaving it to mankind with all its foibles.

First, let us look at a little history to see how we got ourselves into this position. Briefly, one should remember that, in 1945, we had a monopoly on nuclear weapons, and we used two of them. The results were devastating. Later you will hear about the consequences of those explosions; I won't go into detail here.

From my point of view, the important thing was that, at that time, we had a monopoly through the 1940s. The Soviets first tested a nuclear weapon in 1949. In the 1950s, we saw that both sides were not satisfied with the puny 15-kiloton weapons which destroyed Hiroshima, so we both moved into the hydrogen bomb era, where the explosive yield of the weapons was a thousand times as great as that which essentially wiped out the cities of Hiroshima and Nagasaki.

Furthermore, not only did we put greater explosive power in nuclear warheads, we also started to develop new kinds of delivery systems. The United States moved forward quickly on bomber delivery systems and a little slower regarding missiles. This delay, in the long run, aided our security. The Soviets, on the other hand, essentially bypassed the development of modern bombers and went to intercontintental missiles. They tested an ICBM before we did, and it looked as though it was a reliable missile which they could deploy.

In the 1950s, we didn't have any satellites which could take pictures of the entire Soviet Union, and so our intelligence—and I have to plead guilty to this myself, as I was involved—without being able to prove it, believed that the Soviets had developed a reliable ICBM and had deployed at least a small number of them. Of course, the Air Force said there were hundreds, and we in CIA were saying a much more modest number, but there wasn't much argument that some deployment was going forward.

It wasn't until the end of 1960, when we started to get satellite coverage of the entire Soviet Union, that we suddenly realized that the Soviets had never even deployed their first-generation ICBM—or at least no more than a handful of their first-generation missiles. In the meantime, however, we had already reacted to what we thought was a missile gap and had gone ahead with extensive programs for both land-based ICBMs and submarine-based ICBMs. The land-based ICBMs were put in hardened silos, and so we sat with a relatively large, highly survivable deterrent strategic force. There was no risk to that force, no matter what the Soviets did; there was no chance that they could gain anything by trying to launch a first strike against it. Then, of course, the Soviet Union came tagging along behind us; by the end of the 1960s, they had also built up an approximately equal strategic deterrent force, which was also invulnerable.

Actually, for a long time before the end of the 1960s, neither country had the kind of forces that could really contemplate a first strike. But, by the end of the 1960s, there was no question that we were in a position of mutual deterrence. So, at that point, both nations turned to arms control, and we were very fortunate to have Gerard Smith as our negotiator at the SALT 1 talks.

The ABM Treaty was signed in 1972, and that really should have put a cap on the arms race, because it essentially guaranteed that both countries would have a survivable deterrence posture for the foreseeable future. However, it is at that point that both sides went astray, because—instead of profiting from the relatively stable, mutual deterrence situation which we had in 1972—both superpowers went ahead and procured more weapons. Now one hears claims all the time that the Russians are to blame for the arms race since 1972 and that we didn't do anything after SALT 1, because we just relied on arms control for our security. Frankly, nothing could be further from the truth. The United States has to take its share of the responsibility for the continued arms race, which moved in very dangerous directions in the 1970s.

The United States took the lead in the two most destabilizing developments of that decade. One was to develop and deploy Multiple Independently Targeted Reentry Vehicles (MIRVs), which are multiple warheads on a single missile. Each warhead has a separate guidance system so that it can be aimed at separate targets. MIRVs revolutionized the whole strategic balance, because for the first time, there was at least the potential for one missile, if it was fired first, to be able to destroy several missiles on the other side. In other words, we had created a system which gave an advantage to using nuclear weapons first. This was an extremely dangerous development, because what we should have been doing then and should continue to do now is try to create situations where there is no advantage to going first.

There may have been some opportunity for getting MIRVs under control in SALT 1, but our negotiator, Gerard Smith, was never really given a chance to make a good college try to limit MIRVs under SALT 1. The United States government, after a lot of debate, decided to race the Soviets in MIRV development. We went ahead with our MIRV deployments, and as might have been predicted, the Soviet Union came along five years behind us and also deployed MIRVs. Thus, we moved into a situation where both sides had increased the incentives for initiating a nuclear attack.

The second significant U.S. weapons development in the 1970s is directly related to MIRVs; it was the development of more advanced guidance systems for MIRVed warheads, so that each one would have at least a high theoretical probability of being able to destroy a missile silo of the other side. I would stress the term "theoretical," because I don't think this is a real-life capability, but with this development came the culmination of the threat to the land-based portion of the deterrent posture of both sides. In our case, this was not a great disaster, in spite of what you might gather from the press, because in the 1960s and 1970s we had made the proper decision to put only 25 percent of our forces into land-based missiles which were becoming theoretically vulnerable.

However, the Soviet Union put 75 percent of their efforts into land-based missiles, which were becoming vulnerable to our advanced guidance systems. And, as might be expected, the Soviets got better guidance systems, too, so all these technological improvements did was raise the level of the arms race to another more dangerous level. That is the situation in which we see ourselves today. Both sides are deploying, or have deployed, weapons which have theoretical capability of destroying at least the ICBM portion of the deterrent, and, as I said, this is a much more serious problem for the Soviet Union than it is for the United States.

That gets to one point I would like to make which is relevant to the role academia can play in teaching about nuclear-war issues. Today there is a tremendous amount of nonsense passed out about the nature and danger of the Soviet threat. Our politicians have learned over the years that the most effective way of getting money for new weapons is to say that the Russians have better weapons and are about to attack us. They ignore completely what actual security significance those weapons have. For example, even if the Soviets had been first in getting weapons which threatened ICBMs, which they weren't, that is still no reason why we should copy them. By copying them and getting a first-strike capability of our own, we are only providing them with targets and incentives to actually use their weapons. It would be much better for the United States not to have any weapons like that at all; then the Soviets would just have wasted their technological talents in getting this capability.

This concept of a weak United States is used to sell the Congress and the public on buying more weapons. To say that the United States is nuclearly weak, has a vulnerable strategic force—and I have heard the Secretary of Defense say this—and that we don't have a secure deterrent against a Soviet attack, I find to be very, very dangerous. It is essentially playing the Soviet propaganda line, and there is absolutely no truth to this whatsoever. The United States has a much more survivable strategic deterrent force than does the Soviet Union. Granted, both sides' land-based ICBMs may be vulnerable, but we have a much better-balanced force. You never hear about the good sides of our force, only about the bad sides. At all times we have submarines out in the ocean that carry about 3,000 warheads, each of which has a yield three times greater than that of the Hiroshima bomb. They can destroy military targets as well as cities. The only thing that they can't do is destroy missile silos, and that, in my view, is a very good characteristic rather than a bad one.

Therefore, any notion that the United States is weak is just plain misleading and does us a lot of harm. Yet, it is probably the most flamboyant fuel that exists to keep the arms race escalating. It is terribly important that a rational view of the nature of the Soviet threat be taken and that the American public understands that there is no evidence available to suggest that today the Soviets have any incentive to launch a first strike. However, if current trends prevail, the U.S. might push them to the wall in some kind of a situation where they feel so threatened that they might lash out and decide that it is better to launch their weapons than to run the risk that we would launch ours first.

That brings me to the European situation. What we see now in Europe is the United States pressing our Allies to deploy cruise missiles—most importantly, *Pershing II* missiles in West Germany. Now *Pershing II* missiles have several very dangerous characteristics. These are ballistic missiles with such highly accurate guidance systems that they can threaten even the hardest targets, including command and control centers and missile silos. Also, they can probably reach Moscow; you can argue a bit about whether their nominal 1,000-mile range really will hit the Kremlin or the suburbs, but from the Soviet point of view, they certainly look as though they could hit Moscow.

Pershing IIs, therefore, present a very direct threat to the entire Soviet political and military command-and-control structure, but they cannot be made survivable. Thus, we will have this vulnerable target which is a sort of Damocles' sword hanging over the heads of the Soviet political and military command. Now, visualize a situation like Poland in East Germany, where there might be skirmishes across the border, and the Soviet Union could be faced with a problem of actually using its own forces to try and contain the internal problems in East Germany. Before they fire a single shot or move a single soldier, they will be under strong pressure to launch nuclear weapons to destroy the *Pershings* in West Germany; then we are off to the races with a nuclear war. Nobody would know how to contain it or keep it limited; it could be the end of civilization as we know it today.

The last point I would like to make, after all this pessimism about the dangers of nuclear war, is that I, like Gerard Smith, feel much more optimistic today than I did six months ago, or certainly more than I did a year ago, because at last the public is being heard. It has already been heard in Europe. The fears about the deployment of these weapons in Western Europe, together with some of the statements about fighting "limited" wars, which are limited to Europe, haven't gone over very well over there. The anti-nuclear movement in Europe is not, as some people would like you to believe, just composed of Communist-inspired groups; it is a very broad anti-nuclear-war movement that has already demonstrated political clout. I don't think there is a single government, with the possible exception of Great Britain, which can afford to neglect that pressure from the people to try to stop this mad nuclear-arms race. That pressure has been transported across the waters to the United States by political leaders in Europe and is the reason we have the only arms-control negotiation which is going on today, the Geneva talks on intermediate-range weapons.

To date, there has essentially been no real interest by the present Administration in trying to use arms control as a method of controlling the nuclear threat. The only evidence of interest was the agreement to start the negotiations in November on European-theater weapons. At that time, both President Brezhnev and President Reagan set forth what I call sort of extreme starting positions. These are quite all right if they are used as a start for negotiations and a basis to seriously work toward an agreement. However, they are not of any value at all if they are "a take it or leave it" type of position, and I am getting increasingly worried that we are negotiating in Geneva on a take-it-or-leave-it basis. If so, we might as well write off these negotiations.

Unfortunately, we have seen nothing in terms of negotiations on intercontinental systems. Perhaps this summer, before President Reagan goes on his trip to Europe, there may be some statement about starting these negotiations—restarting START instead of SALT—but two and a half years have already been lost in terms of negotiating time, counting the year we tried to get the SALT II Treaty ratified. We simply can't afford that kind of time scale. Weapons development doesn't stop while negotiations are in recess—or even while they are in process. What we are seeing is that every day the situation is becoming harder to control and more dangerous, yet we don't seem to be taking any steps to face up to this threat.

In the last nine months, however, and particularly in the last month, there has been a tremendous ballooning of U.S. public concern about nuclear war. This is certainly a hopeful sign, because without it, we are never going to control this race. All of the careful studies and preparations for SALT or START agreements are not going to solve the problem. What is going to solve the problem and get it addressed seriously is public understanding of what the issues are. If people can't understand the basic issues, they will tend to leave it to the experts, and this is not a problem to be left to the experts. You shouldn't just listen to me or the experts in the United States government. This is a problem which the public can understand, with a little bit of help in stripping away some of the nonsense it is always encumbered with. The *MX* issue was one where the public studied the issue and translated its views into political action. Fostering sensible public education about arms control and nuclear-war issues is the task that I would hope you people could address yourselves to, because I can't think of a more important one than we in this country have to face today.

Question: Are the Soviets' most sophisticated systems, the *SS-18s* and *SS-19s,* any more of a first-strike weapon than the most sophisticated *U.S. Minuteman IIIs* with their guidance systems and warheads, or are they about equal in lethality?

Scoville: They are essentially equal in lethality. The Soviet missiles are larger than ours; therefore they carry more warheads. The *Minuteman III* only carries three warheads, while the *SS-18* can carry ten and the *SS-19* six. Therefore, in the long run, once they complete their deployment, they will have more warheads and have a bigger threat than certainly our *Minuteman.* Nevertheless, when we complete the deployment of the new guidance systems on the *Minuteman III,* which incidentally has the same guidance and warhead that was orginally going to be put on the first-generation *MX,* we will have about 1,650 warheads with this kind of a guidance system and an ability to threaten Soviet ICBMs. This is not enough to destroy their entire ICBM force, which at the moment is about 1,400, but this U.S. force could theoretically destroy a larger fraction of the total Soviet deterrent than they could of ours, since they put so many warheads on land-based ICBMs; thus, we would still have a larger part of our deterrent left and a much more secure force than they would have, even if their *SS-18s* and *19s* could destroy every single ICBM we own.

Question: On the Goldwater-Hart report on the false alert, it would appear that it wasn't all that bad. What is your view?

Scoville: I think it was not that bad in the actual situation that existed, because we don't now have a launch-on-warning policy. I don't think there was ever any real danger that we would launch weapons and that a war would have started by accident. But, had we had a launch-on-warning policy, then the situation would have been much more dangerous. Everyone could be a little more relaxed in the first situation, but in a real launch-on-warning situation, you can't afford to sit by. You just have to set the process in motion within a minimum amount of time, and the chances that we might have launched by accident would have been much greater.

RANDALL FORSBERG

Call to Halt the Nuclear Arms Race — Proposal for a Mutual U.S.-Soviet Nuclear-Weapon Freeze

Randall Forsberg (b. 1943) authored this sweeping arms control proposal. Initially proposed in late June 1982, Freeze Resolution (HJ Res 521) was rejected by the House on August 5, 1982 by a vote of 204–202. The resolution (HJ Res 13) finally passed in the House on May 4, 1983, in a heavily amended version. The Senate rejected a slightly different version of the Freeze Resolution on October 31, 1983, by a 58–40 vote. (Also see p. 74.)

Statement of the Proposal

To improve national and international security, the United States and the Soviet Union should stop the nuclear arms race. Specifically, they should adopt a mutual freeze on the testing, production, and deployment of nuclear weapons and of missiles and new aircraft designed primarily to deliver nuclear weapons. This is an essential, verifiable first step toward lessening the risk of nuclear war and reducing the nuclear arsenals.

The horror of a nuclear holocaust is universally acknowledged. Today, the United States and the Soviet Union possess 50,000 nuclear weapons. In half an hour, a fraction of these weapons can destroy all cities in the northern hemisphere. Yet over the next decade, the U.S. and USSR plan to build over 20,000 more nuclear warheads, along with a new generation of nuclear missiles and aircraft.

The weapon programs of the next decade, if not stopped, will pull the nuclear tripwire tighter. Counterforce and other "nuclear war-fighting" systems will improve the ability of the U.S. and the USSR to attack the opponent's nuclear forces and other military targets. This will increase the pressure on both sides to use their nuclear weapons in a crisis, rather than risk losing them in a first strike.

Such developments will increase hair-trigger readiness for massive nuclear exchange at a time when economic difficulties, political dissension, revolution,

---

and competition for energy supplies may be rising worldwide. At the same time, more countries may acquire nuclear weapons. Unless we change this combination of trends, the danger of nuclear war will be greater in the late 1980s and 1990s than ever before.

Rather than permit this dangerous future to evolve, the United States and the Soviet Union should stop the nuclear arms race.

A freeze on nuclear missiles and aircraft can be verified by existing national means. A total freeze can be verified more easily than the complex SALT I and II agreements. The freeze on warhead production could be verified by the Safeguards of the International Atomic Energy Agency. Stopping the production of nuclear weapons and weapon-grade material and applying the Safeguards to U.S. and Soviet nuclear programs would increase the incentive of other countries to adhere to the Non-proliferation Treaty, renouncing acquisition of their own nuclear weapons, and to accept the same Safeguards.

A freeze would hold constant the existing nuclear parity between the United States and the Soviet Union. By precluding production of counterforce weaponry on either side, it would eliminate excuses for futher arming on both sides. Later, following the immediate adoption of the freeze, its terms should be negotiated into the more durable form of a treaty.

A nuclear-weapon freeze, accompanied by government-aided conversion of nuclear industries, would save at least $100 billion each in U.S. and Soviet military spending (at today's prices) in 1981–1990. This would reduce inflation. The savings could be applied to balance the budget, reduce taxes, improve services, subsidize renewable energy, or increase aid to poverty-stricken Third World regions. By shifting personnel to more labor-intensive civilian jobs, a nuclear-weapon freeze would also raise employment.

Stopping the U.S.-Soviet nuclear arms race is the single most useful step that can be taken now to reduce the likelihood of nuclear war and to prevent the spread of nuclear weapons to more countries. This step is a necessary prelude to creating international conditions in which:

- further steps can be taken toward a stable, peaceful international order;
- the threat of first use of nuclear weaponry can be ended;
- the freeze can be extended to other nations; and
- the nuclear arsenals on all sides can be drastically reduced or eliminated, making the world truly safe from nuclear destruction.

Scope of the Freeze

1. Underground nuclear tests should be suspended, pending final agreement on a comprehensive test ban treaty.
2. There should be a freeze on testing, production, and deployment of all missiles and new aircraft which have nuclear weapons as their sole or main payload. This includes:

U.S. DELIVERY VEHICLES

In Production:

Improved Minutemen ICBM
Trident 1 SLBM
Air-launched cruise missle (ALCM)

In Development:

MX ICBM
Trident II SLBM
Long-range ground- and sea-launched cruise missiles (GLCM, SLCM)
Pershing II IRBM
New Bomber

SOVIET DELIVERY VEHICLES

In Production

SS-19 ICBM
SS-N-18 SLBM
SS-20 IRBM
Backfire bomber

In Development:

SS-17, SS-18, SS-19 ICBM improvements
New ICBM
New SLBM (SS-N-20).

3. The number of land- and submarine-based launch tubes for nuclear missiles should be frozen. Replacement subs could be built to keep the force constant, but with no net increase in SLBM tubes and no new missiles.
4. No further MIRVing or other changes to existing missiles or bomber loads would be permitted.

All of the above measures can be verified by existing national means of verification with high confidence.

The following measures cannot be verified nationally with the same confidence, but an effort should be made to include them:

5. Production of fissionable material (enriched uranium and plutonium) for weapon purposes should be halted.
6. Production of nuclear weapons (bombs) should be halted.

There are two arguments for attempting to include these somewhat less verifiable steps. First, with a halt to additional and new delivery vehicles, there will be no need for additional bombs. Thus, production of weapon-grade fissionable material and bombs would probably stop in any event. Second, the establishment of a universal ban on production of weapon-grade fissionable material and nuclear bombs, verified by international inspection as established now for non-nuclear-weapon states under the Non-proliferation Treaty and the International Atomic Energy Agency, would greatly strengthen that Treaty and improve the prospects for halting the spread of nuclear weapons.

The Agreement to Freeze

The U.S. and Soviet governments should announce a moratorium on all further testing, production, and deployment of nuclear weapons and nuclear delivery vehicles, to be verified by national means. The freeze would be followed by negotiations to incorporate the moratorium in a treaty. The negotiations would cover supplementary verification measures, such as IAEA inspections; and possible desirable exceptions from the freeze, such as an occasional confidence test.

This procedure follows the precedent of the 1958–1961 nuclear-weapon test moratorium, in which testing was suspended while the U.S., USSR, and UK negotiated a partial test ban treaty.

Relation to SALT Negotiations

The bilateral freeze is aimed at being introduced in the early 1980s, as soon as sufficient popular and political support is developed to move the governments toward its adoption.

The freeze would prevent dangerous developments in the absence of a SALT treaty. It would preclude exploitation of loopholes in past treaties and, at the same time, satisfy critics who are concerned that the SALT process may not succeed in stopping the arms race.

The freeze does not replace the SALT negotiating process, but should supplement and strengthen it. The freeze could be adopted as a replacement for SALT II or as an immediate follow-on, with the task of putting the moratorium into treaty language the job of SALT III.

The Case for a Nuclear-Weapon Freeze

There are many reasons to support a halt to the nuclear arms race at this time:

Parity. There is widespread agreement that parity exists between U.S. and Soviet nuclear forces at present.

Avoiding "Nuclear War-fighting" Developments. The next generation U.S. and Soviet nuclear weapons improve "nuclear war-fighting" capabilities—that is, they improve the ability to knock out the enemy's forces in what is termed a "limited" nuclear exchange. Having such capabilities will undermine the sense of parity, spur further weapon developments, and increase the likelihood of nuclear war in a crisis, especially if conflict with conventional weapons has started. It is of overriding importance to stop these developments.

Stopping the MX and New Soviet ICBMs. Specifically, a freeze would prevent the deployment of new and improved Soviet ICBMs, which are expected to render U.S. ICBMs vulnerable to preemptive attack. This would obviate the need for the costly and environmentally-destructive U.S. mobile MX ICBM, with its counterforce capability against Soviet ICBMs. That, in turn, would avoid the pressure for the USSR to deploy its own mobile ICBMs in the 1990s.

Stopping the Cruise Missile. The new U.S. cruise missile, just entering production in an air-launched version and still in development in ground- and sea-launched versions, threatens to make negotiated, nationally-verified nuclear arms control far more difficult. Modern, low-flying terrain-guided cruise missles are relatively small and cheap and can be deployed in large numbers on virtually any launching platform: not only bombers, but also tactical aircraft, surface ships, tactical submarines, and various ground vehicles. They are easy to conceal and, unlike ICBMs, their numbers cannot be observed from satellites. If the United States continues the development and production of cruise missiles, the USSR will be likely to follow suit in 5–10 years; and quantitative limits on the two sides will be impossible to verify. A freeze would preclude this development.

Preserving European Security. A freeze would also prevent a worsening of the nuclear balance in Europe. To date the USSR has replaced less than half of its medium-range nuclear missiles and bombers with the new SS-20 missile and Backfire bomber. The United States is planning to add hundreds of Pershing II and ground-launched cruise missiles of the forward-based nuclear systems in Europe, capable of reaching the USSR. Negotiations conducted *after* additional Soviet medium-range weapons are deployed are likely to leave Europe with more nuclear arms on both sides and with less security than it has today. It is important to freeze before the Soviet weapons grow to large numbers, increasing pressure for a U.S. response and committing both sides to permanently higher nuclear force levels.

Stopping the Spread of Nuclear Arms. There is a slim chance of stopping the spread of nuclear weapons if the two superpowers stop their major nuclear arms race. The freeze would help the U.S. and the USSR meet their legal and political obligations under the Non-proliferation Treaty. It would make the renunciation of nuclear weapons by other countries somewhat more equitable and politically feasible. In addition, a U.S.-Soviet freeze would encourage a halt in the nuclear weapon programs of other countries which are known or believed to have nuclear weapons or nuclear-weapon technology. These are Britain, France, and China, with publicly acknowledged nuclear weapon programs, and India, Israel, and South Africa, without acknowledged programs.

Timing. There is a unique opportunity to freeze U.S. and Soviet nuclear arms in the early 1980s. The planned new U.S. and Soviet ICBMs and the U.S.

Pershing II and ground-launched cruise missile are not scheduled to enter production until 1983 or later. The Soviets have offered to negotiate the further deployment of their medium-range nuclear forces and submarine-based forces. Given the pressure to respond to new weapons on both sides and the existing nuclear parity, an equally opportune time for a freeze may not recur for many years.

Popular Appeal. Campaigns to stop individual weapon systems are sometimes treated as unilateral disarmament or circumvented by the development of alternative systems. The pros and cons of the SALT II Treaty are too technical for the patience of the average person. In contrast, an effort to stop the development and production of all U.S. and Soviet nuclear weapons is simple, straightforward, effective, and mutual; for all these reasons it is likely to have great popular appeal. This is essential for creating the scale of popular support that is needed to make nuclear arms control efforts successful.

Economic Benefits. Although nuclear forces take only a small part of U.S. and Soviet military spending, they do cost some tens of billions of dollars annually. About half of these funds go to existing nuclear forces, while half are budgeted for the testing, production, and deployment of new warheads and delivery systems. A nuclear-weapon freeze, accompanied by government-aided conversion of nuclear industries to civilian production, would yield several important economic benefits:

- About $100 billion each (at 1981 prices) would be saved by the United States and the Soviet Union over the period from 1981 to 1990 in unnecessary military spending.
- The savings could be applied to balance the budget; reduce taxes; improve services now being cut back; subsidize home and commercial conversion to safe, renewable energy resources; or increase economic aid to poverty-stricken Third World regions, thereby defusing some of the tinderboxes of international conflict.
- With the shift of personnel to more labor-intensive civilian jobs, employment would rise. At the same time, the highly inflationary pressure of military spending would be mitigated.

Verification

The comprehensive nature of a total freeze on nuclear weapon testing, production, and deployment (and, by implication, development) would facilitate verification.

Long-range bomber and missile production would be proscribed. The letter of assurance attached to the draft SALT II Treaty that the USSR will not increase its rate of production of Backfire bombers indicates that not only *deployment* but also *production* of the relatively large aircraft and missiles in question can be observed with considerable confidence. While concealed production and stockpiling of aircraft and missiles is theoretically possible, it would be extraordinarily difficult to accomplish with no telltale construction or supply. Any attempt would require the building or modification of plants and the development of new transport lines that are not operational at present. It would also involve high risks of detection and high penalties in worsening relations without offering any significant strategic advantage.

Verification of a ban on *tests* of missiles designed to carry nuclear weapons can be provided with high confidence by existing satellite and other detections systems. Here, too, a comprehensive approach is easier to verify than a partial or limited one.

Verification of aircraft, missile, and submarine *deployments,* by specific quantity, is already provided under the terms of the SALT II and SALT I Treaty language. Verifying *no* additional deployments or major modifications will be considerably easier, in fact, than checking compliance with specific numerical ceilings in a continually changing environment.

Verification of a comprehensive nuclear *weapon test* ban, the subject of study and negotiation for many years, has been determined to be possible within the terms of the existing draft comprehensive test ban treaty.

Initiatives Toward the Freeze

Either the United States or the Soviet Union could initiate movement toward the freeze by taking modest, unilateral steps that would: demonstrate its good faith, start movement in the right direction, and make it easier for the other country to take a similar step.

For example, either country could:

1. Undertake a three-month moratorium on nuclear test explosions, to be extended if reciprocated.
2. Stop further deployment, for a specified period, of one new strategic weapon or improvement of an existing weapon.
3. Draw up and publish comprehensive conversion plans for the nuclear facilities and employment that would be affected by a freeze, as a sign of serious commitment to the goal.

JEROME B. WIESNER

An Attack on "Nuclear Mythology"

Jerome B. Wiesner (b. 1915), whose research in the field of electrical engineering dealt with radar, acoustics, and the theory of communication, was for many years president of the Massachusetts Institute of Technology. He writes widely on the arms race and advocates nuclear weapon reductions. He was Science Advisor to President Kennedy and is greatly respected in the scientific community. This article was written as an editorial for major newspapers.

There are four points which, if widely understood, would give the American people the courage to demand that their government treat the efforts to halt the arms race as serious proposals, rather than as a public-relations problem, as is now the case.

First, we must understand the extent to which the United States has been running an arms race with itself, and, in the process, become a military culture—a society in which the arms race is accepted as a way of life.

Second, we must understand that there is *no* military use for nuclear weapons, and the steady development and accumulation of them increases the danger of ultimate disaster. The only sound role for nuclear weapons is as a deterrent to their use by others. A very few nuclear weapons, certain of delivery, constitute a powerful deterrent. Some analysts believe that large deterrents are needed for psychological reasons, yet we know from experience that even a very few bombs have acted as an effective deterrent.

Third, there are many safe alternatives to the present military policy of achieving security through an all-out nuclear arms race.

Finally, and most important of all, there is no need for expertise or secret knowledge to understand the principal issues of the arms race; every citizen can be knowledgeable and confident enough to insist on a voice in the critical military decisions.

President Dwight D. Eisenhower warned in 1961 about the growing influence of the military-industrial complex in our society. His message reflected his frustration at his inability to control the combined impact of the pressures from the military, industry, Congress, journalism, and veterans' organizations for buying more weapons and against his efforts to seek accommodations with the Russians.

As a member of the President's Science Advisory Committee, I saw first-

---

hand how government officials and industrial suppliers of the military collaborated with members of Congress to defeat his efforts.

As President John F. Kennedy's Special Assistant for Science and Technology, I saw how he, too, had to contend with powerful opposition when he chose to continue Eisenhower's efforts to negotiate a halt to nuclear testing. In fact, the opposition to his efforts became much more intense than that faced by his predecessor when it appeared that he just might succeed. Similarly, pressure from the Congress, Defense Department, and outside groups caused Kennedy to build a much larger Minuteman missile force than was necessary, even after photo reconnaissance made it clear that the anticipated missile gap did not exist.

That was hardly the first or the last time that billions of taxpayers' dollars were spent for political rather than security reasons. President Jimmy Carter yielded on the MX in the hope of getting the SALT II treaty through Congress. President Gerald R. Ford and his secretary of defense, James R. Schlesinger, because of military pressures, proposed to procure what they called "a limited strategic war-fighting capability," which Schlesinger ultimately admitted to Congress was planned for "a highly unlikely contingency."

During the more recent and successful effort to sell the B-1 bomber, the manufacturer carefully placed contracts so widely that almost every state and hamlet had a stake in the B-1's future. According to a report in the *San Francisco Examiner,* the average stake per state on the B-1 was $700 million, and the states of the 20 senators who lobbied hardest for the aircraft were scheduled to get sums ranging from $1 billion to $9 billion.

Even more disturbing is the fact that labor unions and chambers of commerce lobbied vigorously for this marginally useful aircraft, even though economic data show that dollars spent for defense systems produce only half as many jobs as the same amount of money spent on civilian activities.

Such pressures, however, are not a problem for President Reagan. He not only accepts most of the ideas of the groups that Eisenhower warned us against, he has become their most articulate spokesman, espousing an enormous buildup in U.S. military power, especially in nuclear war-fighting capability, while at the same time making a shambles of arms-control efforts. What is more, his Administration is made up largely of like-minded people, so he is not apt to hear a moderating voice from within. And the pressures of the defense community only confirm and enhance this Administration's intent.

More than 30 years of confrontational behavior has created a situation in which it is difficult to talk rationally about how we got here, even among ourselves. A combination of newspeak words, false information, half-baked ideas about successful preemptive attacks and winning nuclear wars, and a phony but authoritative clairvoyance in projections of Soviet forces and objectives have constantly masked the opportunities that exist for exploring alternatives.

Dependence upon such ideas as worstcase analysis, for example, supported by controlled leaks of secret information, has made possible the manipulation of public opinion. It has also made it easy for Americans to deny any responsibility for the arms race, to believe that the Russians are relentless and reckless aggressors and to conclude that there is nothing we can do to stop the catastrophe we see coming.

We need to disenthrall ourselves from a sense of aggrieved innocence and appreciate the extent to which our combination of fears and overwhelming technical and economic strength have caused our country to be a leading force in the arms race. In the future, we must find ways of using these same strengths and energies to take the lead in ending the arms race.

We need to abandon the idea that innovative technology can ever make it possible to win a nuclear war, or protect a nation involved in one from annihilation. Accepting this fact alone will open many options.

We must abandon the belief that there are no reasonable alternatives to the arms race to be seriously considered. A comprehensive nuclear test ban, a freeze on new weapons testing and deployment, a halt to the development of antisatellite and space weapons, reductions in the number of strategic weapons and a weapon-free zone in Europe are some of the suggestions that have been made in recent years that I believe could be safely put into effect.

To achieve a national policy that reflects these alternatives, we must disabuse ourselves of the belief that understanding the forces driving the arms race is beyond the comprehension of "non-expert" citizens. Most of all, we must become convinced that, at this moment in the history of our democratic nation, it has been overtaken by the social cancer of a runaway militarism from which only widespread understanding and decisive action can save it.

My basic point is that no one knows how to use nuclear weapons in warfare. There are thousands of experts on technical matters and on military hardware, but on the critical issues of strategy, deterrence, physical structures, and the environment, there are truly no experts. *None!* No one knows for sure about the actual field performance of missiles, their reliability or their accuracy. Because it is impossible to test nuclear weapons systems in realistic conditions, uncertainty about their performance in combat overrides the knowledge of the performance of individual components.

The layman who argues for a nuclear freeze or a test ban is frequently put down because he lacks secret information on the matter. There are no secrets on the vital issues that determine the momentum of the arms race. Each citizen should realize that on the critical issues of what constitutes enough, what is an adequate deterrent, whether humanity can recover from a nuclear war, and many other such questions, his or her studied judgments are as good as those of a president or a secretary of defense.

The nuclear bomb stubbornly remains the terror weapon wise men saw it to be at its birth. The default solution of the frustrated hordes of so-called experts has been to continue the arms race in the futile hope that a magic technical solution will appear.

Albert Einstein once said that God would not shoot dice with the universe. Man should not play such games either. Waiting for a technical solution is a futile gamble. We need to reevaluate our premises and rethink our priorities. We need to stop amassing nuclear destructive power.

EDWARD ZUCKERMAN

"This Area *Will* Be Evacuated"

Edward Zuckerman (b. 1948) has written for Harper's, *the* New York Times Magazine, New Times, *and* Rolling Stone. *This excerpt is a chapter from his book* The Day After World War III *(New York: Viking Press, 1984); a portion of the book, which was previously published in* Esquire, *won the 1983 Livingston Award in journalism on national affairs.*

If a nuclear attack on the United States ever appears imminent, the Plattsburgh, New York, police department will assign two patrolmen to direct traffic at the corner of Broad and Cornelia. That was one of the decisions made at a series of meetings held in the Emergency Operating Center beneath Plattsburgh police headquarters to plan the evacuation of Plattsburgh, site of a Strategic Air Command base, during a major confrontation between the United States and the Soviet Union. Such an evacuation is expected to cause traffic problems, so two hours were set aside to consider them.

It was Plattsburgh Police Sergeant George Rabideau who said, "You'll need at least two men there," when the intersection of Broad and Cornelia was pointed out on a map. Rabideau was sitting across from a captain representing Plattsburgh Air Force Base and a very bored-looking young man from the Clinton County Highway Department.

New York State civil-defense planner Joseph Hein, at the head of the table, pointed out a number of other intersections likely to be congested on the eve of a nuclear war. He calculated that to keep traffic moving will require two shifts of twenty policemen each, which will strain the resources of the forty-five-man Plattsburgh department.

"Couldn't we use school crossing guards?" suggested the Air Force captain.

"They're too old," said Rabideau. "They couldn't take it. It's hard on the body to direct traffic."

Plattsburgh's part-time civil-defense director, a professional insurance salesman, suggested that civil-defense volunteers be trained for the task.

Rabideau approved. "That will leave us free to cover car accidents," he said, "or fires, or fights between individuals. People will be emotional. I don't know if they're going to be hysterical, but they're definitely going to be emotional."

Indeed they are. The Plattsburgh evacuation plan is part of the national civil-defense program called Crisis Relocation Planning, under which the residents of areas considered to be likely targets for nuclear attack will move to low-risk "host areas" during a period of extreme international tension, such as that which might accompany tactical nuclear warfare between American and Russian forces on a foreign battlefield. On the theory that "there is nothing quite so helpful as being, say, ten miles or more away from a nuclear weapon when it goes off," plans are being made now to move 150 million residents of 400 "risk areas" to several thousand small towns throughout the country.[1] The Federal Emergency Management Agency, which is supervising the planning, predicts that 65 percent of the risk-area population can be evacuated in one day, and more than 95 percent in three days. "No one is in a position to provide an iron-clad guarantee that this kind of time would be available," FEMA acknowledges. "But it is the judgment of the Department of Defense that if the U.S. should ever suffer a nuclear attack, it is much more likely that this would follow a period of intense international tension than occur as a 'bolt from the blue.' "

Crisis Relocation Planning has therefore been designed not merely to save lives if an attack occurs but to play an important role in managing that intense preattack crisis. "Civil defense . . . is an essential ingredient of our nuclear deterrent forces," President Ronald Reagan decreed in a 1982 National Security Decision Directive. As "an element of the strategic balance," the directive says, one of the purposes of civil defense is to "assist in maintaining perceptions that this balance is favorable to the U.S." It will thus "reduce the possibility that the U.S. could be coerced in time of crisis."

So if the Russians ever, say, invade Iran, and the United States replies by dispatching the Rapid Deployment Force, and the Russians reply by increasing the alert status of their intercontinental nuclear forces, and the United States wants to resist the "coercion" implicit in that move by reducing the potential American death toll of a Soviet attack (or by letting the Russians know we're getting ready to reduce it), residents of Plattsburgh will find on their doorsteps, perhaps as a supplement to their local newspaper, a large-format brochure headlined EVACUATION INSTRUCTIONS.

"This area *will* be evacuated," says the brochure, which has already been prepared. "If a nuclear attack occurs, [this area] would be subject to the greatest danger. All persons living in this risk area must evacuate, when ordered, to lower risk portions of Clinton County called 'host areas.' " Printed on the back page of the brochure are seven large letters—A to G—one for each Plattsburgh neighborhood and its designated host area. Plattsburgh residents are instructed to cut out the letters assigned to their neighborhoods and attach them "to the lower left-hand (Driver's Side) corner of your car windshield," so that emergency personnel, including the two policemen at the corner of Broad and Cornelia, will be able to tell at a glance if a given carload of evacuees is driving in the right direction.

If for some reason the brochures are not delivered, Plattsburgh residents will be able to find detailed evacuation instructions in their local telephone directory, where, as part of a pilot public information program, FEMA has taken out a four-page ad. The phone book specifies, among other things, that if you live in the town of Plattsburgh, "north of Saranac River *not* including Cumberland Head," you are in evacuation group C. After placing that letter against your windshield, you will drive north on the Old Military Turnpike to the town of Ellenburg, where you will be received at the Northern Adirondack Central Junior-Senior High School. "When you arrive at the reception center," the phone book instructs, "stay in your car—you will be given a number. When your number is called go inside the reception center where you will be registered and directed to a lodging facility." (A similar Boston-area evacuation brochure, also already prepared, includes a questionnaire to be filled out "in duplicate before arriving in host area." It asks for evacuees' names, ages, sexes, occupations, and Social Security numbers, and leaves room for reception workers to fill in the evacuees' fallout shelter assignments.)

The instructions include a list of things to take along on the evacuation, among them sleeping bags, canned food, radios, toothpaste, extra socks, shovels, toilet paper, credit cards, and your will. (For the youngsters, FEMA is testing a coloring book with a page headed, "Color what you would need in a shelter." Kids are supposed to color in the canned beans and the candle, not the cake or the fish.) The evacuation brochure includes a one-page primer on the effects of nuclear explosions and three pages of instructions for building several types of fallout shelters, ranging from a relatively comfortable basement shelter to one built by digging a ditch under your car and then loading the car with dirt. You sit in the ditch.

During an intense international crisis, while 150 million residents of Plattsburgh and other risk areas are pondering this advice, gathering up their radios and shovels—and waiting—they will be able to pass the time by turning on their television sets and watching *Protection in the Nuclear Age,* a twenty-five minute animated civil-defense film that has been produced (in English and Spanish versions and with captions for the deaf) for showing on just such an occasion. The film opens with a drawing of the planet earth floating peacefully in space as an announcer intones, "We live in a world of tension and conflict. And peace, even where it does exist, does so without guarantees for tomorrow." The view zooms in toward the North American continent. "We must therefore face the hard reality that someday a nuclear attack against the United States might occur. And—equally important—we must also realize that horrifying as that prospect may seem, destructive as such an attack might be, we *can* survive. It would not mean the end of the world, the end of our nation. And you can greatly improve your own chances of survival if you'll remember these facts—about Protection in the Nuclear Age.''

Copies of this, the last film millions of Americans may ever see, have already been distributed to local civil-defense officials, some of whom have in turn already passed copies on to their local television stations.

''Defense Department studies show,'' the film's narrator says, ''that, even under the heaviest possible attack, less than five percent of our entire land area would be affected by blast and heat from nuclear weapons. Of course, that five percent contains a large percentage of our population.''

Red flashes erupt over small target areas on a map of the United States.

''But, even in these high-risk areas, if there's sufficient time to permit evacuation, many millions of lives could be saved.''

Pink radioactive clouds drift out of the red flashes.

''The other ninety-five percent of our land would escape untouched. Except possibly by radioactive fallout.''

The pink fallout spreads across the map.

''Now, here are things you need to know.''

The film proceeds to describe warning sirens, the effects of nuclear weapons, fallout shelter construction, the practicability of evacuation (''after all, we relocate millions of workers from our big cities every evening rush hour''), and other emergency measures. All of them are acted out by animated stick figures. When evacuation is described, a stick-figure family packs up its car and drives past stick-figure policemen to a relocation center, where it is greeted by a stick-figure hostess. Stick figures were selected for the film after many old civil-defense films had to be withdrawn from circulation partly because the old-fashioned clothing on their live actors started to look funny. ''Stick figures don't get obsolete as fashion changes,'' explains an employee of the FEMA audio-visual department.

Protection in the Nuclear Age concludes with a pep talk: ''The greatest danger is hopelessness, the fear that nuclear attack would mean the end of our world, so why not just give up, lie down, and die? That idea could bring senseless and useless death to many—for protection *is* possible.''

A similar pep talk concludes a series of fifteen camera-ready newspaper articles that have been distributed by FEMA to five thousand local civil-defense officials to pass on to local publications in a crisis. The articles include detailed information about constructing fallout shelters, administering first aid, extinguishing flaming curtains ignited by a nuclear explosion (''*prompt* action could save the lives of everyone in the building''), protecting cattle from fallout, and saving industrial equipment from blast damage by covering it with dirt. The fifteenth article is headlined, ''Would Survivors of Nuclear Attack Envy the Dead? . . . Experts Say No.''

"The newspaper articles would be supplemented by the twenty-five-minute television film. . . ." FEMA has explained. "The cost of such materials is very low, and we estimate that the emergency information newspaper articles and television films could add survivors amounting to perhaps 8 to 12 percent of the U.S. population."

And so, merely by watching the film and reading the articles as the United States and Soviet Union head toward nuclear war, the anxious residents of Plattsburgh and other risk areas will be saving no less than eighteen million of their own lives. Or so FEMA figures. The possibility will remain, of course, that the Russians, seeing this material being distributed in the United States, might conclude that the Americans are getting ready to launch a nuclear war and decide that they (the Russians) had better strike first. This irony—that the dissemination of information to save lives in a war might ignite the war—has been taken into consideration by FEMA. It is the reason that the newspaper columns and television film have been predistributed to thousands of *local* civil-defense officials. "One advantage of predistribution," explains FEMA spokesman Russell Clanahan, "is that giving the columns to newspaper will be purely a local decision. We don't have to appear to be escalating the crisis by issuing orders from Washington."

If distributing civil-defense information in a crisis alarms the Russians, then actually ordering the evacuation of hundreds of American cities will terrify them—possibly into launching a preemptive nuclear strike. "If the relocation were executed in the absence of a major move by the other side, it could trigger an unwelcome Soviet response and escalate the crisis," concluded a study of "the potential effect of crisis relocation on crisis stability" sponsored by the Defense Civil Preparedness Agency (a predecessor to FEMA). The report did not worry too much about this scenario, however, because it assumed that the United States would most likely order its cities evacuated only as a countermove to a Russian evacuation of *their* cities or some other provocative first step by the Russians. "Different individual Presidents would undoubtedly have different 'evacuation thresholds' for deciding whether a given move were hostile enough to warrant unilateral U.S. relocation," the study noted. "Most respondents [experts interviewed by the study's authors] felt that a Soviet invasion of Western Europe accompanied by use of theater-nuclear weapons was above their 'evacuation threshold.' "

One guess about what might actually precede the call to evacuate has been hazarded by Massachusetts civil-defense officials, who have prepared a recording, for use in exercises, with the type of announcement that may someday be directed to 150 million nerve-wracked risk-area residents:

> This is President Reagan. You, as well as I, have been carefully following the international events of the past few weeks. As you know, we have been airlifting supplies to West Berlin since the road corridors through East Germany have been closed by the Soviet bloc. Ground and air warfare continues in the Middle East. Three of our supply aircraft have been shot down this morning. Our protest to the Soviet Union

has gone unanswered. The major Russian cities have been ordered evacuated. As a strategic response, I am now ordering the use of our Crisis Relocation Plan, which was distributed nationwide on Monday and Tuesday. An effective relocation of our population to safer areas could demonstrate to the Soviets our national resolve and buy time for further negotiations. If they should launch a limited or general nuclear strike, the relocation would result in survival of most of our people. The nation is not—I repeat not—under attack. But we believe a serious possibility of attack does exist. Following the Crisis Relocation Plan can reduce the possibility of attack. If, God forbid, an attack should be launched, the plan could save millions of lives. We ask you to tune to your local TV station or stay turned to this radio broadcast and carefully follow instructions. We will continue to work for peace and to pray for peace. God bless you.

This is a point that no president will ever want to reach. The mere existence of the evacuation plans is supposed to have a deterrent effect on the Soviets—in the words of Reagan's National Security Decision Directive, to "enhance deterrence and stability in conjunction with our strategic offensive and other strategic defensive forces." If the plans in themselves deter insufficiently (and their deterrent effect rests on the Russians' believing that we believe that the plans really can save tens of millions of lives), a prudent president might decide they are too provocative to implement under any circumstances. FEMA claims that a well-planned and supported evacuation will insure the survival of more than 80 percent of the American people (including about two-thirds of the evacuees) even in a massive nuclear war, but even FEMA recognizes that you will insure the survival of 100 percent by not having the war.

All of this will be on the minds of 150 million risk-area residents as they wait, their cars packed for evacuation, listening to their radios to hear the president say yea or nay. Some of them will have their own "evacuation thresholds." Hearing rumors of war or news of foreign battles, they will head for the hills on their own. (The need to bring order to such "spontaneous evacuation" is one of FEMA's arguments for evacuation planning.) All will surely sense that a centrally ordered national evacuation will bring international tension to a head. As Herman Kahn, the think-tank nuclear war strategist, told the authors of the DCPA report on crisis relocation and crisis stability: "Crisis relocation by both sides . . . would sharply increase the probability that the crisis would be resolved quickly, one way or the other."

One way will be a visit to the country; the other will be nuclear war.

Following the call to begin crisis relocation, to match a Soviet evacuation or some other Soviet move with the evacuation of four hundred American cities, 80 to 85 percent of the residents of those cities will get into their cars or make their way to public transportation to begin the trip out of town, turning back for one last look at the homes they have been told are in the crosshairs of Russian nuclear weapons. The other 15 to 20 percent, FEMA estimates, won't go. They will listen to the president, say good-bye to their neighbors, go back in their houses, and lock the doors. A study conducted for the Defense Civil Preparedness Agency as it was developing crisis relocation planning predicted that those who will insist on staying put "might include disproportionate numbers of the sick, the disabled and handicapped, people with mental problems, alcoholics, drug addicts, and some of the elderly lonely," as well as "professional thieves and burglars" and "some political terrorists." Also likely to stay home, the study predicted, will be "the small proportion of our people who are convinced that no survival in nuclear war is possible . . . and those who feel that even were they to survive an attack, the post-attack world would be unlivable or they would not want to live in it." Finally, there will be those who are convinced that the president has "miscalculated the risks."

"If they don't want to evacuate, that's fine," said Richard Herskowitz, the chief civil-defense planner for New York State, as he drove back to his underground Albany office following the meeting at which traffic control for the evacuation of Plattsburgh was discussed. "That will make it easier for everybody else in the host areas."

Among those who will stay behind with the drug addicts, terrorists, and doomsayers, Herskowitz expects, will be pet lovers; their animals will not be welcome during the evacuation. "We've had a lot of concern about pets at our seminars," Herskowitz said. "We advise people to leave their pets in the basement with a couple of weeks' worth of food. If you come back, your pet is still there. If the area's blasted, he had an easy death."

Many of those who *will* want to evacuate, meanwhile, will not have an easy time of it. The residents of Plattsburgh (population 25,000) will endure a few red lights as they head down Cornelia Street, but what about the residents of New York City? "Nobody's suggesting you could move New York City in fifteen minutes," FEMA director Louis Giuffrida has said. "That's stupid. But we could do New York if we had a plan in place; we could do New York in five days, a week."

Most New Yorkers are skeptical—"Christ Almighty! It took me twenty-five minutes to get through the Brooklyn–Battery Tunnel this morning because there was a little snow," was the reaction of one former chief of the city's Office of Civil Preparedness. In 1982, the New York City Council voted overwhelmingly to join a number of other cities around the country that have refused to have anything to do with crisis relocation planning. Replying to the skeptics, FEMA cites a feasibility study of evacuating New York which concluded that 11.33 million people in the metropolitan area could be evacuated in 3.3 days, using cars, trucks, buses, trains, planes, and boats. This could be done, the study said, by sending 75,000 residents of Manhattan up the Hudson River to Saratoga County on three round trips of five Staten Island ferries. Meanwhile, 300,000 additional Manhattanites would travel by subway to the rail freight yards in Hoboken, where they would board boxcars and ride to Cayuga County; 614,600 people in the Bronx would drive north on Interstate 87 to Ulster County; 43,200 residents of Queens would fly from La Guardia Airport to Bradford, Pennsylvania, in an airlift "with characteristics similar to the Eastern Airlines shuttle." And so on.[2]

To avoid highway congestion during an evacuation of New York, the study envisions dividing the city into small districts and assigning car owners in each district specific evacuation times. To pass instructions on to small groups by radio, the plan proposes addressing them by a combination of their ZIP codes, two digits of their license plates, and birth dates. "The objective," it says, "should be to address instructions and messages to a few hundred people at a time." A resulting broadcast would sound like this: "Group 10020AZ14, start driving up Broadway at four a.m."

The study assumes that each host area will receive five times its own population in New York City evacuees. (Nationwide, the actual ratio of relocatees to host-area residents will range from two to one to five to one.) This will, of course, cause additional problems, not the least of which will be cultural. The sudden news, for example, that half a million black and Hispanic residents of the Bronx are heading for rural Ulster County is likely to create tremors in Ulster County. "How are you going to keep those people there from shooting the people coming in?" a reporter asked Bardyl Tirana, then director of the DCPA, in 1978. Replied Tirana: "That's tough."

"Since you've studied the problem," the reporter offered, "you no doubt have an answer to this."

Replied Tirana: "Don't assume that."

(Such fears are not groundless. In 1961, when evacuation planning was not part of federal civil defense, a Las Vegas official proposed organizing a five-thousand-man militia to deal with nuclear war refugees from California pouring into Nevada "like a swarm of locusts." In 1980, FEMA ordered a special study "to examine the question of whether or not Blacks and other minorities might experience special problems in the event that nuclear war became likely and the President ordered a massive population relocation." It concluded that they would.)

In general, however, the planners predict that host-area residents will be hospitable to the strangers arriving in their towns. "Seventy-three percent of the people surveyed in host areas have indicated they would be willing to take in one or more families in the event of a relocation effort," FEMA says, "and local governments are urged to encourage such assistance." The Plattsburgh evacuation instructions encourage such assistance in a paragraph addressed to host-area residents: "Your neighbors who have evacuated their homes need your help, particularly those families with little children. Volunteer now to bring a family to live with you. . . . You may be saving their lives." A phone number will be provided for those willing to take in a relocatee.

But the planners are not relying on anybody to call. Host-area plans are designed to accommodate *all* relocatees in public and commercial buildings. To figure who will fit where, college architecture and engineering students employed by FEMA have been fanning out through the nation's designated host areas every summer, surveying every nonresidential building in sight. Each building is photographed. Then a form is filled out with the building's name, address, age, size, latitude and longitude, distance from soil that is readily available to be piled up around the building to shield it from fallout, and other relevant data. With this information in hand—more than one million host-area buildings have been surveyed so far—comprehensive host-area plans are devised. The plan for Nogales, Arizona (to which some residents of Tucson will evacuate), specifies, for example, that 200 evacuees will live at Kino Cleaners at 226 Arroyo Boulevard and will eat at the McDonald's at 205 Crawford Street. If war breaks out and bombs fall, they will be joined at Kino Cleaners by 342 of the 530 people living at Elks Lodge #1397, because Kino Cleaners can be more easily converted into a fallout shelter (by packing dirt around it) than can the Elks Lodge.

The present owners and occupants of buildings that will house relocatees have not been troubled with prior notification of any of these plans. A couple of years after the Nogales plan was written, a reporter tried to telephone Kino Cleaners. It took several phone calls to reach the right building, because Kino Cleaners had been converted to a True Value hardware store, but owner Ed Baez was finally contacted and told of the plan to house two hundred refugees in his store.

"Oh?" he said. "That's news to me."

He was told 542 people will live in his store after a nuclear attack.

"Jiminy Christmas!" he exclaimed. "I guess they could live here. It wouldn't be too comfortable. They'd have to stand in line to use the johns. There's only two."

(While he had no objection to housing nuclear war refugees in his store, Baez added, as for himself he'd probably just head over the hills into Mexico.)

The manager of the McDonald's on Crawford Street hasn't been notified yet either to expect a few hundred extra customers on the eve of a nuclear war, but FEMA has begun contacting wholesale food distributors about special arrangements for crisis relocation. "Sixty major food distributors have told FEMA that, with only twenty-five-percent manning, they can reroute food from risk to host areas," says John Dickey of FEMA's Emergency Management Program Office. And more direct measures are envisioned. "One thing that was raised at an exercise we had," says Wyoming civil-defense director Bill Reiling. "was what authority the governor has over interstate commerce. If a food truck is stopped by the crisis, we might have to take it and give the driver a receipt."

Consumer rationing will be imposed in the host areas and so, probably, will a price freeze. Withdrawals from bank accounts will be limited until the crisis is over, but host-area banks will be expected to cash out-of-town checks. One "planning assumption" for crisis relocation is that the federal government will pick up the tab for feeding, housing, and transporting evacuees as well as reimbursing the owners of food trucks seized by local civil-defense officials. Wyoming authorities have already anticipated a formal announcement of this policy by preparing a sample news release for host areas: "The Chairman of the Board of the County Commissioners announced that the Federal Government will accept responsibility for all expenses incurred as a result of Crisis Relocation activities which exceed normal local government or private sector expenditures. All department heads of government agencies and owners/managers of private businesses must maintain complete and accurate records to justify claims submitted after the Crisis Relocation emergency." ("This is an optional release which should reduce anxiety," the Wyoming civil-defense guide advises, "particularly on the part of small businesses and marginal government agencies which probably would not be able to re-open if federal assistance was not available.")

If the federal government does adopt such a policy, it will put an additional strain on a national economy already crippled by the movement of 150 million people away from their homes. FEMA expects crisis relocation to cost the country about two billion dollars a day. To prevent the economy from collapsing, key workers in risk areas will be evacuated to relatively nearby host areas from which they can commute to their regular jobs. Such key workers will include police and firemen guarding the abandoned cities, food industry workers needed to provide food for the relocated population, and defense-industry workers gearing up for the anticipated war that provoked crisis relocation in the first place. Exactly how key workers will be prevailed upon to enter areas they have been told are subject to imminent nuclear attack is not clear. "If things got pretty tough, they could say the hell with running the wholesale food business and get out," acknowledges one crisis relocation planner. "But, if key workers got a half-hour warning of an attack, they could get in their cars and get pretty far away. They wouldn't have to worry about the speed limit." (FEMA has also begun designing and testing blast shelters for key workers caught in town when nuclear war begins.) Similar questions have been raised about people like the bus drivers who are supposed to drive people out of town when the evacuation begins and then return for another couple of runs. "As for the likelihood of police officers, truck drivers, and others carrying out their assigned jobs in a crisis relocation emergency," FEMA says, "there can be no absolute certainty. But in peacetime disasters, most people who have a job to do get it done."[3]

FEMA's optimism extends to every aspect of crisis relocation. Will there be hopeless traffic jams on the highways? "Prepositioned bulldozers" will push disabled vehicles off the roads, says a FEMA official. Will people panic? Riot? Loot? "While no one can guarantee perfect behavior in such an unprecedented situation as crisis relocation," FEMA says, "the judgment of those who have studied peacetime and wartime evacuations is that constructive and law-abiding behavior would be predominantly, indeed overwhelmingly, the case." Will evacuees be able to settle into host areas in a calm and orderly way? Wyoming civil-defense officials have already prepared this news release for relocatees: "Assistance will be needed in food preparation, babysitting, recreational activities, communications, office work and a concentrated effort toward improving fallout shelters. Watch the bulletin board for details on how you can help."

A fuller description of host-area life is provided in a FEMA publication in which a fictional participant describes a fictional crisis relocation: "When

Hamburg fell during the last week in July almost everyone knew that the CRP would soon be implemented. . . . We left our home at 7 p.m. on August 1 and arrived at our off ramp in Fremont at 9:45. . . . The community life was unusual from the beginning. In the first place most stores, food, hardware, etc., and services such as doctors, dentists, laundries were open at least 16 hours a day (and 24 hours, in some cases), and 7 days a week . . . Doctors among the refugees shared offices with the local doctors, as did dentists. Retailers were able to handle the increased load by the extra daily hours and the weekends. The greater the efficiency of these operations, the more labor would there be available for shelter and other preparations as well as for work in the key industrial and commercial firms involved in military requirements, and in stockpiling."

Shelter preparation will in fact be the top priority of the evacuees. They will spend their days piling up dirt around and on top of the True Value hardware stores, schools, churches, and other buildings where they have taken up residence. "Fallout protection," FEMA says, "is dirt cheap. . . . One fallout-protected space can be developed by moving (on the average) about one cubic yard of earth (about 70 to 100 buckets)." Key workers commuting daily back to risk areas will not be available to help with this effort, but the host-area work force will be augmented by convicts guilty of minor crimes, who will be released from host-area prisions to make room for felons from risk-area prisons. All of this shoveling will be rather difficult in much of the country if the nuclear crisis should happen to take place in winter, but FEMA promises that construction equipment will be assigned to assist. FEMA is also developing plans to supply the shelters with sanitation and ventilation supplies.

The digging will continue until the crisis relocation ends. "It is assumed the evacuation period would last from one to two weeks," FEMA says, "though a longer period should not be discounted."

The crisis relocation will end, of course, in one of two ways, with "derelocation" or worse. Wyoming civil-defense officials are already prepared for either eventuality with two alternate public announcements:

1. "The Governor has announced the improvements in diplomatic negotiations has [*sic*] greatly reduced the possibility of an attack on the United States and that it should be safe for the relocated residents of ——— County to return to their homes. Highway control procedures are currently being set up to keep traffic congestion to a minimum. . . ."

2. "A state of war now exists between the United States and———. Nuclear detonations have been reported in ——— states and we can expect attacks in our area at any time. . . ."

Most Americans, relocated or not, will not have to wait for a postattack news release to learn that crisis relocation has failed as a deterrent and nuclear war has begun. Many will figure it out for themselves in the instant before they are burned or battered to death. To get the news out to others a little sooner than that, FEMA maintains a National Warning Center in the Combat Operations Center of NORAD headquarters inside Cheyenne Mountain in Colorado. There, where military controllers constantly monitor satellite and radar data for signs of enemy attack, two FEMA warning officers are also on duty twenty-four hours a day. Upon detection of an attack, while NORAD is conferring with other military commands and the president, the FEMA warning officers will swing into action.

"Alternate National Warning Center, I have an emergency message," one of them will announce over the National Warning System, a nationwide party line leased from AT&T.

"Authenticate," a warning officer at the alternate center (underground in Olney, Maryland) will demand. Nobody wants a false alarm (or a false termination of a real alarm) from an impostor to get out on the system.

"I authenticate," the first warning officer will reply, consulting his secret authentication documents for the correct response. Then (in accordance with the *Procedures Manual for National & Regional Warning Centers*) he will ring the bell on the national party line for exactly seven seconds.

Bells will ring on dedicated phones at ten regional FEMA officers, other underground FEMA facilities, four hundred other federal civilian and military installations, and more than two thousand city, county, and state "warning points," most of them local police and fire dispatching centers.

"Attention all stations," the FEMA warning officer will announce. "This is the National Warning Center. Emergency. This is an Attack Warning. Repeat. This is an Attack Warning. Declaration time———Zulu [Greenwich time]. Alternate Warning Center acknowledge."

The alternate center will do so, and the Colorado center will call the roll of the FEMA regional offices. The regional offices will call the roll of state warning points. Meanwhile, the national warning officer will dial another number on his console to reach the national wire services and broadcast networks. "Attention news agencies," he will announce. "This is the National Warning Center. Emergency. An Attack Warning has been declared. . . ."

The president, if he is not too busy racing for his plane, may elect at this time to activate the Emergency Broadcast System (which replaced CONELRAD in 1963) and deliver a personal message to the American people. The National Oceanic and Atmospheric Administration will be broadcasting the attack warning over its FM Weather Radio System. The Coast Guard will be broadcasting it to ships at sea. The Federal Aviation Administration will be putting it out over its national teletypewriter network (and ordering all commercial airplanes to land).

In Maryland, the Alternate National Warning Center will activate the Washington Area Warning System, a network of outdoor sirens and bells and lights in federal government buildings. All over the country, city and country warning points will turn on their sirens, and Americans will hear a three- to five-minute wavering tone.

Some Americans will, anyway.

"We feel we can get the warning to the state and local levels," says Russ Lawler, who works in the area of warning for FEMA. "The weakness in the system is getting it to the individual."

If the enemy attack comes at 3 a.m. most Americans will be sleeping. Even if it comes at noon, very few Americans will happen to be hanging out in their local police dispatch rooms, or listening to the NOAA Weather Radio, or working in an FAA control tower.

"We ask local emergency operating centers, 'Can you receive attack warning in two minutes?' 'Can you receive it on a twenty-four-hour basis?' and 'What percent of the local population can you reach via public warning?' " says Joseph Mealy, chief of emergency management systems support for FEMA. "The numbers don't read too good. In theory, forty percent of the population can hear the sirens. I don't believe it."

The government has been trying for decades to find a way to overcome this problem. In the early 1960s, a device called NEAR (National Emergency Alarm Repeater) was designed. It was a small black box that individuals would stick into home electrical outlets. In an attack, civil-defense officials would send a signal over the nation's electric lines that would cause the NEAR to buzz and flash. A 1964 survey found that most Americans would welcome having a NEAR in their homes.

"We tested it in Michigan," says Mealy. "It didn't work."

In the late 1960s and early 1970s, the government developed DIDS (Decision Information Distribution System). DIDS was to consist of a nationwide network of low-frequency radio transmitters that, in an attack, would broadcast a signal that could automatically turn on sirens, other alarm systems, and even home television sets that had been fitted with inexpensive receivers. "The technology is there," says Mealy, who has a television set in his office that is fitted with a DIDS receiver. "The signal can turn it on and make it go to high volume. A device to retrofit a home TV would cost about thirty dollars. To install it as you manufacture the TV would only cost ten or twelve dollars." A 1972 survey found that 69 percent of all Americans would be willing to pay fifteen dollars for such a device, and a prototype transmitter was built in Maryland. "We had this thing ready and field-tested," says Mealy.

It has been mothballed. "The unfortunate thing that happened," Mealy explains, "was the downfall of Nixon with some of the things he did. After that, there was no way we were going to tell John Q. Public that we were going to put something in his home TV that was controlled by the government."

In 1982, FEMA Director Louis Giuffrida said he was still dissatisfied with the present system, mainly because the leased telephone line it runs on is unlikely to survive a nuclear attack. (In fact, it was never meant to survive a nuclear attack; its purpose is to get its message out *before* the missiles fall.) FEMA intends, Giuffrida said, to "replace the old system with a new one which will survive a nuclear attack and provide an operational capability throughout the emergency. . . . As equipment and funds become available, we will introduce satellite communications, low-frequency radio, and meteor-burst technology to provide an element of redundancy in the system.''

Even now, with a nonsurvivable system that most people can't hear, Joseph Mealy is confident that the system will work if a war begins during crisis relocation. ''In an international crisis, saberrattling, or ground war in Europe, or initial use of tactical nuclear weapons, the American public will not be too hard to warn,'' he says. FEMA literature suggests that, in a crisis, neighborhood radio watches be established, with neighbors taking turns staying awake and listening for news. ''And then there's the old neighborhood door-knocking routine,'' says Mealy. ''It's human nature. When you get bad news, the first thing you want to do is verify it with someone else.''

And then?

When you hear the warning siren, FEMA says, you should dash to a fallout shelter and take a radio with you. ''It is possible—but extremely unlikely,'' the literature says, ''that your first warning of an enemy attack might be the flash of a nuclear explosion in the sky some distance away. . . . If there should be a nuclear flash—especially if you are outdoors and feel warmth at the same time—take cover *instantly* in the best place you can find. By getting inside or under something within a few *seconds,* you might avoid being seriously burned by the heat or injured by the blast wave of the nuclear explosion.'' The best way to lie, FEMA says, is ''on your side in a curled-up position,'' with your arms wrapped around your head. ''This would give you some additional protection.''

Of course, if you are too close to an exploding nuclear weapon, you will be killed no matter what you do with your arms. Asked what the National Warning System will do for civilians in target areas who will have no time to get away, the vice-commander of NORAD told reporters in 1981: ''I guess they'll die all tensed up.''

Even those who do reach shelters may never be seen again. A shelter in the basement of a twenty-two-story office building, FEMA figures indicate, will be buried beneath thirty-three feet of debris after a nearby blast. Such considerations led New York City's top civil-defense official to propose a few years ago that the city's sirens be disconnected. They were costing six thousand dollars a month in phone bills to maintain, he said, half of them didn't work, and: ''A Russian submarine forty miles off New York can lob missiles at New York City that from launch to detonation will take seven seconds. In that time, the military command has to discern the attack at its headquarters in Colorado, and then notify Albany, and they notify us, and we have to notify fifty-six precincts to turn on the sirens, and the people who hear them will run into buildings and be turned to sand in a few seconds anyway.''

Those who are not turned to sand, advises the narrator of the film *Protection in the Nuclear Age,* should not panic: ''If your home is in an area where the heat wave has started small fires, use the next few minutes to put them out.

Prevent them from growing into big ones. Then shut off your main water valve and other utilities. You'll have at least thirty minutes to do all this—and then find shelter—before radioactive fallout starts coming down."

Finding shelter, of course, will be the most important next step. Blast survivors might find a shelter marked with one of the familiar black-and-yellow signs left over from the ambitious, and now abandoned, shelter-marking program of the early 1960s. "There are more than 227,000 of these shelters coast-to-coast," says the narrator of the film, "enough to shield our whole population if they were perfectly distributed. Unfortunately, they're not." (In fact, more than two-thirds of them are in risk areas and thus unlikely to survive blast damage themselves.)

"Even if you're unable to reach a shelter," the film consoles, "you can still improvise some protection. Set up a strong table or workbench in the corner [of your basement] that's most below ground level—and away from windows. Cover the top with as much heavy materials as it will safely hold—doors, bricks, flagstones, books. Wall it in with heavy bookcases, chests of drawers. Then fill the drawers with earth or sand for added shielding. . . .

"Or you can dig an L-shaped trench in your yard, about four feet deep and three feet wide. Make the longer side of the L big enough to accommodate your family—the shorter leg will serve as the entrance. Shore up the sides of the trench for safety. Cover it with house doors or heavy timbers, then pile two feet of earth on top for protection."

Detailed plans for this "door-over-trench expedient fallout shelter," as well as the similar "car-over-trench" and other models, will be distributed during crisis relocation, on the theory that, if an attack comes, many Americans will have time to dig holes in the ground big enough for their families before dangerous fallout reaches them. FEMA knows such shelters can be built quickly because in 1977 its predecessor, the DCPA, sponsored a test in which average families were paid a fee to build the shelters from the plans. "They were also paid a bonus of $5.00 for every person-hour they could reduce from the anticipated construction time," the study report adds. "The bonus was used to stimulate the stress situation that would exist in an actual emergency."

It is debatable whether a race to finish digging a fallout shelter to earn an extra ten or twenty dollars is as stressful as a race to finish digging a fallout shelter before fallout arrives and you die, but the test did establish that some average American families could build door-over-trench shelters in a day or less. A fatherless black Michigan family consisting of a mother, three sons, and a daughter dug theirs in thirty-one person-hours, earning a twenty-seven-dollar bonus. Two people in Colorado built a car-over-trench shelter in only four person-hours. "If a cross-section of American families will build shelters to earn some money," FEMA concluded, "it's likely that a substantial number of crisis evacuees would work hard to develop fallout shelters that could save their lives."

And so, if all goes well, and the ground's not frozen solid, within a few hours after a nuclear attack, previously unprepared Americans will be sitting in ditches under cars and doors: if all has gone well with the relocatees, they will be sitting more comfortably in church and school basements surrounded by the extra dirt they piled up during the relocation period. Even then, however, the shelterees will not be guaranteed immunity against fallout sickness or death. An especially heavy attack upwind, or just a bad break on wind direction, may bring enough fallout to overwhelm the defenses of dirt-covered churches, not to mention car-covered ditches. (Even if all goes as expected, two federal civil-defense researchers not affiliated with FEMA found in a 1981 study, sixteen of the forty-nine American counties likely to suffer the highest levels of fallout after a large Soviet attack have not been designated risk areas; shelterees in those counties will have a very hot time of it.)

Whether or not they are receiving lethal doses of radiation is something the shelterees will want to know. But that will not be easy. People who start vomiting in their shelters may be exhibiting the first symptom of fatal radiation poisoning, they may be exhibiting the first symptom of mild radiation poisoning, or they may only be nervous and upset. Symptoms specific to radiation sickness, such as loss of hair, will not become apparent until it is too late to take measures to avoid the radiation that caused it.

FEMA is working on this problem now, hiring and training state Radiological Defense Officers, maintaining 237,000 sets of radiation meters deployed in the early 1960s (one-third of which are defective), and manufacturing new radiological defense kits for shelters. Each kit will include one ratemeter (to measure the rate at which radiation is entering the shelter), two dosimeters (to measure cumulative radiation doses), and one charger (to charge the dosimeters). FEMA's goal is to produce seven million kits. FEMA is also working on plans to get the kits to the shelters in time of need.[4]

If the kits don't arrive in time, and shelter residents are out of communication with anyone informed about fallout levels, the shelterees will have to guess, or improvise, FEMA literature suggests that a white plate or cloth be placed outside the shelter. Fallout particles will show up against the white background. "A flashlight beam will illuminate fallout as it descends at night," FEMA adds. People entering the shelter after fallout has begun to descend should remove or shake off their outer clothing. "Later they can be visually inspected for radioactive particles. Use combs and brushes to remove particles, or brush them off, and then sweep these small amounts of fallout out of the shelter."

Then shut the door.

While tens of millions of American shelterees are waiting to emerge into the outside world—a wait, FEMA says, that will not exceed two weeks in host-area shelters—they will spend their sleeping hours laid out head to foot. "A head-to-toe arrangement, as shown in the following diagram," says the comprehensive FEMA guide, *How to Manage Congregate Lodging Facilities and Fallout Shelters,* "is the best position for sleep, in that it decreases the spread of respiratory ailments." But respiratory ailments will not be the only concern when the lights go out. Unmarried men and women will be separated from each other; if everyone is sleeping in one room, family groups will sleep in the middle, with the unmarried men on one side and the unmarried women on the other. "High social standards, particularly for sexual behavior, should be maintained in the sleeping area," the guide specifies. "Management should try to identify *potential* problems and keep them from becoming *actual* problems."

A great deal of responsibility for all sorts of problems will fall on the shoulders of fallout shelter management, and so FEMA has prepared *How to Manage Congregate Lodging Facilities and Fallout Shelters* as a practical guide for people trained as shelter leaders, perhaps during the crisis relocation period. "It is . . . quite feasible to take someone with a strong management background and in a short time give him the technical information required to manage a shelter effectively," says another FEMA publication, the *Attack Environment Manual.* Maturity, leadership experience, and courage are among the qualities that will make a good shelter manager, it says, and it offers a short test—"Rate Yourself as a Potential Shelter Leader"—for curious readers. Excellent physical health earns ten points on the test, as does having been a successful sales manager. Military officers who have led men in combat are awarded eight points, as are high school teachers. Mountain climbers, cave explorers, clergymen, and PTA presidents rate six points. Simply believing that you can manage a shelter effectively earns you five points. "What's that?" the test concludes. "You say you're a middle-aged spinster who teaches English at the high school, scuba dives on weekends, and thinks managing a shelter would be a blast? You'd make a good choice. Take me to your shelter, leader!!"[5]

In case of a shortage of pretrained managers, or if managers can't make it to every shelter, FEMA has prepared a short version of the shelter management guide that will simply be left in designated shelters to be picked up by the first person to run in. A notice is printed on the cover of the booklet: "The safety and well-being of the people in this shelter depend on capable leadership. If a civil defense manager is not present, anyone seeing this handbook who has leadership experience can and should TAKE CHARGE IMMEDIATELY."

Once the shelter manager has taken charge, he (or she) will supervise the entrance of shelter residents, see that they fill out registration forms, confiscate their weapons, and, if possible, collect their perishable food, radios, drugs, and liquor. The manager will then appoint assistants and deputies and organize the shelterees into work teams devoted to radiological defense, supplies, technical maintenance, health, fire control, safety and rescue, communications, administration, water, training and education, security, night watch, psychological first aid, shelter upgrading, recreation, religion, food, sanitation, and ventilation. (Faced with the "threat" of "an emergent leader who has assumed control before Manager and trained staff entered shelter," the guide advises that the manager give the upstart a position in the shelter hierarchy.) The shelter will also be organized into community "units" of seven to twelve friends and/or family members; the units will combine into "sections" of forty to sixty people; the sections will be parts of "divisions" of two hundred to four hundred people; and, if the shelter is really big, the divisions will be organized into "squadrons" of one thousand to fifteen hundred. "Such living groups will provide individuals with the reassurance they receive from group membership," the shelter management guide says, "and (2) will help you run the shelter more effectively."

Even so, it is expected that there will be problems. "Managing a [fallout shelter] is similar in many ways to running a hotel," the guide says. But it points out some differences as well. For example: "If you lack enough medical resources, including drugs, to meet the needs of your total population, and you are unable to increase your supplies, you must decide which patients will receive the scarce drugs, and in what order of priority. . . . It may be necessary to let some people die."

Other problems may arise from the fact that standard fallout shelter designs provide just ten square feet per person. In such close quarters, heat stroke and carbon dioxide poisoning can be fatal unless adequate ventilation is supplied. If nuclear attack has knocked out electrical equipment, shelters will be pitch black. Civil-defense officials have run a shelter living test in which volunteers spent twenty-four hours in the dark and they "apparently adjusted very well," FEMA reports, but a shortage of batteries or generators in a shelter will still make life difficult.

Water will be drinkable after an attack. FEMA says, fallout-contaminated water can be filtered. But there is likely to be a scarcity of water in the shelter, and foraging trips outside during days of heavy fallout will be dangerous. When fallout levels dip to where there is no threat of immediate incapacitation, foragers will be risking getting cancer later. Long-term cancer deaths can, however, be reduced, two federal civil-defense researchers suggested in 1981, by selecting foragers from among the older shelterees. "Older people will come to the end of their natural life spans before reaching the end of the risk [of fallout-induced cancer] . . .," the researchers wrote, "thus, the same exposure may produce fewer total excess cancers in this group than within a younger segment of the population."

It will not be necessary to risk the life of anyone, old or young, to go out searching for food, FEMA shelter literature advises: "Healthy individuals should be physically able to survive a several-week shelter stay without any food. If shelterees are expected to participate in postshelter recovery operations, however, they will require food during the confinement period. Moreover, food has tremendous emotional significance and failure to provide what is commonly perceived as a basic need can make the keeping of people in shelter very difficult." As for other basic needs, regulation shelters will be equipped with one portable sanitation kit (a barrel with a plastic liner and a toilet seat) for each fifty shelterees. "To increase toilet area cleanliness," says the shelter management guide, "it will be necessary for both men and women to perform all toilet functions sitting down. . . . It may be necessary to schedule toilet use at peak hours (early morning, late evening) and you must remember that any illness causing diarrhea or vomiting will increase toilet use."

People will adjust surprisingly well to most odors in the shelter, the guide assures, but one odor that may cause problems will be that of dead bodies. "Death in a Fallout Shelter causes three management problems," the manual advises. "(1) Health (the body might contain disease-producing organisms); (2) Emotional impact of death on your population; (3) Legal problems." The trained manager will see that people who die are really dead ("those who have not been medically trained must use great caution in pronouncing death"), then record the death, wrap the corpse in a sheet or blanket, "quickly remove it from your main area, out of sight of the population," and bury it outside "as soon as external radiation levels allow a short trip."[6] Finally, the manager or "a member of the religious activities team" will "conduct a simple service" and "provide emotional support to family members."

Bereaved family members will not be the only ones needing emotional support. "Maintaining the morale of people confined in close quarters and possibly in semi-darkness for two weeks will not be easy," notes the management guide, "especially if they are worried about the effect of an enemy attack on our nation and their own ways of life." But the well-trained shelter manager will try to keep spirits up. At least one interdenominational religious service will be conducted on the first day in the shelter, with more to follow. Group singing will be encouraged, as will board games. "Improvising checkerboards and pieces, cards, etc., is an important part of your recreational program," the guide says, "and is a team effort that will bring people together." The checkerboards and cards may be made by shelterees during arts and crafts sessions. ("Arts and crafts products can be shown and admired," says the manual.) Special emphasis will be placed on news briefings about the world outside (if any information is getting in): "It is vital . . . that you [the manager] take steps to give your population factual, official information and move swiftly to counter and stifle rumors that will weaken their motivation to adjust and to prepare themselves for the day when they will emerge from the fallout shelter to an uncertain future."

This will be the manager's greatest challenge—to dispel negative thinking among the shelter population. "Some of your population may be upset by the danger in which they think they are placed as the result of the attack or attack threat which forced the move to Fallout Shelters. They may be even more worried than before about the safety of family and friends with whom they have not been able to make contact. They may believe that the attack means the end of their way of life and are afraid of being killed or having to live under impossible conditions."

If these doubts and pressures lead any of the shelterees to commit antisocial or criminal acts, they will be disciplined or confined. (Mock trials and/or expulsion from the shelter, which could be fatal, are specifically not recommended, however.)

For the rest, "discussion groups" and "training-education classes" will be organized. These will teach "survival techniques for the post shelter world." It is also probable, says the shelter manual, that surviving government officials "will at some point provide you with an outline of recovery information which our government wants you to discuss with your population." Despite their importance, such classes will have to be kept short. "Under the stress of a nuclear attack, people will not be able to concentrate easily for extended periods of time." The best time for such sessions will be shortly after meals or coffee breaks, "when your population is most alert."

These sessions will be one of the most important parts of the weeks underground, as they will reach out to those who have concluded that nuclear war leaves them nothing to look forward to. "Such training will shift thinking positively toward the future," promises the shelter management guide. "The best lesson that your population can learn in the Fallout Shelter is to know they can survive and to believe in a future in which our society can be rebuilt."

Notes

[1]Risk areas are defined as those in which nuclear weapons are based, those containing other important military facilities or war industries, and cities with populations of more than fifty thousand. Risk area selection was, however, based on unclassified information, so secret installations of military importance, of which the Soviets may well be aware, are not included in the risk-area list.

[2]In 1981, the New York City Transit Authority solicited bids for equipment to protect the city's subways from being knocked out by "electromagnetic pulse," a nuclear-weapon effect which can destroy electrical systems hundreds of miles away from a nuclear explosion. Such protection would be essential if the subways were to be used in evacuating New York after a nuclear attack on another part of the country, such as the midwestern missile fields. A Brooklyn state senator, however, brought the Transit Authority plan to public attention and attacked it as a waste of money. "The Transit Authority can't keep the trains rolling during an average rush hour," he said. "Why is it worrying about a nuclear attack?" The plan was abandoned the next day.

[3]Exhibiting somewhat less confidence, the Nuclear Regulatory Commission threatened in 1983 to shut down the Indian Point, New York, nuclear power plants partly because of the "questionable availability" of drivers for buses needed to evacuate residents near the plants in case of accident. In hearings on the evacuation plan, bus drivers had testified that they would not enter a radiation zone without monitoring equipment; some said they would walk off their jobs to get their own families out of the area. Ultimately, the commission allowed the plants to stay open, after utility officials began giving a course on radiation to area bus drivers so they could make "informed decisions" on whether to volunteer to drive during an emergency.

[4]Radiation meters will play an important role in preserving fallout shelter morale, Herman Kahn observed in his 1960 book, *On Thermonuclear War*. As a result of "anxiety, unfamiliar environment, strange foods, minimum toilet facilities, inadequate shelters and the like . . . some high percentage of the population is going to be nauseated, and nausea is very contagious," he wrote. "It would not be surprising if almost everybody vomits. Almost everyone is likely to think he has received too much radiation. Morale may be so affected that many survivors may refuse to participate in constructive activities. . . . The situation would be quite different if radiation meters were distributed. Assume now that a man gets sick from a cause other than radiation. Not believing this, his morale begins to drop. You look at his meter and say, 'You have received only ten roentgens, why are you vomiting? Pull yourself together and get to work.' "

[5]In its newer literature, FEMA is resolutely nonsexist. "In the following pages," notes *How to Manage Congregate Lodging Facilities and Fallout Shelters,* "the manager and staff are often referred to as 'he,' which term is intended only as a space-saving convenience, with no implications whatsoever of any sexual discrimination. In the event of nuclear disaster, women will be playing major roles as Managers and other key staff in helping our nation survive and recover."

[6]While waiting for radiation levels to dip, former federal civil-defense researcher Cresson Kearny has observed, "the sickly-sweet stink of a decaying human body is [likely to be] greatly disturbing. Some civil defense workers have theorized that the best way to take care of a corpse in a shelter until the fallout dose-rate outdoors is low enough to allow burial is to seal it in a large plastic bag. A simple test with a dead dog proved this idea impractical: gas pressure caused the bag to burst."

GEORGE F. KENNAN

Cease This Madness

George F. Kennan (b. 1904) is a historian and diplomat who has written about U.S.-Soviet relations over his long and distinguished career. He was U.S. Ambassador to the Soviet Union (1952) and to Yugoslavia, (1961–63). It was Kennan who first proposed that the United States adopt a policy of "containment" toward the Soviets (in 1947). In the last decade or so, Kennan has been an outspoken critic of the excesses to which the United States has gone in pursuit of that policy. Among his recent books is The Nuclear Delusion: Soviet-American Relations *(New York: Pantheon Books, 1982).*

When I glance back over the past fifty years, it seems evident that the East-West relationship has been burdened by certain unique factors that lie in the very nature of the respective societies. When it comes to describing these factors, permit me—so far as the Western side is concerned—to confine myself to my own society.

I have no doubt that there are a number of habits, customs, and uniformities of behavior, all deeply ingrained in the American tradition, that complicate for others the conduct of relations with the American government. There is, for example, the extensive fragmentation of authority throughout our government—a fragmentation that often makes it hard for a foreign representative to know who speaks for the American government as a whole. There is the absence of any collective Cabinet responsibility, or indeed of any system of mutual responsibility between the executive and legislative branches of government. There are the large powers exercised, even in matters that affect foreign relations, by state, local, or private authorities with which the foreign representative cannot normally deal. There is the suceptibility of the political establish-

George F. Kennan, "Cease This Madness," *Atlantic Monthly* (January 1981), pp. 25–28.

ment to the emotions and vagaries of public opinion, particularly in this day of confusing interaction between the public and the various commercialized mass media. There is the inordinate influence exercised over American foreign policy by individual lobbies and other organized minorities. And there is the extraordinary difficulty a democratic society experiences in taking a balanced view of any other country that has acquired the image of a military and political enemy—Democratic societies do very poorly in coping, philosophically, with the phenomenon of serious challenge and hostility to their values.

In the light of these conditions, I can well understand that dealing with our government can be a frustrating experience at times for any foreign representative. I regret these circumstances, as do some other Americans. They constitute one of the reasons I personally advocate a more modest, less ambitious American foreign policy than do many of my compatriots. But these conditions flow from the very nature of our society, and they are not likely to be significantly changed at any early date.

When we look at the Soviet regime, we also encounter a series of customs and habits, equally deeply rooted in history and weighing heavily on the external relationships of that regime. These, strangely enough, seem to have been inherited much less from the models of the recent Petersburg epoch than from those of the earlier Grand Duchy of Muscovy. And they have found a remarkable reinforcement in some of the established traditions of Leninist Marxism itself: in its high sense of orthodoxy, its intolerance for contrary opinion, its tendency to identify ideological dissent with moral perversity, its ingrained distrust of the heretical outsider.

One example is the extraordinary passion for secrecy in all governmental affairs—a passion that prevents the Soviet authorities from revealing to outsiders even those aspects of their own motivation that, if revealed, would be reassuring to others. Excessive secrecy tends, after all, to invite excessive curiosity, and thus serves to provoke the very impulses against which it professes to guard.

Along with this passion for secrecy goes a certain conspiratorial style and tradition of decision-making, particularly within the Party—a practice that may have its internal uses but often inspires distrust. And there is the extraordinary espionomania that appears to pervade so much of Soviet thinking. Espionage is a minor nuisance, I suppose, to most governments. But nowhere, unless it be in Albania, is the preoccupation with it so intense as it appears to be in the Soviet Union. This is surprising, for one would expect to encounter it, if anywhere, in a weak and precariously situated state, not in one of the world's greatest and most secure military powers.

The foreigner who has to deal with the Soviet government often has the impression of being confronted, in rapid succession, with two quite disparate, and not easily reconcilable, Soviet personalities: one, a correct and reasonably friendly personality, which would like to see the relationship assume a normal, relaxed, and agreeable form; the other, a personality marked by a suspiciousness so dark and morbid, so sinister in its implications, as to constitute in itself a form of hostility. I sometimes wonder whether the Soviet leaders ever realize how much they damage their own interests by their cultivation of it.

Finally, there is the habit of polemic exaggeration and distortion, carried often to the point of denial of the obvious and solemn assertion of the absurd—a habit that has offended and antagonized a host of foreigners, and to which even some of the old-timers find it hard to accustom themselves.

These, then, are what I might call the permanent complications of the East-West relationship. There have been others, less permanent but even more serious.

The first, and the one that marked the relationship throughout much of the 1920s and 1930s, was the world-revolutionary commitment of the early Leninist regime, with its accompanying expression in rhetoric and activity. It is true that the period of the intensive pursuit of world revolution was brief. As early as 1921, aims of this nature were already ceasing to enjoy the highest priority in the policies of the Kremlin. Their place was being taken by concern with the preservation of the regime and the agricultural and industrial development of the country. But world-revolutionary rhetoric remained substantially unchanged throughout the twenties and much of the thirties; and Moscow continued to maintain in the various Western countries small factions of local Communist followers over whom it exerted the strictest discipline, whom it endeavored to use as instruments for the pursuit of its policies, and whose unquestioning loyalty it demanded even when this conflicted with loyalty to their own governments. So unusual were these practices, and so disturbing to Western governments and publics, that they formed the main cause for the high degree of tension between Russia and the West.

With the triumph of Hitler in Germany, however, an important change occurred. Beginning about 1935, the menace of Hitler began to loom larger in Western eyes than did the ideological differences with Soviet communism or the resentment of world-revolutionary activities. The result was that the Soviet Union came to be viewed in the West no longer primarily from the standpoint of its hostility to Western capitalism but rather from the standpoint of its relationship to Nazi Germany.

And this had several confusing consequences. For one thing, it tended to obscure from the attention of the Western public the full savagery of the Stalinist purges of the late 1930s. But then, after 1941 the common association of the Western powers with the Soviet Union in the war against Germany gave rise to sentimental enthusaisms in the West and to unreal hopes of a happy and constructive postwar collaboration with Soviet Russia. It was this factor, as the war came to an end, that brought the various Western statesmen to accept without serious remonstrance not only the recovery by the Soviet Union of those border areas of the former Russian empire that had been lost at the time of the Revolution but also the establishment of a virtual Soviet military-political hegemony over the remainder of the eastern half of the European continent; in other words, a geopolitical change of historic dimensions, bound to complicate the restoration, in the postwar years, of anything resembling a really stable balance of power.

It was not surprising that when the war came to an end, and people in the West turned to the construction of a new world order, a reaction set in. There was a sudden realization that the destruction of Germany's armed power and the effective cession to the Soviet Union of a vast area of military deployment in the very heart of the continent had left Western Europe highly vulnerable to a Soviet military attack, or at least to heavy military-political pressures from the Soviet side. Added to this was the growing realization that with the establishment of Communist regimes, subservient to Moscow, in the various Eastern European countries, the relations of those countries with the West had become subject to the same limiting factors that already operated in relations with the Soviet Union. Then came the Korean War—a conflict in which, though Soviet forces were not actually involved, people in the West soon came to see a further manifestation of Soviet aggressiveness. And it was just at this time that the nuclear weapon began to cast its baleful shadow over the entire world, stirring up the fear, confusion, and defensive panic that were bound to surround a weapon of such apocalyptic—indeed, suicidal—implications.

The death of Stalin, the establishment of the dominant position of Khrushchev, and the accompanying relaxations in Soviet policy gave rise to new hopes for the peaceful resolution of East-West differences. Although Khrushchev was crude, he wanted no war; and he believed in human communication. But he overplayed his hand. And such favorable prospects as his influence presented went largely without response in the West. The compulsions of military competition and military thinking were already too powerful.

For, during this entire period, Soviet leaders persisted in the traditional Russian tendency to go too far in the cultivation of military strength, particularly conventional strength. They continued to maintain along their western borders, as their czarist predecessors had done before them, forces numerically greater than anyone else could see the need for. And the situation was not made better by the tendency of Western strategists and military leaders to exaggerate the strength of these forces, with a view to wheedling larger military appropriations out of their own reluctant parliaments, or by the tendency of the Western media to dramatize these exaggerations as a means of capturing public attention.

The Americans, meanwhile, unable to accommodate to the recognition that the long-range nuclear missile had rendered their country no longer defensible, threw themselves headlong into the nuclear arms race, followed at every turn by the Russians. In the U-2 episode and the Cuban missile crisis, the two great nuclear powers traded fateful mistakes, further confirming each other's conviction that armed force, and armed force alone, would eventually determine the outcome of their differences. Out of all these ingredients was brewed the immensely disturbing and tragic situation in which we find ourselves today: anxious competition in the development of new armaments; blind dehumanization of the prospective adversary; systematic distortion of that adversary's motivation and intentions; steady displacement of political considerations by military ones in the calculations of statesmanship; in short, a dreadful militarization of the entire East-West relationship.

This moral and political cul-de-sac represents a basic change, as compared with the first two decades of Soviet power, in the source of East-West tensions. It is not the capacity of the Kremlin for promoting social revolution in other countries that is feared and resented. Rather, the Soviet Union is seen primarily as an aggressive military menace.

But there is no rational reason for the militarization of the Cold War. Neither side wants a third world war. Neither side sees in such a war a promising means of advancing its interests. The West has no intention of attacking the Soviet Union. The Soviet leadership, I am satisfied, has no intention of attacking Western Europe. The interests of the two sides conflict, to be sure, at a number of points. Experience has proven, most unfortunately, that in smaller and more remote conflicts, where the stakes are less than total, armed force on a limited scale might still continue to play a certain role, whether we like it or not. The United States has used its armed forces in this manner three times since World War II: in Lebanon, in the Dominican Republic, and in Vietnam. The Soviet Union now does likewise in Afghanistan. I am not entertaining, by these remarks, the chimera of a total world disarmament. But for the maintenance of armed forces on a scale that envisages the total destruction of an entire people there is no rational justification. Such a practice can flow only from fear, and irrational fear at that. It can reflect no positive aspirations, and it is dangerous.

No one will understand the danger we are all in today unless he recognizes that governments in this modern world have not yet learned how to create and cultivate great military establishments, particularly those that include the weapons of mass destruction, without becoming the servants rather than the masters of what they have created. Modern history offers no example of the cultivation by rival powers of armed force on a huge scale that did not in the end lead to an outbreak of hostilities. And there is no reason to believe that we are greater, or wiser, than our ancestors. It would take a very strong voice, indeed a powerful chorus of voices, from the outside, to say to the decision-makers of the two superpowers what should be said to them:

"For the love of God, of your children, and of the civilization to which you belong, cease this madness. You have a duty not just to the generation of the present; you have a duty to civilization's past, which you threaten to render meaningless, and to its future, which you threaten to render nonexistent. You are mortal men. You are capable of error. You have no right to hold in your hands—there is no one wise enough and strong enough to hold in his hands—destructive powers sufficient to put an end to civilized life on a great portion of our planet. No one should wish to hold such powers. Thrust them from you. The risks you might thereby assume are not greater—could not be greater—than those which you are now incurring for us all.''

But where is the voice powerful enough to say it?

There is a very special tragedy in this weapons race. It is tragic because it creates the illusion of a total conflict of interest between the two societies. It tends to conceal the fact that both of these societies are today confronted with internal problems never envisaged in the ideologies that originally divided them. In part, I am referring to environmental problems: the question whether great industrial societies can learn to exist without polluting, exhausting, and thus destroying the natural resources essential to their very existence. These are not only problems common to the two ideological worlds; they are ones the solution of which requires each other's collaboration, not each other's enmity.

But there are deeper problems—social, and even moral and spiritual—that increasingly affect all the highly industrialized, urbanized, and technologically advanced societies. What is involved here is essentially the question of how life is to be given an adequate meaning, how the quality of life and experience is to be assured for the individual citizen in the highly artificial and overcomplicated social environment that modern technology has created. Neither we in the West nor they in the East are doing well in the solution of these problems. We are both failing—each in our own way. If one wants an example of this, one has to look only at our respective failures in our approach to teenage youth. The Russians demoralize their young people by giving them too little freedom. We demoralize ours by giving them too much. Neither system finds itself able to provide them with the leadership and inspiration and guidance needed to realize their potential as individuals and to meet the responsibilities the future is inevitably going to place upon them.

And this is only one point at which we are failing. Neither here nor there is the direction of society really under control. We are all being swept along, in our fatuous pride, by currents we do not understand and over which we have no command. And we will not protect ourselves from the resulting dangers by continuing to pour great portions of our substance, year after year, into the instruments of military destruction. On the contrary, we will only be depriving ourselves, by this prodigality, of the resources essential for any hopeful attack on these profound emerging problems.

The present moment is in many respects a crucial one. Not for thirty years has political tension reached so dangerous a point as it has attained today. Not in all this time has there been so high a degree of misunderstanding, of suspicion, of bewilderment, and of sheer military fear.

The United States and possibly the Soviet Union will see extensive changes in governmental leadership this year. Will the new leaders be able to reverse these trends?

Two things, as I see it, would be necessary to make possible this transition.

First, statesmen on both sides should take their military establishments in hand and insist that these become the servants, not the masters and determinants, of political action. Both sides must learn to accept the fact that only in the reduction, not in the multiplication, of existing monstrous arsenals can the true security of any nation be found.

But beyond this, we must learn to recognize the gravity of the social, environmental, and even spiritual problems that assail us all in this unreal world of the machine, the television screen, and the computer. We and our Marxist friends must work together in finding hopeful responses to these insidious and ultimately highly dangerous problems.

LEON WIESELTIER

A Defense of "Nuclear Realism"

Leon Wieseltier (b. 1952) is a historian of Jewish history and is literary editor of the New Republic. *He has recently been writing about the nuclear situation, and his book* Nuclear War, Nuclear Peace *shows his attempts to articulate a middle ground position between "hawks" and "doves." Recently, the name "owls" for this middle ground has gained in popularity. This is an editorial written for major newspapers.*

The nuclear debate of recent years has consisted of a contrast between idealism and realism. It is easy to understand that idealism has become the more popular inspiration. All the good rhetoric, and a lot of the bad reality, seem to be on its side.

The threat of nuclear war *is* intolerable. It breeds impatience; and it is idealism in its many forms that most honors that impatience. By idealism, I mean the broad variety of dramatic denouements to the nuclear predicament that have been proposed—the abolition of the arms race, the abolition of nuclear weapons, the abolition of war, the abolition of soverign states, the abolition of the evil in man. These are all solutions that are commensurate with the ultimate scale of the problem. We are contemplating, after all, the possibility that the worlds of culture and nature may someday be destroyed.

Moreover, it is emotionally very difficult to make do with the idea that the

---

Leon Wieseltier, "A Defense of 'Nuclear Realism.' " This article originally appeared in the *Los Angeles Times*, October 7, 1984, IV, p. 1. Leon Wieseltier is literary editor of the *New Republic* and author of *Nuclear War, Nuclear Peace* (New York: Holt, Rinehart, and Winston, 1983). Reprinted by permission.

greatest threat to human history should be met with concepts of management—which is what the idea of deterrence asks. And yet idealism is not the most responsible approach to the nuclear danger. Indeed, it is the very magnitude of the danger that makes idealism the least responsible method of anti-nuclear thought and anti-nuclear action.

Realism—that is, deterrence uncomplacently conceived—deserves to be defended against its idealist critics, for two good reasons: First, if you really respect the horror of a nuclear holocaust, you will think and act very coolly about it. Attempting the abolitions mentioned above could create a whole new class of instabilities that could have the infernal and ironic consequence of setting the whole thing off.

Of no abolitionist is this more true, by the way, than of Ronald Reagan. When he promised to save the United States, and eventually the Soviet Union, from the nuclear situation with a "Star Wars" system of defense, the President placed himself prominently in the camp of the idealists. But even the beginning of an attempt to implement a defense of our cities against their ballistic missiles could shatter the strategic stability that has characterized superpower relations in the nuclear area for decades.

Second, it must be impressed upon the American public how very remote is the realization of any of the nuclear abolitionisms. There are now about 50,000 nuclear weapons in the American and Soviet arsenals. The world will not be safe, we may all agree, until all or most of these weapons are actually dismantled, until the President of the United States and the prime minister of the Soviet Union instruct their subordinates to pass out the screwdrivers. If you believe the "nuclear winter" scenario, at least 49,000 of these deadly devices will simply have to disappear.

Is it really defeatism to suggest that this is not likely to happen? Certainly arms control will not accomplish it. If Reagan and Konstantin U. Chernenko sign a piece of paper written by George F. Kennan, according to which each side will cut its arsenal in half, each side will still possess power to destroy the world.

Deterrence, then, is an accurate description of reality for a very long time to come. We are stuck with it; there are grounds for a certain amount of fatalism about history after Hiroshima. And since we are stuck with it, it is a dangerous thing to discredit. Fatalism, however, is not the same thing as despair. There is deterrence properly managed and deterrence improperly managed. A great deal hangs on the distinction.

In the area of strategy, deterrence properly managed requires a firm and forthright rejection of any notion that a nuclear war can be prosecuted like a conventional war, that it can be limited or controlled. In the area of force structure, it requires a rejection of any weapons system that will upset the tender but tangible nuclear balance; the MX missile deserves the death it is about to meet at the hands of Congress, the precise nature of cruise missiles needs to be more carefully thought out, the D-5 missile of the Trident II submarine should be improved more for its range than for its accuracy, and so on.

In the area of arms control, a "walk in the woods" type of compromise on intermediate-range nuclear forces in Europe should be made (the failure to make it so far lies primarily with the Soviets); the Strategic Arms Reduction Talks (START) should be resumed, this time with a realistic American proposal; the ABM treaty should be reaffirmed, and talks should quickly commence on the banning of weapons from space.

It will be apparent from the above that realism is not exactly the sexiest or the most satisfying way to address the danger. Moreover, even the most devout advocate of deterrence must agree that it may fail. Deterrers are afraid, too; they, too, dream of disarmament. But nobody so far has shown precisely how we get from here to there. And until somebody does, it would be well to lower the intellectual and political temperature and calmly discuss what it is precisely that we *can* do.

I propose a division of intellectual and political labor: Let those who insist that there must be an idea that will end the nuclear era keep searching for the idea. They do not deserve to be scorned. But neither do those who insist that in the interim the danger must also be managed; and frequently they are.

As Irving Howe has observed, there is the politics of the near and the politics of the far. Nuclear politics must allow for both. After all, when it is the destruction of the world that we are talking about, it is an honorable thing to trouble about the here and the now. Somebody has to.

McGEORGE BUNDY, GEORGE F. KENNAN, ROBERT S. McNAMARA, and GERARD SMITH

The President's Choice: Star Wars or Arms Control

McGeorge Bundy (b. 1919) was Special Assistant to the President (Kennedy and Johnson) from 1961 to 1966 and was president of the Ford Foundation from 1966 to 1979. He is currently a history professor at New York University. Robert S. McNamara (b. 1916) was

---

McGeorge Bundy et al., "The President's Choice: Star Wars or Arms Control," *Foreign Affairs* (Winter 1984/85): 277–292. Reprinted by permission of *Foreign Affairs*.

Secretary of Defense from 1961 to 1968 and has written and spoken extensively on national security affairs. Gerard Smith was Chief of the U.S. Delegation to SALT I from 1969 to 1972. (See George F. Kennan, p. 289.) In 1983 the "Gang of Four," as they are called, wrote an article jointly, "Nuclear Weapons and the Atlantic Alliance," on the defense of Europe in which they argue strongly that NATO adopt a policy of "no first use" of nuclear weapons. NATO still has not done so, and the question remains very controversial. The article about SDI, presented here, is one of the most respected critiques of the plan to appear to date.

The reelection of Ronald Reagan makes the future of his Strategic Defense Initiative the most important question of nuclear arms competition and arms control on the national agenda since 1972. The President is strongly committed to this program, and senior officials, including Secretary of Defense Caspar W. Weinberger, have made it clear that he plans to intensify this effort in his second term. Sharing the gravest reservations about this undertaking, and believing that unless it is radically constrained during the next four years it will bring vast new costs and dangers to our country and to mankind, we think it urgent to offer an assessment of the nature and hazards of this initiative, to call for the closest vigilance by Congress and the public, and even to invite the victorious President to reconsider. While we write only after obtaining the best technical advice we could find, our central concerns are political. We believe the President's initiative to be a classic case of good intentions that will have bad results because they do not respect reality.

This new initiative was launched by the President on March 23, 1983, in a surprising and quite personal passage at the end of a speech in praise of his other military programs. In that passage he called on our scientists to find means of rendering nuclear weapons "impotent and obsolete." In the briefings that surrounded the speech, Administration spokesmen made it clear that the primary objective was the development of ways and means of destroying hostile missiles—meaning in the main Soviet missiles—by a series of attacks all along their flight path, from their boost phase after launch to their entry into the atmosphere above the United States. Because of the central position the Administration itself gave to this objective, the program promptly acquired the name Star Wars, and the President's Science Advisor, George Keyworth, has admitted that this name is now indelible. We find it more accurately descriptive than the official "Strategic Defense Initiative."[1]

II

What is centrally and fundamentally wrong with the President's objective is that it cannot be achieved. The overwhelming consensus of the nation's technical community is that in fact there is no prospect whatever that science and technology can, at any time in the next several decades, make nuclear weapons "impotent and obsolete." The program developed over the last 18 months, ambitious as it is, offers no prospect for a leak-proof defense against strategic ballistic missiles alone, and it entirely excludes from its range any effort to limit the effectiveness of other systems—bomber aircraft, cruise missiles, and smuggled warheads.

The President's hopes are entirely understandable. There must be very few Americans who have never shared them. All four of us, like Mr. Reagan, grew up in a world without nuclear weapons, and we believe with passion that the world would be a much safer place without them. Americans should be constantly on the alert for any possibilities that can help to reduce the nuclear peril in which we all live, and it is entirely natural that a hope of safety like the one the President held out should stir a warmly affirmative first response. But false hope, however strong and understandable, is a bad guide to action.

The notion that nuclear weapons, or even ballistic missiles alone, can be rendered impotent by science and technology is an illusion. It reflects not only technological hubris in the face of the very nature of nuclear weapons, but also a complete misreading of the relation between threat and response in the nuclear decisions of the superpowers.

The first and greatest obstacle is quite simply that these weapons are destructive to a degree that makes them entirely different from any other weapon in history. The President frequently observes that over the centuries every new weapon has produced some countervailing weapon, and up to Hiroshima he is right. But conventional weapons can be neutralized by a relatively low rate of kill, provided that the rate is sustained over time. The classic modern example is defense against non-nuclear bombing. If you lose one bomber in every ten sorties, your force will soon be destroyed. A pilot assigned to fly 30 missions will face a 95-percent prospect of being shot down. A ten-percent rate of kill is highly effective.

With nuclear weapons the calculation is totally different. Both Mr. Reagan's dream and his historical argument completely neglect the decisive fact that a very few nuclear weapons, exploding on or near population centers, would be hideously too many. At today's levels of superpower deployment—about 10,000 strategic warheads on each side—even a 90-percent kill rate would be insufficient to save either society from disintegration in the event of general nuclear war. Not one of Mr. Reagan's technical advisers claims that any such level of protection is attainable. They know better. In the words of the officer in charge of the program, Lieutenant General James Abrahamson, "a perfect defense is not a realistic thing." In response to searching questions from Senator Sam Nunn of Georgia, the senior technical official of the Defense Department, Under Secretary Richard DeLauer, made it plain that he could not foresee any level of defense that would make our own offensive systems unnecessary.

Among all the dozens of spokesmen for the Administration, there is not one with any significant technical qualifications who has been willing to question

Dr. DeLauer's explicit statement that "There's no way an enemy can't overwhelm your defenses if he wants to badly enough." The only senior official who continues to share the President's dream and assert his belief that it can come true is Caspar Weinberger, whose zealous professions of confidence are not accompanied by technical support.

The terrible power of nuclear weapons has a second meaning that decisively undermines the possibility of an effective Star Wars defense of populations. Not only is their destructive power so great that only a kill rate closely approaching 100 percent can give protection, but precisely because the weapons are so terrible neither of the two superpowers can tolerate the notion of "impotence" in the face of the arsenal of the opponent. Thus any prospect of a significantly improved American defense is absolutely certain to stimulate the most energetic Soviet efforts to ensure the continued ability of Soviet warheads to get through. Ever since Hiroshima it has been a cardinal principle of Soviet policy that the Soviet Union must have a match for any American nuclear capability. It is fanciful in the extreme to suppose that the prospect of any new American deployment which could undermine the effectiveness of Soviet missile forces will not be met by a most determined and sustained response.

This inevitable Soviet reaction is studiously neglected by Secretary Weinberger when he argues in defense of Star Wars that today's skeptics are as wrong as those who said we could never get to the moon. The effort to get to the moon was not complicated by the presence of an adversary. A platoon of hostile moon-men with axes could have made it a disaster. No one should understand the irrelevance of his analogy better than Mr. Weinberger himself. As secretary of defense he is bound to be familiar with the intensity of our own American efforts to ensure that our own nuclear weapons, whether on missiles or aircraft, will always be able to get through to Soviet targets in adequate numbers.

The technical analyses so far available are necessarily incomplete, primarily because of the very large distance between the President's proposal and any clearly defined system of defense. There is some truth in Mr. Weinberger's repeated assertion that one cannot fully refute a proposal that as yet has no real content. But already important and enduring obstacles have been identified. Two are systemic and ineradicable. First, a Star Wars defense must work perfectly the very first time, since it can never be tested in advance as a full system. Second, it must be triggered almost instantly, because the crucial boost phase of Soviet missiles lasts less than five minutes from the moment of launch. In that five minutes (which new launch technology can probably reduce to about 60 seconds), there must be detection, decision, aim, attack, and kill. It is hard to imagine a scheme further removed from the kind of tested reliability and clear presidential control that we have hitherto required of systems involving nuclear danger.

There are other more general difficulties with the President's dream. Any remotely leak-proof defense against strategic missiles will require extensive deployments of many parts of the system in space, both for detection of any Soviet launch and, in most schemes, for transmission of the attack on the missile in its boost phase. Yet no one has been able to offer any hope that it will ever be easier and cheaper to deploy and defend large systems in space than for someone else to destroy them. The balance of technical judgment is that the advantage in any unconstrained contest in space will be with the side that aims to attack the other side's satellites. In and of itself this advantage constitutes a compelling argument against space-based defense.

Finally, as we have already noted, the President's program offers no promise of effective defense against anything but ballistic missiles. Even if we assume, against all the evidence, that a leak-proof defense could be achieved against these particular weapons, there would remain the difficulty of defense against cruise missiles, against bomber aircraft, and against the clandestine introduction of warheads. It is important to remember here that very small risks of these catastrophic events will be enough to force upon us the continuing need for our own deterrent weapons. We think it is interesting that among the strong supporters of the Star Wars scheme are some of the same people who were concerned about the danger of the strategic threat of the Soviet Backfire bomber only a few years ago. Is it likely that in the light of these other threats they will find even the best possible defense against missiles a reason for declaring our own nuclear weapons obsolete?

Inadvertent but persuasive proof of this failing has been given by the President's science adviser. Last February, in a speech in Washington, Mr. Keyworth recognized that the Soviet response to a truly successful Star Wars program would be to "shift their strategic resources to other weapons systems," and he made no effort to suggest that such a shift could be prevented or countered, saying: "*Let* the Soviets move to alternate weapons systems, to submarines, cruise missiles, advanced technology aircraft. Even the critics of the President's defense initiative agree that *those* weapons systems are far more stable deterrents than are ICBMs [land-based missiles]." Mr. Keyworth, in short, is willing to accept all these other means of warhead delivery, and he appears to be entirely unaware that by this acceptance he is conceding that even if Star Wars should succeed far beyond what any present technical consensus can allow us to believe, it would fail by the President's own standard.

The inescapable reality is that there is literally no hope that Star Wars can make nuclear weapons obsolete. Perhaps the first and most important political task for those who wish to save the country from the expensive and dangerous pursuit of a mirage is to make this basic proposition clear. As long as the American people believe that Star Wars offers real hope of reaching the President's asserted goal, it will have a level of political support unrelated to reality. The American people, properly and sensibly, would like nothing better than to make nuclear weapons "impotent and obsolete," but the last thing they want or need is to pay an astronomic bill for a vastly intensified nuclear competition sold to them under a false label. Yet that is what Star Wars will bring us, as a closer look will show.

III

The second line of defense for the Star Wars program, and the one which represents the real hopes and convictions of both military men and civilians at the levels below the optimistic President and his enthusiastic secretary of defense, is not that it will ever be able to defend *all our people,* but rather that it will allow us to defend *some of our weapons and other military assets,* and so, somehow, restrain the arms race.

This objective is very different from the one the President has held out to the country, but it is equally unattainable. The Star Wars program is bound to exacerbate the competition between the superpowers in three major ways. It will destroy the Anti-Ballistic Missile (ABM) Treaty, our most important arms control agreement; it will directly stimulate both offensive and defensive systems on the Soviet side; and as long as it continues it will darken the prospect for significant improvement in the currently frigid relations between Moscow and Washington. It will thus sharpen the very anxieties the President wants to reduce.

As presented to Congress last March, the Star Wars program calls for a five-year effort of research and development at a total cost of $26 billion. The Administration insists that no decision has been made to develop or deploy any component of the potential system, but a number of hardware demonstrations are planned, and it is hoped that there can be an affirmative decision on full-scale system development in the early 1990s. By its very nature, then, the program is both enormous and very slow. This first $26 billion, only for research and development, is not much less than the full procurement cost of the new B-1 bomber force, and the timetable is such that Mr. Reagan's second term will end long before any deployment decision is made. Both the size and the slowness of the undertaking reinforce the certainty that it will stimulate the strongest possible Soviet response. Its size makes it look highly threatening, while its slowness gives plenty of time for countermeasures.

Meanwhile, extensive American production of offensive nuclear weapons will continue. The Administration has been at pains to insist that the Star Wars program in no way reduces the need for six new offensive systems. There are now two new land-based missiles, two new strategic bombers, and two different submarine systems under various stages of development. The Soviets regularly list several other planned American deployments as strategic because the weapons can reach the Soviet homeland. Mr. Reagan recognized at the very outset that "if paired with offensive systems," any defensive systems "can be viewed as fostering an aggressive policy, and no one wants that." But that is exactly how his new program, with its proclaimed emphasis on both offense and defense, is understood in Moscow.

We have been left in no doubt as to the Soviet opinion of Star Wars. Only four days after the President's speech, Yuri Andropov gave the Soviet reply:

> On the face of it, laymen may find it even attractive as the President speaks about what seem to be defensive measures. But this may seem to be so only on the face of it and only to those who are not conversant with these matters. In fact the strategic offensive forces of the United States will continue to be developed and upgraded at full tilt and along quite a definite line at that, namely that of acquiring a first nuclear strike capability. Under these conditions the intention to secure itself the possibility of destroying with the help of the ABM defenses the corresponding strategic systems of the other side, that is of rendering it unable of dealing a retaliatory strike, is a bid to disarm the Soviet Union in the face of the U.S. nuclear threat.[2]

The only remarkable elements in this response are its clarity and rapidity. Andropov's assessment is precisely what we should expect. Our government, of course, does not intend a first strike, but we are building systems which do have what is called in our own jargon a prompt hard-target kill capability, and the primary purpose of these systems is to put Soviet missiles at risk of quick destruction. Soviet leaders are bound to see such weapons as a first-strike threat. This is precisely the view that our own planners take of Soviet missiles with a similar capability. When the President launches a defensive program openly aimed at making Soviet missiles "impotent," while at the same time our own hard-target killers multiply, we cannot be surprised that a man like Andropov saw a threat "to disarm the Soviet Union."[3] Given Andropov's assessment, the Soviet response to Star Wars is certain to be an intensification of both its offensive and defensive strategic efforts.

Perhaps the easiest way to understand this political reality is to consider our own reaction to any similar Soviet announcement of intent. The very thought that the Soviet Union might plan to deploy effective strategic defenses would certainly produce a most energetic American response, and the first and most important element of that response would be a determination to ensure that a sufficient number of our own missiles would always get through.

Administration spokesmen continue to talk as if somehow the prospect of American defensive systems will in and of itself lead the Soviet government to move away from strategic missiles. This is a vain hope. Such a result might indeed be conceivable if Mr. Reagan's original dream were real—if we could somehow ever deploy a *perfect* defense. But in the real world no system will ever be leak-proof; no new system of any sort is in prospect for a decade and only a fragmentary capability for years thereafter; numerous powerful countermeasures are readily available in the meantime, and what is at stake from the Russian standpoint is the deterrent value of their largest and strongest offensive forces.

In this real world it is preposterous to suppose that Star Wars can produce anything but the most determined Soviet effort to make it fruitless. Dr. James Fletcher, chairman of an Administration panel that reviewed the technical prospects after the President's speech, has testified that "the ultimate utility . . . of this system will depend not only on the technology itself, but on the extent to which the Soviet Union agrees to mutual defense arrangements and offense limitations." The plain implication is that the Soviet Union can reduce the "utility" of Star Wars by refusing just such concessions. That is what we would do, and that is what they will do.

Some apologists for Star Wars, although not the President, now defend it on the still more limited ground that it can deny the Soviets a first-strike capability. That is conceivable, in that the indefinite proliferation of systems and countersystems would certainly create fearful uncertainties of all sorts on both sides. But as the Scowcroft Commission° correctly concluded, the Soviets have no first-strike capability today, given our survivable forces and the ample existing uncertainties in any surprise attack. We believe there are much better ways than strategic defense to ensure that this situation is maintained. Even a tightly limited and partially effective local defense of missile fields—itself something vastly different from Star Wars—would require radical amendment or repudiation of the ABM Treaty and would create such interacting fears of expanding defenses that we strongly believe it should be avoided.

The President seems aware of the difficulty of making the Soviet Union accept his vision, and he has repeatedly proposed a solution that combines surface plausibility and intrinsic absurdity in a way that tells a lot about what is wrong with Star Wars itself. Mr. Reagan says we should give the Russians the secret of defense, once we find it, in return for their agreement to get rid of nuclear weapons. But the only kind of secret that could be used this way is one that exists only in Mr. Reagan's mind: a single magic formula that would make each side durably invulnerable. In the real world any defensive system will be an imperfect complex of technological and operational capabilities, full understanding of which would at once enable any adversary to improve his own methods of penetration. To share this kind of secret is to destroy its own effectiveness. Mr. Reagan's solution is as unreal as his original dream, and it rests on the same failure of understanding.

There is simply no escape from the reality that Star Wars offers not the promise of greater safety, but the certainty of a large-scale expansion of both offensive and defensive systems on both sides. We are not here examining the dismayed reaction of our allies in Europe, but it is precisely this prospect that they foresee, in addition to the special worries created by their recognition that the Star

---

Scowcroft Commission Committee appointed by President Reagan, headed by General Brent Scowcroft, to assess relative strengths of the U.S. and Soviet arsenals and to make recommendations about which weapons systems the United States should build. The "Report of the President's Commission on Strategic Forces" was published by the U.S. Government printing office in 1983.

Wars program as it stands has nothing in it for them. Star Wars, in sum, is a prescription not for ending or limiting the threat of nuclear weapons, but for a competition unlimited in expense, duration, and danger.

We have come this way before, following false hopes and finding our danger greater in the upshot. We did it when our government responded to the first Soviet atomic test by a decision to get hydrogen bombs if we could, never stopping to consider in any serious way whether both sides would be better off not to test such a weapon. We did it again, this time in the face of strong and sustained warning, when we were the first to deploy the multiple warheads (MIRVs) that now face us in such excessive numbers on Soviet missiles. Today, 15 years too late, we have a consensus that MIRVs are bad for us, but we are still deploying them, and so are the Russians.

IV

So far we have been addressing the question of new efforts for strategic defense with only marginal attention to their intimate connection with the future of the most important single arms control agreement that we and the Soviet Union share, the Anti-Ballistic Missile Treaty of 1972. The President's program, because of the inevitable Soviet reaction to it, has already had a heavily damaging impact on prospects for any early progress in strategic arms control. It has thrown a wild card into a game already impacted by mutual suspicion and by a search on both sides for unattainable unilateral advantage. It will soon threaten the very existence of the ABM Treaty.

That treaty outlaws any Star Wars defense. Research is permitted, but the development of space-based systems cannot go beyond the laboratory stage without breaking the Treaty. That would be a most fateful step. We strongly agree with the finding of the Scowcroft Commission, in its final report of March 1984, that "the strategic implications of ballistic missile defense and the criticality of the ABM Treaty to further arms control agreements dictate extreme caution in proceeding to engineering development in this sensitive area."

The ABM Treaty stands at the very center of the effort to limit the strategic arms race by international agreements. It became possible when the two sides recognized that the pursuit of defensive systems would inevitably lead to an expanded competition and to greater insecurity for both. In its underlying meaning, the Treaty is a safeguard less against defense as such than against unbridled competition. The continuing and excessive competition that still exists in offensive weapons would have been even worse without the ABM Treaty, which removed from the calculations of both sides any fear of an early and destabilizing defensive deployment. The consequence over the following decade was profoundly constructive. Neither side attempted a defensive deployment that predictably would have given much more fear to the adversary than comfort to the possessor. The ABM Treaty, in short, reflected a common understanding of exactly the kinds of danger with which Star Wars now confronts the world. To lose the Treaty in pursuit of the Star Wars mirage would be an act of folly.

The defense of the ABM Treaty is thus a first requirement for all who wish to limit the damage done by the Star Wars program. Fortunately the Treaty has wide public support, and the Administration has stated that it plans to do nothing in its five-year program that violates any Treaty clause. Yet by its very existence the Star Wars effort is a threat to the future of the ABM Treaty, and some parts of the announced five-year program raise questions of Treaty compliance. The current program envisions a series of hardware demonstrations, and one of them is described as "an advanced boost-phase detection and tracking system." But the ABM Treaty specifically forbids both the development and the testing of any "spaced-based" components of an anti-ballistic missile system. We find it hard to see how a boost-phase detection system could be anything but space-based, and we are not impressed by the Administration's claim that such a system is not sufficiently significant to be called "a component."

We make this point not so much to dispute the detailed shape of the current program as to emphasize the strong need for close attention in Congress to the protection of the ABM Treaty. The Treaty has few defenders in the Administration—the President thought it wrong in 1972, and Mr. Weinberger thinks so still. The managers of the program are under more pressure for quick results than for proposals respectful of the Treaty. In this situation a heavy responsibility falls on Congress, which has already shown this year that it has serious reservations about the President's dream. Interested members of Congress are well placed to ensure that funds are not provided for activities that would violate the Treaty. In meeting this responsibility, and indeed in monitoring the Star Wars program as a whole, Congress can readily get the help of advisers drawn from among the many outstanding experts whose judgment has not been silenced or muted by co-option. Such use of independent counselors is one means of repairing the damage done by the President's unfortunate decision to launch his initiative without the benefit of any serious and unprejudiced scientific assessment.

The Congress should also encourage the Administration toward a new and more vigorous effort to insist on respect for the ABM Treaty by the Soviet government as well. Sweeping charges of Soviet cheating on arms control agreements are clearly overdone. It is deeply unimpressive, for example, to catalogue asserted violations of agreements which we ourselves have refused to ratify. But there is one quite clear instance of large-scale construction that does not appear to be consistent with the ABM Treaty—a large radar in central Siberia near the city of Krasnoyarsk. This radar is not yet in operation, but the weight of technical judgment is that it is designed for the detection of incoming missiles, and the ABM Treaty, in order to forestall effective missile defense systems, forbade the erection of such early warning radars except along the borders of each nation. A single highly vulnerable radar installation is of only marginal importance in relation to any large-scale breakout from the ABM Treaty, but it does raise exactly the kinds of questions of intentional violation which are highly destructive in this country to public confidence in arms control.

On the basis of informed technical advice, we think the most likely purpose of the Krasnoyarsk radar is to give early warning of any attack by submarine-based U.S. missiles on Soviet missile fields. Soviet military men, like some of their counterparts in our own country, appear to believe that the right answer to the threat of surprise attack on missiles is a policy of launch-under-attack, and in that context the Krasnoyarsk radar, which fills an important gap in Soviet warning systems, becomes understandable. Such understanding does not make the radar anything else but a violation of the express language of the Treaty, but it does make it a matter which can be discussed and resolved without any paralyzing fear that it is a clear first signal of massive violations yet to come. Such direct and serious discussion with the Soviets might even allow the two sides to consider together the intrinsic perils in a common policy of launch-under-attack. But no such sensitive discussions will be possible while Star Wars remains a non-negotiable centerpiece of American strategic policy.

Equal in importance to defending the ABM Treaty is preventing hasty overcommitment of financial and scientific resources to totally unproven schemes overflowing with unknowns. The President's men seem determined to encourage an atmosphere of crisis commitment to just such a manner of work, and repeated comparisons to the Manhattan Project of 1942–45, small in size and crystal-clear in purpose by comparison, are not comforting. On the shared basis of conviction that the President's dream is unreal, members of Congress can and should devote themselves with energy to the prevention of the kind of vested interest in very large-scale ongoing expenditures which has so often kept alive other programs that were truly impotent, in terms of their own announced objectives. We believe that there is not much chance that deployments remotely like those currently sketched in the Star Wars program will ever in fact occur. The mere prospect of them will surely provoke the Russians to action, but it is much less likely that paying for them will in the end make sense to the American people. The larger likelihood is that on their way to oblivion these schemes will simply cost us tens and even hundreds of billions of wasted dollars.[4]

In watching over the Star Wars budget the Congress may find it helpful to remember the summary judgment that Senator Arthur Vandenberg used to offer on programs he found wanting: "The end is unattainable, the means hare-brained, and the cost staggering." But at the same time we believe strongly in the continuation of the long-standing policy of maintaining a prudent level of research on the scientific possibilities for defense. Research at a level ample for insurance against some Soviet surprise can be continued at a fraction of the cost of the present Star Wars program. Such a change of course would have the great advantage of preventing what would otherwise be a grave distortion of priorities not only in defense research but the whole national scientific effort.

V

This has not been a cheerful analysis, or one that we find pleasant to present. If the President makes no major change of course in his second term, we see no alternative to a long, hard, damage-limiting effort by Congress. But we choose to end on a quite different note. We believe that any American president who has won reelection in this nuclear age is bound to ask himself with the greatest seriousness just what he wants to accomplish in his second term. We have no doubt of the deep sincerity of President Reagan's desire for good arms control agreements with the Soviet Union, and we believe his election night assertion that what he wants most in foreign affairs is to reach just such agreements. We are also convinced that if he asks serious and independent advisers what changes in current American policy will help most to make such agreements possible in the next four years, he will learn that it is possible to reach good agreements, or possible to insist on the Star Wars program as it stands, but wholly impossible to do both. At exactly that point, we believe, Mr. Reagan could, should, and possibly would encourage the serious analysis of his negotiating options that did not occur in his first term.

We do not here explore these possibilities in detail. They would certainly include a reaffirmation of the ABM Treaty, and an effort to improve it by broadening its coverage and tightening some of its language. There should also be a further exploration of the possibility of an agreement that would safeguard the peaceful uses of space, uses that have much greater value to us than to the Soviets. We still need and lack a reliable cap on strategic warheads, and while Mr. Reagan has asked too much for too little in the past, he is right to want reductions. He currently has some advisers who fear all forms of arms control, but advisers can be changed. We are not suggesting that the President will change his course lightly. We simply believe that he does truly want real progress on arms control in his second term, and that if he ever comes to understand that he must choose between the two, he will choose the pursuit of agreement over the demands of Star Wars.

We have one final deep and strong belief. We think that if there is to be a real step away from nuclear danger in the next four years, it will have to begin at the level of high politics, with a kind of communication between Moscow and Washington that we have not seen for more than a decade. One of the most unfortunate aspects of the Star Wars initiative is that it was launched without any attempt to discuss it seriously, in advance, with the Soviet government. It represented an explicit expression of the President's belief that we should abandon the shared view of nuclear defense that underlies not only the ABM Treaty but all our later negotiations on strategic weapons. To make a public announcement of a change of this magnitude without any effort to discuss it with the Soviets was to ensure increased Soviet suspicion. This error, too, we have made in earlier decades. If we are now to have renewed hope of arms control, we must sharply elevate our attention to the whole process of communication with Moscow.

Such newly serious communication should begin with frank and explicit recognition by both sides that the problem of nuclear danger is in its basic reality a *common* problem, not just for the two of us, but for all the world—and one that we shall never resolve if we cannot transcend negotiating procedures that give a veto to those in each country who insist on the relentlessly competitive maintenance and enlargement of what are already, on both sides, exorbitantly excessive forces.

If it can ever be understood and accepted, as a starting point for negotiation, that our community of interest in the problem of nuclear danger is greater than all our various competitive concerns put together, there can truly be a renewal of hope, and a new prospect of a shared decision to change course together. Alone among the presidents of the last 12 years, Ronald Reagan has the political strength to lead our country in this new direction if he so decides. The renewal of hope cannot be left to await another president without an appeal to the President and his more sober advisers to take a fresh hard look at Star Wars, and then to seek arms control instead.

Notes

[1]There has been an outpouring of technical comment on this subject, and even in a year and a half the arguments have evolved considerably. Two recent independent analyses on which we have drawn with confidence are *The Reagan Strategic Defense Initiative: A Technical, Political, and Arms Control Assessment,* by Sidney D. Drell, Philip J. Farley, and David Holloway, A Special Report of the Center for International Security and Arms Control, July 1984, Stanford: Stanford University, 1984; and *The Fallacy of Star Wars* (based on studies conducted by the Union of Concerned Scientists and co-chaired by Richard L. Garwin, Kurt Gottfried, and Henry W. Kendall), John Tirman, ed., New York: Vintage, 1984.

[2]Cited in Sidney Drell *et al., op. cit.*, p. 105.

[3]Richard Nixon has analyzed the possible impact of new defensive systems in even more striking terms: "Such systems would be destabilizing if they provided a shield so that you could use the sword." *Los Angeles Times,* July 1, 1984.

[4]The Russians have their own program, of course. But they are not about to turn our technological flank in the technologies crucial for ABM systems. "According to the U.S. Department of Defense, the United States has a lead in computers, optics, automated control, electro-optical sensors, propulsion, radar, software, telecommunications, and guidance systems." Drell *et al., op. cit.*, p. 21.

Long-Range Alternatives

JONATHAN SCHELL

The Choice

Jonathan Schell, see p. 3. This excerpt is the conclusion of Schell's book, The Fate of the Earth.

Four and a half billion years ago, the earth was formed. Perhaps a half billion years after that, life arose on the planet. For the next four billion years, life became steadily more complex, more varied, and more ingenious, until, around a million years ago, it produced mankind—the most complex and ingenious species of them all. Only six or seven thousand years ago—a period that is to the history of the earth as less than a minute is to a year—civilization emerged, enabling us to build up a human world, and to add to the marvels of evolution marvels of our own: marvels of art, of science, of social organization, of spiritual attainment. But, as we built higher and higher, the evolutionary foundation beneath our feet became more and more shaky, and now, in spite of all we have learned and achieved—or, rather, because of it—we hold this entire terrestrial creation hostage to nuclear destruction, threatening to hurl it back into the inanimate darkness from which it came. And this threat of self-destruction and planetary destruction is not something that we will pose one day in the future, if we fail to take certain precautions; it is here now, hanging over the heads of all of us at every moment. The machinery of destruction is complete, poised on a hair trigger, waiting for the "button" to be "pushed" by some misguided or deranged human being or for some faulty computer chip to send out the instructions to fire.

That so much should be balanced on so fine a point—that the fruit of four and a half billion years can be undone in a careless moment—is a fact against which belief rebels. And there is another, even vaster measure of the loss, for stretching ahead from our present are more billions of years of life on earth, all

---

Jonathan Schell, "The Choice." From *The Fate of the Earth* by Jonathan Schell (New York: Knopf, 1982), pp. 151–163. Originally appeared in the *New Yorker*.

of which can be filled not only with human life but with human civilization. The procession of generations that extends onward from our present leads far, far beyond the line of our sight, and, compared with these stretches of human time, which exceed the whole history of the earth up to now, our brief civilized moment is almost infinitesimal. And yet we threaten, in the name of our transient aims and fallible convictions, to foreclose it all. If our species does destroy itself, it will be a death in the cradle—a case of infant mortality.

The disparity between the cause and the effect of our peril is so great that our minds seem all but powerless to encompass it. In addition, we are so fully enveloped by that which is menaced, and so deeply and passionately immersed in its events, which are the events of our lives, that we hardly know how to get far enough away from it to see it in its entirety. It is as though life itself were one huge distraction, diverting our attention from the peril to life. In its apparent durability, a world menaced with imminent doom is in a way deceptive. It is almost an illusion. Now we are sitting at the breakfast table drinking our coffee and reading the newspaper, but in a moment we may be inside a fireball whose temperature is tens of thousands of degrees. Now we are on our way to work, walking through the city streets, but in a moment we may be standing on an empty plain under a darkened sky looking for the charred remnants of our children. Now we are alive, but in a moment we may be dead. Now there is human life on earth, but in a moment it may be gone.

Once, there was time to reflect in a more leisurely way on our predicament. In August, 1945, when the invention of the bomb was made known through its first use on a human population, the people of Hiroshima,° there lay ahead an interval of decades which might have been used to fashion a world that would be safe from extinction by nuclear arms, and some voices were in fact heard counseling deep reflection on the looming peril and calling for action to head it off. On November 28, 1945, less than four months after the bombing of Hiroshima, the English philosopher Bertrand Russell rose in the House of Lords and said:

> We do not want to look at this thing simply from the point of view of the next few years; we want to look at it from the point of view of the future of mankind. The question is a simple one: Is it possible for a scientific society to continue to exist, or must such a society inevitably bring itself to destruction? It is a simple question but a very vital one. I do not think it is possible to exaggerate the gravity of the possibilities of evil that lie in the utilization of atomic energy. As I go about the streets and see St. Paul's, the British Museum, the Houses of Parliament, and other monuments of our civilization, in my mind's eye I see a nightmare vision of those buildings as heaps of rubble with corpses all round them. That is a thing we have got to face, not only in our own country and cities, but throughout the civilized world.

Toward the end of World War II, with the aim of hastening the end of the war, the United States dropped a small atomic bomb on the Japanese city of Hiroshima. Over 130,000 people were killed or injured or were never found, and 90 percent of the city was leveled. [Schell's note.]

Russell and others, including Albert Einstein, urged full, global disarmament, but the advice was disregarded. Instead, the world set about building the arsenals that we possess today. The period of grace we had in which to ward off the nuclear peril before it became a reality—the time between the moment of the invention of the weapons and the construction of the full-scale machinery for extinction—was squandered, and now the peril that Russell foresaw is upon us. Indeed, if we are honest with ourselves we have to admit that unless we rid ourselves of our nuclear arsenals a holocaust not only *might* occur but *will* occur—if not today, then tomorrow; if not this year, then the next. We have come to live on borrowed time: every year of continued human life on earth is a borrowed year, every day a borrowed day.

In the face of this unprecedented global emergency, we have so far had no better idea than to heap up more and more warheads, apparently in the hope of so thoroughly paralyzing ourselves with terror that we will hold back from taking the final, absurd step. Considering the wealth of our achievement as a species, this response is unworthy of us. Only by a process of gradual debasement of our self-esteem can we have lowered our expectations to this point. For, of all the "modest hopes of human beings," the hope that mankind will survive is the most modest, since it only brings us to the threshold of all the other hopes. In entertaining it, we do not yet ask for justice, or for freedom, or for happiness, or for any of the other things that we may want in life. We do not even necessarily ask for our personal survival; we ask only that we *be survived.* We ask for assurance that when we die as individuals, as we know we must, mankind will live on. Yet once the peril of extinction is present, as it is for us now, the hope for human survival becomes the most tremendous hope, just because it is the foundation for all the other hopes, and in its absence every other hope will gradually wither and die. Life without the hope for human survivial is a life of despair.

The death of our species resembles the death of an individual in its boundlessness, its blankness, its removal beyond experience, and its tendency to baffle human thought and feeling, yet as soon as one mentions the hope of survival the similarities are clearly at an end. For while individual death is inevitable, extinction can be avoided; while every person must die, mankind can be saved. Therefore, while reflection on death may lead to resignation and acceptance, reflection on extinction must lead to exactly the opposite response: to arousal, rejection, indignation, and action. Extinction is not something to contemplate, it is something to rebel against. To point this out might seem like stating the obvious if it were not that on the whole the world's reaction to the peril of extinction has been one of numbness and inertia, much as though extinction were as inescapable as death is. Even today, the official response to the sickening reality before us is conditioned by a grim fatalism, in which the hope of ridding the world of nuclear weapons, and thus of surviving as a species, is all but ruled out of consideration as "utopian" or "extreme"—as though it were "radical" merely to want to go on living and to want one's descendants to be born. And yet if one gives up these aspirations one has given up on everything.

As a species, we have as yet done nothing to save ourselves. The slate of action is blank. We have organizations for the preservation of almost everything in life that we want but not organization for the preservation of mankind. People seem to have decided that our collective will is too weak or flawed to rise to this occasion. They see the violence that has saturated human history, and conclude that to practice violence is innate in our species. They find the perennial hope that peace can be brought to the earth once and for all a delusion of the well-meaning who have refused to face the "harsh realities" of international life—the realities of self-interest, fear, hatred, and aggression. They have concluded that these realities are eternal ones, and this conclusion defeats at the outset any hope of taking the actions necessary for survival. Looking at the historical record, they ask what has changed to give anyone confidence that humanity can break with its violent past and act with greater restraint.

The answer, of course, is that everything has changed. To the old "harsh realities" of international life has been added the immeasurably harsher new reality of the peril of extinction. To the old truth that all men are brothers has been added the inescapable new truth that not only on the moral but also on the physical plane the nation that practices aggression will itself die. This is the law of the doctrine of nuclear deterrence—the doctrine of "mutual assured destruction"—which "assures" the destruction of the society of the attacker. And it is also the law of the natural world, which, in its own version of deterrence, supplements the oneness of mankind with a oneness of nature, and guarantees that when the attack rises above a certain level the attacker will be engulfed in the general ruin of the global ecosphere. To the obligation to honor life is now added the sanction that if we fail in our obligation life will actually be taken away from us, individually and collectively. Each of us will die, and as we die we will see the world around us dying. Such imponderables as the sum of human life, the integrity of the terrestrial creation, and the meaning of time, of history, and of the development of life on earth, which were once left to contemplation and spiritual understanding, are now at stake in the political realm and demand a political response from every person. As political actors, we must, like the contemplatives before us, delve to the bottom of the world, and, Atlas-like, we must take the world on our shoulders.°

The self-extinction of our species is not an act that anyone describes as sane or sensible; nevertheless, it is an act that, without quite admitting it to ourselves, we plan in certain circumstances to commit. Being impossible as a fully intentional act, unless the perpetrator has lost his mind, it can come about only through a kind of inadvertence—as a "side effect" of some action that we do intend, such as the defense of our nation, or the defense of liberty, or the de-

---

Atlas A figure in ancient Greek mythology. He was condemned by Zeus, the king of the gods, to hold the world on his shoulders. [Schell's note]

fense of socialism, or the defense of whatever else we happen to believe in. To that extent, our failure to acknowledge the magnitude and significance of the peril is a necessary condition for doing the deed. We can do it only if we don't quite know what we're doing. If we did acknowledge the full dimensions of the peril, admitting clearly and without reservation that any use of nuclear arms is likely to touch off a holocaust in which the continuance of all human life would be put at risk, extinction would at that moment become not only "unthinkable" but also undoable. What is needed to make extinction possible, therefore, is some way of thinking about it that at least partly deflects our attention from what it is. And this way of thinking is supplied to us, unfortunately, by our political and military traditions, which, with the weight of almost all historical experience behind them, teach us that it is the way of the world for the earth to be divided up into independent, sovereign states, and for these states to employ war as the final arbiter for settling the disputes that arise among them. This arrangement of the political affairs of the world was not intentional. No one wrote a book proposing it; no parliament sat down to debate its merits and then voted it into existence. It was simply there, at the beginning of recorded history; and until the invention of nuclear weapons it remained there, with virtually no fundamental changes. Unplanned though this arrangement was, it had many remarkably durable features, and certain describable advantages and disadvantages; therefore, I shall refer to it as a "system"—the system of sovereignty. Perhaps the leading feature of this system, and certainly the most important one in the context of the nuclear predicament, was the apparently indissoluble connection between sovereignty and war. For without sovereignty, it appeared, peoples were not able to organize the launch wars against other peoples, and without war they were unable to preserve their sovereignty from destruction by armed enemies. (By "war" I here mean only international war, not revolutionary war, which I shall not discuss.) Indeed, the connection between sovereignty and war is almost a definitional one—a sovereign state being a state that enjoys the right and the power to go to war in defense or pursuit of its interests.

It was into the sovereignty system that nuclear bombs were born, as "weapons" for "war." As the years have passed, it has seemed less and less plausible that they have anything to do with war; they seem to break through its bounds. Nevertheless, they have gone on being fitted into military categories of thinking. One might say that they appeared in the world in a military disguise, for it has been traditional military thinking, itself an inseparable part of the traditional political thinking that belonged to the system of sovereignty, that has provided those intentional goals—namely, national interests—in the pursuit of which extinction may now be brought about unintentionally, or semi-intentionally, as a "side effect." The system of sovereignty is now to the earth and mankind what a polluting factory is to its local environment. The machine produces certain things that its users want—in this case, national sovereignty—and as an unhappy side effect extinguishes the species. . . .

The terms of the deal that the world has now struck with itself must be made clear. On the one side stand human life and the terrestrial creation. On the other side stands a particular organization of human life—the system of independent, sovereign nation-states. Our choice so far has been to preserve that political organization of human life at the cost of risking all human life. We are told that "realism" compels us to preserve the system of sovereignty. But that political realism is not biological realism; it is biological nihilism—and for that reason is, of course, political nihilism,° too. Indeed, it is nihilism in every conceivable sense of that word. We are told that it is human fate—perhaps even "a law of human nature"—that, in obedience, perhaps, to some "territorial imperative," or to some dark and ineluctable truth in the bottom of our souls, we must preserve sovereignty and always settle our differences with violence. If this is our fate, then it is our fate to die. But must we embrace nihilism? Must we die? Is self-extermination a law of our nature? Is there nothing we can do? I do not believe so. Indeed, if we admit the reality of the basic terms of the nuclear predicament—that present levels of global armament are great enough to possibly extinguish the species if a holocaust should occur; that in extinction every human purpose would be lost; that because once the species has been extinguished there will be no second chance, and the game will be over for all time; that therefore this possibility must be dealt with morally and politically as though it were a certainty; and that either by accident or by design a holocaust can occur at any second—then, whatever political views we may hold on other matters, we are driven almost inescapably to take action to rid the world of nuclear arms. Just as we have chosen to make nuclear weapons, we can choose to unmake them. Just as we have chosen to live in the system of sovereign states, we can choose to live in some other system. To do so would, of course, be unprecedented, and in many ways frightening, even truly perilous, but it is by no means impossible. Our present system and the institutions that make it up are the debris of history. They have become inimical to life, and must be swept away. They constitute a noose around the neck of mankind, threatening to choke off the human future, but we can cut the noose and break free. To suppose otherwise would be to set up a false fictitious fate, molded out of our own weaknesses and our own alterable decisions. We are indeed fated by our acquisition of the basic knowledge of physics to live for the rest of time with the knowledge of how to destroy ourselves. But we are not for that reason fated to destroy ourselves. We can choose to live.

---

biological nihilism . . . political nihilism *Nihilism* in general is the belief that existence is meaningless and without value. By "biological nihilism" Schell means a willingness to annihilate the species, communal suicide. By "political nihilism" he means the view that the social order is so corrupt that its destruction is desirable.

BEYOND WAR
A New Way of Thinking

Beyond War, a citizens' group, believes in a grass-roots educational effort to change what Einstein called our "old habits of thinking" about war. The group was launched by the Creative Initiative Foundation in 1982. Members of the group are dedicated to the prevention of nuclear war and continue to work at changing the conditions that make such a war possible.

> The unleashed power of the atom has changed everything save our modes of thinking and we thus drift toward unparalleled catastrophe.
>
> –Albert Einstein, 1946

The development, deployment and use of nuclear weapons have forever altered our environment. For the first time, a species has the capability of destroying itself and its life support system. Our thinking, however, has not yet caught up with that reality. In order to survive, we must change our mode of thinking. This change requires knowledge, decision, and action.

I. Knowledge

A. War Is Obsolete

Throughout recorded history, war has been used to acquire, to defend, to expand, to impose, to preserve. War has been the ultimate arbiter of differences between nations. War and the preparation for war have become intrinsic to human culture. Now we must accept the reality that war has become obsolete.

We cannot fight a full-scale nuclear war. A full-scale nuclear war would destroy civilization as we know it and would threaten life itself.

We cannot fight a limited nuclear war. Detonation of even a small percentage of the world's nuclear arsenals could trigger a "nuclear winter" and cause the extinction of humanity. It is also highly probable that a limited nuclear war would escalate to a full-scale nuclear war.

We cannot fight a conventional war among the superpowers. Such a war would likely escalate to a nuclear war.

"Beyond War: A New Way of Thinking." Reprinted with permission from Beyond War, 222 High Street, Palo Alto, CA 94301.

We cannot fight a conventional war among the non-superpowers without potentially involving the superpowers. The growing interdependence of nations has produced a network of "vital interests" that the superpowers have pledged to defend. This defense could, in turn, escalate through conventional war to nuclear war.

Today, because war has become obsolete, we must learn to resolve conflict without violence.

B. We Are One

> Once a photograph of the earth, taken from the outside, is available . . . a new idea as powerful as any in history will let loose."
>
> –Sir Fred Hoyle, 1948

The view of the earth from space is a symbol of the interconnectedness of all life. This symbol of oneness is validated by a variety of scientific discoveries of the last century.

Physics demonstrates that nothing exists in isolation. All of matter, from subatomic particles to the galaxies in space, is part of an intricate web of relationships in a unified whole.

Ecology provides the understanding that all parts of a living system are interconnected and that greater stability results from increased diversity.

Biology reveals that, in a totally interrelated system, the principle of survival of the fittest has new meaning. The "fittest" is now seen as that species which best contributes to the well-being of the whole system.

Psychology explains the projection of the dark side of the personality upon an "enemy." That knowledge gives us new tools to understand conflict and to improve relationships between individuals and between nations.

Together these discoveries reveal in a new way the meaning of "One." We are one interconnected, interdependent life-system, living on one planet.

C. The New Mode of Thinking

The knowledge that war is obsolete and that we are one is the foundation of the new mode of thinking. Our mode of thinking is what we identify with. It determines our values, our attitudes, our motivation, and our actions.

Until recently, we had not experienced the earth as one integrated system. We had limited experience of other peoples and other cultures. Therefore, our primary loyalty has been limited to our family, tribe, race, religion, ideology, or nation. Our identification has been restricted and we have often seen those beyond that identification as enemies.

In the nuclear age this limited identification threatens all of humanity. We can no longer be preoccupied with enemies. We can no longer see ourselves as separate. Modern transportation, communication systems, and the discoveries of science have increased tremendously our direct and indirect experience of the world. We now see that all of life is interdependent, that we share a common destiny, that our individual well-being depends on the well-being of the whole system. We must now identify with all humanity, all life, the whole earth. This expanded identification is the new mode of thinking.

It may be that we will never eliminate conflict between individuals or between nations. There will always be different perspectives, different ideas, and different approaches to problems. However, an overriding identification with the whole earth will enable us to resolve conflicts by discovering solutions that benefit all. Diversity will no longer be a cause of war. By changing our mode of thinking, diverse points of view will become a source of creative solutions.

The human species has repeatedly demonstrated the ability to change its mode of thinking. As we have matured and acquired new knowledge, we have expanded our identification beyond the tribe, the clan, and the city-state. As we began to expand our identification beyond race, we abolished the insitution of slavery. Now, by expanding our identification to the whole earth and all humanity, we will build a world beyond war.

> The Age of Nations is past. The task before us now, if we would not perish, is to build the earth.
>
> –Pierre Teilhard de Chardin, 1936

II. Decision

The process of building a world beyond war begins with the acknowledgment that war is obsolete and that we are one. Change then requires a decision to reject totally the obsolete and to commit totally to build upon the new identification.

''Decision'' means to cut (''cision'') away from (''de''), to reject forever an option, to close the door to an existing possibility. Without a decision it is impossible to discover the new. There is always peril in moving into the unknown. We cannot preview all that will happen. We must draw upon our individual and collective experience of making such ''leaps'' in the past.

The decision to change our mode of thinking must be made on an individual basis. Individuals are the basic elements of societies. Without individual change, societal change cannot occur. Each of us must decide to adopt the new mode of thinking as the basis of his or her life.

> To compromise in this matter is to decide; to postpone and evade decision is to decide; to hide the matter is

> to decide. . . . There are a thousand ways of saying no; one way of saying yes; and no way of saying anything else.
>
> –Gregory Vlastos, 1934

III. Action: Building Agreement

Societies generate their own vision of what is possible and draw their behavior from that vision. This nation must renew its commitment to the vision upon which it was founded and build agreement about the implications of that vision in the contemporary world.

> We hold these truths to be self-evident: that all men are created equal; that they are endowed by their Creator with certain unalienable rights; that among these are life, liberty, and the pursuit of happiness; that, to secure these rights, governments are instituted among men, deriving their just powers from the consent of the governed.
>
> –Declaration of Independence, 1776

We have not always lived up to the highest expression of our founding principles. For example, the principle that "all men are created equal" originally meant only white, tax-paying, property-owning males. Clearer understanding of these principles has resulted in creative change. When enough of us agreed that "all men are created equal" meant black and white, we abolished slavery. When enough of us agreed that it meant women and men, we instituted women's suffrage. When enough of us agreed that it meant more than "separate but equal," we recognized civil rights.

When new agreements about principles are reached, laws, treaties, and policies are developed to implement them. That is the only sequence of lasting change: agreement about principle, then law. Law cannot effectively precede agreement. Agreement must spring from new understanding of principles. The action through which agreement is built is education.

Today education must be based upon the knowledge that war is obsolete and that we are one. We now know that the principle "all men are created equal" applies to every human being on the planet. We now know that the unalienable right to life, liberty, and the pursuit of happiness cannot be secured by war. We must now work together to build agreement based on that knowledge throughout our society.

Power comes from individuals who are connected to universal principles and who are working together to build new agreements. The power of this nation has come from the involvement of the people in the unfolding of our founding principles. We have always agreed that such involvement is not the exclusive right of the elite. Truth is self-evident: it is available to all. Power flows not from the top, but from the consent of the governed. Our Great Seal says it clearly: "E Pluribus Unum—Out of Many, One."

We have become a demonstration of that statement on our Great Seal. The possibility that resulted from the process of involving people in the pursuit of truth has been unfolding for 200 years. This process has served as a beacon of hope and inspiration to people around the world. It has drawn the largest diversity of people ever assembled in one nation. We have gathered the "Many"—the religions, the races, the nationalities—working for the well-being of the "One," the Whole, the United States of America.

To fulfill the purpose and vision upon which this nation was founded, we must change our understanding of the principle "Out of Many, One" to include the whole earth and all life. We must now work together to build a world beyond war.

> I know of no safe repository of the ultimate power of society but the people. And if we think them not enlightened enough, the remedy is not to take the power from them, but to inform them by education.
>
> –Thomas Jefferson, 1820

E. P. THOMPSON

Overthrowing the Satanic Kingdom

E. P. Thompson (b. 1924), a British historian and writer, is an outspoken critic of British nuclear policy. He is a leader of the Campaign for Nuclear Disarmament (CND), Britain's nuclear protest group founded in the 1950s by Bertrand Russell and others.

I have sought in these pages to open up the arguments of the defense "experts," to show what is inside them, which premises and what conclusions. I have not been trying to frighten readers but to show the consequences to which these arguments lead.

Although I am myself by conviction a socialist of William Morris's sort, I have not been grounding any arguments upon premises of that kind. And I cer-

---

E. P. Thompson, "Overthrowing the Satanic Kingdom." From *Protest and Survive*, E. P. Thompson and Dan Smith, eds. (New York: Monthly Review Press, 1981), pp. 39–52.

tainly do not suppose that all blame for the desperate situation of the world lies with the ideological malice and predatory drives of the capitalist "West," although some part of it does.

I have based my arguments on the *logic* of the cold war, or of the deterrent situation itself. We may favor this or that explanation for the origin of this situation. But once this situation has arisen, there is a common logic at work in both blocs. Military technology and military strategy come to impose their own agenda upon political developments.

This is an interoperative and reciprocal logic,° which threatens all, impartially. If you press me for my own view, then I would hazard that the Russian state is now the most dangerous in relation to its own people and to the people of its client states. The rulers of Russia are police-minded and security-minded people, imprisoned within their own ideology, accustomed to meet argument with repression and tanks. But the basic postures of the Soviet Union seem to me, still, to be those of siege and aggressive defense; and even the brutal and botched intervention in Afghanistan appears to have followed upon apprehension as to U.S. and Chinese strategies.

The United States seems to me to be more dangerous and provocative in its general military and diplomatic strategies, which press around the Soviet Union with menacing bases. It is in Washington, rather than Moscow, that scenarios are dreamed up for theater wars; and it is in America that the alchemists of superkill, the clever technologists of "advantage" and ultimate weapons, press forward "the politics of tomorrow."

But we need not ground our own actions on a preference for one or the other bloc. This is unrealistic and could be divisive. What is relevant is the logic of process common to both, reinforcing the ugliest features of each other's societies, and locking both together in each other's nuclear arms in the same degenerative drift.

It is in this sense that NATO's modernization program and the Soviet intervention in Afghanistan, taken together, may perhaps be seen as a textbook case of the reciprocal logic of cold war. NATO's plans were certainly perceived by Soviet leaders as menacing, and vigorous efforts were made by Brezhnev and others to prevent them. This perception of menace hardened, on December 12, 1979, when NATO endorsed the full program at Brussels—and when, in the meantime, the U.S. Senate, under pressure from the arms lobby, failed to ratify SALT II. In response, the hard arguments and the hard men had their way among the Soviet leadership and, two weeks later, the Soviet intervention in Afghanistan took place. NATO modernization was not a decisive factor, in the view of the Russian historian Roy Medvedev (to whom I addressed some questions last June), since the intervention of Afghanistan had been mediated and pre-

---

interoperative and reciprocal logic Referring to the previous line, Thompson means that weapons technology, military strategy, and politics interact intricately and exponentially.

pared over a much longer period. But it signaled to those Soviet leaders who favored the military option that, in relation to Europe, they now had nothing to lose.

Throughout this essay I have been attempting to disclose this reciprocal logic of process, which is driven forward by the armorers of both superpowers. And what I have been contending is this: First, I have shown that the premises of nuclear deterrence are *irrational.*

Second, I have been concerned throughout with the use of *language.*

What makes the extinction of civilized life in Europe probable is not a greater propensity for evil than in previous history but a more formidable destructive technology, a deformed political process (East and West), and also a deformed culture.

The deformation of culture commences within language itself. It [the language of deterrence] makes possible a disjunction between the rationality and moral sensibility of individual persons and the effective political and military process. A certain kind of "realist" and "technical" vocabulary effects a closure which seals out the imagination, and prevents the reason from following the most manifest sequence of cause and consequence. It habituates the mind to nuclear holocaust by reducing everything to a flat level of normality. By habituating us to certain expectations, it not only encourages resignation—it also beckons on the event.

"Humankind cannot bear very much reality," T. S. Eliot wrote. As much of reality as most of us bear is what is most proximate to us—our self-interests and our immediate affections. What threatens our interests—what causes us even mental unease—is seen as outside ourselves, as the Other. We can kill thousands because we have first learned to call them "the enemy." Wars commence in our culture first of all, and we kill each other in euphemisms and abstractions long before the first missiles have been launched.

It has never been true that nuclear war is "unthinkable." It has been thought and the thought has been put into effect. This was done in 1945, in the name of allies fighting for the Four Freedoms (although what those Freedoms were I cannot now recall),° and it was done upon two populous cities. It was done by professing Christians, when the Allies had already defeated the Germans, and when victory against the Japanese was certain, in the longer or shorter run. The longer run would have cost some thousands more Western lives, whereas the short run (the bomb) would cost the lives only of enemy Asians. This was perfectly thinkable. It was thought. And action followed on.

What is unthinkable is that nuclear war could happen to *us.* So long as we can suppose that this war will be inflicted on *them,* the thought comes easily. And if we can also suppose that this war will save "our" lives, or serve our self-interest, or even save us (if we live in California) from the tedium of queuing

---

Four Freedoms During World War II, people in the West were told they were defending freedom from fear, freedom from want, freedom of religion, and freedom of speech.

every other day for gasoline, then the act can easily follow on. We *think* others to death as we define them as the Other: the enemy: Asians: Marxists: non-people. The deformed human mind is the ultimate doomsday weapon—it is out of the human mind that the missiles and the neutron warheads come.

For this reason it is necessary to enter a remonstrance against those who use this kind of language and adopt these mental postures. They are preparing our minds as launching platforms for exterminating thoughts. The fact that Soviet ideologists are doing much the same (thinking us to death as "imperialists" and "capitalists") is no defense.

It is therefore proper to ask such experts to resist the contamination of our culture with those terms which precede the ultimate act. The deaths of fifteen million fellow citizens ought not to be described as "disagreeable consequences." A war confined to Europe ought not to be given euphemisms of "limited" or "theater." The development of more deadly weapons, combined with menacing diplomatic postures and major new political and strategic decisions, ought not to be concealed with the anodyne technological term of "modernization." The threat to erase the major cities of Russia and Eastern Europe ought not to trip easily off the tongue as "unacceptable damage."

I am thinking of that great number of persons who very much dislike what is going on in the actual world, but who dislike the vulgarity of exposing themselves to the business of "politics" even more. They erect both sets of dislikes around their desks or laboratories like a screen, and get on with their work and their careers. I am not asking these, or all of them, to march around the place or to spend hours in weary little meetings. I am asking them to examine the deformities of our culture and then, in public places, to demur.

I will recommend some forms of action, although every person must be governed in this by his or her own conscience and aptitudes. But, first, I should offer a scenario of my own.

I have come to the view that a general nuclear war is not only possible but probable, and that its probability is increasing. We may indeed be approaching a point of no return when the existing tendency or disposition toward this outcome becomes irreversible.

I ground this view upon two considerations, which we may define (to borrow the terms of our opponents) as "tactical" and "strategic."

By tactical I mean that the political and military conditions for such war exist now in several parts of the world; the proliferation of nuclear weapons will continue, and will be hastened by the export of nuclear energy technology to new markets, and the rivalry of the superpowers is directly inflaming these conditions.

Such conditions now exist in the Middle East and around the Persian Gulf, will shortly exist in Africa, while in Southeast Asia, Russia, and China have already engaged in wars by proxy with each other, in Cambodia and Vietnam.

Such wars might stop short of general nuclear war between the superpowers.

And in their aftermath the great powers might be frightened into better behavior for a few years. But so long as this behavior rested on nothing more than mutual fear, then military technology would continue to be refined, more hideous weapons would be invented, and the opposing giants would enlarge their control over client states. The strategic pressures toward confrontation will continue to grow.

These *strategic* considerations are the gravest of the two. They rest upon a historical view of power and of the social process, rather than upon the instant analysis of the commentator on events.

In this view it is a superficial judgment, and a dangerous error, to suppose that deterrence has worked. Very possibly it may have worked, at this or that moment, in preventing recourse to war. But in its very mode of working, and in its "postures," it has brought on a series of consequences within its host societies.

Deterrence is not a stationary state, it is a degenerative state. Deterrence has repressed the export of *violence* toward the opposing bloc, but in doing so the repressed *power* of the state has turned back upon its own author. The repressed violence has backed up and worked its way into the economy, the polity, the ideology, and the culture of the opposing powers. This is the deep structure of the Cold War.

The logic of this deep structure of mutual fear was clearly identified by William Blake in his Song of Experience, "The Human Abstract":

And mutual fear brings peace;
Till the selfish loves increase.
Then Cruelty knits a snare,
And spreads his baits with care . . .

Spoon spreads the dismal shade
Of Mystery over his head:
And the Catterpillar and Fly
Feed on the Mystery

And it bears the fruit of Deceit,
Ruddy and sweet to eat;
And the Raven his nest has made
In its thickest shade.

In this logic, the peace of "mutual fear" enforces opposing self-interests, affords room for "Cruelty" to work, engenders "Mystery" and its parasites, brings to fruit the "postures" of Deceit, and the death-foreboding Raven hides within the Mystery.

Within the logic of deterrence, millions are now employed in the armed services, security organs, and military economy of the opposing blocs, and corresponding interests exert immense influence within the councils of the great powers. Mystery envelops the operation of the technological alchemists. Deterrence has become normal, and minds have been habituated to the vocabulary of mutual extermination. And within this normality, hideous cultural abnormalities have been nurtured and are growing to full girth.

The menace of nuclear war reaches far back into the economies of both parties, dictating priorities and awarding power. Here, in failing economies, will be found the most secure and vigorous sectors, tapping the most advanced technological skills of both opposed societies and diverting these away from peaceful and productive employment or from efforts to close the great gap between the world's north and south. Here also will be found the driving rationale for expansionist programs in unsafe nuclear energy, programs which cohabit comfortably with military nuclear technology whereas the urgent research into safe energy supplies from sun, wind, or wave are neglected because they have no military payoff. Here, in this burgeoning sector, will be found the new expansionist drive for markets for arms, as capitalist and socialist powers compete to feed into the Middle East, Africa, and Asia more sophisticated means of killing.

The menace of this stagnant state of violence backs up also into the polity of both halves of the world. Permanent threat and periodic crisis press the men of the military-industrial interests, by differing routes in each society, toward the top. Crisis legitimates the enlargement of the security functions of the state, the intimidation of internal dissent, and the imposition of secrecy and the control of information. As the natural lines of social and political development are repressed, and affirmative perspectives are closed, so internal politics collapses into squabbling interest groups, all of which are subordinated to the overarching interests of the state of perpetual threat.

All this may be readily observed. It may be observed even in failing Britain, across whose territory are now scattered the bases, airfields, camps, research stations, submarine depots, communications-interception stations, radar screens, security and intelligence HQs, munitions works—secure and expanding employment in an economic climate of radical insecurity.

What we cannot observe so well—for we ourselves are the object which must be observed—is the manner in which three decades of deterrence, of mutual fear, mystery, and state-endorsed stagnant hostility, have backed up into our culture and our ideology. Imagination has been numbed; language and values have been fouled by the postures and expectations of the deterrent state. But this is matter for a close and scrupulous inquiry.

These, then, are among the strategic considerations which lead me to the view that the probability of great-power nuclear warfare is strong and increasing. I do not argue from this local episode or that: what happened yesterday in Afghanistan and what is happening now in Pakistan or North Yemen. I argue from a general and sustained historical process, an accumulative logic, of a kind made familiar to me in the study of history. The episodes lead in this direction or that, but the general logic of process is always toward nuclear war.

The local crises are survived, and it seems as if the decisive moment—either of war or of peacemaking and reconciliation—has been postponed and pushed forward into the future. But what has been pushed forward is always worse. Both parties change for the worse. The weapons are more terrible, the means for their delivery more clever. The notion that a war might be fought to "advantage," that it might be "won," gains ground. There is even a tremor of excitement in our culture as though, subconsciously, humankind has lived with the notion for so long that expectations without actions have become boring. The human mind, even when it resists, assents more easily to its own defeat. All moves on its degenerative course, as if the outcome of civilization was as determined as is the outcome of this sentence: in a full stop.

I am reluctant to accept that this determinism is absolute. But if my arguments are correct, then we cannot put off the matter any longer. We must throw whatever resources still exist in human culture across the path of this degenerative logic. We must protest if we are to survive. Protest is the only realistic form of civil defense.

We must generate an alternative logic, an opposition at every level of society. This opposition must be international and it must win the support of multitudes. It must bring its influence to bear upon the rulers of the world. It must act, in very different conditions, within each national state, and, on occasion, it must directly confront its own national state apparatus.

The campaign for European Nuclear Disarmament, which is already gaining active support in many parts of Western Europe, as well as a more cautious attention in some parts of Eastern Europe, has as an objective the creation of an expanding zone freed from nuclear weapons and bases. It aims to expel these weapons from the soil and waters of both East and West Europe and to press the missiles, in the first place, back to the Urals and to the Atlantic Ocean.

The tactics of this campaign will be both national and international.

In the national context, each peace movement will proceed directly to contest the nuclear weapons deployed by its own state, or by NATO or Warsaw Pact obligations upon its own soil. Its actions will not be qualified by any notion of diplomatic bargaining. Its opposition to the use of nuclear weapons by its own state will be absolute. Its demands upon its own state for disarmament will be unilateral.

In the international, and especially in the European, context, each national movement will exchange information and delegations, will support and challenge each other. The movement will encourage a European consciousness, in common combat for survival, fostering informal communication at every level, and disregarding national considerations of interest or security.

It is evident that this logic will develop unevenly. The national movements will not grow at the same pace, nor be able to express themselves in identical ways. Each success of a unilateral kind—by Holland in refusing NATO cruise missiles or by Rumania or Poland in distancing themselves from Soviet strategies—will be met with an outcry that it serves the advantage of one or the other bloc.

This outcry must be disregarded. It cannot be expected that initiatives on one side will be met with instant reciprocation from the other. Very certainly, the strategists of both blocs will seek to turn the movement to their own advantage. The logic of peacemaking will be as uneven, and as fraught with emergencies and contingencies, as the logic which leads on to war.

In particular, the movement in West and East Europe will find very different expression. In the West we envisage popular movements engaged in a direct contest with the policies of their own national states. At first, Soviet ideologues may look benignly upon this, anticipating a weakening of NATO preparations which are matched by no actions larger than "peace-loving" rhetoric from the East.

But we are confident that our strategy can turn this rhetoric into acts. In Eastern Europe there are profound pressures for peace, for greater democracy and international exchange, and for relief from the heavy burden of siege economies. For a time these pressures may be contained by the repressive measures of national and Soviet security services. Only a few courageous dissidents will, in the first place, be able to take an open part in our common work.

Yet to the degree that the peace movement in the West can be seen to be effective, it will afford support and protection to our allies in Eastern Europe and the Soviet Union. It will provide those conditions of relaxation of tension which will weaken the rationale and legitimacy of repressive state measures, and will allow the pressures for democracy and détente to assert themselves in more active and open ways. Moreover, as an intrinsic part of the European campaign, the demand for an opening of the societies of the East to information, free communication and expression, and exchange of delegations to take part in the common work will be pressed on every occasion. And it will not only be pressed as rhetoric. We are going to find devices to symbolize that pressure and dramatize that debate.

Against the strategy which envisages Europe as a theater of limited nuclear warfare, we propose to make in Europe a theater of peace. This will not, even if we succeed, remove the danger of confrontation in non-European theaters. It offers, at the least, a small hope of European survival. It could offer more. For if the logic of nuclear strategy reaches back into the organization and ideologies of the superpowers themselves, so the logic of peacemaking might reach back also, enforcing alternative strategies, alternative ideologies. European nuclear disarmament would favor the conditions for international detente.

When I first sat down to write this essay, in February 1980, it seemed to the handful of us in Britain, France, West Germany, and Eastern Europe who were then discussing such a campaign that we were only whistling in the dark. On every side of us the armorers were having their way. Only in Norway, Holland, and Belgium did it seem that a popular movement of conscience could still bring any influence to bear upon political decisions.

Now we know differently. The movement has taken off, and it is moving rapidly across Europe, west, north, and south. It is, already, too large and too various for any group or interest to manipulate it for sectional ends. No one is going to nobble it: this is a movement of people for themselves.

And we have seen, in the last six months of 1980, another movement of quite extraordinary resilience among the Polish people. There have been all the usual attempts—among the Soviet and NATO military—to translate this movement into the habitual terms of the Cold War. These attempts continue, and I have no doubt as to their dangers. Yet the movement of Polish Solidarity is, in a critical sense, *of the same kind* as the movement in West Europe to resist nuclear rearmament. Both are movements of Europeans for autonomy—away from cold-war cliency—and movements, by Europeans, to resume a political space for themselves.

The Western European initiative for nuclear disarmament is no more "pro-Communist" than Polish Solidarity is "pro-capitalist." These movements, taken together, offer more hope of some way out of the world's appalling impasse than delivery systems, megatonnage, or throw-weight can ever do. They offer a very difficult—barely possible—path forward, whose ultimate end would be, not only the dismantling of some nuclear weapons but the dismantling of the blocs which would throw them. A more limited success might offer, at the least, a nuclear-weapons-free space, in the heart of Europe, holding the superpowers apart—a space of quiet within which alternatives could grow.

I cannot see how such an outcome could be against the true interests of either the American or the Russian people. The rising mood in Europe is neither "anti-American" or "anti-Soviet": it is antimilitarist, and it is opposed to the militarism of both blocs. For militarism, in its rivalry and even more in its reciprocity, is bringing out the worst features in both superpowers. It is containing the forces making democratic transition in the East, so that the aging old guard of Stalinism is now propped up by the weaponry of the West and given fresh transfusions of legitimation by the Western threat. I will not say what I consider that militarism is doing to the political and cultural life of the United States. That is a problem which readers of the *Nation* know only too well.

I promised to conclude by returning you from European perceptions to yourselves. But there is nothing that I can say that readers do not already know. I have described a militarist logic whose outcome must be terminal for civilization in the Northern Hemisphere. The absurd scenarios of counterforce menus and options and theater wars are quite as menacing to Americans as they are to Europeans: only a day or a week will divide us in our common fate. What happens then will make the worst possible outcome of Three Mile Island appear as no more than a pistol shot.

This is what is being prepared, steadily, year by year, and I think it probable that it will come to its conclusion—through accident or miscalculation, through the paranoia of the Russian old guard or the brash theatricals of American preemptive deterrence and, above all, through the steady growth in influence, in both superpowers, of the military-industrial forces and their Satanic "experts"—and that the conclusion will be in the next two or three decades.

On July 25, 1945, President Truman scrawled in his personal notebook: "We have discovered the most terrible bomb in the history of the world. It may be the fire destruction prophesied in the Euphrates Valley era, after Noah and his fabulous ark." The President's literal biblical reference is touching, and touching also was his confidence that his instructions to the Secretary of War that the weapon be used on a "purely military target" only, and not "women and children," would be obeyed by the military executors. For from that very moment it is the logic of weaponry which has been in the saddle, and which has been riding the horse of the Apocalypse remorselessly into the Valley of the Shadow of Death.

What deterrence has done has been to strike into immobility every normal political process of human negotiation or reconciliation. For decades the rival military blocs, like inadequate personalities, have postponed dealing with the problems of today, and, in the name of deterrence, have tied these problems to the backs of missiles and sent them on into the future. Which future we are now fouling up today, just as the experts of the late 1950s fouled up our own present day.

The R and D for the weapons which will kill our children and grandchildren in the twenty-first century is now in hand and is being paid from our current taxes. The leaders of your country and of mine have no political remedy of any kind. None. Nor have those immensely expert contributors to *Daedalus*. From all of them—nothing. They show a process without end, except the terminus of nuclear war.

We offer, cautiously, a possible politics of protest and survival: the different END of European Nuclear Disarmament. It is a politics which commences, not at the top with diplomats and abortive SALT negotiations but with popular movements and with scores of less formal lateral exchanges. As we proceed we may build around the small nonaligned core of Europe (Sweden, Austria, Yugoslavia) a more influential alliance of political parties and of governments.

I doubt whether we can succeed: nothing less than a worldwide spiritual revulsion against the Satanic Kingdom would give us any chance of bringing the military riders down. What might make it just possible that we could succeed would be if the "we" become not just European but truly international—if there should be, first of all, a profound shift in American public opinion, and then, and alongside this, by all our combined efforts and skills, an extension deep into Russian opinion also.

Impossible? It may seem so. That is not the way things are going in the West just now. Dominant American policy appears to be intent upon freezing Europe in the postures of war forever, while enhancing daily the means of that war's final execution. Europeans watch your new administration enter into Washington and await the outcome with fear.

MICHAEL NAGLER

Redefining Peace

Michael Nagler (b. 1937) is professor of classics at the University of California at Berkeley, where he teaches in the Peace Studies Program. Living over twenty years in a community dedicated to Gandhian nonviolence, Nagler thinks deeply about alternatives to violence. He has recently written a book, America without Violence: Why Violence Persists and How You Can Stop It *(Ithaca, N.Y.: Island Press, 1982).*

A basic disparity in modern civilization came into stark relief two summers ago when Mother Teresa of Calcutta rushed into the rubble of West Beirut to rescue orphaned children. Mother Teresa had recently received the Nobel Peace Prize. So had Israeli Prime Minister Begin, whose operation had reduced the city to rubble and orphaned those children.

What is peace? Two contradictory definitions seem to have coexisted since antiquity without causing confusion, until recent times. Modern peace science—a fledgling discipline—knows them as *negative* peace, adequately defined as the absence of war, and *positive* peace.[1] Positive peace has yet to be adequately defined at all.

Futurist Willis Harman reminds us that "we human beings have an awesome ability to deceive ourselves," and the question of peace, with its emotional urgency and denotational vagueness, is where this capacity is most devastatingly exercised.[2]

A May 25, 1984, letter to the highly conservative *Washington Times* complains that Rudolph Hess, "prisoner of peace," is being deprived of his freedom "all because he tried to stop large scale war." The writer might be dismissed as a crank, but in fact his negative definition of peace is unquestioned throughout society. The corrugated iron barricades between Protestant and Catholic neighborhoods of Belfast are called "peace lines." They are now being rebuilt permanently in brick. The artillery barrage of Beirut was part of an operation called "Peace for Galilee." And of course, one of the most dangerous first-strike nuclear weapons has been dubbed "Peacemaker."

My aim is not to stigmatize adherents of the negative definition who are found in many lands and at all levels of officialdom. Rather, it is in the spirit of Freeman Dyson's attempt to bring the "two worlds" of pro-defense and anti-nuclear thinking into contact—words sundered largely by their unexamined ad-

---

Michael Nagler, "Redefining Peace," *Bulletin of the Atomic Scientists* (November 1984): 36–38. Reprinted by permission of the *Bulletin of the Atomic Scientists,* a magazine of science and world affairs.

herence to negative and positive peace ideals.[3] I would show that the thinking of each group is perfectly logical, given its assumption about the nature of peace, and that a clearer articulation of the positive side could help bring about an open and fruitful debate.

At present, all operational terms in the debate mean opposite things, depending on whether one's overriding definition of peace is negative or positive: Is "security" dominating one's enemies, or learning to live so that one does not have enemies? Is "strength" the power to hurt others, or to make appropriate sacrifices and undertake necessary corrections in one's own course?

It is not possible—fortunately—to reduce the emotional charge carried by the concept of peace. But though we cannot, and should not, make the term less emotional, we should certainly be able to make it less confusing.

About 12 years ago Heinrich Schneider, co-director of the Vienna Institute for Peace Research, summarized much of what recent peace research has gained by stating that if we must have a definition by negatives, the opposite of peace is not war, but violence.[4] "Non-war" would be achieved in the Middle East if the enemies of Israel were driven out, in the East-West confrontation if the Soviets would accept perpetual inferiority; in Central America if the peasant population were completely subdued and terrorized. But none of these conditions would be peace, because all of them contain violence of body, mind, and spirit.

"Violence" itself, however, requires definition. The well-known Norwegian peace research scholar, Johann Galtung, has defined violence as, simply, that which inhibits the fulfillment of a human being.

Perhaps this only brings us to a third unknown: What is a human being? How is he or she to be fulfilled? But in fact we gain much clarity by taking on these two logical questions, because they rescue the ancient problem of war and peace from the technosphere and reground the contemporary debate in human realities. Beneath the technological face of our civilization and its dilemmas lie unresolved human problems which have changed only in appearance over many thousands of years. This is particularly poignant in the area of arms control and the larger task of building a stable peace system, for it is here that attempts at technical and scientific solutions have most dishearteningly eluded us.

For the technologically-minded, it may be self-evident that the job of science is to determine how the forces of nature can "serve the human will."[5] But more than a thousand years ago St. Augustine, in his *Confessions,* exposed the fallacy of this argument: "My will was captured by the Enemy." By "Enemy" Augustine meant the dark, chaotic forces of hatred, fear, and greed that then as now lurk beneath the surface of human consciousness. Edward Teller,°

Edward Teller (b. 1908) A nuclear physicist often called the father of the hydrogen bomb; was active in early attempts to develop the atomic bomb. He pressed hard against scientific, political, and military opposition to the hydrogen bomb; the H-bomb became a reality in 1954. More recently, Teller had a major role in President Reagan's decision to press for the Strategic De-

. . . cavalierly declar[es] it the job of science to place the catastrophic powers of nature at the disposal of these psychic forces. The relationship between a negative definition of peace and a non-human sense of how to achieve peace are not coincidental, nor is the policy result.

Johann Galtung argues that there is something essential about the value of *each* human life which cannot be violated if we are to speak of peace.[6] Thus the challenge is to the entire notion of sacrificing the few for the many, as well as that of terrorizing one group for the advantage of another—cornerstones of every peace edifice civilization has built down the centuries. In this spirit Gandhi himself, in a rare comment on international peace, defined it as that state in which every person is fully realized.

Peace in its own right; peace, not the absence of something else; peace, a system in which no one need be sacrificed—the concept may strike us as rather visionary. But it should be. "Where there is no vision," runs the rediscovered text of Proverbs 29:18, "the people perish." Without the vision of a remote condition like peace how can we know which steps would lead us there?

I accept Gandhi's definition, and one of St. Augustine in *The City of God*—"Peace is the ordered tranquility of all parts of a system." But I have also been experimenting with another: that state in which all parties spontaneously desire one another's welfare. Any truly positive definition tells us immediately not only that the "Peacemaker missile" cannot bring positive peace—if it is not, indeed, some kind of grotesque joke—but that the deterrent concept itself cannot be equated with building peace.

Until we have such a positive definition, "arms control" is doomed to remain, as experienced negotiators have learned, a euphemism for creating conditions in which the numbers of arms in fact increase and are more swiftly deployed. Conversely, the potential of many good ideas, doomed to remain muffled in the present confusion, could suddenly emerge in a positive peace perspective. Nonviolent "social defense" comes immediately to mind, or interventionary "peace brigades," like those having unheralded successes against severe violence right now in Guatemala, Costa Rica, and Nicaragua.[7]

These methods of conflict resolution are completely victimless. They do not mortgage society to the services, and ultimately the values, of a military cadre. They could be safely instituted as long- and short-term measures. Because they call upon values and social skills out of which a distant order of stable peace could grow, even where there are no more overt conflicts to resolve, they are not desperate holding measures but seeds of future. Because they are entirely

---

fense Initiative, (SDI). He has held highly influential and prestigious positions in nuclear weapons research and development, including the assistant directorship of Los Alamos laboratory (1949–1952) and assistant directorship and directorship of Lawrence Livermore laboratory (1954–1958); Livermore is where most of the research on the hydrogen bomb was conducted. Teller is still active in nuclear weapons research and development through the Hoover Institute at Stanford and the phsyics department at the University of California at Berkeley, both of which have direct involvement in weapons research at Livermore.

non-threatening to the true well-being—as opposed to the malevolent purposes—of any adversary, they can be classified, without irony, as peace measures.

Before the scientific community today is the idea of an "oath of Pythagoras," like the Hippocratic oath of physicians, under which its members could pledge to refrain from working on clearly destructive projects. Initiated 15 years ago by a Berkeley-Stanford group, it has recently been embraced by International Student Pugwash° and has gained moral support in the Pope's remarkable address to the Pontifical Academy of Sciences in November 1983.

From a positive peace perspective this is an excellent but incomplete idea. Scientists and engineers should, of course, have the option of non-participation in the design, testing, or development of destructive weapons, without facing sanctions or being professionally disadvantaged. But they should also pledge to become engaged in constructive works badly needed for human survival in many parts of the world. This would replace whatever loss might accrue to national defense from such abstention, since severe underdevelopment problems are not only an active cause of conflict, but such problems are inherently forms of violence. Pope Paul VI once said that "development is the new name for peace." (I would say, "appropriate development.")

Most importantly for the future of science and society, scientists and engineers should pledge part of their time to learning and teaching the structure of stable peace. In the eloquent words of Carl von Weizsäcker, the real job of science "does not lie in abandoning research or suppressing scientific information but in transforming the political order of the world, which in its present form makes the misuse of scientific knowledge almost inevitable."[8]

Like the drawings used in perception tests, where figure and ground keep switching back and forth as the perceiver stares at them, how we look at the whole world can be turned inside out between two ways of viewing. In the old way, history always unfolds as "between two wars." In the new, as Gandhi said, peace is the even process of history and wars are its breakdowns. In the old way, as Richard Barnet put it, "nuclear war is unthinkable, but tens of thousands of people are paid to think about it every day." In the new way, at least as many people will be employed to work out the structure of peace, in at least as enthusiastic detail.

In a sense, either view is perfectly valid. But in a tragic and immediate sense, they are terribly unequal. The idealistic response and emotional charge released by the word "peace" will always be strong and this is as it should be. "Peace" awakens one of the deepest aspirations of the human spirit. Again to cite St. Augustine, "Man by the very laws of his nature seems, so to speak, forced into

---

International Student Pugwash An organization for science students interested in reducing the potential for nuclear war. It is a spinoff of the International Pugwash Movement (see "The Russell-Einstein Manifesto" on p. 70).

fellowship and, as far as in him lies, into peace with every man.'' In our own world, in Gallup polls taken from 1947 on, most Americans have consistently listed peace—whatever they understood by it—as the issue most important to them.

Yet most human energy today is mobilized by negative peace—often, as with ''Peace for Galilee,'' a concept hardly distinguishable from war. That energy belongs by right of idealism to the positive peace vision and program. It should be repossessed by those of us who hold this vision, for the benefit of mankind.

This will require the moral courage to cling to a positive vision of peace, unsentimentally, in a cynical age. It will also require that we define clearly and work out in reasonable detail the emotional, political, economic, and social structure of such a peace.

Notes

[1] Gerardo Zampaglione, *The Idea of Peace in Antiquity,* trans. Richard Dunn (South Bend, Indiana: Notre Dame University Press, 1973); Kenneth E. Boulding, *Stable Peace* (Austin: University of Texas, 1978), Chap. 1.

[2] Willis Harman, ''Consciousness Research and Nuclear War'' (unpublished paper, Dec. 1983).

[3] Freeman Dyson, *Weapons and Hope* (New York: Harper and Row, 1984).

[4] Heinrich Schneider, ''Freidensverständnis in Vergangenheit und Gegenwart,'' in Rudolph Weiler and Valentin Zsifkovits, *Unterwegs zum Frieden* (Vienna: Herder, 1973), p. 149.

[5] Edward Teller as quoted in Barton J. Bernstein, ''Truman and the H-bomb,'' *Bulletin* (March 1984), p. 14.

[6] Johann Galtung, ''Self-Reliance: an Overriding Strategy for Transition,'' in Falk, Kim, and Mendlowitz, *Toward a Just World Order* (Boulder: Westview, 1982), pp. 602–22.

[7] Current information on alternative defense can be obtained from the Program on Nonviolent Sanctions, Center for International Affairs, Harvard University. For developments in Central America contact Peace Brigades International, 4722 Baltimore Ave., Suite 2, Philadelphia, PA 19143.

[8] Carl von Weizsäcker, *The Unity of Nature,* trans. Francis J. Zucker (New York: Farrar, Straus and Giroux, 1980) p. 17.

RUTH LEGER SIVARD

Opportunities

Ruth Leger Sivard, director of World Priorities, a nonprofit research organization, was formerly chief of the economics division of the U.S. Arms Control and Disarmament Agency. Her broad background of experience as an analyst of economic-social issues includes executive positions with Dun & Bradstreet in New York, the United Nations Relief and Rehabilitation Administration in Austria, the Interna-

---

tional Refugee Organization in Switzerland, and the Marshall Plan in France. Her annual publication, World Military and Social Expenditures *(Published by the World Priorities Institute, New York), is an accessible, fascinating source of economic and demographic information around the world.*

In the poverty-scarred, tension-filled world of 1983, it is essential to explore alternatives to the uncontrolled military competition no matter how difficult and remote they may seem to be at this time. The cost of the arms race, whether measured in social underdevelopment or threat of annihilation, is now beyond the ability of any country to bear. The community of nations has for years officially recognized the need for restraint. The efforts made, including an enormous sacrifice of man-hours in international negotiations, have failed to stop the race or even slow its momentum. The result is the emergency of universal and dangerous proportions which now confronts us.

Emergency situations sometimes evoke solutions that under normal conditions would not be foreseen. Just as a person in extreme need may experience a surge of superhuman physical power, political authorities may suddenly be blessed with the strength to achieve what has seemed in the past to be an impossible task. But if this ever occurs, it will surely be because the public had demanded it. In many countries the demand can already be heard.

A Time for Change

The difference between the perilous state of the world today and a few years ago is less in the size of the danger threatening it—although this continues to increase—than in the public awareness of it and active response to it, both of which have grown much faster.

Various factors came together to precipitate this growth. One was the decision in both the Warsaw Pact and NATO alliances to base still more nuclear weapons in Europe. The plan for deployment, even in the democratic countries of western Europe, had been a purely military decision, not subject to confirmation by the elected legislative bodies. With other military-related developments it began to ring alarm bells which attracted more and more public attention.

The accident at the Three-Mile Island nuclear plant in the U.S. in 1979, official plans for a neutron bomb, an escalation of belligerent rhetoric between the superpowers, the upward thrust of budgets for nuclear weapons in the face of cutbacks in social programs—all of these pieces began to fit together into a picture of nuclear recklessness. To a public already sensitized by a new awareness of unresolved environmental and social problems, it appeared that major life-or-death decisions were entirely out of their control. The danger of nuclear annihilation in a sense became the public issue around which others coalesced.

The anti-nuclear, pro-peace movement has now become an articulate social force of major political importance. In Western Europe and North America especially it is significant in the size as well as the breadth of its constituency, and in the range of issues it is prepared to address. In the U.S., where a mutual freeze on nuclear weapons has become the rallying issue, it was endorsed by over 10 million voters in 44 localities in the largest referendum ever held on a single issue. A public opinion poll in 1983 showed 80 percent of Americans in favor of a nuclear freeze.

The physical presence of the independent peace movements in western countries—repeatedly demonstrated in rallies, marches, and non-violent actions—does not yet have a counterpart in the communist countries. So far the Soviet Union has not allowed any non-official peace movement to flourish. Leaders of the only known non-official group, The Group To Establish Trust Between the USSR and USA have been repeatedly threatened, jailed, or exiled. Yet Sergei Batovrin, one of the former leaders, now exiled and in the U.S., says that the movement is growing and that he is confident that it will continue to grow.

In East Germany the independent peace movement has considerably more strength, although its leaders have also been harassed and sometimes exiled. It is not allowed by the government to have direct-action protests or hold demonstrations but, with the strong support of the Protestant Church, works quietly through forums and exhibits and a wide grass-roots movement of small groups. This appears to be the most firmly rooted of the organized efforts in eastern Europe.

At present the western public has to speak loudly enough for both sides—a task as difficult as it is vital.

Reducing Military Overload

The entry of the public into the disarmament debate has already brought official negotiations under closer scrutiny and raised pressures for progress. In view of the numbers of people involved and the diversity of their views, any generalizations about their attitudes are necessarily over-simplifications, but the main thrust can perhaps be identified as follows:

Impatience and Evident Dissatisfaction with the Results Achieved So Far in Formal Negotiations. Despite years of effort and an impressive list of agreements . . . disarmament has been achieved in only one category of weapons of war, biological and toxin weapons. Nuclear weapons, the principal focus of negotiating efforts since 1945, are not yet under effective controls . . . nor has their use in war been banned.

Narrowing the scope of negotiations to piecemeal measures and to an emphasis on numerical balances in limited categories of weapons has been counterproductive. If the arms competition is reduced in one area, it is merely channeled to others.

While negotiations in themselves can be useful instruments for peace, providing a forum for dialogue and exchange of views, they are no substitute for determined purpose. So far they seem designed to create order in the competition, allowing each side to protect its own advantage, rather than to stop the arms race. Unfortunately they give the impression that disarmament is officially seen to threaten, as Lord Hankey put it half a century ago, "a decrease in national virility."

A Renewed Emphasis on Basic Principles, Particularly with Respect to Nuclear Weapons. Many of the churches in formal statements have challenged the morality of nuclear weapons. In the U.S., three major church councils, the National Conference of Catholic Bishops, the National Council of Churches (representing Protestant and Orthodox churches), and the Rabbinical Assembly, are on record condemning nuclear war and supporting a nuclear weapons freeze. In a break with NATO tradition there is also a call for a declaration against the first use of nuclear weapons. At a conference in Sweden of 150 church leaders from all parts of the world, a majority of participants went a step further to state a clear condemnation of the *possession* as well as the *use* of nuclear weapons. The involvement of the churches in the anti-nuclear movement has become one of the most important influences for fundamental change.

From associations of lawyers, including most recently the Law Council of Australia, have come new reminders that existing international convenants prohibit weapons and tactics that cause wanton or indiscriminate destruction. The universally-accepted Hague Conventions of 1949 also specifically require all belligerents to ensure the safety of civilians. On the basis of these principles and evidence provided by scientific testimony on the consequences of nuclear war, a majority of countries in the United Nations has repeatedly declared the use of nuclear weapons to be "contrary to the law of humanity and . . . a crime against mankind and civilization."

Scientists have also become more vocal about the uncontrollable destruction implicit in any use of nuclear weapons and in particular about the threat to the ecosphere on which all life depends. In an unusual convocation assembled by the Pontifical Academy, scientists from 30 countries in every area of the world issued a forceful declaration on the prevention of nuclear war, declaring *inter alia,* "nuclear forces must be reduced, with the ultimate goal of complete nuclear disarmament."

A Call for Alternatives to the Present Stalemate in Negotiations, Stressing More Comprehensive Disarmament Approaches. Nuclear weapons are the first priority, with public proposals favoring approaches that would immediately move away from the fragmented official efforts and the details in which negotiations have been hopelessly enmeshed for years. People want to see clear, fast progress leading to reductions of nuclear forces. There is also growing support for steps to prevent the outbreak of nuclear war, especially through a general renunciation of the first use of nuclear weapons (a principle to which China and the USSR already publicly subscribe).

Of the organized efforts underway in the U.S., the nuclear freeze appears to have first place in public support. Its proponents envision this as a bilateral (U.S.-USSR) and varifiable halt to testing, production, and deployment of nuclear weapons. Conceivably it could be led off by a moratorium on deployment, followed promptly by formal agreements to be concluded within a year or so.

Joined with the freeze is a variety of measures, including elements of the "strategy of suffocation" earlier enunciated by Prime Minister Trudeau of Canada, and measures that have already been the subject of extensive study and negotiation. High on the list are: a comprehensive ban on nuclear testing, a ban on flight-testing of missiles and aircraft which carry nuclear weapons, and a cut-off of production of weapons-grade fissionable material.

In a most instructive series of public hearings on the freeze proposals, the Federation of American Scientists assembled leading scientists and other specialists to explore the technical feasibility, including verification, of specific measures and of comprehensive programs of disarmament. The extensive testimony produced in these hearings not only enlightens the public debate but firms the ground for political initiatives and should encourage them as well.

In western Europe, there is strong public support for the freeze concept, but the organized effort at present is primarily directed towrad the immediate goal of preventing the new deployment of NATO missiles and getting *reciprocal* Soviet withdrawal of their land-based SS-20 missiles. A further objective is the removal of all nuclear weapons from Europe. Several concepts of nuclear-free zones are under discussion, including proposals for the Arctic, Balkans, and Northern and Central Europe. The CND° appeal for a nuclear-free Europe "from Poland to Portugal" has popular support in the western countries but has not yet attracted the endorsement of the official peace councils in eastern Europe.

Enhancing Security

Disarmament alone is not enough. Advocates of faster progress on disarmament and the adoption of universal and comprehensive approaches to it have long recognized that effective control over the world arms race cannot by itself increase world security. The reduction of national military forces, in fact, will not proceed far unless there is a simultaneous strengthening of the instruments for peace. And even before the process begins, a major effort must be focused

---

CND Campaign for Nuclear Disarmament, Great Britain's nuclear-protest group.

on improving the political climate and building confidence and trust between nations.

The peace process calls for a decisive change of direction, a movement away from the resolution of conflicts by means of war toward a system that provides workable and attractive substitutes. In addition to disarmament, the basic requirements of such a system have been identified by many thoughtful observers over the years. A quick summary fo the points they have stressed—grouped here under four headings—may help to stimulate further discussion of the broad framework required for world peace and security.

***Civilian-based defense*—**The idea of an entire population mobilized for military defense is not new. Tiny Switzerland, for example, depends on it; Cuba has a highly organized citizen army; Nicaragua is reportedly training its population for armed resistance against invaders.

But there is an alternative possibility: the training of a whole population in *non-violent* defense. Sweden and the Netherlands have been studying it.

Professor Gene Sharpe of Harvard, after reviewing the history of past actions of this nature, argues that with advance planning and training countries could rely on a civilian-based defense to prevent, deter, and defend against attacks. The concept emphasizes massive non-cooperation and defiance by the entire population. The struggle against an opponent would be fought by undermining the opponent's authority and making the country unrulable. A civilian-based defense, armed not with guns but with training in organized tactics of non-cooperation, conceivably could be started as an addition to armed forces and gradually replace them.

***Legal system*—**Essential to a peace system is a body of law forbidding the use of force and backed by judicial tribunals for the settlement of disputes. The legal system would extend to a global basis those principles and procedures that we have come to accept as natural components of government in civilized nation-states.

The International Court of Justice already exists. The addition of regional courts appears desirable, and the acceptance of the International Court's authority over all states essential.

Mediation before the outbreak of conflict is within the purview of the UN Secretary General and the Security Council. In carrying out this authority two major problems recur: (1) the decisions of the Security Council must be unanimous but are often victims of the East-West split and (2) nations frequently ignore the resolutions. The Secretary General has called for a review of ways to strengthen the UN's ability to deal with threats to peace and the Security Council at present has this underway.

Outside observers sometimes see the problem as the need to mobilize world support for negotiated solutions as well as the need to strengthen the institutional framework. One proposal, outlined by Professor Thomas Saaty, University of Pittsburgh, is for a specialized International Center for Conflict Resolution. Beginning in the very earliest stages of a conflict situation, it would attempt to bring the parties into structured negotiations, drawing on the abilities of retired world leaders both to negotiate the conflict and attract world attention to the developing problem.

World police force—UN peacekeeping forces have been used in the Congo, Yemen, Indonesia, Cyprus, Sinai, Syrian Golan Heights, and Lebanon. In Lebanon alone, soldiers from 18 countries have participated in the UN force and 89 have lost their lives there. As the "symbol of the international community on patrol for peace," these forces have clearly demonstrated the need for effective and impartial peacekeeping while solutions to the causes of the conflict are being worked out.

The UN forces, however, operate under especially difficult conditions. They carry only light arms for self defense, are stationed only with the consent of the parties concerned, and can be effective only with their continued support. They cannot operate, as originally foreseen under Article 42 of the UN charter, as a force to prevent aggression. They are not equipped to halt a major military movement such as the Israeli invasion of Lebanon in 1982.

Alternatives to the present structure, in the form of a world police force within the framework of the United Nations, are ultimately dependent on agreement among the major powers. In their seminal work on world law, Clark and Sohn° saw the necessity for a permanent UN Peace Force, to be built up parallel with disarmament, so that at the end of the process it would be the only military force permitted.

The Social Condition—A fourth element of the peace system is a cooperative international effort to strengthen security through broad social progress. The focus here is not on military and legal controls but on the conditions that foster the need for them.

Disarmament can release the resources needed for a concerted attack on economic and social problems. Whether it is poverty or diminishing energy resources, illiteracy or a polluted environment, adequate food, water, and health care or the disposal of growing piles of radioactive and other dangerous wastes—no major problem stops these days at national borders. Their solutions do not require institutional changes or particular kinds of national political systems. They do require an understanding of the interdependence of the world economy and the importance of an effort to seek ways of accommodation and cooperation.

Grenville Clark and Louis B. Sohn. *World Peace Through World Law: Two Alternative Plans*, 3rd ed. Cambridge, Mass.: World Without War, 1966.

In awakening society to its peril, nuclear weapons have made a contribution to global sanity. They have demonstrated, perhaps more effectively than anything else could have, how fragile, and how interdependent in its vulnerability, the world community is. Now what is needed, as Professor [George F.] Kennan has said so eloquently, is the will to proceed.

APPENDIX 1

Writing a Research Paper

This appendix is intended to help you grapple with the challenge of writing a research paper on a topic related to nuclear weapons. Perhaps you expect to base your paper entirely on the essays in this book; or perhaps you will be using the book as one of several sources. In either case, the process of planning, reading, researching, and writing will be less formidable if you read these suggestions before you begin.

Experienced writers know that any project looks daunting when it is contemplated all at once. Therefore, the first order of business is to break the job down into manageable steps. In this respect, writing a paper is something like planning a long trip or choosing a college: challenging to confront but exciting and fairly easy to do if you take it one step at a time.

For a research paper, the steps you take are likely to resemble these:

1. Choose a topic.
2. Read to get a more precise idea of what you want to write about.
3. Write up a tentative outline and thesis statement.
4. Read for research, taking detailed notes.
5. Revise the thesis statement and outline in preparation for writing.
6. Draft the paper.
7. Revise the paper.
8. Document the sources.
9. Type the final draft and proofread the paper.

There are two advantages to starting at the top of this list and proceeding step by step to the end. One is that each item in itself is a manageable task that you can accomplish without too much difficulty. The other is that if you begin at the beginning rather than somewhere in the middle, you have to deal with only one aspect of the process at a time. In the long run, this makes the job go more quickly and smoothly.

1. Choose a topic.

When you first consider what subject you might want to write about, you need not be too specific. A good tactic is to start with a general area or question that interests you. You might begin by skimming through some of the essays in this book or by consulting the Further Research Sources on pp. 381–388. Or you might see an item in a newspaper or magazine that you want to pursue. You may also find it helpful to reread the book's Contents and Introduction for ideas. Or look at the contents and the index in other books on the subject.

Two criteria are important in choosing a topic for a research paper. First, your subject should be one that interests you. If you are curious about the technology of nuclear weapons, you might decide to write about a particular weapons system or the difference between early and current guidance systems. If you like history, you could trace the political controversy about the hydrogen bomb or focus on an individual who has been influential in some aspect of weapons development or arms control. (Many people who participated in the Manhattan Project that produced the first atomic bomb are now central figures in the arms control debate.) If you expect to do research beyond the essays in this book, you might try to see some of the films listed in the filmography in Appendix 3 and analyze their techniques for presenting a case. You can explore the issue of nuclear weapons from the perspective of almost any discipline: political science, medicine, sociology, psychology, physics, even literature. The issue is large enough so that, no matter what your interests, you can find some aspect of it that will stimulate your curiosity. This is important because it is hard to hold your readers' attention if you yourself are bored.

The second characteristic of a good topic is that it rewards exploration. That is, both you and your audience should finish your paper knowing something new. Your job as the author of a research paper is not only to assemble facts but to interpret them—to ask (and answer) the question, "What does all this mean?" If your topic is either too narrow or too broad, this will be difficult to do.

For example, suppose you want to write about the National Security Council. In itself this is a broad topic. You would need to narrow it (probably by reading and thinking about it further) to something more specific, such as, "What role does the National Security Council play in shaping U.S. nuclear policy?" or "What is the official function of the National Security Council, and how well does it accomplish this function?" On the other hand, you would not want to narrow the topic so far that neither you nor your readers learn anything of interest. If you chose the topic "Who are the members of the National Security Council?" your role as an investigator would be reduced simply to reporting facts from some other source. Such a paper would not repay either your effort in writing it or your audience's effort in reading it.

Other topics to avoid are ones that are too subjective or too technical for your skills as a researcher. Any topic that asks you to do no more than state your opinion is not a research topic. At the other extreme, topics that ask you to master a great deal of difficult technical information will probably not allow you to absorb the material quickly and fully enough to present a coherent research paper. For example, a technical report on the discoveries in physics that led up to the making of the atom bomb might be too difficult for a student who has had no training in physics.

Finally, if you choose a controversial topic, learn the arguments of both sides. You may strongly favor one side; however, as a researcher your task is to present information as carefully as possible. This does not mean that you cannot argue for one side; it means that you must present all the evidence accurately.

Your clear reasoning and judicious presentation of all positions on an issue will be your most useful persuasive strategy.

2. Read to get a more precise idea of what you want to write about.

Having picked a general subject, you now begin to explore it. At this stage the goal is to establish the scope and essential elements of your topic in just enough depth to set guidelines for your research. You might start by jotting down whatever ideas come to mind—facts you already know; questions you want to look into; relevant individuals, events, and organizations. You can then skim through the essays in this book and note the ones that seem likely to shed light on your topic. (Even if you plan to do library research, it may be best to limit yourself to this book until you reach the outline stage.)

This kind of initial reading helps you identify what you need to find out in order to discuss the subject effectively. To clarify what that means, let's look again at the five questions mentioned in the Introduction. These questions indicate basic areas of information that should be considered in any investigation of a complex topic. Here, they are applied specifically to nuclear weapons:

1. What are nuclear weapons?
2. How have they come about?
3. How do we (as a culture) justify them?
4. How do we (as a culture) criticize or assess them?
5. How can we reduce the risk of their annihilating our world?

Recall that in the Introduction each of these questions represents an increase in complexity over the one before. This becomes more evident when we rephrase the questions in a general form applicable to any subject:

1. What is it? (Definition, identification, description, classification)
2. How has it come to be? (Chronology, sequence, analysis of causality or process)
3. What is its purpose? Why is it considered important? (Conceptual analysis, analysis of justifications)
4. How should we assess it? (Functional or moral analysis; critique, evaluation, reflection)
5. What should we do about it? (Policy formulation, advocacy)

The terms that follow the questions describe the kinds of thinking we do when we attempt to answer them. As you can see, each set of thinking processes depends on and builds on the one that preceded it. Why should we notice this? Because noticing it can help us to judge the complexity of any issue we might want to write about, identify its key elements, and anticipate the kinds of thinking that will go into our paper.

For example, suppose we are concerned about the question, "Should Congress grant funding for one hundred MX missiles requested by the Reagan administration?'' A quick glance at our five questions places this one at the end of the list. That marks it as a very complex question indeed, one asking us to formulate a position (and advocate it). Before we can begin to do this, we must identify a number of simpler questions that will bring us information on which to decide our position.

1. *What is it?* To begin with, we will need a definition and description of the MX missile. What can it do (and not do)? How does it differ from other missile systems?
2. *How has it come to be?* At this level we would want to know something about the MX's history—why it was developed, what debates preceded the present controversy over funding.
3. *What is its purpose? Why is it considered important?* Here we are asking for facts about the MX's role as a solution to particular military and political problems. How does it fit into our nation's existing nuclear arsenal? into our strategy of deterrence?
4. *How should we assess it?* Now we shift from facts and concepts into opinions. The advocates and opponents of this missile system have very different views of its value. What are their main arguments? How valid do these arguments seem to be?
5. *What should we do about it?* On the basis of our answers to the preceding questions, we can recommend an informed course of action.

This five-part paradigm can be a helpful tool throughout the research and writing process, as we shall see. During the initial reading stage, it is useful mainly as a means of gauging the complexity of the chosen topic and of ensuring that the right types of questions are asked. Notice that the emphasis is on asking questions, not on answering them. Answers come in the research phase. At this point your purpose is threefold: (1) to clarify exactly what you want to write about, making sure your subject is appropriate in scope for your assignment; (2) to decide on your approach to the subject: Are you taking a position on a controversy, proposing a course of action, or merely surveying available information? (3) to identify what you will need to find out in order to discuss the subject effectively in a research paper.

3. Write up a tentative outline and thesis statement.

The goal of your initial reading was to set the scope and probable direction of your paper. Now you can summarize your paper's purpose in a thesis statement: a sentence or two describing the topic in terms of your approach to it, and you can outline your paper's basic structure. Your thesis may be a question you propose to answer: ''Should Congress grant funding for one hundred MX missiles requested by the Reagan administration?'' If you have already decided on an answer, you might phrase your thesis statement declaratively: ''Congress should (or should not) grant funding for one hundred MX missiles requested by the Reagan administration.'' If your ideas about the subject are still vague, your working thesis could be as general as "The MX missile: Do we need it?" or "Congress versus Reagan on current weapons systems."

If you ended your preliminary reading with a fairly specific idea of your subject and your approach to it, your tentative thesis statement may be quite close to the final thesis statement that will appear in your paper. In this case, your outline will show any arguments you need to support and rebut, as well as the central facts that provide a basis for your position. If you are not yet sure of your paper's thrust, your thesis statement will undergo revision as your ideas become clearer. In this case, your outline may simply identify the major areas of controversy and the information you expect will be relevant. As you make up your outline, the accumulating evidence may help you define your approach and refine your thesis statement. It is not unusual for a thesis statement to change shape a half-dozen times or more during the process of outlining and research.

Your outline provides you with a "road map" to follow toward the destination described in your thesis statement. At this point, you probably will find that a working outline suits your needs better than a formal one. Many of the items in your outline are likely to be questions, noting gaps you need to fill or information you need to check. Once you track down these missing pieces, you will have a more precise sense of how each item relates to the others and how to arrange your material in a logical sequence. Outlines, like thesis statements, often go through several revisions before they become final.

Some writers like to use a visual diagram for an outline, placing their thesis statement in the center of a blank sheet of paper and connecting it with lines radiating outward to its major subtopics (Figure 1). On one side of the page these subtopics typically focus on *analysis,* or the factors that have made the subject what it is: a definition and description, causes and influences, the subject's current role and purpose. The other side of the page is *projection,* or the subject's effects: how people perceive it and are affected by it, what impact it has had on the culture's institutions and systems, its likely future impact, and recommendations. The types of question generated during the reading stage usually fit well into this diagrammatic type of outline. Another advantage to such a format is that you need not arrange the subtopics in any particular order until you have laid them all out and can see how they are connected. Also, you can add new items as they arise without having to redo the whole outline.

Or you may prefer to follow a traditional outline format, starting with your thesis statement and listing the subject's major and minor subtopics in the order you plan to cover them. In a formal outline, subheadings are indented under major headings. The following example shows the pattern:

I. Current purpose and role of the MX missile
   A. Definition of the MX
      1. Capabilities of the MX
      2. Limitations of the MX
      3. Differences between the MX and other weapons systems

FIGURE 1 Diagramming an Outline

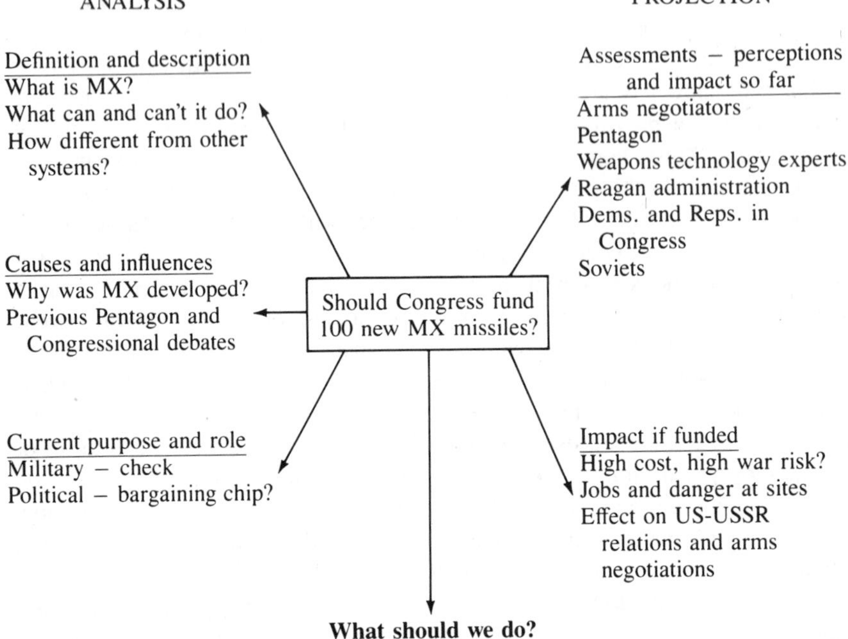

a. Other land-based systems
b. Air-based and sea-based systems
c. Equivalent Soviet land-based systems

B. Military role of the MX (deterrence)
C. Political role of the MX

4. Read for research, taking detailed notes.

The more you know about the purpose of your research, the more efficiently you can proceed. You should begin the research stage with a thesis statement, an outline, and some notes about which essays in this book apply to your topic. If your paper is to be based entirely on material in the book, your research process will be fairly straightforward. If you plan to use other sources, you will need to think about what types of information can be helpful and where you are most likely to find them.

In either case, you should start your research with a large supply of index cards. Index cards are preferable to notes collected on sheets of paper because they enable you to record each fact or idea separately, along with its source. When you have gathered as much information as you need, you can arrange

FIGURE 2 Sample Note Card and Bibliography Card

NOTE CARD

Aldridge
First Strike
p. 104

History of MX

In 1979 the National Security Council advised against full-scale development of MX because it could "upset the military balance between Russia + U.S."

BIBLIOGRAPHY CARD

U263.A43
1983

Aldridge, Robert C.
First Strike: The Pentagon's Strategy for Nuclear War. Boston: South End Press, 1983.
illustrations throughout

the cards in accord with your outline. Then, as you write, you can proceed from one major topic or subtopic to the next in order, without having to search through pages of notes.

Using Note Cards

As you read, record each relevant point you discover on a clean index card. Write the card's topic at the upper right (see Figure 2). Ideally, this topic heading should come from your outline, to help you keep track of where the card fits into your paper.

On the upper left side of the card, record the source of the information. Your source note will ultimately become a footnote or reference in your paper and an entry in your bibliography; for that you will need the author's full name, the correct title of the work, its publisher, the place and year of publication, and the page number(s) of the information you want to use. Most people find it useful to write the full source reference on a separate list or index card (3 × 5-inch cards are very good for this purpose). Then only an abbreviated form of the source—author's last name, key words in the title, and page number—is needed on note cards from that source. On the source card (also called a bibliography card; see Figure 2) record the call number of a book as well as the publication information for easy retrieval.

In deciding how much information to put on a note card, keep in mind the way you might use it.

Quoting

A research paper gains its authority from its sources. The most emphatic way of presenting a source's position (or showing a source's support for your own position) is to quote. But a research paper it not a string of quotations; it is your own interpretation of a body of material. Choose your quotations wisely, and as you take notes copy the exact words and punctuation of passages you think you will quote in your final paper.

The most effective quotations make their point in a few well-chosen words. The ideal quotation is one that says what you want to say in vivid or unforgettable language. Quoting is also useful when your source is a noted expert on the subject and you want to show your familiarity with his or her position, whether or not you share it. Occasionally you may want to quote a source you disagree with in order to point out a flaw in the argument. If your source is important but long-winded, you can quote the most relevant phrases or sentences and use ellipses (. . .) to show where material has been omitted. Whenever you use a quotation be careful that you do not distort the author's meaning by taking statements out of context.

You may need to insert words into a quotation to clarify it or to make it fit smoothly and grammatically into your paper. Use brackets whenever you insert something of your own into a quotation:

> The White House stated that "the purpose of SDI [Strategic Defense Initiative] is to strengthen deterrence and lower the level of nuclear forces."

Paraphrasing. When you give the essence of a source's comments rather than his or her exact words, you are paraphrasing. This is usually appropriate when the source's position is important but is not stated impressively or concisely enough to quote. Often a paraphrase will have roughly the same number of words as the original, but the words and sentence structure of the paraphrase will be your own. The more you put information into your own words as you take notes, the easier it will be to write your paper. Remember, though, whenever you paraphrase you must cite the source in your paper. See p. 357 for an example.

Summarizing. If you want to cite only the point a source has made without any reference to his or her phrasing, you can summarize by writing down the gist of the source's remarks. A summary will have fewer words than the original. You can summarize an article or the information from charts or graphs in a few sentences. You can even summarize an entire book, depending on your purpose. See p. 357 for an example. Again, you must cite the source of any information you summarize.

In addition to recording your sources' observations, be sure to write down any questions they raise in your mind or points you want to pursue further. You may find it helpful to keep a separate set of note cards listing questions to yourself. These questions can be checked off as the answers emerge from your research; or you can create a numbering or lettering system to cross-reference your questions with your notes.

As you complete each note card, put it in order among the others according to your outline. If you find that your research is changing your ideas about what your paper will cover, or changing the relative priority of your subtopics, you may stop and revise your outline.

Avoiding Plagiarism. Plagiarism is the use of another's work without proper acknowledgment. In many cases, plagiarism is the result of carelessness at the notetaking stage. Be sure to write down sources and page numbers on your note cards and enclose any quoted words or statements in quotation marks. For a fuller discussion of plagiarism with examples, see p. 358.

Using the Library

Now let's consider how you might proceed if your research takes you to the library. Suppose that during your initial reading you were struck by the fact that the United States' fundamental nuclear weapons strategy (our ''strategic doctrine,'' generally referred to as *deterrence*) has changed very little since Robert S. McNamara was secretary of defense in the early 1960s. You're puzzled or intrigued by that, and you'd like to find out why the policy hasn't changed much. How would you do it?

First, you would need to formulate a thesis statement: ''Why has U.S. strategic doctrine changed so little since McNamara?'' Looking back at the list of five questions on p. 345, you conclude that your preliminary thesis is a fairly complex question, calling for analysis of concepts and justifications (see question 3). Obviously, you cannot begin your research at that level. Questions 1 and 2 suggest some more basic points you need to investigate first:

1. What is it? Your starting point will be to establish a working definition of your key terms, *deterrence, strategic doctrine,* and *national security policy.* Does everyone agree on what these words mean? If not, what are the important differences? Can you identify the main strategies for deterrence? What does the United States have today?

2. How has it come to be? Perhaps the origins of today's strategy may be found in the Kennedy administration (McNamara was secretary of state under President John F. Kennedy), or they may go back to the end of World War II or even earlier. It makes sense to start with the Kennedy years and work backward and forward as necessary from there. On your outline you might note some possible historical influences: the cold war; attitudes toward the Soviets; roughly equal capabilities; technological changes.

Once you have answered these questions, you can proceed to question 3:

3. What is its purpose? Why is it considered important? Here you would be likely to compare justifications for countervailing strategies today and in McNamara's time. Are they still seen in the same way, for the same purpose? Have any alternatives been seriously considered? If so, why (and by whom) were they rejected?

In adapting these questions into an outline for your research, you draw on the most readily available sources: your own thoughts and knowledge, the essays in this book, the book's glossary, and perhaps your instructor or a textbook or dictionary. Make use of the information at hand before proceeding to the library, to save yourself time and effort. Also, look through the bibliography in this and any other relevant books you have and make a list of likely references.

Once you are in the library, you will probably move back and forth between the reference room and the card catalog. Different topics require different sources of information. Some will be primary sources, original pieces of writing such as speeches, legislative bills, stories, eyewitness accounts, interviews, and historical documents. (Many of the pieces in this book are primary sources.) Others will be secondary sources, works that have already distilled information from primary sources.

A good place to begin is with a dictionary, if you have not already consulted one. Even if you have, you may find that the dictionaries in the library (specialized as well as general) can give you more complete definitions of your key terms. The *McGraw-Hill Dictionary of Scientific and Technical Terms* or the *Dictionary of Scientific Biography* might be very useful for a project on nuclear weapons.

Your next step might be an encyclopedia, where you can look up these terms for a fuller description of what they mean and perhaps find some clues to their origins. The *Encyclopedia Americana* and the *Encyclopaedia Britannica* are probably your best bets, but other general encyclopedias may also contribute helpful information. Check publication dates to be sure the information you find is as current as possible. An encyclopedia's index is especially valuable for steering you to relevant articles, and to other terms that relate to your project. You will also want to look up the people you have identified as as influential in creating specific strategies for deterrence, such as Robert McNamara.

Next, look for a specialized encyclopedia that relates to your subject. One that might work for this topic is the *International Encyclopedia of the Social Sciences*. Here, and in most other encyclopedias, you can scan the suggested readings at the ends of the articles for further sources.

From these general reference works you will want to move on to books related specifically to your subject. The *Library of Congress Subject Heading* guide *(LCSH),* usually kept near the card catalog or at a reference desk, will provide the correct terms and cross-references to check in the card catalog to find works on deterrence, national security policy, nuclear strategy, and other subjects you have listed as applicable to your topic. Then you can use the card catalog to find promising titles. Copy the titles and call numbers of books on bibliography cards, using a separate card for each title. Once you know where in the stacks to look, browse through the area—there may be other books you can use besides the ones you have identified from the card catalog.

The card catalog in a library lists only those books owned by the library.

You can find these and other books on your subject by checking in bibliographies such as the *Bibliographic Index: A Cumulative Bibliography of Bibliographies.* This general reference tool lists by subject bibliographies that are included in books, parts of books, and periodicals. You might find more specific bibliographies listed in the card catalog for your subject. *Science Technology and Public Policy: A Selected and Annotated Bibliography* and *Political Science Bibliographies* are only two of the specific bibliographies that might be useful for a project on some aspect of nuclear weapons. If you find promising titles not owned by your library, your reference librarian can suggest others and can advise you on borrowing books from other libraries through interlibrary loan.

Periodicals as well as books will aid your research. The *Readers' Guide to Periodical Literature* indexes articles by author and subject in many popular magazines, such as *Time, Newsweek,* and the *Nation,* and is updated every few months. The *Readers' Guide* has a good cross-referencing system and includes articles by, as well as about, the people it mentions. The *Social Sciences Index* lists scholarly articles by author and subject in the fields of sociology, psychology, law, economics, and others and is more useful than the *Readers' Guide* for many topics on nuclear weapons. A specialized index that is valuable for issues related to nuclear weapons is the *Public Affairs Information Service Bulletin (PAIS).* It contains references to three kinds of publications related to public policy issues: periodicals; books; and some government publications, including printed transcripts of congressional testimony. Transcripts can be a valuable source of information and arguments about nuclear weapons, since they often include overviews of specific problems as introductions to congressional or committee hearings. Like the *Readers' Guide,* which is more broadly based, *PAIS* comes out several times a year and is consolidated annually.

Newspapers are also a good source of information about nuclear issues. The *New York Times Index* gives a brief summary of the articles it indexes along with detailed information about the location of the articles. The *Newspaper Index* provides subject and author indexes to the *Washington Post, Chicago Tribune, Los Angeles Times,* and *New Orleans Times-Picayne.* The *Wall Street Journal,* along with a number of other newspapers, has its own index. Again, your reference librarian can direct you to the most useful indexes for your topic.

You might also want to have a computer search done for books and articles on a topic. A fee is often charged for this service, and it may be impractical for many topics. A reference librarian can help you decide if a computer search would be appropriate for your topic, and if it is, the librarian will ask you to define the topic as specifically as possible by giving a list of terms that can be used to search various data bases for articles on the topic. In most cases the librarian will choose which data bases to search.

Depending on the topic you choose, different approaches and different works will be appropriate. Volumes such as the *Encyclopedia of Science and Technology,* the *Dictionary of American Biography, American Men and Women of Science,* the *Congressional Weekly* and *Congressional Digest* are only a few that could be valuable in research on issues related to nuclear weapons. Ask your librarian for suggestions—he or she can direct you to publications you might never think to look for on your own.

How do you know when you have done enough research? Your outline is an important gauge. If you have kept it current, you should be able to see when all its gaps are filled and its questions answered, or when what originally appeared as gaps are now areas outside your redefined topic. Your note cards to yourself can serve as a double check. Another clue is your running list of sources to consult. Remembering that a research paper gains its authority from its sources, you will not want to skip any book or article that may contain essential information. When you have gathered enough material to substantiate your thesis thoroughly, and to document your findings, it's time to stop reading and get ready to write.

5. Revise the thesis statement and outline in preparation for writing.

Your purpose at this stage is to organize your information so that writing your paper will proceed as smoothly as possible. Your final outline and thesis statement represent the road map and destination of your paper. At this point you should check your note cards against your working outline and make a formal outline showing each topic and subtopic in the order you plan to cover it. As you generate your final outline, you may discover additional gaps or questions you want to check. Once you are satisfied that your research is adequate, your outline will provide you with detailed guidelines for the writing process.

Part of creating a final outline is deciding how your information fits together. You may find that some subtopics are not as important as you thought, whereas others have become more central to your thesis than you expected. Using the formal outline format, with topic headings followed by supporting ideas and facts, enables you to sort out your priorities. Are all your major headings parallel in weight? Does each section include enough details to make it convincing? Have you left out anything that could strengthen your thesis? (If so, it is better to reorganize your outline than to omit a valuable point.) Have you found adequate counterarguments to positions that disagree with yours? Think also about transitions: Does each new idea proceed logically from the previous one? Is your material organized in a sequence that will build from your initial statement of your thesis to its confirmation at the end of your paper?

This is also the time to put your thesis statement into final form. Now that you know where your paper will start and finish, you can settle on a phrasing that fits with your outline. (It may be necessary to make slight changes as your paper comes together; but a clear thesis statement at this stage will help you write a coherent draft.) Perhaps you want to open with your thesis statement, to tell your readers immediately what you intend to discuss:

> The question of funding for one hundred new MX missiles affects not only Congress and the Reagan administration but everyone in the United States.

Or you may want to talk about the issue for a paragraph before introducing your thesis:

> Twenty years ago, Congress depended on the Pentagon to tell it how the United States could best be defended in case of attack. Today, with the arms race absorbing *x* percent of the national budget, members of the House and Senate are more skeptical. . . .

You might decide to present your thesis as a controversy to be resolved:

> One of the hottest nuclear weapons debates in recent history has been the fight between Congress and the Reagan administration over funding for one hundred new MX missiles.

Or you could state it as a question to be answered either in your opening paragraphs or at the end of your paper:

> Should Congress grant funding for the one hundred new MX missiles requested by the Reagan administration?

The wording and placement of your thesis statement will influence your readers' attitude toward your subject. More important than its form, however, is its content. Once you have formulated your thesis statement, ask yourself again whether it accurately sets the direction for your paper. Many writers have found that, after their research was done, the evidence pointed to a somewhat different conclusion from the one they had in mind when they started. Before you begin writing, review your outline and thesis statement one more time to make sure that they are firmly on the same track.

6. Draft the paper.

Ideally, someone who has done thorough research, outlined carefully, and devised a thesis statement that encapsulates his or her purpose should be able to sit down and write a first draft almost without effort. But in reality this seldom happens. Even the most experienced writers hesitate a little when faced with the prospect of turning the data they have gathered into prose. Fortunately, getting started is usually the hardest part. Don't be too concerned at first with the brilliance of your sentences. Concentrate on putting down what you want to say—you can always go back later to work on saying it as clearly as you can. Your early paragraphs are likely to change, anyway, once the whole draft is finished.

If your outline is orderly and detailed, writing the paper should not be too difficult. When in doubt, trust the work you have already done—stick with the plan represented by your outline and read over your note cards before you begin writing. Many people find that they can write a first draft in their own words more easily and smoothly if they write from their outline and refer to their note cards only occasionally (e.g., when they need a fact or a quotation). Cover each subject fully and connect one topic to the next with transition sentences at the end or beginning of your paragraphs. When you hit a snag, stop and ask yourself: What am I really saying here? Most writers progress smoothly in some places and haltingly in others. Only after your first draft (or a good-sized chunk of it) is done can you see which sections are well expressed and which ones need more work. Then you can go back over your outline and your notes to revise and develop these sections.

A research paper, like any piece of writing, is addressed to an audience. You probably noticed a variety of styles among the sources you read, depending on whether their target audience was made up of specialists or general readers. And you undoubtedly found some styles more appealing than others. Many authors, especially the less experienced, fall into the trap of trying to impress readers with their command of complex language and syntax instead of simply communicating information. Any essay, article, or book aimed at a nontechnical audience is most impressive when it is most direct. You should assume (unless instructed otherwise) that your audience consists of people much like yourself: interested in your subject, but not informed about it in any detail. Part of your job is to explain any idea, term, or event with which they may not be familiar in language that makes your meaning clear.

In transforming a collection of notes into a unified presentation, you will also make decisions about what to quote, what to paraphrase, and what to summarize. You should use your sources in whatever way best suits the goals of your paper. If the language of a source is vivid, or if a writer states a position directly and that position is important to your discussion, then quote the source. But remember, when you quote, you divert attention from your own words to someone else's. Sometimes this is useful; sometimes it is merely distracting. If you wish to draw on another person's ideas without spotlighting the source, it is generally preferable to paraphrase or summarize.

Your quotations should be brief—from a phrase to a few sentences—and there should not be so many that they dominate your paper. You may want to use more quotations if your paper centers on other people's positions or if your sources are highly articulate. You can use fewer if your paper does not rely heavily on expert commentary or if you haven't found many remarks worth quoting. If two quotations are equally appropriate and you have room for only one, choose the more authoritative source.

Using Sources

The following examples illustrate the various ways of using sources.

LONG QUOTATION

If you quote more than four typed lines, indent the quotation ten spaces from the left margin and double-space throughout. Integrate the quotation into your own writing by introducing it fully. You can give the author's name and credentials in this introduction. The parenthetical information in the examples that follow use the Modern Language Association (MLA) system of citation which is described later in this appendix. Your instructor will tell you which documentation style is preferred for your subject.

In his defense of nuclear realism, author and editor Leon Wieseltier demands that both sides of the nuclear debate be taken seriously:

> Let those who insist that there must be an idea that will end the nuclear era keep searching for the idea. They do not deserve to be scorned. But neither do those who insist that in the interim the danger must also be managed; and frequently they are. (297)

MEDIUM-LENGTH QUOTATION

E. P. Thompson points out that "It is in Washington, rather than Moscow, that scenarios are dreamed up for theater wars" (321).

SHORT QUOTATION

We should remember that the unresolved human problems that have haunted us for centuries are the ones that haunt us still "beneath the technological face of our civilization" (Nagler 331).

PARAPHRASE

Original: In the area of strategy, deterrence properly managed requires a firm and forthright rejection of any notion that a nuclear war can be prosecuted like a conventional war, that it can be limited or controlled. In the area of force structure, it requires a rejection of any weapons system that will upset the tender but tangible nuclear balance. (Wieseltier 296)

Paraphrase: Wieseltier says that if deterrence is to work, we must reject the notion that nuclear war can be limited, and we must object to any weapons systems that will change the balance and allow one side to gain significant advantage over the other (296).

SUMMARY

In discussing the psychological obstacles to coping with nuclear weapons, Jerome Frank explains that nuclear weapons are unreal to most of us, including the leaders who have to make decisions about these weapons. Treating nuclear arms as if they were conventional weapons, leaders feel that outarming their rivals will ensure their safety as it did in the past with other kinds of weapons (172–74).

COMBINATION

Many of the Soviet children interviewed by Eric Chivian and others said that they learned about nuclear weapons when they were seven or eight years old. They learned of them through television programs and through newspapers and conversations. When asked what would happen if there were a nuclear war, one thirteen-year-old from Moscow showed a sad wisdom. He responded: "Many casualties, many, many casualties. And they will principally be people who want peace, children, old people" (International Physicians 180–81).

Avoid Plagiarism

Information that is common knowledge, such as facts or dates that are widely known, or particular information about a topic that is available in many different sources, does not have to be documented. But whenever you quote or paraphrase another writer, or cite an idea you found in someone else's work, you must say so with a source reference. The purposes of documenting your research are to give credit where credit is due, to strengthen your case by showing that it has the support of other authorities, and to enable your readers to look up any outside comment or information they may be curious about. If you do not document your sources, you are guilty of plagiarism. If you document the source but do not enclose borrowed words in quotation marks, you are also guilty of plagiarism. In the following example, a student borrows the wording of a source without enclosing the words in quotation marks.

> *Original:* ''In the last nine months, however, and particularly in the last month, there has been a tremendous ballooning of United States public concern about nuclear war'' (Scoville 257).
>
> *Plagiarized version:* Recently there has been a tremendous ballooning of concern about the issues of nuclear war and weapons—particularly in the last month (Scoville 257).

In the next example, the words are the student's own, but the sentence structure is borrowed from the source.

> *Plagiarized version:* In the last year and especially in the last few weeks, there has been a dramatic increase in United States public concern about nuclear war (Scoville 257).
>
> *Proper use of the source:* Scoville notes a ''tremendous ballooning'' of concern in the United States about nuclear war (257).

Notice that the way you introduce ideas taken from an outside source is just as important as the kind of punctuation you use. The charge of plagiarism in the second example would have been avoided had the paraphrase been introduced by something like: ''Herbert Scoville feels that in the last year. . . .''

7. Revise the paper.

When you have finished writing your paper, let it sit for at least a few hours. If possible, spend some of that time getting exercise, listening to music, talking with friends about subjects totally unrelated to your paper, or doing something else that will divert your mind from your paper. Then you can come back to it later with a fresh perspective. The best way to spot any problems that need fixing is to read your draft as if another person had written it. This is difficult to do after you have been working on a paper for a long time, but any break away from the paper will help.

If you reread your paper and think it is either perfect or terrible, you are probably not being objective enough. Nearly every piece of writing needs some revision before the final draft; but in very few cases is it necessary to throw the whole thing out and start over. First, look at the whole paper to see that it is unified, complete, and coherent. Then move to paragraphs and finally to sentences and particular words. Ask yourself the following questions are you go through the different stages of revision: (1) Is the entire paper unified, starting with a clear thesis and using subordinate ideas and details to support that thesis? (2) Does the paper reach a conclusion that reiterates its opening statement on the basis of adequate evidence? (3) Is each paragraph coherent? Does each make a valid and essential point? (4) Are quotations and paraphrases integrated into the text? (5) Finally, look for specific flaws to correct in sentence structure, spelling, grammar, and punctuation.

If you aren't sure whether your paper is successful, two tactics may help. One is to read it aloud and see how it sounds. Another is to ask someone else to look at it and make suggestions. You need not follow every recommendation a reader gives you, but you should pay attention to anything he or she finds difficult to follow or understand.

8. Document the sources.

There are several different styles of documentation, including traditional footnotes (which most of the essays in this book use), the MLA (Modern Language Association) style, and the APA (American Psychological Association) style. Your instructor can tell you where to find detailed guidelines on whichever format he or she has assigned. Here we will focus on the basics of parenthetical citation in the MLA style. See p. 365 for basic information about footnotes and endnotes.

Parenthetical References

MLA utilizes a parenthetical reference in the text giving enough information so that the source can be identified in the "Works Cited" section at the end of the paper. Usually, the author and page number are sufficient:

> In January 1980, Carter asked the Senate to "delay consideration" of the Treaty (Talbott 290).

If you mention the author's name in the text of your paper, you need not repeat it in the parenthetical reference:

> Talbott notes that in January 1980, Carter asked the Senate to "delay consideration" of the treaty (290).

If you have drawn on more than one work by the same author, your parenthetical reference in the manuscript should indicate which work you mean: (Steiner, *Treblinka* 20). Steiner's works would then be alphabetized under his name by their titles in the "Works Cited" section. Similarly, if you mention the author and the title of the work in the text, you need only include the page number in the parenthetical reference.

Ordinarily the reference immediately follows the quoted or cited material, or where a pause would naturally occur.

> According to DeGrasse, the 1973 oil crisis ''forced many manufacturers to invest heavily in new, energy-efficient plant and machinery'' (165).

Note, however, that the parenthetical reference comes before the final punctuation when quotations are incorporated in the text.

For indented quotations the reference is placed two spaces after the final punctuation, as in the following example:

> DeGrasse argues that
>
>> a diversion of government resources to the military on the scale planned by the Reagan Administration will seriously weaken the nation's ability to meet the challenges of unemployment, foreign market losses, diminishing technological leadership and industrial obsolescence. (171)

For a work with two or three authors, give all the authors' last names in your citation:

> This situation has not changed since the 1950s (Greb and Johnson 223).

For works with more than three authors, give the last name of the first author followed by the Latin abbreviation *et al.* (which means ''and others''): (Franck et al. 119).

If you cite an entire work and you give the author's name in the text of your paper, you need not include a parenthetical reference:

> Noam Chomsky's *Language and Responsibility* is a useful study of ideological control.

If you don't mention the author, include the name in a parenthetical reference.

The following examples illustrate other common variations of parenthetical references.

CORPORATE AUTHOR

> When asked whether nuclear war between the U.S. and the USSR can be prevented, 93.3 percent of the Soviet children answered yes (International Physicians 184).

GOVERNMENT DOCUMENTS

> Over 50% of U.S. aeronautical engineers worked primarily on national defense in 1978 (U.S. National Science Found. B-13).

WORK CITED BY TITLE

If the author of a work is not known, cite the work by an abbreviated form of the title:

> Courses on nuclear war are showing up on college campuses across the country (''Colleges'' 33).

MULTIVOLUME WORK

Cite the volume used in the parenthetical reference:

Stillwater argues for international control of nuclear testing (2: 335).

Nuclear testing should be under international control (Stillwater 2: 335).

INDIRECT SOURCE

It is always best to quote from the original source of a comment, but if this is impossible, use the abbreviation "qtd. in" to indicate that you have quoted from an indirect source:

Kaufman complained that "no more costly method of keeping a limited number of airplanes at a forward base has ever been devised by the mind of man" (qtd. in Wicklein 85).

MORE THAN ONE WORK IN A PARENTHETICAL REFERENCE

Cite each source separated by a semicolon:

The White House believes that the Strategic Defense Initiative provides our only hope for credible deterrence (White House 4; Reagan 6).

ONE-PAGE ARTICLES OR ENCYCLOPEDIAS

"A number of British scientists did join the weapon design effort at Los Alamos" (Frank).

Unless an article from an encyclopedia is longer than one page, you need not give page numbers. If the article is unsigned, give a brief form of the title in the parenthetical reference.

Content Notes with Parenthetical Citation

Content notes can be used to explain information in the paper, to mention additional sources, and to give the original publication data for sources quoted indirectly. The presence of such a note is indicated with a raised number in the paper. All the notes are then typed at the end of the paper.

In 1976 the Committee on the Present Danger[1] put out a pamphlet arguing that the Soviet Union was the "principal threat to our nation, to world peace, and to the cause of human freedom" (2).

The note at the end of the paper would read:

[1]Ronald Reagan was one of the founding members of the Committee.

Works Cited

The list of works cited is typed double-spaced on a separate page and included after content notes (if there are any) at the end of the paper. The first line of each entry is typed flush with the left margin; subsequent lines are indented five spaces. Authors are listed alphabetically. The entry for a book should include the author(s), title, edition number (if any), editor or translator (if any), place and year of publication, and volume number (if any). Page numbers will be included in the parenthetical citation in the text. For a magazine, journal, or newspaper article, you need all of the following information that is available: the article's author(s) and title, the name of the publication, the volume, number (in some cases), date of publication, and the page numbers of the article. (In the examples that follow, the words in italics would be underlined in a typed or handwritten paper.)

If more than one work by a single author is included in the "Works Cited," list the titles alphabetically and type three hyphens in place of the author's name in the second entry:

Chomsky, Noam. *American Power and the New Mandarins.* New York: Pantheon, 1969.

- - -. *For Reasons of State.* New York: Random House, 1973.

The following examples give the format for the most common types of entries in a list of works cited. If you are citing pieces from this book, you can do so in one of two ways: (1) Use the format for a work in a collection of pieces by different authors (see p. 363); here you give the original publication information, which can be found in the copyright notice, along with the publication information for *The Nuclear Predicament;* (2) Use the format for cross-referencing a number of articles from the same anthology (see p. 363). Ask your instructor which of these two formats is preferred.

BOOK WITH ONE AUTHOR

White, William D. *U.S. Tactical Air Power: Missions, Forces and Costs.* Washington: Brookings Institution, 1974.

BOOK WITH TWO OR THREE AUTHORS

Enthoven, Alain C., and Wayne K. Smith. *How Much Is Enough? Shaping the Defense Program 1961–69.* New York: Harper, 1972.

Note that only the first author's name is reversed.

BOOK WITH MORE THAN THREE AUTHORS

Adams, Robert F., et al. *A History of Détente.* Washington: Institute for Policy Studies, 1984.

CORPORATE AUTHOR

Glasgow Media Group. *Bad News.* London: Routledge & Kegan Paul, 1976.

GOVERNMENT DOCUMENTS

U.S. National Science Foundation. *Characteristics of Experienced Scientists and Engineers, 1978, Detailed Statistical Tables.* Washington: GPO, 1978.

The abbreviation *GPO* means Government Printing Office.

Cong. Rec. 28 Mar. 1977: 9269.

In citing the *Congressional Record,* you need give only the date and the page number.

WORK IN MORE THAN ONE VOLUME

Jain, J. P. *Nuclear India.* 2 vols. New Delhi, India: South Asia Books, 1981.

If you want to cite only part of a set, include the number(s) of the volume(s) you used at the end of the entry:

Jain, J. P. *Nuclear India.* 2 vols. New Delhi, India: South Asia Books, 1981. Vol. 2.

To cite a single volume of a multivolume set that has separate titles, use the following format:

Tolgyessi, J., et al. *Introduction to Nuclear Analytical Chemistry.* Vol. 1 of *Nuclear Analytical Chemistry.* 5 vols. Baltimore: Univ. Park, 1981.

WORK BY THE SAME AUTHOR IN A COLLECTION

Simmons, J. L. "Deterrence." *A History of Nuclear Weapons.* By Simmons. New York: Harvest Press, 1982. 29–37.

WORK BY DIFFERENT AUTHORS IN A COLLECTION

Freeman, Patricia. "Balancing Terror." *The World Waits.* Ed. Mark Johnson. New York: Winston Books, 1984. 64–98.

If the piece was reprinted from another source, give the original publication date (which can usually be found in a copyright notice), following by the publication data for the source in which it is reprinted:

Greb, G. Allen and Gerald W. Johnson. "A History of Strategic Arms Limitations." *Bulletin of the Atomic Scientists* Jan. 1984. Rpt. in *The Nuclear Predicament: A Sourcebook.* Ed. Donna Uthus Gregory. New York: Bedford Books of St. Martin's Press, 1986. 96–108.

EDITOR OF AN ANTHOLOGY

Reed, MaryEllen, ed. *The Survival Manual.* New York: Westend Books, 1984.

CROSS-REFERENCES

When you are using a number of pieces from one collection, you can list the complete publication information for the collection and then cross-reference the individual pieces to the collection. Note the following example:

Oe, Kenzaburo, ed. *The Crazy Iris and Other Stories of the Atomic Aftermath.* New York: Grove Press, 1985.
Hara, Tamiki. "Summer Flower." Oe 37–54.
Sata, Ineko. "The Colorless Paintings." Oe 113–125.

ENCYCLOPEDIA

Frank, W. J. "Nuclear Weapons." *The New Encyclopaedia Britannica.* 1981 ed.

If the article is signed, list by author. If it is not signed, list by title.

EDITION

Friedlander, Gerhart, et al. *Nuclear and Radio Chemistry.* 2nd ed. New York: Wiley, 1981.

TRANSLATED BOOK

Zampaglione, Gerardo. *The Idea of Peace in Antiquity.* Trans. Richard Dunn. Notre Dame: U of Notre Dame P, 1973.

INTRODUCTION, PREFACE, FOREWORD, OR AFTERWORD

Peavitt, Francis L. Introduction. *Arms Control.* By Susan Jameson. Philadelphia: Reed, 1983.

This entry cites the introduction itself. In citing the author, use the following format:

Jameson, Susan. *Arms Control.* Intro. Francis L. Peavitt. Philadelphia: Reed, 1983.

PAMPHLET

Committee on the Present Danger. *Common Sense and the Common Danger.* Washington, 1976.

Berringer, Carla. *Where We Go from Here.* Boston: Writers for Social Responsibility, 1985.

ARTICLE IN A JOURNAL WITH CONTINUOUS PAGINATION

If a journal numbers its pages continuously through the year rather than numbering each issue separately, include the author, title, name of the journal, volume, year, and page numbers:

Kondratieff, Nikolai. "The Major Economic Cycles." *Review of Economic Statistics* 18 (1935): 78–96.

ARTICLE IN A JOURNAL WITH SEPARATE PAGINATION

If a journal numbers each issue separately, include the author, title, name of the journal, volume, month or season of publication, year, and page numbers:

Frank, Jerome D. "Psychological Causes of the Nuclear Arms Race." *Chemtech* 12 (Aug. 1982): 466–69.

If the journal does not designate a month or a season, type the volume number followed by a period and then by the issue number: 5.2 (1985): 29–36.

MONTHLY MAGAZINE

Pringle, Peter. "Political Science." *Atlantic* Oct. 1985: 67–81.

WEEKLY MAGAZINE

Kittle, Robert A. "Behind Sudden Threat to Midgetman Missile." *U.S. News & World Report* 23 Sept. 1985: 38–39.

ANONYMOUS ARTICLE

If the author is not known, list the article by its title:

"The Bishop at Ground Zero." *Life* July 1982: 62–66.

NEWSPAPER ARTICLE

Farrell, Michael. ''Leader Talks Détente.'' *National Catholic Reporter* 15 July 1983: 45+.

The + sign indicates that the article, which begins on page 45, does not appear on consecutive pages. If a newspaper is divided into sections, with each section numbered separately, include the section letter before the page number.

EDITORIAL

Marks, Robert. ''Teach Our Children.'' Editorial. *Boston Globe* 18 Aug. 1985, sec. B:15.

LETTER TO THE EDITOR

Meyers, Barbara. Letter. *Philadelphia Inquirer* 14 Jan. 1984: 19.

PUBLISHED INTERVIEW

Walters, Vernon. ''Why the U.N. Has Been a 'Measured Disappointment.' '' *U.S. News & World Report* 23 Sept. 1985: 29.

LECTURE

Forsberg, Randall. ''A Nuclear Freeze.'' Waging Peace Conference. Harvard Univ., 4 Apr. 1982.

FILM

Dr. Strangelove or: How I Learned to Stop Worrying and Love the Bomb. Dir. Stanley Kubrick. Columbia Pictures, 1964.

TELEVISION PROGRAM

''Civil Defense.'' *Weekly Report.* PBS. WGBH, Boston. 18 Sept. 1983.

PERSONAL INTERVIEW

Evans, Joseph. Personal interview. 12 June 1985.

Footnotes or Endnotes

If you are using footnotes or endnotes to document your sources, the first step is to insert a raised number after each use of source material. These numbers should be sequential all the way through the paper. The notes are then listed in numerical order on a separate page labeled ''Notes'' at the end of the paper (unless your instructor prefers that each one appear as a footnote on the page of citation).

The first time you refer to a given source, your note should describe it in full. For a book this means author(s), title, edition number (if any), editor (if any), place and year of publication, volume number (if any), and page number(s). For a magazine or newspaper you should include all of the following information that is available: the aritcle's author and title, the name of the publication, the volume, number (in some cases), date of the issue, and page number(s). Subsequent references need to contain only a shortened form of this information.

In various styles of endnotes and footnotes, the Latin abbreviation *Ibid.* is used to indicate that a subsequent reference is the same as the preceding reference. The abbreviation *op. cit.* with the author's name is used to indicate that the reference is to a work that has already been cited. You may see these abbreviations in the notes to pieces in *The Nuclear Predicament* that use styles of documentation other than the note style recommended by MLA, or in references in older publications. For subsequent references MLA recommends including the author's last name and the page number(s), unless you are referring to more than one book by the same author. In this case, include a shortened form of the title in later references. The following examples illustrate the format for the most common types of notes.

FIRST REFERENCE TO A BOOK BY A SINGLE AUTHOR

[1]William D. White, *U.S. Tactical Air Power: Missions, Forces and Costs* (Washington: Brookings Institution, 1974) 85.

SUBSEQUENT REFERENCE

[2]White 109–17.

BOOK WITH TWO OR THREE AUTHORS

[3]Alain C. Enthoven and Wayne K. Smith, *How Much Is Enough? Shaping the Defense Program 1961–69* (New York: Harper, 1972) 223.

BOOK WITH MORE THAN THREE AUTHORS

[4]Robert F. Adams et al., *A History of Détente* (Washington: Institute for Policy Studies, 1984) 54.

CORPORATE AUTHOR

[5]Glasgow Media Group, *Bad News* (London: Routledge & Kegan Paul, 1976) 104.

GOVERNMENT DOCUMENTS

[6]United States, National Science Foundation, *Characteristics of Experienced Scientists and Engineers, 1978, Detailed Statistical Tables* (Washington: GPO, 1978) B-13.

[7]*Cong. Rec.*, 28 Mar. 1977: 9269.

WORK IN MORE THAN ONE VOLUME

[8]J. P. Jain, *Nuclear India,* 2 vols. (New Delhi, India: South Asia Books, 1981).

The above citation refers to both volumes of Jain's work. To cite only one volume, use the following format:

[9]J. P. Jain, *Nuclear India,* 2 vols. (New Delhi, India: South Asia Books, 1981) 2: 329.

To cite a single volume of a multivolume work that has individual titles use the following format:

[10]J. Tolgyessi et al., *Introduction to Nuclear Analytical Chemistry,* vol. 1 of *Nuclear Analytical Chemistry,* 5 vols. (Baltimore: Univ. Park, 1981) 27.

WORK BY THE SAME AUTHOR IN A COLLECTION

[11]J. L. Simmons, "Deterrence," *A History of Nuclear Weapons* by Simmons (New York: Harvest Press, 1982) 29.

WORK BY DIFFERENT AUTHORS IN A COLLECTION

[12]Patricia Freeman, "Balancing Terror," *The World Waits,* ed. Mark Johnson (New York: Winston Books, 1984) 64.

If the piece was reprinted from another source, give the original publication data (which can usually be found in a copyright notice), followed by the publication information for the source in which it is reprinted:

[13]Greb, G. Allen and Gerald W. Johnson, "A History of Strategic Arms Limitations," *Bulletin of the Atomic Scientists* Jan. 1984: 9; rpt. in *The Nuclear Predicament: A Sourcebook,* ed. Donna Uthus Gregory (New York: Bedford Books of St. Martin's Press, 1986) 96–108.

EDITOR OF AN ANTHOLOGY

[14]MaryEllen Reed, ed., *The Survival Manual* (New York: Westend Books, 1984) vi.

ENCYCLOPEDIA

[15]W. J. Frank, "Nuclear Weapons," *The New Encyclopaedia Britannica,* 1981 ed.

If you are citing from only one page of an article that is longer than a page, you can give the page number.

PAMPHLET

[16]Carla Berringer, *Where We Go from Here* (Boston: Writers for Social Responsibility, 1985) 3.

ARTICLE IN A JOURNAL WITH CONTINUOUS PAGINATION

[17]Nikolai Kondratieff, "The Major Economic Cycles," *Review of Economic Statistics* 18 (1935): 80.

ARTICLE IN A JOURNAL WITH SEPARATE PAGINATION

[18]Jerome D. Frank, "Psychological Causes of the Nuclear Arms Race," *Chemtech* 12 (Aug. 1982): 468.

MONTHLY MAGAZINE

[19]Peter Pringle, "Political Science," *Atlantic* Oct. 1985: 67.

WEEKLY MAGAZINE

[20]Robert A. Kittle, "Behind Sudden Treat to Midgetman Missile," *U.S. News & World Report* 23 Sept. 1985: 39.

ANONYMOUS ARTICLE

[21]"The Bishop at Ground Zero," *Life* July 1982: 64.

NEWSPAPER ARTICLE

[22]Leon Weiseltier, "A Defense of Nuclear Realism," *Los Angeles Times* 7 Oct. 1984, part IV: 1.

EDITORIAL

[23]Robert Marks, "Teach Our Children," editorial, *Boston Globe* 18 Aug. 1985, sec. B: 15.

PUBLISHED INTERVIEW

[24]Vernon Walters, "Why the U.N. Has Been a 'Measured Disappointment,' " *U.S. News & World Report* 23 Sept. 1985: 29.

LECTURE

[25]Randall Forsberg, "A Nuclear Freeze," Waging Peace Conference, Harvard University, 4 Apr. 1982.

FILM

[26]*Dr. Strangelove or: How I Learned to Stop Worrying and Love the Bomb,* dir. Stanley Kubrick, Columbia Pictures, 1964.

TELEVISION PROGRAM

[27]"Civil Defense," *Weekly Report,* PBS, WGBH, Boston, 18 Sept. 1983.

PERSONAL INTERVIEW

[28]Joseph Evans, personal interview, 12 June 1985.

9. Type the final draft and proofread the paper.

If your instructor does not provide specific guidelines for preparing your manuscript, you can use the following suggestions. Type the paper on one side of 8½ × 11-inch typing paper (not onionskin), doublespacing throughout (including long quotations, endnotes (if any), and list of works cited). Leave margins of at least one inch on all sides. You do not need a separate title page unless you are handing in a formal outline along with the paper. Type your name, the instructor's name, the course name, and the date, each on a separate line beginning about one inch from the top of the page and flush with the left margin. Double-space between each of these lines. Skip two spaces after the heading and center the title of the paper between the left and right margins. Capitalize the first letter of the first and last words of the title and all other words except articles, prepositions, and conjunctions. Do not underline the title or put it in quotation marks unless you mention the title of another work. In this case underline the title of the work if it is a book or pamphlet, or enclose it in quotation marks if it is the title of an essay or other short piece.

Number all pages with arabic numerals at the top right corner about one-half inch from the top of the page. From page 2 on, type your last name before the page number (in case pages are misplaced). If you include an outline, you can number its pages with lowercase roman numerals (i, ii, and so on).

Proofread the paper carefully before handing it in. Make corrections with liquid correction fluid. You can insert small corrections by typing them above the line and using a caret (∧) to indicate where they go.

If you need additional information on how to document sources or prepare the final manuscript, consult your instructor, a handbook, or Joseph Gibaldi and Walter S. Achtert's *MLA Handbook for Writers of Research Papers,* 2nd ed. New York: Modern Language Association of America, 1984.

APPENDIX 2
Suggested Research Topics

The following questions are arranged under five topic headings; in condensed form they are: ''Arsenals''; ''Historical Questions''; ''Foreign Policy, Deterrence, and the Soviet Threat''; ''Language and Ethics''; and ''Proposals''. The question topics do not correspond to the four part sections into which the readings are divided. Instead, in a loose way, these headings reflect the kinds of question posed in the Introduction: definition, process analysis, conceptual analysis, evaluation, and advocacy. The questions are much more specific than these in the Introduction, however. Thus, though the first two topics—the nature of the weapons arsenals and the history of arms developments—are the same as the ones discussed in the Introduction, here the third topic includes both justifications and critiques, the forth topic consists of special kinds of evaluation—ethical, logical, rhetorical, and literary, and various proposals are discussed in the fifth topic.

The questions under each topic heading are divided into two kinds, one that can be answered from the text alone and another that calls for library research. You shouldn't draw a hard line between these two categories, however. If you have access to a library, intend to do research, and are intrigued by one of the questions limited to *The Nuclear Predicament,* the question can be the basis of your research plan. Similarly, the library segment of many of the questions under ''For Further Research'' can be omitted, providing you with an interesting problem to research in this reader. Appendix 1, Writing a Research Paper, will help you if you intend to use the library.

Nuclear Arsenals: What's in Them? What Can They Do?

1. Detail both the numbers of weapons the United States and the USSR possess today and the ways the U.S. and Soviet arsenals are configured—their ''force structures.'' Explain how the asymmetrical force structures of the two countries complicates assessments of ''who's ahead.'' (See ''Factual Information on Present Nuclear Arsenals'' (p. 18) and Appendix 5.)
2. Drawing from the information about the effects of nuclear weapons, write a fictional account—perhaps in the form of a news release from an unaffected country—about the effects of a nuclear attack today. You may assume either (1) a strike on selected military installations in the United States, such as the Minuteman missile fields in North and South Dakota or on a variety of strategic military bases; (2) an attack on either a single city or several cities in the United States or (3) a strike in the Middle East (e.g., Israel, Syria, Iraq), or in West Germany. If your fictional situation targets cities, assume that 5 megatons are likely to be used on a small city (under 1 million) and 20 megatons on a big city.

For Further Research

3. Several films, short stories, and novels treat the potential effects of a nuclear attack at several levels of intensity. Read or view one or more of these: *Warday* by Whitley Strieber and James Kunetka (New York: Holt, Rinehart, and Winston, 1984); "Charlottesville" by Nan Randall, available in *The Nuclear Almanac,* compiled and edited by MIT faculty (Reading, Mass.: Addison-Wesley, 1984); films: *Threads, Testament,* or *The Day After.* Write an essay discussing the work's accuracy based on the information in these books or films.
4. The nuclear winter effect has stimulated some controversy. What is this controversy about? Find recent discussions of the nuclear winter issue. (The findings of the Sagan group were published in *Science* on December 23, 1983; the debate began after that.) You might want to read Carl Sagan's article in *Foreign Affairs* (Spring 1984) on the policy implications of the nuclear winter effect; then find out in what ways others agree or disagree. Newspaper articles appearing during 1985 are good sources for information on continuing research on this issue.
5. While the number of weapons has continued to increase, total megatonnage has decreased by about half since it reached its peak in 1962. (See Albert Carnesale *et al, Living with Nuclear Weapons* (New York: Bantam Books, 1983, pp. 74–77.) Which is more important, the number of weapons, the type, or their blast force? What other factors must you take into account to assess whether the arsenals today threaten more or less or differently than they did some time ago? Research the weapons and their effects, and answer the question, "Are we safer now than we were in 1970? In 1960? In 1945?" Most important, explain your criteria for answering the question. The Stockholm International Peace Research Institute (SIPRI) publications are good sources for this question, as is the U.S Congress Office of Technology Assessment publication, *The Effects of Nuclear War* (Washington, D.C.: G.P.O., 1978) and the UN publication excerpted in Part 1 of this book.
6. How is a hydrogen warhead made? Find out what actually goes into its detonator; where the uranium is mined and processed; what plutonium is and where it comes from; where and how the warhead is assembled; and, if you like, where and how such warheads are connected to guided missiles and shipped to their destinations. Consult *The Nuclear Almanac* and the special issue of *Physics Today* (March 1983) to get started. "Hydrogen bombs" would be a likely Library of Congress subject heading.

Historical Questions: Weapons Development, the Arms Race, Arms Control, Scientists and Politics

1. In Michael Farrell's interviews with Soviet scholars, Georgy Arbatov says that it is not the Soviet Union that is introducing new weapons systems; Zhurkin agrees, saying that the United States designed all the major weapons systems since 1945 and that the Soviets just followed suit. Is this contention true? What have you learned from the readings in this book? (See United Nations Secretary-General in Part 1;

Randall Forsberg, and G. Allen Greb and Gerald W. Johnson in Part 2; and Herbert Scoville, Jr., in Part 4.)

2. Mary Kaldor, Robert DeGrasse, and Lisa Peattie (and, to some extent, Paul Chilton) discuss domestic causes of the arms race. Explain how bureaucratic and economic factors within the United States help maintain weapons development and production.
3. Characterize the elements of the "decision-making" process that Barton Bernstein describes. Is it logical to assume that the same kind of unexamined assumptions and unimpeded momentum he examines may have influenced weapons development or U.S.-Soviet negotiations? Find essays in this book to support your view and take into account any that contradict your view.
4. The Russell-Einstein Manifesto of 1955, an appeal to end war, was enthusiastically received by people all over the world. Yet it failed. Based on your understanding of the memorandum by Niels Bohr, "The Franck Report," Henry L. Stimson's letter and memorandum, and "The Baruch Plan," explain why the Russell-Einstein attempt failed. If Russell had heeded the experience of his predecessors, what might he have done differently? Consider how an appeal to the people was a new approach.
5. "The Baruch Plan" was initiated and influenced by the same scientists who were primarily responsible for designing the first nuclear weapons. Many people, both within and outside the scientific community, believe strongly that science should be kept separate from politics. (The scientists who wrote to Presidents Roosevelt and Truman and lobbied for a disarmament proposal have been severely criticized for those actions.) Others point out, however, that by engaging in weapons research in the first place the scientists were already involved in a political project. Moreover, it was scientists who initiated the bomb project—recall Einstein's letter.

   Write an essay in which you take a position on the thesis that "Scientists should/should not assume responsibility for the way society uses their discoveries." Explore some arguments that support scientists' involvement in political issues and some that oppose this view. Draw from the readings in Part 2. The book by Robert Gilpin listed in Appendix 3 is a good starting point for researching this question.

For Further Research

6. Gen. Dwight D. Eisenhower, in his "Letter to Bernard Baruch, June 14, 1946," iterates a common theme in U.S. arms control negotiations. He says several times that the United States must not "recede from its position of advantage." Research this proposition. Has the United States ever receded from its position of advantage?
7. "The Franck Report," in its concern about how the atomic bomb was to be used, argued that "It may be very difficult to persuade the world that a nation which was capable of secretly preparing and suddenly releasing a new weapon . . . is to be trusted in its proclaimed desire of having such weapons abolished by international agreement." Find some detailed histories of the Baruch Plan negotiations, which lasted about three years. What measures, if any, did Baruch take to reassure the Soviet Union that our "proclaimed desire" to abolish these weapons was sincere?

   A good overview of arms control history appears in the Stanford Arms Control Group's *International Arms Control: Issues and Agreements* listed in Appendix 3. Another good starting point might be an overview of arms control negotiations in an encyclopedia article, which may suggest further readings. The Library of Congress subject heading, "Atomic weapons and disarmament," would indicate where to look in your subject card catalog.

8. Construct a history of the hydrogen bomb debate in the late 1940s and early 1950s focusing on Edward Teller and J. Robert Oppenheimer. Begin with Herbert York's *The Advisors* (see Appendix 3). What were the key points of conflict? You might want to extend this to compare the H-bomb debate with the MX debate: here you would start with Herbert Scoville's *MX: Prescription for Disaster*, (Cambridge, Mass.: MIT Press, 1981).
9. The authors of "The Franck Report" argued against using the bomb on civilian targets in Japan on the ground that the American public would not approve of such an act. Barton Bernstein, in "The Dropping of the A-Bomb," in Part 2, finds that quite the opposite happened: American public opinion overwhelmingly supported the bombings. Read some accounts in popular magazines and try to characterize the public's reaction to the bombings; an interesting account appears in an August 1945 issue of *Life* magazine. Try to answer the question of why the public reacted as it did. (Does Paul Chilton's analysis of language in "Nukespeak" in Part 3 explain why?)
10. The scientists who developed the atomic bomb worked in the field where the most sophisticated science and the most pressing international tensions converged. Some of the challenges and conflicts they faced epitomize the challenges and conflicts our culture as a whole faces in the nuclear age. Do a biographical study of one of these scientists. Focus your report on some point in this person's life at which he had to confront a difficult choice, one that represents some of our fundamental choices as a people. Much has been written about Albert Einstein, Neils Bohr, J. Robert Oppenheimer, Leo Szilard, and Edward Teller; an appropriate encyclopedia article might point you to useful sources. In fact, a Library of Congress subject card specifically designates the names of most of the atomic scientists; they are covered as well in early histories of atomic energy such as York's *The Advisors*, already mentioned; Robert Jungk's *Brighter than a Thousand Suns* (New York: Harcourt, Brace, 1958), and Gregg Herken's *The Winning Weapon* (New York: Knopf, 1980). Biographical dictionaries can be a good starting point.
11. Play detective: Could Bernard Baruch have wanted unimpeded nuclear weapons development rather than a treaty? Who was he? Who were his friends and associates? What were his values and his political attitudes? Start with a recent biography of Baruch; research some of its references and look up some of his friends in a *Who's Who* for the period.
12. What is the history of the early U.S. Atomic Energy Commission? Who were its first directors? How was it involved in the political tensions of the time? What was its unique relation to private industry? Several histories of the AEC have appeared recently.

American Foreign Policy, Deterrence, the Soviet Threat

1. Beginning with Jerome Frank's "Psychological Causes of the Nuclear Arms Race," explain what he means of the "image of the enemy" and the fear—or hate—that

image engenders. Find examples of our images of the USSR in Part 2, ''Early History: Manhattan Project to A-Bomb'' and in later writings in Part 4, ''What Should We Do? Prospects for the Future'' (e.g., those by President Ronald Reagan, Caspar Weinberger, and George F. Kennan). What different images of the USSR and its military intentions do you find? Account for the differences.

2. Many of the documents in Part 2, ''Early History,'' stress the need for mutual trust. Reflect on how individuals develop and maintain trust, both in low-tension situations and in more intense conflicts. In what ways might the behavior of individuals illuminate the behavior of nations, and in what ways is the analogy insufficient? Drawing on the materials in this section, write an essay on this question.
3. Is our concept of ''individualism'' or ''individual freedom'' equivalent to what Zanoshkin, in Michael Farrell's interview, means by ''humanistic ideals''? How do differing U.S./Soviet conceptions of ''materialism'' bear on this question? You might consider reading about materialism in a philosophical encyclopedia.
4. Jeffrey Porro defines *deterrence* and gives examples of two different schools of thought about how to deter. Drawing from other essays as well, construct a definition of *deterrence*. Note the divergences you find and try to account for them. (One scholar has found twenty-six different ways the term is used in discussions of strategic doctrine.)
5. Some people believe that nuclear weapons both can and should be used as ''a means of political pressure in peace'' (''The Franck Report''). Does this seem to you to be a justifiable basis for the use of nuclear weapons? Find some writers who approve of this use and others who disapprove of it and compare their reasons. Be sure to include readings from Part 4.

For Further Research

6. Read Stimson's proposal carefully (Part 2). Based on the kinds of arguments Stimson raises and tries to counter, infer what he knows about President Harry S. Truman's position. Then read Truman's account of this period in his memoirs, *Memories,* listed in Appendix 3. Write a memo from Truman to Stimson, explaining why you reject Stimson's proposal.
7. Keeping in mind the working definition of *deterrence* you contructed in question 4, go to the library to seek a fuller understanding of the term. Start with the index to the *Encyclopedia of the Social Sciences.*
8. After sufficiently understanding the term, explain how deterrence, in seeking stability—that is, invulnerability of second-strike forces—gives a huge impetus to the arms race.
9. Catch up on weapons developments. Find out about the Trident III D-5, the Midgetman missile, and recent cruise missile technology. Answer the question, ''Why do some people believe these weapons will be 'destabilizing'?''
10. Richard Pipes, David Holloway, and George F. Kennan have written books on the Soviet Union (see Appendix 3). Their pictures of the Soviet threat differ significantly. (Pipes takes a very different view from that of both Holloway and Kennan, whose perspectives are more alike.) Read two of these books and determine some key elements of their positions. Then show how some of the writers in this book resemble one author or the other. Try to account for the fundamental differences in perspective.

11. Do some research on *realpolitik,* the theory that power politics must regulate relations between nations. The *Encyclopedia of the Social Sciences* might give you a good overview and some reading suggestions. Alternatively, try the *Encyclopaedia Britannica*'s *Micropaedia,* which may send you to a good survey of theories of international relations and another bibliography. Some people believe that the United States began to accept the theory of realpolitik in the mid-1940s and cite our nuclear forces as one example of this. Based on issues surrounding the atomic bombings of Japan and the conflicts attending the possibility of international control of nuclear weapons (the material in Part 2), what do you think: Should we or should we not agree that realpolitik is inevitable in international politics?
12. What is *containment?* Find the *Mr. X* article, "The Sources of Soviet Conduct," in *Foreign Affairs* (July, 1947). How does George F. Kennan today explain how his term has been so differently applied from the way he meant it?
13. What was *détente?* How do some people today see it as a possible way to lessen East-West tensions?
14. What is the *military-industrial complex* (MIC)? Begin with Mary Kaldor's essay. Then choose one major defense contractor, find out something about its history, and identify ways it does/does not typify the bureaucratic processes of the MIC. Bruce Russett and Gordon Adams are good scholars to read on this subject (see Appendix 3).

Language and Ethics: Some Cultural Contexts for Evaluation

1. Today many people assume that "deterrence has worked"—that is, nuclear arsenals have prevented a major conflict between the United States and the USSR. This contention cannot be proved, however. The claim "deterrence has worked" is based on a faulty kind of causal reasoning that philosophers call a *post hoc* fallacy. The reasoning about deterrence says, "We have had peace for forty years *after* the advent of nuclear weapons; therefore, we have had peace *because of* nuclear weapons." Examine this assumption in some detail. Explain what we would have to know to prove that "deterrence has worked."
2. Lisa Peattie begins her essay by reflecting on civil defense plans. The *Shelter Management Handbook* is one example of the kind of effort she is thinking about. Edward Zuckerman, too, is worried about civil defense plans and what they might portend, but his treatment of the issue is very different from Peattie's. Remembering that Zuckerman's essay is just one chapter from a book that considers the subject, nevertheless, some fruitful comparisons can be made regarding these two very different treatments of the same topic. Explain how the *meaning* of the problem changes according to each different *treatment* of the problem.
3. Peattie talks about ways the division of labor in Nazi concentration camps prevented people from getting some perspective on what their work was all about. She seems to intend her article to be, at least in part, an allegory of our own culture. Trace the ways that the blindness in the concentration camps might be like our blindness toward the danger of nuclear war. How far can you go with the analogy? How do other writers in this book help you assess this analogy? (Consider the essays of

Bernstein, Frank, and Chilton; perhaps read Chapter 2 of Jonathan Schell's *The Fate of the Earth,* listed in Appendix 3.)

4. What is connoted by the term *arms race?* That is, what does the "race" metaphor reveal about the way we perceive the military competition between the United States and the USSR? Think of as many kinds of races as you can and examine some of their qualities. Consider the difference in attitude expressed by the phrase, "a *race* toward oblivion" and the statement, "The arms *competition* is the best form of arms control."
5. Analyze President Reagan's "National Security: Address to the Nation"—the "Star Wars" speech—as a speech. What is its purpose? To whom is it addressed? What are the devices by which the speaker tries to achieve his purpose? Are statistics and examples keyed to the general knowledge of the audience? Is the logic fair and straightforward, or does the speaker draw false conclusions or make questionable inferences? Does the speaker use words and phrases designed to elicit an emotional response? If so, is such a response appropriate to the topic or does it cloud the audience's reasoning? Do you think he succeeds in his purpose? What causes his success or failure?
6. Many of the pieces in this book were written to persuade. Analyze two or three of them: compare their structures of reasoning and identify the ways they try to convince their readers to adopt their position or proposed course of action.

For Further Research

7. Read Hannah Arendt's *Eichmann in Jerusalem: A Report on the Banality of Evil* (New York: Penguin, 1964). This book seems to have influenced Peattie, though she emphasizes some aspects of it and not others. Arendt's main point is that there is another kind of human evil than the evil committed through greed, envy, or desire for revenge. Adolf Eichmann, she argues, could commit the crimes he did because he never reflected on what he was doing. He put his actions into no context but the immediate one, and he thought with only the most superficial and conventional of formulations. Write a paper on the question, "How is the inability to think deeply about issues, such as Eichmann demonstrated, related to our nuclear predicament?"
8. Recently, the National Council of Catholic Bishops issued a detailed statement about the presence of nuclear weapons in our culture (see Appendix 3; the statement has been reprinted in many sources). The bishops examined both the mainstream Christian tradition of the "just" war and the minority, pacifist tradition that rejects all war, in order to determine the ethical status of nuclear weapons. They found that, even within the tradition that holds some wars to be just, nuclear weapons must be condemned on two grounds: first, they cannot discriminate sufficiently between soldiers and civilians; second, even if they could, the potential for escalation puts both civilians and civilization itself at a risk disproportionate to any possible "justification." They conclude that nuclear deterrence—that is, the threat to use nuclear weapons—can be considered moral *only if deterrence is a step toward nuclear disarmament.*

   Read the bishops' "Letter" and some of the material cited in its bibliography on the just war and the pacifist traditions. Write a well-focused paper on a single issue. One of the following topics might work for you:

8a. Some people believe that matters of state—particularly national defense—ought not to be bound by the same kinds of moral consideration that ought to bind individuals. What does the "just war" theory say about this? What does the pacifist theory say? What do you think?

8b. The policy of the Reagan administration is to maintain nuclear deterrence and to use arms control only to make deterrence stable; there is no official policy that sets nuclear *disarmament* as a goal. Furthermore, the president receives much pressure from political groups and individuals who prefer no arms control negotiations at all; they believe either that the United States can win the arms race or that the arms competition itself will continually create enough stability. Write a letter from the Bishops to the president (or to his special assistant for national security affairs) explaining the position the bishops would take toward his administration's policy. Include special consideration of whether there should be arms control efforts and, if so, what their goals should be.

8c. You will notice that the bishops support a freeze on nuclear weapons as the first step toward arms reductions and ultimately disarmament. Therefore, the Nuclear Freeze movement has been perceived as being a moral approach. Recently, however, Dr. George Keysworth, President Reagan's science advisor, said that the Strategic Defense Initiative (SDI or Star Wars) "takes the moral highground away from the supporters of the Nuclear Freeze Initiative," supposedly by making nuclear weapons less effective and therefore less needed and by being defensive, not offensive, in purpose. Research the arguments that support SDI and the arguments that oppose it. Current periodicals are good places to look. Then write a paper in which you argue that SDI is a moral/immoral proposal.

8d. In addition to the bishops' "Letter," read two or three of the philosophers' articles (distinguish them from the strategists' articles in the same volume) in the April 1985 issue of *Ethics*. Then evaluate the moral argument made by Colin S. Gray and Keith Payne in Part 3 of this book. Or evaluate the moral argument in the final chapter of *Living with Nuclear Weapons,* listed in Appendix 3.

9. The heart of the Lawyers Committee on Nuclear Policy, "Statement on the Illegality of Nuclear Weapons," in Part 3 is the perception that all the existing laws of war are designed to set limits on permissible violence. The heart of the bishops' "Letter" is similar: force, when used, must be proportional and discriminative. Compare these two fundamental premises and the ways they are developed. Why are they so similar?

10. Louis Ridenour (1911–1959) was a physicist who worked on atomic fission in the 1940s. In 1946, while working at the Radiation Laboratory at MIT, he wrote a one-act play set in a future time, "some years after all the industrialized nations have mastered the production and use of atomic power." He called the play "Pilot Lights of the Apocalypse." The play is darkly satirical, casting a worried eye on the possibility of controlling a runaway arms race and of preventing a subsequent nuclear holocaust. It was printed in a volume edited by Morton Grodzins and Eugene Rabinowitch, *The Atomic Age: Scientists in National and World Affairs* (New York: Basic Books, 1963); you may also find it in other sources. Read the play and respond to one of the following questions.

10a. Why did Ridenour write this play? Did he think that the play depicts what will happen *if* we fail to prevent an arms race or what is going to happen because we *will* fail to prevent an arms race? In other words, what was his attitude toward his subject? How can you tell? Justify your position with clear reasoning and solid evidence, including evidence drawn from this book about other scientists' attitudes at the time.

10b. If you have seen Stanley Kubrick's film *Dr. Strangelove* (1963), write an essay comparing it with "Pilot Lights." Take some of these questions into account: How are the works thematically similar? Identify the authors' attitudes toward their subject matter and compare them. How do you think both pieces would affect an audience—move them to action, to disgust, to scorn, to laughter, to a sense of hopelessness, or what? What do these works say about American and/or Soviet culture? How does each work view human nature? Does either consider anything aside from the immediate subject of nuclear weapons and policies governing their use?

11. Read some feminist writing about nuclear weapons, such as Helen Caldicott's *Missile Envy* (New York: Morrow, 1984), an anthology entitled *Reweaving the Web of Life,* edited by Pamela McAllister (Philadelphia: New Society, 1982); "Feminism and Militarism" in *Beyond Survival: New Directions for the Disarmament Movement,* edited by Michael Albert and David Dellinger (Boston, South End Press, 1983); or Dorothee Soelle's *The Arms Race Kills Even Without War* (Philadelphia: Fortress Press, 1983). To what extent do you find a common perspective in these works? Identify their common assumptions toward nuclear weapons and try to account for them.

12. Paul Chilton argues that media language helps societies to accommodate nuclear weapons. Find and explain examples from the media—television news or shows, films, magazines, advertising—of ways either nuclear weapons or nuclear deterrence is being represented (or not represented). Do you agree with Chilton? Why or why not?

13. Robert J. Lifton, a psychiatrist, is interested in nuclear language in ways that resemble Chilton's. Read Lifton's *Indefensible Weapons* (New York: Basic Books, 1982). What do both say about the way language works, particularly in its "religious" aspects? What do you think of their arguments?

Proposals: Technology, Negotiation, Alternatives

1. Read President Reagan's speech and Caspar Weinberger's letter to Congress carefully, noting any similarities you find in their attitudes and their language about national defense and foreign policy issues. Then find two other essays that express different views. How would you characterize the contrasting views? Set up a fictional debate between President Reagan (or Secretary Weinberger) and the author of another essay on the question, "What defends?"
2. It is sometimes said that conservatives believe that the preeminent threat is the Soviets, whereas liberals hold that the nuclear arsenals themselves pose the greatest threat. What evidence do you find throughout this book to support this assertion? What evidence contradicts it? To the extent that this generalization accurately characterizes conservatives and liberals, what does it reveal about the current debate?
3. What are the arguments favoring continued nuclear deterrence—that is, why do we continue to construct and deploy nuclear weapons? What are the official explana-

tions of the claim that nuclear weapons are necessary to our national security? Do you agree or disagree with these explanations? What evidence would you have to provide to support or to refute them?

4. Jerome Frank believes that we will make little headway on arms control until we abandon our "Us *versus* Them" attitude in favor of "Us *and* Them." Explore this idea. Russell, Greb and Johnson, Kennnan, Beyond War, Nagler, and Schell express this idea in one form or another. Do you generally agree or disagree with this assertion? Why?
5. Zhurkin, in Michael Farrell's interview, says that the ABM treaty of 1972, which prohibited ABM systems, was a good one, because we would all live in a very dangerous world if we insisted on building such systems; that is, *not* building them helps keep us safer. From what you know about strategy—not politics—explain Zhurkin's opinion. Why did both sides agree to ban ABM systems? Read Greb and Johnson's history of arms control negotiations: On what grounds do they argue that ABM prohibitions are so important?
6. The material in Part 4 is representative of the complicated dialog presently being conducted between roughly three different factions: those who emphasize primarily technological and military solutions; those who emphasize arms control and diplomacy; and those who emphasize alternatives to nuclear deterrence. Most of the supporters of the "Star Wars" ABM system have also supported new technological developments and have been generally against arms control negotiations. When they have supported them, they have held that we must always negotiate from a position of strength—not equality or inferiority.

   Based on your reading of the materials in Part 4 explain why the essays in the second section of Part 4 do not support "Star Wars," whereas those in the first section of Part 4 do support the "Star Wars" strategy. Choose specific authors, and base your analysis on actual positions they take on *other* issues.

For Further Research

7. Learn about the content of the nuclear weapons treaties between the United States and the USSR and about the process of arriving at these agreements. (The piece by Greb and Johnson is a good place to start; then consult Appendix 3.) If SDI is implemented, it will abrogate the ABM treaty, which is universally considered to be the finest treaty the United States and the Soviet Union have made. If the space-based lasers should be activated by internal nuclear explosive devices, the Outer Space Treaty would be abrogated, and if any of these devices were tested, the Test Ban Treaty might also be violated. Many people consider the violation of treaties between the United States and the USSR extremely serious and dangerous. Others disagree with this view and believe that going ahead with space-based technology is the safest policy.

   After carefully reading the White House Paper, "The President's Strategic Defense Initiative," and the essay by McGeorge Bundy et al., imagine that you are an advisor to the president on arms control. The president, dedicated to SDI, believes that it would provide the world with more security than adhering to the ABM treaty would. Draft a memo to the president detailing several arguments in support of continued U.S. adherence to the treaty and several arguments against it. Consider the issue in the broader context of the role of arms control negotiations and treaties in U.S.-Soviet relations. Come to a final position yourself. (Alternatively, write the letter to your senator or representative.)

8. What are the arguments favoring a massive civil defense effort in the United States, and what are the arguments opposing it? Find out how civil defense fits into deterrence strategy. You will need to know about "deterrence by denial," sometimes called *nuclear warfighting* or *prevailing*. The essays by Porro and by Gray and Payne will be helpful on this subject. Richard Smoke's *National Security and the Nuclear Dilemma,* listed in Appendix 3, will also be helpful.
9. You are a member of Congress about to present the freeze proposal, "A Call to Halt the Nuclear Arms Race," before the House. In your presentation, argue for the freeze in particular by responding to the arguments against it. Or speak against the proposal but respond to specific arguments for it.
10. What are the arguments favoring the public's influence as a viable means of altering U.S. foreign and defense policy? Find out about the legislative process and public input into that process. Identify some of the specific public debates over weapons procurement and illustrate how they have or have not influenced the ultimate decisions. You might want to look at some books on the legislative process or read an essay by J. B. Hehir, "Can Nuclear Protest Change Policy?" in *Commonweal,* 18 (June 1982). What do you think: Can public opinion affect U.S. policy?

APPENDIX 3

Further Research Sources: Books, Periodicals, and Films

Books and Articles

History: The Arms Race, Technology, Foreign Policy

Ambrose, Stephen E. *Rise to Globalism: American Foreign Policy 1938–1980*. 2nd ed., rev. New York: Penguin, 1980. A balanced presentation, intended for the general reader.

Gaddis, John Lewis. "Containment: Its Past and Future." *International Security* 5:4 (Spring 1981): 74–102. An excellent overview and analysis of the history of our policy toward the Soviet Union. Somewhat complex.

———. *The United States and the Origins of the Cold War, 1941–1947*. New York: Columbia University Press, 1972. A widely respected assessment of the question of how the cold war began.

Gilpin, Robert. *American Scientists and Nuclear Weapons Policy*. Princeton: Princeton University Press, 1962. Examines the role scientists played in attempts to influence national security policy.

Halle, Louis. *The Cold War as History*. New York: Harper and Row, 1967. The classic treatment of the cold war, interesting reading and often referred to.

Jervis, Robert. *Perception and Misperception in International Relations*. Princeton: Princeton University Press, 1976. A very important discussion of the role of communication, understanding, and misunderstanding in international affairs.

Kennan, George F. *The Nuclear Delusion: Soviet-American Relations in the Atomic Age*. New York: Pantheon, 1982. A former ambassador to the Soviet Union and distinguished historian laments the militarization of U.S. foreign policy.

Kennedy, Robert. *Thirteen Days*. New York: Norton, 1969. An exciting firsthand account of the Cuban missile crisis—an important test of American nuclear strategy in a crisis.

Smoke, Richard. *National Security and the Nuclear Dilemma: An Introduction to the American Experience*. New York: Random House, 1984. The best introduction to national security affairs to date; Smoke covers the history of deterrence doctrine, arms control negotiations, and the weapons buildups on both sides. Good bibliography.

Spanier, John W. *American Foreign Policy Since World War II*. 8th ed. New York: Holt, Rinehart and Winston, 1980. A standard text.

Truman, Harry S. *Memories*. Vol. 2, *Years of Trial and Hope, 1946–1952*. New York: Doubleday, 1956. Truman explains how his administration understood the early nuclear age.

York, Herbert. *The Advisors: Oppenheimer, Teller, and the Superbomb*. San Francisco: W. H. Freeman, 1976. A history of the H-bomb debate from a scientist-insider.

Deterrence: Nuclear Weapons Strategy

Aldridge, Robert. *The Counterforce Syndrome: A Guide to U.S. Nuclear Weapons and Strategic Doctrine.* Washington, D.C.: Institute for Policy Studies, 1978. Aldridge's work is a classic explanation for a popular audience. It is written from a perspective critical of U.S. policy. See Utgoff and Wohlstetter, below, for contrasting views.

Ball, Desmond. "Can Nuclear War Be Controlled?" *Adelphi Paper No. 169.* London: International Institute of Strategic Studies, 1981. The classic argument against the possibility of a controlled nuclear exchange.

Brodie, Bernard. *Strategy in the Missile Age.* Princeton: Princeton University Press, 1959. A classic essay on nuclear strategy by one of the earliest and most respected students of the issue.

Freedman, Lawrence. *The Evolution of Nuclear Strategy.* New York: St. Martin's Press, 1981. A discussion of the history of U.S. nuclear strategy, resembling Smoke, above, but more advanced.

George, Alexander L., and Richard Smoke. *Deterrence in American Foreign Policy: Theory and Practice.* New York: Columbia University Press, 1974. Analyzes how nuclear weapons have played a role in major crises between the superpowers.

Harvard Nuclear Study Group. *Living with Nuclear Weapons.* New York: Bantam Books, 1983. An introduction to nuclear history and strategy, the book is often distorted by a strong interest in discrediting Jonathan Schell and the disarmament movement.

Schelling, Thomas. *Strategy of Conflict.* Cambridge, Mass.: Harvard University Press, 1960. One of the most important works on deterrence.

Utgoff, Victor. "In Defense of Counterforce." *International Security* 2:4 (Spring 1982). A well-respected statement advocating counterforce strategy.

Wohlstetter, Albert. "The Delicate Balance of Terror." *Foreign Affairs* 37 (January, 1959): 211–234. The classic statement explaining why stable deterrence depends on a secure second-strike force.

Soviet Defense Policy and Force Structures

Cockburn, Andrew. *The Threat: Inside the Soviet Military Machine.* New York: Random House, 1983. A journalistic and lively account of the Soviet defense establishment.

Halloway, David. *The Soviet Union and the Arms Race.* New Haven: Yale University Press, 1983. A well-respected study of the arms race from the Soviet side.

International Institute of Strategic Studies. *The Military Balance;* also *Strategic Survey.* London: IISS (annuals). Together with *SIPRI World Armaments* (below), these are definitive sources for information on the world's arsenals.

Kaplan, Fred. *Dubious Specter: A Skeptical Look at the Soviet Nuclear Threat.* Washington, D.C.: Institute for Policy Studies, 1980. A critique of the Soviet buildup.

Pipes, Richard. "Why the Soviet Union Thinks it Could Fight and Win a Nuclear War." *Commentary* 64:1 (July 1977). An important and much-debated argument that is thought by many to base its hypothesis on very narrow data.

Ulam, Adam. *Expansion and Coexistence: Soviet Foreign Policy 1917–1973.* 2nd ed. New York: Praeger, 1974. A dependable and balanced description of Soviet foreign policy through the early 1970s.

Defense Budget and Defense Industry

Adams, Gordon. *The Politics of Defense Contracting: The Iron Triangle*. New Brunswick, N.J.: Transaction Books, 1981.

Dellums, Ronald V. *Defense Sense: The Search for a Rational Military Policy*. Cambridge, Mass.: Ballinger Publishing Co., 1983. An anthology of articles, aimed at informing the concerned citizen about defense budget issues. Takes an activist position.

Sivard, Ruth Leger. *World Military and Social Expenditures*. Washington: World Priorities (annual). As the SIPRI publications are to weapons data, Sivard's annual publication is the invaluable source of financial data. Covers expenditures on food, medicine, education, etc., in addition to weapons costs.

U.S. Department of Defense. *Annual Report to Congress*. Washington: U.S. Government Printing Office (annual). Written at the time the secretary of defense presents his annual budget to Congress, the report also contains budget projections for the next five years. The justifications are an important clue to classified U.S. defense strategy.

Assessments of Deterrence

Fallows, James. *National Defense*. New York: Random House, 1981. Engaging presentation that takes up general issues. A good, but biased, introduction to the national security debate.

Mandelbaum, Michael. *The Nuclear Question: The United States and Nuclear Weapons, 1946–1976*. New York: Cambridge University Press, 1979. A history that argues for a middle ground: despite its costs and risks, deterrence is our best hope.

Panofsky, Wolfgang, and Spurgeon M. Keeny, Jr. "Mad versus Nuts: Can Doctrine or Weaponry Remedy the Mutual Hostage Relationship of the Superpowers?" *Foreign Affairs* 60:2 (Winter 1981/82): 287–304. A well-known article assessing new developments in deterrence doctrine.

Russett, Bruce. *The Prisoners of Insecurity: Nuclear Deterrence, the Arms Race, and Arms Control*. San Francisco: W. H. Freeman, 1983. Russett has studied the domestic and international sources of the arms race.

Schell, Jonathan. *The Fate of the Earth*. Boston: Houghton Mifflin, 1982. An intelligent polemic favoring disarmament, Schell's book is still unique in drawing from the humanistic tradition of western culture rather than from social-scientific sources.

Thompson, E. P., and Dan Smith, eds. *Protest and Survive*. New York and London: Monthly Review Press, 1981. Thompson, a British historian, founded the campaign for European Nuclear Disarmament (END). These are essays from a radical perspective.

Wieseltier, Leon. *Nuclear War, Nuclear Peace*. New York: Holt, Rinehart and Winston, 1983. Frustrated with the polarization between "the party of war," which advocates technological solutions coupled with little or no arms control, and "the party of peace," which seems to him composed of naive dreamers, Wieseltier argues for a middle ground.

Ethics, Religion, Alternative Defense

Ethics 95:2 (April 1985). Special issue devoted to essays on the morality of nuclear deterrence written by philosophers and strategists.

Gandhi, Mohandas K. *Nonviolence in Peace and War*. New York: Garland, 1971. All discussions of nonviolence begin here.

Merton, Thomas. *The Nonviolent Alternative*. Edited by Gordon C. Zahn. New York: Farrar, Straus and Giroux, 1980. The preeminent interpretation of Gandhi's thought in American political contexts. The intellectual center of the peace movement.

National Council of Catholic Bishops. ''Pastoral Letter on War and Peace—The Challenge of Peace: God's Promise and Our Response.'' *Origins* 13:1 (May 19, 1983). The official position of the Catholic church on the ethical status of nuclear deterrence. A rich resource for ethical reflection with extensive bibliographic references.

Sharp, Gene. *The Politics of Nonviolent Action*. 3 vols. Boston: Porter Sargent, 1973. Gene Sharp has made important attempts to develop civilian-based defense systems.

Wallis, Jim, ed. *Waging Peace: A Handbook for the Struggle to Abolish War*. New York: Harper and Row, 1983. A handbook for the disarmament movement coming from a religious perspective.

Walzer, Michael. *Just and Unjust Wars: A Moral Argument with Historical Illustrations*. New York: Basic Books, 1977. A classic statement of the ''just war'' argument.

Woito, Robert S., ed. *To End War*. New York: Pilgrim Press, 1982. A rich compilation of essays and annotated bibliographies; indispensable to disarmament efforts or to anyone who wants to understand war better.

Arms Control

Bechhofer, Bernard G. *Postwar Negotiations for Arms Control*. Washington, D.C.: Brookings Institution, 1961. A detailed history of arms negotiations through the 1950s.

Independent Commission on Disarmament and Security Issues (Palme Commission). *Common Security: A Blueprint for Survival*. New York: Simon and Schuster, 1982. A Swedish-sponsored study with detailed suggestions for reducing the possibility of nuclear war.

SIPRI (Stockholm International Peace Research Institute). *SIPRI Yearbook of World Armaments and Disarmament*. London: Taylor and Francis (annual). An indispensable source for weapons data and current analyses of political issues. (Comes also in an abbreviated edition.)

Smith, Gerald. *Doubletalk: The Story of the First Strategic Arms Limitations Talks*. New York: Doubleday, 1980. A controversial report on SALT I by a SALT negotiator.

Stanford Arms Control Group. *International Arms Control: Issues and Agreements*. 2d ed. Edited by Coit D. Blacker and Gloria Duffy. Stanford: Stanford University Press, 1984. A useful and thorough textbook.

Talbott, Strobe. *Deadly Gambits*. New York: Knopf, 1984. Here Talbott discusses, in detail, the intricate maneuverings that frustrated the START negotiations.

———. *Endgame*. New York: Harper and Row, 1979. A journalist's account of the SALT negotiations.

Psychology

Frank, Jerome D. *Sanity and Survival in the Nuclear Age.* 2nd ed. Introduction by James Muller. New York: Random House, 1982. A well-known psychologist studies the dynamics of negotiations and conflict resolution. Frank's many articles on the nuclear arms race are well worth reading.

Lifton, Robert Jay. *Death in Life: Survivors of Hiroshima.* New York: Random House, 1967. A moving study of Hiroshima survivors by a noted psychiatrist.

Mack, John E. "Psychosocial Effects of the Nuclear Arms Race." *Bulletin of the Atomic Scientists* 37 (April 1981): 18–23. Mack is concerned with the effects on us of living under the shadow of annihilation.

Literature

Hersey, John. *Hiroshima.* New York: Bantam Books, 1946. A true account, in fictional form, based on interviews with Hiroshima survivors.

Hoban, Russell. *Riddley Walker.* New York: Washington Square Press, 1980. Brilliant allegorical account of the world 2,000 years after a nuclear holocaust that leads us to reflect on our actions today.

Miller, Walter M. *A Canticle for Leibowitz.* London: Weidenfeld, 1959. A science-fiction classic.

Periodicals

General and International Affairs Periodicals

ACADEMIC PERIODICALS

Current History, 4225 Main Street, Philadelphia, PA 19127 (Monthly, $18.85/year)

Foreign Affairs, Council on Foreign Relations, 58 East 68th Street, New York, NY 10021 (5 times/year, $22/year)

Foreign Policy, Carnegie Endowment for International Peace, 11 Dupont Circle, Washington, DC 20036 (Quarterly, $15/year)

International Studies Quarterly, International Studies Association, University of South Carolina, Columbia, SC 29208 (Quarterly, membership required)

Orbis: Journal of World Affairs, Foreign Policy Research Institute, 3508 Market Street, Suite 350, Philadelphia, PA 19101 (Quarterly, $15/year)

POPULAR PERIODICALS

The Atlantic, 8 Arlington Street, Boston, MA 02116 (Monthly, $18/year)

Harper's Magazine, 2 Park Avenue, New York, NY 10016 (Monthly, $14/year)

Newsweek, 444 Madison Avenue, New York, NY 10022 (Weekly, $32.50/year)

Time, Time and Life Building, Rockefeller Center, New York, NY 10020 (Weekly, $35/year)

U.S. News & World Report, 2400 N Street NW, Washington, DC 20037 (Weekly, $32/year)

GOVERNMENT PERIODICALS

Congressional Record, U.S. Government Printing Office, Washington, DC 20402 (Daily, $75/year)

Department of State Bulletin, Department of State, Washington, DC 20520 (Monthly, $19/year)

Subject Periodicals

MILITARY STRATEGY

Aviation Week and Space Technology, 1221 Avenue of the Americas, New York, NY 10020 (Weekly, $35/year)

International Security, MIT Press, 28 Carleton Street, Cambridge, MA 02142 (Quarterly, $15/year)

WEAPONS CONTROL

Arms Control Today, Arms Control Association, 11 Dupont Circle NW, Washington, DC 20036 (Monthly, $20/year)

Defense Monitor, Center for Defense Information, 122 Maryland Avenue NE, Washington, DC 20002 (10 issues/year, $15/year)

INTERNATIONAL ORGANIZATIONS AND INTERNATIONAL LAW

Christianity and Crisis, 537 West 121 Street, New York, NY 10027 (Biweekly, $15/year)

Commonweal, 232 Madison Avenue, New York, NY 10016 (Biweekly, $22/year)

Friends Journal, 152A North 15th Street, Philadelphia, PA 19102 (Semimonthly, $10.50/year)

National Catholic Reporter, P. O. Box 281, Kansas City, MO 64141 (Weekly, $18/year)

INSTITUTIONAL AND SOCIAL REFORM

Fellowship, Fellowship of Reconciliation, 523 North Broadway, Nyack, NY 19060 (8 times/year, $8/year)

Peace News: For Nonviolent Revolution, 8 Elm Avenue, Nottingham 3, England (Biweekly, $13/year)

Sojourners, 1309 L Street NW, Washington, DC 20005 (Monthly, $12/year)

Working Papers for a New Society, Center for the Study of Public Policy, Transaction Periodicals, Rutgers University, New Brunswick, NJ 08903 (Bimonthly, $15/year)

PEACE STUDY AND EDUCATION

Bulletin of Peace Proposals, Box 258, Irvington-on-Hudson, NY 10533 (Quarterly, $20/year)

Journal of Peace Research, International Peace Research Institute, Oslo, Box 258, Irvington-on-Hudson, NY 10533 (Quarterly, $24/year)

Peace Research Reviews, 25 Dundana Avenue, Dundas, Ontario, Canada L9H 4E5 (6 times/year, $20/year)

OPINION AND POLITICS

Congressional Digest, 3231 P Street NW, Washington, DC 20007 (Monthly, $18/year)

Perspective-setting Periodicals

Alternatives: A Journal of World Policy, 777 United Nations Plaza, New York, NY 10017 (Quarterly, $15/year)

The American Spectator, P. O. Box 1969, Bloomington, IN 47402 (Monthly, $15/year)

The Center Magazine, Box 4068, Santa Barbara, CA 93103 (Bimonthly, $15/year)
Commentary, 165 East 56th Street, New York, NY 10022 (Monthly, $27/year)
Dissent, 505 Fifth Avenue, New York, NY 10017 (Quarterly, $12/year)
The Guardian: The Independent Radical Newsweekly, 33 West 17th Street, New York, NY 10011 (Weekly, $17/year)
Inquiry, 1700 Montgomery Street, San Francisco, CA 94111 (20 times/year, $16/year)
Mother Jones, 625 Third Street, San Francisco, CA 94107 (Monthly, $18/year)
Nation, 72 Fifth Avenue, New York, NY 10014 (Weekly, $30/year)
The National Review, 150 East 35th Street, New York, NY 10016 (Biweekly, $24/year)
New Republic, 1200 19th Street NW, Washington, DC 20036 (Weekly, $32/year)
New York Review of Books, 250 West 57th Street, New York, NY 10019 (Biweekly, $20/year)
The Progressive, 409 East Main Street, Madison, WI 53703 (Monthly, $17/year)
The Washington Spectator, P.O. Box 442, Merrifield, VA 22116 (22 times/year, $10/year)

Films

Here is a short list of some excellent films about nuclear weapons that are all available for rental. Not included on the list are feature films like *Dr. Strangelove, Testament,* or *Threads,* all of which are superb for educational purposes but are quite expensive to rent; however, all college media libraries will have rental information for films like these. The best source of continuing information and reviews on nuclear-related films appears in the *Bulletin of the Atomic Scientists* each month in a column by John Dowling; the column also provides information about special summary lists and updates which are available for a nominal charge.

Armaments: The War Game (24 min.; color). University of California Extension Media Center, 223 Fulton Street, Berkeley, CA 94720. Includes both liberal and conservative views.

The Atom Strikes (31 min.; black and white). U.S. Army Training and Audio-Visual Center, Fort Devens, MA 01433. U.S. Army training film useful for exemplifying military language and perspectives.

The Atomic Cafe (88 min.; color). New Yorker Films, 16 West 61st Street, New York, NY 10023. Depicts U.S. government propaganda in the 1950s and 60s, using clips from government civil defense educational films.

Countdown for America (27 min.; color). American Security Council Foundation, Boston, VA 22713. The Peace Through Strength campaign's film opposing the nuclear freeze, and favoring an arms buildup.

Daniel Ellsberg Speaks on America's Secret Nuclear Policy (55 min.; color video). Original Face Video, P.O. Box 447, Grass Valley, CA 95945. Ellsberg details numerous ways the U.S. has used its nuclear arsenal coercively.

The Day After Trinity (60 min.). Pyramid Films, 2801 Colorado Avenue, Santa Monica, CA 90404. Documentary on J. Robert Oppenheimer and the internal impetus to build and use the bomb.

Decision to Drop the Bomb (82 min.; black and white). Films Incorporated, 1144 Wilmette Avenue, Wilmette, IL 60091. Interesting complement to the article by Barton J. Bernstein in Part 2.

Dr. Strangelove (93 min.; black and white). Swank Motion Pictures, 201 S. Jefferson Avenue, St. Louis, MO 63166. Dark satire on U.S. national security policy. Director Stanley Kubrick interviewed nuclear strategists, and the film reflects some accurate language.

Eight Minutes to Midnight (20 min.). Direct Cinema, Ltd., P.O. Box 69589, Los Angeles, CA 90069. Portrait of the dynamic feminist Dr. Helen Caldicott, former president of Physicians for Social Responsibility.

George Kennan, A Critical Voice (58 min.; color). Blackwood Productions, 251 West 57th Street, New York, NY 10019. Portrait of a man at the center of U.S.-Soviet affairs since before World War II.

Hiroshima: A Document of the Atomic Bombing (28 min.; black and white, some color). American Friends Service Committee, 15 Rutherford Place, New York, NY 10003. A stark documentary.

How Much is Enough? Decisionmaking in the Nuclear Age (60 min.; color). Michigan Media, University of Michigan, 400 Fourth Street, Ann Arbor, MI 48103. Examines the history of the arms race, including both U.S. and Soviet developments.

If You Love This Planet (26 min.; color). American Friends Service Committee, 2161 Massachusetts Avenue, Cambridge, MA 02140. An impassioned lecture by Dr. Helen Caldicott on the medical effects of a nuclear war.

The Last Epidemic: Medical Consequences of Nuclear Weapons and Nuclear War (36 min.; color). Resource Center for Nonviolence, P.O. Box 2324, Santa Cruz, CA 96063. The primary educational film produced by Physicians for Social Responsibility presents a symposium of experts and some footage of Hiroshima victims.

Management of Mass Casualties (24 min.; black and white). U.S. Army Training and Audio-Visual Center, Fort Devens, MA 01433. U.S. Army training film showing unrealistic attitudes about stress in nuclear war.

Nuclear Strategy for Beginners (52 min.; color). Time-Life Video, 100 Eisenhower Drive, Paramus, NJ 07652. A PBS/NOVA production that examines the history of the arms race and the ways nuclear strategy have adapted to these changes.

The War Game (49 min.). Federation of American Scientists, 307 Massachusetts Avenue NE, Washington, DC 20002. An outstanding fictional drama produced by the BBC in the early 1960s and gripping still in 1986. Could be viewed with *Threads* or *Testament*.

War Without Winners (28 min.; color). American Friends Service Committee, 2161 Massachusetts Avenue, Cambridge, MA 02140. Interviews with arms control and disarmament leaders.

APPENDIX 4

What Can You Do? Directory of Organizations

Many people want to help lessen the threat of a nuclear war and wonder what they can do. Whether you decide generally that we need a military buildup or that we need to stop the arms race, the paths of potential action are as numerous and varied as individuals and their imaginations. What you can do depends on your abilities, interests, and situation. But whoever you are, your own plan of action will start from an informed analysis of the situation. This book and its suggested further research sources will have given you such a background.

In order to give some structure to what is an amorphous set of possibilities, let's divide potential action into four groups: political, educational, international, cultural. These are not tidy and consistent categories; they all overlap in several respects.

Political refers to actions aimed primarily at influencing our political process, such as writing to legislators, campaigning for or against a particular weapons system, attempting to shape public opinion on a candidate or an issue, raising money to support a campaign, protesting, or demonstrating.

Educational includes attempts to inform others either about the situation in general, about some aspect of the current situation, or about some proposal for the future. Educational efforts may take place in formal classrooms, including colleges or secondary schools; in church and community groups; or in your own living room, dorm room, or employees' lounge. Consider, for example, forming an informal talk group among people you live or work with, sharing arrangements to schedule films, or planning to discuss a short list of books or essays. Invite people to come and talk with your group. Education can be adapted to whatever you do. Are you a psychologist? Try some group sessions on conflict and ways to resolve it. Are you in business? Find out about groups attempting to influence trade with Eastern bloc countries and share the information with others. What are your hobbies? Consider playing some of the strategy games like "Diplomacy" or some of the nuclear war games and discussing with friends how these games fit in with what you know about nuclear weapons in our culture. Similarly, play with some video games with this in mind—perhaps you can design some alternative video games and convince or educate others about their value. More learning about the Soviet Union and life in Eastern Europe is greatly needed; some people even think it may be the answer to the present risk. This is a fascinating and endless subject for individuals or groups to pursue.

International activities would include any attempt at creating a more cooperative and interdependent world—including creating the vision that makes such a world seem possible. For example, a group of students at the University of California, at San Diego recently decided to try a joint project with a group of Soviet students. When they conceived the idea, they had no idea whether such an activity was even possible. They succeeded; here's roughly what happened. They found a corresponding group of college students studying communications in Russia and agreed on a topic, United States and Soviet recollections of World War II. Both groups of students made a half-hour film. They met in the Soviet Union and edited the two films together. The resulting film then was broadcast via satellite simultaneously in the United States and the USSR, with live studio audiences in both nations. The two groups plan a second film, the next one perhaps on nuclear energy. Exciting projects like this one are possible if we only imagine richly enough.

Increasing numbers of people concerned about nuclear war think that building bridges across the ocean could prove a very fruitful step. Consider the efforts of businesspeople to increase trade with Eastern bloc countries, for instance: if we become mutually dependent, it makes less and less sense to be enemies. Similarly, the more that private citizens in both East and West travel and meet people in the countries of their enemies, the less cause, goes this reasoning, for blind conflict. One thing you can do, then, is take a trip and make as many new friends as possible. Many groups—Physicians for Social Responsibility, for instance—are trying to encourage exchange programs for both physicians and students to and from the Eastern bloc. Could you work on developing exchanges between, say, students at your school and students at a school in Kiev or Prague?

Cultural here actually means creative: creating institutions and pathways that make cultural change possible. Are you a talented writer or filmmaker? Then pave the way for a better world by showing us some visions of what might be possible if we thought of conflict or power or enemies in some different ways. Do you read for fun, say, science fiction or poetry or a naturalist's writings like the works of Loren Eiseley? Why not compile and annotate a list of books that help you create pictures of a different world, and then get your essay published. Teachers could use it to build exciting classes; individuals could become inspired and enriched by it, and perhaps they could add to it. What is the place where you work like? Can you find ways to make it a more humane place where people can appreciate that there are many ways to deal with conflict or with enemies? Perhaps finding potential causes of violence in the workplace will help us better understand the causes of violence in the world as a whole.

The list of organizations that follows includes groups with very diverse interests. People tend to make the mistake of thinking of all "peace groups" as composed of activists who primarily stage demonstrations. While such activist groups are included here, they are hardly typical or representive of the varied memberships, aims, and activities pursued by other peace organizations. Joining a group that is already organized is often a good way to meet people with similar concerns and to get moving on some meaningful action.

Finally, as a supplement to all these categories of suggestions, you will find some stimulating ideas in two publications. One is a pamphlet published by the Center for Defense Information (its address is given among the groups listed below) called *Nuclear War Prevention Kit: What Can You Do?* The other is a book entitled *To End War: A New Approach to International Conflict* by Robert Woito (New York: Pilgrim Press, 1982) that is a rich compendium of ideas for both long-term and short-term activities. It contains an annotated list of hundreds of peace-oriented groups, of which the list that follows is a very small sample.

American Committee on East-West Accord, 227 Massachusetts Avenue NE, Washington, DC 20002. Corporate executives seeking to reduce U.S.-Soviet tensions primarily by promoting arms control, non-political trade, and exchange programs.

American Friends Service Committee, 1501 Cherry Street, Philadelphia, PA 19102. A Quaker organization promoting public education and political activities, all from a nonviolence perspective. Has many local groups all open to concerned people. A major peace organization.

Arms Control Association, 11 Dupont Circle NW, Suite 900, Washington, DC 20036. Nonpartisan, public education group aiming to promote understanding of arms control measures. Publishes *Arms Control Today,* a monthly newsletter and a valuable source of information.

Business Executives Move for New National Priorities, 900 North Howard Street, Baltimore, MD 21201. An organization of business owners and executives favoring decreased military spending and conversion to domestic production.

Catholic Peace Fellowship, 339 Lafayette Street, New York, NY 10012. A Catholic disarmament group aiming to educate people about Christian nonviolence and to undertake action programs. Areas include Central America, the draft, nuclear weapons. Most major denominations have a similar fellowship: Baptists, Buddhists, Lutherans, Unitarians, and others.

Center for Defense Information, 122 Maryland Avenue NE, Washington, DC 20002. CDI provides useful information about defense issues. Like the Arms Control Association, it is nongovernmental. Publishes *The Defense Monitor,* a very important monthly.

Clergy and Laity Concerned, 198 Broadway, New York, NY 10038. Invites participation of citizens, corporations, and religious groups. Works for international conditions promoting peace and justice.

Coalition for a New Foreign and Military Policy, 120 Maryland Avenue NE, Washington, DC 20002. Coalition of over 40 religious, labor, peace, and public interest organizations working to shape a peaceful, noninterventionist foreign policy.

Committee on the Present Danger, 1800 Massachusetts Avenue NW, Suite 601, Washington, DC 20036. A conservative group promoting a strong military to counter what is believed to be a Soviet drive for world dominance. Publish informational booklets. Many CPD members received appointments in the Reagan administration.

Common Cause, 2030 M Street NW, Washington, DC 20036. Citizens lobby group concerned generally about government accountability.

Council for a Livable World, 11 Beacon Street, Boston, MA 02108. A citizens group that informs members of the U.S. Senate about nuclear issues and helps elect senators who support rational arms control policies.

Council on Economic Priorities, 84 Fifth Avenue, New York, NY 10011. Clearinghouse for information on military production and spending, and on attempts at military conversion.

Federation of American Scientists, 307 Massachusetts Avenue NE, Washington, DC 20002. Composed of engineers and scientists, offers educational materials for professional, college, and high-school audiences.

Fellowship of Reconciliation, Box 271, Nyack, NY 10960. International pacifist organization, concerned about world hunger and injustice as well as nuclear issues. Publishes *Fellowship.*

Friends of the Earth, 72 Jane Street, New York, NY 10010; 620 C Street SE, Washington, DC 20003; 124 Spear Street, San Francisco, CA 94105. International conservation organization committed to rational use of the earth and its resources. Active against MX and on other issues. Has many local grass-roots groups.

Institute for Defense and Disarmament Studies, 251 Harvard Street, Brookline, MA 02146. Developed the original nuclear weapons freeze proposal; serves as clearinghouse for research on military/disarmament issues.

Institute for Policy Studies, 1901 Q Street, NW, Washington, DC 20009. A scholarly research center. Publishes books on alternative strategies for national security, human rights, and related subjects.

Institute for World Order, 777 United Nations Plaza, New York, NY 10017. A scholarly center that produces materials for college courses and for public education. Publishes *Alternatives: A Journal of World Policy.*

International Seminar on Training for Nonviolent Action, 148 N Street South, Boston, MA 02127. Like the American Friends Service Committee, the Mobilization for Survival, and the California Alliances for Survival, Seminar supplies training in nonviolent action and resistance.

Mobilization for Survival, 853 Broadway, New York, NY 10003. A primary coalition of local activist groups focusing on nuclear weapons issues. Write to find the group nearest you.

Movement for a New Society, 4722 Baltimore Avenue, Philadelphia, PA 19143. A loose network of small, local groups who each work collectively in direct political action, Movement for a New Society also does organizing work and tries to create alternative institutions within local communities.

NARMIC (National Action/Research on the Military-Industrial Complex), 1501 Cherry Street, Philadelphia, PA 19102. A project of the American Friends Service Committee that produces both printed and audiovisual educational materials on nuclear issues.

Northern California Alliance for Survival, 944 Market Street, San Francisco, CA 94102. A California version of the Mobilization for Survival. Write for local information.

Southern California Alliance for Survival, 5539 West Pico Boulevard, Los Angeles, CA 90019. See previous description.

National Council for a World Peace Tax Fund, 2111 Florida Avenue NW, Washington, DC 20008. Works for the passage of legislation that would permit those morally opposed to military violence to deposit the military percentage of their taxes in a special fund.

Nuclear Transportation Project/AFSC, 92 Piedmont Avenue NE, Atlanta, GA 30303. A project of the American Friends Service Committee, organizes against transport of nuclear wastes and weapons components.

Nuclear Weapons Facilities Project, 1660 Lafayette Street, Denver, CA 80218. Coordinates demonstrations around weapons facilities. A project of the American Friends Service Committee.

Nuclear Weapons Freeze Campaign National Clearinghouse, 4144 Lindell Boulevard, Suite 201, St. Louis, MO 63108. Provides information and coordinates grass-roots activist groups working for a nuclear freeze.

Pax-Christi USA, 3000 North Mango, Chicago, IL 60634. International Catholic group working for disarmament, peace education, and a just world order.

Physicians for Social Responsibility, P.O. Box 144, 56 North Beacon Street, Watertown, MA 02177. Composed of physicians and medical workers wishing to halt the arms race and promote international peace. Has fine educational films and speakers bureau.

Riverside Church Disarmament Project, 490 Riverside Drive, New York, NY 10027. Gives an outstanding course in nuclear issues and makes its syllabus—with photocopied readings included—available to groups and individuals around the country. Write for information.

SANE, 514 C Street NE, Washington, DC 20002. A national educational group that also works with unions and lobbies against excessive military allocations. Has many local grass-roots canvas groups.

Union of Concerned Scientists, 1384 Massachusetts Avenue, Cambridge, MA 02138. Politically active group of scientists who conduct research on nuclear weapons issues, often challenging Pentagon studies.

United Nations Association, 300 East 42nd Street, New York, NY 10017. Provides films and literature on international dimensions of the arms race and alternative solutions. Also provides information on specific UN agencies involved in disarmament and arms control.

War Resisters League, 339 Lafayette Street, New York, NY 10012. A nonreligious pacifist organization with local branches in twenty cities. Does effective work regarding disarmament, social justice, the draft, and tax resistance.

Women's International League for Peace and Freedom, 1213 Race Street, Philadelphia, PA 19107. An international group organized in 1915, seeking peace and justice by nonviolent means.

Worldwatch Institute, 1776 Massachusetts Avenue NW, Washington, DC 20036. Newsletter and publications aimed to inform concerned citizens about global issues such as energy, the environment, nuclear weapons.

World Without War Council, 175 Fifth Avenue, New York, NY 10010. Research, publications, internships focusing on alternatives to violence.

APPENDIX 5

The Nuclear Arsenals of the United States and the USSR

Nation	System	Date Deployed	Number Deployed	Weapons Load; CEP	Range (km)	Total Warheads
Intercontinental Ballistic Missiles (ICBMs)						
U.S.	Titan II	1962	52[a]	1 × 9 Mt; CEP 1.3km	11,500	52
	Minuteman II	1966	450[b]	1 × 1–2 Mt; CEP 0.4km	9,000	450
	Minuteman III/Mk-12	1970	250	3 × 170 kt MIRV; CEP 0.3km	9,000	750
	Minuteman III/Mk-12A	1979	300	3 × 350 kt MIRV; CEP 0.3km	9,000	900
	Peacekeeper-MX (forthcoming)	1986(?)	100(?)	10 × 335–500 kt MIRV; CEP 0.1km	11,000	1,000
USSR[c]	SS-11	1966	580	1 × 1 Mt, CEP 1.0–1.8km; or 3 × 500 kt MIRV, CEP 1.0–1.8km	10,500	n.a.[d]
	SS-11 (Model 3)	1973				
	SS-13	1969	60	1 × 1 Mt; CEP 1.3km	8,000	60
	SS-17 (Model 1)	1977	130	4 × 200–750 kt MIRV; CEP 0.4km	10,000	520
	SS-17 (Model 2)	1977	20	1 × 3 Mt; CEP 0.3–0.6km	10,000	20
	SS-18 (Models 1 & 3)	1975/76	308	1 × 25–50 Mt; CEP 1km	12,000	n.a.
	SS-18 (Model 2)	1977		8 × 1–2 Mt MIRV; CEP 0.2km	12,000	n.a.
	SS-18 (Model 4)	1979		10 × 1–2 Mt MIRV; CEP 0.2km	12,000	n.a.

	SS-19 (Model 1)	1976	300	6 × 200 kt–1 Mt; CEP 0.3–0.45km	9,600	n.a.
	SS-19 (Model 2)	1976		1 × 10–25 Mt; CEP 0.4km	10,000	n.a.
China	CSS-3	1976	2–4	1 × 10–25 Mt; CEP n.a.	7,000	2–4
Submarine-launched Ballistic Missiles (SLBMs)						
U.S.	Poseidon C-3	1970	304	10 × 40 kt MIRV; CEP 0.5km	4,600	3,040
	Trident C-4	1979	240	8 × 100 kt MIRV; CEP 0.5km	7,500	1,920
	Trident D-5 (forthcoming)	1990s(?)	240–264	8 × 350 kt MIRV; CEP 0.2km	11,500	1,920–2,112
USSR[e]	SS-N-5	1964	18	1 × 1 Mt; CEP 1.5km	1,200	18
	SS-N-6 (Models 1 & 2)	1968	n.a.	1 × 1 Mt; CEP 1–2.5km	2,900	n.a.
	SS-N-6 (Model 3)	1973	n.a.	2 × 200 kt MIRV; CEP 1–2.5km	2,900	n.a.
	SS-N-8	1973	346	1 × 1 Mt; CEP 1–1.5km	7,900	346
	SS-NX-17	1979	12	1 × 1 Mt; CEP 0.8km	n.a.	12
	SS-N-18	1978	144	3 × 200 kt MIRV; CEP 0.5–1km	7,500	432
	SS-NX-20	1981	20–24	7–12 × 200 kt MIRV; CEP n.a.	7,500	140–288

Table reprinted by permission of Westview Press from *Toward Nuclear Disarmament and Global Security,* edited by Burns H. Weston (Boulder, Colo.: Westview Press, 1984).

Nation	System	Date Deployed	Number Deployed	Weapons Load; CEP	Range (km)	Total Warheads
France	MSBS M-20	1977	80	1 × 1 Mt; CEP n.a.	3,000	80
	MSBS M-4 (forthcoming)	1985(?)	16(?)	6–7 × 150 kt MIRV; CEP n.a.	4,000	96–112
Britain	Polaris A-3	1967	64	3 × 200 kt MIRV; CEP n.a.	4,600	192
Long-Range Sea-launched Cruise Missiles (SLCMs)						
U.S.	BGM-109 Tomahawk (forthcoming)	1980s	1,720	1 × 200 kt; CEP 0.1km	2,500	1,720
USSR	SS-N-3 Shaddock	1962	100	1–? kt; CEP n.a.	700	100
Long-Range Strategic Bombers						
U.S.	B-52 C/D/E/F	1956	83	27 tons of bombs	18,500	
	B-52 G/H	1959	265	34 tons of bombs, SRAMs, and Hound Dog ALCMs	20,000	3,100 bombs, SRAMS, and Hound Dog ALCMs
	FB-111A	1970	65	17 tons of bombs and SRAMs	n.a.	
	B-1B (forthcoming)	1989(?)	100(?)	30(?) Tomahawk ALCMs	n.a.	n.a.
USSR	M-4 Bison	1955	45	9 tons of bombs and ALCMs	10,000	n.a.
	Tu-95 Bear	1956	100	18 tons of bombs and ALCMs	12,500	n.a.

Air-launched Strategic Weapons						
U.S.	Bombs	early 1950s	n.a.	200 kt–1 Mt; CEP 0.1km	n.a.	n.a.
	Hound Dog ALCM	1961	400	1 × ? kt; CEP n.a.	1,000	400
	Tomahawk ALCM (forthcoming)	1980s	3,300	1 × 200 kt; CEP 0.1km	2,500	3,300
	SRAM	1972	1,020	1 × 170 kt; CEP n.a.	150	1,020
USSR	Bombs	1950s	n.a.	Mt range; CEP 0.1km	n.a.	n.a.
	AS-3 Kangaroo ALCM	1961	n.a.	1 × ? Mt; CEP n.a.	650	n.a.
	AS-4 Kitchen ALCM	1962	800	1 × ? Mt; CEP n.a.	700	800
	AS-5 Kingfish ALCM	1977	n.a.	1 × ? kt; CEP n.a.	n.a.	n.a.
Ballistic Missiles Defenses (BMDs)						
USSR	ABM-1 Galosh	1967	64	1 × 2–3 Mt; CEP n.a.	300	64
Medium-Range Bombers						
U.S.	FB-111 E/F	1970	300 (165 in Europe)	17 tons of bombs and SRAMs	6,000	n.a.
USSR	Tu-16 Badger	1955	600–700 (Tu-16 and Tu-22 combined)	9 tons of bombs and ALCMs	4,800	n.a.
	Tu-22 Blinder	1961		10 tons of bombs and ALCMs	2,250	n.a.
	Tu-22M Backfire	1974	150	9 tons of bombs and ALCMs	3,400	n.a.
Britain	Vulcan B2	1960	40	10 tons of bombs	3,500	n.a.

Nation	System	Date Deployed	Number Deployed	Weapons Load; CEP	Range (km)	Total Warheads
China	Tu-16	n.a.	less than 300	n.a.	n.a.	n.a.
	Tu-4	n.a.		n.a.	n.a.	n.a.
France	Mirage IV-A	1964	35	n.a.	1,600	n.a.
Long-Range Theater Missiles						
U.S.	Pershing II (forthcoming)	1983(?)	108(?)	1 × ? kt; CEP 0.04km	1,800	108[f]
	Tomahawk GLCM	1983(?)	464(?)	1 × ? kt; CEP 0.05km	2,500	464(?)
USSR	SS-4	1959	340	1 × 1 Mt; CEP 2.4km	1,800	340
	SS-5	1961	40	1 × 1 Mt; CEP 1.2km	3,500	40
	SS-20	1977	324	3 × 200 kt MIRV; CEP 0.3km	5,000	972[g]
China	CSS-2	n.a.	50–70	n.a.	2,600	n.a.
	CSS-1	n.a.	40–50	n.a.	1,000	n.a.
France	SSBS S-3	1980	18	1 × 1 Mt; CEP n.a.	3,000	18
Strike Aircraft						
U.S.	F-4	1962	1,400 (250 in Europe)	n.a.	1,100	n.a.
	A-6E	1963	150	n.a.	n.a.	n.a.
	A-7E	1966	720 (360 active, 48 in Europe)	n.a.	n.a.	n.a.
	F-16	1979	380	n.a.	n.a.	n.a.

USSR	Su-17	1970	850	n.a.	n.a.	n.a.
	Su-24	1974	600	n.a.	n.a.	n.a.
	MiG 23/27	1971	2,000	n.a.	n.a.	n.a.
Short-Range Theater Missiles						
U.S.	Lance	1972	900 (36 in Europe)	1 × 1–100 kt; ERW capable; CEP n.a.	1,900	900[h]
	Pershing 1A	1962	108	1 × 60–400 kt; CEP n.a.	700	108
USSR	FROG-series	1965	680 (est.)	1 × 15 kt; CEP n.a.	30–70km	680 (est)
	SS-1c Scud B	1965	620	1 × ? kt; CEP n.a.	300	620
	SS-12 Scaleboard	1969		1 × 1 Mt; CEP n.a.	800	
	SS-22	1979	100–120	1 × 1 Mt; CEP n.a.	900	100–120
France	Pluton	1974	32	1 × 15–25 kt; CEP n.a.	120	32
Artillery						
U.S.	M-110 203mm howitzer	1962	1,000 (est.)	1 × 1–2 kt; CEP n.a.	15–30km	n.a.
	M-109 155mm howitzer	1964	1,000 (est.)	1 × 1–2 kt; CEP n.a.	15–30km	n.a.
USSR	M-55 203mm gun	1950s	n.a.	1 × 15 kt; CEP n.a.	15–45km	n.a.

[a] All Titan II missiles are expected to be deactivated by the end of 1986.
[b] Fifty single-warhead Minuteman IIs are scheduled for conversion to three-warhead MIRVed Minuteman IIIs.
[c] The number of total warheads associated with single- and multiple-RV versions of the SS-11, SS-18, and SS-19 are subject to substantial variation in the public literature. The total number of Soviet ICBM warheads generally is placed at 5,100, which means that more than 75% of these weapons are deployed in their multiple-RV versions.
[d] The abbreviation "n.a." means "not readily available."
[e] The total number of SS-N-6s is 274. Publicly available information does not break the number down into separate counts of single- and multiple-RV versions.
[f] The Pershing II launch vehicle has a rapid reload/refire capability that enables it to store a second missile on board. Thus, it is likely that the number of Pershing IIs finally deployed will total 216.
[g] The SS-20, like the Pershing II, is a rapid reload/refire system, which means that the total number of SS-20 missiles may actually add up to 1,944.
[h] The number of Lance warheads in active inventory may be twice the number cited, as the United States Government is stockpiling enhanced radiation warheads compatible with this missile.

APPENDIX 6

Glossary of Nuclear Terms

ABM Antiballistic Missile. A missile intended to destroy an incoming ballistic missile reentry vehicle.

ACDA Arms Control and Disarmament Agency. The principal agency of the U.S. government for arms control affairs.

AEC Atomic Energy Commission. For about three decades following World War II, the federal agency responsible for the design and manufacture of atomic weapons. Subsequently absorbed into the Federal Energy Agency, which was absorbed into the Department of Energy.

ALCM Air-launched cruise missile. Any cruise missile designed to be carried by, and launched from, an airplane.

APC Armored personnel carrier. A heavily armored vehicle that carries a small number of troops.

assured destruction The American name for the policy, pursued by both the U.S. and USSR, of deterring the opponent from striking one's homeland by threatening to devastate his own in retaliation.

ASW Antisubmarine warfare. All measures intended to identify, track, and destroy enemy submarines.

ballistic missile A missile that rises on a steep trajectory to a high altitude and then plunges back very fast, also at a steep angle.

bias The tendency for a ballistic missile RVs to drift to the side of its intended target because of anomalies in the earth's shape and gravitational field, and other factors.

catalysis A process by which a small-scale conflict, such as one among Third World nations, ignites a much larger conflict, usually one between the superpowers.

CBW Chemical and biological warfare. (Weapons of these kinds, if grouped together with nuclear weapons, are also called ABC weapons, for atomic-biological-chemical.)

CIA Central Intelligence Agency. The best-known of many U.S. intelligence agencies, charged, among other things, with synthesizing the information gathered by the others together with its own.

COIN Counterinsurgency warfare. Warfare against guerrilla forces.

counterforce The targeting of one's missiles and other forces against enemy strategic forces, especially missile silos. Also, an American strategic doctrine of the early to mid-1960s, revived less formally in the late 1970s and since, the goal of which was and is to destroy the bulk of Soviet ICBM forces.

countervalue The targeting of one's missiles and other forces against what the enemy values most: usually cities.

crisis stability A condition in which the superpowers are not much tempted, in a crisis, to escalate to nuclear warfare, in part because most or all of their strategic forces are relatively secure.

---

cruise missile A missile which flies a roughly horizontal trajectory, like an airplane.

damage limiting An American strategy during the 1960s, intended to reduce the damage suffered by the United States in the event of nuclear war, by both offensive and defensive means.

decapitation A strategy of destroying an enemy country's leading governmental officials, on the premise that this will make it impossible thereafter for the country to carry on the war coherently.

DIA Defense Intelligence Agency. The principal intelligence service of the Defense Department. It includes the separate intelligence agencies of the military services.

DOD Department of Defense.

DOE Department of Energy. Branches of this department, not DOD or the military services, design and manufacture U.S. atomic weapons.

first-strike capability Not the capability to strike first, but to largely or entirely disarm one's opponent in a first strike.

Flexible Response A loose doctrine that emphasizes the creation and maintenance of "multiple options" and the flexible decision making and communications that go with them, for managing crises and conflicts. Flexible Response holds that strategic nuclear, theater nuclear, and conventional forces will all be maintained to deter the opponent's use of equivalent forces.

Flexible Targeting An American strategic doctrine since the mid-1970s, emphasizing the ability to strike either Soviet cities and/or Soviet military targets, including missile silos.

forward-based systems (FBS) A term, originally introduced by the Soviets, for the American systems located in Europe, Asia, and on ships around the Soviet periphery, capable of delivering nuclear weapons into the USSR.

fratricide Destruction or deflection of incoming warheads by the nuclear explosion of other warheads that have just preceded them.

general purpose forces A generic term for all combat forces other than those armed with nuclear weapons. Synonymous with "conventional forces."

Graduated Deterrence An American strategic doctrine of the late 1950s, which sought to supplement the threat of Massive Retaliation with the additional threat that relatively large conventional attacks on U.S. allies might be met with nuclear strikes in the local theater.

horizontal escalation Enlarging a conflict by bringing in nations previously uninvolved, or by attacking the opponent's forces or interests elsewhere in the world. (See, by contrast, "vertical escalation.")

IAEA International Atomic Energy Agency. A United Nations-related agency that monitors compliance with prescribed safeguards against the misuse of nuclear materials; and also promotes peaceful applications of atomic technology.

ICBM Intercontinental ballistic missile. A ballistic missile with a range sufficient to travel from the United States to the USSR or vice versa.

IRBM Intermediate-range ballistic missile. A missile with a range from 1,500 up to five thousand kilometers.

JCS Joint Chiefs of Staff. The four senior officers of the four American military services, plus an elected chairman drawn on a rotating basis from the services.

kiloton Equivalent to a thousand tons of TNT. Used as a measure of the yield of nuclear weapons. The Hiroshima bomb, for instance, was about 15 kilotons, or the equivalent of 15,000 tons of TNT.

LRTNF Long-range theater nuclear forces. Weapons with ranges from 1,000 to 5,500 kilometers.

MAD See Mutual Assured Destruction.

Massive Retaliation An American strategic doctrine of the 1950s, which threatened the USSR and China with large-scale atomic strikes on their homelands in the event they sponsored a military attack on U.S. allies, of not precisely defined magnitude.

megaton Equivalent to a million tons of TNT. Used as a measure of the yield of thermonuclear weapons.

Minuteman The backbone of U.S. ICBM forces since the mid-1960s. The Minuteman I was phased out in favor of the more modern Minuteman II (deployed starting in 1966) and the MIRVed Minuteman III (deployed starting in 1970).

MIRV Multiple independently targetable reentry vehicle. Multiple warheads for missiles, in which each warhead can be aimed at a separate target.

MRTNF Medium-range theater nuclear forces. Weapons with ranges from 200 to 1,000 kilometers.

MRBM Medium-range ballistic missile. In some usage, a missile roughly synonymous with MRTNF. In other usage, a missile with range up to about 1,5000 kilometers.

Mutual Assured Destruction The principle that the United States and Soviet Union, each possessing an assured destruction capability against the other, mutually deter each other from launching a nuclear war.

NIE National Intelligence Estimate. A formal, systematic assessment of a foreign nation's capabilities and intentions, or of other questions, prepared on the basis of all available data.

NPT Nonproliferation Treaty. Completed in 1968 and signed by over a hundred countries, this treaty obliges nuclear powers not to transfer, and non-nuclear powers not to receive or manufacture, nuclear weapons or the immediate components thereof.

NSC National Security Council. A legally instituted group of senior advisors to the president on national security issues, including the secretaries of state and defense.

OSD Office of the Secretary of Defense. The analysts and other staff serving the secretary.

PNEs Peaceful nuclear explosives. Atomic explosive devices intended for civilian purposes such as digging canals.

preemption To strike an adversary quickly, before he strikes and in the expectation that he is about to.

RV Reentry vehicle. The warhead, and some associated parts, of a ballistic missile.

ride out To absorb an enemy's strike before responding.

SAC Strategic Air Command. The branch of the USAF that includes ICBMs, strategic bombers, and their command and control.

SAM Surface-to-air missile.

saturating In the context of ABMs, the process of sending so many warheads against the defensive system that its interceptor missiles are exhausted.

second-strike capability The ability to ride out an enemy attack and then retaliate effectively.

SIOP Single Integrated Operations Plan. The basic American war plan for general nuclear war.

SLBM Submarine-launched ballistic missile. A ballistic missile, of intermediate or intercontinental range, launchable from a submerged submarine.

SLCM Ship- or submarine-launched cruise missile. A cruise missile launchable from a ship or a submerged submarine; usually "strategic," that is, intended for use against the enemy's homeland.

SRAM Short-range attack missile. A U.S. missile carried by B-52 and FB-111 bombers, enabling them to avoid flying over the most densely defended targets.

thermonuclear Pertaining to hydrogen (fusion) rather than uranium or plutonium (fission) weapons or processes.

throw weight The total weight that can be carried by a missile to the target.

TNF Theater nuclear forces.

triad The long-standing American strategic doctrine that the United States must maintain three kinds of strategic forces: ICBMs, SLBMs, and long-range bombers.

USAF United States Air Force.

USN United States Navy.

vertical escalation Intensifying a conflict by bringing new forces to bear, employing new types of weapons, or in the extreme case by attacking the enemy's homeland.

yield The explosive force of a nuclear blast, measured in kilotons or megatons.

To the Student

We regularly revise the books we publish in order to make them better. To do this well we need to know what instructors and students think of the previous edition. At some point your instructor will be asked to comment on *The Nuclear Predicament: A Sourcebook;* now we would like to hear from you.

Please take a few minutes to rate the selections and complete this questionnaire. Send it to Bedford Books of St. Martin's Press, 29 Commonwealth Avenue, Boston, Massachusetts 02116. We promise to listen to what you have to say. Thanks.

School ______________________________

School location (city, state) ______________________________

Course title ______________________________

Instructor's name ______________________________

		Definitely Keep	Probably Keep	Uncertain	Drop	Not Assigned
1	Schell (Hiroshima)	___	___	___	___	___
	Arms Control Association	___	___	___	___	___
	Sagan	___	___	___	___	___
	Secretary-General	___	___	___	___	___
2	Einstein	___	___	___	___	___
	Bohr	___	___	___	___	___
	Franck et al.	___	___	___	___	___
	Szilard	___	___	___	___	___
	Stimson	___	___	___	___	___
	Eisenhower	___	___	___	___	___
	Baruch	___	___	___	___	___
	Russell	___	___	___	___	___
	Forsberg (Brief History)	___	___	___	___	___
	Bernstein	___	___	___	___	___
	Ellsberg	___	___	___	___	___
	Greb and Johnson	___	___	___	___	___
	Porro	___	___	___	___	___
	Gray and Payne	___	___	___	___	___
3	Chilton	___	___	___	___	___
	Kaldor	___	___	___	___	___
	Peattie	___	___	___	___	___
	DeGrasse	___	___	___	___	___
	Frank	___	___	___	___	___
	International Physicians	___	___	___	___	___
	Farrell	___	___	___	___	___
	Lawyers Committee	___	___	___	___	___
4	Comm. on Present Danger	___	___	___	___	___
	Reagan	___	___	___	___	___
	White House Paper	___	___	___	___	___
	Weinberger	___	___	___	___	___
	Dept. of Defense	___	___	___	___	___

	Definitely Keep	Probably Keep	Uncertain	Drop	Not Assigned
Fed. Emerg. Mgt. Agency	___	___	___	___	___
Scoville	___	___	___	___	___
Forsberg (Proposal)	___	___	___	___	___
Wiesner	___	___	___	___	___
Zuckerman	___	___	___	___	___
Kennan	___	___	___	___	___
Wieseltier	___	___	___	___	___
Bundy et al.	___	___	___	___	___
Schell (The Choice)	___	___	___	___	___
Beyond War	___	___	___	___	___
Thompson	___	___	___	___	___
Nagler	___	___	___	___	___
Sivard	___	___	___	___	___

Did your instructor assign any or all of the appendices? If so, which ones? Did you find them useful? How can we improve them? (Please use additional paper if necessary.)

Did you find the appendix on writing a research paper particularly helpful?

Any other comments?

Name ______________________________ Date ____________

Address ____